Manual of Corporate Governance

Manual of Corporate Governance

THEORY AND PRACTICE FOR SCHOLARS, EXECUTIVE AND NON-EXECUTIVE DIRECTORS

Duarte Pitta Ferraz
Manish Adhikari

Dedication

*To my professors, for my students, to my loved ones,
especially for my granddaughter Alexia
Duarte*

*To my father Krishna Prasad Adhikari,
and my mother Lata Devi Dahal
Manish*

Contents

Contents

List of Figures

List of Tables

Key Abbreviations

ACCA	Association of Chartered Certified Accountants
ADB	Asian Development Bank
AfDB	African Development Bank
ADIA	Abu Dhabi Investment Authority
AIIB	Asian Infrastructure Investment Bank
AML	Anti-Money Laundering
5AMLD	Fifth Anti-Money Laundering Directive
ALM	Asset Liability Management
BCBS	Basel Committee on Banking Supervision
BIS	Banks for International Settlements
CIC	The China Investment Corporation
CIIA	Chartered Institute of Internal Auditors
CMVM	Comissão do Mercado de Valores Mobiliários
COSO	Committee of Sponsoring Organizations of the Treadway Commissions
CRA	Credit Rating Agency
CRD	Capital Requirements Directive
D&O	Directors and Officers Liability Insurance
DAO	Decentralized Autonomous Organization
DJSI	Dow Jones Sustainability Index
DTA	Double Taxation Agreement
EBA	European Banking Authority
ECAI	External Credit Assessment Institutions

ECB	European Central Bank
EEA	European Economic Area
EIB	European Investment Bank
EIOPA	European Insurance and Occupational Pensions Authority
EMR	Enterprise Risk Management
ESG	Environment, Social, and Governance
ESMA	European Securities and Market Authority
EU/EC	European Union/European Commission
EWoB	European Women on Board
FCA	Financial Conduct Authority (UK)
FDI	Foreign Direct Investment
FDIC	Federal Deposit Insurance Corporation
FISCMA	Financial Investment Services and Capital Markets Act (Korea)
FRC	Financial Reporting Council (UK and Ireland)
FS Act	Financial Services Act (UK)
FSB	Financial Stability Board
FSMA	Financial Services and Markets Act (UK)
FRS	Federal Reserve System (US)
FTSE	Financial Times-Stock Exchange
G20	Group of 20
GAAP	Generally Accepted Accounting Principles (US)
GDP	Gross Domestic Product
GDPR	General Data Protection Regulation (EU)
GPF	Government Pension Fund (Norway)
HQLA	High-Quality Liquid Assets

IAASB	International Audit and Assurance Standards Board
ICSA	Institute of Chartered Secretaries and Administrators
IFC	International Finance Corporation
IFI	International Finance Institutions
IFRS	International Financial Reporting Standards
IIA	Institute of Internal Auditors
IMA	Investment Management Association
IMF	International Monetary Fund
IoT	Internet of Things
IRMI	International Risk Management Institute
ISA	International Standards on Auditing
ISO	International Organization for Standardization
JST	Joint Supervisory Committee
KAM	Key Audit Matters
KPIs	Key Performance Indicators
LCR	Liquidity Coverage Ratio
LGBT+	Lesbian, Gay, Bisexual, Transgender, +
M&A	Mergers and Acquisitions
NAS	Non-Audit Services
NCA	National Competent Authorities
NRSRO	Nationally Recognized Statistical Rating Organizations
NYSE	New York Stock Exchange
OECD	Organisation for Economic Co-operation and Development
PIE	Public Interest Entities
PR	Public Relations
PRI	Principles for Responsible Investment

ROC	Revisor Oficial de Contas
SASAC	State-owned Assets, Supervision and Administration Commission (China)
SASB	Sustainability Accounting Standards Board
SDG	Sustainable Development Goals
SEBI	Securities and Exchange Board of India
SEC	US Securities Exchange Commission
SOE	Stated Owned Enterprise
SPV	Special Purpose Vehicle
SROC	Sociedade de Revisores Oficiais de Contas
SSM	Single Supervisory Mechanism
SWF	Sovereign Wealth Fund
UBO	Ultimate Beneficiary Owner
UN	United Nations
ViSTO	Vision—Strategy—Tactics—Operational
WBCSD	The World Business Council for Sustainable Development
WBG	World Bank Group

Foreword

When people hear corporate governance, they tend to think of codes such as the Cadbury Code, which recommends that companies change their board structures and procedures to make the company more accountable to shareholders. In reality, however, governance goes well beyond just board processes and procedures. It involves the full set of relationships between a company's management, its board, its shareholders, and its other stakeholders, such as its employees and the community in which it operates. And these relationships matter. They have been shown to be closely correlated with corporate performance, financial stability, and a perception of public legitimacy. Many of the big corporate scandals and stock market exuberances that we have experienced in the past 50 years can be directly traced back to poor corporate governance.

Governance is also key to the effective functioning of public policy instruments. As president of the European Investment Bank, the world's biggest multilateral financial institution by assets, this is an issue close to my heart—not just for the day-to-day operation of the institution and decision taken on the bank's strategic course, but also for the design of effective policy interventions. I look at the European Fund for Strategic Investments (EFSI), or Juncker Plan, for example, not just as a financial marvel that supported over €500 billion of badly needed investment following the global financial crisis, but also as a triumph of good governance. The lean, efficient set-up of this stimulus program laid the foundation for its success. Beyond its economic impact, EFSI also illustrates the interaction of governance with contemporary issues, such as gender, mandating in its regulation that its Investment Committee should be comprised of an equal number of men and women.

Good governance matters: *Manual of Corporate Governance—Theory and Practice for Scholars, Executive and Non-executive Directors* is a textbook on how to get it right; for use by everyone, from academics and students to policymakers, bankers, directors, and family businesses. The authors address classical aspects of governance and risk management—as well as current ones, such as issues of environmental and social sustainability and even the question of how effective governance can work under COVID-19 conditions. I am greatly impressed by its breadth and depth and delighted to provide a foreword to such an important work.

Dr. Werner Hoyer, President of the European Investment Bank

Introduction to the First Edition

We kindly welcome our readers to the first edition of the textbook *Manual of Corporate Governance—Theory and Practice for Scholars, Executive and Non-executive Directors*. It is targeted to both in the financial and nonfinancial enterprises. Its purpose is to offer a comprehensive and holistic compilation of themes and topics affecting the corporate governance arena, a branch of study within the business administration field. As a textbook, it is addressed to educators and students, as well as to decision-makers, notably executive and non-executive directors as well as to company secretaries and first-line managers to assist in understanding corporate governance standards and concepts to better contribute to a robust corporate governance framework that makes their board highly efficient.

First, we fully disclose to our readers that this textbook is not a guideline for the development of a new policy or framework in corporate governance, but a comprehensive aggregation of several topics in corporate governance domain. The textbook is developed by sourcing and referencing the contents from several institutions and authors—in the European Union (EU), the United Kingdom (UK), the United States of America (USA), Asia, amongst others. Although the content about banking and financial institutions is significant in the textbook, we believe that the same can be leveraged by nonfinancial institutions and therefore adjusted to their own needs or requirements. As the guidelines, rules, laws, regulations, and directives vary with jurisdictions and regions and continuously evolve with time and new developments, we are committed to incorporate such changes in the subsequent editions of the textbook.

We draw your attention to the fact that the perspectives presented and discussed in the textbook often refer to legal frameworks or corporate governance guidelines—which often vary among jurisdictions—but the textbook focuses on the impact in the corporate governance framework elements of this science in public and private organizations. We emphasize that reading or studying this manual does not substitute the consultation of the applicable legislation to the jurisdiction and professional legal counsel in the decision-making process within the framework of corporate governance of public and private institutions.

The textbook is developed with an intent that directors and managers in any kind of public or private companies or even start-ups should know about corporate governance. We kindly suggest our readers to feel free to skip any specific topics that are found to be irrelevant to their area of interest or operation and jump to the next. For example, some of the topics can be quite relevant to financial institutions and perhaps not so for nonfinancial institutions. Nonetheless, we believe it can be worthwhile to know the rules or regulations concerning banking and financial institutions, as there is a general understanding that if the banks fail, the economy fails.

The textbook is divided into 8 parts and 23 chapters.

Part I is essentially an introduction to corporate governance. The topics include the history and relevance of corporate governance; corporate governance theories such as the agency theory and the models of corporate governance incorporated in different jurisdictions; dynamics of governance models; among others. This part also covers the topics of strategy, business model, and sustainable growth.

Part II discusses family business governance. The topics ownership and management, governance structure in family business, governance mechanism model, and the role of the board and of senior management in a family business. Succession planning in a family business is also discussed.

Part III comprises the organizational management and governance framework, including models such as The IIA Three Lines Model, The Four Lines of Defense, Internal Control Framework (ICF), Enterprise

Risk Management (ERM), among others. The topics of internal control functions in an institution, such as risk management function, compliance function, and audit functions are detailed. Risk concepts, risk types, risk appetite, and their relevance to the institution are also discussed. Compliance concepts including anti-money laundering and taxation are detailed. This part also includes Supervisory Mechanism, so that directors or managers in any institutions—not just banks—are aware of how regulators and supervisors like European Central Bank (ECB) and NCA (National Competent Authorities) monitor the institutions. Supervisory mechanisms such as Single Supervisory Mechanism (SSM), and Culture and Behavior Supervision are discussed and compared. Additionally, topics such as Asset and Liability Risk Management (ALM) are believed to come handy to directors or managers involved in banking and financial institutions.

Part IV is all about the board. It begins with the Fit and Proper principles—the essential principle for the selection of board members, incorporating guidelines from Banks for International Settlements (BIS) and ECB, as we believe they constitute a framework of the corporate governance best practice. The concept of diversity and inclusion has never been so relevant; this part adequately captures the topic. The guidelines on board effectiveness are detailed, with accordance to the guidelines from the European Banking Authority (EBA), Basel Committee on Banking Supervision (BCBS), Financial Reporting Council (FRC, UK), among others. The decision-making dynamics in the board are discussed and an example of a decision-making framework is demonstrated. The traps and biases in decision-making, particularly in board meetings, are elaborated. The relevance of the roles of the chair, independent/non-executive directors, and executive directors as well as the importance of board committees (e.g., audit committee, risk committee, nomination committee, remuneration committee, governance committee) are fairly discussed. The view on the evaluation of the board members and the board as a whole is discussed. The concepts of independence, conflicts of interest, and crisis management are provided.

Part V presents the current trend of deglobalization and the new kind of geopolitics that board members or directors must be aware of and examine in their agendas for consideration and decision-making. Some of the well-known geopolitical cases in the international context are presented. The case of COVID-19 and globalization is examined. The theory and relevance of Foreign Direct Investments (FDIs) and internationalization is well discussed.

In Part VI, the concept of corporate credit rating and why credit rating matters for corporate is discussed, incorporating guidelines from global credit rating agencies. The credit rating methodology is also fairly discussed. Acknowledging that sustainability—ESG (Environment, Social and Governance)—is particularly important to businesses in current times, this part also discussing extensively topics regarding the business model and sustainable growth. This part also discusses activism by individual shareholders and by institutional shareholders. The content about activist investors, the essence of proxy voting services, and the recent flavors in activism are presented.

Part VII discusses reporting. The concept of corporate reporting is presented comprehensively, along with its importance in maintaining robust communication among stakeholders. The difference in annual reporting of the two main governance models—monist model and dualist model—is discussed. The paradigm shift in corporate reporting to shareholders or/and stakeholders is also discussed, including the evolution of sustainability reporting and integrated reporting.

Finally, Part VIII encapsulates the main topics and drivers discussed in the preceding parts and chapters, presenting the framing and main conclusions.

The authors plan to have the textbook available, separately, as a set of PowerPoint slides to support professors of Corporate Governance courses to prepare and deliver classes. It will be possible to edit and tailor the slides to the syllabus.

The authors wish the manual is useful for scholars, students, decision-makers, notably executive and non-executive directors, corporate secretaries, as well as managers that have to prepare and provide data and information to the board, on a structured and intelligible fashion, to allow for robust decisions managing an organization.

About the Authors

This textbook is perhaps one of the best outcomes of Professor—Student rapport. Duarte Pitta Ferraz and Manish Adhikari stem from different background; yet find a common goal to author this textbook titled *Manual of Corporate Governance—Theory and Practice for Scholars, Executive, and Non-executive Directors*.

Duarte Pitta Ferraz holds a Doctorate of Business Administration (DBA) from Nottingham Business School—Nottingham Trent University, being qualified as a Portuguese chartered accountant (ROC—*Revisor Oficial de Contas*) and a lawyer (*Advogado*). Experience in consulting, banking, and financial institutions, working in countries such as Portugal, USA, Angola, Greece, Turkey, Luxembourg, and the United Kingdom, spanning over a period of 30 years. Professor of Governance and Banking at Nova School of Business and Economics—Executive Education, Portugal, and Visiting Fellow at Nottingham Business School. Experienced Non-executive Director (NED), having held positions at institutions such as European Investment Bank (Chairman of the Audit Committee), Infraestruturas de Portugal (Supervisory Board and Audit Committee), and Grupo Manuel Champalimaud (Audit Board). He was a member of the Privatization Oversight Committees of TAP Air Portugal and CTT—Correios de Portugal Postal Services. Worked at Deloitte and at Philip Morris USA. Has been a speaker at conferences held In Austria, USA, the United Kingdom, Brazil, Hong Kong, Canada, Japan, Germany, South Africa, The Netherlands, and Austria.

Manish Adhikari has Professional experience working in Portugal, UAE, and Nepal. Manish is an Engineer with management and governance qualifications. Manish holds Master of Science in Management from Nova School of Business and Economics, Portugal, and Bachelor of Computer Engineering from Kathmandu University, Nepal. Manish also attended the executive level course, Corporate Governance: The Board Leadership, at Nova SBE Executive Education, Portugal. After his bachelor's, Manish worked as an IT personnel in Dubai, UAE, before moving to Portugal for master's. Manish concluded his master dissertation under the supervision of Duarte, titled *The impact of the merger law wave era (2012–2015) in the performance of commercial banks in Nepal*. Thereafter, Manish worked as a consultant in Capgemini before moving to collaborate with Duarte again as an Associate Researcher at IVENS | Governance Advisors, a consultancy firm focused on the corporate governance arena. Since then, both Manish and Duarte have found a common shared vision in corporate governance.

The authors are extremely excited to welcome their readers in this governance journey's textbook.

Acknowledgments

We would like to acknowledge the fellow professors, colleagues, and Doctoral candidates, master of science and MBA students without whom this textbook would have not been completed.

To Dr. Werner Hoyer, President of European Investment Bank (EIB)—an advocate of robust corporate governance structures—for writing the foreword of this textbook targeted at scholars and decision-makers, notably executive and non-executive directors. Also, to Rui Maximino and Duarte Júlio Pitta Ferraz for being available to discuss the content over its development, as well as to João Dinis Gomes and Catarina dos Reis Almeida for reading and developing the figures.

To Duarte's Nothingham Business School's Doctoral Students, Drs. Issam Al Bulushi, Rania Itani Traboulsi, and Wilson Tawodzera who completed their doctorates in the corporate governance arena, as well as to Sara Costa Araújo currently at the doctoral program at ISCSP—Universidade de Lisboa. To those with expertise in specific areas of knowledge and management, as well as their time, patience, and feedback in reviewing specific sections or chapters: Alexandra Abreu Loureiro, André São Marcos Barbado, Duarte J. Pitta Ferraz, Gonçalo Moura de Figueiredo, João Oliveira, Joaquim Grade da Encarnação, and Pedro Miguel Mendes.

To Duarte's fellow Professors: Alistair Mutch, Baback Yazdani, Carole Tansley, Colin Fisher, Daniel Traça, António Silva Ribeiro, Florencio Lopez-de Silanes, Heitor Barras Romana, João Carvalho das Neves, José António Ferreira Machado, José Manuel Neves Adelino, Michael W. Zhang, Miguel Ferreira, Manuel Meirinho, Miguel Pina e Cunha, Nuno Severiano Teixeira, Paulo Matos Costa, Ricardo Teixeira de Gouveia, and Teodora de Castro for the support, enthusiasm, and counseling along the career in academy, as well as for their teachings in the area of corporate governance. To Professor Ilídio Tomaz Lopes and Professor Teodora de Castro, Andrea Nannicini, Ardit Kopliku, and Simon Hitzelberger—co-authors—for having accepted to jointly research and publish scientific papers and articles, namely about corporate governance.

Alain Godard, António Vitorino, Frank Schuster, Jens-Henrik Laursen, João Talone, Jorge Jardim Gonçalves, Jorge Magalhães Correia, Luís Amado, Luís Todo Bom, Michael Kaiser, Margareth Pitta Ferraz, Mindaugas Macijauskas, Paolo Lombardo, Paulo Abrantes Lopes, Pedro Rebelo de Sousa, Richard H. Bogan, Uldis Cerps, Vitor Bento, William T. Cunningham, and William Smiy for their teachings and reflections about governance topics in the business administration arena, as well as for their wisdom in addressing challenging issues and developing balanced solutions for decision.

To Manish's friends Aakriti Lamsal, Bishal Thapa, Dier Lohani, Dilli Odari, Gita Adhikari, Gayatri Dahal, Joakim Neergård, Manish Basnet, Mayanath Bhattarai, Sanjay Shah, Simon Kolhoff, Surendra Humagain, and Susan Subedi for encouraging and motivating me to be involved in this textbook.

We are grateful to all the organizations and publications that gave us permission to make use of their published materials, and we assure that we have made all our effort to reference them properly.

Last but not least, our Readers' continued support is the determining criteria to encourage us further and come with up an improved future edition.

We want to thank Amnet Systems for preparing the manuscript for publication. We have tried the best to make this textbook free from factual or typographical errors, but even with good intentions mistakes do sometimes occur. In such cases, we kindly request our reader to notify the error and the corresponding page number to the following e-mail: manualcg@ivensadvisors.com.

Part I—Corporate Governance History, Theories, Models, and Sustainability

Chapter 1

Introduction to Corporate Governance

With the continuous development and growth of new economies and corporates (hereafter colloquially referred to as companies, firms, organizations, or institutions) over the past decades, the topic of corporate governance has evolved accordingly.

The legal structure of the company depends on whether the entity is:

1. Publicly traded corporation (shares)
2. Private corporation (e.g., family-owned, venture-backed, and others)
3. Limited liability company
4. Partnership
5. Non-profit corporation
6. Foundation
7. State-owned enterprise (SOE)

This textbook primarily deals with the topics, guidelines, best practices, and regulations concerning publicly listed companies, which in fact should be seen as the recommended guidelines for any other types of company.

The core narrates the control and supervision of corporates through appropriate rules and regulations (i.e., how effectively corporates are managed toward sustainability, performance, efficiency, growth, structure, audit, regulation, stakeholder and shareholder relations), as well as the emergence of trends related to sustainability, society, governance, and climate. As geographies across the world have diverse historical, social, economic, political, and cultural aspects, the development of corporate governance structures encompasses several forms, such as shareholder-centric and unitary board structure in the United States (US), the United Kingdom (UK), and other Anglo-Saxonic countries with a strong focus in capital markets, and stakeholder-centric two-tiered board (dual model) structure in Germany, Scandinavia, Portugal, France, among others.

Nonetheless, independent of the formal structure, their governance objectives are the same. On top of well-known corporate scandals that often led companies to bankruptcy, negatively impacting stakeholders, and as the 1997 Asian Financial Crisis, 1998 Russian Financial Crisis, 1999 Brazilian Financial Crisis, and 2008 Global Financial Crisis unfolded over the period, the significance and importance of corporate governance have never been as paramount.

An annual corporate directors' survey conducted in 2019 by PwC US,[1] a global consulting and audit firm, highlighted some of the crucial findings in the US. Essentially, institutional investors own around 80 percent[2] of US-based public companies, and the board members are increasingly challenged by them. Traditionally, the boards have valued collegiality, consensus, and the status quo over innovation and fresh thinking. However, the behavior in boardrooms is now showing signs of change. Some of the topics that need attention include corporate culture, ESG (Environment, Social, and Governance), diversity and inclusion, pay gap, strategy, high tech and rapid digital transformation, cybersecurity disconnect, globalization and geopolitics, and economic uncertainty and pandemics such as COVID-19.

In the later chapters, the aforementioned topics are adequately considered. The contents are widely borrowed from banking and financial regulations and best practice prevalent across the world.

Undoubtedly, if the banks fail, the wider economy is susceptible to fail, and regulations encircling these institutions are believed to be very stringent. It should be considered a good opportunity for non-financial sector's companies, beyond banks and financial institutions, to customize such regulations to meet their own needs and compliance requirements, protecting value creation, sustainability, shareholders and stakeholders.

1.1 MODERN CORPORATE GOVERNANCE HISTORY

The 1929 US Wall Street Crash and the 1930s Great Depression augmented the global need for the development of robust governance models.

During the 1920s, the US economy expanded rapidly, and the stock price at the New York Stock Exchange (NYSE) grew wildly, reaching much higher than the actual value in August 1929. As industrial production gradually went down and unemployment rose, this triggered a collapse of the stock price, as nervous investors began selling overpriced stocks *en masse*. Other reasons for the 1929 crash were the proliferation of debt, a struggling agricultural sector, low wages, and an excess of large bank loans that could not be liquidated. The crash subsequently led to the economic downturn in the industrialized world from 1929 to 1939, also known as the Great Depression. Over this period, consumer spending and investment dropped, causing steep declines in industrial output and employment. The effect of depression was not only felt in the US, but also in countries such as the UK, Germany, France, and Portugal.

In 1933, the then newly appointed 32nd US President Franklin D. Roosevelt passed legislation that aimed to stabilize industrial and agricultural production, create jobs, and stimulate recovery. The Roosevelt administration reformed the financial system by introducing the Federal Deposit Insurance Corporation (FDIC) to protect depositors' accounts and establishing the Securities and Exchange

Commission (SEC) to regulate and supervise the stock market. Subsequently, new accounting standards were adopted, and the need for independent external auditors to verify the authenticity of financial statements became the norm.

The real concept of modern corporate governance came into existence after two American authors Adolf Berle and Gardiner Means published a textbook named *The Modern Corporation and Private Property*[3] in 1932 (the second revised edition in 1967). The textbook advocated the concept of separation of ownership and control (further discussed in Section 1.3: "Corporate Governance Definition and Concept"). Later, the textbook evolved as a foundational stone for cultivating US corporate governance model, corporate law, and institutional economics.

The article *The Nature of the Firm*[4] (1937), authored by Nobel Prize-winning author and British economist Ronald Coase, elaborated the concept of establishment of firms by explaining the theory of transaction costs. Coase argued that obtaining goods or services from the market for the firm adds more cost than just the price of the goods or services, including search and information costs, bargaining costs, enforcement costs, and other equivalent costs, and the author labeled all these kinds of costs as transaction costs. Thus, the necessity of firms is realized such that they can produce goods or services internally to avoid the unnecessary transaction costs from the market.

In 1960, Coase published another article named "The Problem of Social Cost"[5] which explains the economic problem of externalities. The article turned out to be instrumental in the field of law and economics. Externalities is the concept from economics regarding the positive or negative consequences of economic activities experienced by unrelated third parties. For example, loud noise from a factory that affects public health is an example of a negative externality, and increased productivity of factory from skilled labor is an example of a positive externality. Because of the consequences arising from externalities, the government must regularly come up with appropriate regulations for robust compliance and governance.

Paul Samuelson, the first American to win the Nobel prize in economic sciences, authored the book named *Foundations of Economic Analysis*[6] (1947), demonstrating a common mathematical structure underlying multiple branches of economics from two basic principles: maximizing behavior of agents, such as of utility by consumers and profits by firms, and stability of equilibrium as to economic systems, such as markets or economies. Samuelson co-authored another book named *Economics: An Introductory Analysis*[7] in 1948 with William Nordhaus, which is often touted as one of the best-selling economics textbooks and has been translated into many languages over several editions. Samuelson defined economics as the study of how men and society choose, with or without the use of money, to employ scarce productive resources which could have alternative uses, to produce various commodities over time and distribute them for consumption now and in the future amongst various people and groups of society.

In the mid-1960s and early 1970s, American economist Eugene Fama developed a hypothesis about the *behavior of stock markets and efficient market.*[8] Fama argued that stocks should always trade at their fair value, thus making it impossible for investors to buy stocks at undervalued prices or sell at inflated prices. As a result, the impact is seen in the transparency of corporate financial reporting. Authors Michael Jensen and William Meckling published a paper titled "Theory of the Firm: Managerial Behavior, Agency Costs and Ownership"[9] (1976) that integrates elements from the agency theory, property rights theory, and finance theory to develop a theory of the ownership structure for the firm. The paper detailed the *principal-agent problem* observed in firms. The paper has been very popular in both the academic and professional worlds. The concept of agency theory is detailed in Section 2.1: "The Agency Theory."

In 1977, American business historian Alfred Chandler published a popular book named *The Visible Hand: The Managerial Revolution in American Business*[10] that established the theory about the visible hand of management through eight propositions, such as the status quo about multiunit businesses, managerial hierarchy, accountability, and monitoring by the board of directors.

1.2 CORPORATE GOVERNANCE GUIDELINES

As managers started to have more influence in corporate decision-making, procedures and structures to check these actions equally became crucial. Therefore, the development of corporate governance guidelines has been continuously ongoing since the 1990s.

1.2.1 CADBURY CODE AND COMBINED CODE (UK 1992 AND 2003)

The first proper discretionary code of corporate governance—the *Cadbury Code*[11]—was published in 1992. As a result of increasing lack of investor confidence in the honesty of the corporates and the accountability of listed companies due to the sudden collapse of two UK-based companies (wallpaper group Coloroll and Asil Nadir's Polly Peck consortium), Cadbury Committee (Committee on the Financial Aspects of Corporate Governance) was established in 1991 by the British Financial Reporting Council, the London Stock Exchange, and the accountancy/auditing profession. Furthermore, the collapse of the Bank of Credit and Commerce International and the Maxwell Group in 1992 due to misappropriation of funds and bad governance practices pushed the committee members to expedite the publication of the code, which was eventually published in December 1992.

In 2003, Sir Derek Higgs contributed to the revised version of the Cadbury Code, also known as *Adjusted Cadbury Code/Combined Code.*[12] The adjusted code enhanced the role, quality, and effectiveness of senior independent director, non-executive or independent directors, and executive directors in the board. The code laid down the standard process for executives' selection and remuneration. Within the periphery of the code, The London Stock Exchange required listed companies, or any companies that want to be listed, to *comply or explain*, thereby requiring companies to conform to the code, and if they do not, explain to what extent and why. The current best practice demands that if a promise of complying is made, then a deadline for its implementation should be included in the annual report.

At present, the combined code is also known as *UK Corporate Governance Code*, which is overseen by Financial Reporting Council (FRC), an independent regulator in the UK and Ireland responsible for regulating auditors, accountants, and actuaries, and setting the UK's Corporate Governance and Stewardship Codes.

Comply or Explain
The Institute of Chartered Accountants in England and Wales (ICAEW)[13] mentions,

> "(…) the effectiveness of comply or explain depends on mutual trust but institutional arrangements are also important to provide a communication channel between the board and shareholders. Shareholders play a key role in monitoring the quality of explanations, to see whether they are a credible alternative to regulatory and legal enforcement. These arrangements relate to shareholder rights and engagement, patterns of ownership, and legal and regulatory traditions. Together, these arrangements create incentives for shareholders to play the stewardship role, by scrutinizing and challenging companies' explanations."

Instead of forcing the corporate to adopt a one-size-fits-all approach, the comply or explain approach offers flexibility to adjust according to the corporate structure and eventually explain to the shareholders the propriety of the arrangements. In this approach, the directors being in a unitary board are supposed to promote the long-term sustainability of the corporate and generate value to shareholders and to the society as a whole. It is also important that the board identifies and regularly reviews the key stakeholders' relationships and communications. Should the board engage directly with the key stakeholders or should it be the management team, the board has the flexibility to decide. In the end, the chairperson, being supported by the board, the management, and the company secretary, must determine how best to ensure the decision-making processes of the board remain proper and ultimately communicate the same with the shareholders when making decisions.

The comply or explain approach was not only adopted by the UK but also by several European countries to some degree such as Germany, the Netherlands, and Sweden. Because comply or explain is a discretionary measure, it is supposed to work superlatively in the background of trust, shared beliefs, and effective communication between board, shareholders, and stakeholders.

1.2.2 DOT-COM BUBBLE AND SARBANES–OXLEY ACT (US 2002)

During the 2000s, the US economy took a strong hit after the burst of the *Dot-Com Bubble*.[14] Stock value in billions of dollars was destroyed as a result of corporate and accounting scandals, including the bankruptcy of big companies such as Enron and WorldCom. Dot-Com Bubble is remembered as the period of involuntary stock price speculation of corporates from 1997 to 2000. The bubble was stimulated by the extreme growth in the usage and adoption of newly born *Internet Technology* at the time. To address the dodgy behaviors of the corporates at the time and promote transparency, the US Congress passed the act Sarbanes–Oxley Act[15] in 2002. The act set the customary governance requirements for all US public company boards and management and public accounting firms. While the Cadbury Report was more about the recommendations and voluntary measures for corporates to become compliant, the Sarbanes–Oxley Act was enshrined as law and compulsory requirement for corporates to become compliant. Hefty fines were levied on incompliant corporates.

1.2.3 Global Financial Crisis 2007–2008 and Increased Governance

As the 2007–2008 financial crisis rocked the global economies, financial regulators across the world stepped up with increased governance measures for reinforcing strong financial stability. The financial crisis stimulated the importance of board-level procedural safeguards and subsequent introduction of new board-level committees on top of the audit committee, such as risk and compliance committee under the guidance of a CRO (Chief Risk Officer) or any executive director in a position to oversee risk management issues within the legally binding rules.

The UK government passed the Financial Services Act (FS Act)[16] in 2010, amending some of the provisions of the Financial Services and Markets Act 2000 (FSMA). The revised act gave the UK Financial Services Authority (FSA) heightened responsibilities and powers. In 2011, The Financial Reporting Council (FRC) in the UK and Ireland published a document named *Guidance on Board Effectiveness.*[17] It outlined some of the very important added measures in corporate governance practices such as the role of the board and directors, board composition, remuneration, and risk management. The FRC is an independent regulator in the UK and Ireland. It is responsible for regulating the auditors, accountants, and actuaries, and maintaining the UK's Corporate Governance and Stewardship Codes. FRC remit is aimed at investors that rely on annual reports, audit, and high-quality risk management. In 2018, FRC published a fully revised version of Guidance on Board Effectiveness. The guidance is detailed in Section 14.3: "Understanding Board Effectiveness."

In 2014, Bank for International Settlements (BIS) published the revised principles about *Fit and Proper Principles,*[18] the assessment of the fitness of directors, control functions' managers (risk, compliance and internal audit), and shareholders whose holdings are above specified thresholds or who exercise a material influence on their operations (key shareholders) meet the fitness, propriety, and other qualification tests of their supervisors (central banks or any other equal entities). The concept of fit and proper is detailed in Chapter 11: Board Selection.

The Basel guidelines are coined after Basel, the city in Switzerland. Basel hosts the main office of BIS (Bank of International Settlements), also sometimes known as the central bank for central banks. The participating member nations in BIS intend to nurture cooperation to achieve a shared goal of global financial stability and common standards of banking regulations. Basel Committee for Banking Supervision (BCBS), an international forum for financial regulation, is a separate entity from BIS, but it is very closely associated with BIS and is housed in the same office as BIS in Switzerland.

In 2014, the European Union (EU) passed a new directive on nonfinancial reporting—*Disclosure of Non-financial and Diversity Information*.[19] The directive is applicable to large public-interest companies also named Public Interest Entity (PIE) with more than 500 employees across the EU, including listed companies, banks, insurance companies, institutions with securities, namely bonds issued in the market and other companies designated by national authorities as public-interest companies, notably because of their significant public importance (e.g., business, size, number of employees) or holding assets under a fiduciary capacity. The directive was passed with an intention of public interest such that investors, consumers, policymakers, and other stakeholders could assess the nonfinancial performance of large companies and encourage those companies to demonstrate an example of good corporate citizenship by developing a responsible approach for the business.

In 2015, the BCBS published the revised guidance about *Corporate Governance Principles for Banks*.[20] Comparable to the guidelines published by Financial Reporting Council (FRC) in the UK and Ireland, the

BCBS principles extensively elaborated on the board's overall responsibilities, qualification, and composition including executive and non-executive or independent directors, board practices, governance of group structures, risk management, internal audit, compensation, and disclosure of information. Later, in 2015, the same was followed by the Organisation for Economic Co-operation and Development (OECD) publishing the revised and updated *G20/OECD Principles of Corporate Governance*,[21] incorporating corporate governance best practices with a purpose to support policymakers in evaluating and improving the legal, regulatory, and institutional framework for corporate governance. OECD is an intergovernmental economic organization of developed economies to stimulate economic progress and world trade, headquartered in Paris, France.

European Banking Authority (EBA), a regulatory agency of the EU that conducts stress tests of the European Banks, published comprehensive *Guidelines on Internal Governance* (EBA/GL/2017/11)[22] in order to further harmonize institutions' internal governance arrangements, processes, and mechanisms within the EU in line with the requirements introduced by Directive 2013/36/EU. The guidelines take into account the principle of proportionality, namely influenced by the complexity of the business model, by specifying the tasks, responsibilities, and organization of the management body, and the organization of institutions, including the need to create transparent structures that allow for supervision of their activities. The guidelines also specify requirements aimed at ensuring the sound management of risks across all three lines[23] and, in particular, set out detailed requirements for the second line (functions that oversee risks—the independent risk management and compliance function) and the third line (function providing independence assurance—the internal audit function and general inspection, as often set up in multilateral financial institutions).

In 2020, the COVID-19 (coronavirus) pandemic brought the whole world to a standstill. Many people died across the world, and the financial and economic impact brought by the pandemic has often been compared to the great depression. As such, policymakers started to coin the term *agile governance*, which potentially encapsulates the diverse risk scenarios on a holistic level.

The objectives of all these governance frameworks boil down to the one common point: good governance and risk practices. Corporates are free to choose or customize the frameworks in their own best inferences as there is no mandatory one-size-fits-all approach in line with the suggestion of the Cadbury Code. We can also expect that over time, corporate governance principles will continually be updated as times often change fast, and there is no doubt that change is being fueled by rapid hi-tech digital transformation and innovative thinking. The case of the COVID-19 pandemic was unprecedented, and many corporates were caught with the sovereign policy of massive lockdown and social distancing. The lesson learned is that boards must be strategically prepared to deal with such unseen challenges that may drastically impact the business environment and revenues.

1.2.4 CORPORATE GOVERNANCE—LEGAL MANDATE OR VOLUNTARY?

As discussed above, the repeated financial scandals have forced the G-7 and the G-20 to request and recommend governments to legislate and also recommend regulators and mainly supervisors, both in the financial and nonfinancial system, to enforce stringent regulatory measures, such as the US imposing mandatory governance rules by adopting the Sarbanes–Oxley Act. On the contrary, other jurisdictions have implemented variants of Comply or Explain governance regimes to some degree to improve their governance system. As comply or explain is a voluntary measure, through which corporates must demonstrate their compliance with best practice governance rules adopted, and if that cannot demonstrated, substantiate it with the proper explanation and indicate deadlines for its implementation, if that is the plan. At the end of the day, the framework of voluntary measures is sustained with trust, shared beliefs, and effective communication among stakeholders. Ultimately, the need for legal mandate or voluntary governance rules depends on the values rooted in the society and the market but ultimately on the shareholders' expectations and the board's leadership in the governance arena.

1.3 CORPORATE GOVERNANCE DEFINITION AND CONCEPT

1.3.1 DEFINITION

Starting by the concept of governance—both "Good Governance" and "Corporate Governance," The World Bank introduced the "Good Governance" concept for the public sector,[24] advocating that "(...) good governance is an essential complement to sound economic policies and is central to creating and sustaining an environment which fosters strong and equitable development," while the IMF added more elements and vectors to it, arguing that "(...) promoting good governance in all its aspects, including by ensuring the rule of law, improving the efficiency and accountability of the public sector, and tackling corruption, as essential elements of a framework within which economies can prosper."[25]

The World Bank also established that the mandate relating to the corporate governance arena—governance of the private sector—would be part of the FMI (Financial Market Integrity) remit, which is focused on the improvement of corporate governance for emergent and developing countries (e.g., technical assistance, support to mandates and programs), with commitments involving organizations operating under the corporate governance arena, recommending the use of guidelines published by the above mentioned institutions. Teodora de Castro and Duarte Pitta Ferraz advocate that decision-making benefits from the World Bank Group concept of "Good Governance" best practice, as well as that the Fit and Proper standards applicable to the financial system, are an opportunity to be considered by the nonfinancial sector that could similarly benefit from equally demanding standards, creating a culture that ensures the sustainability of organizations.[26]

In order to achieve effective corporate governance, a sound legal, regulatory, and institutional framework is required on which the participants in the market can potentially rely to establish their own private contractual relations. As the structure of corporate governance differs from one jurisdiction to another jurisdiction—unitary board structure in most Anglo-Saxonic countries and dual board structure in Continental Europe—there is no conclusive definition of corporate governance models. Therefore, the definition and principles of corporate governance are formed to mutually embrace and respect all the models, while sharing the fundamental common elements that are applicable to all governance structures across jurisdictions.

However, it could be said that the definition of the concept of corporate governance is fairly aligned in its conceptual cornerstone elements—organizational structures, set of processes and systems, and decision-making process. The focus of the definition may add additional elements, which include for example the access to markets, making informed decisions, how corporate decisions are made, definition of authority and responsibility, growth boosts? and sustainability, investor confidence, capital formation, and allocation, stakeholders' expectations or development of employment opportunities.

Several organizations and institutions have outlined their own definitions of corporate governance. The Cadbury Committee (1992) referenced in Section 1.2.1: "Cadbury Code and Combined Code," defined corporate governance as "the system by which companies are directed and controlled," which eventually became one of the most widely used worldwide definitions. The system can be inferred as the structures and processes.

The BIS Corporate Governance Principles for Banks (2015), referenced in Section 1.2.3: "Global Financial Crisis 2007–2008 and Increased Governance," maintains:

"Corporate governance is a set of relationships between a company's management, its board, its shareholders and other stakeholders which provides the structure through which the objectives of the company are set, and the means of attaining those objectives and monitoring performance. It helps define the way authority and responsibility are allocated and how corporate decisions are made."

International Finance Corporation (IFC),[27] a sister organization of the World Bank, states:

"(…) good corporate governance helps companies operate more efficiently, improve access to capital, mitigate risk, and safeguard against mismanagement. It makes companies more accountable and transparent to investors and gives them the tools to respond to stakeholder concerns. Moreover, corporate governance also contributes to the development and economic growth as good corporate governance practices lead to increased access to funding which ultimately boosts economic growth and provides employment opportunities."

OECD[28] mentions:

"(…) the quality of corporate governance affects the cost for corporations to access capital for growth and the confidence with which those that provide capital—directly or indirectly— can participate and share in their value-creation on fair and equitable terms."

The G20/OECD Principles of Corporate Governance were developed with an understanding that governance policies have a critical role in achieving the broader economic objectives in relation to investor confidence, capital formation, and allocation. Ultimately, governance rules and practices help reduce the gap between the household savings and investment in the real economy, and reassure shareholders and other relevant stakeholders that their rights are well protected and therefore allow the corporations to decrease the cost of capital and to facilitate their access to the capital market.

In a unitary structure, the corporate governance principles are related to all members of the single board composed of both executive and non-executive directors. In a dual board structure, the principles are primarily related to the supervisory board (supervisory function) composed of only independent directors or at least with a majority of independent directors, as non-independent directors like shareholders, family business owners, or other directors often do not qualify as independent, and the executive board (executive function) is the management board composed of executives or executive directors.

Fundamentally, the principles are supposed to provide a robust yet flexible reference for policymakers and market participants to establish their own innovative governance framework and so to remain competitive in the current landscape of disruption and sustainability to meet new demands and grasp new opportunities. As a result, the definition and principles of corporate governance are evolutionary, often altering with the changing scene in order to maintain their role as a leading instrument for policymaking in the area of corporate governance.

For the companies and countries to access financing from a much larger pool of investors (shareholders and bondholders), obtaining the full benefits of the global capital market, and attracting long-term patient and dormant capital, corporate governance arrangements must be demonstrated, must be credible, well understood across borders, and adherent to internationally accepted principles and best practices. Even for corporations that do not rely on foreign investment, a good, credible corporate governance mechanism will invoke the confidence of domestic investors, reduce the cost of capital, demonstrate the integrity of financial markets, induce stable sources of financing, and may eventually drive to create a good investment destination for foreign investors and ultimately attract talent to the organization.

1.3.2 CONCEPT

The concept of corporate governance primarily involves three dimensions—bodies, governance, and management.

Bodies

Corporate governance deals with a variety of bodies for a series of purposes to achieve a corporate's vision and mission. As corporate governance commands the entire conduct of the corporate, it should strive to strike the balanced chord with all involved bodies (i.e., board, management, shareholders, talent pool, suppliers, customers, lenders, government, and other relevant stakeholders, see Figure 1.1).

Figure 1.1: Bodies of corporate governance

Modern corporate governance model advocates the formation of committees from the selected members of the board of directors, such as governance committee, audit committee, remuneration committee, nomination committee, risk committee, strategy committee, or ESG committee in order to achieve the governance Key Performance Indicators (KPIs). For example, *Financial Times* (FT)[29] states, "audit committee provides independent review and oversight of a company's financial reporting processes, internal controls and independent auditors. It provides a forum separate from management in which auditors and other interested parties can candidly discuss concerns." In most jurisdictions, corporate law requires the establishment of an audit committee.

Governance and Management

Separation of ownership and control in publicly listed companies is one of the core fundamentals of modern corporate governance (see Figure 1.2).

Figure 1.2: Structure of corporate governance

BOD   Board of Directors; NED—Non-executive Director

Effective governance is achieved through the proper assembly of qualified and experienced executive and independent non-executive directors, with the board having an appropriate mix of skills, gender diversity, age, nationality, and quotas with the objective of ensuring a board that is globally fit for the tasks and challenges. Robust management is achieved through the collaboration of executive board directors and management team comprising of nonboard senior managers. In a family business, one more major stakeholder comes to the play, namely often family and family members. Therefore, the governance model in a family business exceeds the complexity of a normal governance model in a publicly listed company, as the family adds a complex third element to the framework—the family component. More about family business governance model is discussed in Chapter 5: Family Business Governance.

1.4 STRUCTURE AND DEVELOPMENT

As regions across the world are influenced by their own social, economic, political, and cultural values, different models of governance evolved. Countries and businesses often learn from their own negative corporate and economic disasters or from other countries where different models have evolved. Thus, corporate governance has always been an evolutionary process adjusting to trends and best practices.

There are two main models: the Anglo-Saxon *Shareholder-centric* model and the Continental European *Stakeholder-centric* model. The Anglo-Saxon board structure is also known as monistic board structure and that of Continental is known as dualistic board structure. The combination of both is sometimes known as the mixed board structure. The corporate governance models in four different countries are illustrated in Table 1.1, demonstrating the different requirements and corporate governance best practices:

Table 1.1: Corporate governance models in different countries

US	UK
• Shareholder-centric model • Unitary board: executive and non-executive directors • Board composition: majority non-executive directors; selected based on expertise/knowledge • Board responsibilities: advisory and compliance roles • Audit Committee composition: independent outside directors, including a minimum of one person who qualifies as a financial expert • Requirements: SEC and NYSE (or Nasdaq)	• Shareholder-centric model • Unitary board: executive and non-executive directors • Board composition: at least half + 1 non-executive directors (majority independents) • Board responsibilities: advisory and compliance roles • Audit Committee composition: at least three non-executive directors (majority independent, with an independent chairperson) • Requirements: UK Corporate Governance Code
Germany	**Japan**
• Stakeholder-centric model • Two-tiered board: supervisory and management • Board composition: no managers on supervisory board; one-third or half labor representatives, founding family members, national banks or insurance companies in the supervisory board • Board responsibilities: management and oversight • Audit Committee composition: established within the supervisory board • Requirements: German law	• *Keiretsu* model • Unitary board: executive and non-executive directors • Board composition: few outside directors; non-executive directors often include banks, suppliers or customers representatives • Board responsibilities: management, with strong influence from the banks • Audit Committee: no specific requirements • Requirements: scarce regulation

1.5 THE RELEVANCE OF CORPORATE GOVERNANCE IN RAISING CAPITAL

The importance of companies to operate under well-functioning corporate governance practices has gained precedence in recent decades, following the revelation of several company scandals and outright economic crises that left shareholders and bondholders out of pocket and other stakeholders negatively affected. Specific markets can have investors perceive corporate governance standards as weak and thus not relevant when considering investment strategies. A company with good corporate governance standards in place signals a positive sign for investors. Credit rating agencies take governance metrics as an important criterion when rating the corporate. Corporates with a high credit rating can raise the capital in global financial markets at a low cost (further discussed in Section 19.2: "Credit Rating Agency"). Investors can pay a higher price for the shares or invest in lower yield corporate bonds of companies with sound governance that act in compliance with corporate governance guidelines and best practices when setting up the governance framework, organizing the work of the board of directors and its committees ensuring a prominent level of disclosure, while simultaneously respecting the shareholders', investors', and stakeholders' rights.

Corporate governance also tries to steer a company into sustainable development practices. Institutional investors (entities that pool money to purchase securities, corporate bonds, real estate, and other investment assets) and minority shareholders are more often deciding their vote in shareholders' meetings guided by a due diligence process and the resulting recommendations of specialized agencies (further discussed in Chapter 20: Proxy Voting Services). The latter is constantly analyzing the quality of the corporate governance of the company in which it owns a stake. Over time, investors are increasingly creating portfolios based on criteria such as sustainable development indexes and nonfinancial factors such as ESG (Environment, Social, and Governance) criteria, named ESG Ratings. Other investors that are involved in project financing, mainly international and multilateral financial institutions, are also growingly concerned about robust corporate governance practices, including them as a relevant item of the decision-making process. As such, corporate governance standards and requirements tend to be included in the investment contract. In other words, the recipient of the cash must comply with the agreed corporate governance standards with penalties to be applied in case of noncompliance. The corporate governance model that meets the requirements of international investors is based on several basic principles.

In the later chapters, the following concepts are discussed and explained:

- The rights and interests of the shareholders, investors and stakeholders.
- Separation of powers and responsibilities among management units.
- Efficient board including the structure of the board of directors, operating committees, absence of conflict of interest.
    - o Usually, there is no one-size-fits-all model. In other words, the organization has to understand what the best ratio of executive directors to non-executive directors for its business (expertise vs independence) is, how directors are nominated, appointed and remunerated, along with several other tactical issues.
- A well-established system of management accounting and reporting.
- Formalized and transparent policy and process of electing directors and board members.
- Formalized and transparent policy and process of compensation for directors and company management.
- Financial and operational information transparency for shareholders and other stakeholders, including nonfinancial information about corporate social responsibility, ESG.
- Transparent dividend policy.
- Efficient internal control framework and internal audit systems.
- Sustainability measures.

1.5.1 COST OF IMPLEMENTING GOOD GOVERNANCE

The implementation of corporate governance standards requires investment. Some of the costs include:

- Extensive financial disclosures require a great deal of time and money to prepare, and independent audits.
- Independent board of directors may interfere with management's decision-making authority.
- Internal compliance and monitoring mechanisms have the company incur start-up costs, such as legal and consulting fees.
- Reallocation of staff, as they may focus on shifting the business toward the compliance code and its details instead of the vision of business.

However, these costs are controllable if corporates' boards and directors follow and maintain the best practices of corporate governance principles as they are relevant to ensure a robust governance framework, ensuring effective control functions—risk management, compliance, and internal audit—and provide assurance to investors and other stakeholders about the robustness of their governance practices. The benefits of robust governance significantly outweigh the cost—attracting talent and capital, reducing the cost of capital, assuring robust internal controls, improving strategic planning and decision-making, among others. The textbook attempts to adequately cover the benefits of good governance.[30]

1.5.2 SOVEREIGN WEALTH FUNDS

A Sovereign Wealth Fund (SWF) is a state-owned investment fund investing in real and financial assets such as stocks, bonds, real estate, precious metals, or in alternative investments such as private equity fund or hedge funds. Sovereign wealth funds invest globally and are set aside for investment purposes to benefit the country's economy and citizens.[31] The type of investment criteria varies from country to country. The practices of corporate governance also have a strong impact on investment decisions by SWFs.

SWFs often have the following or similar structure:

- Governing bodies composed externally by the members of the parliament and ministry of finance, auditor general, and external audit, and internally by an executive board, CEO, and managers.
- Supervisory bodies.
- Internal audit, risk management, and compliance units.

In many situations,

- The owner of the SWF is typically a central government; in some cases, the national parliament that approves the laws regulates the SWF.
- The executive board is the governing body that sets internal rules and regulates within the mandate and legal constraints; it also appoints the CEO.
- Managers can be external or internal, and they operate within risk limits set by the CEO and respective staff, under the limits decided by the supervisory body.
- Investment policy is decided at the highest level.
- Often, SWFs limit the sectors they can invest in, excluding some sectors (e.g., defense or defense related industries, tobacco, environment, fossil fuels) or the minimum investment grade (e.g., credit rating, ESG Rating) of the investing target.
- Jurisdictions involved in aggressive tax planning, tax optimization, money laundering, poor labor practices, among others, are also usually excluded, as well as institutions involved in poor corporate governance practices.

- The auditor general is often appointed by the parliament, and it makes sure the formal owner is operating within the already defined laws and regulations.
- The ministry of finance appoints the independent external auditor and monitors the behavior of the SWF and if it operates within the law, rules and regulations, and supervisory board decisions.
- The internal auditor, risk management, and compliance unit control the activity of the SWF, and they are usually appointed by the executive board and the CEO, respectively.

Because SWFs are perceived as long-term investors and are under scrutiny (both political and regulatory), they are less likely to sell their position. This turns SWFs' investment into captive capital. Consequently, protecting long-term returns through oversight of corporate governance is a priority for many SWFs. Nevertheless, SWFs can exert influence simply through their voting rights due to big equity investment, though they are not believed to act like a hawkish activist investor.

Sovereign credit rating refers to the credit rating awarded to a sovereign state that is considered independent and administers its own government and takes into consideration notably the rigor of the sovereign fiscal policy (further discussed in Section 19.4: "Sovereign Credit Rating"). The rating notations are similar to corporate credit ratings. As governments in advanced and emerging markets borrow money by issuing *government bonds*, a good sovereign credit rating is a condition of relative assurance for individual and institutional investors (including SWFs) to invest in the sovereign governments' bonds. Usually, high sovereign credit rating brings a low cost of financing. Some of the prominent SWFs are discussed in the next section. The amount of the assets indicated as of mid-2020 are taken from Sovereign Wealth Fund Institute (SWFI) website.[32]

1.5.3 THE BIGGEST SOVEREIGN WEALTH FUNDS

Norway

The Government Pension Fund (GPF) is made up of two separate investments funds with different mandates, one focusing on the worldwide investments (Global), and the other focusing solely on the country (Norway).[33] GPF Global is a SWF derived mainly from Norway's oil wealth whereas the GPF Norway was associated with the country's social security systems but later transformed into a SWF that invests solely on national companies. Norges Bank Investment Management, a part of the Norwegian Central Bank, manages the Global SWF. The GPF Global is valued more than one trillion dollars as of mid-2020 and is considered the biggest fund in the world under management. GPF Global invests in a wide array of asset classes. GPF Domestic is rather small in comparison and is limited to investment allocation to domestic firms. Though these investments have been restricted by an ethical council that has the power to remove firms engaged in malpractices since 2009, such as excluding producers of nuclear weapons (and defense industry in general), tobacco, and others from its portfolio. Any violation of human rights immediately puts the company in the excluded list. Due to its focus as an engaged and responsible shareholder, the quality of corporate governance in the target's top management is a major factor when investing.

China

The China Investment Corporation (CIC) is a SWF from China valued around one trillion dollars as of mid-2020. The fund is responsible for managing part of China's foreign exchange reserves. It was established in 2007 by special bonds (specifically long-term treasury bonds) issued by the Chinese Ministry of Finance. This SWF primarily focuses on equity, income, and alternative investment strategies such as hedge funds. CIC is a vehicle for investing the huge trade surplus of China and for receiving regular inflows of capital. China has been a large investor in American Treasuries for many years with the objective of earning a higher return on its foreign investments. Nevertheless, the current trade tariffs and globalization quarrel between China and USA may change the paradigm and raises concerns, namely in the trade and geopolitical arenas.

United Arab Emirates: Abu Dhabi

Abu Dhabi relies on oil exports for building wealth and SWF, namely, Abu Dhabi Investment Authority (ADIA). To shield the economy from oil-related risk, it tends to invest in diversified assets. The fund is valued around 580 billion dollars as of mid-2020. ADIA invests in international markets, namely equities (public and private), fixed income, treasury, infrastructure, real estate, and alternatives such as hedge funds and commodity trading advisers. ADIA does not tend to seek active management of the companies it invests in. Even though ADIA does not disclose what specific corporate governance standards they desire, it is generally understood that their risk management analysis considers operational due diligence and compliance risk.

Some other examples of the biggest SWFs as of mid-2020 are mentioned below, in alphabetical order:

- China—SAFE Investment Company
- China—National Council for Social Security Fund
- Dubai, UAE—Investment Corporation of Dubai
- Hong Kong—Hong Kong Monetary Authority Investment Portfolio
- Kuwait—Kuwait Investment Authority
- Qatar—Qatar Investment Authority
- Saudi Arabia—Public Investment Fund
- Singapore—GIC Private Limited
- Singapore—Temasek Holdings

Topics of the Chapter

The following topics that impact a board's agenda and should be monitored by the board of directors or the supervisory board, has been discussed within this chapter:

- Corporate governance is broadly defined as "the system by which companies are directed and controlled."
- The brief history of modern corporate governance, including:
  i. The US Wall Street Crash (1929) and the following Great Depression (1929–1939)
  ii. Publication of several seminal works regarding the concepts of corporate governance (1930s–1970s)
  iii. Publication of the first proper discretionary code of corporate governance—the Cadbury Code (1992)
     o Further revised into Adjusted Cadbury Code/ Combined Code (2003)
  iv. The burst of the *Dot-Com Bubble* (2000)
     o Subsequent passage of Sarbanes–Oxley Act (2002)
  v. Global Financial Crisis (2007–2008)
     o Increased corporate governance on a global scale
- Modern corporate governance model advocates the formation of committees from the selected members of the board of directors.
- Separation of ownership and control in publicly listed companies is one of the core fundamentals of modern corporate governance.
- Two main models of governance:
  i. Anglo-Saxon Shareholder-centric model (unitary board, monist)
  ii. Continental European Stakeholder-centric model (dual board, two-tiered board, dualist)

Chapter 2

Corporate Governance Theories

There are several prevalent theories regarding corporate governance. Among them, the Agency Theory is one of the most notable, rooting from Anglo-Saxon countries where corporates have dispersed ownership. Other suggested theories include Stewardship Theory, Stakeholder Theory, and Political Theory.

This chapter discusses agency theory in detail while other theories are briefly presented.

2.1 THE AGENCY THEORY

The very core and fundamental principle of the agency theory stems from the disciplines of political science and economics. In the introductory chapter, Modern Corporate Governance History, the referred paper "Theory of the Firm: Managerial Behavior, Agency Costs and Ownership Structure" (1976) described the concept of agency theory. In general, agency theory is the philosophy employed to understand the relationship between the agents and principals in the business.

In firms, there are three generic agency problems:

1. *Conflict between the firm's owners and hired managers.* The owners/shareholders are the principals, and the managers are the agents. The main challenge is to ensure the managers are

acting in the owners' interests rather than pursuing their own personal interests.

2. *Conflict between the majority or controlling owner/shareholder and the minority or noncontrolling owner/shareholder.* In this case, the minority shareholders are considered as the principal, and the majority ones are considered as the agent. The problem here is to ensure the minority are not expropriated by the majority. However, if the minority enjoy veto rights in relation to particular decisions affecting the whole class of owners, it can give rise to a new species of agency problem.

3. *Conflict between the firm's owners and the third parties with whom it has contracts, such as employees, creditors, suppliers, manufacturers, and customers.* Here, the firm is the agent, and the third parties are the principal. The problem lies in assuming that the firm does not behave opportunistically toward other principals, such as by expropriating creditors and suppliers, exploiting employees, and misleading customers.

In the corporate world, the three generic agency problems discussed above may fall into two categories, but not limited to, (i) transfer of corporate resources to the insider, including taking corporate property, self-dealing (insider), asset stripping, executive compensation, and other mixed motives; and (ii) diluting outsiders' share in the firm, namely going private and dilution. Most of the primitive companies go through multiple rounds of private financing and this often results in a "down round," which entails a disappointing price per share.

Self-dealing may take several forms, but it generally involves an individual benefiting, or attempting to benefit, from a transaction that is being executed on behalf of another party, and it may involve misappropriation or usurpation of corporate assets or opportunities, such as asset sale or deceptive transfer pricing within the different divisions of same corporate. The term *tunneling* is used very often.

Tunneling is considered financial fraud, and it involves the transfer of assets and profits out of corporates for the benefit of those who control them, such as large shareholders and managers. In other words, selling assets at lower valuation to the second company owned by the same shareholders and managers. The key feature of tunneling is that the stakeholders, who engage in the activity, usually act in accordance with the relevant legal procedures for personal gains. Tunneling may also involve asset stripping, that is, justifying that selling off the corporate's assets is to improve returns for equity investors, but the real motive may be different.[34] As public firms' shareholders have the right to vote on the remuneration of executives, also known as *Say on Pay*, it may become less important if directors perform the fiduciary duties in the best interests of the firm. However, history has shown that this is not always the case, and shareholders have voted to contain excessive executive compensation. The topic of executive compensation is further discussed in Section 17.4.1: "Designing Executive Compensation."

The process of tunneling may also involve diluting the outsider's share in the firm. A prominent example of tunneling through private transactions is the case of *Velcro Industries*, the producer of the famous touch fastener. Two-thirds of the shares of Velcro Industries were controlled by the Cripps family at the time. *The New York Times* reported that the company reduced dividends, delisted itself from the Montreal Stock Exchange, and took other measures that essentially reduced stock price.[35] Then, it eventually made an attempt to make the company private on the cheap through a buyback. Minority shareholders, being felt cheated, sued in New York court, and the judge ruled that the US was the proper jurisdiction for prosecuting Velcro.[36] The Cripps then decided to call off their offer rather than go under the light of the US law. Subsequently, the company resumed its dividend payments.

In another situation, the collusion of share dilution can take place when the CEO and the controlling shareholder of the holding company is the same. As the holding companies tend to have many subsidiaries, one subsidiary may increase the number of shares to dilute the outsider's share while the other subsidiary may benefit from an excessively high discount to repurchase the share. As a result, an insider can increase his share of the firm without transferring any assets.

2.1.1 THE CASE OF PRINCIPAL-AGENT PROBLEM IN THE CORPORATE

In an ideal situation, the agent is expected to work in the best interests of the principal without any regard for self-interest. As discussed above, that it is not always the case, which may lead to the problem widely known in literature as *principal-agent problem* (see Figure 2.1).

Figure 2.1: Principal-agent problems in the corporate

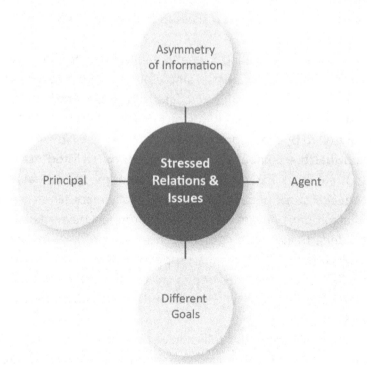

Although the agents are the main decision makers in the organizations, they bear little to no financial risk in comparison to the principal (shareholders). This is because the shareholders are the primary investors. Therefore, the uneven distribution of financial risk may lead to a different level of risk tolerance and risk culture between the agent and the principal. Such anomalies may constitute a precarious business situation when both agent and principal have diverging goals and/or objectives. In another situation, the agent may need to establish a contractual relationship with third parties to render goods or services to operate the business of which the principal may not always be aware. This could potentially induce the situation known as *asymmetry of information*. Other situations often emerge in processes of mergers and acquisitions or restructuring, with potential for the agent to manipulate in favor of self-interests if the conditions of the operation will not produce benefits, either financial or maintaining/securing a relevant position in the new company.

Misstatement of financial statements, accounting policies applied with aggressive interpretations of accounting principles, as well as lack of transparency in annual reports are tools used to introduce asymmetry of data and information by agents in relation to principals. *Enron*, once ranked as one of the biggest and most innovative companies in the US, collapsed and filed for bankruptcy in 2001 as their executives were involved in several malpractices, including misstatement of financial statements, such as publishing inflated earnings and complex non-transparent financial statements, which were confusing for both shareholders and analysts,[37] including not consolidating large amounts of debt used notably in acquisitions, parked in opaque offshore centers, interestingly enough with the support of large investment banks. Other similar situations were brought to light in WorldCom in the US and Parmalat in Italy that also involved misstatement of financial statements and hiding debt in offshores. The German-based WireCard fintech—with a market cap larger than Deutsche Bank—forged fraudulently the financial statements, to cheat investors in raising capital, with shareholders and bondholders and other stakeholders taking the fintech into bankruptcy.[38]

2.1.2 MECHANISM TO ALIGN STAKEHOLDERS' INTERESTS

The mechanism to align the interests of the agent with those of principal should be fostered unequivocally upfront, that is, before the agent is hired, as well as reviewed periodically and adjusted if required. This process should encompass a formal process, and therefore the organization should incorporate legal strategies and formalism adequate to the agreement. The legal strategies can be broken down into two components: regulatory strategies and governance strategies. Below, the strategies are detailed from the paper *Agency Problems, Legal Strategies, and Enforcement* jointly authored by John Armour, Henry Hansmann, and Reinier Kraakman.[39]

Regulatory strategies are prescriptive, that is, they dictate substantive terms that govern the content of the principal-agent relationship, tending to constrain the agent's behavior directly. This includes compliance with the prevalent regulations framed by lawmakers as enforced rules and setting the terms of entry and exit with a legal mandate. *Governance strategies* seek to facilitate the principals' control over their agent's behavior. This textbook primarily deals with governance strategies in the corporate. Three aspects are very important in governance strategies:

1. Selection and Removal: The appointment rights and the power to select or remove directors and relevant managers (e.g., those holding responsibilities for the control functions of risk management, compliance and internal audit) are key strategies for controlling the firm and are at the very core of corporate governance.
2. Initiation and Ratification: Decision rights, granting principals the power to initiate or ratify management decisions, and

expanding the power of principals to intervene in the firm's management.

3. Trusteeship and Reward: These are incentives given to agents rather than expanding the powers of principals.

The first incentive strategy, *reward strategy*, is to reward the agents for successfully advancing the interests of their principals. There are two types of reward strategy—sharing rule and pay for performance. The *sharing rule* motivates loyalty by tying the agent's monetary returns directly to those of the principal. For example, the minority shareholders benefit from the equal treatment norm that strictly requires a pro rata distribution of dividends and, consequently, controlling shareholders (here deemed as agents) have an incentive to maximize the returns of the firm's minority shareholders (here deemed as principals) to the extent that corporate returns are paid out as dividends. *Pay for performance*, though less popular in the corporate law, is where an agent (here deemed as managers) is paid for successfully advancing the interests of the principal (here deemed as shareholders) without sharing their returns. Some jurisdictions may be more open to pay for performance than others while some others continue to limit them. For example, the law in the US has embraced incentive compensation vehicles such as stock option plans.

The second incentive strategy, the *trusteeship strategy*, seeks to remove the conflict of interest wherein the agent may not obtain personal gain from disserving its principal. In the absence of high-powered monetary incentives to behave opportunistically, this strategy assumes that agents will respond to the low-powered incentives of conscience, pride, and reputation and would thus be more likely to function in the interests of their principals. The concept of *independent director* is an example of a trusteeship strategy. It is observed that independent directors will not personally profit from actions that disproportionately benefit the firm's managers or controlling shareholders and are therefore guided strongly by conscience and reputation in decision-making. Another example of trusteeship strategy is a reliance on *auditors* to approve financial statements, as auditors are primarily motivated by the reputational concerns.

In correspondence with the governance strategies, the solutions for implementing incentives and monitoring mechanism are discussed below, both inside and outside the corporate (see Figure 2.2).

Figure 2.2: Incentives and monitoring in the principal-agent conflict

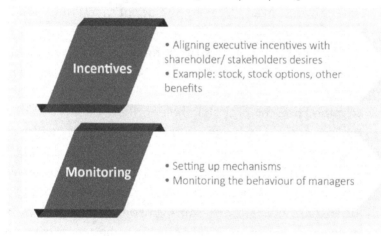

Within the corporate, independent-minded board of directors are highly accountable to implement the governance code. In many jurisdictions, the board has the power to hire and fire the top management and develop a mechanism to monitor the behavior of the managers; other jurisdictions require a decision of the shareholders' meeting, which makes the process usually longer and more complex, as it may require the call of an extraordinary shareholders' meeting for that end and alignment of positions among shareholders. Therefore, appropriate corporate code, policies, and procedures should be developed in correspondence with any prevalent standards. Other details such as performance measurement and profit-sharing should depend on the performance of the firm (Figure 2.3). Incentives such as stock,

stock options, and other benefits should be properly aligned with the shareholders' interests.

Figure 2.3: Issues to consider within the company and outside the company in agency conflict

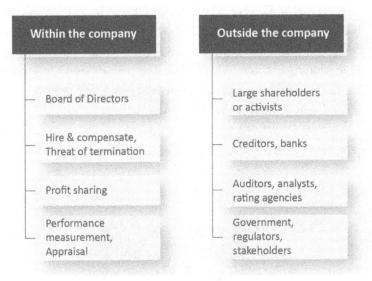

Outside the corporate, a proper mechanism should be developed to cooperate and communicate with large shareholders, activists, creditors, employees' representatives in some jurisdictions, and any other important external stakeholders. Analysis from credit rating agencies, proxy agencies (read further in Chapter 19: Overview of Credit Ratings), and independent external audit enhances the transparency of the firm. Communication with regulators and governmental authorities must be coherent.

The development of the process of *Governance strategies* requires an active involvement of the committee of remunerations and nominations, as well as the involvement of the chairperson and/ or the shareholders, depending if this committee (or committees) is appointed directly by the shareholders' meeting or emerges from the board/supervisory board. The corporate law of different jurisdictions influences this process, although philosophically, the idea is to achieve the objectives that regulate in a clear, transparent, and equitable the principal-agent's relations.

2.1.3 MONITORING THE STAKEHOLDERS' INTERESTS IN CORPORATE GOVERNANCE

Monitoring the stakeholders' interests is fundamentally influenced by the four market forces in market-based economy,[40] depicted in Figure 2.4. The corporate board and senior management are required to align accordingly with such forces.

Figure 2.4: Four forces for monitoring stakeholders' interests

The force, including markets for corporate control, is meant to achieve a greater shareholder orientation among corporate

management. There exists a relation between the performance of managers and share price. Shareholders often respond to poor managerial performance by exiting, which may impact the share price negatively. As a result, outsiders have an incentive to buy shares at lower price, restructure the board, and therefore, accumulate the control rights.

Another force, stock market and price evolution, may potentially value the corporation below their real and fair value. It is argued that the takeovers-raiders can be motivated by the profit seeking behavior of shareholders—notably activist investors—which does not constitute long-termism and sustainability. To defend from takeover threats, managers may react negatively by implementing costly defensive strategies, such as executives' golden parachutes or poison pills and, therefore, seeking legal protection from a takeover or a raider to protect the agent's self-serving interests. An example can be influencing the share price at the expense of long-term projects and investments.

Labor markets are one of the major components of the economy, inherently linked to markets for capital, goods, services, and talent. At general shareholders' meetings, investors—notably shareholders—have a *say on pay* of executives and may raise reservations regarding their qualifications or reputation, that is the fit and proper profile of individuals and the board as a whole. Proxy agencies often facilitate on such arrangements, as they provide due diligence services regarding proposals to the shareholders' meetings about a wide range of issues, namely related to the business model, remuneration of executives, business development, among others. Different jurisdictions, regions, or political unions (e.g., European Union) have developed guidelines or regulations regarding the selection of executives and remuneration policies and packages.

A fourth force relates to product and markets' competition and regulation, often considered a relevant aspect of corporate governance. This issue is related to the business model—stream of revenues and a cost structure—and the way executive directors monitor and develop it but also the role played by the non-executive directors in supervising that the strategic plan is based on the business model and that executive directors respect the board decision on both issues that are intimately interconnected. This should take into consideration the product development and the markets targeted by the organization as well as the changes or new regulation about the organization products and developments of direct competitors in the market but also in the international arena as well as from other industries that may develop products impacting their business model. There are numerous examples of products being launched outside direct competitors (iPhone's impact in manufacturers of cameras, digitalization in the photography industry) or demanding regulation with which a company is not prepared to deal with. Firms that are not competitive and have not implemented or followed corporate governance standards or regulations are susceptible to be replaced by the competitors or other players or even be pushed out of the market by regulators and supervisory bodies (e.g., tobacco industry, asbestos, financial institutions). To some degree, product and markets' competition and regulation are believed to reduce the scope for managerial inefficiency and opportunism, imposing on agents a permanent attention and awareness on these issues. The boards must play a major role in this.

2.1.4 CRITICISM OF THE AGENCY THEORY

Unquestionably, agency theory has been the core rationale for establishing management and governance practices in the domain of corporate governance. However, it has raised criticisms too. One critic is that the agency theory does not discuss the ethical standards that directors and managers should observe when performing their roles and responsibilities in order to maximize the shareholder's value. Critics also argue that a company's health should be the primary concern for the directors and managers who run the company and not the shareholder's health, because it may make companies less vulnerable to, namely, activist investors, as managers should actively focus on the long-term propositions. Another criticism is that the agency theory does not make shareholders accountable or responsible, even though they are considered the owners of the company. The agency theory may, therefore, be seen the other way around, that is, the principal not awarding the agents the fair share of their performance or profile. Essentially, each monetary unit paid to the agent is one less monetary unit in profits and, eventually, dividends. This may emerge namely at moments of a reputational crisis, which may impact the reputational profile requirements of a manager to solve reputational issues. There are qualitative aspects that should also be taken into consideration when determining the remuneration.

As the companies may have several types of shareholders—large with or without influence, minority, institutional investors, sleeping partners, yield—with varying intentions and investment objectives, the shareholders may not be treated as a "single owner" of the corporate. And, at odds with the existing corporate law in most jurisdictions, shareholders do not have the full rights of being corporate owners, such as not having access to the corporate premises or use of corporate assets. Investors are currently also focusing on topics emerging from social value, long-term views, as well as in environment, social, and governance, instead of a sole focus on a shareholder-centered model, usually a characteristic of the Anglo-Saxon countries.[41] The debate about constructive opinion and criticism is very open, and, depending on the jurisdiction, corporates are free to adjust the fundamentals of agency theory to meet their own standards.

In 2019 Business Roundtable, a group of chief executives of around 200 major US corporations, issued a statement with a new definition of the purpose of the corporation, effectively proposing to abandon the historical shareholder-first ideology. They issued a statement committing to all relevant stakeholders that investing in employees, delivering value to customers, dealing ethically with suppliers and supporting outside communities, sustainability practices, and long-termism are now at the forefront of American business goals.[42]

There are views arguing that this move from US CEOs goes toward the corporate governance philosophy defined as the stakeholders-centric model that is used in Continental Europe. However, another line of thought argues that the purpose of companies should be set by their owners, not directors or managers. This view questions how the chief executive would know what the society and stakeholders want—vision and strategy—from their companies without assimilating the ordinary people's voice. This may further cause the small group of executives to accumulate immense power to set goals for the other stakeholders and society that could have far-reaching consequences beyond the company. Sustainability issues, notably climate change—ESG—are real, constituting a high priority trend, but ultimately, the purpose of companies may be better defined by incorporating owners' and relevant stakeholders' views in the decision-making process.

2.2 THE STEWARDSHIP THEORY

Steward refers to someone who is responsible to take care of something. Thus, in this theory, it is believed that company executives and managers are stewards who work on the best interests of the shareholders in order to maximize their wealth by increasing firm's performance. The stewardship theory is built on the notion of trust and shared values, this being different from agency theory. The agency theory puts shareholders' concern at the center of the discussion, while the stewardship theory focuses on the role of top management acting as stewards and eventually integrating stakeholders' (including shareholders') goals as part of the organization. The stewardship theory advocates for an autonomous position of executives and managers, and the stewards are satisfied and motivated when organizational success is achieved, which eventually will make profits for the shareholders. The theory seems to offer a more positive perspective on the relationships between principals and agents.

The stewardship theory advocates the unification the role of the CEO and the chair. The theory argues that unification reduces the agency costs and fosters a greater role as stewards in the organization. The critics of stewardship theory argue that executives and managers are in fact managing their own careers in order to be seen as effective stewards of their firm, and managers thus aim to return profitability to investors to foster a good reputation so that they can have easy access to finance or capital again.

However, the Chair-CEO position held by the same individual has been questioned, notably in the US, where this practice was predominant a decade ago. The trend to separate the positions is based on the rationale that a standalone chair can act as a counterweight to a standalone CEO, as well as regulators and supervisors—notably in the financial system—demanding the separation of the positions, a trend that the US is following,[43] as from around 85 percent a decade ago, the number of corporates with this model has reduced to approximately 40 percent.

This change aligns US organizations with their European peers, also because one of the non-executive directors' responsibilities as board members is to supervise and monitor the executive directors—executive committee.

The keiretsu model in Japan is perhaps one of the best examples of stewardship theory, as the Japanese model is built on trust values. Apparently, observers have noted that the normal workers in Japan tend to take the work ownership seriously as a steward and execute them very effectively, showing loyalty to both the organization and the stakeholders. Keiretsu model is further discussed in Chapter 3: Models of Corporate Governance.

2.3 THE STAKEHOLDER THEORY

A stakeholder is a group or individual that has an interest in a firm and who can affect or is affected by the achievement of the organizational objectives. The examples of stakeholders include investors, shareholders, bondholders, employees, customers, suppliers, among others. In Continental Europe, the notion of the stakeholder theory is particularly strong, and stakeholders may further include unions, community, government, or trade associations that are usually represented in the board/supervisory board. The corporate governance model in Continental Europe is discussed in Chapter 3: Models of Corporate Governance. This theory is built on the network on relationships among stakeholders like employees, suppliers, and shareholders, unlike the owner-manager relationship in agency theory. Nevertheless, critics argue that the network of relationships with many stakeholders can affect the decision-making process, as well as capturing the interests of all stakeholders can be difficult to achieve and handle efficiently.

2.4 THE POLITICAL THEORY

In political theory, the government is the central component. Political theory is an unapologetically mongrel subdiscipline, with no dominant methodology or approach. The allocation of corporate power, privileges, and profits among owners, managers, and other participating stakeholders are determined through the government's favor. China and Russia are obvious examples, where state-owned big enterprises are common. On the contrary, countries with strong democratic socialism or even social democracies (e.g., France, Portugal, Spain), where any unexpected government reform or measures may possibly be met with strikes or blockades by the labor unions. The corporate governance models in Continental Europe, China, and Russia are discussed in Chapter 3: Models of Corporate Governance. Critics argue that the entry of politics in corporate governance may disqualify independence status and exert immense influence and that other stakeholders' interests may not be adequately assured.

Topics of the Chapter

The following has been discussed in this chapter:

- The prevalent theories regarding corporate governance include:

     i.   Agency Theory
     ii.   Stewardship Theory
     iii.   Stakeholder Theory
     iv.   Political Theory

- The agent is expected to work in the best interests of the principal without any regard for self-interest. Failure to do so leads to *principal-agent problem.*
- Common problems in an agency occur due to conflicts between:
  i. Owners and manager
  ii. Controlling owner/shareholder and non-controlling owner/shareholder
  iii. Owners and third parties such as employees, creditors, suppliers, manufacturers, and customers
- The development of the process of governance strategies requires an active involvement of the committee of remunerations and/or nominations, as well as the involvement of the chairperson and/or the shareholders and other relevant stakeholders.
- Governance strategies seek to facilitate the principals' control over their agent's behavior through:
  i. Selection and Removal
  ii. Initiation and Ratification
  iii. Trusteeship and Reward
- Specific models of corporate governance mentioned in this chapter are further discussed in Chapter 3: Models of Corporate Governance.

Chapter 3

Models of Corporate Governance

Corporate governance models across the world are influenced by their own social, economic, political, and cultural values, as well as framed by specific legal frameworks. However, principles evolve and change with time and technological advances and developments, and countries often learn from each other's models, especially from exceptional negative events. Historical evidence of corporate disasters in different countries helps understand gaps in the accounting principles and reporting, regulatory environment, risk culture, conflicts of interest, or even moral fabric of corporate governance (Figure 3.1).

This chapter discusses and summarizes the main models of corporate governance observed in different parts of the world, discusses in detail the two commonly employed models—*unitary board* and *dual board*—and elaborates on the best practices of corporate governance.

Figure 3.1: Functioning of corporate governance models

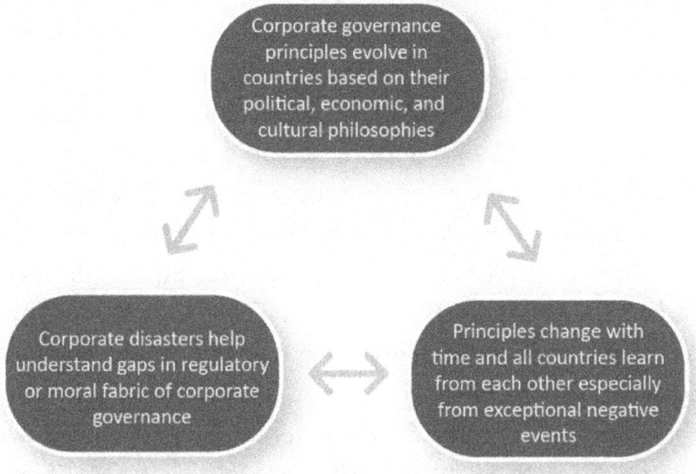

3.1 USA, UNITED KINGDOM, AUSTRALIA, HONG KONG

The corporate governance model employed in countries such as USA, United Kingdom, Australia, Hong Kong is also known as the *Anglo-Saxon* model. The model is very *market-centered*—capital markets—and *shareholder-centric*. Essentially, capitalism is at the heart of Anglo-Saxon management philosophy. Its priority concentrates on value creation and increasing the wealth of shareholders. As a consequence, market forces play a crucial role in the Anglo-Saxon model. Nonetheless, the trend commitment to all relevant stakeholders is increasingly gaining importance. The best practices of governing corporates are either defined by a legal mandate or a discretionary code, such as the Sarbanes–Oxley Act in the USA or Corporate Governance Code in the United Kingdom. The publicly listed companies in the USA must comply with rules and regulations of the Securities Exchange Commission (SEC) and the New

York Stock Exchange (NYSE) or Nasdaq. As the UK Governance Code advocated the concept of *comply or explain* (discussed in Section 1.2.1: "Cadbury Code and Combined Code"), London Stock Exchange requires all publicly listed companies to demonstrate their adherence to the code through comply or explain regulation, should they wish to list in the exchange (see Table 3.1). On top of these, regulators and supervisors in Europe like the European Central Bank (ECB), European Banking Authority (EBA), European Insurance and Occupational Pensions Authority (EIOPA), European Securities and Markets Authority (ESMA), and NCA—National Competent Authorities are particularly demanding notably on the financial system, regarding prudential and conduct regulation. Other regulatory bodies like ESA—European Space Agency or commercial aviation agencies are very active in their fields of industry. The EMA (European Medicines Agency) is in charge of the evaluation and supervision of medicinal products in European Union.

Table 3.1: Corporate governance models in the US and the UK[44]

US	UK
• Shareholder-centric model • Unitary board: executive and non-executive directors together • Board composition: majority non-executive directors, selected based on expertise/knowledge • Board responsibilities: advisory and compliance roles • Audit Committee composition: independent outside directors, including a minimum of one person who qualifies as a financial expert • Compliance Requirements: SEC and NYSE (or Nasdaq)	• Shareholder-centric model • Unitary board: executive and non-executive directors together • Board composition: at least half non-executive directors • Board responsibilities: advisory and compliance roles • Audit Committee composition: at least 3 non-executive directors (2 for companies below FTSE 350 index), at least one member having recent and relevant financial experience • Compliance Requirements: UK Corporate Governance Code (comply or explain)

The Anglo-Saxon comprises a *unitary board of directors* with a mix of executive and non-executive or independent directors in the same board. The board of directors is responsible for appointing the CEO, as well as forming the different governance board committees to fulfill their advisory and compliance roles. The board of directors is also obliged to prudently evaluate the corporate strategy, operational execution (tactics and operational), capital structure, and financial statements and financial reporting. As the model is overly sensitive to capital markets, financial health of the corporate—including the generation of cash-flows to keep the company sustainability—is the prime concern of shareholders and specifically the board of directors. Similarly, compliance with applicable laws (e.g., embargos, sanctions, corporate law), tax legislation, foreign direct investment legislation, controls over foreign exchange transactions, or the establishment of special purpose vehicles (SPV) in jurisdictions that may create reputational issues and regulations must be frequently monitored by the board, as they may affect reputation. New trends in corporate governance about diversity, pay gap, whistleblowing, ESG or potential conflicts of interest are also topics increasingly being regulated and are target of legislation and guidelines.

3.2 CONTINENTAL EUROPE

In Continental Europe, the *stakeholder-centric model* has flourished overtime (Table 3.2). The model is very *bank centered*. Usually, banks, investment funds, insurance companies, family stakes, and conglomerates hold major financial stakes in corporates. Therefore, it is common for firms to have either a dominant shareholder (banks, insurance companies, state-owned companies) or a few dominant shareholders (banks, family stakes, conglomerates), although they may be listed companies.

Table 3.2: Corporate governance model in the Continental Europe

Continental Europe

• Stakeholder-centric model
• Two-tiered board: Supervisory Board and Executive Board
• Board composition:
  • The Supervisory Board includes non-executive directors, that may include shareholders, labor representatives, founding family members, banks, insurance companies, or other relevant stakeholders in the supervisory board
  • The Executive Board includes the executive directors
• Boards responsibilities:
  • Supervisory Board: Governance, strategy and supervision/oversight
  • Executive Board: Strategy development, Tactics and supervision of Operational
• Audit Committee composition: established from within the supervisory board
• Compliance requirements: Country-specific law of Germany, France, and other EU countries

Corporates in Continental Europe tend to have a two-tiered board structure—*management* and *supervisory*. Corporate law differs among countries, some allowing both the unitary and the dualist models or only one of them, which often is the unitary model. Usually, the option for the dualist model is followed by companies with a higher concentration of ownership like family companies, state-owned companies, or other having shareholder concentrations. While the primary responsibility of the management board is to manage and run the corporate, the responsibility of the supervisory board is to supervise, control, and monitor the management board, including governance, strategy and sustainability of the business model. There are no managers on the supervisory board or in the committees of the board, although a committee can hire advisors to assist in a specific topic or challenge; an advisor should not be a permanent member of a committee. The shareholders' meeting elects the supervisory board and executive management board, although there are corporate law models that allow the nomination of the executive board by

the supervisory board. The latter model clearly grants more powers to the supervisory board, as the executive management board
or an executive director can be dismissed without the need to call a
shareholders' meeting. Essentially, the supervisory power in the latter
model is clearly stronger.

The influence of government, national interests (*nationalism*
often emerges in cross-border operations), and job preservation are
strong in the continental model. Dominant shareholders have both
the incentive and the power to supervise, monitor, and discipline
executive management. Nonetheless, there is also a risk that highly
concentrated ownership may create a new agency problem, as the
interests of controlling shareholders and minority shareholders may
not always be aligned. It is paramount that the management body
with the supervisory role—supervisory board—notably the independent non-executive directors, ensure that minority shareholders'
interests are protected. Another agency issue emerged as a result
of the 2007–2008 economic crisis, particularly in the financial sector,
related to conflicts of interest between the interests of depositors and
shareholders. The legislation to address this particular issue includes
the guidelines on internal governance—EBA/GL/2017/11, discussed
in Section 1.2.3: "Global Financial Crisis 2007–2008 and Increased
Governance"—states clearly that the depositors have a higher priority than the shareholders, basically because customers' deposits
represent a much larger amount of money than the share capital of
a bank.

A certain level of influence from other corporate governance models could also be seen in some of the European countries. For example, the Netherlands is more inspired by the Anglo-Saxon model to
conduct business. Germany, the Netherlands, and Sweden are motivated by the comply or explain approach (discussed in Section 1.2.1:
"Cadbury Code and Combined Code") for publicly listed companies.
France and Portugal have incorporated a more social-democrat and
socialist-democracy model.

3.2.1 THE NORDIC MODEL

The Nordic model, incorporated in Scandinavian countries of Denmark, Norway, and Sweden, lies somewhere between the unitary board structure and the dual board structure. The board is usually one-tier in small companies, but if the private or public company crosses a certain number of employees, they should establish the supervisory board, also colloquially known as the corporate assembly. For example, in Norway, the board structure in small companies usually unitary, but the legal framework[45] mandates that if the number of employees exceeds 200 in public or private company, the company must establish corporate assembly, whose primary tasks are to elect the board members and supervise the management of the board, the chair, and the CEO. The Nordic model often gets highlighted[46] that despite having very concentrated ownership by stakeholders, the exploitation by key stakeholders for private benefits is low. The wealthy Nordic countries are primarily driven by trust values and social status, and therefore, the corporate ownership and control tend to be heavily influenced by the social, political, and industrial environment.

3.3 CHINA

In People's Republic of China (PRC), most of the big corporates such as banks, energy, commodities, and transports are *state-owned enterprises* (SOE), as the ultimate beneficiary owner (UBO), even in seemingly private groups, are state-owned through holdings. China is home to over 100 corporations listed on the Fortune Global 500, but only approximately 15 percent of those are privately owned.[47] PRC has adopted various laws and regulations for governing state-owned enterprises alone. The State-owned Asset Supervision and Administration Commission (SASAC), established in 2003, is aiming to restructure SOE into profit-oriented corporations—that in practice are overseen by SASAC—structured as legal entities separate from the government, having their own boards of directors, and projecting a perception of delegating more authority to the executives. However, there are views that believe this does not happen in practice due to a strong political cultural influence and control over the corporate boards.

As Chinese politics is rooted in socialism, communism, geopolitics, and national identity and influence, the government's decision-making ability has a heavy influence in large corporates. Government ensures control over the corporates by some sort of mechanism, such as preserving most of the shares or by special voting rights. For example, PetroChina is one of the biggest Chinese oil and gas companies. However, most of the shares are held by the Chinese government through state-owned China National Petroleum Corp (CNPC). Since China represents a big economy at the global stage, largely as a result of increased global trade and foreign direct investment, the Chinese government had never before been more open to capitalization and Foreign Direct Investments (FDI). Nevertheless, governmental decision-making is still dominant.

The corporates in PRC tend to have a *two-tiered structure*—the board of directors and the board of supervisors. While the board of directors comprises both executive directors and independent directors, the board of supervisors comprises representatives of shareholders and at least one-third of employees' representatives. Because People's Republic of China has some degree of concentrated ownership, the primary responsibility of independent directors is to monitor large controlling shareholders on behalf of minority shareholders. Unlike in western countries, the board chairperson is the top executive manager rather than the Chief Executive Officer (CEO). In PRC, General Manager (GM) is often colloquially called as CEO.[48] For publicly listed companies, code of corporate governance for regulations, measures, and guiding opinions are mandated by the Securities Regulatory Committee.[49]

3.4 RUSSIA

Like in People's Republic of China, the big enterprises in the Russian Federation are normally held by *state* or within the vicinity of *state-related members.* National identity and influence are strongly prevalent in state-owned corporates. Gazprom, one of the largest Russian oil producers in the world, is often considered as a national champion, meaning that big corporates are often leveraged to pursue national strategic interests, often beyond profitability. However, as a result of privatizations, corporates tend to have dispersed ownership. In 2014, the central bank of the Russian Federation approved revised and improved corporate governance discretionary measures—Corporate Governance Code (colloquially known simply as the "Code"). A company that decides to be listed in the stock exchange should comply with the Code. However, for private joint stock companies, its adoption is voluntary. Therefore, few Russian private companies comply with the code. The publicly listed corporates in Russia have a *unitary board of directors*, with the inclusion of both executive and independent directors.[50]

Observers agree that the corporate governance environment in Russia has formally improved in recent years, as the government has enhanced the legal and policy framework, and key institutions have grown in sophistication and maturity. Thus, many major Russian companies have also voluntarily improved their financial and ownership transparency, although the influence from the political establishment is regarded as being present. Several reform initiatives are currently underway.[51]

3.5 JAPAN

The corporate governance model adopted in Japan is termed as *keiretsu model* and is highly *bank centered*. The root of the development of corporate governance model in Japan stems from post-World War II reconstruction efforts and is deeply inherited in traditions and business relationships. Normally, a bank would own small percentage of shares of keiretsu affiliated companies, and at the other end, keiretsu affiliated companies would own small percentage of shares of a bank, entering into a cross-ownership arrangement. This eventually forms an interlocking relationship, and this is supposed to aid in controlling and monitoring organizational governance. Cross-ownership arrangements—also common in Germany—Involve a business culture that may raise corporate governance malpractices, as one board may accommodate decisions in exchange for the same in a similar situation from their side, on top of other criticisms. The keiretsu model takes two forms—horizontal and vertical. For example, Mitsubishi has horizontal businesses such as MUFG Bank, Mitsubishi Motors, and Mitsubishi Electric.[52] However, Mitsubishi Motors may also have vertical businesses in the supply chain that supply parts of the vehicle. MUFG is the controlling bank and may own a small portion of stocks in all horizontal and vertical keiretsu member Mitsubishi business, and in return, keiretsu member businesses would own a small percentage of the bank's shares.[53] Thus, the keiretsu model is a kind of conglomerate-based model where a corporation has an interdependent relationship between industry, suppliers, and banks.

The keiretsu model usually follows a *unitary board structure* with executive and non-executive directors, which in its board composition has few outside or independent directors. Nonetheless, the Japanese Companies Act put forward three governance systems—Companies with the Board of Directors, and an Audit and Supervisory Board; Companies with the Board of Directors and three designated Committees: Audit Committee, Nomination Committee, Remuneration Committee; Companies with Board of Directors and an Audit and Supervisory Committee.[54]

The board members often come from banks, suppliers, or customers' representatives, considered relevant stakeholders and, therefore, contributing to the business development from inside the board. The board should engage in the establishment of corporate goals and essentially the setting of strategic direction through constructive discussion with respect to specific business strategies and business plans, therefore ensuring that major operational decisions are based on the company's strategic direction following the

Corporate Governance Code 2015, revised in 2018. Keiretsu corporate governance model is highly protective of executive management, as a result of very few outside independent directors in the unitary board (see Table 3.3). As banks are often loaded with cash and investments (e.g., MUFG Bank, Soft Bank), minority shareholders may not be able to compete or be protected under that governance structure. Hence, banks are very powerful in the keiretsu model because of their role as very relevant providers of financial advice and loans, and as a result, the demands of a bank are quite prominent in most of the decision-making process.

Table 3.3: Corporate governance model in Japan

Japan
• Keiretsu model
• Unitary board: executive and non-executive directors (although not mandatory)
• Board composition: few outside independent non-executive directors; directors often include banks, suppliers, or customers representatives
• Board responsibilities: executive management, with strong influence from the banks
• Audit Committee: depends on the governance model
• Compliance requirements: Corporate Governance Code 2018

Historically, the keiretsu model has been successful within Japan, being deeply embedded in its high-growth economic engine. However, to achieve sustainable growth in the current era of global digital transformation, Japanese companies are progressively focusing on modern corporate governance reforms. To facilitate such reforms, in 2018, Corporate Governance Code was revised.[55] Leading Japanese companies have adopted reforms, but Japanese practices still show relevant gaps when compared to western governance practices. However, the strong characteristics of the Japanese business culture apparently have successfully impacted the performance of many corporates.

3.6 SOUTH KOREA

The South Korean model of corporate governance is known as *chaebol model*. Like the keiretsu model in Japan, it is a conglomerate-based model, but the ownership is generally held by powerful families. Two big corporates—Samsung and Hyundai—are examples of the chaebol model. Both corporates have established horizontal and vertical businesses globally. As the economy of South Korea has been largely driven by the chaebol model of business, the South Korean government and the chaebol businesses have always maintained a very symbiotic relationship. Like Japan, Korean companies need to focus on enhancing corporate governance reforms, although the Commercial Act for controlling commerce has been prevalent in South Korea since 1963. Despite that, top executives of Samsung and Hyundai have been found guilty of corruption in the past, and their closeness with governmental representatives has been questioned.[56]

In South Korea, corporate governance is regulated by the Korea Commercial Code, which was lately amended in December 2015 with improved governance measures. The code does not restrict short-termism, but any violation by the management may form a ground for dismissal, civil liability, or criminal liability. Also, any shareholders conspiring with management or instructing management may be equally liable. It is understood that the Korean government is restructuring the code for further improvement in the incorporation of corporate governance best practice, as well as the securities' market.[57] The Ministry of Justice is the enforcing authority of the code. The publicly listed companies are subject to rules and regulations of Financial Investment Services and Capital Markets Act (FISCMA).[58]

3.7 INDIA

Prevalent large Indian corporates follow the *family-centric* model. Like Continental Europe, the corporate governance model is more *bank-centered* within reach of powerful families. Banks' finance is based on capital needs and job creation. The corporate accounting scandal of publicly listed Satyam Computer Services in 2009 to the tune of a billion dollars, manipulated by its then CEO and founding member, demonstrated the level of minority shareholders' protection at the time and also evidence of family and founding members' dominance in corporate decision-making.[59] Since then, the Indian government has introduced a series of reforms, guidelines, and regulations for incorporating sound corporate governance practices. The reformed act, Companies Act 2013, covered provisions relating to the board constitution, board meetings, board processes, independent directors, general meetings, audit committees, related party transactions, disclosure requirements in financial statements, among others.[60]

Indian firms are also partially influenced by the Anglo-Saxon model, but the incentives for shareholders' protection and return are not often as protected. Corporates tend to have a *unitary board structure*. Independent directors are represented in the board. The publicly listed companies in India must comply with rules and regulations of the Securities and Exchange Board of India (SEBI). In recent years, shareholders' activism has been gradually rising in India, thus raising the stake in improving the corporate governance standards. As Indian economy is considered as one of the emerging economies and posed to take the heightened stage in the global economy, the importance and awareness of corporate governance has grown. Many companies in India still tend to take corporate governance for granted and only focus on monetary gains and profits, and this approach often generates lack of trust in corporate governance and investors' sentiments.[61] Nevertheless, after several corporate scandals, corporates have started to realize the importance of corporate governance and its impact on raising the capital in global markets. As a result, corporates are increasingly promoting the concept of value creation over the longer term than short-termism, as well as slowly adopting governance best practice.

3.8 UNITARY BOARD (MONIST) VS DUAL BOARD (DUALIST)

Anglo-Saxon countries are fundamentally influenced by the unitary board structure, and others such as Continental Europe and People's Republic of China are generally influenced by the dual board structure. Critics have long argued that both boards have their own advantages and disadvantages. Sometimes, the combination of the unitary board and the dual board is also known as mixed structure board, where the CEO usually sits also in the supervisory board, and the chair in the executive board; the chair, in most jurisdictions that allow the dual board structure, can attend the executive board at own discretion. Nevertheless, the mixed structure is rarely adopted.

3.8.1 UNITARY BOARD

The main *advantages* of the unitary board are:

1. Superior flow of information.
2. Swift decision-making abilities.
3. Effective understanding and participation in the business by the board.
4. Reduced bureaucracy, as separate approval from the supervisory board is not required.
5. Independent non-executive directors and executive directors under the same roof leads to frequent meetings; constant contacts; better understanding; corporate business profile, and strategy; and a greater prominence of the supervisory function of the board in management decision-making, reducing the asymmetry of information and data.
6. Allows non-executive directors to advise and challenge executive directors when a matter is discussed.
7. Skilled independent directors, being optimistically skeptic, are believed to bring experiences and expertize to the board, helping alignment and often coaching of executive directors,

which in return may also constitute the effectiveness of reward strategy in corporate governance.[62]

The main *disadvantages* of the unitary board are:

1. Possibility of increased agency conflict between the shareholders and the board, as there is no supervisory board to oversee the board.
2. Simultaneously making and monitoring the same decision.
3. Increased potential for collusion among board members, due to personal relationships not limited to appointment, compensation, and monitoring.
4. Questionable neutrality and independence of non-executive board members.
5. Reduced willingness of non-executive directors to discuss issues openly.
6. Compensation of the board members based on corporate performance, which may induce agency conflict with the shareholders.
7. The tone of the board overexposed to the personality of the chairs.
8. The concept of serial director (i.e., the independent director being on several boards), may cause his/her effective monitoring process to fade.

3.8.2 DUAL BOARD (TWO-TIER)

The *advantages* of the dual board are:

1. Effective monitoring through separation (i.e., separate board with power to influence management through consent, advise, and incentives).
2. Greater focus on stakeholder inclusion, possibly reducing the agency conflict.

3. Allows for a more open discussion.
4. More clearly defined roles and responsibilities of directors in each board and strict separation between the chair and the CEO roles, which is eventually believed to lead to greater independence.
5. Transparent distinctions of liabilities shared between the supervisory board and the management board.
6. Functional report of the control function—risk management, compliance, and internal audit—maintaining more robust independence.

The *disadvantages* of the dual board are:

1. Increased probability of information and data asymmetry between the uninvolved supervisory board and the executive management board, especially if the supervisory board is solely dependent on the management for its information.
2. Increased possibility of inefficient monitoring due to a lack of information flow between the boards.
3. Increased bureaucracy in achieving decisions due to excessive protectionism measures incorporated by stakeholders, thus constituting operational hindrance, which can even put the firm at threat in a competitive market where decisions need to be taken swiftly and continuously.

3.9 DYNAMICS ON SELECTING A GOVERNANCE MODEL

The choice between a monist or dualist governance model should consider which is fit for purpose, considering several characteristics of the company and its shareholdings and stakeholders. Choosing either model brings consequences and creates risks that must be mitigated in order to protect shareholders and stakeholders. However, the choice of one or another has the same objective, which is to have a robust governance model.

In a monist structure, all board members are in one main collegial body, led by a chairperson, and are all responsible for governance, vision and strategic functions. The executive directors then belong to a subgroup specifically responsible, additionally, for the developing the strategy under the direction of the supervisory board, as well as deal with the tactics and operational responsibilities.

In a dualist structure, there are two main collegial organs—the supervisory and the executive—each with its own members and own functions: Supervisory with vision and strategy, and executive with strategic development, tactics and operational. The executive organ may be subordinate to the supervisory or be a peer of it.

3.9.1 BOARD MEMBERS' TIME DEDICATION

Our previous description demonstrates the first aspect to consider when choosing between a monist and dualist structure. In a monist model, members of the executive body are also responsible for—and thus need to dedicate a significant portion of their time to—the vision and Strategic functions. In a dualist model, each organ's members dedicate the vast amount of their time—not all of it, given both bodies should consult each other when forming their main decisions—to the functions they are specifically responsible for, respectively supervisory on vision and strategy and executive on the development of strategy, tactics and operational.

This would mean in a monist model, executive directors would have to dedicate a smaller proportion of time to the tactics and operational functions than in a dualist model, where the time dedication of the members in charge of their particular functions would be higher. In a monist model, additionally, board members must avoid falling into the *Short-Term Trap*. Tactics and operational matters, due to their "urgency" and impact in a short-term time frame, often lead to the postponement of medium and long-term decisions that form the basis of vision and strategic functions. Under a monist model, the board as a whole should avoid being diverted into executive decisions and maintain its focus on **governance,** vision and strategic responsibilities**.**

In a dualist model, segregation of the responsibilities for functions should not lead to **an isolation in the** decision-making process. A best practice in this regard is that members of the supervisory body engage with executive directors in order to obtain relevant business insights and their inputs into the **vision** and strategic decisions being made, as well as adhering to the business model. These inputs should be collected during strategy creation checkpoints and at least quarterly as part of the supervisor body's mandate of monitoring and control of the business. Assessment of time commitment is discussed in Section 17.5: "Board and Committee Evaluations."

3.9.2 COMPLEXITY OF THE UNDERLYING BUSINESS

The issue of proportion of time dedication in the previous section leads to the following consideration: how much time does the underlying business require from board members? Internationalization, globalization, diversification, mergers and acquisitions, talent pool, ESG, control functions monitoring, or consolidation are some of the trends that make businesses more complex to manage:

- Higher turnover: more transactions, more payments, more cash and debt.
- Larger staff: more teams/departments, more managers, more recruitment, evaluation, and performance management.
- Expanding to foreign markets: more exposure to different rules and regulations, exchange currency risks, foreign direct investment challenges, longer and more complex logistics, customs procedures and conflict resolution jurisdictions.
- Increasing product/service range: more complex supply chain, sales staff capacity development.

Depending on the way business growth is pursued, a larger business would require a greater time dedication from board members. A small, simple business would require less time for board members to perform the basic governance functions—vision, strategic, tactical, and operational—than a large, multi-departmental business with staff spread and trained across multiple countries.

Similarly, a company with a simpler, smaller business would be better placed to work under a monist model until the time when the complexity of the underlying business increases and justifies segregating the functions of supervisory and executive amongst the board members, thus moving to a dualist model.

3.9.3 RELATIONSHIP BETWEEN EXECUTIVE AND NON-EXECUTIVE DIRECTORS

Under a monist model, the relationship between Executive Directors (ED) and Non-executive Directors (NED) should be closer than under a dualist model, as a result of:

- Group identity from all members belonging to the same board.
- Increased frequency and intensity of interactions.
- Joint decision-making process.

With the eventual increase of members' interactions, consciously or unconsciously, personal relationship building, negotiations, trade-offs and favors between each other, members' interests, motivations, red lines, and allegiances become clearer, and decision-making processes become increasingly foreseeable.

Especially with long-serving members, this could lead to more consensus and alignment in decision-making, which may seem efficient and desirable but raises a question of "Arm's length" evaluation of decisions. A strong, established relationship between NED and EDs can erode the quality of NEDs' oversight, thus increasing the Agency risk toward stakeholders outside the board, namely unpresented or under-represented shareholders, as well as minority shareholders.

A dualist model would provide a more arm's length framework for decision-making by mitigating risk by:

- Separating NEDs and EDs into different groups.
- Reducing the frequency and intensity of their interactions.
- Focusing NEDs more on supervisory functions.
- Limiting EDs' voting power on supervisory decisions.

Term limits, and diversity and inclusion are other governance best practices in this regard. Limiting members' terms provides a regular and steady inflow of new members, which bring a *blank-slate* (*Tabula rasa*) dynamic. Incorporating members with diverse backgrounds and giving them adequate participation and influence brings different perspectives, helps the rethinking of conservative ways-of-working, and opens the stage for healthy debate and challenge. The scrutiny of existing ways-of-working under new or different perspectives and the identification of more options of how to do business should lead to more solid decision-making. Staggered boards—unitary or supervisory—can be of idiosyncratic in nature, and a policy dictum applied to all firms may not be appropriate.

More about the role of board directors is discussed in Chapter 16: Role of Board Members.

3.9.4 DECISION-MAKING SPEED AND ACCESS TO INFORMATION

Under a monist model, since all board members are within one single organ, the decision-making process takes within that body is therefore shorter and more efficient, as well as carries fewer formalities than in a dualist model, which would require organizing separate groups of people and introduce checks and balances to allow an appropriate level of consultation between each.

In terms of access to information, both under a monist or dualist model—but more in the second, given the higher degree of separation between bodies—added care should be taken in mitigating data asymmetry between members belonging the other group. Decision-making is further discussed in Section 15.3: "Decision-making Dynamics in Board."

3.9.5 RELEVANCE OF THE BUSINESS TO SHAREHOLDERS

When the underlying business is relevant to a particular shareholder, whatever the reason, but usually when their income's dependency on the return from that investment (e.g., dividends, share value) is high, they are an activist shareholder or private equity, and their wish to be more involved and exert a higher degree of influence on the business would be higher. The most extreme example is a shareholder having physical presence in its board, a phenomenon common in family businesses.

This increases agency risk, which should be mitigated. The higher the involvement of one or several particular shareholders in the supervisory or executive boards, the larger the concern in mitigating the risk between shareholders present/controlling and non-present or noncontrolling shareholders.

In case of a higher shareholder involvement, a dualist model, with its higher degree of separation and higher degree of independent members and function of oversight, should be more appropriate to protect the interests of less-involved shareholders.

3.10 THE ESSENCE OF DIFFERENT CORPORATE GOVERNANCE MODELS

Regardless of the market-centered model or bank-centered governance model, the essence of corporate governance and its objectives remain the same, being the same philosophy extended to the different structures—monist or dualist. It is inevitable that the codes of corporate governance are periodically updated to meet with new compliance requirements and emerging corporate governance trends. The examples of good corporate governance practices could be completely different from one another, but they all agree on one thing: valuable incentives to the stakeholders—such as shareholders, employees, bondholders, banks, management, customers, suppliers, financiers, government—and proper alignment to avoid conflicts of interest that could potentially lead to biased behavior of stakeholders. In general, the essence of governance models is realized in three aspects: Controlling a company, System of Structuring, and System of Operating (see Figure 3.2).

Figure 3.2: Essence of different corporate governance models

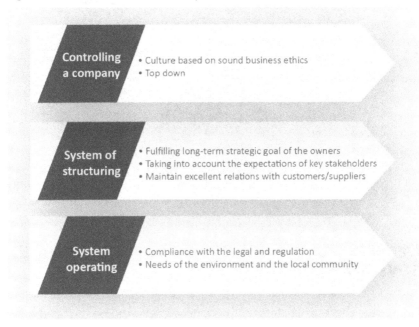

Furthermore, as countries have enacted their own act and code for assimilating best practices, the monitoring mechanisms and incentives employed to achieve the highest level of compliance normally depend on five factors (see Figure 3.3):

1. Model adopted in terms of being bank-oriented or market-oriented
2. Legal environments, guidelines, and frameworks
3. Compensation contracts
4. Institutional investment environments
5. Accounting standards

Figure 3.3: Types of monitoring and incentives used

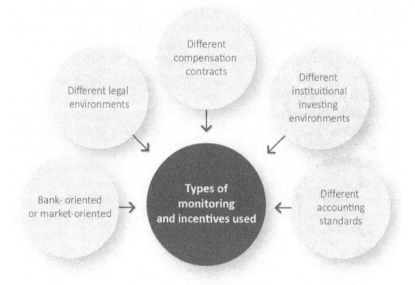

3.11 FIVE GOLDEN RULES FOR BEST CORPORATE GOVERNANCE PRACTICES

As the philosophy regarding corporate governance is often a subjective matter, there exist different ways to achieve the best governance practices. Below are summarized five typical golden rules authored by Applied Corporate Governance:[63]

1. *Business Ethics*, which form the basis of the business:
   o Long-term growth: Sustainability comes from an ethical long-term vision that takes into account all stakeholders.

Smaller but sustainable profits long term must be preferred over higher but riskier short-lived profits.

o Cost and risk reduction: Companies that recognize the importance of business ethics will need to spend less protecting themselves from internal and external behavioral risks, especially when supported by sound governance systems and independent research.

o Anti-capitalist sentiment: The financial crisis marked another blow for the credibility of capitalism, with resentment toward bank bailouts at the cost of fundamental rights such as education and healthcare.

o Limited resources: The planet has finite resources but a growing population; without ethics, those resources will be depleted for purely individual gain at a huge cost both to current and future generations.

2. *Business Goals* that are aligned to create a suitable stakeholder decision-making model

o Do you have clear business goals physically (or electronically) documented and distributed within the organization?

o Are your employees aware of and do they agree with the long-term business goals?

o Is the outward expression of the goal a factor that helps or hinders sales?

o Do you establish goals with your suppliers and trading partners?

o Is the community in which you operate aware and supportive of your business goals?

3. *Strategic Management* that incorporates stakeholder value:

o Set a goal that matches the duly considered expectations of the stakeholders.

o Work out a feasible strategy to achieve that goal.

o Put in place an organization that can carry out the strategy and attain the goal.

     o Set up a control and reporting function to permit management to drive the organization effectively and make necessary adjustments to the strategy or even the goal.

     o Ensure adherence of tactics to the business model and strategy.

4. *Organizational Effectiveness* structured to good governance:
     o Clear-headed logic about the natural way to organize effectively, disregarding the baggage of current practices.
     o Paying due regard to the experience of the past in assessing what appears to work well and what appears to cause problems.
     o Putting in place the mechanism to deliver the agreed strategy, with whatever modifications and additions are needed.

5. *Corporate Communication*, reporting systems structured to provide transparency and accountability.
     o Ensure all stakeholders are happy with the proposed strategy.
     o Monitor progress from point A to point B in the strategy.
     o Ensure stakeholders are receiving all the information they require.

Topics of the Chapter

The following has been discussed within this chapter:

- Models of corporate governance adopted in different parts of the world.
- The two commonly employed corporate governance models:
  1. Unitary Board: Model with a single board composed of executive and non-executive directors, combining executive management and supervisory functions in the same board

2. Dual Board: Model with a board of executive directors handling management functions and another board of non-executive members handling supervisory functions
    o   Combinations or intermediates of the two are also discussed
- Governance model should be based on considerations regarding the characteristics of the company and its shareholders; regardless, the rules for best practices should be followed:
1. Business Ethics
2. Business Goals
3. Strategic Management
4. Organizational Effectiveness
5. Corporate Communication

Chapter 4

Strategy, Business Model, and Sustainable Growth

Strategy and business model are very relevant topics for a corporation and its board, which is why any aspiring or current board member or senior manager must understand the business value chain incorporated in the business model. The business model is interconnected to the concept of sustainability and to the principle of an organization's ongoing concern, and it should be periodically reviewed, along with its impact on the strategic plan. Vision, strategy, tactics and operations are the fundamental basis to business model. This chapter defines vision, strategy, tactics, operations, and business model; how it is built; how it affects the board; and how it connects to the sustainability of the business.

4.1 VISION, STRATEGY, TACTICS, AND OPERATIONAL

A board should have included in the global agenda the periodic evaluation of the business model as a cornerstone of their functions and decision-making process, both in their supervisory (non-executive directors) and management functions (executive directors)—an idea beforehand about the expectations of stakeholders, capital markets, and regulatory entities and their relevance to ensure the sustainability of the organization. It is relevant to ensure that the organizational structure and the allocation of responsibilities and roles among shareholders, non-executive directors, executive directors, and senior management, as well as to middle management, are well established and clear to themselves—which is often not the case.

One of the major challenges to the board in terms of responsibilities and roles is related to the unfocused definition and understanding by those players regarding the scope of their responsibilities. This can lead to situations that are not performed and monitored by a director as well as complex misunderstandings of each one role, for example, between executive and non-executive directors. Often, executive and non-executive directors do not fully understand their main role—governance, strategy, and supervision of executive directors—and executive directors in their management function do not understand that they are supervised by non-executive directors, that the latter should be involved end-to-end in the strategic process, and that they are mainly responsible to exercise monitoring and control over the governance framework of the organization. The role of an executive directors includes the preparation and supply of complete, comprehensive, and transparent data and information to the board while participating in the board meeting, as well as seek advise from non-executive directors. However, the data and information should also take into consideration an active input from non-executive directors in their management supervisory capacity.

A way to frame this distribution of functions and its purpose to split responsibilities and roles could be to allocate the main blocks of responsibility—within the governance framework—to the different hierarchical levels of an organization: vision, strategy, tactics, and operational (ViSTO). The process of allocating responsibilities and roles will be influenced by several factors that include, among others, the business model, size, complexity, segmentation by product and market, and the nature of the business, which will require cascading down into a different substructures within each level. The structure is depicted in Figure 4.1.

Figure 4.1: "IVENS ViSTO Framework"

Vision
What Business should look like in an **appropriate long-term**

NED with inputs from ED
NED responsible for delivery

Strategy
How to **achieve the Vision** on the short and medium term

Driven by **ED** with inputs from Directors/ Managers
ED responsible for delivery

Tactics
How to **implement** the Strategic objectives

Driven by **Directors/Managers** with inputs from their teams
D/M responsible from delivery

Operational
Making Objectives **real**

Driven by **Team Leaders**
TL and **Team Members** responsible for delivery

Source: (IVENS | Governance Advisors–www.ivensadvisors.com)

The "IVENS ViSTO framework" is a conceptual framework around the dynamics of the roles and responsibilities of board members in leading their companies, as well as the lower levels of an organizational pyramid of a company. This acronym is based on the sequence above: **Vi**sion, **S**trategy, **T**actics, and **O**perational. This framework is structured for the different decision-making levels of the pyramid above. While dynamics in the social bodies may vary as a result of the legal structure, it is vital to guarantee that its objective is to ensure a robust and proper governance framework and an effective decision-making process. An element of this framework relates to the governance model adopted by the organization, including the governance structure under a monist (usually in common-law countries) or a dualist system (often adopted in large or listed companies in

Continental Europe like Germany, Scandinavia, or Portugal), or even a mixed system.

Focusing on the allocation of responsibilities among the different levels of the pyramid varies depending on several factors, realities, and the current organization structure. These factors include the size, listed or non-listed, family business (with the founder still in activity), concentrated ownership (start-ups or businesses founded by friends still in the first generation), the geographical presence, the area of activity (financial or nonfinancial sector), complexity, relations with the capital markets and the banking system, and regulated and supervised activity. The idea boils down to the need to have a clear allocation of responsibilities and roles down the pyramid to ensure that the social bodies—shareholders' meeting, board of directors/supervisory board, and executive board/committee—and organizational structures do not step into the roles of others, as well as to ensure that all areas of the business model are covered by a layer of the pyramid. This may seem obvious, but it often presents a challenge for organizations, especially ones that are less structured, notably small and medium-sized enterprises, and family businesses or businesses with high concentration of ownership.

The IVENS ViSTO framework fosters an alignment across directors—executive and non-executive—management and staff considering the fashion the different organizational levels contribute to setting and achieving the direction of a company. It can be used for the development of the strategic plan, its execution or even the preparation of a meeting:

- **Vision** involves creating the *purpose* of the organization to achieve in the medium term in a sustainable fashion, thus making the directors who establish it also accountable for its delivery. It should be balanced neither to stretch the organization in light of reality and achievability nor be too easy to require the organization to rise to the challenge.

- **Strategy** is related to defining the *objectives* to be reached to realize and achieve the Vision. This phase should start to materialize milestones and therefore clarify challenges, which will require overcoming to realize the Vision, notably the allocation of scarce resource—namely Capital and Talent—and whether the organization is able to deliver them as-is or seek partnerships, or perform acquisitions and disposals.
- **Tactics** encompass materializing policies and ways-of-working to reach the *strategic objectives*, considering specific knowledge about the context's premises and/or assumptions as well as anticipating scenarios of potential outcomes, consequences, and ways to deal with them.
- **Operational** relates to the organization's base, responsible for the deployment of the strategic plan under the established business model. This is intimately dependent on individuals' skills, including speed and focus on action and execution as well as engagement influence and deliver the objectives.

The IVENS ViSTO framework should neither be a top-down nor a bottom-up exercise but rather a co-creation. Co-creating the way forward requires involving, engaging, challenging, and aligning all levels of the organization to create a shared commitment on the way forward. It requires an underlying culture of active participation, risk, growth mindset, and humility, especially amongst its leadership. When the Titanic set off for its inaugural voyage, passenger cruise lines were focused on delivering their passengers on schedule, with courses drawn and operations managed based on achieving full speed to deliver the voyage plan efficiently. Before leaving port, the Captain was warned of the presence of icebergs on the route. However, based on a widely held belief at the time—that large ships, in particular the Titanic, were indestructible even when hitting icebergs—the Captain and other leaders involved did not review, adjust, or change their operating method and, therefore, procceded based on business as usual: "full steam ahead."

In the aftermath of the Titanic disaster, several measures were implemented. A less known one among those measures was the creation of International Ice Patrols to monitor shipping lanes for the presence of icebergs to allow launching early warnings to traveling sea vessels to be able to slow down and keep watch to detour when required. Despite the historical increase of icebergs in shipping lanes, the only collision to date in over the hundred years since the Titanic's sinking has been one vessel that did not heed such warnings.

At an institutional level, Vision should be led and approved by the board of directors/supervisory board, adopting an interactive process of engagement of non-executive and executive directors. The non-executive directors should have an involvement end-to-end in the strategy, while the executive directors should prepare the development of the strategy, eventually to be approved by the board or by the supervisory board. The roles of non-executive and executive directors are clearer in the dualist model. Once established, non-executive directors should supervise and oversee its execution and adherence to the business model. Tactics should be led, set, and overseen by the senior management, who should involve and supervise its Operational implementation.

As Talent reaches top hierarchical levels, especially in a large and complex organizations, those executives and non-executive directors are not be expected to know in detail all the areas they oversee, and instead focus on harnessing the collective knowledge of the leaders in the structure and identify the most adequate decisions. To perform the latter, leaders should consider: (i) Empowering—fostering a culture where knowledgeable individuals contribute actively with data, insights and recommendations, to help reducing and mitigating the asymmetry of data and information; (ii) Humble listeners—recognizing they are not as knowledgeable in all the areas they oversee as the managers and staff reporting to them and thus receiving and considering the latter's inputs; and (iii) System thinkers—assembling the various views and perspectives, together with their own, into a complete, appropriate and working outcome which fits the organization's best interests.

Follows the discussion of the vision, strategy, tactics and operational, presented for the different levels of the pyramid and the roles and responsibilities.

Vision

The development and design of a business model initiates (or updates) with setting (or adjusting) the Vision, which may be expanded or detailed into a *Mission*, and emphasize values linked to the strategy, tactics, and operational components of a business model. The vision is expressed in a short or very short (ideally up to three words) statement that should be clearly understood by internal and external stakeholders. For internal stakeholders, it should express the way an organization acts in its business and therefore as a *supreme guide* in driving the stance of the organization.

The vision represents the anchor of an organization, as it should express the aspiration and dream providing the inspiration for developing the strategy—the second layer of the organizational structure—and should ultimately answer the question: "Where do we want to go?"[64] It should also support the direction of the organization, impacting the decision-making process in the scarce resource's allocation, notably talent, and capital. The vision statement should make it easy for internal stakeholders how to better respond to challenges, leverage best practices, and share scarce resources to fulfill the vision. The vision focuses on the future drive and mission on its current presence set by the board with an end-to-end involvement. It must be purpose-driven, realistic, sustainable, and explicitly tied to the economic theory focused on optimal allocation of scarce resources (notably talent and capital), the cost structure, and the stream of revenues embodied by the characterization of the model.[65] Concerns have often been raised about the agility of the board to adapt to change or disruption. Critics argue that organizations that function in "stable mode" are usually unable to adapt to change, because they see change as a threat, reflecting "closed systems" that reject information that implies their partial failure, as this impacts their perception of stability. Nonetheless, the business model should describe the logic behind the ability of an organization to create, deliver, and generate value aligned with the organizational vision, under a statement creating a concept that the stakeholders understand, however not over-simplify the complexities involved in it.

Examples of vision statements include:

- *Unilever:* Feel good, look good, and get more out of life
- *Procter & Gamble:* The consumer is the Boss
- *American Express:* Don't leave home without it
- *IKEA:* To create a better everyday life for the many people
- *TED:* Spread ideas
- *Coca-Cola:* It's the Real Thing; Coke Adds Life; or Have a Coke and a Smile
- *Tesla:* To accelerate the world's transition to sustainable energy
- *Amazon:* To be earth's most customer-centric company, to build a place where people can come to find and discover anything they might want to buy online
- *Universal Health Services Inc.:* To provide superior quality healthcare services
- *Cradle Crayons:* Provide children from birth through age 12, living in homeless or low-income situations, with the essential items they need to thrive—at home, at school, and at play
- *McDonald's:* The Simpler the Better
- *Ronald McDonald House Charities:* Keeping families close
- *Red Cross and Red Crescent Day:* #Love

Strategy

Moving into the second layer of the pyramid, Strategy—allocation of scarce resources to achieve the vision—focuses on what shapes the value proposition of the business model that is the *purpose-driven strategy*. The current best practices for the strategy development (notably in the financial system, as required by the EBA/GL/2017/11—Internal Governance for Banks) requires an involvement of the full board [or the supervisory board] in a process end-to-end, contrary to the previous practice of *rubber stamp process* involving only the final approval of the plan presented by the executive board. Currently, the non-executive directors are required to give input, discuss assumptions, review and give feedback on the first output, and then approve the strategic plan. The concept of strategy applied to the business world can be linked and interlocked to the concept of *Economy* and considered under the *Corporate Governance Framework*, as advocated by the OECD (G20/OECD Principles of Corporate Governance—www.oecd.org) in its definition, which should promote transparent and fair markets (linked to raising capital) and the efficient allocation of scarce resources (linked to the concept and definition of economy) involving notably capital and talent. It should be consistent with the rule of law and support effective supervision and enforcement (linked to the processes and structures' integral part of the concept of corporate governance). The economy can be defined as social science that studies the fashion how society uses limited resources, focused on the four factors of production: land, labor, capital, and enterprise.[66] Economics is usually split into two broad categories: macroeconomics and microeconomics. The first focuses on the overall working of a national economy, including growth, inflation, interest rates, unemployment, fiscal policy and taxation. The latter studies decision-making in businesses and households, including purchasing, savings, pricing, and competition. Current trends also show the emergence of societal concerns related to environment, governance, and sustainability, including giving back to society. While microeconomics focuses on the individual level, macroeconomics focuses on decisions that may affect countries or regions under economic and/or political unions.

Although several authors rendered different definitions, a common feature of strategy is the proper allocation of scarce resources—notably capital and talent, as discussed in the preceding paragraph—in order to achieve the organizational vision and motivate and unify the relevant stakeholders with broadening impact. The board and the senior management need to think also how to make societal purpose a core part of their strategy. Often, boards—notably non-executive directors responsible to supervise the executive board—do not dedicate enough time to discuss and reflect about this topic, which should be included in the board's global agenda and reviewed periodically to ensure the business model does not require adjustments. Also, boards may hire advisors or consultants to help in the reflection and also consider conducting off-site meetings with that purpose.

The purpose can be designed through two approaches—*retrospective* or *prospective*.[67] The retrospective approach essentially comprises of an existing organization's reason for being and requires looking back to codify organizational and cultural DNA. This approach allows the organization to leverage the past experience for the introduction of adjustments. The board should take an optimistically skeptical approach questioning itself, particularly about the kind of business the organization did in the past, how the organization reached its current status, or where the organization wants to go. On the contrary, the prospective approach neglects the historical status and takes a forward-looking approach with the stock of the broader ecosystem in which the organization wants to work and assesses its potential for impact in the ecosystem. The prospective approach is about the sense of the future with a strong external focus. Those who adopt this approach would need to answer questions about where the organization can go; which trends affect the business of the organization; what kind of emerging new needs, opportunities, and challenges lie ahead for the organization, or what role can the organization play, so that they can open up future opportunities for the organization.

The purpose can be generic or narrowed, such as Samsung's broad vision purpose, "inspire the world, create the future," compared to Wells Fargo's narrowed vision purpose, "we want to satisfy our customers' financial needs and help them succeed financially." However, the notion of the existence of corporates just to reward shareholders is slowly fading, and many large corporates have signaled to transition to purpose-based commitments to relevant stakeholders and the society favoring long-termism and sustainable growth. This trend is emerging in the United States and other Anglo-Saxon countries, as the corporate governance philosophy is historical strongly focused on the shareholders and therefore profits. In Continental Europe, the philosophical approach for governance has been generally oriented toward the stakeholders for a long time. Two approaches emerging in the corporate world to achieve that include the transformation of the leadership agenda and the dissemination of the purpose through-out the organization, affecting the culture stance toward sustainable growth and society. As the approach to design the purpose is not a kind of one-off, the board should periodically—if not constantly—assess how the purpose can guide strategy and should be willing to adjust or redefine this relationship as conditions change. This certainly requires a sustained focus, but it can also render dramatic advantages. Figure 4.2 illustrates purpose-driven strategy as adapted from Barclays.

Figure 4.2: Purpose-driven strategy

Source: (Barclays Bank 2019–2020)[68]

Three components of the purpose-driven strategy—*strategic analysis, strategic planning,* and *strategic management*—are funda-mentally important (see Figure 4.2). Strategic planning is the process of defining strategy or direction and making decisions on allocating the scarce resources to pursue the purpose of the defined strategy to achieve the vision.[69] The decision to achieve proper allocation is often done through operations research in the corporate world, an advanced analytical and statistical method of problem-solving useful in the management of organizations. Strategic planning generally occurs at the beginning of a year, a quarter, or a month. Strategic plans need to be reviewed every quarter or semester—depending on the size and complexity of the business—responding to trends such as globalization, climate and urbanization which must be included in the core agenda.

The strategic management component relies on strategic analysis and strategic planning (essentially the board and executive management's role on setting goal and objectives to achieve the purpose), directly responsible individuals, goal implementation, and decision-making process to achieve the representative corporate vision, which ultimately culminates into *tactics*.

As the strategic component usually looks at the longer horizon (three years or more), the risks or potential fallout—notably in corporates with an international footprint—such as operational risks, geopolitical risks, sovereign rating, political risk, legal framework instability, idiosyncratic risk, macro and micro risks, systemic and nonsystemic risks, foreign exchange rate and interest rate risks, war, demonstrations that result into tumults, natural disaster, or any opportunity cost to untapped markets must be carefully analyzed and monitored with adequate business continuity and contingency plans. These risks require agile boards demanding quick definition and redefinition of the risk appetite that frames the strategic plan. The concept of sustainability is further discussed in Section 4.3: "Corporate Sustainability."

Tactics

The third layer of the responsibilities and roles within the global governance framework belongs to executive committee relating to the implementation of the strategy defined by the board, moving into the tactics. The *tactical plan* is developed after crafting the strategic plan.

Executive directors and first-line managers use tactical planning to draw what several segments or divisions of the organization must do for the organization to be successful at some point, usually for one year or less into the future. Tactical planning is deployed as a short-term tool and measured on a frequent basis (such as weekly or monthly) to meet the compliance standards of the long-term purpose-driven strategic plan. Notwithstanding, tactical planning does carry some degree of uncertainties. Unlike strategic plan, tactical planning lies closer to the control of executive directors, which usually lie—depending on the jurisdiction corporate law framework—under a structure of an executive committee, depending on the size and complexity of the business.

In other words, tactical planning comes with clear guidance from a higher level of management, tends to be directive in nature, and is more concerned with the responsibility and functionality of lower-level departments to fulfill their respective contributions toward the strategic plan. For example, if the strategic plan initiated by the top-level management of a manufacturing company is to achieve growth and profitability by boosting productivity, then middle management must ensure the accomplishment of strategic plan through the proper implementation of tactical plans, such as testing a new productivity process in order to decrease the time taken for production or investing in new machine that can boost productivity and consider other measures required to achieve it.

Operational

Operational planning is simply the process of linking strategic plan goals and objectives to tactical plan goals and objectives, and it should be placed under the supervision and direct responsibility of the first-line managers. The operation plan often describes the milestones and conditions for success and explains how, or what portion of, a strategic plan will be put into operation through tactical plan during a given operational period.[70] Operational planning focuses on aspects such as the production, equipment, personnel, inventory, and processes of a business and also on financial ratios to analyze profitability. With the operational plan being initiated by a low-level production manager, it may include creating a monthly budget; developing employees schedule every week, as well as their performance goals; assessing, ordering, and stocking inventory; and other such tasks.

Operational plan can either be a one-off or reusable. One good example of a one-off plan is an advertisement operational plan in order to increase the sale of certain product in a month or quarter within the scope of a monthly budget, while creating a monthly budget and employee schedules are reusable plans. In another case, if a corporation's sales team is struggling to hit a monthly sales target (monthly operational measure) for three consecutive months and does not reach the target in three months (tactical plan of three months), then it might be necessary to review the tactics (i.e., tactical plan of hitting targeted sales' quota in three months). Also, if considered necessary, the overall target sales strategy (strategic plan) may be reviewed to adjust to more realistic terms (see Table 4.1).

Table 4.1: Differences between strategic, tactical, and operational plan

Vision	Strategic Plan	Tactical Plan	Operational Plan
Top of the Organization	Board of Directors/ Supervisory Board	Executive Committee or Directors	First Line & Middle Management
Defining Purpose	What is our purpose?	How can we achieve our purpose?	What can we do to achieve our purpose?
Examples: • *Samsung*: Inspire the World, Create the future • *Tesla*: To accelerate the world's transition to sustainable energy	Examples: • Boosting productivity • Increasing profitability • Reducing greenhouse gases • Reducing the non-performing loans level	Examples: • Investment in a new machine • Pricing optimization • Investment in an electric machine • Increasing the minimum income requirement for a house loan	Examples: • Employee scheduling • Monthly budget allocation • Inventory management • Credit analysis plan of source and income

4.2 DEFINITION AND CONCEPT OF A BUSINESS MODEL

The term business model has different meanings depending on the area of activity to which it relates, in summary, it contrasts the revenues' stream and the cost structure of an organization. The cost-to-income ratio shows the efficiency of an organization, being a demanding and cruel ratio that essentially projects a corporation into the future and warns for a sustainable balance between the two streams, that require strong action—monitoring and challenging executive board and supervision—from the board, notably the non-executive directors. The overall ratio may hide relevant symptoms for the need of correction or changes in the global business model—relevant business segments or products should develop a structured business model that provide inputs into the global one—of an organization, which is why a refined and more granular analysis may be required to properly and timely identify areas for action, ensuring that profitable streams of revenues do not subsidize loss-making ones as well as that the cost structure is being leveraged properly. The main objective of the cost structure stream is to generate flows for the revenues' stream.

The definition of a business model has been debated. Some define it as a concept supporting the logic of doing business,[71] and others consider it a link between strategy, business processes, and information systems, embracing a broad spectrum of organizational activities, from the operational to the strategic. Nonetheless, the business model should articulate the value proposition, provide a solution and a process to get it done, and ultimately, present the offer.[72] The board and the senior management must be intrinsically associated with the presented offer. Also, the business model should encompass a set of operating practices to generate profits, being culturally ingrained across functions and reflecting what a company does to generate revenues and profits. In most cases, the business model reflects the vision, the mission statement and strategy, that is the allocation of the scarce resources of an organization to achieve the vision; shows knowledge of the target market; knows its value proposition, the resources required, and key activities; and shows a cost and revenue model as well as providing the value chain. Some see the business model as the link between strategy (including competition and implementation) and business organization and systems (how the elements of the business concept fit together). Often, the term *entrepreneurial management* is thrown around: the implications of theory and practice on strategic management and promoting a culture of knowledge-sharing by working in synergy within an organization and even leveraging other stakeholders' skills and research, thus adding value to the current business model by stimulating and meeting customer demand. Successful firms fulfill customer needs with an effective and sustainable business model.

Customer relationship management (CRM) has given corporates the advantage to leverage the relationship management with customers by crafting a customer strategy; working with employees, counterparts, and suppliers; and demonstrating an ability to negotiate and manage cultures. CRM can be seen as a coordination tool that recognizes the customer throughout channels and across products from purchase and service lines and relies on customer feedback to support decisions about customer needs. Essentially, the key resources of a business lie within its assets and capabilities, seen in its employees, technology, products, channels, and brands, all of which are identified in order to deliver the value proposition to customers. Once deployed effectively, they create value for the customer and the company. However, the key to the success of the business model is the interaction between these values. Research has revealed that corporations often have many of the key resources in place, but the interaction among them as well as the fashion they are leveraged to service customers was lacking. A successful firm fulfills customer needs with an effective business model and challenges "orthodoxies" to meet unsatisfied and hidden customer needs. Whether that model is explicit or not is defined by its interlocking elements that, when articulated, create and deliver value. Within this, the customer value proposition is the most important, because successful businesses create value for customers by providing solutions to their needs. An understanding of the need is required to define the solution and carry out the processes to design and market it. Others view business models as a set of operating practices built around the idea of generating profits.[73] It is the embodiment of an ingrained approach to business—a cultural ethos—that crosses functions and technology and reflects corporate behavior. Often, many business segments do not identify and address the specific needs of customers and thus do not recognize their inherent business potential.

Therefore, a business model should link business strategy as a plan to determine where an organization aspires to be within a predetermined time frame and to satisfy customer needs—reflected in the vision—by defining the customer segment it seeks to serve. The design of the business model is thus built around a strong understanding of customer needs according to the customer segment. Whether to build a new business model or adjust an existing one is a strategic decision that demands management awareness and board involvement, as well as particular attention from non-executive directors. Models may be adjusted in order to disrupt competitor advantage, or a new business model may be introduced to reinforce and complement the core business; deciding the objective of the business model is, therefore, foremost to its design, implementation, and success. Lack of executive management and board awareness are common gaps that go unaddressed and impact profitability negatively and are shown to limit recognition of the potential profitability of leveraging revenues through addressing the business segments. Often, most businesses segments' executive management have the view of a product instead of the customer and conclude that this could greatly affect how value proposition is delivered.

The lack of creativity, proactivity, and entrepreneurial risk-taking may be a part of the reason why the board and senior management have not been informed about the potential, unleveraged, and unextracted value of the desired business segment. It could also be due to the proximity and integration of the personnel responsible for the business model, as responsibility for business model innovation is usually remote from the business and operational areas (within the tactics of the governance pyramid—Figure 4.2), or excessively close, generating low incentives to readdress and change the business model. Innovation can be impaired by an organizational mind-blindness, constituting a barrier such that innovation is not only internal to a particular organization but also a process demanding a high level of inter-firm integration (networking), as a company does not operate in isolation. The dynamics of speed and quick market availability are also key factors in successful product innovation. These gaps seem to provide possible explanations for the existence of lack of communication, planning, creativity, and innovation among stakeholders in the business world. Business models often evolve by themselves, requiring regular review and update, as they are defined through a dynamic network of stakeholders,[74] making it inevitable for businesses to evolve quickly in their structures, research, and prospective thinking, having in mind the sustainability of their business models.

Business strengths and opportunities support and consider the theoretical components of a business model. A SWOT analysis indicates the strengths and weaknesses—as seen from two perspectives: the internal world of the company and the external world of the company—and the market's business opportunities and threats. In relation to business, opportunities are defined as the result of one's action to change, improve, or take advantage of a situation or paradigm. Opportunities are apparent to those who recognize them, using knowledge, experience, and behavior to create a new venture within an industry that is already known and understood. In as much as this relates to the business model, a tool fundamental to the efficiency of an organization, it reflects what it does and why it does it and essentially echoes the notion of the opportunity often being there, if only it is recognized. Thus, it seems relevant to focus on the opportunities that complement the strengths and redesign the business model to eliminate the weaknesses to exploit the opportunities presented by business segments. These items should be of the utmost concern and focus of boards, being included in their global agenda.

Yet, there could be some threats that relate mainly to macroeconomic policies, legal environments, regulation, internationalization, and cultural environments that may limit business development in certain countries, although they are related intimately to services and product development. There is also a relevant threat related to the customer view, linked to corporations' reputational risk, as stakeholders—but rarely corporations—are critical of the lack of leadership and vision shown to the needs of customers. Another line of thought would be that it may not make sense to change a business model when it generates profits, unless it is foreseen that a social element might damage corporate image and reputation; as this contributes to long-term profitability,[75] this threat requires the consideration of boards of directors and senior management regarding the business model.[76] The challenge is to devise an innovative business model to anticipate the need to adapt or change current practice and bring about the sustainable positive benefits envisaged for both society and businesses. A popular way to approach this challenge could be the structured approach proposed by Alexander Osterwalder titled the Business Model Canvas,[77] (Figure 4.3) based on his book titled Business Model Ontology, outlining nine segments that constitute building blocks for a business model.

4.2.1 BUSINESS MODEL CANVAS
The business model canvas theorized by Osterwalder includes nine blocks, each one with the business's essential components organized under the Revenue Streams and the Cost Structure (see Figure 4.3).

The revenue streams include customer segments, channels, and customer relationships, while the cost structure focuses on key activities, key resources, and key partnerships. The value propositions are split between the revenue streams and the cost structure. Osterwalder advocates that the business model canvas reflects systematically on a business model, allowing the process to be prepared segment by segment. The process can be initiated with a brainstorming and the transferring (brain-dump) of knowledge and/or a large quantity of information about a particular subject or business from the brains of management and staff to other storage medium, such as the business model canvas in the figure below. This would allow the development of a structured process to fill the segments of the teams' minds and then develop empty segments to close the gaps. Alexander Osterwalder suggests a list of basic questions to brainstorm and compare the variations and ideas for your next business model innovation.

Figure 4.3: Osterwalder's business model canvas

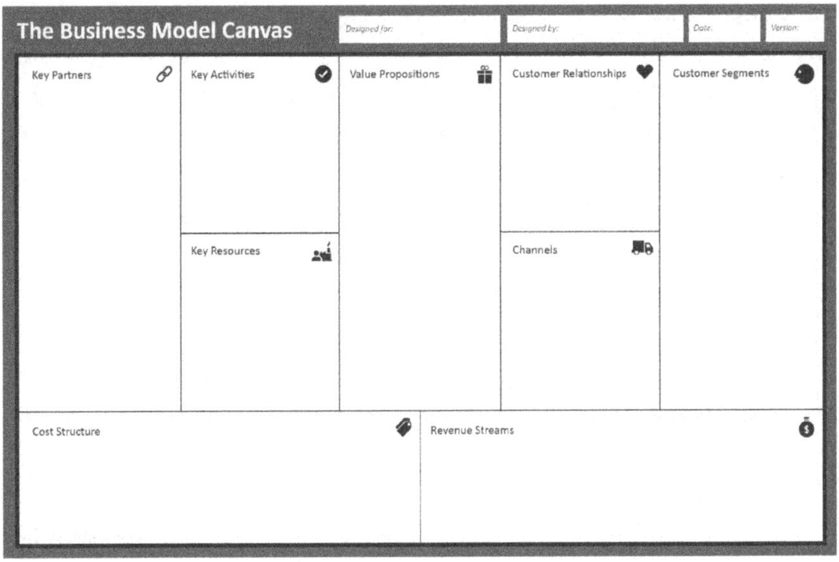

Source: (Business Model Canvas—Alexander Osterwalder)[78]

The value proposition—stream of revenues and the cost structure—relates to the core value a business must have about the vision to deliver to the customers, as well as the needs the business model should address and satisfy. Under the cost structure block, the canvas addresses the costs of the business—which key resources and activities are most expensive—and identifies the key partners for the business, the suppliers, and the motivations for the business partnerships. For the key activities, the canvas proposes to list the one that is indispensable or critical to the value propositions as well as the activities pivotal to the distribution channels, customer relationships, and revenue streams. The block of key resources should identify the resources that the value proposition requires, ponting out the important ones to the distribution channels, customer relationships, and revenue streams.

The revenue stream should cover the pricing: what value are customers willing to pay, what and how do they recently pay, alternatives to the current method to understand how they would prefer to pay, as well as a critical question related to how much (margin) every revenue stream contributes to the overall revenues to ensure that some revenue streams do not subsidize loss-making segments or products. The revenues stream block should also deal specifically with the customer relationship, identifying the target customer and segment that a business expects to establish as well as how to integrate efficiently them into the business, considering both cost and format. The customer segment should identify the classes for whom the business creates values and identify the most important customers' segment. As it relates to the distribution channel, the model should identify the channels to reach customers, the ones that work best, their cost, and the way they are integrated into the business and the customers' routines.

Below is the short summary of the business model canvas:[79]

1. **Infrastructure:**
   i. *Key Partners*: Organizations may cultivate buyer-supplier relationships to optimize operations and reduce the risks

of a business model. This essentially allows them to focus on their core activity.

ii. *Key Activities:* The most important activities in executing a value proposition. Activities must address sustainability concerns (i.e., ESG, the current business model).

iii. *Key Resources:* Talent, financial, intellectual, or other important scarce resources necessary in the corporate to create sustainable value for the customers.

2. **Offering:**

Value Propositions: This should distinguish it clearly from its competitors. Value comes from several qualitative and quantitative elements such as novelty, performance, customization, design, brand/status, price, cost reduction, and others. While qualitative elements look at the subjective assessment of customer experience, quantitative elements oversee price and efficiency. For example, the value propositions of a quartz watch, and a Rolex luxury watch are certainly not the same.

3. **Customers:**

i. *Customer Segments:* Company must categorize the customer segment it is trying to serve. Customer segments include mass-market (no specific segmentation, i.e., product marketed to the masses), niche market (specialized needs segment, such as luxury products), diversified (multiple customer segments with different needs and characteristics, such as Toyota, which offers both regular and luxury car segments), or any other identified segments.

ii. *Customer Relationships:* Without building a very good rapport with customers, the business can never thrive. Companies need to identify what kind of relationships they want to create and maintain with their desired customer segments, such as automated service, personal assistance, VIP service, self-service, communities, and others.

iii. *Channels:* The channel to deliver the value proposition and the offerings, such as own channel (storefront), partner channel (distributors), or a combination of both. E-commerce (online mediums such as Amazon and Alibaba) has never been as dominant in Western and emerging economies such as People's Republic of China and has been laterally expanding to other emerging economies across continents.

4. **Finances:**

   i. *Cost Structure*: The cost structure defines the monetary (e.g., cash-flows) consequences of operating under different business models and purpose-driven strategic plans. The two classes of cost structure are cost-driven (model focused on minimizing the costs, such as low-cost airlines) and value-driven (model less concerned with cost, and focused on creating value for products and service, such as luxury products). The characteristics of cost structures fall in the following categories: fixed costs (such as building, machinery), variable costs (such as wages, utilities), economies of scale (cost per unit of output decreasing with increasing scale), economies of scope (efficiencies formed by variety, not volume such as a gas station that sells gasoline can also sell other products such as lubricants, food, water, newspapers).

   ii. *Revenue Streams*: The revenue streams that the corporate is expected to generate from each customer segment through desired channels. The revenue stream models include, but are not limited to, asset sale (selling ownership rights to a physical good, i.e., selling a product in a physical store or online channel, such as Amazon), interest revenues (such as banks charging interest on housing loans, personal loans, vehicle loans), subscription fees (monthly subscription fees such as Netflix, Spotify), licensing (fees for the use of a protected intellectual property such as Arm Holdings develops the computing architecture and licenses it to other companies such as Apple, Samsung Electronics), advertising (revenue generated for advertising the product in the provided platform such as Google). Regarding the pricing, the company may employ fixed pricing or dynamic pricing aligned with the targeted segment.

4.2.2 BUSINESS MODEL EVALUATION—LEVERAGING THE BANKING SECTOR PRACTICES' PROCESS

The business model evaluation should be a structured process in any organization to ensure full knowledge and awareness of the board regarding the sustainability of an organization in any sector of activity and, therefore, ensure timely and adequate decision-making about measures to correct it. The lack of this structured process usually results in surprises in terms of its sustainability, as non-executive directors—and often directors other than the CEO and the CFO—are not aware of the minimum levels of detail by business segment, a phenomenon that emerges from asymmetric information and data reporting provided to the board and, very often in reality, not being demanded by the board. The evaluation of the business model is a clear example of a topic that has advanced well in the financial sector and from which the nonfinancial sector can get inspiration to leverage the process to a particular nonfinancial industry.

The banking system tool to evaluate the business model, named SREP (Supervisory Review and Evaluation Process, further discussed in Chapter 9: Supervisory Mechanism) could be adopted as a best practice to evaluate and challenge business models with adjustments to other industries and services—as the process is very rigorous and challenging—while stressing the statements of economic and financial positions, as well as the cash flows statement. The SREP building block that adopts the EBA (European Banking Authority) guidelines objectives can be summarized into three areas: (i) Quantitative capital measures, (ii) Quantitative liquidity measure, and (iii) Other measures. An overall assessment named "holistic approach" is performed within these areas, including a score, the rationale, and the main conclusions.

Within the SREP framework,[80] the ECB (European Central Bank) requires the eurozone banks to develop a robust strategic plan to be incorporated in the business model within acceptable risk appetite boundaries. The business model is assessed both qualitatively and quantitatively through five broad themes:

1. *Business Environment:* Reasoning of strategic assumptions on the basis of macroeconomic conditions, market trends, and strategic intents of the competitors
2. *Current Business Model:* Organizational strategy, financial drivers, and internal and external profitability dependencies
3. *Strategy and Financial Plans:* Challenging the viability and riskiness of organizational strategy and strategic assumptions to be successful
4. *Business Model Viability:* Covering the current business environment, financial drivers and dependencies, the business model's ability to generate acceptable returns over the following years
5. *Strategic Sustainability:* Under the current business model and strategic assumptions, relating to the organization's strategy sustainability over three years or more

This overall assessment is focused on four pillars:

1. *Business Model Assessment,* involving reviewing the viability and sustainability of the business model.
2. *Governance and Risk Management Assessment,* covering the adequacy of the governance framework and the risk management.

3. *Assessment of Risks to Capital*, focusing mainly on credit, markets, operational risk, and IRRBB (Interest Rate Risk in the Banking Book).

4. *Assessment of Risks to Liquidity and Funding*, covering the assessment of risks that may affect liquidity in terms of availability or resulting from non-expected withdrawals, as well as access to funding—either from shareholders, bondholders, or the financial system—which is a major reason for bankruptcy and a factor that affects any industry in the financial or nonfinancial sectors.

The results of this structured exercise to evaluate and actually stress the business model of an organization should be included in the global agenda of any board and monitored by the committees of the board—namely the strategy, the risk, and/or the audit committee—not only to assess the results more granularly but also to ensure implementation of corrective measures. This process should also involve the control functions—risk, compliance, and internal audit—to ensure an independent review of the methodologies and adherence to best practices. The outcomes and decisions should be structured in action points and an agreed action plan including milestones for implementation by the executive committee or senior management or executive board, thereafter, monitored by an internal audit and reported back to the board. The review and evaluation process should include an intense dialogue at the board level to keep it informed of key aspects of the strategic (*strategy*) and operational plan (*tactics*), including capital (Capital Adequacy Ratio) and liquidity vectors (Liquidity Coverage Ratio), having a view of the components of the profit and loss account, the components, trends and idle assets of the balance sheet, as well as the cash-flows statement. The board should also review the sustainability, risk appetite and internal control frameworks' capacity, and limits and buffers for the risk appetite framework, all of which should be framed within a criterion that responds to stakeholders' expectations and business managed prudently by the board.

In summary, the criteria for a business model evaluation adapted from the ECB would include namely the following (Table 4.2):

Table 4.2: Criteria for business model evaluation

Qualitative Analysis	Quantitative Analysis	Business Model Sustainability Evaluation (More than three years)
• Evaluation of any changes made to the business model and strategy to achieve the vision and reset objectives. • The ability of the organization to implement the plans. For example, the historical record of the management, past record of plan-to-actual deviations, the complexity of the goals to be achieved with relation to the current business model.	• Analysis of estimated figures for the income statement, balance sheet, cash-flows, business development, and other financial quantitative information such as financial and economic ratios. • Assumptions on which future estimations are made are checked for plausibility such as the macroeconomic conditions, market trends, sales growth, margin growth, geopolitical arena.	• The plausibility of the planning considering the assumptions and the forecasted values. The forecasts calculated by an organization compared with supervisors' forecasts. • The difference and impact of supervisors' projections on the financial figures and other planning estimates of the organization in cases when the supervisor and institution's estimates vary. • The risk of the strategy measured by the complexity of the strategy compared to the current business model, and the probability of success of the strategy as measured by the ability of the organization to implement the plans.

Source: (ECB—www.ecb.europa.eu)

4.2.3 THE RELEVANCE OF BUSINESS MODEL TO THE BOARD

The business model is a critical element of sustainable growth of an organization, as it ensures the framework within which an organization ensures that the stream of revenues leverages and extracts the maximum value of the cost structure, as well as allows monitoring of threats and opportunities. Often, the board and the senior management may lose sight of the importance of the business model and its business potential or obsolescence, rendering the current business model ineffective since it has not responded to the change in the paradigm—still the "old" in their minds and culture—and either not considering its review and reflection on the board's agenda or simply lacking the vision and strategy necessary to leverage the business and the cost structure installed to generate the stream of revenues. Major reasons for this relate to the lack of monitoring and supervision of the business segment, changes that have occurred in the landscape, distractions, inertia, and the fact that the weight of revenues from important or strategic items and elements of the balance sheets, profit and loss statements, and cash-flows statements have been overlooked. The dismay of Nokia mobile phones cannot be forgotten. Critics often mention that Nokia mobile phones' failure was as a result of management decisions, dysfunctional organizational structures, growing bureaucracy, and deep internal rivalries, resulting in the organization forgetting and not generating and applying the philosophy of the vision set up by the board, titled "Connecting People," that led their mobile phones to the top.[81] As a result, Nokia's phone market business model components related to its vision lost ground and, very likely, the importance for the board and staff to growing competitive forces and accelerating market changes, fueled by Apple, Huawei, and Samsung was not taken as a real threat to the business model segments of value proposition and customer segments. Also, companies that did not regard the latter as direct competition were affected significantly in their business models (e.g., cameras manufacturers, social media moving from computers to mobile phones).

In many organizations, management often lacks information—notably due to information asymmetry between non-executive and executive directors—as well as not following up and monitoring the recommendations published by international institutions, politicians, regulators, and supervisors, as well as governance trends emerging in the landscape. This is often partly due to the fact that middle management fails to prioritize strategic business segment, failing to inform senior management and the board of relevant changes in the landscape, namely those that are taking place in the market or resulting from the change in technology, but also the absence of a challenging stance of the board toward executive directors about the sustainability of the business model. Furthermore, there is a risk of middle management not being sufficiently knowledgeable about the recommendations and changes in the paradigm themselves. It is the culmination of those factors that results in the lack of awareness about changes in the paradigm, which may require the prevalent business model to be redefined. A way to circumvent and mitigate the unawareness of the non-executive directors is the inclusion in the global agenda of the board topics related to issues that are not dealt on a regular basis. This may include geopolitics; ESG (environment, social, and governance); capital markets and capital raising; internationalization; trends in products and services; competition benchmarking (local, regional, and international) from within and outside the same area of business; cybersecurity and data warehouse; talent; pay gap, among others. Some of these areas may require the involvement of advisors and, potentially, consulting services, having in mind the objective of providing the board independent and updated advice.

Another aspect is the corporate relations with all relevant stakeholders toned by the board, aiming to have an understanding of the stakeholders' expectations, which may or may not be aligned with the board's expectations, and which should be considered in the risk appetite framework as well as in the way the criterion for the IIA three lines (further discussed in Section 6.2: "IIA Three Lines of Defense Model and Its 2020 Successor") is built and developed. Most stakeholders demonstrate low concern about communicating with each other, assuming that the communication initiative is the responsibility of other stakeholders offering different reasons for this stance. This poses a question about who should break this vicious cycle and turn it into a virtuous cycle. One common sense solution could be that whoever produces the information should ensure it reaches all interested parties, a paradigm that should carefully managed, notably because of the risk of copying everyone on every document, which may represent a "technique" of managing asymmetry of information providing so much that it is not possible to cope with it. However, the corporate business model should advocate that the corporate initiate the change in culture, because it is in the corporates' interest to attend to the business segment, and they also already own structures that can monitor macro- and microeconomic situations and manage financial information. Furthermore, corporates should ensure that recommendations from international institutions, such as G20 directives, UN SDGs (UN Sustainable Development Goals), financial system directives are adopted and assimilated, as this not only relates to their social responsibility obligations but also to the very survival and sustenance of growth.

4.2.4 ASSURING SUSTAINABLE GROWTH

A purpose-driven strategy is a prerequisite to confirm the existence of a sustainable business model, which not only helps generate commercial success in the future but also make future-ready and ethically allowed to submerge in the next generation of a sustainable society. Within the boundary of purpose-driven strategy, sustainable business strategy may experiment then. One of the ways to create a sustainable business strategy is discussed below.[82]

1. Assess the challenges and define objectives

The first thing to consider is that what sustainability means to the team, company, industry, and client, and ask questions like:

i. How much waste is the organization creating?
ii. Is our company culture struggling?
iii. Are our hiring practices attracting diverse, qualified and best job candidates?
iv. Is our product targeted to help a certain audience?
v. What impact does our company have on the local community?
vi. What is our environment, social, and governance objectives and contribution?

Answers to the above indicative type of questions help build an understanding of the sustainability position of the corporate and aid in establishing the sustainability objectives.

2. Establish Your Mission

After setting concrete objectives, it is important to establish a corporate mission within the context of the vision statement. A distinct mission statement is an important part of becoming a more sustainable business and should define corporate's five Ws: Who, What, When, Where, and Why.

3. Craft Your Strategy

After having a mission aligned with sustainability, it is required to craft a sustainable business strategy within the boundary of a purpose-driven strategy. It is very important to analyze whether corporate remains profitable after implementing a sustainable business strategy to achieve the vision.

4. Results

With proper vision, mission, and strategy, achieving sustainable business objectives is certainly plausible. In the end, the corporate may benefit holistically, as the sustainability reputation of the corporate may largely cut the cost of raising the capital.

4.3 CORPORATE SUSTAINABILITY

In the age of disruption and more recent generations (e.g., Gen X, Millennials, Gen Z), and also considering the challenges resulting from COVID-19, sustainability must be part of the corporate DNA and be very core to the business model. However, it should be noted that Corporate Social Responsibility (CSR) and Corporate Sustainability involve two different concepts. CSR constitutes the demonstration of social, economic, environmental, or any other helpful contribution to society in order to enhance corporate reputation.[83] Corporates often perform CSR activities to show societal compliance and principally target opinion groups, such as journalists, politicians, and activists, to fetch positive reviews and favorable public relations with investors and the masses. On the other hand, sustainability is about the very survival of the corporate with regard to ESG (Environment, Social, and Governance).[84] The sustainability efforts target the whole value chain network and seek to reward investors (or stakeholders) in the longer term. Nevertheless, CSR measures may be encapsulated under the sustainability goals.

Traditionally, corporates and investors have focused on the governance aspects, such as the role of the board, financial reporting practices and transparency, executive compensation, size of boards, industry expertise, independence profile, or diversity. However, in the current landscape, aside from governance, corporate sustainability originates in two broad themes: (i) the effect the corporate business has on the environment and (ii) the effect the corporate business has on the society. Issues such as climate change, pollution, sexual harassment, unethical job conduct, gender pay gap, employee well-being, reputation, rapid technological transformation, cybersecurity, privacy, scientific advancements, or pandemics such as COVID-19 may pose an inherent threat to the corporate sustainability. For example, The Weinstein Company, an independent American film studio, went into bankruptcy a couple of weeks into 2018 after its joint founder and chief executive Harvey Weinstein was accused and condemned of sexual harassment, assault, or rape by several women.[85] This subsequently led to the rise of the *Weinstein Effect*, wherein many people (largely women) came forward to accuse the famous men of sexual misconduct. This eventually became termed as the "#Me Too" movement across the world. The movement not only rocked the film and fashion industries but the business world. Another example, the COVID-19, led to dramatic business slowdown. Several industries suffered, but, ironically, no one would have thought about such a level of consequences, and very few companies considered it as a significant risk in the contingency plan.

The Committee of Sponsoring Organizations of the Treadway Commission (COSO—www.coso.org), a joint initiative to combat corporate fraud, published standard guidelines about applying enterprise risk management to ESG-related risks (Table 4.3). The COSO enterprise risk management to ESG-related risks and sustainability is further discussed in Section 6.6.2: "Enterprise Risk Management to Environmental, Social, and Governance Risks."

Stakeholders and investors are increasingly making use of ESG ratings. A study conducted by Governance & Accountability Institute, a New York consultancy, found that between 2011 and 2019, the proportion of S&P firms' ESG reporting increased dramatically from 20 percent to 90 percent.[86] More about ESG ratings is discussed in the Section 19.3.5: "ESG Ratings."

Table 4.3: ESG themes

3 Pillars	10 themes	37 ESG Key Issues
Environment	Climate Change	Carbon emissions Product carbon footprint Financing environmental impact Climate change vulnerability
	Natural Resources	Water stress Biodiversity and land use Raw material sourcing
	Pollution and waste	Toxic emissions and waste Packaging materiality and waste Electronic waste
	Environmental opportunities	Opportunities in clean tech Opportunities in green building Opportunities in renewable energy
Social	Human Capital	Opportunities in clean tech Opportunities in green building Opportunities in renewable energy
	Product Liability	Product safety and quality Chemical safety Financial product safety Privacy and data security Responsible investment Health and demographic risk
	Stakeholder opposition	Controversial sourcing
	Social opportunities	Access to communications Access to finance Access to health care Opportunities in nutrition and health
Governance	Corporate governance	Board Pay Ownership Accounting
	Corporate behavior	Business ethics Anticompetitive practices Tax transparency Corruption and instability Financial system instability

Source: (MSCI—www.msci.com)

4.3.1 SUSTAINABLE DEVELOPMENT GOALS

The United Nations (UN) has listed 17 Sustainable Development Goals (SDGs)[87] in *The 2030 Agenda for Sustainable Development*, adopted by all UN Member States in 2015, which is supposed to provide a shared blueprint for peace and prosperity for people and the planet, now and into the future.

The 17 goals are:

1. No poverty
2. Zero hunger
3. Good health and well-being
4. Quality education
5. Gender equality
6. Clean water and sanitation
7. Affordable and clean energy
8. Decent work and economic growth
9. Industry, innovation, and infrastructure
10. Reduced inequalities
11. Sustainable cities and communities
12. Responsible consumption and production
13. Climate action
14. Life below water
15. Life on land
16. Peace, justice, and strong institutions
17. Partnerships for the goals

The goals are meant to act by all the countries, developed, emerging, and developing, in a global partnership. The UN mentions that all the countries must recognize that ending poverty and other deprivations must go hand in hand with strategies that improve health and education, reduce inequality, and spur economic growth, and corporates or businesses should find a common ground to drive the path of a good corporate citizen by incorporating sustainable goals in their business strategies. The COVID-19 pandemic has high potential to impact these conditions. The World Business Council for Sustainable Development (WBCSD—www.wbcsd.org), a CEO-led organization of over 200 major international companies is pursuing the realization of the SDGs through six work programs to achieve systems transformation: Circular economy, Cities and mobility, Climate and energy, Food and nature, Redefining value and People. In a corporate survey conducted by McKinsey,[88] 70 percent of respondents stated that their companies have formal governance of sustainability in place. While the figure is itself not bad, the other corporates are also expected to incorporate a sustainable business model.

4.3.2 PRINCIPLES FOR RESPONSIBLE INVESTMENT

In addition to the sustainable development goals, the UN has published the six principles for responsible investment allied to environmental, social, and governance factors, also known as UN Principles for Responsible Investment (UNPRI—www.unpri.org). Corporates, investors, or businesses that are deemed as signatories must follow these principles to meet their sustainable development goals in order to facilitate in developing a sustainable financial ecosystem, and therefore serving for broader interests of the society. The principles are mentioned below:

- *Principle 1:* We will incorporate ESG issues into investment analysis and decision-making processes.
- *Principle 2:* We will be active owners and incorporate ESG issues into our ownership policies and practices.
- *Principle 3:* We will seek appropriate disclosure on ESG issues by the entities in which we invest.
- *Principle 4:* We will promote acceptance and implementation of the Principles within the investment industry.
- *Principle 5:* We will work together to enhance our effectiveness in implementing the Principles.

- *Principle 6:* We will each report on our activities and progress toward implementing the Principles.

Large institutional investors such as Fidelity Investments, BlackRock, and The Vanguard Group are signatories to the UN PRI. As of mid-2020, more than 2000 financial institutions have already signed to the principles.

4.3.3 EU TAXONOMY FOR SUSTAINABLE ACTIVITIES

In order to achieve the sustainable financial growth and facilitate sustainable investment in line with the UN Sustainable Development Goals, the European Union (EU) came up with the EU taxonomy, a classification system for sustainable activities. The EU's policy for sustainable finance has a long-term strategy to reach carbon neutrality by 2050. The taxonomy is a detailed guide with benchmarks and metrics to educate business and society about sustainable activities and risk management for sustainable business. Essentially, the taxonomy is a tool that can facilitate corporates, businesses, and investors to become voluntarily compliant with the sustainable taxonomy regulation. The EU Taxonomy Regulation was officially published on 22 June 2020—*Regulation (EU) 2020/852 on the establishment of a framework to facilitate sustainable investment and amending Regulation (EU) 2019/2088.*[89]

The taxonomy is based on the six environmental objectives.[90]

1. Climate change mitigation
2. Climate change adaptation
3. Sustainable use and protection of water and marine resources
4. Transition to a circular economy, waste prevention, and recycling
5. Pollution prevention and control
6. Protection of healthy ecosystems

The objectives are aligned to:

1. Reorient capital flows toward sustainable investment, in order to achieve sustainable and inclusive growth
2. Manage financial risks stemming from climate change, environmental degradation, and social issues
3. Foster transparency and long-termism in financial and economic activity.

At present, the EU taxonomy covers the following industries:[91]

- Agriculture, forestry, and fishing
- Manufacturing
- Electricity, gas, steam and air conditioning supply
- Water, sewerage, waste and remediation
- Transportation and storage
- Information and Communication Technologies (ICT)
- Buildings (construction and real estate activities, with application to other sectors where appropriate)

The EU is also in the process to facilitate the green bonds, by issuing bonds for sustainable and green business. The European Investment Bank (EIB) issued in 2007 the world's first Green Bond, labeled Climate Awareness Bonds (CAB), remaining a world leader issuer of Green Bonds in 13 currencies, gradually building green reference yield curves.[92] The funds are earmarked to projects contributing to climate action in the fields of renewable energy and efficiency sectors.

4.3.4 SUSTAINABILITY ACCOUNTING AND NONFINANCIAL REPORTING

Financial Accounting Standards Board (FASB—www.fasb.org), a private, non-profit organization standard-setting body to establish and improve Generally Accepted Accounting Principles (GAAP) in the United States (US),[93] and the International Accounting Standards Board (IASB), an independent, accounting standard-setting body of the International Financial Reporting Standards (IFRS) Foundation,[94] are taking initiatives to work on the standardization of nonfinancial reporting (including ESG). While the obvious challenge is to improve the quality of ESG-related data, there is no doubt that the standardization of nonfinancial reporting worldwide would profoundly aid in nurturing the sustainability ecosystem.

Additionally, many organizations have voluntarily developed the sustainability reporting framework. For example, SASB (Sustainability Accounting Standards Board), a board formed to disseminate sustainability accounting standards, provides an interactive and detailed materiality map on five dimensions:[95]

1. Environment
2. Social capital
3. Human capital
4. Business model and innovation
5. Leadership and governance

It is meant to enable the corporate to identify sustainability issues that have potential or are likely to affect their profitability and financial stability. The materiality map may be useful to identify financially material issues—the issues that are reasonably likely to impact the financial condition or operating performance of a company (see Figure 4.4).

Other sustainability reporting frameworks include Global Reporting Initiative (GTI–www.globalreporting.org), Task Force on Climate-Related Financial Disclosures (TCFD–www.fsb-tcfd.org), Climate Disclosure Standard Board (CDSB–www.cdsb.net), and Climate Disclosure Project (CDP–www.cdp.net).

Figure 4.4: SASB materiality map dimensions and categories

Environment
• GHG Emissions
• Air Quality
• Energy Management
• Water & Wastewater
  Management
• Waste & Hazardous
  Materials Management
• Ecological Impacts

**Leadership &
Governance**
• Business Ethics
• Competitive Behavior
• Management of the Legal &
  Regulatory Environment
• Critical Incident Risk
  Management
• Systemic Risk Management

Social Capital
• Human Rights &
  Community Relations
• Customer Privacy
• Data Security
• Access & Affordability
• Product Quality & Safety
• Customer Welfare
• Selling Practices &
  Product Labeling

Human Capital
• Labor Practices
• Employee Health &
  Safety
• Employee Engagement,
  Diversity & Inclusion

Business Model & Innovation
• Product Design & Lifecycle Management
• Business Model Resilience
• Supply Chain Management
• Materials Sourcing & Efficiency
• Physical Impacts of Climate Change

4.3.5 SOME EXAMPLES OF SUSTAINABILITY INITIATIVES

HSBC Bank, one of the largest banking and financial services organizations in the world, has set out high standards regarding its sustainable business vision, goals, and objectives. In its ESG report,[96] the bank mentions that it has facilitated the first green sovereign sukuk (Islamic bond) in Indonesia. Under the Paris Agreement (UN framework convention on climate change), Indonesia pledged to reduce carbon emissions up to 41 percent by 2030 and adopted the green sukuk framework to support its commitment in line with sustainable finance policy. Similarly, it facilitated the first green loan for the United Kingdom commercial buildings to make them energy efficiency through reduction of greenhouse gas emissions, as direct greenhouse gas emissions from buildings in the United Kingdom account for 19 percent of the country's total emissions. It has also developed sustainable strategies toward climate risk management (exposure to coal mining), supplier ethical code of conduct, and sustainable operations. It has operational goals to reduce carbon emissions, renewable electricity challenge, waste challenge, and high commitment to communities supporting the sustainable supply chain.

EDP, one of the largest Portuguese electric utility company, states that sustainability is in its core DNA. Evidently, for more than 10 consecutive years, it has been included in the Dow Jones Sustainability Index (DJSI). In order to achieve sustainable development and growth, EDP has fundamentally incorporated the following guidelines in its strategy:

1. Economic and social value
2. Eco-efficiency and environment
3. Innovation
4. Integrity and good governance
5. Transparency and dialogue
6. Human capital and diversity
7. Energy access
8. Social development[97]

The Paris Agreement,[98] also known as UN framework convention on climate change, signed by more than 190 state countries, deals with greenhouse-gas-emissions mitigation, adaptation, and finance to determine, plan, and report on the contribution it makes in the effort to mitigate the global warming. For example, France announced a plan to ban all petrol and diesel vehicles by 2040 and to no longer use coal to produce electricity after 2022. Norway announced the ban on the sale of petrol and diesel-powered cars by 2025. The Netherlands announced the same to reach the target by 2030.

Topics of the Chapter
The following has been discussed within this chapter:

- A business model should link the vision to the business strategy as a plan to determine where an organization aspires to be within a predetermined time frame and to satisfy customer needs by defining the customer segment it seeks to serve.

- The "Osterwalder business model canvas" is a tool that can be used to develop a structured process for building a business model segment by segment (see Figure 4.3).

- The business model is a structured process that offers the supervisory board/board of directors and senior management a framework to ensure sustainable growth of the business segments and the organization as a whole.

- Corporate sustainability refers to a corporation's intent to have a positive impact of the corporate on the environment and the society, which in turn affects its reputation and—by extension—sustained growth.

Part II—Family Business Governance and Succession

Chapter 5

Family Business Governance

Most large corporations were initially set up as family businesses by one or more founders, constituting the bedrock of most economies' industrial fabric. Their sustainable growth and success were based on several elements and factors linked to the scope of business itself. The success the founders were able to achieve—structured or unstructured until a certain point—is a critical vector for those initial businesses to become relevant for the family and for society as a whole, all done within a conscious or unconscious governance framework of responsibilities and roles for the different levels within the network of family and the business. This chapter discusses in detail the role of family businesses in an economy, the aspects commonly seen, the need for corporate governance, and the structures and governance models that can be employed.

The topic of family business framework is also discussed, notably because of the importance and role family businesses have in most regions of the world. Family businesses pose additional Governance challenges, because aside from Ownership and Management of the business, its dynamics involve a family or families, and the concept of "Legitimacy" emerges as critical. A family includes stakeholders who are members of the family, but may neither be shareholders nor management, be one of the two, or both. The challenges vary depending on the stage of Generational Control the business is in—Founder,

Siblings' Partnership, or Cousins' Consortium phases—as well as on the business's lifecycle phase and its complexity.

Succession is one of the major challenges in a family business, as it should not be an automatism that empowers the eldest rather than the most fit and proper to drive the business's sustainable value creation. Succession is a process that has to be addressed with time and structure, as is done, for example, in a monarchy—preparing the potential successors ahead of time for the responsibilities they are designated to bear. However, in a Family Business, succession need not have a birth-defined rule of succession, and rather the leadership succession decision should incorporate some flexibility and take into consideration several possible alternatives. Only members of the family that are fit and proper for the job should sit in managerial positions. In the case of shareholders of a family business who are not deemed as fit and proper for positions in the Family Business or otherwise choose other interests and professional careers outside the family business, they must be respected, which implies their entitlement to receive dividends. The textbook presents frameworks—the "eagle approach" versus the "ostrich approach"—to consider different vectors to address these challenges.

The approaches that may be adopted toward corporate governance in family businesses include:

1. A structured process segregating clearly—and often sensitively—property and management at a point in time; usually, when the business starts growing, wishes to enter the capital markets, or succession issues emerge; and,
2. Using the business's success to provide income and/or employment to family members, taking the stance that when the leadership cannot be involved in the business anymore, the successors will have to decide how to proceed.

The first approach has the main objective of anticipating the development needs future potential leaders may have, setting and following a plan to develop them, ensuring the business's sustainable growth, and regular payment of dividends. The latter creates a high degree of uncertainty in accomplishing these objectives. Also, the fact that the inheritance process will, in most situations, disperse the controlling stake amongst successors creates a situation where such strategic decisions will go through tough negotiations, compromises, and trade-offs to make decisions, which will typically be slower and more complex than when control is still concentrated.

Therefore, the definition of the vision of the founder or founders for the family business should constitute a priority, establishing a family governance framework and a business governance framework. The family governance framework should consider the inclusion of independent members in key organization bodies, including individuals not known or related to the family to ensure independent and objective advice to the decision-making family bodies or shareholders. Its structure should take into consideration several factors that include the size and complexity of the business model and the definition of the approach to take to the family governance framework (see Figure 5.1).

Figure 5.1: Aspects of family business

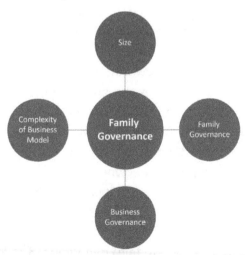

Family businesses (or family enterprises) are often considered the cornerstone of modern economic organization. The scope of family businesses may extend from small mom-and-pop stores to publicly listed multinational companies. Family businesses are not to be confused with the companies having the same owner (major stakeholder) and manager (chief executive). The concept of the family business is inherited from the inclusion of multiple generations of family members related by blood, marriage, or adoption. Usually, the family members are strongly represented in the board or/and management team in a family business, and they exhibit stark company presence and decision-making abilities to influence the dynamics of the business. Publicly listed family businesses may have external shareholders or owners beyond family members, and the governance of such publicly listed family entities falls within the same regulatory landscape as other public firms, in addition to the existing complexity of family governance. A family business may also be managed by others—professionals—who are not considered as family members, but the family members may still exert operational influence in some capacity, such as being the major shareholder. In privately owned family businesses (i.e., not listed on the market), the influence can be much higher. Nevertheless, it is widely agreed that family firms must implement sound family business governance mechanisms to become successful down the generations and ensure/ or /, ensuring sustainable survival.

The succession process down the generations viewed top-down dilutes the initial shareholder stake percentage along each successive generation. It is common to be faced with a shareholder structure that, having started from 100 percent, will be down to 12.5 percent each shareholder at the third generation (grandchildren). If the starting point is 50 percent, then the ownership percentage will be down to 6.25 percent. Statistics suggest that family businesses typically have successful transitions at the rate of 30 percent per generation, meaning that 30 percent make it in the family from first to second generation, 10 percent from second to third generation, 3 percent from third to fourth, and fewer than 1 percent from fourth to fifth and beyond.

These figures show that in one or two generations, the ownership control is diluted to a point that one or two shareholders together will be unable to "control and dictate alone" the rules due to the dispersion of wealth and control over the shareholders' structure, not even considering the influence that descendants and relatives—notably daughters or sons-in-law—have in succession processes that may impact strongly the business. The risks that emerge from this situation are serious and threaten the sustainability of the business, the regular payment of dividends, and the growth of the family wealth. Certainly, it is challenging to control this process along the generations. However, having a governance structure that addresses the issue is paramount to have a healthy, productive, and stable environment to return wealth, notably through the payment of regular dividends.

The percentage of family business across Europe is illustrated in Figure 5.2, referenced from European Family Businesses (EFB) (see Table 5.1).

Figure 5.2: Family businesses across Europe

Source: (European Family Business—www.europeanfamily businesses.eu)[99]

Table 5.1: List of successful family firms across the world

Country	Some Family Business Firms (Public or Private)
Germany	Volkswagen, BMW, Aldi, Henkel, Heraeus Holding, Bertelsmann, Boehringer Ingelheim, Otto Group
France	PSA Peugeot Citroen, Auchan Group, Bouygues, LVMH, L'Oréal, PPR, Michelin
US	Walmart, Berkshire Hathaway, Ford Motor, Koch Industries, Cargill, Comcast, Dell Technologies, Tyson Foods
UK	Wittington Investments, Liberty Global, Arnold Clark Automobiles, Pentland Group
Italy	Fiat, Exor, Edizone, Luxottica Group, Saras, Esselunga, Parmalat
Spain	Mercadona, Industria de Diseno Textil, El Corte Ingles, Ferrovial
Portugal	Jerónimo Martins, Sonae, Grupo Amorim, CIN, SEMAPA
Switzerland	Gunvor, Roche Holding, MSC, Ineos, Tetra Laval International, Swatch
Netherlands	Louis Dreyfus, Altice Europe, Randstad, BCD, Heineken, Shv Holdings
Belgium	Frere-Bourgeois Holding, Colruyt, UCB, Bekaert, Dleteren, Etex
Denmark	Maersk, Danfoss, Lego, Grundfos Holding
Sweden	H&M, Axel Johnson, Investor, Stena

One of the main reasons of differences in family businesses across the world can be attributed to cultural differences. For example, the Indian concept of *jugaad*—frugal, flexible, and inclusive approach to problem-solving and innovation—is deeply rooted in the Indian mindset and not only limited to the family business. Recently, western companies are increasingly seen adopting the same concept. Other differences include that the emerging markets are often community-oriented, and the concept of family may be understood in broader terms with more hierarchy and less individualism than seen in most of the developed economies. As the global revenues' turnover generated from family-owned business is in excess of billions of dollars, the importance of corporate governance in these businesses has gained even more significance. In most family business firms in Europe, the family ownership usually exceeds more than 50 percent. Nonetheless, in the era of technology, platforms such as Amazon or Alibaba taking markets from traditional family retailers such as Walmart and Nordstrom should be of concern. Therefore, for any family businesses to survive and become sustainable, they must innovate over time, stay up to date on technology and incorporate a sustainable business model (see Table 5.2).

Table 5.2: What does family businesses constitute?

GDP	Constitute 60–90% of non-governmental GDP in many countries
Jobs	Constitute 50–80% of all private sector jobs in many countries
Start-ups	Constitute 85% of start-ups with family money
Job Growth	Constitute more than 75% of job growth in the US, and in many countries
Weighting	Constitute between 70% and 95% weight of all businesses in many countries

Source: (European Family Business—www.europeanfamily businesses.eu)

According to the Global Family Business Index 500 (FB500), an index that measures the performance of the top 500 family-owned businesses across the world based on several criteria including data on board composition and characteristics, published jointly by the professional services company EY and Switzerland-based University of St. Gallen, both new and existing firms are increasingly having boards comprising a majority of nonfamily members, and the younger companies are more flexible to hire external directors from outside the family in order to benefit substantially from their expertise and perspectives in the current disruptive landscape. However, the board in most of the family-owned firms is still dominated by the male members, which explains the source of criticism regarding gender equality.[100]

5.1 OWNERSHIP AND MANAGEMENT ISSUES IN A FAMILY BUSINESS

In addition to the principal-agent problem seen in the public firm (discussed in Section 2.1: "The Agency Theory"), a family-owned firm could potentially face prior family issues within the ownership and management structure. As the family business starts with the founder's individual drive and in tight controllership, once it reaches the third generation, it becomes very hard to govern without a proper framework as a result of the growth of family members, and the physical distance and cultural differences among family members.[101] Particularly, cousins may exhibit different traits from their grandparents, as they are highly likely to have become geographically distant and grown up in culturally diverse or disruptive environments, which may naturally give rise to family conflicts between the older generation and the newer generation. International Finance Corporation (IFC), a member of the World Bank Group, explains the ownership and management issues in a family business in a handbook named *IFC Family Business Governance Handbook*.[102]

Figure 5.3: Stages of family business

| Controlling Owner | Sibling Partnership | Cousin Consortium |

At the initiation stage of the family business, the founder(s) are usually the prime owners or controlling shareholders as they own the business and are very committed for the growth of the business (Figure 5.3). While they may seek expert advice from outsiders to achieve business growth, the major decision-making abilities still remain with them. Thus, the notion of ownership and management may not be very important at this stage. However, the founder(s) may address the succession plan initiatives in order to drive the business in successive generations, regardless of the size of the family business. This stage is known as the *controlling owner* stage. Assuming the family business becomes successful, the ownership and management will be transferred to the children of the initial founders(s). This is where complexity starts. Possible family governance challenges include maintaining the harmony between siblings, avoiding inheritance conflicts, formalizing the business processes and procedures, establishing coherent communication channels between family members, and ensuring succession planning for key management positions. This stage is known as the *sibling partnership* stage. Assuming that the family business thrives through generations, more family members (such as children of the siblings, cousins, in-laws) will be directly or indirectly engaged in the family business activities. These family members may come from different branches of the family ranging across generations. The generational gap may constitute different sets of ideas and opinions, and this may further raise the corporate governance challenges in addition to the challenges discussed in the previous stage. Possible family governance challenges include family vision and mission, development of strategy, allocation of corporate capital (dividends, debt, and profit levels), family ownership rights, family member employment, family role in the business, and family conflict resolution. This stage is known as the *cousin consortium* stage, defined as cousins who share ownership of a joint business, generally involving the third-generation members' business.

Research has shown that most of the family businesses do not last more than two generations due to the power struggles among successors and dispersion of wealth and control. Family businesses that managed to overcome these family governance challenges are the ones that survived over the generations and are considered profitable. As family businesses trace back a long history, and since no standard regulations or rules prevailed in the older times, successful family business came up with their own governance mechanism and family charter. Later, the governance mechanism that the family business incorporated became one of the sources of corporate governance model in respective jurisdictions, which eventually became influenced by their own social, political, economic, and regulatory climate. The family governance model incorporated by successful family firms is discussed in the subsequent section.

5.2 FAMILY BUSINESS GOVERNANCE STRUCTURE

To understand the fundamental definition and concept of modern corporate governance, refer to Section 1.3: "Corporate Governance Definition and Concept." However, in a family business, another major stakeholder needs to be considered—the family (and generations of family members). Therefore, the corporate governance mechanism incorporated, or to be incorporated, in family businesses is typically formed in such a way that the influence of the family is preserved in the firm while complying with the prevalent standard corporate governance mechanism. The content presented below is influenced by the case study developed by John A. Davis about the fundamentals of family business system governance (see Figure 5.4).[103]

A corporate governance model involves two distinct components:

1. *Management Supervisory Function*: Governance, supervision, vision and strategy definition conducted under the guidance of non-executive directors in the unitary board or supervisory board in the dual board.
2. *Executive Management Function*: Strategy execution, and tactics' supervision conducted under the command of chief executive and senior management.

Figure 5.4: Comparison of governance and management in public firm and family-owned public firm

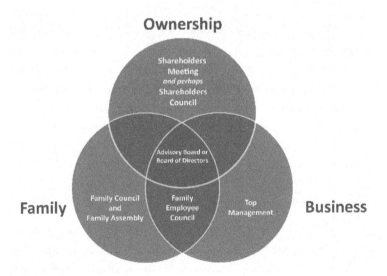

Source: (second figure from Fundamentals of Family Business System Governance—John A. Davis)

From the entrance of the "family" component to the supervisory function and executive management component in a family business emerges the need to incorporate two more constituents to defend family interests and the sustainability of the business: *Family Constitution* and *Family Institutions*.

5.2.1 FAMILY CONSTITUTION

A Family Constitution is a family charter, protocol, or principles. The constitution needs periodical update aligned with business growth over time. Depending on the nature and scope of the family businesses and family members' involvement, the constitution may vary from one business to other, but they all agree to rules for important components to be included in the family constitution.

The components of a family (based on IFC) constitution are:

- Family vision, mission, and strategy
- Family institutions, such as the family assembly, the family council, the family office, and others
- Board of directors (and also board of advisors, if considered necessary)
- Senior management
- Authority, responsibility, and relationship among the family, the board of directors, and the senior management
- Policies regarding important family issues such as succession plan, family members' employment policy, family members' shareholding policy, among others

5.2.2 FAMILY INSTITUTIONS

The governance organizational structure of a family business depends on its size, stage of development, and complexity. However, whatever facts and realities a family business faces, it is an issue related to the management and sustainability of a relevant source of wealth, which is why the approach to take should be the *eagle approach*, defined as a person or organization with far-sighted vision committed to sustainable behaviors and growth strategies, instead of the *ostrich approach*, defined as a person or organization failing to see or act upon the need to a sustainable growth strategy, also known as the *head in the sand*. The approach that is considered adequate should be ingrained into the family business culture.

Family governance institutions such as *Family Council* and *Family Assembly* should be considered to be established and aligned accordingly with the ownership and management structures in order to reduce internal family disputes and conflicts of interests (discussed further in Section 8.1: "Business Ethics and Conduct"), and principally preserve family interests among all participating stakeholders and shareholders. Figure 5.5 explains the detailed structure of a family enterprise.

Figure 5.5: Structure of a family enterprise

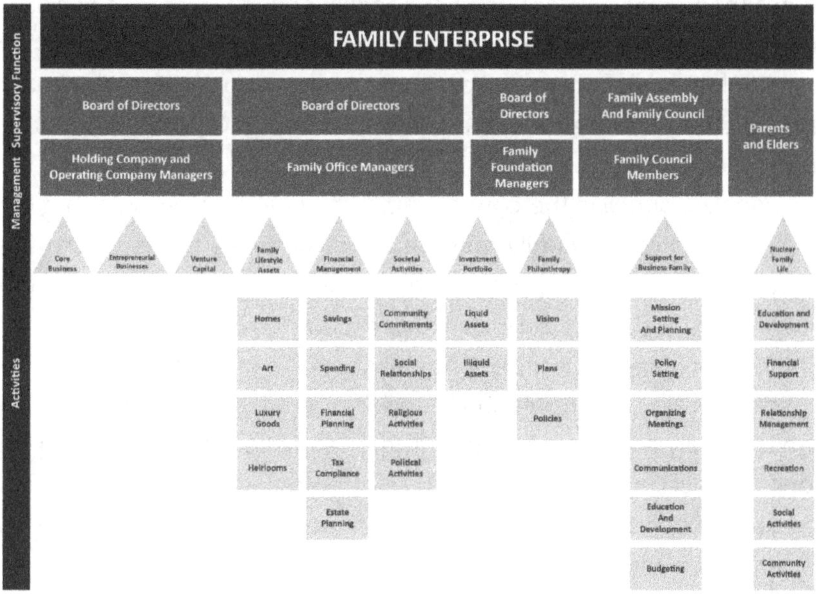

Source: (Fundamentals of Family Business System Governance—John A. Davis)[104]

Family Assembly is the consortium of family members with the authority to set family plans and policies. Usually, the family assembly elects the members of the family council and meets once or twice a year to review and approve the work done by the family council on the family assembly's behalf. Separate annual family assembly meeting in addition to shareholders meeting may be conducted in the publicly listed family firms. By contrast, in private family firms, the meetings are often seen conducted together, as the distinction between shareholders and family members ownership may not be as large. However, it is recommended to carry these meetings separately, because they are supposed to hold different agendas.

The assembly meeting is considered a venue for landing constructive dialogue about the business and ownership, other family activities, discussions and approval of family business plans and policies developed by the family council, educating family members about the business, election of the family council in order to appoint new family members, and other such important matters. Both family and nonfamily managers make a presentation about the business and lead discussions. Normally, the leader of the family council moderates the assembly meeting.

Family Council is the council formed by family members that carries interests of the family members, drafts family policies, and nurtures family business communications and bonds. The family council determines the family business mission and goals, provides support to the board and other relevant stakeholders in order to implement defined mission and goals, and conducts regular family meetings and annual family assembly meeting. Other activities include developing consensus-based policies (such as shareholder agreements), harnessing harmony, maintaining effective communication and positive relationships among family members, educating family members about family business system, maintaining the family discipline, and budgeting and financing of family activities. The employment and development of talent within the family should be a priority for the family assembly in terms of policies and rules to follow, as this decision would impact the sustainable growth of the family business. There are different models including unstructured or structured ones—namely empowered with a degree of independence that may include a veto power—which can be adopted, depending on the vision developed by the founder(s) or the family bodies established.

One alternative would be the constitution of a *family employee council* to protect equitably and in a balanced fashion the family employees' interests and concerns regarding the company and the development of their careers in the family business by developing rules, policies, agreements, and plans that can be proposed to top management. Another alternative, aligned with a more demanding governance model to extend employment to family members, would be to constitute a *family employee committee* or hire a consultant to ensure that only family members with the adequate profile *Fit and Proper* (further discussed in Section 11.1: "Fit and Proper") are hired as employees. This should include considering professionals—both internally and externally—for the position. Also, the committee should be independent, even having a veto power on hiring a family member that the committee decided is not fit and proper for the job. The process can be structured to result into a short list, including—or not—family candidates for position. This selection process would ensure a structured independent and strict process for the family members, leading to the hiring of only the best to carry the duties entrusted to the executive management to ensure sustainable growth and the payment of dividends to the shareholders. In large family business enterprises, it can also be considered that the jury would be constituted by talent search professionals, academics, psychologists, medical doctor, and/or a specialist in the area of activity—business, foundation, family office, social affairs—with the decisions of the family employee committee being unappealable. This issue is also linked to the succession process of the family members in all bodies of the family business as well as at the level of executive management bodies. A similar structured process should be adopted if the objective is to ensure a sustainable growth and the regular payment of dividends.

Also, a *shareholder council* on the top of the board may be established to recognize "all owners" to discuss family business financial and ownership interests, enhance relations with family members and shareholders, coordinate with the board to determine the appropriate dividend distributions, and any other relevant activities (see Table 5.3).

Table 5.3: Summary of family constitution and family institutions

Family Constitution	Family Governance Institutions	
	Family Assembly	**Family Council**
Also known as family charter, protocol, or principles to be followed in running the family business, promoting clarity and transparency. Includes guidelines for family vision and strategy, family institutions, board of directors or/and advisors, senior management, succession policies, shareholding policies, among others. Is supposed to aid in strengthening the family glue (i.e., emotional cohesion), and essentially to nurture the relationship between the family members and the company (i.e., emotional ownership). May not be legally binding but is the key factor to mandate family governance framework, sustainability, and survival.	A family institution that endorses formal annual discussion forum for all family members about family business and issues. Nonfamily managers or employees are often invited. The topics discussed include business & ownership issues, family activities, discussions and approval of family business strategy, plans and policies (drafted or revised by the family council), employment and compensation policies, education of family members about their rights and responsibilities, and election of the family council in order to appoint new family members. Constituted primarily to bring family members together to reflect on family and family business issues. Usually, the leader of the family council moderates the family assembly meeting.	The working governing body; its members are elected by family assembly body. Act as the facilitator between the family, board of directors, and senior management to implement the family vision and goals. Drafts or revises family vision, plans, policies, cultivate family business communications, and bonds. Provides support to the board and other relevant stakeholders to implement the approved mission and goals from the family assembly. Conducts regular family meetings and annual family assembly meeting in order to harness transparency and harmony among all participating stakeholders. Internal sub-council may be established, such as *family employee council*, to protect family employees' interests equitably and in a balanced fashion, and essentially draft or revise a robust succession plan in accordance with Fit and Proper.

5.3 FAMILY BUSINESS GOVERNANCE MECHANISM MODEL

As the family business adds two more governance structures—family council and family assembly—the governance mechanism follows a variant of the modern governance model, regardless of a unitary or dual board structure. Table 5.4 demonstrates the governance structures and plans for a family enterprise and how the key family members and directors interact within the internal and external scope of the family business.

Table 5.4: Family governance structures and plans

Plan or Agreement	Structure or Role			
	Family CEO	Senior Management	Board of Directors	Family Council and Family Assembly
Strategic Plan (e.g., sustainability strategic plan)	Leads and approves	Generates	Consults and approves	Consults and supports
Family Constitution	Consults and supports	Consults and supports	Consults and approves only business policies	Generates
Succession Plan	Generates	Consults and supports	Consults and approves or supports	Consults and supports
Family Business Leader's Retirement Plan	Generates	Is aware	Consults to the extent that the retirement plan affects the business	Consults and supports
Family Inheritance Plan	Helps to generate immediate family	Is aware	Encourages	Encourages and supports
Shareholder's Agreement	Usually leads and helps to generate	Is aware	Is aware	Is aware and supports

Source: (Fundamentals of Family Business System Governance—John A. Davis)[105]

5.4 ROLE OF BOARD IN A FAMILY BUSINESS

Due to the addition of the more stakeholders than usual, namely family council and family assembly, and to uphold the family influence in the board and the firm, many family businesses advocate the concept of two boards—*Advisory Board* and *Board of Directors*.

5.4.1 ADVISORY BOARD

IFC mentions that in a family business an advisory board is a group of experienced and respected individuals that many family businesses form when their own board of directors is only composed of family members and company senior managers. In other words, the advisory board is the voluntarily formed board without family members, offering an opportunity to gather expertise from outsiders without diluting the family members' influence in the real board of directors. The advisory board can be of ceremonial nature—as the advisory board is supposed to bring expertise and value from the outside members perspective, such as international expansion, human resources management, capital management, and other strategic areas, which otherwise could not be found in the existing real board—but the expertise and value are not legally binding to the real board and senior management, and the members in advisory board carry no legal responsibilities.

While the real board is often dominated by family members, the advisory board is deemed to be an independent board with outsiders, not be confused with independent non-executive directors in a real board. Usually, the advisory board is made up of three to seven members, and the fit and proper principle (discussed in Section 11.1: "Fit and Proper") can be voluntarily—or not depending on the established vision by the shareholders—applied to the required degree to select the advisory board members.

In order to respect the independent status and integrity of the advisory board, there are individuals whose profile is not considered suitable for an advisory board:[106]

- Suppliers or vendors.
- Friends of the owners with no relevant expertise to offer.
- Existing providers of service to the company, such as bankers, lawyers, external auditors, consultants; their advice is already provided in other forms, and their objectivity and independence might be in jeopardy, as they are paid by the company.
- Individuals who have a potential or a conflict of interest in being advisors.
- Individuals who are already overcommitted in terms of time and would not be able to dedicate enough time and focus to perform their role.

Advisory board best benefits the business if independent board members take their position and status seriously, despite being systemically less important, with their advice and expertise being valued by the real, decision-making board. Otherwise, the existence of ineffective advisory board is just a waste of time and money.

5.4.2 BOARD OF DIRECTORS

The concept of board of directors in a family business is the same as the board in public listed companies, except that the board of directors in a family business tends to be dominated by the family members and family interests delegated through family council and family assembly.

Nonetheless, if the family business is publicly listed, compliance with standard rules or regulations must be demonstrated like any other publicly listed business. Depending on the jurisdictions, the board can be a unitary board or dual board structure. The NED (non-executive directors or independent directors) should not be confused with members of the advisory board. The unitary board structure usually comprises both NED and ED (executive directors), and if the family business is publicly listed, it is mandatory to have NED in most of the jurisdictions, including a requirement that the independent NED outnumber the rest of the board. It is a good practice not to hire family members as a NED to respect the independence status, unless the society and business values trust, such as in Scandinavia; however, they can be appointed as an ED. The Chief Executive Officer (CEO) is often a member of the core family, known as "Family CEO," though the CEO can also be a professional hired from outside the family circle.

The most crucial aspects are to maintain a healthy mix of both NED and ED to avoid potential conflicts of interests through proper coordination and cooperation with the family council, family assembly, senior management, advisory board, and key stakeholders (or shareholders). The corporate tone should be set at the top. The selection of board members must be conducted according to the fit and proper principle (discussed in Section 11.1: "Fit and Proper"). The successful families in business understand that in the longer term, the family members who are not as competent or do not have the profile including outside professional experience as outsiders in the constantly evolving current business landscape, should step down and instead recruit professional and skilled outsiders that should ensure the sustainability and payment of dividends, as well as mitigate negative outcomes of the Agency Theory. This process is not often easy to accept, and its governance should therefore be defined clearly within the best practices.

Regarding the guidelines on board effectiveness, refer to the guidelines detailed in Chapter 14: Fiduciary Duties, Board Effectiveness, and Dynamics. The board dynamics and the concept of independence and NED in the real board are explained in Section 14.4: "Board Dynamics" and Chapter 13: Independence and Conflicts of Interests, respectively.

5.4.3 ROLE OF SENIOR MANAGEMENT IN A FAMILY BUSINESS

The senior management, or the team of executive directors in a management board, are the ones who run the company. Therefore, in a family business, it is natural that family managers may occupy vital positions inherited through generations. Notwithstanding, the hiring spree of non-family managers has also been on the rise in recent times, because family businesses started to realize that skilled and specialized outside managers can add substantial value to the firm. IFC, in the same family business governance handbook, points out the following steps so that family business can ensure that they have the right mix of senior managers from both inside and outside the family.

- Analyzing the organizational structure and contrasting the current and optimal roles and responsibilities (compared to peer companies) of each senior manager.
- Designing a formal organizational structure that clearly defines the roles and responsibilities of all senior managers. This should be based on the company's current and future business operations' needs.
- Evaluating the skills and qualifications of the current senior management based on the new organizational structure.
- Replacing and/or hiring senior managers.
- Decentralizing the decision-making process and approval levels as necessary. Decision-making powers should be linked to the roles/responsibilities of managers and not to their ties to the family.
- Establishing a clear family employment policy and making its content available to all family members.
- Developing an internal training program that allows skilled employees to be prepared for taking on senior assignments in the future.

- Establishing a remuneration system that provides the right incentives to all managers depending on their performance and not their ties to the family.

Another important spectrum in the family business is the difference between family-first companies and business-first companies. A family-first company has an open door for all family members, favorable employment policies and generous resources allocation to family members and is more hierarchical. A business-first company only intakes qualified family members, salary and leadership are based on performance, and business resources are allocated strategically.

The concept of family member needs to be defined, circumscribed and ring-fenced, although this may represent a challenge, depending on matrix of the phase of the family business—Founder, Siblings' Partnership or Cousins' Consortium—and the complexity of the business model.

5.4.4 SUCCESSION PLANNING IN A FAMILY BUSINESS

Since family members naturally have business interests in the family business, many family businesses take the appointment of CEO or senior management for granted within their vicinities. However, a successful CEO or manager would be the one who is very competent and drives the growth, profitability, and very survival of the business, regardless of being a family member or not. Also, some of the well-governed family businesses require younger family members to gain experiences in other institutions before joining the business, learning and bringing back lessons in professionalism, growing less insecure and more accepting of failure with no shame, earning respect but not assuming it, building humility, and essentially exploring new territories that family business does not offer.[107] Therefore, considering such things, a family business must draw up a prior succession plan, and it is very crucial to engage family members, the board, key senior managers, and relevant stakeholders in the selection process under the direction of the nomination committee formed within the real board. The nomination committee is responsible for drawing the final succession plan not only for the selection of CEO or senior management but also for the board member. The roles of the nomination committee and succession planning are further discussed in Section 17.3: "Role of Nomination Committee" and Section 17.3.1: "Succession Planning."

Topics of the Chapter

The following has been discussed within this chapter:

- Family businesses (or family enterprises) are often considered the cornerstone of modern economic organization. (see Table 5.2)
- While tackling growing scope, complexity, and competition, successful family businesses have established their own governance mechanisms and structures.
- The two components of a corporate governance model are:
  1. Management Supervisory Function
  2. Executive Management Function
- The concepts of family constitution and family governance institutions—including family assembly and family council are discussed (summarized in Table 5.3).
- The structure of family business governance is discussed in Table 5.4.
- In family businesses, a dual structure of Advisory Board and Board of Directors is employed to balance the interests of the family and the interests of the business.

Part III—Control Functions, Risk Concepts, and Supervision

Chapter 6

Control Functions and Related
Frameworks

The three typical control functions of an organization are: Risk
Management, Compliance, and Internal Audit. Framed under a
governance framework and an Internal Control Framework (ICF), the
control functions comprise a structure [organizational] system and a
set of processes and systems that govern the decision-making process of an organization. This chapter discusses the rise of the prevalence of the control functions, the organizational risk management
framework, models applied within a corporation and externally, and
how a well-functioning governance framework and internal control
framework can be achieved to lead to informed decisions.

There are several reasons for the existence and raising importance
(notably after the 2007–2008 financial crisis) of the control functions,
which include the mitigation of risks contemplated in the internal
control framework that may affect the sustainability of the business
model, reputation, or even the risk of penalties for noncompliance.

Other relevant reasons are linked to asymmetry of data and
information between non-executive and executive directors as well
as with the audit board. Some jurisdictions require the audit board
to be an independent board separated from the board of directors,
while in others, such as the UK, the audit committee may be formed

within the board of directors. The audit board is responsible for performing auditing and issuing opinions on matters that may involve transactions with related parties, and, in banks, involving loans to be extended to shareholders and members of social bodies. The audit committee should have an independent stance, as firstly, it should be chaired by an independent non-executive director, other than the chair; secondly, its remit should adopt appropriate policies in line with best practice and guidelines; and thirdly, its composition should include only or majority of independent directors.

Usually, the control functions are monitored and supervised by the audit committee, also referred to as the financial matters committee in the dual model structure in some legal frameworks. In most jurisdictions, the audit committee is formed by independent non-executive directors and always chaired by an independent director while the audit board is formed by members not belonging to the supervisory board/board of directors, one of which should be professionally qualified as a statutory auditor and/or chartered certified accountant. The maintenance of a close, intense working relationship of the audit committee or audit board, if applicable, with the control functions is critical to reduce the asymmetry of data and information. The same principle should apply to the non-executive directors not sitting in the audit committee, who should find mechanisms in the organization to be properly updated by the heads of the control functions—risk management, compliance, and internal audit. Board committees are further discussed in Chapter 17: Board Committees.

Within the executive committee or executive board, the CEO and the CFO usually have information and data of higher quality and detail than their colleagues, which places them in a privileged position. The executive committee members or/and the senior management may also have a greater detail and information that may not be shared, therefore introducing another source of asymmetric data and information within the organization. The control functions play a major role as a tool, notably for non-executive directors, in reducing the risks of asymmetric data and information, but also within the executive committee and senior management. Additionally, in regulated industries—notably in the financial system—the heads and staff members of control functions have an independence statute, as well as particular responsibilities and roles in reporting directly to the regulators and supervisors, even without communicating previously (or at all) to the supervisory board/board of directors, or even to their hierarchy.

The control functions—risk, compliance, and internal audit—as well as external auditors can play a major role in reducing the asymmetry of data and information. As organizations are always susceptible to known or unknown risks (further discussed in Section 7.1.1: "Risk Types") from both external and internal sources, whether linked or not linked directly to their business fundamentals, functions to check those risks must be established robustly throughout the organization at all levels, processes, and functions under a robust umbrella of risk culture with the "tone from the top" and clear established policies. Control functions have gained relevance and prominence after the 2007–2008 financial and economic crisis, as mainly regulators and supervisors of the financial system empowered control functions and their leaders with special duties, responsibilities, and obligations as well as protection functional features from undue pressure within the institutions employing them as managers or staff. The measures and rules enforced, not only in the financial system, but also in other regulated and supervised nonfinancial system institutions, significantly changed the paradigm of the internal control framework (ICF) and the governance framework's landscape, mainly the reinforcement of the role of the board of directors/supervisory board with senior management, notably in their involvement and relations with them, often acting as their "eyes and ears."

Additionally, the relevance of the control functions grants them a statute of full independence as well as a position of privilege in the organizational chart, one of the drivers of the corporate governance definition. The models vary among organizations, depending on financial or nonfinancial, size, international footprint, and nature and complexity of the business model. However, it is paramount that the reporting model is not tainted by potential conflicts of interest. For the control functions, a way to avoid potential conflicts of interest is to split the reporting model's structure between *functional reporting* and *administrative reporting*. The first relates to the activity itself, which involves a status of independence, and the latter deals with the day-to-day areas related to administrative matters. Additionally, in organizations, notably ones with an international footprint, the reporting and organizational model for the control functions should follow the same principles of independence as well as the segregation of the functional reporting and administrative reporting within the group. The control functions of the subsidiaries should report functionally—the "administrative report" can be to the subsidiary—to the group's respective heads, and ultimately to the group's supervisory board/board of directors. This reporting system is required by the guidelines in the banking system, notably in Europe. The Bank of International Settlements—Principle 5: Governance of Group Structures—states that in "a group structure, the board of the parent company has the overall responsibility for the group and for ensuring the establishment and operation of a clear governance framework appropriate to the structure, business, and risks of the group and its entities. The board and senior management should know and understand the bank group's organizational structure and the risks that it poses."[108]

For internal audit—third line of defense (further discussed in Section 6.2: "IIA Three Lines of Defense Model and Its 2020 Successor")—the most common models under functional reporting are the direct report to the audit committee of the supervisory board/board of directors, which should be constituted by a majority of independent non-executive directors, or in few instances to the Chairperson. Administrative reporting to the CFO is the most common. Internal audit function should not report administratively to anyone responsible for any of the other two control functions (risk and compliance, i.e., second line of defense). As discussed above, some legal frameworks may also include an audit or fiscal board responsible for auditing *a posteriori*. In this case, there is also a mitigated reporting function of the internal audit to the audit board, as well as an overlap of activities performed under the scope of the audit committee of the board (a responsibility primarily linked to management supervision in its supervisory role) and the audit board (a responsibility linked to audit, i.e., an *a posteriori* activity and responsibility).

As it relates to risk, the most common functional reporting is to the Chief Risk Officer (CRO), the second line of defense, although some organizations report this to a risk and compliance committee of the supervisory board/board of directors. The administrative reporting of risk management is usually accumulated by the Chief Risk Officer. It is relevant to mention that the credit analyses and approval process (first line of defense) should be segregated from the risk control function (second line of defense), since the latter is part of the second line of defense, while the credit analysis and approval process are part of the first line of defense.

As it relates to compliance, the models vary significantly. Recently, two discussions have emerged. The older approach, advocating compliance (second line of defense) at the same hierarchical level and importance of the other two control functions, is still more prevalent, and the new approach argues that compliance is related mainly to reputational and financial risks and should therefore report to risk control. However, it still seems arguable that having the compliance function report to the supervisory/board of directors would provide a more robust framework, as the specificity and complexity of the risks— including reputational, behavioral, regulations regarding Anti-Money Laundering (AML), Combating the Financing of Terrorism (CFT) and Proliferation Weapons of Mass Destruction (WMD), dealings with FIU (Financial Intelligence Units)—as well as the different staff profiles' skills involved in compliance presents a strong argument to have compliance as a stand-alone unit reporting to the board/supervisory board. In spite of its importance and relevance, since the compliance function being a relatively new function in organizations, there is still a temptation—voluntarily or not—of compliance officers—second line of defense—to step into performing functions that are reserved to the internal audit—third line of defense. This is an area that involves often challenging issues, but compliance officers should be aware of situations that should be passed to internal audit instead of being handled by themselves (Figure 6.1), except when the law or regulators dispose differently. This is an area that the audit committee of the supervisory board/board of directors should monitor carefully and intensely.

Figure 6.1: Aspects of internal control framework and functions

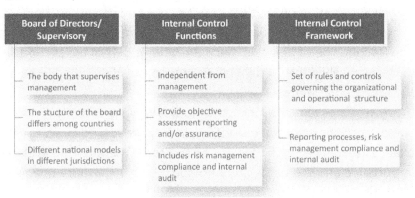

The implementation of robust control functions contributes to prudent control and supervision of risks and compliance, as well as to a robust risk culture. The internal control system enables the institution to appropriately identify, evaluate, and manage their business risks, considering the risk profile, risk capacity, risk appetite, risk buffers as well as risk tolerance. It must promote a strong risk culture: a sound, responsible, and prudent attitude toward risk. Institutions must have an internal control framework that is adequately resourced to fulfill its functions completely and timely, wherein the control functions are operationally independent of the operational units under their control, and with the necessary internal statutes to significantly influence the institution's analysis and decision-making process."[109]

The Chief Executive Officer (CEO) is ultimately responsible and should assume "ownership" of the system by[110]

1. Setting "the tone at the top," which affects integrity and ethics and other factors of a positive control environment.
2. Fulfilling duties by providing leadership and direction to senior managers.
3. Reviewing the way the business is controlled.

Senior managers assign responsibility for establishment of specific internal control policies and procedures. Therefore, the management is responsible for the effectiveness of the internal control framework (ICF), while internal auditors should perform assurance audits to ensure its evaluation and make recommendations for improvements as well as ensure that changes in the business model, systems, and processes are adequately reflected in an update of the ICF.[111]

6.1 EMERGENCE AND EMPOWERMENT OF THE INTERNAL CONTROL FUNCTIONS

The internal control functions were always relevant. However, after the recent financial and economic crisis, they gained added relevance and importance within the governance framework of an organization. In spite of regulation about the control functions and their role in organizations, several factors contributed to the fact that many organizations did not regard them as critical tools in their daily management, notably in risk monitoring, not granting it the relevance they should have in the governance framework. On the other hand, notably in the financial system, regulators and supervisors were performing supervision under a paradigm of "remote control supervision mode," which resulted in the absence of a rigorous and robust supervisory process.

As a result of the impact of the financial and economic crisis in corporations, and society in general, the control functions' relevance emerged in the view of the stakeholders—notably in the financial system, G7 and G20, international institutions like OECD, European Commission, regulators, supervisors, and professional bodies, notably the ones related to financial reporting—as a critical tool to monitor institutions' prudential financial and economic vectors and behavior components, including risk culture, behavior, and transparency with depositors and investors as well as other factors and elements that have emerged as relevant trends for society. Governments and regulators improved the frameworks under which internal control functions operated in practice, imposing demanding criteria and standards on institutions, notably in the financial system. This included the recruitment and profiling of the heads and staff of control functions for supervised institutions, institutionalizing a Fit and Proper process for members of boards and other social bodies that should, in terms of best practices, be also applied to the nonfinancial system, especially to ones that are regulated and supervised. An innovation in the improvement of the process is the clarification and empowerment of the role of directors (the board in its management function and role) and non-executive directors (the board in its supervision function and role), the latter being responsible and accountable for the supervision of the executive directors. The relations of the non-executive directors, executive directors, and the heads and staff of control functions with regulators and supervisors also changed the paradigm. Now it imposes a closer and potentially intense relation when these figures identify issues or challenges that may impact reputation or financial stability. The board of directors must discuss with senior management the state of the art of the internal control framework and system, provide oversight, and duly seek input from both the internal and external auditors.

The asymmetry of data and information is a challenge that board members—notably the non-executive directors—have to overcome, as the data and information provided to the supervisory board/board of directors are often incomplete, not provided on a structured fashion, or even presented in excessively long documents or including relevant information and data filtered by management or even executive directors. Although there could be good reasons for this, like the purpose of providing objective and summarized data and information, matters that should come to the attention of non-executive directors could potentially get lost in the process of preparation of documents addressed for their review. These matters may be relevant for non-executive directors to supervise risks the institution is exposed to or even to challenge executive directors and management in their decisions, taking a stance under an optimistically skeptical approach. Boards should set up procedures and roles relating to the standards for documents presented to the board.

One of the important components of the concept and objectives of the internal control functions is to assist the board of directors and management—and by extension the stakeholders—to ensure a company is properly run. However, experience shows that it is not unusual for the control functions to suffer pressures, notably to enter into commercial transactions outside the risk appetite defined or involving risky jurisdictions to which they have to resist with their statute of independence as well as to report the results of audits that identify weaknesses in the control systems and the internal control framework transparently to the supervisory board/board of directors. Because of their independent stature, the control functions should play a pivotal role in assisting the non-executive directors in their management supervisory role. It is relevant for directors to understand the organizational risk management and control framework, also known The Three Lines Model, which encapsulates the internal control functions—risk, audit, and compliance—under specific lines of defense.

6.2 IIA THREE LINES OF DEFENSE MODEL AND ITS 2020 SUCCESSOR

The *IIA Three Lines of Defense model*[112] is one of the important models for organizational risk management and control introduced nearly 20 years ago, updated in 2020—to reflect changes of paradigm in this landscape—by the Institute of Internal Auditors (IIA–www.theiia.org), one of the most respected entities in internal audit standards and guidance. The three lines of defense model may be solely applied to design the holistic organizational control framework and functions, or it may also be customized by taking some leverage from other available frameworks such as COSO Internal Control Framework (ICF). In plain concept, the first line deals with operational management, overseeing functions that own and manage risks; the second line deals with compliance, which are functions that oversee risks; and the third line provides assurance, which includes functions that provide independent assurance. The Bank of International Settlements (BIS) further advocates for the fourth line of defense, including the regulators, supervisors, and external auditors, which is discussed in Section 6.5: "Four Lines of Defense Model."

The three lines of defense framework is considered to be simple, easy to communicate, and easy to understand. Its design should be based on the main drivers of the expectations from stakeholders. It describes the respective responsibilities and roles of the board or the governing body, senior and operational management, risk and compliance functions, internal audit functions, as well as their connection with regulators, supervisors, and external auditors. In 2020, IIA introduced a major update—dubbed *The Three Lines Model*.[113]

Previously, the first and second lines of defense were managed by senior management, while the governing bodies, board, and audit committee supervise the second and third lines of defense. Commentators observed that the previous model was limited and restrictive and focused only on defensive actions rather than taking a more proactive approach. The financial crisis and corporate scandals demonstrated that corporates need to further enhance their governance structures and measures. In addition to macro-prudential rules, there are talks about micro-prudential rules and robust internal control systems relating to the frequent misconducts at the corporates. On the other hand, the three lines of defense model does not include the role of the board and the audit committee in the first line of defense, where the business model fundamentals reside. Today, the role of non-executive directors should involve a monitoring role in the supervision of the business model of an organization, which includes control over the revenue stream and the cost structure.

The IIA's updated three lines of defense model associates role-based functions with clearly defined roles for governing bodies and management within an organization, including holistic oversight by the governing body or board of directors, risk and compliance incorporation through management and operational roles, and independent assurance through internal audit. The revised model follows the principles-based approach and adopting the model to suit organizational objectives and circumstances; achieving objectives and creating value through effective risk management, also to the matters of "defense" and protecting value; understanding the roles and responsibilities represented in the model and the relationships among them; and implementing measures to ensure activities and objectives are aligned with the prioritized interests of stakeholders.

Regulators and supervisors have started to value the corporate tone, culture, and risk behavior very highly. Hence, the best of a model can be implemented with both a proactive and a reactive approach; recognition of the overlapping areas of activities and further clarity to the roles and responsibilities with tone at the top; agile, scalable, and incremental model; and incorporation of all-important internal and external stakeholders to governance without blurring the lines of defense in organizational structure. As recommended, COSO's Internal Control Framework (ICF) can be potentially leveraged. Also, COSO and IIA together have published a comprehensive guideline titled *Leveraging COSO Across the Three Lines of Defence*,[114] mapping the functions of the three lines of defense to COSO principles from which corporates can benefit freely (Figures 6.2 and 6.3). Although mapping with new IIA Three Lines Model is expected to come in the future. In this textbook, the guidelines from the Institute of Internal Auditors are largely adapted to explain the three lines model. In addition to three lines model, the concept of four lines of defense model is discussed in Section 6.5: "Four Lines of Defense Model."

Figure 6.2: IIA's 2020 three lines of defense model

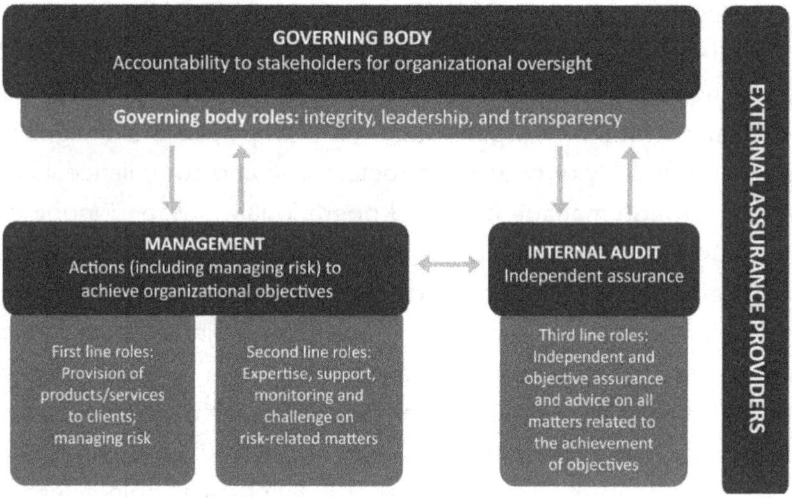

Source: (IIA—www.na.theiia.org)[115]

6.2.1 THE GOVERNING BODY

The governing bodies are accountable to stakeholders—not only to shareholders—for the oversight of the organization, having as an umbrella role the assurance of integrity, leadership, and transparency, notably in financial and nonfinancial reporting.

The board or the governing body oversees the organization by defining the vision, mission, values, strategic plan, and organizational appetite for risk and risk culture. The governing body's relationship with management and internal audit is essentially critical. As the body receives reports from management on planned, actual, and expected outcomes, as well as reports on risk and the management of risk. Internal audit is meant to achieve the reasonable assurance on such reports. Depending on the jurisdictions, the board may be single-tiered or two-tiered; nonetheless, the governing body has the main following roles:

- Accept accountability to stakeholders for oversight of the organization.
- Engage with stakeholders to monitor their interests and communicate transparently on the achievement of objectives.
- Nurture a culture promoting ethical behavior and accountability.
- Establish structures and processes for governance, including auxiliary committees as required.
- Delegate responsibility and provide resources to management for achieving the objectives of the organization.
- Determine organizational appetite for risk and exercises oversight of risk management (including internal control).
- Maintain oversight of compliance with legal, regulatory, and ethical expectations.
- Establish and oversee an independent, objective, and competent internal audit function.

Figure 6.3: Different functions of three lines model

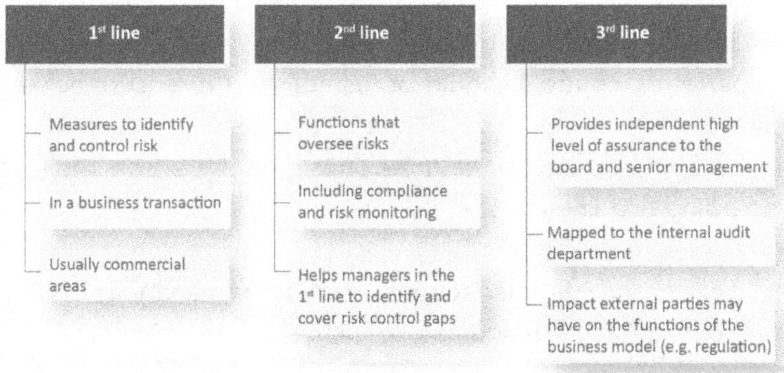

6.2.2 MANAGEMENT—FIRST LINE ROLES AND FUNCTIONS

Roles and functions that support the provisions of products or services to clients own and manage risks. At the first level, the operational management has ownership, responsibility, and accountability for directly assessing, controlling, and mitigating risks. Operational managers not only own and manage risks but are also responsible for implementing corrective actions to address process and control deficiencies in the revenue-generating units. The controls executed in this line are supposed to be very granular because of execution of individual transactions, as it assumes that the operational level employees are involved in the process daily, thus being familiar with the workplace and any possible control weaknesses. This subsequently allows operational level staff to provide immediate notifications to the operational management. Operational managers need to ensure the timely implementation of necessary measures. With the introduction of automated controls, comprehensive control activities may be achieved with exceptional situations requiring immediate management review.

Operational management assists in identifying, assessing, controlling, and mitigating risks through the development and implementation of internal policies and procedures, and it essentially ensures that the actions are aligned with strategic interests, goals, and objectives. For example, the mid-level managers design and implement important procedures (known as "control") and supervise the execution of those procedures by staff. Therefore, adequate managerial and supervisory controls should be established to ensure achieving compliance.

The 2020 IIA update of the three lines model presents the following regarding first line roles:

- Leads and directs actions (including managing risk) and application of resources to achieve the objectives of the organization.

- Maintains a continuous dialogue with the governing body, and reports on: planned, actual, and expected outcomes linked to the objectives of the organization; and risk.
- Establishes and maintains appropriate structures and processes for the management of operations and risk (including internal control).
- Ensures compliance with legal, regulatory, and ethical expectations.

6.2.3 MANAGEMENT—SECOND LINE ROLES AND FUNCTIONS

These are roles and functions that provide expertise, support, challenge, and oversee risk-related matters. The second line establishes the added layer for monitoring and supervising the first line controls. If the controls in the first line are absent, the controls in the second line of defense may apply to eliminate or at least mitigate the possibility of the corporation entering into unacceptable risks. IIA mentions the following typical functions of the second line:

- A *risk management function* that facilitates and monitors the implementation of effective risk management practices by operational management and assists risk owners in defining the target risk exposure and reporting adequate risk-related information throughout the organization. The risk management function has seen its role enlarged, now covering a range of risks affecting a corporation, notably the monitoring of the levels of risk capacity, risk buffers, and risk appetite defined at board level.
- A *compliance function* to monitor various specific risks such as noncompliance with applicable laws and regulations and control risks involving reputational issues that usually also have a financial impact (such as fines, additional taxation). In this capacity, the best practice for this stand-alone function is

to report directly to the board in their functional duties. In the banking sector, the compliance function must report directly to a committee (such as audit committee) of the supervisory board/board of directors. Multiple compliance functions often exist in a single organization, each responsible for specific types of compliance monitoring including health and safety, supply chain, environmental, or quality monitoring. There is also a model, prevalent particularly in the banking system, where the compliance function has antennas residing within the first line of defense and it responsible for compliance with regulations and laws.

- A *controllership function* that monitors financial risks and financial reporting issues.

The second line functions are essentially established to ensure the effectiveness of the first line by defining *preventive* and *detective* control requirements. Contrary to operational functions in the first line, second line functions are regarded as management functions, having the power to intervene in changing and developing improved internal and risk control measures. The second line of defense functions are effectively positioned for risk management and internal controls. Second line functions should be independent of the first line and apply controls either on an ongoing (such as daily) or periodic basis. In the 2020 updated model, IIA mentions the following responsibilities of second line.

- Provides complementary expertise, support, monitoring, and challenge related to the management of risk, including:
  o The development, implementation, and continuous improvement of risk management practices (including internal control) at a process, systems, and entity level.
  o The achievement of risk management objectives, such as: compliance with laws, regulations, and acceptable ethical

behavior; internal control; information and technology security; sustainability; and quality assurance.
- Provides analysis and reports on the adequacy and effectiveness of risk management (including internal control).

6.2.4 INTERNAL AUDIT—THIRD LINE ROLES AND FUNCTIONS

The third level ensures full independence for internal audit functions, although the risk and compliance functions are also supposed to be independent. Internal audit is not only supposed to deliver a reasonable level of assurance on the effectiveness of applied governance, risk management, and internal controls but also to be aligned to the way first- and second-line functions achieve risk management and control objectives. Therefore, internal auditors cater to the board and senior management with comprehensive assurance, based on the highest level of independence and objectivity within the organization. The board is primarily responsible for the independent audit function (involving the audit committee), and measures should be taken to ensure a high level of independence in meeting with the board in the absence of senior management.

The scope of audit assurance reported to the governing body (in its functional role) and senior management (in its administrative role) covers:

- A broad range of objectives, including efficiency and effectiveness of operations, safeguarding of assets, reliability and integrity of reporting processes, and compliance with laws, regulations, policies, procedures, and contracts.
- All elements of the risk management and internal control framework, which includes internal control environment, all elements of an organization's risk management framework (i.e., risk identification, risk assessment, and response), information and communication, and monitoring.

- The overall entity, divisions, subsidiaries, operating units, and functions, including business processes such as sales, production, marketing, safety, customer functions, and operations, as well as supporting functions such as revenue and expenditure accounting, human resources, purchasing, payroll, budgeting, infrastructure and asset management, inventory, and information technology.

The 2020 IIA's updated three lines model mentions the following roles of internal audit:

- Maintain primary accountability to the governing body and independence from the responsibilities of management.
- Communicate independent and objective assurance and advice to management and the governing body on the adequacy and effectiveness of governance and risk management (including internal control) to support the achievement of organizational objectives and to promote and facilitate continuous improvement.
- Report impairments to independence and objectivity to the governing body and implements safeguards as required.

In addition, BCBS's Principle 10—Internal audit states that "the internal audit function should provide independent assurance to the board, support board and senior management in promoting an effective governance process and the long-term soundness of the bank."[116]

6.2.5 EXTERNAL ASSURANCE PROVIDERS

These are the independent entities outside the organization; however, these entities play an essential role in the governance and control structure of the organization and therefore constitute an added layer of defense, sometimes also called the *fourth line of defense* (further discussed in Section 6.5: "Four Lines of Defense Model") (see Table 6.1).

Table 6.1: Relevance of external assurance providers viewed in three perspectives

Stakeholders	Board of Directors (BoD)/Management	Supervisory Board
• The auditor provides credibility and reliability • The auditor reduces uncertainty • Risk associated to the shareholders' decision-making process	• The auditor helps the BoD/Management on the fulfillment of their responsibilities against the shareholders and other stakeholders • Better understanding of the applicable accounting framework, law, and regulation	• The auditor provides relevant information that enable the supervisory board to develop their monitoring activities • Risk overseeing and supervision of internal control framework (ICF) system and financial reporting process

External audit's primary responsibility is to issue an independent opinion about the correctness and financial statements—statement of financial position, profit and loss statement, statement of cash-flows, and notes to the financial statements—assist in identifying any loopholes and vulnerabilities, and therefore prompt to take necessary measures to correctively address those weaknesses. Regulators may enforce mandatory compliance requirements, and companies must demonstrate their compliance status. All of these are designed to improve the risk profile and risk appetite of the organizations. The management representation letter written by an external auditor and signed by the executive board and often by senior management depending on the jurisdiction—particularly CEO and CFO—attests to the accuracy of the financial statements, as well as financial and nonfinancial reporting usually included in the annual report or in a separate specific report (e.g., sustainability report, governance report, supervisory board report). The letter is usually signed following the completion of external audit activities such that the financial statements are issued along with the auditor's opinion.

The concept of *"four lines"*[117] is targeted at financial institutions, although it is applicable to any regulated and audited institution mention that since the 2008–2009 financial crisis. The design and implementation of internal control systems has attracted attention, notably about the effectiveness and characteristics of internal audit functions and on the effectiveness of corporate governance processes. Based on these, the authors have developed the concept of the four lines to cover the supervisors and external auditors—who are formally outside an organization—that the updated IIA's three lines model names External Assurance Providers. This concept, though not incorporated with the designation of fourth line of defense in the IIA 2020 update, is also very relevant because of the duty and responsibility, notably in the financial system, of the governing bodies, namely non-executive directors and the audit committee, as well as the staff of the independent control functions—risk, compliance, and internal audit—or reporting and interact namely with the supervisors and external auditors, as well as with judiciary authorities in certain situations, notably the ones related to money laundering and financing to terrorism and weapons of mass destruction. Section 6.5 details the fourth line. Chapter 9 discusses regarding the role of the regulators, for example, ECB (European Central Bank) and SSM (Single Supervisory Mechanism) in the eurozone.

6.2.6 THE EFFECTIVE COORDINATION OF THE THREE LINES

As it is known that no one-size-fits-all, there is no definitive approach to design the functions of the three lines of defense. Corporations are big, medium, and small, and they may have different requirements, goals, and objectives. Therefore, corporations are free to design their own risk management framework, but they should adequately incorporate the fundamentals of three lines model practices.

The recommended practices of IIA are:

- The governing body, management, and internal audit have their distinct responsibilities that are aligned with the objectives of the organization.

- The basis for successful coherence is regular and effective coordination, collaboration, and communication.
- Risk and control processes should be structured in accordance with the three lines model.
- Each lines should be supported by appropriate policies and role definitions.
- There should be proper coordination among the separate lines of defense to foster efficiency and effectiveness.
- Risk and control functions operating on the different lines should appropriately share knowledge and information to assist all functions in better accomplishing their roles in an efficient manner.
- Lines of defense should not be combined or coordinated in a manner that compromises their effectiveness.
- In situations where functions of different lines are combined, the governing body should be advised of the structure and its impact. For organizations that have not established an internal audit activity, management and/or the governing body should be required to explain and disclose to their stakeholders how adequate assurance on the effectiveness of the organization's governance, risk management, and control structure will be obtained.

6.3 INTERNAL CONTROL CONCEPTS

In order to achieve a functioning framework designated through five internal control structural components at different lines of defense:

1. Environment
2. Risk Assessment
3. Control Activities
4. Information and Communication
5. Monitoring

These are elaborated on the basis of the tone set at the top, namely ethical values, management and operating philosophy, empowerment and responsibility. Thus, the risks need to be continuously assessed. A precondition to risk assessment is the establishment of control objectives that are linked at different levels and are internally consistent. Appropriate basis and mechanisms may be established to identify and analyze the relevant risks to achieve desired control objectives. Essentially, internal control functions are meant to achieve assurance in three objectives:

1. *Effectiveness and Efficiency* of performance and profitability goals focused on safeguarding of tangible and intangible resources involved in the business vision, strategy, and objectives, as well as reporting to supervising authorities in companies operating in regulated financial and nonfinancial industries.
2. *Reliability* of financial and economic reporting, nonfinancial and noneconomic events and thematic (such as ESG, UN Sustainable Goals), financial statements, transparency, external auditors, and sustainability reporting.
3. *Compliance* with laws, tax laws, regulations (such as foreign direct investment, exchange controls, labor, AML-CFT-WMD) in all respective jurisdictions.

The mechanisms are also required to deal with risks that may arise from the changing landscape such as changes in politics, economic, industry, regulatory, geopolitical environment, legal and taxation frameworks, exchange controls, technology, or operating conditions such as the COVID-19 pandemic. Ultimately, this is achieved through the tone of the corporate control environment set at the top, influencing the control consciousness of staff and serving as the foundational stone for implementing components of internal control functions and provide discipline and structure. The factors that affect control environment include integrity, ethical values, competence of the entity's people and resources, direction provided by the board of directors, management's philosophy and operating style of the executive committee, the way management assigns authority and responsibility, and organization and development of human resources or talent.

Control functions and activities, inherited from control environment, are departments operating under an independent regime but are part of an institution that ensures objective assessment, reporting, and assurance in corporations, notably risk control, compliance, and internal audit, although it is common to find areas like inspectorate general—common in IFI (International Financial Institutions) and focusing particularly on fraud and corruption—also serve as a control function. Control activities are designed within the boundary of control environment and control functions. Control activities encompass policies and procedures to ensure management directives are executed and necessary actions are taken to address emerging risks to achieve the control objectives. The range of activities include approvals, authorizations, verifications, reconciliations, reviews of performance, security of assets, segregation of duties, among others. Control functions can be detective, preventative, and/or corrective.

Setting up a division to effectively implement the control functions and develop an updated internal control framework is a viable option. Proper information and communication in the corporate control environment is equally important, especially to ensure:

1. Pertinent information is identified, captured, and communicated.
2. People and staff are enabled to carry out responsibilities and are able to produce operational, financial, and compliance information in their job position and capacity.

3. Clear communication and directive from the top of management that the staff take control responsibilities seriously and be accountable.

4. Analysis of internally generated control and compliance information dealing with external events, activities, and conditions to form the basis for informed decision-making and external reporting.

Monitoring of internal control framework is crucial to achieve continuous assurance. The following four elements of control functions require continuous monitoring, namely, Effectiveness, Synergies, Relationships, and Transversal.[118]

1. *Effectiveness*, as the effectiveness of internal control systems need continuous monitoring and communication of the processes and results with all participating personals, which is usually facilitated by the internal audit (conducted internally) and subsequently external audit (conducted by an external auditor).

2. *Synergies* and linkage among these components, thus forming an integrated system that reacts dynamically to changing conditions. As the internal control system is intertwined with the entity's operating activities and exists for fundamental business reasons, it is most effective when controls are built into the entity's infrastructure and are a part of the essence of the enterprise. Undoubtedly, "built in" controls support quality and empowerment initiatives, avoid costs, and enable quick response to changing conditions.

3. *Relationships* need to be monitored between the three categories of objectives to ensure what an entity strives to achieve and between the five components of internal control functions to ensure what is needed to achieve the control objectives' is principally important.

4. *Transversal*, with all five control components being relevant to each objectives' category, and thus to conclude that internal control over operations is effective. Any internal control deficiencies should be reported to the top management and the board.

6.3.1 INTERNAL CONTROL FRAMEWORK (ICF)

The recommended guidelines—European Banking Authority (EBA) Guidelines on Internal Governance under Directive 2013/36/EU (EBA/GL/2017/11)[119] and COSO (Committee of Sponsoring Organizations) of the Treadway Commission's ICF (Internal Control Framework)[120]—help structure and explain the fundamental concepts.

The five integrated components of COSO must be assessed and monitored by the supervisory/board of directors, a challenging task whose effective and efficient operation can be ensured by directors with the support and contributions of the control functions and the external auditors. The ICF is supposed to capture the adequate control functions advocated by three lines model functions, or four lines, when regulators, supervisors and external auditors are considered the fourth line of defense (discussed in Section 6.5: "Four Lines of Defense Model"). These guidelines on internal governance are structured and detailed in a best practice fashion, which is why they can be easily adopted by the nonfinancial industry.

EBA, the European Union (EU) agency tasked with implementing a standard set of rules to regulate and supervise banking across EU countries, states that institutions should develop and maintain a culture that encourages a positive attitude toward risk control and compliance within the institution and a robust and comprehensive internal control framework. Under this framework, institutions' business lines (first line of defense) should be responsible for managing the risks they incur in conducting their activities and should have controls in place that aim to ensure compliance with internal and external requirements. As part of this framework, institutions should have internal control functions with appropriate and enough authority (independence privileges), stature and direct access, and actually functional reporting to the management body in its supervisory function (non-executives) or management (executive directors) capacity to fulfill their mission and a risk management framework. The ICF should ensure effective and efficient operations; prudent conduct-of-business; adequate identification; measurement and mitigation of risks; reliability of financial and nonfinancial information, reported both internally and externally; sound administrative and accounting procedures; compliance with laws, regulations, supervisory requirements, and the institutions; and a set of internal policies, processes, procedures, rules, and decisions.

COSO, a commission established to combat corporate fraud, published the Standard Internal Control Framework (ICF)[121] and has been widely used by the corporations for designing, implementing, and monitoring the internal control framework and functions as well as to support the enterprise risk management integrating with strategy and performance. Moreover, COSO has developed a detailed and robust *Enterprise Risk Management (ERM) framework*, integrating with corporate strategy and performance, which itself expands on the foundations of ICF. COSO states that the internal control is not a serial process but a dynamic and integrated process. The framework applies to all entities: large, mid-size, and small; for-profit, not-for-profit, and government bodies. However, each organization may choose to implement internal control differently. For instance, a smaller entity's system of internal control may be less formal and less structured and yet have effective internal control (see Figure 6.4).

The framework provides for three categories of objectives (as discussed earlier in Section 6.3: "Internal Control Concepts"): (i) Operational Objectives, (ii) Reporting Objectives, and (iii) Compliance Objectives.

Relationship of Objectives and Components
COSO mentions a direct relationship between objectives (which is what an entity strives to achieve), components (which is what is

required to achieve the objectives), and the organizational structure of the entity (the operating units, legal entities, and others).

- Categories of objectives (i.e., operations, reporting, and compliance) are represented by the columns.
- Five components are represented by the rows.
- Entity's organizational structure is represented by the third dimension.

Figure 6.4: Internal Control Framework

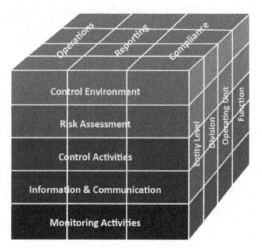

©2013, Committee of Sponsoring Organizations of the Treadway Commission (COSO). Used by permission.

Source: (COSO—www.coso.org)

Principles

The COSO ICF sets out 17 principles based on 5 integrated components. The principles are as follows:

A. Control Environment

1. The organization demonstrates a commitment to integrity and ethical values.

2. The board of directors demonstrates independence from management and exercises oversight of the development and performance of internal control.
3. Management establishes—with board oversight—structures, reporting lines, and appropriate authorities and responsibilities in the pursuit of objectives.
4. The organization demonstrates a commitment to attract, develop, and retain competent individuals in alignment with objectives.
5. The organization holds individuals accountable for their internal control responsibilities in the pursuit of objectives.

B. Risk Assessment
6. The organization specifies objectives with sufficient clarity to enable the identification and assessment of risks relating to objectives.
7. The organization identifies risks to the achievement of its objectives across the entity and analyzes risks as a basis for determining how the risks should be managed.
8. The organization considers the potential for fraud in assessing risks to the achievement of objectives.
9. The organization identifies and assesses changes that could significantly impact the system of internal control.

C. Control Activities
10. The organization selects and develops control activities that contribute to the mitigation of risks to the achievement of objectives to acceptable levels.
11. The organization selects and develops general control activities over technology to support the achievement of objectives.
12. The organization deploys control activities through policies that establish what is expected and procedures that put policies into action.

D. Information and Communication

13. The organization obtains or generates and uses relevant, quality information to support the functioning of internal control.
14. The organization internally communicates information, including objectives and responsibilities for internal control, necessary to support the functioning of internal control.
15. The organization communicates with external parties regarding matters affecting the functioning of internal control.

E. Monitoring Activities

16. The organization selects, develops, and performs ongoing and/or separate evaluations to ascertain whether the components of internal control are present and functioning.
17. The organization evaluates and communicates internal control deficiencies in a timely manner to parties responsible for taking corrective action, including senior management and the board of directors, as appropriate.

6.3.2 INTERNAL CONTROL FUNCTIONS—EBA

In the usual scenario, the internal control functions are established on the basis of objectives, components, and principles of a control framework such as COSO framework or another corporate customized framework. EBA (European Banking Authority) illustrates three important internal control functions agreeing with the control functions advocated by three lines of defense.[122] EBA states that the internal control functions should include a *risk management function* (second line of defense), a *compliance function* (second line of defense), and an *internal audit function* (third line of defense). The risk management and compliance functions should be subject of review by the internal audit function. The heads—and staff, when deemed necessary—of internal control functions should have direct access or report directly (currently emerging as the best practice) to the management body in its supervisory function (non-executive directors) to raise concerns and warn the supervisory function, where appropriate, when specific developments affect or may affect the institution.

For the internal control functions to be regarded as independent, the minimum following conditions should be met:

- Internal audit staff do not perform any operational or consulting tasks (although internal audit may participate as an observer in relevant committees, as long as it does not impair its independence) that fall within the scope of the activities the internal control functions are intended to monitor and control.
- They are organizationally separate from the activities they are assigned to monitor and control.
- In spite of the overall responsibility of members of the management body for the institution, the head of an internal control function should not be subordinated—only administratively—to a person who has responsibility for managing the activities monitored and controlled by the internal control.
- The remuneration of the internal control functions' staff should not be linked to the performance of the activities the internal control function monitors and controls.

Essentially, internal control functions should have adequate resources. They should have an adequate number of qualified staff, both at the parent level and at subsidiary level. Staff should remain qualified on an ongoing basis and should receive training as necessary.

Risk Management Function (second line of defense)

EBA states that institutions should establish an independent RMF (Risk Management Function) covering the whole institution (EBA/GL/2017/11). The RMF should have, where and when necessary, direct access to the management body in its supervisory function and its committees and have access to all business lines and other internal units that have the potential to generate risk. The RMF should be a central organizational feature of the institution, structured such that it can implement risk policies and control the risk management framework. Staff within the RMF should possess enough knowledge, skill, and experience in relation to risk management techniques and procedures, markets, and products.

Significant institutions—defined in Article 131 of Directive 2013/36/EU: Global Systemically Important Institutions G-SII—may consider establishing dedicated RMFs for each material business line. The RMF should provide relevant independent information, analyses, and expert judgment on risk exposures, advise on proposals and risk decisions made by business lines or internal units, and inform the management body whether they are consistent with the institution's risk appetite and strategy. The head of the RMF should be responsible for providing comprehensive and understandable information on risks and advising the management body, enabling this body to understand the institution's overall risk profile. In most cases, RMF is guided under the direction of the CRO (Chief Risk Officer).

Compliance Function (second line of defense)

EBA states that the institutions should establish a permanent and effective compliance function to manage compliance risk and should appoint a person to be responsible for this function across the entire institution (EBA/GL/2017/11). This function can be combined with the head of the RMF or can be performed by another senior person (e.g., head of legal), provided there is no conflict of interest between the functions combined. However, due to the characteristics and growing complexities of the issues covered by the compliance function—which impacts the profile of its staff and therefore a very specific training program to keep them fit for the job—the best practice would recommend maintaining it as an autonomous control function, i.e., reporting to the same hierarchical level as internal audit and risk management. The compliance function, including the head of compliance, should be independent of the business lines and internal units it controls and should have enough authority, stature, and resources. The management body in its supervisory function should oversee the implementation of a well-documented compliance policy, which should be communicated to all staff.

The compliance function should advise the management body on measures to be taken to ensure compliance with applicable laws, rules, regulations, and standards, and should assess the possible impact of any changes in the legal or regulatory environment on the institution's activities and compliance framework. The compliance function should ensure that compliance monitoring is carried out through a structured and well-defined compliance monitoring program and that the compliance policy is observed. Institutions should take appropriate action against internal or external fraudulent behavior and breaches of discipline. Institutions should ensure that their subsidiaries and branches take steps to ensure that their operations are compliant with local laws and regulations. In most cases, compliance is guided under the direction of the CCO (Chief Compliance Officer) from compliance department.

There are areas that require particular expertise, notably taxation and Foreign Direct Investment (FDI). These areas have high potential reputational risk. Tax issues and related compliance deserve focused attention from boards—both from executive and non-executive directors—particularly because boards often do not include directors with taxation and FDI experience and/or expertise. The position of the board about tax issues should be clearly defined with a stance set up at the top, involving deep consideration to tax planning practices, especially ensuring that the institution does not adopt aggressive tax planning and/or tax optimization practices or mechanisms that often may involve reputational risk like the use of SPV (Special Purpose Vehicles, colloquially known as offshores) in jurisdictions that are not considered adopting transparent practices. Potentially reputational issues, namely in terms of Anti-Money Laundering/Combating the Financing of Terrorism/Weapons of Mass Destruction (AML-CFT-WMD), may emerge from those practices.

On the opportunities side, a corporation should leverage conventions for the Avoidance of Double Taxation (DTA) but deal within an arms' length criteria, particularly with issues related to inter-company pricing and management fees.

Internal Audit Function (third line of defense)

The internal audit function should provide independent assurance to the board and support the board and senior management in promoting an effective governance process and the long-term soundness of an institution. EBA states that the institutions should set up an independent and effective internal audit function (IAF) and should appoint a person to be responsible for this function across the entire institution EBA/GL/2017/11). The IAF should be independent of the audited activities. Therefore, the IAF should not be combined with other functions. The IAF should, following a risk-based approach, independently review and provide objective assurance of the compliance of all activities and units of an institution—including outsourced activities—with the institution's policies and procedures and with external requirements. The IAF should not be involved in designing, selecting, establishing, and implementing specific internal control policies, mechanisms and procedures, and risk limits.

In particular, the IAF should assess:

- Appropriateness of the institution's governance framework.
- Whether existing policies and procedures remain adequate and comply with legal and regulatory requirements and with the risk appetite and strategy of the institution.
- Compliance of procedures with the applicable laws and regulations and with decisions of the management body.

- Whether procedures are correctly and effectively implemented (e.g., compliance of transactions, the level of risk effectively incurred).
- Adequacy, quality, and effectiveness of the controls performed, and reporting done by the defense business units and by risk management and compliance functions.

Also, an internal audit plan should be drawn up at least once a year based on the annual internal audit control objectives. The internal audit plan should be approved by the management body, after the input of the audit committee. In most cases, the audit function is guided under the direction of the CAE (Chief Audit Executive) from audit department. The audit plan is an end-to-end process with the involvement of the audit committee and the board of directors/supervisory board.

6.3.3 CAPTURING RISK UNDER THE INTERNAL CONTROL FRAMEWORK

The Risk Management Framework is itself derived from ICF (Internal Control Framework); the framework evolves from the tailored use of internal control framework and functions. Companies are free to develop their own version of risk management framework; however, the framework must ensure that it captures control functions adequately. Risk concepts are further discussed in Chapter 7: Risk Concepts and Risk Appetite.

The internal control framework should be adapted individually to the specificity of the business, complexity and associated risks, considering the group (EBA/GL/2017/11). The exchange of the information should ensure that each management body, business line, and units, have the resources to carry their responsibilities, as well as exchange of information among businesses and the heads of the control functions at the group level and the social bodies body of the institution. The ICF should cover the organization on a consolidated basis.

EBA states that the risk management framework should enable the institution to make fully informed decisions on risk-taking. The risk management framework should encompass on and off-balance sheet risks as well as actual risks and future risks that the institution may be exposed to. Risks should be evaluated both from the bottom up and from the top down, within and across business lines, using consistent terminology and compatible methodologies throughout the institution and at the consolidated or sub-consolidated level. All relevant risks should be encompassed in the risk management framework with appropriate consideration of both financial and nonfinancial risks including credit, market, liquidity, concentration, operational, IT, reputational, legal, conduct, compliance, and strategic risks.

The risk management framework should be subject to independent internal review (i.e., performed by the internal audit function), and it should be reassessed regularly against the institution's risk appetite, considering information from the risk management function, and, where established, the risk and compliance committee. When identifying and measuring or assessing risks, an institution should develop appropriate methodologies, including both forward-looking and backward-looking tools. Institutions should be fully aware of the limitations of models and metrics and use not only quantitative but also qualitative risk assessment tools (including expert judgment and critical analysis). In addition to the institutions' own assessments, institutions may use external risk assessments (including external credit ratings or externally purchased risk models). Regular and transparent reporting mechanisms, along with effective communication and awareness regarding risks and the risk strategy, are crucial for the whole risk management process.

6.4 INTERNAL AUDIT

6.4.1 INTRODUCTION—CHANGE IN INTERNAL AUDIT PARADIGM

The changes in regulation and the reinforcement of the role of risk management and compliance as well as the need for stronger scrutiny over the business model of an organization impacted internal audit strongly shifting the paradigm for internal auditors' soft and hard skills required to perform their duties in a robust fashion. This change is a result of the need to deal with challenges in risk management, compliance, and credit approval process, which have been objects of major regulatory changes.

Training programs and new hiring policies should be established to answer the new required set of skills, which should include a demand for professional qualifications. This should include, for example, certification as internal auditor, IT auditor, compliance certifications, risk management certification, or others equivalent to those required by external auditors (e.g., statutory auditor). Also, it should be required that internal audit performs and delivers audit reports to protect the business and the stakeholders and, eventually, deliver measurable value, ensuring an internal audit department remains fit to keep up with the changes. Internal auditors' skills should also include the capacity to challenge issues emerging in the strategic plan linked to the business model and should therefore be able to challenge the ability of a company to deliver the vision and mission defined by the board.

EBA states that institutions should have an independent and effective internal audit, taking into account the proportionality criteria. One individual should be responsible for internal audit across the institution, including subsidiaries, therefore the named consolidation perimeter of a group. Internal audit should be independent and have authority, stature, and resources as well as ensure that the qualification of its staff members and the resources are adequate considering the institution's size, locations, the nature, scale, and complexity of the risks associated of the business model, risk culture, and risk appetite.

The International Professional Practices Framework (IPPF) is the conceptual framework that sets up the guidelines promulgated by The Institute of Internal Auditors (IIA), a global guidance-setting body that provides internal audit professionals with guidance organized in the IPPF as mandatory.[123] An updated framework was introduced in 2015, and the IPPF of Internal Auditing—known as the Red Book—approved it in 2016. IPPF Internal Auditing Standards determine that as internal audit is conducted in diverse legal and cultural environments and as organizations vary in purpose, size, complexity, and structure (including staff within and from outside the organization), differences may affect the practice, but conformance with International Standards is critical to meet responsibilities of internal auditors and their internal audit duties.

The new paradigm also suggests room for the scope of cooperation of other areas—notably risk management and compliance—with internal audit. However, although this may be welcome, it should be taken into consideration that the autonomy and independence of parties cannot be affected, maintaining clear boundaries of responsibilities and confidentiality regimes. EBA (2018) indicates that the internal audit function should be independent of the audited activities and, consequently, should not be combined with other functions.

6.4.2 INDEPENDENCE AND OBJECTIVITY OF INTERNAL AUDIT PLAN

Internal audit work should be performed in accordance with an audit plan and detailed audit programs following a risk-based approach. The audit plan should be drawn annually on the basis of the control objectives in line with the guidance of the management body in its supervisory functions or the unitary board. Internal audit reports are subject to a formal follow up to ensure and report their effective and timely resolution. There are fundamentally two elements that underline the characteristics of internal audit plan: *Independence* and *Objectivity*.

The Institute of Internal Auditors (IIA)[124] states:

"(...) independence is the freedom from conditions that threaten the ability of the internal audit activity to carry out internal audit responsibilities in an unbiased manner. To achieve the degree of independence necessary to effectively carry out the responsibilities of the internal audit activity, the CAE (Chief Audit Executive) has direct and unrestricted access to senior management and the board, as well as to the supervisors if operating in a regulated industry. This can be achieved through a dual-reporting relationship—functional and administrative. Threats to independence must be managed at the individual auditor, engagement, functional, and organizational levels. Objectivity is an unbiased mental attitude that allows internal auditors to perform engagements in such a manner that they believe in their work product and that no quality compromises are made. Objectivity requires that internal auditors do not subordinate their judgment on audit matters to others. Threats to objectivity must be managed at the individual auditor, engagement, functional, and organizational levels."

The concept includes elements like unrestricted access to the board, regulators, and supervisors, as well as a dual-reporting governance structure—functional and administrative. Objectivity is a predicate that ensures the performance of engagements resulting in an audit report without quality compromises or unbiased political views, therefore not subordinating judgment to others' views. Threats to independence and objectivity must both be dealt with by the individual auditor at any required organizational level to address the issue. Actually, as control functions, the concepts of independence and objectivity should both also apply to risk management and compliance. An issue that may emerge relates to the length of time a CAE (Chief Audit Executive) is responsible for internal audit, linked to the potential loss of independence and objectivity. Therefore, the tenure of a CAE and the potential need for rotation after a reasonable number of years is relevant to consider when an institution applies professional standards and adopts best practices for the control functions.

The discussion around the compulsory rotation of CAEs emerged from the mandatory rotation of external auditors. The benefits of rotation include enhancing independence and objectivity; bringing fresh outlooks or views that strengthen the internal audit role in challenging the executive management; bringing new or more sophisticated skills and different experiences or viewpoints; and removing the danger of a shareholder or the public perceptions of close relationships between the CAE and management. On the other hand, the drawbacks of rotation include the potential loss of continuity, loss of specific experience, as well as the potential reduction of the internal audit effectiveness. The standards and implementation guidelines do not state a period for automatic or recommended rotation of the CAE, although a rotation every 5–7 years appears to be the best practice. Both standards and implementation guide as well as the IIA position paper[125] recommends that the tenure of the CAE should be considered in the annual individual appraisal and external quality assurance processes on the basis of performance, effectiveness, independence, and objectivity. The annual appraisals should be led by the Chair of the audit committee.

Independence

The internal audit activity must be free from interference in determining the scope of internal auditing, performing work, and communicating results.[126] Organizational independence is achieved when the CAE directly and functionally reports to the board, and the board shows a proactive approach to undertake the following actions:

- Approving the internal audit charter
- Approving the risk-based internal audit plan
- Approving the internal audit budget and resource plan
- Receiving communications from the CAE on the internal audit activity's performance relative to its plan and other matters
- Approving decisions regarding the appointment and removal of the CAE
- Approving the remuneration of the CAE
- Making appropriate inquiries of management and the CAE to determine whether there are inappropriate scope or resource limitations

Depending on the jurisdictions, corporate law usually defines, with different levels of demand, the legal concept and factors that impart independence, notably to the non-executive directors, when that quality is required to be nominated to board.

Individual Objectivity

Internal auditors must be competent and trained, have an impartial, unbiased attitude, and avoid any conflict of interest—or even potential conflict of interest—to give any audit opinion, as they often arise when an internal auditor, who is in a position of trust, has a competing professional or personal interest. This could essentially undermine the confidence of internal auditor, the audit activity, and the profession, and may consequently impair the auditor's ability to perform his/her duties and responsibilities objectively. Impairments may include scope limitations; restrictions on access to records, personnel, and properties; and resource limitations such as funding. Therefore, any impairment compromising independence or objectivity must be disclosed immediately to the appropriate parties.

Also, the status of objectivity is presumed to be impaired if an internal auditor provides assurance services for a specific activity for which the internal auditor had responsibility within the previous year. Internal auditors are not expected to be involved in developing, implementing, or operating the risk management function or another line of defense. They may be requested to attend committees' meetings as observers, with the objective of detecting—at an early stage—changes in policies or procedures that may negatively affect the internal control framework of the institution. In these circumstances, these facts or risks resulting from the discussions should be documented and reported. The assurance engagements for functions over which the CAE has responsibility must be overseen by a party outside the internal audit activity, preferably an external auditor acting as a consultant, and not in its function as statutory auditor that issues an opinion on the financial statements.

Nonetheless, internal auditors may provide consulting services relating to operations for which they had previous responsibilities, but any potential impairments must be communicated upfront and disclosed to the board and the audit committee.

6.4.3 BIS STATURE OF INTERNAL AUDIT FUNCTION

BIS has published a comprehensive consultative document about the internal audit function in banks regarding the supervisory expectations to the internal audit function (Figure 6.5).[127] Nevertheless, the same can be efficiently applied for any regulated industries or nonfinancial sectors. Essentially, BIS advocates the same concept of independence and objectivity promulgated by the IIA and, with regard to corporate governance considerations, also proposes the following for internal audit function's communication channels. It is highly recommended for directors to be familiar the papers and guidelines published by those entities.

Figure 6.5: Internal audit function's communication channels

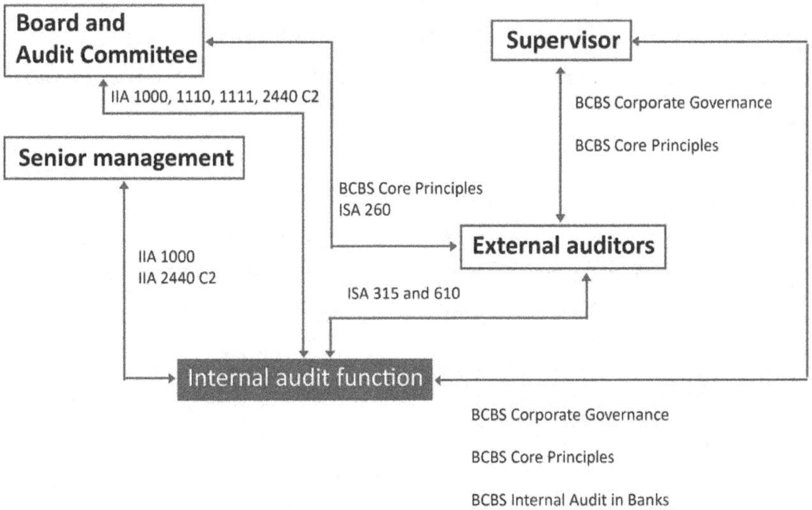

Source: (BIS—www.bis.org)[128]

Basel Committee on Banking Supervision (BCBS):

- BCBS Core Principles for Effective Banking Supervision
- BCBS Principles for Enhancing Corporate Governance
- BCBS Internal Audit Function in Banks

Institute of Internal Auditors (IIA): Standards starting at 1xxx (e.g., IIA 1000) are Attribute Standards and Standards starting at 2xxx are Performance Standards.

- IIA 1000—Purpose, Authority, and Responsibility
- IIA 1100—Independence and Objectivity
- IIA 1110—Organizational Independence
- IIA 1111—Direct Interaction with the Board
- IIA 2440—Disseminating Results

International Standards on Auditing (ISA): ISA Standards starting at 2xx (for example—ISA 260) deal with the overall objectives and responsibilities of the external auditor, standards starting at 3xx deal with risk assessment and response to assessed risk by the external auditor and standards starting at 6xx deal with the external auditor's use of the work of others.

- ISA 260—Communication with Those Charged with Governance—deals with the auditor's responsibility to communicate with those charged with governance in an audit of financial statements; does not establish requirements regarding the auditor's communication with an entity's management or owners unless they are also charged with a governance role.[129]
- ISA 315—Identifying and Assessing the Risks of Material Misstatement through Understanding the Entity and Its

Environment—deals with the auditor's responsibility to identify and assess the risks of material misstatement in the financial statements, through understanding the entity and its environment, including the entity's internal control.[130]

- ISA 610—Using the Work of Internal Auditors—deals with the external auditor's responsibilities relating to the work of internal auditors when the external auditor has determined, in accordance with ISA 315, that the internal audit function is likely to be relevant to the audit.[131]

6.4.4 INTERNAL AUDIT PLANNING FRAMEWORK

As internal audit is not a stand-alone or isolated activity, it involves quite a standard process. Within the scope of internal control framework, the flow process starts with developing an internal audit charter, the internal audit strategy, the internal audit strategic plan, and finally the annual internal audit plan. As discussed earlier, no one size fits all. There is no right or wrong way to define the internal audit coverage. However, Chartered Institute of Internal Auditors (CIIA–www.iia.org. uk), the entity that represents internal auditors in the UK and Ireland, mentions that the following elements can be considered when developing the annual internal audit coverage plans: The risk profile and risk appetite (discussed in Chapter 7: Risk Concepts and Risk Appetite)[132]

- The structure and geographical spread of the organization.
- The internal auditor's experience of the organization and the sector more generally to identify other areas of risk which may warrant attention.
- The prevailing legal and regulatory regime; for example, in some sectors such as financial services a number of audits might be scheduled specifically to address legal or regulatory requirements, some of which may have been requested by the regulator.

- Stakeholders' requirements.
- *Ad hoc* areas that do not feature as a high or medium risk but where the organization would benefit from an internal audit review.
- To provide assurance to the audit committee and external auditors regarding operation of the key financial and management information systems.
- The work of other assurance activities, such as first and second lines of defense.

According to BIS,[133] the audit charter should be drawn up and reviewed periodically by the CAE and approved by the board of directors or/ and the audit committee. At a minimum, it must include:

- The internal audit function's position, its authority, its responsibility, and its relations with other control functions.
- The purpose and scope of the internal audit function.
- The key features of the internal audit function.
- The obligation of the internal auditors to communicate the results of their engagements and a description of how and to whom this should be done (reporting line).
- The criteria for when and how the internal audit function may outsource some of its engagements to external experts.
- The terms and conditions according to which the internal audit function can be called upon to provide consulting or advisory services or to carry out other special tasks.
- The responsibility and accountability of the head of internal audit.
- A requirement to comply with sound internal auditing standards.
- Procedures for the coordination of the internal audit function with the statutory or external auditor.

Figure 6.6: Internal audit planning framework

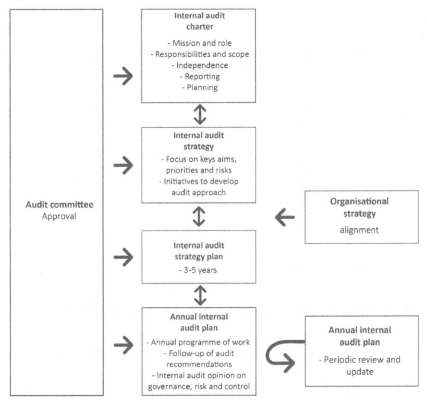

Internal audit charter
- Mission and role
- Responsibilities and scope
- Independence
- Reporting
- Planning

Internal audit strategy
- Focus on keys aims, priorities and risks
- Initiatives to develop audit approach

Audit committee Approval

Organisational strategy
alignment

Internal audit strategy plan
- 3-5 years

Annual internal audit plan
- Annual programme of work
- Follow-up of audit recommendations
- Internal audit opinion on governance, risk and control

Annual internal audit plan
- Periodic review and update

Source: (CIIA—www.iia.org.uk)

Often, corporates have insufficient resources to perform the internal audit function, and this may potentially constitute significant pressure in CAE to provide the same value with limited resources (Figure 6.6). Therefore, a way to achieve the most with limited resources is by defining the severity of risks from high priority to low priority but not being complacent. As a result, communication with board is vital, respecting both independence and objectivity. An example of internal audit plan adapted from CIIA is illustrated in Figure 6.7.[134]

Figure 6.7: Risk-based internal audit plan

Business area or activity	Key risk description	R1	Treatment	Monitoring and/or 2 line assurance	R2	Responsibility	Date of last audit	IA narrative	IA Plan allocation
Governance	Failure to comply with new regulatory code of conduct on fair customer treatment resulting in fines, complaints and loss of income.	25	Re-design of customer charter and sales manual. Check-point controls within sales process. Sales team training.	Compliance team set up of testing checklist. Complaints KPIs and reporting.	20	Head of Compliance and Complaints team.	None to date.	This is a new code of conduct which becomes operation in April. IA will liaise with Compliance team and will review checklist approach. IA will verify accuracy of KPI complaints handling report.	10 days
Business continuity	A major IT outage that denies access to front line systems and use of central hardware.	25	Full scale 'hot site' business continuity plan. IT back-up and support. Emergency planning training	Schedule of plan testing IT Team Monitoring of down time and incidents.	15	Director of IT.	June 2012. Review of business continuity prep.	In June this year there will be a full test of back-up restoration with off-site PC set up. IA will observe and validate IT team report to senior man. IA review of the downtime & incident log with trend analysis and examination of responses.	6 days
Purchasing	Purchases of raw materials into the manufacturing cycle are unsuitable, too expensive and/or delivered too late.	25	Sample material testing by product design. Tendering plan as per purchasing strategy. Price increases above 5% reviewed and approved purchasing manager.	Exception reporting upon price variations to contracts by Finance. Review of outstanding orders by Buying team.	12	Head of Product Design. Purchasing Manager.	Sept 2011 review of tendering procedure.	2012 saw major over spend in the raw material purchasing budget. IA will compare invoiced prices to contract prices using IDEA software and review any major variations. This will involve exception report production and management responses.	10 days

R1 Inherent risk score impact x likelihood on 5 by 5 matrix before risk treatment & monitoring
R2 Residual risk score impact x likelihood on 5 by 5 matrix after risk treatment & monitoring

Source: (CIIA—www.iia.org.uk)

6.4.5 FIT AND PROPER—NEW DEMANDS ON INTERNAL AUDITORS

The CAE plays a pivotal role in ensuring a fit internal audit department, being accountable for the internal audit standards used. Resource Management (IIA Standard 2030) should be a permanently monitored to ensure that the internal audit resources are appropriate, sufficient, and effectively deployed to achieve the plan, meaning that internal audit be equipped with the right mix of knowledge, skills, and other competencies, with the adequate headcount, and that resources are effectively deployed when they are used in a way that optimizes the achievement of the approved audit plan. The IIA indicates that the standards apply to individual internal auditors and the internal audit activity, with internal audit being accountable for conforming to the standards related to individual objectivity, proficiency, and due professional care and the standards relevant to the performance of their job responsibilities.

IIA establishes Proficiency and Due Professional Care (#1200) that internal auditors must possess the knowledge, skills, and other competencies, and that internal audit collectively must possess or obtain the knowledge, skills, and other competencies to perform its responsibilities.[135] Considering the current activities, trends, and emerging issues, internal auditors are therefore encouraged to demonstrate their proficiency by obtaining appropriate professional certifications and qualifications to enable recommendations. Continuing Professional Development (#1230) is a critical process to maintain and develop internal auditors, who must enhance their knowledge, skills, and other competencies through continuing professional development. Internal audit staff must ensure the qualification of the internal audit function and its resources, mainly by monitoring tools and risk analysis methods according to its size, locations, and the nature as well as the scale and complexity of risks associated with the business model and activities and the risk culture and risk appetite framework (EBA/GL/2017/11).

However, one line of thought argues that external auditors greatly benefit from prudent activities performed by internal auditors, but the incentive internal auditor receive is very less compared to the external auditors. Essentially, many companies fail to offer appropriate incentive to internal auditors, especially now that the role of internal auditors has become even more crucial.

6.5 FOUR LINES OF DEFENSE MODEL

The functions of fourth line of defense were previously called *supervision functions*, updated in the 2020 IIA review of the model to *external assurance providers*. The fourth line of defense concept is discussed in a paper published by BIS (Bank for International Settlements) authored by Arndorfer and Minto titled the "Four Lines of Defence"[136] model addressed to financial institutions, essentially feeding the inputs from the three lines of defense model to elaborate further on specific governance features of regulated financial institutions. The model suggests a fourth line of defense involving external assurance providers—regulators, supervisors, external auditors. However, the model may not be understood as to replace the original model developed by IIA (updated in 2020). It should be seen as another model by introducing the fourth line, not only being relevant to banking and financial institutions, but also to be considered and leveraged by any regulated industries such as energy, transportation, oil and gas, defense, pharmaceutical, communications, among others. Although IIA made a major update in 2020 to the three lines of defense model, the relevance of the fourth line of defense was introduced in the revised framework.

The four recommendations for improvement pointed out in the paper are as follows:

1. Misaligned incentives for risk-takers in the first line of defense

As the first line is often the revenue-generating unit, management may often put more emphasis on the achievement of financial objectives than control-oriented objectives. Nevertheless, this may constitute a bigger challenge. For example, several banks in the US faced financial penalties when the staff in the first line expanded derivatives trading positions on US residential mortgage-backed securities. However, the same information did not reach the board and even top management levels, as was limited to general reports. The insufficient controls and financial reporting systems concealed the exposure to the US mortgage market. Thus, the important point relates to how banks or corporates can incentivize the first-line risk-takers—managing risks' responsibilities—who meet the control objective but fail to generate revenue for the organization. One way is to introduce a compensation system comprising of a variable bonus scheme, coupled with the achievement of a mandatory control objective before being paid out. At a higher level, the achievement of the control objective must be coherently communicated.

2. Lack of organizational independence of functions in the second line of defense

In line with the best practices, the risk management functions report formally to the board. However, the day-to-day reporting lines and communication may fall to senior management rather than to the board. This way, critical control functions may lose independence and objectivity by being embedded in the organization through engagement and exchange of information with other functions of the first—managing clients' risk—and second line of defense—expertise, support, monitor, and challenge on risk related matters—and eventually being assumed as a risk-taking unit rather than acting as a control unit. Remuneration in the second line has also become an important topic, mainly as banks are faced with the challenge of setting objectives for the control units that compensate sufficiently for risk and control awareness while still allowing the organization to generate steady profits and sustainable growth.

3. Lack of skills and expertise in second line function
Despite the second line of defense being organizationally independent, it may not have enough skills and expertise to challenge the practices and controls in the first line, such as the validation of complex models like interest rate risk in the banking book (IRRBB).[137] Also, the experience and remuneration in first line functions are still considerably higher than in second line functions, despite the tighter regulation of variable compensation practices. Ultimately, the larger question is how banks can lure highly qualified staff to work in second line functions rather than in first line or risk-taking functions.

4. Inadequate and subjective risk assessment performed by internal audit
The annual audit plan is based on the holistic risk assessment framework and may be performed by individuals who have a good grasp of the risk profile of the organization. However, the failure in detecting high-risk areas may lead to audits focusing on the wrong risk areas and undermine the effectiveness of the third line of defense. For example, UBS internal audit performed a review of the critical trading desk for US mortgage-backed derivatives and subsequently detected control weaknesses but failed to finalize the audit report in due time.

The delay in validating and finalizing the audit report became very critical and therefore weakened the otherwise good quality of the report. However, the integration of external auditor's role in the lines of defense may address the shortcomings of the traditional model. Another challenge for internal audit relates to the ability of its staff to audit areas of high complexity that require particular levels of expertise, notably in risk management and compliance, especially the knowledge of algorithms and artificial intelligence that would ensure a knowledgeable audit of issues related to money laundering and financing to terrorism and weapons of massive destruction, taxation, and issues linked to foreign direct investment.

6.5.1 FOURTH LINE OF DEFENSE (EXTERNAL AUDIT AND SUPERVISOR)

International standard setters did not require a close relationship between supervisors and corporate control functions for a long time. However, the landscape is changing very fast, raising the need for an enhanced dialogue with the board and senior management regarding the governance of risk, development of risk appetite framework, and an assessment of the risk culture, as well as with compliance and internal audit. Essentially, for the latter, a BCBS (Basel Committee on Banking Supervision) paper on internal audit function mentions the relationship between internal audit and supervisors, an overview of supervisory expectations relevant to the internal audit function including quality assessment, and benefits of enhanced communication between supervisors and internal audit function.[138] Accordingly, the fourth line of defense advocates the assignment of a specific role to external auditors and banking regulators and supervisors in relation to the monitoring the internal control system, acknowledging that they remain outside the organization but become instrumental in defining assurance and governance systems (Figure 6.8). Figure 6.8 shows in the left side the superseded model of the IIA three lines of defense model—current model in Figure 6.2—and, on the end right side of the figure, the "triangular concept" advocated by the fourth line of defense.

Figure 6.8: Four lines of defense (based on the IIA superseded model)

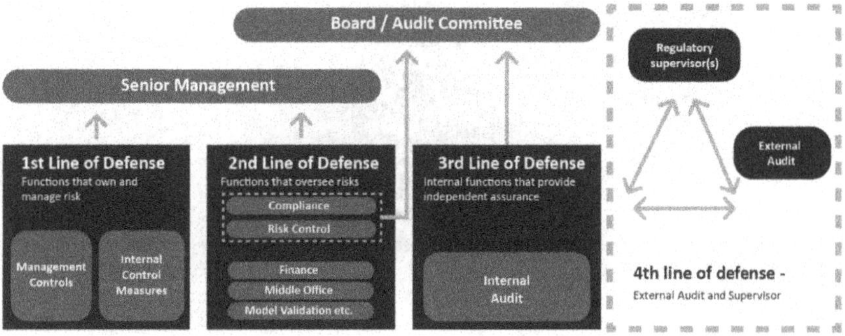

Source: (BIS—www.bis.org)

Communication between the internal auditor, external auditor, and supervisors—both prudential and behavior—are very relevant (Figure 6.9). Good communication certainly works by reducing, if not eliminating, asymmetric information among the parties involved, provided that the treatment of information is to make risk control system more effective. The audit committee of the board, often in coordination with the audit board when it exists (as some countries such as Portugal require the existence of an independent audit board formed by individuals not belonging to the supervisory board/board of directors), may identify and nominate suitable candidate firms to act as external auditors and approve their appointment. If required, a new set up of harmonized rules for sharing information between internal audit and external parties can be facilitated and, because of internationalization, the same entity may be subject to different regulations in different jurisdictions. However, when a group has cross-border operations, the best practice is to adhere to the most demanding standard, as they conform with lower standards in a particular jurisdiction.

Figure 6.9: The triangle of external assurance providers

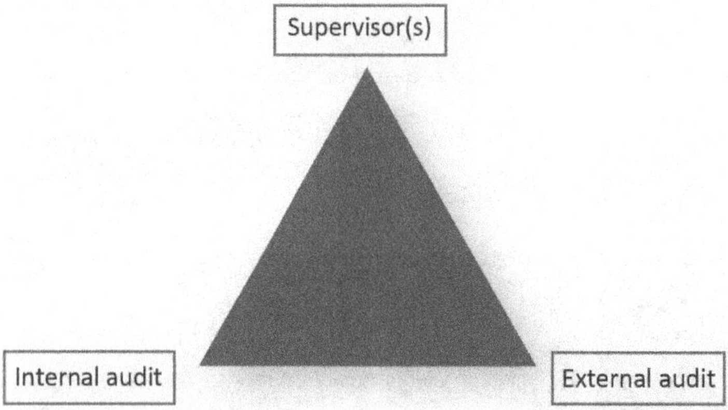

Source: (BIS—www.bis.org)

In EU, the participation of external supervision has become even more important, as European Central Bank (ECB) has a direct responsibility to supervise more than 110 significant banking and financial institutions in the eurozone within the framework of Single Supervisory Mechanism (SSM), further discussed in Section 9.2: "Single Supervisory Mechanism," while outside the eurozone, each NCA (National Competent Authority) has that role and responsibility. The additional fourth line of defense is believed to contribute to the mitigation of the information data and asymmetries with both the board—notably the non-executive directors—and regulators, supervisors, and external auditors. Essentially, ECB may benefit from the internal audit work of a bank as well as take any supplementary information from the external auditor, thereby forming a triangular relationship where all parties benefit each other.

Also, the fourth line advocates that external auditors may provide an autonomous assessment of the three lines of defense, wherever relevant to the audit of the organization's financial reporting and to compliance with regulatory requirements. Supervisors in countries such as the UK, the USA, and Switzerland have already shown the initiative.

6.5.2 TRANSITIONING FROM THE THREE LINES TO FOUR LINES

The shift from three lines to four lines should be accompanied by closer interactions with internal auditors, external auditors, and supervisors. It may also be considered that a stronger relation with non-executive directors and the committees of the board is another vector contributing to the same end. An organization should always seek to maintain a periodic dialogue with the auditors as well as prudential and behavior supervisors with proper incentive mechanism in place, and vice versa. It should be taken into consideration the several models for supervision that show differences in their structures and duties, mainly whether to combine prudential and behavior supervisions, or even banking and insurance. The external auditor could indeed be a valuable ally for the supervisory authorities, particularly in areas where skills and resources are scarce. In the end, the proper and closer interaction and communication between internal auditors, supervisors and external auditors can result in a control system capable of capturing deficiencies and weaknesses in the first and second lines. When establishing and implementing the four lines of defense model, the following features of the relationship should be duly taken care of while understanding that there is no one-size-fits-all approach and should be in line with the corresponding case. The "fourth lines of defense" designation advocated by Arndorfer and Minto was not adopted in 2020 Institute of Internal Auditors review of the three lines of defense model, although the concept is considered in the theoretical framework.

Regularity of information provide

- Definition of the terms and scope of the interaction.
- Exchange of information before and during the audit engagement, allowing flexibility (e.g., ad hoc meetings whenever necessary).

Quality of interactions

- Ex post feedback on the quality of interactions and information sharing.
- Regular assessment of independence and objectivity of each party involved (e.g., the conditions of an external auditor's appointment).

Clear definition of authority and scope

- Supervisors should have the power to request access to any type of information retained by external/internal audit.
- All three parties should jointly set the audit scope of the subject matter to be reviewed (e.g., joint discussion of financial statements).
- All three parties should share their audit methodology and discuss critical action plans.

6.5.3 OTHER REGULATORS AND SUPERVISORS—FOREIGN DIRECT INVESTMENT

When a corporation is involved in activities related to Foreign Direct Investment (FDI), a matter that is strongly linked to internationalization, which is impacted by geopolitical issues, reason why governmental institutions that oversee and approve FDI should be considered a part of the mechanism of the fourth line of defense. There are numerous examples of FDI attempts that fail under this process. Many countries also require the involvement of national defense authorities in FDI processes (e.g., energy, telecommunications, defense equipment). Example of competition authorities include DG COMP (Directorate-General for Competition) in EU, CMS (Competitions and Markets Authority) in UK, FTC (Federal Trade Commission) in the US, among others. The objective of competition authorities is to ensure that markets work better by providing better quality goods and services at lower prices as well as ensuring that companies compete fairly. This should result in efficiency, create a wider choice for consumers, reduce prices, and improve quality. These are the reasons why the EU and other countries' competition authorities fight anticompetitive behavior, review mergers and acquisitions and state aid, as well as encourage liberalization.

In the European Union, competition policy aims to:

- Ensure low prices for all, as it encourages businesses to produce and boosts the economy.
- Deliver better quality, as competition is believed to encourage improving quality of goods and services.
- Offer wider choice, with firms making their products different and better and presenting a better ratio price and quality.
- Innovate to deliver this choice and produce better products, as businesses need to be innovative to improve product concepts, design, and production techniques.
- Ensure better competitors in global markets.[139]

Competition authorities investigate companies that violate or could potentially violate competition rules to safeguard competitive markets. Authorities act both to prevent and to punish competition violations. Usually, decisions are binding, although they can be appealed to courts, varying among countries, depending on legal frameworks. Both FDI and competition issues should be included in the global agenda of boards with cross-border operations, as they have potential to affect reputation.

6.6 OTHER STANDARD RISK MANAGEMENT FRAMEWORKS

6.6.1 ENTERPRISE RISK MANAGEMENT
Besides the Internal Control Framework (ICF), COSO has also produced an *Enterprise Risk Management (ERM) framework*[140] to support effectively in identification, assessment, and management of risk. The ERM framework expands on internal control, providing a more robust

and extensive focus on the broader subject of enterprise risk management. It is not meant to replace the Internal Control Framework but rather act as a guideline to the demands of an enlarged scope. Essentially, the ERM framework aims to capture the risk in both the strategy setting process and in driving the performance of organization, because in the current landscape, organizations need to strategically consider how to manage the increasing volatility, uncertainty, complexity, and ambiguity (VUCA concept) of the world, notably in areas that are new for boards like geopolitics, cyber security, interest rates level, foreign exchange depreciation and/or controls, pandemics such as COVID-19, emerging barriers to world trade, or even having to deal with the recent landscape of demanding regulation and supervision, notably for the financial system. This must be done appropriately at the senior management level as well as in the boardroom, where the stakes should always be the highest.

ERM for Senior Management

Senior managers are the ones who are responsible for identifying, manage, and mitigate any kind of corporate risks. It is equally important to enhance the communication with the board and the stakeholders, thereby leveraging the principles of ERM. Managers may use ERM to understand risk considerations and their impact on choice of strategy aligned with vision and mission. In the end, it may support managers with alternative strategies and hedge the risks, which should later be presented and addressed by the board of directors.

ERM for Board

The board has an oversight and supervisory role, framing the vision, helping to support in value creation for the stakeholders, and hence prevent and/or mitigate risks. The conventional nature of boards is changing from a supporting role to the prudential oversight and supervision of ERM. The ERM considerations for board include an end-to-end involvement (governance and culture); strategy and objective setting; performance; the review and revision of practices to enhance entity performance; and information, communications, and reporting.

The board is supposed to review, challenge, and concur with management on the following challenges:

- Proposed strategy and risk appetite
- Alignment of strategy and business objectives with the entity's stated mission, vision, and core values
- Significant business decisions including mergers, acquisitions, capital allocation, funding, and dividend-related decisions
- Response to significant fluctuations in entity performance or the portfolio review of risk
- Responses to instances of deviation from core values
- Approving management incentives and remuneration
- Participating in investor and stakeholder relations

The Enterprise Risk Management framework advocates the concept of five components and 20 principles, integrating with strategic planning and embedding it throughout an organization with an assumption that risk influences and aligns strategy and performance, considering the business model, across all departments and functions (Figure 6.10).

Figure 6.10: Enterprise risk management framework

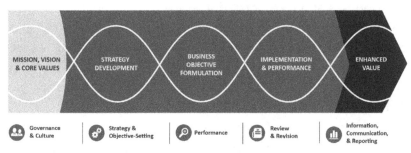

Source: (COSO—www.coso.org)

Governance and Culture

Governance and a robust culture set the organization's tone, rein-forcing the importance of, and establishing oversight responsibilities for, enterprise risk management. Culture pertains to ethical values, desired behaviors, and understanding of risk in the entity, which is why in the financial system it is called "risk culture." According to EBA (European Banking Authority), institutions are required to consider their size and internal organization and the nature, scale, and com-plexity of their activities when developing and implementing internal governance arrangements (EBA/GL/2017/11).

Strategy and Objective Setting

Enterprise risk management, strategy, and objective setting work together over the strategic planning process and the business model. The risk appetite—that should be set within the boundaries of the stakeholders' expectations and the risk capacity of an organization—is established and aligned with strategy, business model, and busi-ness objectives put strategy into practice, while serving as a basis for identifying, assessing, and responding to risk.

Performance

Risks that may impact the achievement of strategy and business objectives need to be identified and assessed. Risks are prioritized by severity in the context of risk appetite. The organization then selects risk responses and takes a portfolio view of the amount of risk it has assumed. The results of this process are reported to key risk stake-holders and should be considered to include in the annual report of the company to inform the stakeholders.

Review and Revision

By reviewing entity performance, an organization can consider how well the enterprise risk management components are functioning over timo and in light of substantial changes, and what revisions are needed.

Information, Communication, and Reporting

Enterprise risk management requires a continual process of obtaining and sharing necessary information, from both internal and external sources, that flows up, down, and across the organization.

The principles aligned with the five components are depicted in Figure 6.11. COSO mentions that the principles cover everything from governance to monitoring. They are manageable in size, and they describe practices that can be applied in different ways for different organizations regardless of size, type, or sector. Adhering to these principles can provide management and the board with a reasonable expectation that the organization understands and strives to manage the risks associated with its strategy and business objectives.

Figure 6.11: Components and principles of ERM

Governance & Culture	Strategy & Objective-Setting	Performance	Review & Revision	Information, Communication, & Reporting
1. Exercises Board Risk Oversight	6. Analyzes Business Context	10. Identifies Risk	15. Assesses Substantial Change	18. Leverages Information and Technology
2. Establishes Operating Structures	7. Defines Risk Appetite	11. Assesses Severity of Risk	16. Reviews Risk and Performance	19. Communicates Risk Information
3. Defines Desired Culture	8. Evaluates Alternative Strategies	12. Prioritizes Risks	17. Pursues Improvement in Enterprise Risk Management	20. Reports on Risk, Culture, and Performance
4. Demonstrates Commitment to Core Values	9. Formulates Business Objectives	13. Implements Risk Responses		
5. Attracts, Develops, and Retains Capable Individuals		14. Develops Portfolio View		

Source: (COSO—www.coso.org)

6.6.2 ENTERPRISE RISK MANAGEMENT TO ENVIRONMENTAL, SOCIAL, AND GOVERNANCE RISKS

Section 4.3: "Corporate Sustainability" discusses why sustainability issues have been the core front for the very survival of the corporate today. To aid risk management and sustainability practitioners, COSO published guidelines about applying Enterprise Risk Management to Environmental, Social and Governance (ESG) related risks.[141] As COSO mentions that entities—including businesses, governments and non-profits—face an evolving landscape of ESG-related risks that can impact their profitability, success, and even survival. Essentially, there is no universal or agreed upon definition of ESG-related risks, which may also be referred to as sustainability, nonfinancial, or extra-financial risks. The environmental dimension examines how a company complies with the natural concerns. The social dimension evaluates the relationship amongst the customers, suppliers, employees, and other relevant stakeholders. The governance part deals with the details of a company organizational structure—corporate governance.

The COSO ESG framework is built on the five pillars of existing enterprise risk management reporting:

1. Governance and culture for ESG–related risks
2. Strategy and objective-setting for ESG–related risks
3. Performance for ESG–related risks
   a. Identifies risk
   b. Assesses and prioritizes risks
   c. Implements risk responses
4. Review and revision for ESG–related risks
5. Information, communication and reporting for ESG–related risks

As global investors are increasingly making use of ESG-related indices and ratings (e.g., DJSI, MSCI ESG ratings), large corporates have actively started to report on ESG-related activities, although that is not mandatory in many jurisdictions. Some small and medium-sized companies are also adopting the same best practices. It has been observed that the corporates with high ESG ratings tend to become more successful than the lower ones, able to raise capital—from shareholders and bondholders—at lower cost and build their reputation with stakeholders. *Financial Times* reported that assets in the ESG sector, although still being small compared to the market sector, are expanding very rapidly.[142] Figure 6.12 and Table 6.2 demonstrates an example of the governance of ESG-related risk from COSO ESG guidelines.

Figure 6.12: One example of governance of ESG-related risks

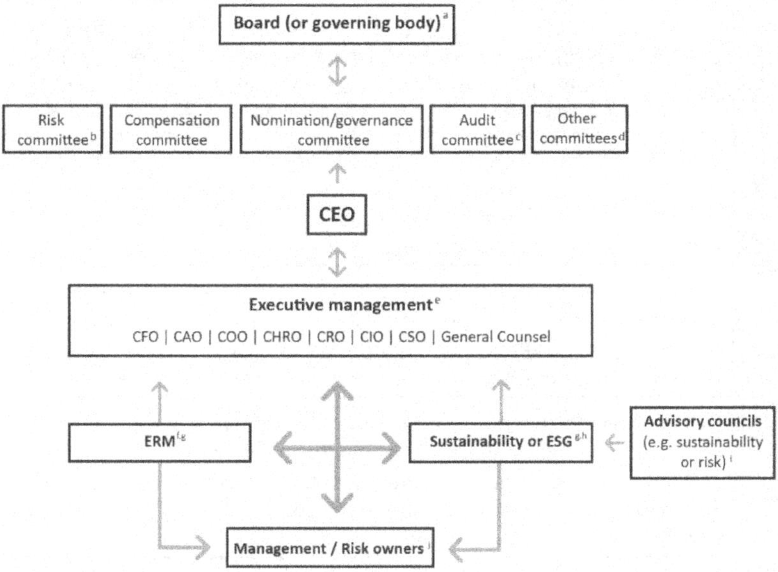

Source: (COSO guidelines—www.coso.org)
Note: CEO (Chief Executive Officer), CFO (Chief Financial Officer), CAO (Chief Administrative Officer), COO (Chief Operating Officer), CHRO (Chief Human Resource Officer), CRO (Chief Risk Officer), CIO (Chief Information Officer), CSO (Chief Strategy Officer), ERM (Enterprise Risk Management)

Table 6.2: Description of governance of ESG-related risks

A	The board is responsible for overseeing and, where appropriate, challenging management's approach to ESG-related risk ownership as well as ensuring there is a program in place to effectively identify, assess, manage, and monitor ESG-related risks.
B	The risk and compliance committee establishes the direct oversight of enterprise risk management. The focus of the risk and compliance committee is entity-wide in nonfinancial areas that go beyond the authority of the audit committee and its available resources (e.g., operational, obligations, credit, market, technology).
C	The audit committee assists the board of directors in fulfilling its corporate governance and overseeing responsibilities in relation to an entity's financial reporting, internal control, risk management, and internal and external audit functions.
D	Some companies have additional board committees, such as a sustainability committee, separate from the risk and compliance committee and the audit committee, comprising of cross-functional representatives to identify, monitor, and review ESG-related risks.
E	Connections to strategic planning and operations personnel are also critical to linking sustainability to new strategies and risk responses. These connections support timely assessment of new and emerging ESG-related risks so that the organization is better prepared to identify risks and related opportunities.
F	The ERM function or director is responsible for coordinating and consolidating ERM activities and will typically report into the CRO or other C-suite as well as lead the process for managing enterprise-wide risks in an integrated, systematic manner.
G	The sustainability director should maintain a close relationship with the ERM director.
H	The sustainability director may report to the CFO, CSO, or COO and provides support in coordinating ESG-related activities. This includes monitoring megatrends as well as identifying, assessing, and monitoring risks.
I	Cross-functional or multi-stakeholder advisory councils (either internal or external) can provide perspective on particular aspects of ESG issues or other risks.
J	Although management collectively "owns" the entity risks, a "risk owner" is frequently designated as the point person with accountability for ensuring specific risks are appropriately managed.

Source: (COSO—www.coso.org)

6.7 ACHIEVING A WELL-FUNCTIONING INTERNAL CONTROL FRAMEWORK

Before applying any control framework, corporates must identify and understand their risk profile. As the control functions are considered the key functions to influence business decisions, the control functions that prepare for emerging and other key risks and essentially provide actionable reporting are the clear winners. In contrast, the control functions that only focus on the next compliance initiative with no pri-oritized controls for capturing risks are doomed to be losers. In many institutions, the internal control framework is established on common prevalent standards, tools, and processes for minimum alignments, such as risk taxonomy, business process review, common risk appe-tite logic, and board-level reporting of control assessment results. While such a mechanism in often based on legacy standards that may provide enough ceiling, the best practice of modern control frame-work should include a review of the activity landscape with regards to governance, inherent risks, required controls, and residual risks with the tone set at the top. The documented process, risk ownership, accountability, iteration, and continuous monitoring are important fundamentals. Also, it distinguishes the fundamental restructuring of governance, process, and responsibilities (IIA three lines model) with an introduction to common, comprehensive, and tool-supported landscapes. There are some good guidelines to achieve a well-func-tioning ICF, and one such example is explained below. The content is adapted from the consulting firm Oliver Wyman.[143, 144]

- **Define risks along with risk taxonomy**

It is crucial to identify and define any possible risks with different lev-els of granularity to ensure adequate use, for example, in risk assess-ment. The taxonomy should be based on MECE (mutually exclusive and commonly exhaustive) taxonomy, meaning that risks incidents should appear appropriately in their own defined risk event category (i.e., one incident is strictly one event type), but the captured risks incidents across the categories should form the basis for the collective definition of the risks' taxonomy.

Environmental and social risks were traditionally ignored by institutions, but the scene has recently been constantly changing. In order to promote sustainable finance and to deal with the threat culminating from climate change and environmental systems, the EU published the EU Taxonomy (further discussed in Section 4.3: "Corporate Sustainability"), being aligned with the UN Sustainable Development Goals and climate-related goals through the Paris Agreement framework—*Regulation (EU) 2020/852 on the establishment of a framework to facilitate sustainable investment, and amending Regulation (EU) 2019/2088.*[145] The EU Taxonomy is supposed to be an implementation tool that can enable capital markets to identify and respond to investment opportunities that contribute to environmental policy objectives. The taxonomy promotes sustainable finance by design, and for those who intend to be compliant, facilitates with a list of economic activities that can make a substantial contribution to climate change mitigation and criteria to do no significant harm to other environmental objectives and fundamentally encourage capital markets to reorient capital flows. Institutions are encouraged to use the taxonomy report[146] published by the EU or any other equivalent entities to get a prior notion about environment and social risks and therefore prepare the steps toward sustainable finance.

After developing event-based risk taxonomy, it is important to define the risk ownership and responsibilities for taxonomy items (Table 6.3). As common risk taxonomy sharpens the understanding of scope and responsibilities and can reveal any potential gaps in coverage, this also aids in the articulation of potential risk events in a systematic approach. Nevertheless, some corporates may make a mistake by delegating the risk ownership only at board or committee level, limiting the expertise at the operational level involving management and staff.

Table 6.3: Example of event-based risk taxonomy

Risk Events: Operational Risks	Event Examples
Internal fraud	Online channels, cyber security, non-online channels, unauthorized activity
External fraud	Online channels, non-online channels, physical, business operations
Employment practices and workplace safety	Employee relations, workplace safety
Clients, products, and business practices	Breach of duties to customers, product, and servicing failures
Execution, delivery, and process management	Reporting an error, non-client counterparty failure
Risk Events: Compliance Risks	Event Examples
Financial crime	Money laundering, financing to terrorism and weapons of massive destruction, sanctions breach, tax evasion, aggressive tax planning, tax optimization
Product and customer	Customer needs, product pricing, customer communication, marketing and disclosure, barriers to exit, complaints mismanagement, product deterioration
Employee Behavior	Remuneration, licenses and regulatory accreditation, competence and knowledge, conflicts of interest, bribery and corruption, internal fraud
Market Behavior	Market manipulation, insider trading, regulated market practices, competition law
Organizational Behavior	Data protection and privacy, record keeping, cross-border rules, regulatory requests, compliance adequacy, whistleblowing
Risk Events: Environment Risks	Event Examples
Pollution (air/water)	High amount of carbon/greenhouse gases emitted, use of outdated production machinery, nuclear waste dissolved in water
Environment Ecosystem	Death of aquatic animals, infertile soil, pollution of soil/rivers/sea, spread of disease

Source: (Oliver Wyman–www.oliverwyman.com)

The bowtie methodology is often used to distinguish risk causes, control, events, and impacts and to define the cause of the risk, the event that leads to the risk, and the potential impact from the risk event (see Figure 6.13 and Table 6.4). The bowtie method is a risk assessment method that can be used to analyze and communicate how high-risk scenarios develop. Risk events are identified, threats that directly leads to the top events independently are listed, and the consequences that can constitute unwanted scenarios are recognized—realistic and specific in nature.[147]

Figure 6.13: Illustration of bowtie methodology

Table 6.4: Example of risk cause, event, and impact

Cause	Event	Impact
Compliance failure	Sanctions breach	Hefty Fines
Lack of detailed description of the roles and responsibilities of employees at all levels	Unauthorized activity by the employee	Fines, Reputational Damage
Lack of environment guidelines and methodology	High amount of carbon emitted	Hefty fines, Reputational Damage, Survival

Source: (Oliver Wyman–www.oliverwyman.com)

• **Map business process**

The assessment of the business process requires ensuring the right level of granularity and aggregation, as too much aggregation may make the processes meaningless; on contrary, too much mapping may cause the work to be very tedious and inefficient. The business process should be end-to-end with a logical initiation and a conclusion, and relationships with other processes should be easily understood by the relevant stakeholders. Holistically, it must be ensured that the mapping of business processes covers the range of activities performed by all the respective entities within the business, such as the business process and mapping of a manufacturing standard process, sales documentation, data protection and privacy guidelines, and complaint handling process. Organizations often have a divergence between written rules and practical activities, a challenging issue that is intimately linked to the culture of the organization resulting often from an ambiguous, dubious, or inappropriate tone from the top. Corporates should review and update existing procedure manuals to ensure a philosophical stance toward a deterministic approach in terms of procedures and rules as well as sanctions, minimizing room for interpretation in its application, therefore ensuring a robust culture.

- **Prioritize and assess risks**

After identifying the risks based on risk events taxonomy and adequately considering the elements defined in the Taxonomy Regulation (EU Taxonomy, for example),[148] they should be prioritized according to the expected level of threat (high, medium, or low) and the likelihood or probability of threat. When probability value is not quantifiable, subjective probability assessment can be assigned, implying the degree of confidence or belief that often comes from the expertise and experiences. Some of the risks could be inherent risks. Based on risk prioritization most-to-least-critical importance ranking, different control measures and governing approaches could be applied to the degree and frequency of threat. A common mistake is to neglect quantifying nonfinancial or sustainable risks and not providing to the board of directors enough information and awareness for the level of potential harmful risks.

- **Define controls and measures to manage risks**

Depending on the types of risk—such as inherent risk, residual risk, or any identified risks—it is necessary to ensure sufficient control and measures. For controllable risks, it is important to define the controls that help reduce inherent risk exposures to residual risk levels that are deemed acceptable. Risk mitigation mechanisms such as avoid, accept, share, or transfer may be applied for each identified risk (Figure 6.14).

Figure 6.14: Risk control and mitigants

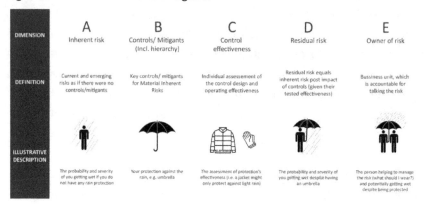

DIMENSION	A Inherent risk	B Controls/ Mitigants (incl. hierarchy)	C Control effectiveness	D Residual risk	E Owner of risk
DEFINITION	Current and emerging risks as if there were no controls/mitigants	Key controls/ mitigants for Material Inherent Risks	Individual assessement of the control design and operating effectiveness	Residual risk equals inherent risk post impact of controls (given their tested effectiveness)	Bussiness unit, which is accountable for talking the risk
ILLUSTRATIVE DESCRIPTION	The probability and severity of you getting wet if you do not have any rain protection	Your protection against the rain, e.g. umbrella	The assessment of protection's effectiveness (i.e. a jacket might only protect against light rain)	The probability and severity of you getting wet despite having an umbrella	The person helping to manage the risk (what should I wear?) and potentially getting wet despite being protected

Source: Oliver Wyman (www.oliverwyman.com)

- **Monitor, test, and assess risk**

Having appropriate risk taxonomy, mapping, process, and procedures, it is necessary to monitor, test, and assess the risk on a regular basis. *COSO's Guidance on Monitoring Internal Control* mentions that the foundation for monitoring is achieved through setting a proper tone at the top; the effectiveness of organizational structure assigning monitoring roles to people with appropriate capabilities, objectivity and authority; designing and executing monitoring procedures focused on a persuasive information about the operation of key controls; assessing and reporting results that evaluates the severity of any identified deficiencies and reporting the monitoring results to the appropriate personnel and the board for timely action and follow-up if determined necessary.[149]

And the breadth of monitoring, testing, and assessing risk encompass periodic evaluation and testing of controls by internal audit; continuous monitoring programs built into information systems; analysis of, and appropriate follow-up on, operating reports or metrics that might identify anomalies indicative of a control failure; supervisory reviews of controls, such as reconciliation reviews as a normal part of processing; self-assessments by boards and management regarding the tone they set in the organization and the effectiveness of their oversight functions; audit committee inquiries of internal and external auditors; and quality assurance reviews of the internal audit department. When necessary, any adjustments must be done in an agile, interactive, and incremental manner, and, eventually, that concerns any new regulations or rules. Any noncompliant issues must be reported through a dedicated channel to the level of threat.

Topics of the Chapter

The following has been discussed within this chapter:

- After the 2007–2008 financial crisis, the relevance of control functions emerged as a critical tool to monitor the financial and economic vectors and behavior components of a corporation.
- The Three Lines Model—updated by IIA in 2020—for organizational risk management and control is based on:
  1. First Line Roles and Functions: Operational Management
  2. Second line Roles and Functions: Risk Management and Compliance
  3. Third Line Roles and Functions: Internal Audit
- The updated model associates role-based functions with clearly defined roles for governing bodies and management within an organization.

- The Four Lines of Defense Model adds external auditors, regulators, and supervisors—external assurance providers—for enhanced organizational risk management and control.
- Enterprise Risk Management framework expands on internal control and acts as a guideline for organizational risk management and control through a robust, extensive focus on the topic.
- Before applying the internal control framework, companies must identify and understand their risk appetite framework—stakeholders' expectations, risk capacity, risk appetite, and risk buffers—as well as the way risk is handled within the business model.
- The ERM framework supports in identification, assessment, and management of risk.

Chapter 7
Risk Concepts and Risk Appetite

The risk concepts, risk capacity, and risk appetite are fundamentally framed within the scope of broader organizational control framework and functions, as discussed in Chapter 6: Control Functions and Related Frameworks. The tone for a healthy risk culture should be set right from the very top, and the same kind of risk culture should cascade down the organizational structure. Therefore, the concept of risk must always be forward-looking, under the monitoring of the risk management officer, within the constant oversight and supervision of the board and the senior management. This chapter discusses the concept of risks, how risks are classified, how an organization should prepare for them within the business model, and how an organization should have operating tools to mitigate risks.

7.1 RISK CONCEPTS
International Organization for Standardization (ISO)[150] states:

> "(…) risk is now defined as the 'effect of uncertainty on objectives,' which focuses on the effect of incomplete knowledge of events or circumstances on an organization's decision-making. This requires a change in the traditional understanding of risk, forcing organizations to tailor risk management to their needs and objectives—a key benefit of the standard."

Figure 7.1: Concept of risk limit, risk management, and risk profile

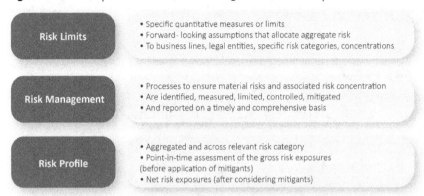

In general, the risk concepts revolve around three topics—*Risk Limits, Risk Management*, and *Risk Profile*—that are intimately linked to Risk Capacity of an organization, which should be determined upfront (Figure 7.1). This issue is also linked to the business model of an organization, as the stream of revenues may be based on businesses' vectors that have embedded higher or lower risks. The terminologies and definitions are adapted from the guidelines *Corporate Governance Principles for Banks* (reference in Section 1.2.3: "Global Financial Crisis 2007–2008 and Increased Governance") published by the Basel Committee on Banking Supervision (BCBS).

Table 7.1: Risk capacity and risk culture

Risk Capacity	Risk Culture
• **The maximum amount of risk able to assume** • **Based on the capital base, risk management, and control capabilities** • **Regulatory constraint**	• Norms, attitudes, and behaviors; tone set from the top • Related to risk awareness, risk-taking, and risk management, and controls that shape decisions on risks • Risk culture influences the decisions of management and staff in day-to-day activities that impact the risks they assume

A robust risk management framework is meant to ensure adherence to compliance to sound risk management principles, compliance, healthy risk governance and culture, proper implementation and oversight of risk policies, procedures, limits, and controls. Content from the consulting company Oliver Wyman is borrowed to further explain the risk concepts and risk appetite.

7.1.1 RISK TYPES

To depict the types of financial and nonfinancial risks in a real case scenario, the following content borrowed from Barclays Bank illustrates a way to report[151] them to stakeholders.

1. Financial and Nonfinancial Risks

Table 7.2 summarizes financial and nonfinancial risks at Barclays Bank and how they are managed and mitigated.

Table 7.2: Types of risks

Examples of how risks are managed		
Financial Principal Risks		
Credit Risk	The risk of loss to the Group from the failure of clients, customers or counterparties—including sovereigns—to fully honor their obligations to the Group, including the whole and timely payment of principal, interest, collateral, and other receivables.	Credit risk teams identify, evaluate, sanction, limit, and monitor various forms of credit exposure, individually and in aggregate.
Market Risk	The risk of loss arising from potential adverse changes in the value of the firm's assets and liabilities from fluctuation in market variables including—but not limited to—interest rates, foreign exchange, equity prices, commodity prices, credit spreads, implied volatilities, and asset correlations.	A range of complementary approaches to identify and evaluate market risk are used to capture exposure to market risk. These are measured, controlled, and monitored by market risk specialists.

Treasury & Capital Risk	**Liquidity risk** The risk that the firm is unable to meet its contractual or contingent obligations or that it does not have the appropriate amount, tenor, and composition of funding and liquidity to support its assets. **Capital risk** The risk that the firm has an insufficient level or composition of capital to support its normal business activities and to meet its regulatory capital requirements under normal operating environments or stressed conditions (both actual and as defined for internal planning or regulatory testing purposes). This includes the risk from the firm's pension plans, interest rate risk in the banking book, the risk the firm is exposed to capital or income volatility because of a mismatch between the interest rate exposures of its (non-traded) assets and liabilities.	Treasury and capital risk are identified and managed by specialists in Capital Planning, Liquidity, Asset and Liability Management, and Market Risk. A range of approaches are used appropriate to the risk, such as limits, plan monitoring, and stress testing.
Nonfinancial Principal Risks		
Operational Risk	The risk of loss to the firm from inadequate or failed processes or systems, human factors, or external events (e.g., fraud or cybercrime) where the root cause is not due to credit or market risks.	Operational risk comprises the following risks: data management and information, execution risk, financial reporting, fraud, payments processing, people, physical security, premises, prudential regulation, supplier, tax, Technology, and transaction operations. It is not always cost effective or possible to attempt to eliminate all operational risks.

		Operational risk is managed across the businesses and functions through an internal control environment with a view to limiting the risk to acceptable residual levels.
Model Risk	The risk of the potential adverse consequences from financial assessments or decisions based on incorrect or misused model outputs and reports.	Models are independently validated and approved prior to implementation and their performance is monitored on a continual basis.
Reputation Risk	The risk that an action, transaction, investment, or event will reduce trust in the firm's integrity and competence by clients, counterparties, investors, regulators, employees, or the public.	Reputation risk is managed by embedding our purpose and values and maintaining a controlled culture within the Group, with the objective of acting with integrity, enabling strong and trusted relationships with customers and clients, colleagues, and broader society.
Conduct Risk	The risk of detriment to customers, clients, market integrity, competition, or Barclays from the inappropriate supply of financial services, including instances of willful or negligent misconduct.	The Compliance function sets the minimum standards required and provide oversight to monitor that these risks are effectively managed and escalated where appropriate.
Legal Risk	The risk of loss or imposition of penalties, damages, or fines from the failure of the firm to meet its legal obligations including regulatory or contractual requirements.	The Legal function supports colleagues in identifying and limiting legal risks.

Source: (Barclays Bank)[152]

The section below discusses selected risks—reputational, cyber, and misconduct—because they have emerged as unidentified risks in many organizations, although in the current paradigm, they represent risks with potentially high impact in an organization and therefore requiring planning and establishment of tools and processes to mitigate them and thus their impact on the sustainability of an organization. However, all the risks should be identified, mapped, and addressed in a structured fashion. Also, an organization should have procedures and norms to allocate the monitoring of those responsibilities to either risk management or compliance (control functions) and establish a good model for coordination of risks that overlap with the control functions and the operational area.

Managing the reputational risk has been increasingly relevant due to the rise of social media, heightened geopolitics, and increased focus on sustainability issues, namely ESG (Environment, Social, and Governance). For example, in 2019, the general managers of an NBA (National Basketball Association) team tweeted in favor of Hong Kong protests. This immediately drew criticism from Chinese authorities, leading to the subsequent withdrawal of Chinese NBA sponsorship and reduction in coverage of NBA matches in China putting, billions of dollars of value at risk.[153] When the NBA did try to address the issue, it was reprimanded by US politicians regarding their weak stance on the protests. As a result, the NBA was caught in a sticky situation in their attempt to maintain the neutrality. In the Hong Kong protests issue, not only the NBA, firms such as Starbucks, ESPN, Disney, and others were also dragged in some level of fallout.

On the other hand, inherent risks arising from pandemics such as COVID-19 are inevitable although the latter represents a *black swan* event, which is why organizations must have a contingency plan to mitigate pandemic risks. The global economy slowed down significantly after the pandemic as many countries across the world took stringent measures to combat the influence of COVID-19. Even though many sovereigns supported firms and self-employed workers with fiscal stimuli and relief packages, these subsidies and other measures should be considered temporary. Therefore, firms should thoroughly identify such kinds of risk events in order to prevent damaging financial losses, as well as develop risk mitigants to maintain them sustainable. Risk scenario planning identifies and lists risks with impact (high, medium, and low) as well as probability (if statistical long series are available to project them, which otherwise represents a challenging exercise), and severity. Its effective integration with risk management function should be prudently implemented to decrease the fallout from reputational risk exposure.

2. Cyber Risk

Cyber risk has become increasingly important and should be considered one of the top operational risks—excluding a financial risk—that may exhibit substantial financial and reputational damage. Often computer viruses such as malware (software that is specifically designed to disrupt, damage, or gain unauthorized access to a computer system) and ransomware (a type of malicious software designed to block access to a computer system until a "compensation" in money is paid) are featured in the headlines. The cyber risk may also lead to a systemic risk due to the interconnection of IT systems, meaning that cyber risk should be considered an inherent risk, and appropriate measures and contingency plans should be always present. Remarkably, cyber-attacks may be initiated not only by the nonethical hackers but also by sovereign countries to influence in geopolitical matters. For example, in response to the missile attack by Iran on a drone owned by the US, the US Cyber Command unit conducted a retaliatory digital strike, reportedly hitting Iranian targets.[154]

Another example was when Facebook was apparently fined to the tune of 5 billion dollars by US Federal Trade Commission for failing to protect user data privacy in the light of the so-called Facebook–Cambridge Analytica data scandal,[155] while facing a variety of similar and other probes in the European court. In Europe, General Data Protection Regulation (GDPR)—arguably one of the most stringent data protection regulations—came into effect in 2018 to ensure data protection and privacy for all individual citizens of the European Union and the European Economic Area (EEA). The main purpose of GDPR is to give control to individuals over their personal data, and their rights to access, and to forgot, records of processing personal and sensitive data; basically, it can translate to: "The data is mine. It must not be shared without my consent. When I give my consent, that must not be abused."

Eventually, an organization needs to demonstrate data protection by design and by default, and if not, should have measures to address data protection. A major feature of the legislation is its self-regulatory system instead of a hetero-regulatory one. This means that the responsibility lies exclusively on the organization to ensure that its controls ensure full compliance. Therefore, regulators, supervisors, and other entities responsible to ensure that organizations comply with GDPR are not obliged to answer questions, clarify doubts, or certify that the systems comply with the law. Otherwise, corporates are susceptible to hefty fines (up to four percent of global turnover) like Facebook, which not only causes financial damage but also significant reputational damage.

Hotel group Marriott International is facing a lawsuit in London's High Court for its alleged failure to protect the personal data of millions of former guests between July 2014 and September 2018.[156] In 2019, British Airways faced a fine of 183 millions of pounds for breach of its security systems. British Airways was accused of poor security arrangements at the company, including log in, payment card, and travel booking details as well as name and address information.[157]

In June 2019, Facebook unveiled the business model of a cryptocurrency (digital currency) called Libra,[158] supposed to be backed by assets denominated in global currencies, promising to make money online cheaper and faster and thereby removing the need of intermediaries. However, this was met with strong skepticism from the US Congress, lawmakers, and the public. One of the possible reasons is a potential risk of a lack of trust in Facebook which may result from the previous reputational damage incident. While it may be premature to assess the viability and success of Facebook's Libra project, Facebook already generates revenues in billions of dollars worldwide from its current business model and is considered profitable, and subsequently it was able to cope with the levied fines and penalties. This underlines the relevance of a company to have developed, monitored, and supervised by the board the risk appetite, both in the financial and other regulated sectors, where regulation imposes usually demanding procedures and controls, and non-regulated sectors, where the issue is left on the hands of the board.

Hence, cyber risk has everyone at stakes, such as the board—notably under the supervision of non-executives—the CEO and the management, the risk manager, suppliers, operations, communication, and compliance. Cyber risk must be considered among the important topics to discuss in the board. Many organizations still neglect cyber risk control measures. *Cyber insurance* for risk mitigation or risk transfer is one of the ways for the board to show an initiative in reducing the impact of cyberattacks, because it is possible that directors' and officers' liabilities insurance (further discussed in Section 16.8: "Directors and Officers Liability Insurance") may not be enough to fulfill the sufficient insurance in a major cyberattack claim, possibly one of the reasons why the board and the management don't make enough investment in information security. Other things that the board and the management should ensure are the robust cyber policies, the availability of pre-approved cyber experts 24/7, such as IT expert, legal expert, and crisis management expert—including the communication area—in order to mitigate the potential loss of any unprecedented cyber damage.

3. Misconduct Risk

Although misconduct risk is deemed as nonfinancial risk, the vulnerabilities from misconduct by board members, managers, employees, or relevant stakeholders may potentially lead to systemic risks and undermine the trust in institutions and their reputations. This can also hinder the sustainable growth envisaged for the future. Sanctions, fines, penalties, or similar measures are the established measures to contain the misconduct. However, the need for preventative approaches that can mitigate the risk of misconduct through improved market organization, structure, and behavior of relevant actors has been identified.

Financial Stability Board (FSB)[159] mentions that establishing a more direct, transparent, and immediate link between conduct issues and the award of variable remuneration may potentially aid in reducing the probability of misconduct. In one of the FSB conducted roundtables, the participants from financial institutions emphasized that conduct remains a collective issue that affects the business unit, individual, and supervisor. Board should not only focus on appropriate compensation policies for staff that potentially may have low adherence or awareness to values—although this should be target of intense training programs to change the culture—but also on how to adjust compensation to encourage positive behavior. Additionally, firms and supervisors agree that compensation is not the only tool for executive committee or senior management to address misconduct and demand a combination of strong leadership and governance processes, incorporating robust and independent control functions, and when taking decisions for promotion, effectively analyzing conduct-related performance in a 360-degree evaluation process.

The governance framework determines the allocation of authority and responsibilities in a company, namely board and senior management. It also aids in monitoring the performance, including incentives and decision-making, at all levels of the firm, which is critical to ensure that employees in all parts of the institution conduct business in a legal and ethical manner. The G20/OECD Principles of Corporate Governance for any publicly listed organizations or BCBS Principles of Corporate Governance aimed specifically for financial institutions provide the guidelines for incorporating a robust governance framework. In both guidelines, ethical conduct is given high importance and place responsibility and accountability on the board and senior management. Appropriate mechanisms to ensure individual accountability for misconduct and the role and responsibilities of the board of directors (both executive and non-executive) and management should be established within the scope of governance framework. Therefore, transparent standards of conduct, accountability, and enforcement mechanisms at all levels are vital to effective operation of governance frameworks. Supervisors or regulators must examine the adequacy of an organization's management of conduct risk. However, the size of the financial institutions may bring extra complexity of oversight, management, and decision-making processes within the institutions. Under such circumstances, the enforcement sanctions related to misconduct may fall on the organization, its shareholders, or other stakeholders rather than the individuals who are accountable for it. Therefore, for regulators or supervisors, it is important that they strengthen the focus on individual accountability within the prudential framework and address measures to misconduct by individuals in the context of enforcement actions against firms.

Other than the misconduct by the board or directors, market misconducts are also discussed as standards of behavior in market practices. It is agreed that market misconduct has been difficult to monitor, as markets are often opaque, dispersed, and cross-border, and different jurisdictions essentially have their own rules or laws, with some being strongly compliant and others less compliant. The case of manipulation of interest rate (LIBOR, EURIBOR, and TIBOR) and FX (Foreign Exchange) benchmarks highlighted the weaknesses of market conduct standards. Regulators in the UK, US, and EU have been continuously publishing recommendations or advice to improve market practices and market behaviors and seeking the clarity on financial indicators. For example, reforms to interest rate benchmarks often involve key market participants working with relevant authorities; in foreign exchange markets, central banks often work closely with industry-based foreign exchange committees. Essentially, strong regulation and sanction regimes are required to deter market misconduct while promoting public confidence and development of efficient markets and economies.

A sound and consistent risk culture should be a part of the key DNA of institutions. The risk culture should be institution-wide and be developed with a full understanding and incorporation of the holistic view of the risks faced by the institutions and how those risks are managed within the institutions' risk appetite. Risk culture is fundamentally developed through policies, communication and staff training regarding institutions' activities, strategy, and risk profile. This should adapt communication and training, considering the staff's responsibilities regarding risk taking and risk management.

According to EBA internal governance guidelines (EBA/GL/2017/11), a strong risk culture is articulated through:

1. *Tone from the top:* The tone of the corporate cascades from the top to bottom level. Therefore, the board is responsible for setting and communicating the institutions' core values and expectations.
2. *Accountability:* Board and staffs must be aware of their role, values of the institution, and its risk appetite and risk capacity. The staff should be made aware that they can be held accountable for their actions in relation to the institution's risk-taking behavior.
3. *Effective communication and challenge:* A sound risk culture should promote an environment of open communication and

effective challenge, which leads to a decision-making process that encourages a broad range of views and allows for testing of current practices and constructive critical attitude among staff, and essentially promotes a fair, open, and constructive engagement, instead of limited one.

4. *Incentives:* The incentives should be set according to the risk-taking behavior that aligns with the risk profile and long-term interest of the institutions. Ultimately, the board should have clear and documented policies on how the standards of corporate values and the code of conduct are met.

7.2 RISK APPETITE

Institute of Risk Management (IRM)[160] defines risk appetite as:

"(...) the amount and type of risk that an organisation is willing to take in order to meet their strategic objectives. Organisations will have different risk appetites depending on their sector, culture and objectives. A range of appetites exist for different risks and these may change over time."

European Banking Authority (EBA) in GL/2017/11 defines risk appetite as:

"(...) the aggregate level and types of risk an institution is willing to assume within its risk capacity, in line with its business model, to achieve its strategic objectives. And risk capacity as the maximum level of risk an institution is able to assume given its capital base, its risk management and control capabilities, and its regulatory constraints."

The risk appetite concepts explained in the subsequent sections are primarily influenced from banking and financial institutions (Figure 7.2). However, the same methodology is applicable to other institutions.

Figure 7.2: Risk appetite graphical concept

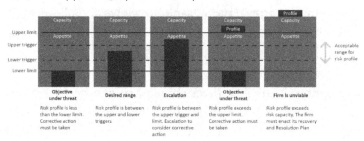

Source: (Deloitte)[161]

Without any doubt, risk capacity, risk appetite, and tolerance (e.g., buffers) should be a core consideration in the risk management function with the active involvement of the board of directors and monitoring by the risk and the audit committees. The risk tolerance is the level of risk an organization can withstand and tolerate.

Measures to mitigate adverse effects of risk include *avoid, control, accept, and transfer (ACAT)* considering risk probability and priorities.

- *Avoid:* Risk must be avoided, and the benefits do not justify potential damage if it is too difficult to protect against a risk. Robust risk management should be present to circumvent the problem.
- *Control:* The threat impact of a risk can be controlled by incorporating appropriate prudent measures.
- *Accept:* A risk that is considered of negligible impact but more expensive to protect against the risk can be accepted.
- *Transfer:* Risk can be outsourced to third parties who are able to manage the outcome.

7.2.1 RISK APPETITE FRAMEWORK

Although the risk appetite framework is a tool to establish, monitor, control, and supervise risk in financial institutions, there are many companies operating in the nonfinancial sector that adopt the same approach in terms of risk framework, as it can be observed in many annual reports. This section refers mainly to guidelines and literature focused on the banking system, although it can be leveraged by the nonfinancial system. The risk appetite framework is also linked to the IIA second line of defense framework.

European Central Bank (ECB)[162] mentions that banks must know how much risk they have capacity to support and set their appetite for risk, accordingly, considering upfront the stakeholders' expectations. Naturally, this takes more than guesswork; it requires comprehensive and well-developed risk appetite frameworks. These frameworks are a core element to determine the risk capacity, establish a risk culture, and therefore manage, control, and supervise risk. Regarding the risk appetite framework, the board should be involved from the start in an end-to-end fashion and process. Banks' risk management and internal control functions can and should contribute to develop and monitor the risk appetite framework.

Bank for International Settlements (BIS) in SRP30: Risk Management,[163] indicates as responsibility of the board of directors and senior management the definition of the institution's risk appetite and to ensure that the risk management framework includes detailed policies that set specific firm-wide prudential limits on the bank's activities that are consistent with its risk-taking appetite and capacity. In order to determine the overall risk appetite, the board and senior management must first determine the risk capacity and then understand a comprehensive risk exposures map on a firm-wide basis. Thus, the Risk Appetite Framework (RAF) should be properly aligned with the strategic interests of the company and profoundly embedded within the risk management framework and the business model.

The overall approach, including policies, processes, controls, and systems, should:

- Establish, communicate, and monitor the risk appetite, taking as first considerations the expectations of the stakeholders.
- Include a clear risk appetite statement, as well as risk limits and respective buffers.

- Outline the roles and responsibilities of those overseeing the implementation and monitoring of RAF, notably the first line of defense, managing risk through a provision of products and services profiles for clients, and the second line of defense, through the expertise, support, monitoring, and challenging on risk-related matters.
- Consider material risks, as well as to its reputation vis-à-vis policyholders, depositors, investors, and customers.
- Align with the strategy and strategic plan, as well as with the business model.

An embedded and robustly established risk appetite framework provides a tool to link risk management, strategic planning, balance sheet, profit and loss, and cash-flows' management within the scope of ICF (Internal Control Framework). Figure 7.3 explains the relationships among risk capacity, the risk appetite, strategic planning, and financial statement management holistically.

Figure 7.3: Essentials of risk appetite framework

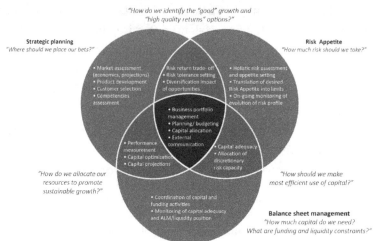

Source: (Oliver Wyman)

7.2.2 RISK APPETITE STATEMENT

Within the embedded scope of Internal Control Framework (ICF) and Risk Appetite Framework (RAF), the organization should articulately develop a clear *Risk Appetite Statement* (RAS). RAS must correspond to all applicable risks in each unit/department with both quantitative and qualitative criteria assessments. The end measures should be well defined to accept, avoid, share, or transfer the risk. In banks— but also outside the financial system (e.g., oil companies, energy sector, commercial airlines, shipping companies, public transportation, telecommunications)—the RAS must emanate from the board and at least cover four key dimensions to capture all material risks of the bank.[164]

(1) *Solvency/Loss Protection:* This reflects the level of protection/buffer against significant losses that could lead to default. They can be both regulatory and/or economic. Healthy organizations usually have the top-of-the-house of capital deployed without creating excessive leverage.

(2) *Liquidity & Funding:* This means the level of protection/buffer against a period of prolonged funding stress (e.g., impact of COVID-19 on cash-flows and sustainability) that could lead to illiquidity and eventually to insolvency. Proper alignment of liquidity and funding constrains the funding mix, keeping the cost of funds at risk optimal levels. In the banking system, there are minimum levels of liquidity to be maintained, monitored namely through the liquidity coverage ratio (LCR).

(3) *Earnings Volatility/Business Mix:* This applies that the earnings/business mix statements constrain excessive up and downside volatility arising from specific portfolios and/or risk types. Proper alignment provides protection against "surprises," and essentially serves to deliver predictable returns

to shareholders, as well as being able to service debt and ensure the protection of depositors. Also, it should be used to address/constrain specific areas of concern for the board/management.

(4) *Franchise & Reputation:* This dimension fundamentally articulates the appetite for risks that are difficult to measure but can pose a substantial threat to an organization overall franchise and reputation, as well as solvency and/or liquidity. For example, operational risks (e.g., cyber risk, supply-chain), reputational risks, ethical behavior, customer treatment. Sustainable measures must be incorporated to address/constrain these kinds of risks, a process that should be permanently updated considering changes in the risk profile or the potential for the emergence of new risks; this challenge is particularly higher in corporates with an international footprint.

The board risk and compliance committees—and the audit committee—play a key role in setting and managing risk appetite, and they must be supported by executive teams in doing so.

7.2.3 DESIGNING RISK APPETITE STATEMENT
An example of setting RAS in a universal bank is demonstrated in Table 7.3. At the end, it all depends on the corporate business risk profile and respective jurisdiction. As regulators demand the demonstration of a robust risk appetite approach from banking and financial institutions, other business corporations may essentially leverage the same risk appetite dimensions to customize the risk appetite statement according to their needs.

Once the appropriate RAS has been identified in line with the abovementioned dimensions, measurable risk appetite metrics must be defined (Table 7.4). Also, it is important that the metrics are periodically updated and measured against the prevalent standards.

Table 7.3: Risk appetite dimensions and statement

Dimension	Possible Risk Appetite Statement
Solvency/Loss Protection	Generally, a board should target a medium–low risk profile to ensure preserving capital adequacy (Liquidity Coverage Ratio) and security mechanisms to strengthen position as a sound institution.
Liquidity & Funding	Ensure that it is permanently able to meet its obligations and funding needs timely, including under adverse economic conditions and aiming at a stable and diversified funding base while preserving and protecting the interests of its depositors.
Business Mix	Maintaining the position in their market segments and targets should ensure a balanced and diversified earnings and capital generation—stream of revenues.
Franchise & Reputation	Commitment to the highest ethical and governance standards in all its business dealings, enforcing sustainability, and responsible social action.

Source: (Oliver Wyman)

Table 7.4: Risk appetite dimensions and measurable metrics

Dimension	Metrics
Solvency / Loss Protection	Expected Loss Cost of Risk Market Risk to Risk-Weighted Assets (RWA) Interest Rate Risk to RWA Common Equity Tier 1 (CET 1) Ratio Other Capital Ratios Leverage Ratio
Liquidity & Funding	Liquidity Coverage Ratio (LCR) Net Stable Funding Ratio Wholesale Funding
Business Mix	Single Name Exposure Sector Concentration Geographic Concentration Non-core Business Sustainable Business (ESG Index)
Franchise & Reputation	Operational Losses Reputational Risk Indicator Cyber Risk

Source: (Oliver Wyman)

7.2.4 REVIEWING RISK APPETITE

Usually, the risk appetite framework (RAF) review process is performed semi-annually or annually but permanently monitored and adjusted. The board risk and compliance committee are pivotal in shaping the risk culture and risk appetite, which should be reviewed, monitored, and supervised by the boards' audit committee, and, depending on the jurisdictions, by the independent audit board. External auditors are also heavily involved in reviewing and auditing the risk appetite framework, as it is critical to ensure a proper risk management of an organization and its potential impact in the financial statements. The set risk appetite statement gets approved after the board and the senior management reaches a common consensus on risk management issues, always considering the risk capacity of an organization.

The CRO (Chief Risk Officer) is the top executive officer, in charge of risk management directly reporting to the CEO (Chief Executive Officer). The role of board members and board committees is described in Chapter 16: Role of Board Members. Earlier, in Section 4.2.2: "Business Model Evaluation," we discussed the evaluation process of business model assuring sustainable growth, which should also form the basis when reviewing risk appetite. The risk management function (a function of the second line of defense) should independently assess the robustness and sustainability of the risk strategy and appetite under the guidance of CRO. On the other hand, internal audit function (a function of third line of defense) should assess whether the existing policies and procedures remain adequate and comply with legal and regulatory requirements and with the risk appetite and strategy of the institution. If necessary, a new/remodeled risk appetite statement may be set following the same procedure discussed above.

Topics of the Chapter

The following has been discussed within this chapter:

- The risk appetite framework is strongly linked to the IIA second line of defense framework.

- The risk appetite framework (RAF) is a tool to manage and supervise risk in both the financial and nonfinancial sectors, although the framework is developed mainly under the guidelines focused on the banking system.
- Risk is defined as the effect of uncertainty on objectives and strategic plan.
- The types of risk include:
  1. Financial and nonfinancial risks
  2. Cyber risk and related risks
  3. Misconduct risks
- Adverse effects of risk can be mitigated by applying the following:
  1. Avoid
  2. Control
  3. Accept
  4. Transfer
- Risk capacity is the amount of risk an organization can support to ensure its sustainability—even in challenging times of financial stress or others—while risk appetite refers to the amount and type of risk that an organization is willing to take in order to meet their strategic objectives.
- The board risk and compliance committee(s) are pivotal in shaping the risk culture and risk appetite. External auditors also assess the RAF. The board is ultimately responsible for this process in an end-to-end fashion.

Chapter 8

Compliance

According to the Three Lines Model (discussed in Section 6.2), the compliance functions hold a crucial role in the IIA second line of defense framework. However, while many corporations already had compliance functions, its importance emerged after the 2008 financial crisis, notably in the financial system, although currently expanding rapidly within the nonfinancial system, as a result of a wider responsibility imposed to many business arenas (e.g., external auditors, lawyers, public notaries, real estate agents, public authorities, not-for-profit institutions) after its publication in many jurisdictions and the enforcement of anti-money laundering and financing to terrorism and weapons of massive destruction. The lack of experience in the area led organizations to adopt different models for the compliance function. In most models, compliance functions transversely ensure ethics and conduct, regarding matters of inside information and market abuse and the area of prevention of money laundering and financing terrorism and weapons of massive destruction. These functions are fundamental to managing risks related to noncompliance with applicable laws and regulations. Therefore, controlling risks involving such issues may bear a significant reputational and financial impact. This chapter discusses the compliance concepts under four (non-exhaustive) themes—business ethics, financial institutions and markets, taxation, and money laundering.

8.1 BUSINESS ETHICS AND CONDUCT

Business ethics are transversal to a corporate and the most important driver is the tone at the top. In Section 3.11: "Five Golden Rules for Best Corporate Governance Practices," business ethics are the very first mentioned. As business ethics are the basis of the company growth, sustainability ultimately comes from long-term ethical vision that encapsulates all relevant stakeholders. Corporates that are compliant with business ethics and values need to spend less protecting themselves from internal and external behavioral and reputational risks, especially when supported by sound governance systems and independent research. Essentially, the resources in the world are finite, but the population is growing. Therefore, without ethics, those resources could be depleted for purely individual gain at huge cost to both current and future generations.

Code of conduct is an essential component to guide the companies to commit to the principles they have set. The code of conduct may not be limited to company itself, and it could potentially extend to suppliers, subcontractors, third parties, among others. For example, Norway's Government Pension Fund-Global (GPF-G) considers ethical instance when it comes to investment. It has maintained guidelines or conduct for organizations about children rights, climate change, or water management and does not invest in any company that does not meet its ethical standards. Banks, for example, have developed sustainable strategies toward climate risk management (e.g., coal mining, shale gas, tar sands, forest protection, pollution), supplier ethical code of conduct, and sustainable operations not financing projects or companies that do comply with the best practices in terms of climate. The code of conduct is not only meant to meet compliance requirements but is very core to the existence of the corporation for serving the better purpose of the society.

Conflicts of interests—and potential conflicts of interests—is another topic that requires attention. The agency theory, as discussed in Section 2.1, primarily discusses the conflicts of interest in the corporate and the incentives mechanism to deal with the conflicts. Also, as humans, we often experience some degree of deficiency, and to deal with such varying deficiency, humans often choose to work on colluding to understand deficiency and underlying motives for colluding. Organizations should have a conflict-of-interest policy to be followed by the directors and the entire organization (internal and external stakeholders), including subsidiaries in geography. Conflicts of interest that may arise in the corporate can be primarily divided into the main four categories:[165] (i) Corporate vs Board, (ii) Stakeholders vs Board, (iii) Shareholders vs Other Stakeholders, and (iv) Corporate vs Society.

Corporate vs Board

Potential conflicts between a corporate member (e.g., a manager of the company) and the board (e.g., director of the board) is common. In a family businesses, this probability is even higher. The source of potential conflicts of interest or conflict of interest can be—though not limited to—self-dealing, insider trading, remuneration, pay gap, abusing corporate assets, or nepotism. Directors should always be obliged to their fiduciary duties and never take inappropriate advantage of the position. They should maintain high ethical standards to the position which they were appointed to, and take prudent measures to forgo any cases of potential conflict. Even so, in the possible occurrences of conflict, they should abide by the corporate's conflict of interest policy and take any corrective actions.

Stakeholders vs Board

The stakeholders may include (though not limited to) shareholders (owners or principals), creditors, suppliers, regulators, or other organizations belonging to the supply-chain. The conflict of interest arises when the board member does not perform namely the fiduciary duty of loyalty to stakeholders, including shareholders. In the event of not being obliged to independence, the board member may exercise influence through cronyism, compensation, tricks, and manipulation.

Showing loyalty to a group of stakeholders while ignoring others can generate an enormous conflict of interest in a corporate. Sometimes, independent non-executive directors are forced to accept the decision of an assertive board member, ignoring stakeholders' and shareholders' concerns, notably minority shareholders' interests, which already is the inception of conflict of interest or potential conflict of interest before it could go viral, affecting reputation. Therefore, the concept of independence of a director (further discussed in Chapter 13: Independence and Conflicts of Interests) is particularly important.

Stakeholders vs Other Stakeholders

As board members are appointed by the general assembly meeting, shareholders expect the duty of care, loyalty, and obedience. Nonetheless, board members also need to deal with several other stakeholder groups, both within and outside the corporate. One example of a stakeholder inside the corporate is the labor union and outside is a creditor or lender (e.g., bondholder, capital markets, and banks). To manage the interests of all stakeholders is evidently very difficult, but board members are expected to address any potential or existent conflicts of interests sensibly, balancing the interests of all participating stakeholders.

Corporate vs Society

This kind of conflict arises when the corporate acts for its own benefit and ignores the interest of society, such as manufacturing companies seeking profits at the expense of non-climate friendly activities or business models. Other examples include evasion of corporate taxes, aggressive tax planning, tax optimization schemes, even when using double taxation agreement (DTAs), theft of intellectual property, treating employees as commodities, misappropriation of material prices, and choking suppliers. Such corporates are seen as value extractors, and their survival to existence is predictable. Even so, the board members can perform the turnaround to manage the conflicts of interest by following their fiduciary duties with high ethical standards and making sensible decisions, thus holistically benefitting both the corporate and the society.

Different jurisdictions define in their corporate law codes the concept of independence and situations that disqualify an individual as nonindependent, a quality that is required notably for non-executive directors. BCBS Principles of Corporate Governance (referenced Section 1.2.3: "Global Financial Crisis 2007–2008 and Increased Governance") include guidelines for developing and implementing the conflict-of-interest policy. It mentions that the policy should include:

- Members' duty to avoid—to the extent possible—activities that could create conflicts of interest or the appearance of conflicts of interest or even potential conflicts of interest.
- Examples where conflicts can arise when serving as a board member.
- Rigorous review and approval process for members to follow before they engage in certain activities (such as serving on another board) to ensure that such an activity will not create a conflict of interest.
- Members' duty to promptly disclose any matter that may result—has already resulted—in a conflict of interest.
- Members' responsibility to abstain from voting on any matter where the member may have a conflict of interest or where the member's objectivity or ability to properly fulfill duties to the bank may be otherwise compromised.
- Adequate procedures for transactions with related parties so that they are made on an arm's length basis.
- Methodology for the board will deal with any noncompliance with the policy.

European Banking Authority (EBA) in GL/2017/11, compiling the guidelines for the best practice in the internal governance of banks, states that the management body should be responsible for establishing, approving, and overseeing the implementation and maintenance of effective policies to identify, assess, manage and mitigate, or prevent actual and potential conflicts of interest at institutional level and staff level, including members of management body. Essentially, the conflicts of interests' policy should set out procedures, measures, documentation requirements, and responsibilities for the identification and prevention of conflicts of interest or potential conflicts of interest, for the assessment of their materiality and for taking mitigating measures.

Conflicts of interests is a very relevant and often a challenging issue when it involves "Related Parties." A related party transaction can be a deal or agreement between parties that find agreement through a preexisting relationship or through shared common interests. It can be transfer of resources, services, or obligations, such as a contract between the corporation and a major shareholder agreeing that the major shareholder would sponsor the annual meeting costs. This can be very controversial, as there exists quite a risk regarding the misappropriation of corporate funds.

Therefore, the standards of IAS 24 Related Party Transactions[166] require disclosures necessary to draw attention to the possibility that the corporate financial position and profit or loss may have been affected by the existence of related parties and by transactions and outstanding balances, including commitments, with such parties. If such compliance requirements are not met, companies often risk their sustainability. This is a reason for many organizations to set up a committee emanating from the board to issue opinions on transactions with related parties before approval, which many companies require to be done by the board. The example of private transactions in Velcro Industries is discussed in Section 2.1: "The Agency Theory," which aggressively wrote down assets to slash earnings in the book to cheaply buy shares of Velcro minority holders.[167]

Whistleblowing (employee/board member or related stakeholders reporting an activity that is dishonest or illegal) must be fair and appropriate. It is crucial to oversee the integrity, independence, and effectiveness of whistleblowing processes and policies to ensure a free and secure environment for stakeholders to complain and/or inform, protecting both ends of the process. Because the board members and directors are the fiduciary to corporates, they must also be strictly guided by the fiduciary duties of care, loyalty, and obedience at all times. It is critical that the policy protects both the whistleblower and the accused individual until an analysis and investigation is performed. Currently, many corporates are observed to maintain their own whistleblowing policy to manage their own reputational risk and can be compulsory requirement in some jurisdictions. To ensure that potential whistleblowers feel secured from being discovered, the policy—notably the people with access to the complaint—should be clear and ensure an unchallenging level of protection. One way many organizations are ensuring the robustness of this process is by outsourcing this function to a third party (e.g., consultant, law office) that has a reliable process to screen and report it to the highest level of the hierarchy. Senior management in their executive function should keep the board regularly and adequately informed of material or relevant matters, including the whistleblowing policy.

8.2 FINANCIAL INSTITUTIONS AND MARKETS

As history has shown, market can fail or be imperfect at times. Misconduct by the board or by certain board members may cause systemic risks and undermine the trust in institutions and its reputation, as discussed in Section 7.1.1: "Risk Types" (Misconduct Risk). It is crucial to establish a more direct, transparent, and immediate link between conduct issues, and a variable remuneration may potentially aid in reducing the probability of misconduct and setting the standards of behavior in market practices. The manipulation of interest rate (Libor, Euribor, and Tibor) and FX (Foreign Exchange) benchmarks by the market participants opened the eyes of regulators to publish recommendations or advice to improve market practices and market behaviors and to seek the clarity on financial indicators.

Section 2.1: "The Agency Theory" discusses two core domains of agency problems:

1. Transferring the corporate resources to the insider, including taking corporate property, self-dealing (insider), asset stripping, executive compensation, and other mixed motives.
2. Diluting outsiders' share in the firm, particularly by going private and dilution.

The two domains, when not handled properly, can bear significant market risk, in addition to other risks, and can undermine trust and integrity. Therefore, an ethical code of conduct is critical to meet the compliance requirements and, when possible, should be designed by default. On the other hand, there are specific conflicts of interest emerging from financial markets, namely issues related to *Market Abuse* and *Inside Information*. These issues should be properly controlled and mitigated, as failure to do so may lead organizations to incur sanctions imposed by regulators and/or complaints by customers, jeopardizing the trust of the stakeholders.

An organization's compliance function must ensure compliance with the legislation, thus guaranteeing the defense of the market and not allowing, nor being conniving, with situations of market abuse, nor that any stakeholders (notably shareholders) make illicit profits by accessing privileged information.

As discussed earlier, Norway's sovereign fund (GPF-G) only invests in company that meet its ethical standards, and companies should follow the robust sign-off process. For example, suppliers may need to provide answers relating to compliance requirements about their company and how they meet the ethical standards or business conduct requirements such as minimum liquidity requirements, health and safety requirements, climate change instance, among others. Therefore, a compliance sign-off process for products or services should be set up. A managerial level employee can be designated as compliance sign-off process owner and therefore be made responsible for identifying, documenting, and compiling all the compliance standards that the entity that supplies materials or the entity that seeks investment should meet.

Effective and transparent complaint handling rules are important to handle the clients' complaints promptly, which is also meant to reduce the risk of further litigations. Corporates should allow complaints to be made by any reasonable medium and recognize complaints as requiring resolution. Financial Conduct Authority[168] (FCA), UK, states that complaints can be any oral or written expression of dissatisfaction, whether justified or not, from or on behalf of a person about the provision of, or failure to provide, a financial service, claims management service, or a redress determination, which:

1. Alleges that the complainant has suffered (or may suffer) financial loss, material distress, or material inconvenience.
2. Relates to an activity of that respondent, or of any other respondent with whom that respondent has some connection in marketing or providing financial services or products or claims management services.

Not dealing with complaints effectively can bring huge fines for the corporate. Therefore, the board must ensure that the corporate has robust complaint handling policy, procedures, or methods. Additionally, there is high potential to leverage synergies between a product sign-off process and the complaints' process, as companies can learn from customers' complaints, make relevant improvements to specifications of a product or procedures, thus avoiding the repetition of situations and better servicing customers.

8.3 TAXATION

The area of taxation involves challenges to executive and non-executive directors, mainly because it is an area that requires detailed and specific skills and qualifications to be able to understand and monitor the real reach at stake. The challenge is aggravated by factors that may eventually impact reputation negatively and have a financial impact, either by the requirement of the payment of additional taxes and related penalties. This is a topic that should be included in the global agenda of a board/supervisory board as well as one that may require the audit committee of the board to supervise, with an option being contracting external consultants to periodically review the taxation area and the compliance with tax law. The complexity increases significantly when a company operates in multiple geographies, due to the need to comply with local tax codes and regulation, but also with the individual taxation of expatriates, to which the social security arena adds additional need for planning. Complying with local tax law does not include only compliance itself but also taking advantage of tax benefits offered and available in the legislation, notably in foreign direct investment specific benefits and leveraging double taxation agreements. The complexity of legislation on exemptions and tax benefits as well as practices that have the potential to qualify as aggressive tax planning (notably the use of tax heavens, tax shields, or aggressive interpretations of tax law) or even tax optimization are practices that are currently not considered acceptable and often involve issues related to money laundering and financing of terrorism.

Tax obligations and compliance are important to make sure a corporate has paid all applicable taxes, interest, penalties, and costs of collection. Traditionally, corporate governance codes were primarily designed to attract the investment and discussion about tax matters considered as too technical in the board. However, the traditional notion is gradually shifting, and the issue of taxation now plays an essential role in corporate governance, therefore impacting boards. The degree of implementation of the principles of corporate governance very much affects the way how a corporate will fulfill its tax obligations. One of the objectives of a good corporate governance is the integrity of financial reporting. Since companies are accountable to national treasuries and tax authorities, reliable financial reporting is the fundamental basis of tax compliance. Therefore, the board and the management must ensure the tax compliance environment by implementing and monitoring the appropriate set of corporate strategies with leadership and commitment. High-level tax compliance environment requires the robust implementation of internal control functions across the entire business and operations, which gains additional importance in companies with an international footprint.

OECD member countries' tax administrators are involved in a program named cooperative compliance program, aimed to ensure tax compliance through the voluntary enhancement of internal control and corporate governance.[169] For example, the National Tax Agency of Japan (NTA) is conducting a program to enhance tax corporate governance of large enterprises. During the tax audit stage, a tax auditor delegated by NTA evaluates the effectiveness of tax corporate governance, and an audit executive of a regional taxation bureau subsequently holds a dialogue with the senior management of the company. NTA tax authorities evaluate on the following criterion during tax audit:

- Engagement and guidance of top management
- Organization and functions of accounting and audit divisions
- Tax and accounting procedures with internal checks and balances
- Dissemination of information and recurrence prevention measures
- Measures to control inappropriate acts

In case of positive evaluation result (i.e., company has sound tax corporate governance and low priority for audit) the NTA will mitigate the burden of audit and extend the interval between audits by one year. During the audit-free year, it is the responsibility of the company to disclose transactions with which the tax authority is liable to disagree, such as the reporting of extraordinarily large losses.

When a company has sources of income outside the residence, Double Taxation Agreements (DTA) are conventions for the avoidance of double taxation play a relevant role in legitimately saving taxes, as those treaties are signed between two or more countries to avoid international double taxation on income and property.[170] It divides the right of taxation between the contracting countries to avoid differences, to ensure taxpayers' equal rights and security, and to prevent tax evasion. Double taxation involves taxing the same income twice, both at the country of origin and at the country of destination. This can happen when a company pays corporate tax at the origin country and, when consolidating the financial statements, again pays corporate taxes on the profits already taxed at origin. Other examples include the payment of dividends when the same income is taxed in two different countries during international trade.

Tax benefits[171] under DTA can be claimed in two ways:

1. Upfront exemption from tax payments or a reduced tax rate on the respective payments.
2. Refund of deducted withholding payments.

Usually to benefit from a DTA, a foreign taxpayer—individual or organization—must be subject to full and unlimited tax liability in the other contracting country with respect to his permanent residence or the source of income, or even to other circumstances, depending on the agreed between two countries or a supranational organization in the double taxation agreement.

DTA between countries or supranational organizations, intercompany pricing, transfer pricing, management fees, and others must be carefully studied as well as considered and monitored by boards. Exchange rate risk management and interest rate risk management are other important aspects. Base erosion and profit shifting (BEPS) refers to tax planning strategies that exploit gaps in the architecture of the international tax system to artificially shift profits to places where there is little or no economic activity or taxation.[172] US-based big tech companies, including Amazon, Facebook, Google, Netflix, Apple, and Microsoft, often face complaints regarding aggressive tax planning. *The Guardian*[173] reports that these companies have been accused of avoiding taxes by shifting revenue and profits through tax havens or low-tax countries and of also delaying the payment of taxes they do incur. For example, Amazon maintained an effective tax rate of 12.7 percent over the decade when the corporate tax rate in the US has been 35 percent for most of that period (until 2019).[174] Amazon has defended its actions, but observers argue that the accounting method employed by big companies are often complex. Facebook and other tech companies have opened European headquarters in Ireland, taking an advantage of reduced corporate tax as low as 12.5 percent, which is about half the average of other countries in the OECD.[175] Seemingly, the EU officials raised questions over Irish corporate tax practices, and Ireland has been at loggerheads with the EU thereafter over its unfair tax treatment. The European Commission established the fight against aggressive tax planning as a priority, notably because of revenue losses, unfair competitive advantages, and lower tax morale.[176]

Companies may potentially use several tax optimization methods, namely transfer pricing; the setup of intragroup loans to transfer the income; use of tax asymmetry methods that facilitate avoiding double taxation, including the exploitation of the loopholes of tax rulings— large companies often negotiate with tax authorities for tax benefits when they set up in another country, usually through foreign direct investment.[177] Tax optimization is the process of reducing or optimizing the tax burden through informed decisions and tax efficient choices within the available legal tax framework.[178] Tax optimization can lead to making choices that would bring the optimal outcome to current and future tax liability. Tax optimization methods, when conducted legally and ethically, probably constitute less risk than aggressive tax planning that exploits gaps in the architecture of the international tax system to artificially shift profits where there is little or no economic activity or taxation. Nonetheless, tax is a national or a regional matter—e.g., European Union—and is a subject where boards must be involved and careful while dealing with it, mainly due to potential reputation issues, notably of not paying taxes at the source of profits but instead at the lowest taxed jurisdiction, as well as the impact of stronger scrutiny from society in general about the requirement of paying a reasonable and acceptable level of taxes. Otherwise, both the reputational and financial risks emerge as inevitable. Apple has ongoing dispute with European Commission because of the concentration and transfer of profits to Ireland—with a much lower corporate tax rate than most EU jurisdictions—allowing Apple to pay substantially less tax than other businesses over many years, concerning 13 billion euros in Irish taxes.[179] The French court ordered UBS to pay record 4.5 billion euros in fines, ruling that UBS solicited clients in France illegally and laundered the proceeds of tax evasion.[180]

OECD drafted principles that can increase tax revenues by approximately 100 billion dollars of corporate taxes under a new tax framework and for which OECD is negotiating a political agreement—expected to be concluded in 2021—among approximately 140 countries. The aim of this new tax framework is to ensure—notably US and European Union groups—that corporates are taxed in the countries where they operate (source of profits) and not in jurisdictions where they are able and allowed to shift taxable profits to tax havens or jurisdictions of lower taxation, a practice that has been advocated by a line of thought of involving aggressive tax planning.[181] There is also a line of thought that considers the concept of tax optimization at a different level of the aggressive tax planning. However, authorities, governments, stakeholders, and the public in general are increasingly aware and are scrutinizing these types of structures, even with most of them designed within a jurisdiction law framework, which may or may not involve taking advantage of loopholes in the legislation. The European Commission's study on aggressive tax planning indicators groups them into four categories:[182] (i) Country-level and bilateral indicators, involving corporate tax rates and revenues, FDI and market structure, royalty flows, bilateral import prices, and treaty shopping indicators; and (ii) multinational enterprises' group-level indicators, namely its geographical structure and relative tax burden, consolidated tax burden, and profitability; (iii) firm-level indicators by corporate types, including specific indicators such as profitability, debt shares, interest payments, intangible assets, patent applications by relative tax rate situation; and (iv) the combination of firm-level indicators, notably shares of target firms, lower tax or conduit entities.

The EU Council Directive 2011/16, also known as DAC6,[183] in relation to cross-border tax arrangements, has come into force since 2018. DAC6 applies to cross-border tax arrangements that meet one or more specified characteristics (hallmarks), in order to foster transparency and fairness in taxation. It concerns either more than one EU country or an EU country and a non-EU country. The directive mandates a reporting obligation for these tax arrangements, if in scope, no matter whether the arrangement is justified according to national law. Failure to comply with DAC6 may bring significant sanctions under local law in EU countries, and corporates therefore need to make sure they are compliant by the deadline in 2020. The major consequence, apart from EU member states sharing cross-border tax information, is that it can also be shared with a third country (when necessary) and taxpayers ensuring, that what is disclosed to tax authorities under DAC6 rules is consistent with their other filings such as country-by-country reporting.

The European Commission researched evidence of aggressive tax planning in EU, based on economic indicators at macro-level and firm-level. Although none of the indicators provides per se an irrefutable causality toward aggressive tax planning, when considered together, they may be regarded as a "body of evidence."[184] Aggressive tax planning structures are grouped into three channels: via interest payments, via royalty payments, and via strategic transfer pricing. Those indicators classify entities within multinational enterprises (MNEs) into three target entities: (i) where the tax base is reduced, (ii) lower tax entities where the tax base is increased but taxed at a lower rate, and (iii) conduit entities which are in a group with ATP activities, but no clear effect on the tax base is identified. Smaller European Union Member States including Cyprus, Malta, and Luxembourg raise more corporate taxes as a percentage of GDP, while Ireland attracts a sizable amount of corporate tax base. On the other hand, The United Kingdom, Luxembourg, Estonia, and the Netherlands are central to tax optimal repatriation routes, enabling tax efficient repatriation of dividends to and from countries outside the EU.

Other jurisdictions may have similar arrangements, and the board members are therefore required to be adequately aware and knowledgeable in taxation issues, if not possible in detail. Particularly, the audit committee and risk and compliance committee members should be knowledgeable about applicable directives and laws regarding the taxation.

As a result of globalization, many multinationals have significant international footprints. Transfer pricing has been on the rise, which includes the price one division in a corporate charges another division for goods or services provided. It can be performed between subsidiaries, affiliates, or companies that are commonly controlled. Big corporates may use transfer pricing as a tool to reduce the tax burden on the parent company by charging a higher price to divisions in high-tax countries, thus reducing profit, while charging a lower price to increase profits in low-tax countries, often dubbed tax havens. Countries or states such as Luxembourg, Bermuda, Switzerland, Ireland, Singapore, Cayman Islands, and British Virgin Islands are some included in the quasi-category of "tax havens" due to their lower-than-average taxation levels or even because of specific tax benefits that apply to companies and individuals that qualify for the applicable tax regime. Tax havens are often criticized for not sharing tax information statistics with foreign tax authorities. However, many sovereigns put constant pressure on tax havens to release information regarding offshore investment accounts. Common standards, transparency, and data sharing are some of the tested methods to combat the tax haven fraud.

When it comes to cross-border transactions, the complexity grows significantly, and board members must therefore ensure that the transfer pricing is fair and legal within the scope of market price and essentially compliant with directives and rules in the respective jurisdictions, such as DAC6 in the EU. Tax authorities in many jurisdictions have endorsed strict rules regarding transfer pricing to prevent corporates fraud related to tax evasion.

A variation of transfer pricing may involve over invoicing whereby profits can be retained in a jurisdiction with a lower level of taxation. Usually, this scheme occurs when a party dealing with trade (export and import of goods and services) invoices a company or SPV (special purpose vehicle), and this intermediary (that may be or not a related party) then re-invoices the importer at a higher or lower price. This scheme, dubbed "triangulation," does not add any value to the goods or services exported. The acid test to detect these types of transactions is to analyze if the goods or services followed the same physical route of the papers and documentation supporting the transaction, such as an export being from a European country to a country in North America, with the goods being shipped from Europe to North America, and the correspondent invoice being issued first to an SPV in the Caribbean Islands and then from there to the destination country. Under invoicing is also considered an illegitimate practice, which usually has the objective of reducing the payment of customs on goods imported from an affiliated party.

The compliance officer or designated employee who holds accountability should fervently engage in any matters encompassing registration of Foreign Direct Investments (FDIs), repatriation of dividends, repatriation of proceeds, or expropriation of assets. Other sensitive tax issues may include topics such as corruption, equalization for expatriates, the purpose of creation of the SPV (being tax havens in most of the cases), offshoring and outsourcing, corporate ethics, among others. In the case regarding tax equalization for expatriates, in the international context, the employer may need to send some of their employees abroad for work purpose. Therefore, it is the responsibility of the employer to make sure that the expatriates are not in a disadvantageous state. Otherwise, if the personal expatriate tax burden increases as a result, the individual should be equalized as if was based at the home country. Matters such as social security tax and income tax must be carefully reviewed in both home and abroad, if any taxation agreement exists. The hypothetical tax that the expatriate pays are usually withheld at the source of income country with the employer bearing any other extra tax costs abroad.

8.4 MONEY LAUNDERING—"THE 5 VECTORS"

This section is adapted from the paper[185] co-authored by Teodora de Castro and Duarte Pitta Ferraz, published in 2019 in InforBanca 117, titled "The International Governance in Corporate Governance— Closing the Fence to Besiege Crime" ("*O Governance Internacional No Corporate Governance—Closing the Fence to Besiege Crime*").

Simply put, money laundering is an illegal process to make "black-money" generated from illegal or criminal activities, from drug trafficking to terrorist funding, corruption, breaking foreign exchange controls to corporate and individual tax evasion, aggressive tax planning, or other fashions to seem to appear originated from a legitimate source.[186] Other no exhaustive examples include an individual committing an offense by concealing criminal property; disguising, transferring or removing criminal property; entering into arrangements that are suspected to facilitate the control of criminal property by or on behalf of another person or firm; and acquiring, using, or possessing of criminal property. A key aspect of laundering is to make a criminal property blend in with normal financial practices, ensuring the system that would trace it back to a crime loses its track. Also, an organization does not need to be aware that they have been involved in a crime to become legally involved.

Deutsche Bank was fined 150 million dollars by US authorities for its financial dealings with Jeffery Epstein, a sex offender, and for its relationship with two banks that were behind large-scale money laundering scandals.[187] One of the research report says that the regulators in Europe and US have imposed 342 billion dollars of fines on banks since 2009 for misconduct behavior, including money laundering cases and that is likely to go above 400 billion dollars by 2020.[188] Commonwealth Bank of Australia paid fine around 700 million dollars (AUD) to Australian authorities for breaching anti-money laundering and counter-terror financing laws—the case of 53,000 suspect transactions that the bank did not immediately report to authorities.[189]

There are five basic vectors involving concepts and mechanisms relevant to consider on the evolution of the fight against the money laundering:

1. Anti-money Laundering (AML)
2. Terrorism Financing (TF)
3. Proliferation of Weapons of Mass Destruction (WMD)
4. Ultimate Beneficiary Owner (UBO), which is linked to the concepts of KYC (Know Your Customer) and PEP (Politically Exposed Person)
5. Special Purpose Vehicles (SPV), which serves as a protection shield to the UBO

The European Commission promulgated the Fifth Anti-money Laundering Directive (5AMLD),[190] amending the Fourth Directive to enhance transparency by:

- Setting up publicly available registers for companies, trusts, and other legal arrangements; enhance the powers of EU

Financial Intelligence Units and provide them with access to broad information for the carrying out of their tasks.

- Limit anonymity related to virtual currencies and wallet providers, and also for prepaid cards.
- Broaden the criteria for the assessment of high-risk third countries and improve the safeguards for financial transactions to and from such countries.
- Set up central bank account registries or retrieval systems in all Member States.
- Improve the cooperation and enhance of information between anti-money laundering regulators and supervisors and between them and prudential supervisors.

The legislation is not consistent, notably in its application but also in its translation to local language into the different legal frameworks of the European Union.[191] Selected relevant acts that govern the fight regarding AML-CFT-WMD in the European Union are listed in Section 14.1.2 "BCBS Principles of Corporate Governance."[192] Intergovernmental organization FATF (Financial Action Task Force), headquartered in Paris, develops policies to combat money laundering, terrorist financing, and other related threats to the integrity of the international financial system.

The first vector regarding money laundering, AML deals with concealing the origin or the actual owner of the funds, with the proceeds resulting from illicit activities becoming reusable capital under the law, giving them an appearance of legality. The money laundering process encompasses three phases:

1. *Initial/placement phase*, where goods and/or money are introduced into the formal financial circuits, usually through the financial system when involving cash, securities, and financial transactions. The FATF[193] mentions that can be characterized by breaking up large amounts of cash into less conspicuous

smaller sums that are then deposited directly into a bank account, or by purchasing a series of monetary instruments (e.g., credit cards, checks, money orders) that are then collected and deposited into accounts at another location.

2. *Layering*, where the launderer engages in a series of conversions or movements of the funds to distance them from their source, channeling them through the purchase and sales of investment instruments or simply wiring the funds through a series of accounts at several financial institutions across the world.

3. *Integration* comes after the successful execution of the first two phases, when the laundered funds become available in the legitimate economy, where the launderer may invest the funds into real estate, luxury assets, paintings, bankrupt companies, social institutions, or other kind of investments.

The second vector, TF, consists of any and all forms of supplying finances and other resources to activities concerning individual or collective terrorism, which is interconnected to the third concept, the financing of proliferation of (WMD). The terrorism financing concept has different characteristics from money laundering, notably because it may not use the formal financial system for the introduction and circulation of money. Traditionally, financing of terrorism moves small amounts while money laundering is mostly associated with large sums of money. Also, in financing of terrorism, the origin and source of the funds can masquerade as lawful (such as donations, small businesses involving cash transactions), while in money laundering, it is always within the concept of illegality. In the financing of terrorism, the transaction has the objective of hiding the destination of the funds destined to commit a crime through the use of local networks or isolated individuals.

The proliferation of WMD—third vector—is often defined as the transfer and export of the CBRN Weapons (Chemical, Biological,

Radiological, and Nuclear), respective forms of delivery, and related materials. It is worth highlighting that the use of methods or means include the suicide terrorism and lone wolf terrorism, cyberterrorism, the CBRN related terrorism with religious motivations, left-wing terrorism, right-wing terrorism, ethnonationalism, separatist terrorism, among others. Proliferation can take many forms, commonly involving the transfer or export of technology, goods, software, services, or knowledge that can be used in programs that involve CBRN weapons, delivery systems that may involve sophisticated technology such the case of missiles, or simple devices. Understanding the risks of proliferation of this kind of funding, which may not seem obvious to ordinary citizens, can elevate the ability of a state to prevent people and entities involved in proliferation of weapons.

The fourth vector, UBO, is defined by FATF as the individual who ultimately owns or controls a customer, company, or entity and/or the one on whose behalf a transaction is conducted. It includes those who exercise effective control over a person, entity, or legal agreement. The concept also includes situations where ownership and/or control is exercised through a chain (such as cascading SPV) instead of direct control as well as the beneficiary of investments linked to insurance policies such as life insurance. Interconnected with the fourth concept should be considered the concept of KYC (Know Your Customer, or nowadays Know Your Counterparties and Know Your Transactions). The process is also known as Due Diligence with respect to obligations that companies have in verifying the identity of their customers, suppliers, or even staff, before and/or during the relationship with them. Crimes with different dimensions, risks, and involving reputational risk are often committed through collusion of internal staff in the organizations, a practice that is facilitated when an organization is not aware of the importance of the internal control framework of having implemented control procedures with demanding stands to address the KYC skills and profile. Also, an UBO is usually linked to a PEP—Politically Exposed Person. Individuals who perform—or have performed—functions in prominent public positions in the last 12 months, in any country or jurisdiction, with the immediate family ascending and descending in first degree, also qualifying as PEP. Thus, the qualification as PEP can raise a dilemma regarding ethics and generation conflicts of interest or potential conflicts of interest in the individuals referred. A PEP generally presents a higher risk of potential involvement in bribery or corruption due to the position and influence that individual can exert. To mitigate those challenges, the process requires an enhanced process of identification and diligence for individuals, the origin of their funds, and their source of wealth. The qualification of an individual as a PEP in most situations implies that the PEP status qualifies their ascendants, descendants, and the likes in first degree as well as others with whom they are especially related in professional terms. Thus, qualification as a PEP can raise an ethical dilemma and the generation of conflicts of interest in those individuals as well as in the limitations and requirements that may to affect them. Therefore, it seems relevant that the acceptance of a position that qualifies someone as a PEP is consensual in family and personal circle affected directly by the PEP statute so that those involved have a sense of its meaning, restrictions and limitations emerging to that status. A question debated regarding PEPs is the definition of the time when a PEP is not linked anymore to the PEP statute. A line of thought requires that a reasonable number of years elapse, while another view that advocates a much more restrictive interpretation that "PEP once ... PEP forever," based on the argument that reputational risk continues after the termination of the service that led to the qualification of a PEP.

The fifth vector relates to Special Purpose Vehicles (SPV), is the formal legal structure used for the creation of fronting companies, assigning an aspect of legal credibility, being even more sophisticated if set up through SPVs (companies, investment funds) in chain and/or cascade. This is criminalized by law in some jurisdictions. The goal is to hinder access to the UBO, because they are spread over several jurisdictions in different geographies and regions where costs and administrative processes for obtaining data and information can be very complex; certain regimes or jurisdictions may be designed specifically to hide SPVs.

Thus, having in mind the objective of controlling the 5 *Vectors*, an organization must perform an examination duty via KYT's (Know Your Transaction) concept. It is critical to analyze the nature, purpose, frequency, complexity, unusualness, and atypical nature of the conduct, activity, transaction, or operation, comparing it with the profile of the players—namely the originator, possible intermediaries, and beneficiary of the funds—to become familiar with and understand the circuit of the funds at all times. This process involves the origin and destination of the funds and validation of the economic objective or lawful purpose associated with the conduct, activity, transaction, or operation. The examination duty is a responsibility transversal to the IIA three lines model of the organization. A potential argument using unawareness or ignorance does not relieve either the organization or its staff. In the due diligence process emerges another concept named KYP (Know Your Process) that requires all employees and staff of an organization to exhibit and have knowledge of its control processes, systems, and procedures as well as the best practices instituted, even recommending adjustments, corrections, and changes to improve the robustness of the internal control framework. Organizations must define control processes and systems as well as procedures, notably based on risk models (Risk-based Approach), investing significantly in the training duty (punctual or specific and continuous), in order to enable their staff members with the adequate skills to perform their jobs under the cultural risk environment defined for the organization to operate.

The AML-CFT-WMD framework promulgated by the European Commission—coordinated with many other jurisdictions and judicial and criminal authorities—significantly impacts the governance of the entities' internal control and governance framework, implying the sophisticated use of information technologies and data warehouse. It also places a strong fiduciary responsibility on the members of the governing bodies and some first-line managers, but also in staff with key duties such as in the control functions—compliance, risk management, and internal audit—and also in operations and back-office and middle-office departments assuming monetary responsibility or prohibiting the exercise of professional functions and/or integrating social bodies. In terms of corporate governance, the framework represents a test of the effectiveness of the IIA three lines model of organizations, with a line of thought considering a fourth line of defense involving the corporate bodies and the control functions with regulators, supervisors, and external auditors.

The organizations' compliance function throughout the establishment should be based on the three concepts—KYP, KYC, and KYT—and governed by robust principles of ethics, rigor, transparency, independence, risk, and strengthening their autonomy when making decisions; exercising the duties of abstention, refusal, collaboration, and communication to the judicial and police authorities; and when preparing and submitting the organization's SAR (Suspicious Activity Report).

8.4.1 REFLECTION FOR DIRECTORS ABOUT THE CHALLENGES OF AML-CFT-WMD

This section is based on an article[194] co-authored by Teodora de Castro and Duarte Pitta Ferraz, published in 2019 in InforBanca 117, in a separate volume titled *Portugal—O Combate ao Branqueamento de Capitais, Financiamento do Terrorismo, e Proliferação de Armas de Destruição em Massa—Desafios e Reflexões da Lei n° 83/2017* (*Portugal—Fighting Money laundering Laundry, Financing to Terrorism, and Weapons of Massive Destruction—Challenges and Reflections about [Portuguese] Law 83/2017*), annex to the article *O Governance Internacional No Corporate Governance—Closing the Fence to Besiege Crime* (*The International Governance in Corporate*

Governance—Closing the Fence to Besiege Crime), published in InforBanca 117.

Directors and boards should ensure, through the study and training programs, that they possess adequate knowledge about the challenges, responsibilities, and role they play in this arena, which is becoming very challenging in terms of the acquisition of skills. The overall conclusion that the main legislative framework constitutes to combat the AML-CFT-WMD (Anti-Money Laundering-Counter Financing of Terrorism-Weapons of Mass Destruction) also poses relevant challenges for new players including directors and the board and supervisory boards as a whole. The financial system stands out, as it is a powerful platform to process monetary transactions involving high volume of money and a high number of transactions, but other activities are also players involved in this process. The training requirement and the sophistication of computer systems in the effective identification of suspicious operations is critical in this fight.

The five basic concepts that frame the development and evolution of the legislation and regulation regarding money laundering are discussed earlier. An area of high sensitivity and vigilance—where reinforced measures are required—is correspondent banking, its chain or intermediaries and/or subsidiaries, and the knowledge of the circuit of funds entrusted to counterparties. Another aspect concerns the control procedures over branches, subsidiaries, and international operations—even if there are no members representing the shareholders in the governing bodies—related to recent AML-CFT-WMD (Anti-Money Laundering-Combating the Financing of Terrorism-Weapons of Mass Destruction) scandals in participating companies.

BCBS[195] considers consolidated supervision to be an essential element of supervision over banking groups. It establishes that the obligated entities have in common 10 general duties:

1. Duty of control
2. Identification and diligence

3. Communication
4. Abstention
5. Refusal
6. Preservation
7. Examination
8. Collaboration
9. Nondisclosure
10. Duty of training

Their violation subjects them, as well as the sectorial authorities, to a matrix of relevant fines and sanctions, which are applied to collective legal entities or similar entities and to individuals motivated by a common issue, interest, or objective. The special responsibility of the corporate bodies as a collective and of its members as individual should be highlighted. New actors involve nonfinancial public entities and nonfinancial entities like statutory auditors, lawyers, auditors, public notaries, conservatories, and real estate agents that are faced with a new paradigm that, in general, they have not incorporated in their operational models and relations with customers and stakeholders. The legislation in general has a relevant impact on the risk and surveillance culture of nonfinancial entities, changing the current paradigm. It may even represent an ethical-cultural impact in the fashion they consider the new paradigm, considering issues linked to professional secrecy and confidentiality as well as the need to apply a structured risk approach. It seems that the adaptation process requires training, especially universities including it in their programs such as in law, finance, and management.

Decision-making structures and processes are closely linked to the governance framework. The assessment of risk factors is critical in the decision-making process and, of course, at the hierarchical level, which, given its importance, must lead by the social bodies and not only at the managerial and/or technical and operational level. The decision—apparently simple and technical—on the application of simplified measures or aggravated measures should be taken at the highest level of the hierarchy, as it involves the approach and decision on three of the risk factors: (i) customer, product, or service, (ii) operation and distribution, and (iii) geographical location. Those factors should be interpreted, qualitatively and quantitatively, in either simplified or aggravated measures. The responsibility of defining the model's criteria and risk classification should be highlighted and should include common minimum risks and specific risks of the sectors as well as the action plan for their mitigation and monitoring.

The suspicions associated with the AML-CFT-WMD are to be reported to the country's Financial Intelligence Unit (FIU) for the sanctioning and criminal aspects. The European Union Member States have created the FIUs with the characteristic of being operationally independent and autonomous but have to coordinate topics of mutual interest within the Egmont Group. The entities with operational competences are the FIUs and the judicial, police, and sectorial authorities, which also include the tax administration, border control services, intelligence services, and other public services considered relevant. 5th AMLD—Fifth Anti-Money Laundering Directive (https://ec.europa.eu) identifies the subject entities (obliged entities), the obligations that generate illicit acts, as well as those related to supervisors and regulators (i.e., sectorial authorities). This framework significantly impacts the governance of the entities' internal control and governance system, implying the sophisticated use of information technologies. It also places a strong fiduciary responsibility on the members of the governing bodies and some first line directors, namely the control functions (compliance, risk management, and internal audit), taking monetary [fiduciary] responsibility or prohibiting the exercise of professional functions or integrating social bodies.

Policies applicable to the employees of the entities were defined without exception in a paradigm that facilitates a permanent state of alert regarding the AML-CFT-WMD, as well as improving the risk culture, which constitutes a significant challenge that must have a structured response. Policies range from:

- adoption of codes of ethics and conduct, customer acceptance policy, conflict of interest policy.
- establishment of decision-making models, the redefinition of delegated competences, segregation of functions and automated decisions (STP—Straight-Through Processing).
- definition, control, and formal processes of capturing, processing, and archiving information.

The entities have to designate one individual among the senior management team to monitor the effectiveness of the controls of compliance with the AML-CFT-WMD prevention framework, and an executive board member serves the function of analyzing and deciding operations identified at the frontier of the communication decision to the Financial Intelligence Unit (FIU), carrying out a critical review in order to ratify—or make—the decision to communicate to the FIU. In terms of corporate governance, this framework also represents a test of the effectiveness of the IIA three lines of defense model of organizations, with a scientific line of thought from Arndorfer and Minto that advocates the existence of a fourth line of defense involving social bodies and control functions with regulators, supervisors, and external auditors—external assurance providers. The effectiveness of the first line of defense (including business and operational units involved in customer management), which is the entry point for suspicious AML-CFT-WMD transactions, and the third line of defense (internal audit) must ensure that the ICF (Internal Control Framework) operates effectively and efficiently.

The role of the fourth line of defense assumes particular relevance in this new paradigm, concerning the involvement—which is often high in intensity—of the members of the governing bodies with the external auditors, regulators, and supervisors. It must ensure that the governance (Governance Framework), risk in its multiple aspects (Risk Appetite Framework), and internal control (Internal Control Framework) guarantee the social and supervisory bodies—particularly non-executive or independent directors, who have responsibility of supervising executive directors—a robust basis for the exercise of their duties and obligations. This requirement of EBA/GL/2017/11 regarding the internal governance of financial institutions remains a challenge. In general, there is a lack of mutual understanding of responsibilities between executives and non-executives and, on their side, the permanence of a culture that has great difficulty in challenging executives, in getting involved in end-to-end development and strategic plan, and in controlling the governance framework of the institutions. This area requires significant cultural change and must be considered critical in the Fit and Proper process.

The concept of the three lines of defense, launched by The Institute of Internal Auditors (www.theiia.org) was reviewed in 2020 to integrate changes and evolution of the paradigm of the landscape, especially considering legislative changes, regulation, supervision, and governance of obliged financial companies. One point of view respects the fact that the governing bodies and senior management have functions that were not reflected within the current paradigm, as it only suggested the intervention of the governing and supervisory bodies takes place only after the second line of defense; the IIA 2020 update indicates that the governing body—accountable to stakeholders for organizational oversight—having the roles of integrity, leadership, and transparency. The updated model seems adequate in the current governance framework, as the business model is intricately linked to the first line of defense and the impact on prudential ratios, particularly capital and liquidity, notably in the financial system. These topics were managed in a non-intrusive fashion by the boards of directors/supervisory boards, as well as by regulators and supervisors, especially regarding behavioral supervision and particularly regarding the protection of the interests of depositors, who have first priority in terms of stakeholders and who are placed ahead of shareholders in the chain of importance by the law.

Sophisticated crime with international targets has no borders or jurisdictions, focusing incessantly on the vulnerabilities of organized societies (i.e., states and companies). They exploited vulnerabilities of PEPs in governments, companies (being an easy target for those facing financial difficulties), as well as NGOs (many dependent on donations for their finances) in search of the weakest link to exert pressure. The techniques include the criminals domination of the law and customs and sometimes resort to reputable law firms, consultants, tax consultants, financial institutions, among others as part of social events, having sophisticated ways of posting news that ensure initial credibility, necessary to the first phase of integration into the formal system (initial/placement phase), then preparing criminal operations.

Sectorial authorities have sanctioning power, including the ability to inhibit the exercise of voting rights and other beneficial ownership and the application of sanctions for noncompliance. Regarding the competence and suitability of people (Fit and Proper), the competent entities can take several measures. They may include setting deadlines for the adoption of measures that comply with the requirements, suspension of authorization to exercise functions, deadline for changing responsibilities or composition of governing bodies, and even withdrawing authorization for the exercise of functions, when measures are not adopted to ensure compliance with the missing requirements.

Topics of the Chapter
The following has been discussed within this chapter:

- Compliance for each of the four themes can be enforced by considering the following:
  1. Business Ethics and Conduct
     - Code of conduct
     - Conflict of interest
     - Whistleblowing

2. Financial Institutions and Markets
   o Maintaining internal transparency
   o Accept and address complaints.
3. Taxation
   o Engagement and guidance of top management
   o Organization and functions of accounting and audit divisions
   o Tax and accounting procedures with internal checks and balances
   o Dissemination of information and recurrence prevention measures
   o Measures to control inappropriate acts
4. Money Laundering
   o Anti-money Laundering
   o Terrorism Financing
   o Proliferation of Weapons of Mass Destruction
   o Ultimate Beneficiary Owner
   o Special Purpose Vehicles

Chapter 9

Supervisory Mechanism

Supervision refers to the act of monitoring the financial performance and operations of banking and financial institutions—or any other equivalent entity—ensuring that they are soundly run, following the prudential rules and regulations enforced by the regulators with the objective of guaranteeing financial stability and protecting taxpayers. This chapter discusses and compares the major models and mechanisms for supervision of banks and other business entities operating under their umbrella (e.g., bancassurance, pension funds, and investment funds).

There are four main types of supervision models[196]—institutional, functional, integrated, and twin peaks—each presenting advantages and disadvantages, with the supervision structure usually being stable and built on historical precedent, politics, and cultural aspects. The models adopted by the countries may or may not take as a common base the legal status of the entity or entities involved as well as the complexity of the institutions, namely the different business models and businesses' segments, such as a conglomerate including only banking industry or banking, insurance, and wealth management, with an international footprint.

This is a first element of complexity for both the supervisors and institutions, namely in relation to the execution of a proper supervision of different business models and business segments. A second element of complexity emerges from the inconsistency among National Competent Authorities (NCAs) and other supervisors in the adopted model, an issue that makes supervision more complex, notably in terms of communication and potentially not covering all elements that should be covered by the NCA. It also relates to the footprint of an institution, especially in terms of different "rule books" applied. If within the eurozone and considering ECB (European Central Bank) banking supervision, there is consistency. However, that cannot be assured for the full EU, not even considering the additional complexity when the footprint extends over one or more continents, which may have less strict regulatory and supervision rules. These elements represent a challenge firstly to the board of the holding company as well as to the regulatory and supervisory authorities. However, if the holding company is based in a geography with lower standards, then a new element of complexity emerges relating the need to decide the enforcement at the subsidiary of the more stringent standards or, alternatively, the competent authority such as the ECB banking supervision not accepting the results of supervision in that particular country as robust enough, thus impacting the supervisory procedures in relation to that particular subsidiary.

Institutional Model

In the institutional approach, a firm's legal status determines which regulator is tasked with overseeing its activity from a safety and soundness as well as a business conduct perspective. A firm's legal status (for example, registered as a bank, a broker-dealer, or an insurance company) determines the regulator tasked with overseeing its activity, both from a safety and soundness and a business conduct perspective. One of the criticisms this model faces is that financial and banking institutions and their peripheral subsidiaries are not adequately guided, with the continuous evolution of financial markets and players and essentially the blurring of product lines across sectors. For example, a single entity can provide banking and insurance services.

Effective coordination mechanisms can still be implemented, but implementation of new changes remains slow. Today, things change fast, and supervision should therefore remain forward-looking, agile, and incremental. China, Hong Kong, and Mexico follow the institutional approach model.

Functional Model

The functional approach is one in which supervisory oversight is determined by the business that is being carried by the entity, without regard to its legal status. Each type of business may have its own functional regulator. For example, a single entity providing banking and insurance services would be overseen by two distinct functional regulators; in some systems, it is even possible that both prudential and behavior supervisions are carried by a particular National Competent Authority while the other may deal only with part of the behavior supervision. However, it is still not considered optimal, as it requires great coordination between regulators or supervisors. France, Portugal, and Brazil follow a functional approach.

In eurozone, common European System of Financial Supervision (ESFS) recently came into existence. Nonetheless, it does not specify the type of supervision approach that each individual country may adopt. The European System of Financial Supervision (ESFS) is a network of three European Supervisory Authorities (ESAs), the European Systemic Risk Board, and national supervisors (NCA—National Competent Authorities), having as remit ensuring consistent and appropriate financial supervision throughout the European Union. The ECB (European banking supervisor) closely cooperates with the ESAs, notably the European Banking Authority (EBA).[197]

Integrated Model

This approach can be effective and efficient in smaller markets, where oversight of the broad spectrum of financial services can be successfully conducted by one regulator. There is a single universal regulator that conducts both safety and soundness oversight and conduct-of-business regulation for all the sectors of the financial services business. For example, an entity providing banking and insurance services is overseen by a single regulator. It has also been adopted in larger, complex markets where it is viewed as a flexible and streamlined approach to regulation. The integrated approach has the advantage of a unified focus on regulation and supervision without confusion or conflict over jurisdictional lines that can occur under both the institutional and functional approaches; this approach tends to eliminate redundancies. One of the criticisms this approach faces is that there is a single point of failure, as it depends on one regulator. Countries such as Canada, Germany, Japan, and Qatar follow the integrated approach.

Twin Peaks Model

The twin peaks approach is based on the principle of regulation by objective and refers to a separation of regulatory functions between two regulators:

- One performs the safety and soundness supervision function (usually named prudential supervision).
- Another focuses on conduct-of-business regulation (usually named behavior).

For example, in the UK, Bank of England's Prudential Regulation Authority (PRA) is responsible for prudential supervision whereas Financial Conduct Authority (FCA) focuses on the regulation of conduct by both retail and wholesale financial services firms, including marketing of financial products. Essentially, this approach balances the trade-off between efficiency and conflict of objectives between prudential and behavioral supervision. The UK, Australia, and Holland follow the twin peaks approach.

The case of the US is seen as quite complex. The supervision structure in the US is strongly guided by historical precedent, politics, and culture. The model incorporated at the US is said to be a functional approach, with the added complexity of several state-level agencies and actors. The supervisors for banks are the Federal Reserve System (Fed), the Office of the Comptroller of the Currency (OCC), the Federal Deposit Insurance Corporation (FDIC), the National Credit Union Administration (NCUA), and the individual regulator in each state.

- The Fed regulates the state member banks (i.e., members of the Federal Reserve System and bank holding companies in the US).
- The OCC regulates national banks.
- The FDIC regulates nonmember state banks.
- The NCUA regulates credit unions.
- At the state level, the New York State Department of Financial Services is one of the examples that regulates financial services and products in New York state in coordination with other national agencies.
- Financial markets in the US are regulated by the Securities and Exchange Commission (SEC) and the Commodity Futures Trading Commission (CFTC).
- The banking regulators employ a prudential regulatory approach while the Securities and Exchange Commission (SEC) is enforcement oriented.

Nonetheless, the weakness exposed during 2007–2008 financial crisis and related financial institution failures pushed the US Treasury toward advocating a modified twin peaks approach as a long-term goal.

9.1 EUROPEAN SYSTEM OF FINANCIAL SUPERVISION

The European System of Financial Supervision (ESFS) is a network centered around three European Supervisory Authorities (ESAs), the European Systemic Risk Board (ESRB), and national supervisors. All of them work closely with European Central Bank (ECB), the eurozone central bank, comprising 19 member states of the eurozone and banking supervision entity. The eurozone is a monetary union of 19 out of the 27 EU member states which have adopted the euro as their common currency and sole legal tender. Regulators of other EU member states out of the eurozone, such as Denmark, Sweden, and Poland, which do not use euro as currency, may closely cooperate and coordinate with the ECB. The task of ESFS is to ensure consistent and appropriate financial supervision in the EU. Individual countries may customize with integrated or twin peaks approach of supervision, abiding with the common principles of ESFS. The legal framework of ECB's Single Supervisory Mechanism (SSM) directive does not specify the type of supervisory procedure to adopt.

European Supervisory Authorities (ESAs)

The European Supervisory Authorities include the European Banking Authority (EBA), European Securities and Markets Authority (ESMA), and European Insurance and Occupational Pensions Authority (EIOPA). ECB states that the ESAs work primarily on harmonizing financial supervision in the EU by developing the single rulebook—a set of prudential standards for individual financial institutions. The ESAs help ensure the consistent application of the rulebook to create a level playing field. They are also mandated to assess risks and vulnerabilities in the financial sector. The ESAs work closely with ECB for micro-prudential supervision of individual institutions such as banks, insurance companies, or pension funds.

ESRB

The ESRB is responsible for macro-prudential supervision of the financial system in the EU. ESRB is not a part of the ECB, but the ECB ensures its Secretariat. ECB[198] states that ESRB is responsible for:

- Collecting and analyzing relevant information to identify systemic risks.

- Issuing warnings where systemic risks are deemed to be significant.
- Issuing recommendations for action in response to the risks identified.
- Monitoring the follow up of warnings and recommendations.
- Cooperating and coordinating with ESAs and international fora.

National Supervisors—National Competent Authorities (NCAs)
ECB classifies the banks into two categories—significant banks and less significant banks (difference discussed in Section 9.2: "Single Supervisory Mechanism"). While ECB directly supervises the 117 significant banks (2020) in Eurozone, less significant banks are supervised by national supervisors (i.e., central bank of each participating country). However, national supervisors are still within the oversight of ECB.

9.1.1 RATIONALE FOR THE BANKING UNION
The eurozone sovereign debt crisis was fueled by countries such as Greece, Portugal, Ireland, Spain, and Cyprus. As a result, the banks in these countries were caught in a downward "death" spiral, even though some of the banks were still healthy in these countries. The cut in the credit ratings of those countries "automatically" pushed the cut—or downgrading—in credit ratings for the banking and financial institutions, as well as for corporates in the nonfinancial system.

As a result, the need to establish a *Banking Union* emerged from the sovereign debt crisis downgrade, accelerating the financial crisis of 2008 and the need to break the perceived and actual link between the sovereigns and the banks, basically because some sovereigns did not have the means to help the financial system. This was resolved in the eurozone through a coordinated intervention of European Commission, International Monetary Fund (IMF), and the European

Central Bank (ECB), dubbed "Troika," that injected money in those sovereigns, at the same time making money available to the financial system through a financial instrument named Coco's (Contingent Convertibles[199]), which are based on the concept of a traditional convertible bond, incorporating a strike price that is convertible into stock or equity when defaulted. Coco's modify the conversion terms, stating specific triggers for its conversion into stock. A relevant trigger could be the requirement to meet regulatory capital levels (e.g., Core-Tier 1 and others) established by regulators, as well as newly defined, more demanding levels of liquidity—liquidity coverage ratio. Usually, they have high yield, reflecting their high-risk profile. Essentially, this was the mechanism used by the Troikas to capitalize banks in the financial crisis in the eurozone, as Coco's amount is used for the calculation of Core-Tier 1 prudential ratio. Sometimes, Coco's are also used outside Europe.

ECB[200] states that the purpose of banking union is to make European banking:

- *More transparent* by consistently applying common rules and administrative standards for supervision, recovery, and resolution of banks.
- *Unified* by treating national and cross-border banking activities equally and by delinking the financial health of banks from the sovereigns where they are located.
- *Safer* by intervening early if banks face problems in order to help prevent them from failing and—if necessary—by resolving banks efficiently.

The Banking Union has essentially three pillars:

1. *Single Supervisory Mechanism* (SSM)
2. *Single Resolution Mechanism* (SRM)
3. *Single Rulebook and Deposit Guarantee Scheme*

9.2 SINGLE SUPERVISORY MECHANISM—SSM

The Single Supervisory Mechanism (SSM) is a legislative and institutional framework introduced by European Commission in 2014 to ensure robust prudential banking supervision over all the banks in the current participating 19 eurozone member states (as well as other countries in EU that decide to adhere to the ECB—Banking Supervision), excluding the branches of banks from non-EEA (European Economic Area) countries, unless they choose to be supervised.[201] The EEA enables the extension of the European Union's single market to non-EU member parties, being governed by the same basic rules that enable free movement of labor, goods, services, and capital within the European Single Market, including the freedom to choose residence in any country within this area. Also, the EEA links all the EU 27 member states with the three European Free Trade Association (EFTA) states: Iceland, Liechtenstein, and Norway. The EFTA members do not participate in the Common Agricultural Policy or the Common Fisheries Policy.

The 19 eurozone countries that use euro as their currency must participate in SSM. EU countries such as Sweden and Denmark that are part of the EU but not part of eurozone are not obliged to participate in SSM; however, they can choose to participate. Therefore, national supervisors should enter into close cooperation with the ECB. In the EU countries not participating in SSM, the ECB and the relevant national supervisors may codify in a memorandum of understanding how they can cooperate on the supervisory matters.

In general, the SSM comprises:

- *European Central Bank (ECB):* The central prudential supervisor of the largest banks in each country.
- *National Competent Authorities (NCAs)* of the participating EU countries: The national supervisors that monitor the remaining least significant banks; the structure of the supervision systems varies among countries, even in the eurozone.

Table 9.1: Criteria for classifying the significant institutions by ECB

Size*	Total value of its assets exceeds €30 billion
Economic importance	For the specific country or the EU economy as a whole
Cross-border activities	Total value of its assets exceeds €5 billion, and the ratio of its cross-border assets/liabilities in more than one other participating Member State to its total assets/ liabilities is above 20%
Direct public financial assistance	Has requested or received funding from the European Stability Mechanism or the European Financial Stability Facility
*A supervised bank can also be considered significant if it is one of the three most significant banks established in a particular country	

Significant institutions are defined as the ones with total assets exceeding 30 billion euros (Table 9.1). If a country does not have any bank above that size of assets, then the three largest banks of that particular country are considered systemic banks. A systemically important bank or financial institution is a bank, insurance, or other financial institution whose failure might trigger a financial crisis. Financial Stability Board (FSB), an international body that monitors and makes recommenda-tions about the global financial system and its financial stability, regu-larly publishes a report about the Globally Systemic Important Banks (G-SIBs). In the eurozone, Santander, ING Bank, Société Générale, UniCredit, BNP Paribas, Deutsche Bank, among others, are considered as G-SIBs, while banks headquartered outside the eurozone such as Agricultural Bank of China, Bank of New York Mellon, Morgan Stanley, Sumitomo Mitsui FG, among others, are considered as G-SIBs. As of 2020, ECB directly supervises approximately 117 significant banks.[202]

The ECB and the NCAs work collaboratively to prudently ensure that banks are compliant with the EU most current banking rules. NCAs supervise more than 2,400 least significant banks in euro-zone (2020).[203] ECB states that the aim of SSM is to ensure the safety and soundness of the eurozone banking system, increase financial integration and stability, as well as ensure consistent supervision. Essentially, SSM is one of the *three pillars* of the EU Banking Union, along with the Single Resolution Mechanism (SRM) and the Single Rulebook with the Deposit Guarantee Schemes (DGS).

9.2.1 GOVERNANCE OF SSM

The execution of the SSM's supervisory powers is conducted by the supervisory board, and the board is responsible to bring and present the new draft measures for adoption by the Governing Council of the ECB, the main decision-making arm of ECB. The supervisory board consists of a chair, a vice chair, four representatives of ECB, and some Representatives from NCAs.

The ECB directly supervises the 117 significant banks of the participating eurozone countries in 2020. Most importantly, these 117 banks hold almost 82 percent of banking assets in the Eurozone. The supervision of the significant institutions is carried out by a Joint Supervisory Team (JST), as each significant bank must have a dedicated JST, including staff from both ECB and NCA. The banks that are not significant (2,453 in 2018) must be supervised solely by NCA in close cooperation with ECB.

9.3 SINGLE RESOLUTION MECHANISM

ECB states that the Single Resolution Mechanism (SRM) applies to banks covered by the SSM. It is the *second pillar* of the Banking Union. If a bank fails despite stronger supervision, the SRM allows bank resolution to be managed effectively through:

- a single resolution board (SRB)
- a single resolution fund that is financed by the banking sector in the country of the bank that failed

The purpose of the SRM[204] is to ensure an orderly resolution of failing banks with minimal costs for taxpayers and to the real economy. The mission of SRB is:

- to ensure the orderly resolution of failing banks with minimum impact on the real economy and the public finances of banking union countries
- to manage the single resolution fund

9.4 SINGLE RULEBOOK AND DEPOSIT GUARANTEE SCHEMES

Single Rulebook is the set of rules that provides legal and administrative standards to regulate, supervise, and govern the financial sector in all EU countries more efficiently. It includes rules on capital requirements, recovery, and resolution processes and a system of harmonized national *Deposit Guarantee Schemes (DGS)*. The package of EU laws under the single rulebook applies to all EU countries. The banking union ensures these rules are implemented consistently across the eurozone and in other participating countries. DGS reimburse a limited amount to compensate depositors whose bank has failed. A fundamental principle underlying DGS is that they are funded entirely by banks and that no taxpayer funds are used.

The EU adopted Directive 2014/49/EU in 2014, which requires EU countries to introduce laws setting up at least one DGS that all banks must join. Thus, EU countries must ensure a harmonized level of protection for depositors and produce lists of the types of deposits that are protected. DGS that are set up and officially recognized in one EU country must cover the depositors at branches of their members in other EU countries. The directive maintains the deposit protection of €100,000 but includes a gradual reduction of the repayment times of deposit guarantees. It also restates the principle of resolving bank failures with the use of funds provided by financial institutions and not by taxpayers.

Basically, all participating banks in SSM must become members of a DGS and pay contributions based on their risk profile and other factors. When deposits become unavailable as a failure of the bank, the guarantee schemes must be in a position to reimburse the depositors. Depositors are to be reimbursed within a maximum of 20 working days; this will be gradually reduced to 7 working days by 2024. Stress test of DGS is to be performed every three years. As the deposit covers all depositors, up to €100,000, other protected deposits include:

- Pension schemes of small and medium-sized businesses.
- Deposits by public authorities with budgets of less than €500,000.
- Deposits of over €100,000 for certain housing and social purposes.
- Also, able to finance resolution of banks.

9.5 STRESS TEST

After the financial crisis 2007–2008, regulators across the world tightened the stress testing procedure. Stress tests are hypothetical simulations to determine the institution's ability to cope with economic crises. A stress test is often conducted on a scenario basis.

Examples of stresses include the so-called what if scenarios model:

- What happens if interest rates go by x%?
- What happens if oil price increase by y%?
- What happens if the Gross Domestic Product (GDP) decreases by z%?

Nonetheless, stress can also be brought by some unprecedented situations, such as COVID-19, which affected the global economy. In such situations, regulators tend to come up with fiscal stimuli and work together with industries in easing the stress collectively.

The fundamental goal of the stress test is to ensure the financial stability, ultimately ensuring financial stability of notably the eurozone banking system. Stress testing is integral to banks' risk management and banking supervision, as it informs bank management and supervisory authorities about unexpected adverse outcomes arising from a wide range of risks and provides an indication to banks and supervisory authorities of the financial resources that might be needed to absorb losses, should large shocks occur. In 2018, BIS published the updated principles named Stress testing principles[205] to meet the demands of continuous evolution in stress testing methodology. The principles are apparently set at a high level so that they may be applicable across many banks and jurisdictions, remain relevant as stress testing practices evolve over time, and be used by jurisdictions to guide all elements of a sound stress testing framework. In general, the principles cover sound stress testing practices and are formulated with a view toward application to large, internationally active banks and to supervisory or other relevant financial authorities.

In the EU, European Banking Authority (EBA) publishes the stress test draft methodology, templates, and template guidance in close cooperation with the European Systemic Board (ESRB), Competent Authorities (including the SSM), the European Central Bank (ECB), and also feeding the inputs from industries. Scenarios,[206] methodology, minimum quality assurance guidance, templates, and template guidance will be agreed upon by the EBA's Board of Supervisors. The macroeconomic adverse scenario and any risk type specific shocks linked to the scenario will be developed by the ESRB and the ECB, in close cooperation with Competent Authorities and the EBA. EBA mentions that the objective of the EU-wide stress test is to provide supervisors, banks, and other market participants a common analytical framework to consistently compare and assess the resilience of EU banks and EU banking system to shocks and to challenge the capital position of EU banks. EBA conducts stress test every two years, and in 2018, all 48 banks analyzed beat the common tier ratio of 5.5 percent under adverse stress, benchmarked against a core tier ratio of 8 percent in the baseline scenario and 5.5 percent in the adverse scenario.[207]

9.6 CULTURE AND BEHAVIOR SUPERVISION

The Financial Stability Board (FSB—www.fsb.org) Guidance on Supervisory Interaction with Financial Institutions on Risk Culture[208] mentions that culture can be a complex issue, as it involves behaviors and attitudes. While the definition of culture may differ across the world, the fundamentals of institution norms, attitudes, and behaviors remain the same. EBA defines risk culture as an institution's norms, attitudes, and behaviors related to risk awareness, risk-taking, and risk management and the controls that shape decisions on risks. Risk culture influences the decisions of management and employees during the day-to-day activities and has an impact on the risks they assume (EBA/GL/2017/11).

The risk culture of an institution often plays a crucial role in influencing the actions and decisions taken by individuals within the institution and essentially in shaping the institution's attitude toward the stakeholders and supervisors. The corporate culture evolves in parallel with the risk culture over time. The subcultures within the institutions and the employees depend on the contexts where and which parts the institution operates. Nevertheless, subcultures must adhere to the high-level values and elements that support the institution's overall risk culture. Thus, an environment that promotes integrity should be created across the institution and focus on fair outcomes for customers.

The indicators of sound risk culture are as follows:

- *Tone from the top:* The tone comes from the board and the senior management, which ultimately cascades down the whole organization over time. The board and senior management are discussed in Chapter 16: Role of Board Members. The chair of the board plays an important role in setting the tone at the board. The leaders promote, monitor, and assesses the risk culture of the financial institution; consider the impact of culture on safety and soundness; and make changes where necessary.
- *Accountability:* All the employees must understand the core values of the institution and its approach to risk. They must be

capable of performing their designated roles and be aware that they are accountable for their actions in relation to the institution's risk-taking behavior.

- *Effective communication and challenge:* Sound risk culture adheres to open communication and effective challenge in which decision-making processes encourage a range of views; allow for testing of current practices; stimulate a positive, critical attitude among employees; and promote an environment of open and constructive engagement.
- *Incentives:* As performance and talent management encourage and reinforce maintenance of the institution, financial, and nonfinancial incentives support the core values and risk culture at all levels of the institution. The concept of incentives is discussed in Section 2.1: "The Agency Theory."

9.6.1 THE CASE OF DE NEDERLANDSCHE BANK

Culture and Behaviour Supervision[209] came into light after the Dutch banking regulator De Nederlandsche Bank (DNB) successfully implemented it. As a supplement to traditional forms of supervision and being influenced from FSB guidelines, the supervision of behavior and cultural aspects targets the causes of behavior that impact the performance and risk profile of financial institutions. The behavior and culture supervision were added to the supervisory duties of the DNB to contain risks arising from risk-seeking behaviors of bank board members and managers. The approach aims at crisis prevention in the long run in a forward-looking manner. It identifies risks that may emerge from culture and behavior at an early stage and consequently implements the adequate measures to prevent risks from materializing. The supervision of behavior and culture is based on the following assumptions:

- In order to prevent future crises, it is required to more than just tighten up rules and legislation.

- Public trust in financial institutions and financial stability are related.
- Board members' behavior and decision-making largely determines the culture and performance of financial institutions.
- Financial institutions are responsible for their own behavior and culture; DNB does not take on the directors' position in this respect.
- Behavior and culture are an integral part of operational management; effective management is only feasible if organizational structure and culture go hand in hand.
- There is no blueprint for an "ideal" culture; every culture may, however, give rise to risks, and supervision works toward identifying and managing these risks.
- Supervision of behavior and culture applies to all groups in an organization, not only to the executive management.

The DNB expert center in charge is composed of specialists from a broad range of backgrounds, such as psychologists and change and governance experts. These experts examine boardroom effectiveness by observing and evaluating their meetings. Their examinations focus on behavior and culture at the top but also investigate, along with the Netherlands Authority for the Financial Markets, whether organizations can absorb organizational and cultural changes.

They follow a three-stage process:

- *Identification Stage:* Compilation of a risk score based on governance, behavior, and culture of the bank.
- *Assessment Stage:* The board's effectiveness, change culture and risk culture are assessed on-site.
- *Mitigation Stage:* Application of a range of mitigates, from raising awareness up to enforcement action, depending on where they find evidence of clear breaches.

To initiate explicit opposition, control functions such as compliance and risk management are installed in the decision-making process at an early stage. Furthermore, the role of independent board members may be strengthened. Additionally, behavior and culture are strategically embedded in change and restructuring processes. As a result, the assessments have identified key issues in the areas of leadership, decision-making, and group dynamics, such as:

- Unsatisfactory adherence to strategic objectives, resulting in opportunistic decision-making and lack of strategic direction.
- Decisions are insufficiently challenged at executive and board level, leading to dominant leadership and submissive board.
- Insufficient change effectiveness due to the absence of a clear change strategy or delegation of change agenda to those with too little authority to grant full implementation.

Incorporating the DNB model, the Dutch banks have increased their awareness of the effects and risks of behavioral patterns. This is believed to result in an enhancement of constructive challenging during board meetings, increase risk awareness, and foster discussion of risk and more organized reflection on complex group dynamics. Also, the ECB has been continuously addressing the relevance of the supervision of behavior and culture to the SSM.[210]

9.7 SSM—CULTURE AND BEHAVIOR SUPERVISION

Some of the differences between SSM, and Culture and Behavior supervision are mentioned in Table 9.2. SSM together with Culture and Behavior Supervision complements the twin peaks approach of supervision.

Table 9.2: Comparison—SSM vs Culture and Behavior Supervision

	SSM	Culture and Behavior Supervision
Goal	• Strengthen and stabilize the European banks and promote the stability of the European financial system • Greater financial integration and a level playing field for European banks	• Supplement the traditional forms of supervision • Improve behavior and culture of financial institutions to decrease risk profile by addressing root causes and targeting sustained change
Scope	• Europe-wide (EU)	• National (Netherlands)
Measurements	• Supervision is risk-based • Supervisory reviews, on-site inspections, and investigations • Authorize and withdraw banking licenses • Assess banks acquisition and disposal of qualifying holdings • Ensuring compliance with EU prudential rules • Setting capital requirements	• Supervision is risk-based and by incorporating behavioral risks at an early stage • Monitoring supervised institutions over a long period of time until the envisaged change has been achieved • Topics include decision-making, board effectiveness, capacity for change, risk culture, search for yield, root causes of supervision problems.
Organizational Structure	• *Supervisory board:* chair, vice chair, 4 ECB representatives, and representatives from national supervisors (NCAs) participating in SSM • The Governing Council of the ECB is the main decision-making arm	• Expert center of professionals from various disciplines, such as governance, risk, change management, organizational psychology

Topics of the Chapter

The following has been discussed within this chapter:

- The four main models of supervision are:
    1. Institutional Model
    2. Functional Model
    3. Integrated Model
    4. Twin Peaks Model
- The European System of Financial Supervision (ESFS) is a network centered around three European Supervisory Authorities (ESAs), the European Systemic Risk Board (ESRB), and national supervisors.
- The Banking Union is required to make European banking:
    1. More transparent
    2. Unified
    3. Safer
- The following three pillars of Banking Union are discussed briefly:
    1. Single Supervisory Mechanism (SSM)
    2. Single Resolution Mechanism (SRM)
    3. Single Rulebook and Deposit Guarantee Scheme
- Stress tests are hypothetical simulations to determine the institution's ability to cope with the economic crisis.
- By contrast, Culture and Behavior Supervision aims to reshape an institute's risk culture by creating an environment that promotes integrity should be created across the institution.

Chapter 10
Asset and Liability Risk Management (ALM)

I n banking and finance businesses, Assets and Liabilities Management (ALM) is the practice of managing risks that may arise due to mismatches between the assets and the liabilities due to liquidity (e.g., deposits versus loans' portfolio), the volatility of interest rates, foreign exchange risk, and capital management. Banks tend to borrow in the short term and lend for the longer term, which can cause a mismatch when maturities arise. Thus, the bank must address the mismatch risk through the structuring of its assets and liabilities or with the use of derivatives (i.e., swaps, swaptions, options, and futures) to ensure that it can satisfy all of its liabilities. Earlier, the awareness for the importance of ALM (notably of executive committees and boards of directors) was almost nonexistent; the issue was usually left to first and second lines of management. It has gained relevance since the financial crisis, with many banks living through stressful times and even going bankrupt. This chapter discusses the banking standards published in regard to ALM, followed by a detailed discussion of its concepts, scope, and governance.

10.1 BASEL ACCORDS, CRD IV, AND CRD V

The Basel Accords are the series of banking regulations (Basel I, II, and III)[211] set by the Basel Committee on Bank Supervision (BCBS). The accord provides recommendations on banking regulations with relation to capital risk, market risk, and operational risk.

Basel I, published in 1988, focused on credit risk, capital, and structure of risk weights (RWA—Risk Weighted Assets) for banks. It primarily emphasized the capital adequacy ratio and risk-weighted assets. The minimum capital requirement was stipulated at 8 percent of risk-weighted assets. The improvement of Basel I led to Basel II, enforced in 2004.

Basel II introduced the concept of three pillars:

1. *Capital Adequacy:* Minimum capital adequacy requirement set to 8 percent of risk-weighted assets determined through credit, market, and operation risk areas.
2. *Supervisory Review:* Review of capital adequacy (CAR— Capital Adequacy Ratio) and internal assessment process, as banks are required to develop a resilient risk management approach to monitor and manage the credit risk, market risk, and operational risk.
3. *Market Discipline*: Disclosing necessary information such as capital adequacy and risk exposure to the follow the market discipline and encourage the norms of sound banking and supervisory practices.

Figure 10.1 shows the main vectors of evolution and requirements from Basel II to Basel III.

Figure 10.1: From Basel II to Basel III

Pillar 1	Pillar 2	Pillar 3		Pillar 1	Pillar 2	Pillar 3
Minimum Capital Requirements	Supervisory Review Process	Disclosure and Market Discipline	→	Enhanced Minimum Capital & Liquidity Requirements	Enhanced Supervisory Review Process for Firm-wide Risk Management & Capital Planning	Enhanced Disclosure and Market Discipline

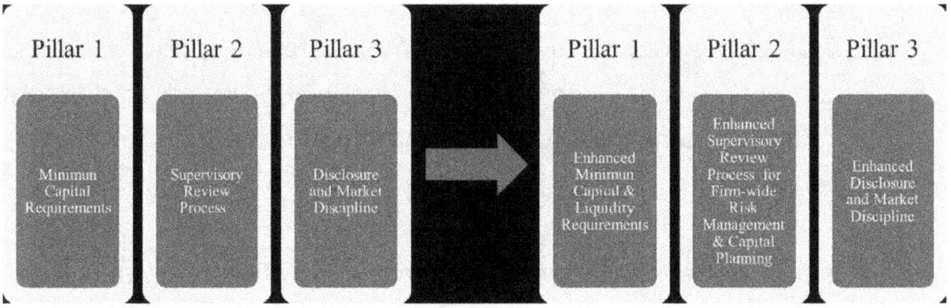

The global financial crisis of 2007–2008 led to the publication to *Basel III* in 2013 to further strengthen prudential banking supervision and regulation. The following are the main changes:

1. Pillar 1 of Basel II only included capital requirements; In Basel III, the requirements are extended to liquidity.
2. Pilar II in Basel II related to the supervisory review process; Basel III imposed more demanding standards and ratios for that process, notably including risk management and capital planning for the full group and interconnected businesses (such as banking, insurance, asset management) on a consolidated basis.
3. Pillar III of Basel II covered disclosure and market discipline; Basel III requires particular standards for enhanced disclosure while stressing the risk component and market discipline.
4. Other elements are included in the Supervisory Review and Evaluation Process (SREP) to ensure that the three pillars are reviewed and controlled.

Essentially, Basel III is built under a more conservative approach to risks, correcting two vectors not considered in Basel II:

1. The recognition that banks should develop and build liquidity and capital ratios to become more resilient to financial and economic crisis, as well as the disclosure and transparency to the markets.
2. A drastic reduction of room for interpretation of critical issues, namely the way in which certain financial products and assets could be computed as part of equity and liquidity for of critical ratios.

Also, Basel III adds the following additional requirements and safeguards, as it further sets the standards for banks to ensure a minimum amount of common equity and a minimum liquidity ratio:

1. Improved quality of capital.
2. Increased quantity of capital.
3. Reduced leverage by introducing the concept of backstop leverage ratio.
4. Increased short-term liquidity coverage.
5. Stable long-term balance sheet funding.
6. Increased risk capture measures such as capturing counter-party credit risk.

The standards of Basel III were phased from 2013 to 2019. Banks must mandatorily maintain minimum capital requirements and leverage ratios. For the most significant financial institutions or systemically important banks, further requirements were levied. For example, the minimum amount of equity, calculated as a percentage of assets, increased from 2 percent to 4.5 percent, and an additional 2.5 percent buffer is required, bringing the total equity requirement to 7 percent. A buffer is introduced as an additional layer such that banks can be resilient during financial crises and stressful times. The minimum CAR (Capital Adequacy Ratio) that the banks must always maintain is 8 percent of RWA (Risk-Weighted Assets); 10.5 percent including the capital conservation buffer. CAR is calculated by adding *Tier 1* capital (bank's core capital and disclosed reserves), and *Tier 2* capital (bank's supplementary capital such as undisclosed reserves, subordinated term debts, and hybrid financial products). Common equity and retained earnings should be the dominant capital (more than 50 percent) in Tier 1 capital instead of debt-like instruments, and more harmonized rules for Tier 2 capital are introduced. The leverage limit is set at 3 percent, which implies a bank's total assets should not exceed 33 times the bank's capital. It is expected that the introduction of a leverage limit aids in reduced lending and strengthens the capital position. The supplementary leverage ratio is the US implementation of Basel III Tier 1 leverage ratio. In the US, banks with more than $700 billion in consolidated total assets or more than $10 trillion in assets under management must maintain an additional 2 percent buffer—thus raising the minimum leverage ratio to 5 percent, and if any insured financial institutions are being covered by corrective action framework because of the capital deficiencies in the past, they must demonstrate at least 6 percent leverage ratio.[212]

Therefore, Basel III places higher pressure and demands on shareholders and management. It is relevant to note that before the financial and economic crisis of 2007–2008, those requirements were significantly less demanding, largely because of the lower level of Tier 1 required and the room for interpretation of the rules stated in Basel II. With Basel III, shareholders have to be prepared to provide more capital if the loans portfolio are riskier, and management should be able to manage the balance sheet, notably the loan portfolio, in a fashion that ensures safer types of loans, as riskier loans would consume equity faster due to their risk weight. This issue is intimately linked to the business model banks adopt, namely in the definition of its vision and the strategic plan, ensuring these two elements are developed and build considering the risk appetite and capital limitations.

Basel III requires banks to meet specific liquidity targets that are set out in the Liquidity Coverage Ratio (LCR) and Net Stable Funding Ratio (NSFR). LCR is a measure of whether the bank has enough High-Quality Liquid Assets (HQLA) to endure 30 days of stress, such as voluntary (e.g., crisis of reputation may lead to waves of withdrawals dubbed "below the line" when processed through internet banking) or involuntary withdrawal of assets by customers or investors, high market volatility, and big loan payments. HQLA only includes those assets with a high potential to be converted into cash easily and quickly and are categorized according to the levels of liquidity—Level 1 HQLA, Level 2 HQLA, among others. Basel III stipulates that assets in Level 1 are not discounted when calculating LCR while that of Levels 2A and 2B can be haircut by 15–50 percent, depending on the class of assets.

- Examples of Level 1: Securities issued or guaranteed by specific sovereign entities

- Examples of Level 2A: Securities issued or guaranteed by specific multilateral development banks such as The World Bank or government sponsored companies
- Examples of Level 2B: Publicly traded equity and investment-grade corporate debt securities issued by nonfinancial sectors.

Basel III expects the LCR to reach 100 percent in an ideal case. In eurozone, banks must maintain LCR of 100 percent (Figure 10.2). Banks are classified into Group 1 and Group 2, according to their systemic importance. According to European Banking Authority (EBA), in December 2016, the average LCR across banks was 139 percent. On average, Group 2 banks have a higher LCR (169 percent) than Group 1 banks (134 percent). Medium Group 2 banks have a higher LCR than large and small Group 2 banks.[213] If the LCR conditions are not met, it is the responsibility of the bank to communicate the same with the national supervising entity or/and European Central Bank (ECB) in line with the prevalent regulation.

Figure 10.2: Basel III requirements for LCR

Items	Factor
Stock of Highly Qualified Liquid Assets (HQLA)	
A. Level 1 assets:	
• Coins and bank notes • Qualifying marketable securities from sovereigns, central banks, PSEs, and multilateral development banks • Qualifying central bank reserves • Domestic sovereign or central bank debt for non-0% risk-weighted sovereigns	100%
B. Level 2 assets (maximum of 40% of HQLA):	
Level 2A assets:	
• Sovereign, central bank, multilateral development banks, and PSE assets qualifying for 20% risk weighting • Qualifying corporate debt securities rated AA- or higher • Qualifying covered bonds rated AA- or higher	85%
Level 2B assets (maximun of 15% of HQLA):	
• Qualifying Residential Mortgage-Backed Securities (RMBS)	75%
• Qualifying corporate debt securities rated between A+ and BBB-	50%
• Qualifying common equity shares	50%

Source: (BIS—www.bis.org)

On the other hand, NSFR (Net Stable Funding Ratio) measures the proportion of the available amount of the bank's stable funding over the required amount of stable funding that will remain in the institution for more than one year. For example, in good economic conditions, it is possible that banks can expand their books quickly by relying on relatively cheap and abundant short-term wholesale funding (i.e., holding deposit/cash from banks, governments, and other large institutions). NSFR aims to limit this and seeks to ensure banks maintain a stable funding structure over the longer horizon (at least a year). Therefore, stable funding is a long-term prospect, as they are funded by long-term stable funding measures such as customer deposits, interbank lending, and equity. In an ideal case, NSFR beyond 100 percent is expected.

The capital requirements directive (CRD) published by the European Council in 2013—CRD IV (Directive 2013/36/EU)[214]—follows a similar line as recommended by the Basel accords, including selected expanded measures. Furthermore, the European Central Bank (ECB) floated the concept of the internal capital adequacy assessment process (ICAAP) and the internal liquidity adequacy assessment process (ILAAP) in CRD IV. ECB[215] states:

"(...) the aim of the ICAAP and ILAAP is to encourage banks to reflect on their capital and liquidity risks in a structured way, using bank-specific approaches to measure and manage those risks. Both processes are required to ensure that banks identify, effectively manage, and cover their capital and liquidity risks. The Supervisory Review and Evaluation Process (SREP), discussed next, recognizes that good ICAAPs and ILAAPs reduce uncertainty for both banks and supervisors about the actual risks that banks are or may be exposed to. They also give supervisors an increased level of confidence in a bank's ability to remain viable by maintaining adequate capitalization and effectively managing its risks. The insights from both processes feed into all SREP assessments and supervisors' decisions about capital and liquidity requirements. The ICAAP and ILAAP are expected to play an even greater role in the SREP, which should encourage banks to continuously improve these processes."

In 2019, the European Commission introduced CRD V[216] to further reinforce the eurozone banks' ability to withstand any potential shocks in addition to the Basel III guidelines:

1. Reducing excessive leverage
2. Addressing long-term funding risk
3. Addressing market risks by increasing the risk sensitivity of existing requirements and enhancing the proportionality of the relevant prudential framework for institutions
4. Easing the compliance burden for smaller and noncomplex banks without compromising their stability
5. Improving banks' lending capacity to support economic growth, in particular for Small and Medium Enterprises (SMEs)
6. Increasing Global Systemically Important Institutions (G-SIIs) loss absorption and recapitalization capacity

The accords and directives are always subject to be revised with the time and the economic conditions.

10.2 SUPERVISORY REVIEW AND EVALUATION PROCESS (SREP)

Supervisory Review and Evaluation Process (SREP)[217] is a holistic process introduced by the ECB (European Central Bank). The concept of SREP was ignited after the introduction of the Basel II accord. ECB mentions that SREP reports the supervisor's findings of the review and requires a particular bank to introduce corrections to close the weaknesses identified, notably in terms of capital requirements and the way it should deal with inherent risks resulting from their business model as well as potential internal and/or external events. The bank receives a SREP assessment and decision from a supervisor at the end of the process, indicating the objectives set to address the identified gaps that must be corrected these within a determined timeframe. Therefore, SREP forms the building block for the Single Supervisory Mechanism (SSM). SSM is further discussed in Section 9.2: "Single Supervisory Mechanism." Figure 10.3 illustrates the ECB's holistic approach for SREP.

Figure 10.3: SREP methodological framework

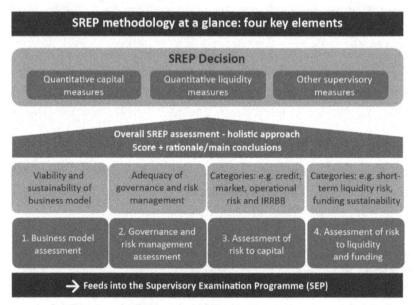

Source: (ECB[218]—www.ecb.europa.eu)

Interest rate risk in the banking book (IRRBB) is part of the pillar two requirements of the Basel's framework and very important criteria for asset-liability management in the banking books as well as SREP assessment. BCBS[219] states:

"IRRBB refers to the current or prospective risk to the bank's capital and earnings arising from adverse movements in interest rates that can affect the bank's banking book positions. When interest rates change, the present value and timing of future cash flows change. This, in turn, changes the underlying value of a bank's assets, liabilities, and off-balance sheet items and hence its economic value. Changes in interest rates also affect a bank's earnings by altering interest-rate-sensitive income and expenses, affecting its net interest income. Excessive IRRBB can pose a significant threat to a bank's current capital base and/or future earnings if not managed appropriately."

BCBS has also published the detailed guidelines for managing interest rate risk within the scope of the supervisory review process, namely SRP98: Application Guidance on Interest Rate Risk in the Banking Book.

10.3 ASSET AND LIABILITY MANAGEMENT—ALM

Asset and liability management is a framework that typically is applied to financial institutions. However, any enterprise should leverage this concept in a structured fashion—as often it is not organized within a framework that allow the board to properly supervise the area and ensure the sustainability of an organization.

As organizations are required to pay the liabilities on time, there should be a process to ensure a healthy, timely, and sustainable transaction of cash flows. This is achieved by making the availability of assets to pay the liabilities (e.g., debts, notably deposits, and bonds) when they become due, and such that assets or earnings can be quickly liquidated to cash, qualifying as liquid or highly liquid assets. An Oracle whitepaper[220] about ALM (Asset and Liability Management) mentions the need for a comprehensive ALM policy framework that focuses on bank profitability and long-term viability by targeting the net interest margin (NIM) ratio and Net Economic Value (NEV), subject to balance sheet constraints. The low or negative level of interest rates on the balance sheet places additional pressure on the net interest margin, making ALM an even more challenging issue in some type of banks.

NEV is the difference between the sum of the present values of all the assets' cash flows and the sum of the present values of all the liabilities' cash flows. NEV may be seen as an indicator depicting the actual economic book value of the company. Essentially, ALM stands at the crossroads between risk management and strategy. The good practices of ALM identify the solutions to mitigate or hedge the risks arising from the interaction of assets and liabilities as well as focus on a long-term perspective to maximize assets in order to meet complex liabilities to increase profitability. ALM was first pioneered by the Anglo-Saxon financial institutions during the 1970s, when interest rates became increasingly volatile. The exact roles and perimeter around ALM can vary significantly among banks and companies, depending on the business model, and can encompass a broad area of risks. In terms of controls by the board of directors, ALM requires a strong coordination at least between the risk and compliance committee and the asset and liability committee of the board, with a direct strong involvement of the CEO, CFO, CRO or/and Chief Economist.

10.4 SCOPE OF ALM

Figure 10.4 below illustrates the scope of ALM, which is then summarized.

Figure 10.4: Scope of asset and liability management

Liquidity Risk

Liquidity risk may constrain the bank's ability to meet its obligations in stress times (e.g., when depositor withdraw a significant amount of money), thus affecting the financial conditions and stability. Therefore, there must be a clear focus on liquidity funding such that there exists a robust ability to meet current and future cash flows demand, obligations and collateral needs, liquidity's benchmark price, and others. In the preceding sections, it has already been discussed that systemically important banking and financial institutions should at least maintain LCR of 100 percent to meet short-term financial obligations. However, banks should maintain liquidity requirements for long-term obligations too. In other words, banking and financial institutions are required to maintain fiscal solvency by discouraging them from excessive lending of short-term debt. Therefore, the importance of liquidity ratio boils down to adsorption of market wide shocks by ensuring banks have enough capital preservation to deal with any liquidity disruptions.

Interest Rate Risk

The interest rate in the market can go up and down, depending on several macroeconomic conditions. Fixed-income securities such as bonds are directly affected by the unexpected changes in the interest rates. The movement of interest rates may have a direct impact on cash flows. Mismatches between interest rate in deposits and loans are also contributing factors to disproportionate amounts. Due to the fact that retail banks earn significantly from the spread of interest accrued to deposits and interest charged to borrowers, they are highly exposed to interest rate risk. Deposits being of shorter maturity are often repriced faster than longer period loans. Moreover, loans cannot be repriced easily, and it is possible for the rate of deposit to go up or down when repricing, which eventually causes the mismatch between the interest rates than the original rates. As banks depend significantly on interest income, maintaining net interest margin is fundamentally crucial, with proper monitoring framework, for hedging interest rate risk within the holistic ALM framework. Usually, banks manage the interest rate risk by pricing a large percentage of loans at variable interest rates that move in tandem with market rates. Fixed-rate loans are usually priced at higher interest rates than the market rate to hedge any volatility.

Currency Risk

Currency may appreciate or depreciate with the market sentiments and the economies of the sovereign states. Cross currency basis risk is the risk that an organization incurs when its lending and funding activities in foreign currency do not match in terms of maturity and/or currency due to change in foreign currency exchange rates determined by the markets. For example, Turkish Lira depreciated heavily in 2018, which led to high inflation, rising borrowing costs, and rising loan defaults. Banks and institutions exposed to Turkish Lira were under stress. Therefore, the rate of exchange in the international market directly affected the companies' cash flows. Companies that operate globally and have assets and liabilities denominated in different currencies are more susceptible to currency exchange risk. Thus, currency risk monitoring and management is crucial.

Funding and Capital Management

The maintenance of adequate capital must be a continuous, dynamic, and ongoing process. It should be considered for both shorter and longer-term capital needs and must be coordinated with the overall strategy and planning cycles, usually within a prospective time horizon of two to five years.

BBVA,[221] the Spanish lender, maintains a two-fold aim in funding and capital management:

1. To maintain levels of capitalization appropriate to the business targets in all the countries in which it operates.
2. At the same time, to maximize return on shareholders' funds, through the efficient allocation of capital to the various units, good management of the balance sheet, and proportionate

use of the various instruments that comprise the Group's equity (such as common stock, preferred securities, conditional convertible bonds, and subordinated debt).

Profit Planning and Growth

There must be proper mechanisms in place to control the forecasts and develop the scenarios and prospective to ensure the profitability and sustainability of the corporate business. Sustainable finance has never been so important. The concepts of sustainability and sustainable business are further discussed in Section 4.3: "Corporate Sustainability." Most of the banks publish sustainable reporting separately from the annual report. Modern day investors value sustainability, social dynamics, and business purpose in addition to the profitability. Therefore, banks should strive to achieve sustainable growth enduring profitability further in the horizon.

Credit Risk

The credit risk (i.e., the loan portfolio), is normally managed by a separate risk management function. Risk management function is discussed in the Section 6.2: "IIA Three Lines of Defense Model and Its 2020 Successor." It manages the impact of the credit portfolio on the balance sheet such as cash, investments, and loans. A structured, strong, and robust ALM department has the objective of reducing the risk of mismatches, supports a sustainable growth organically and by acquisition, and ensures focus on the business model by the management bodies, both in their executive and supervisory functions.

10.5 ALM: GOVERNANCE

The Asset Liability Committee (ALCO) supervises ALM. The ALCO is usually formed within under the executive committee and supervised by the board of directors/supervisory board. The responsibility of ALM is often divided between the Treasury and CFO (Chief Financial Officer). It can also be addressed by one or two key persons (e.g., CEO, CFO, or Treasurer). The majority operate in a centralized ALM model such that it enables oversight of the consolidated balance sheet, and the lower-level ALM units focus on business units or legal entities.

10.5.1 ASSET AND LIABILITY COMMITTEE—ALCO

The objective of ALCO is to attain the goals defined by the short and long-term strategic plans ensuring adequate liquidity while managing the spreads between the interest income and interest expense. Sometimes, ALCO is also known as surplus management committee. ALCO is established to provide an oversight for effectively evaluating on and off-balance sheet risk for banking and finance business or most nonfinancial entities. Liquidity risk, interest rate risk, and currency exchange risk are largely incorporated in the discussion as well as business model, and ALCO members are required to ensure that the institution has adequate liquidity and proper spread between the interest income and interest expense. Strategies and policies should be aligned with the corporate and board's goals and therefore address the extent to which the elements of funds management are centralized or delegated in the institution. ALCO meetings can be conducted weekly, biweekly, monthly, or quarterly (depending on the importance), and the strategies and fund management must be reviewed at least annually.

In a summary fashion, ALCO must approve a contingency plan, approve the liquidity and funds management policy, link the funding policy with needs and sources via a mix of liabilities or sale of assets, and oversee fixed versus floating rate funds, namely the wholesale versus retail deposit, money market versus capital market funding, as well as domestic versus foreign currency funding. This process should be conducted in cooperation with the chief economist, contribution from advisors or consultants depending on the complexity and footprint of the business. Scenarios and prospective are tools used to assist the ALM function.

10.6 CONTINGENCY PLAN

A contingency plan is a backup plan for the outcome other than the expected. As banks are a high-risk candidate to any severe disruption, a contingency plan should be duly established by defining clear lines of responsibility, rules, internal and external communication, and mitigation mechanism not just for liquidity crisis but also for information technology or pandemics such as COVID-19. Some of the internal risk events are rating downgrade (more in Section 19.3.4: "Rating Trigger and Death Spiral"), default by the large borrower, interest default, high withdrawal by the clients, downing of IT infrastructure, among others. External risk events are natural disasters, terrorist attack, bad macroeconomic conditions (such as COVID-19), systemic cyber hack, liquidity shortfall in the interbank market, among others.

As such, the contingency plan must be developed with regard to three elements in consideration:

1. *Liquidity contingency:* Must address risk measures that any possible future event—internal or external—could lead to larger liquidity outflows. It should also take into consideration events that may lead to less than expected liquidity inflows; both situations have potential to affect the financial stability of a bank.

2. *Intraday contingency:* Must address the risk that may cause larger than expected liquidity outflows or less than expected inflows within the same day. For example, customers withdrawing deposits significantly in one possible day.

3. *IT continency:* Should be there, in any case the IT infrastructure fails, which may potentially bring constraints to liquidity needs. For example, a contingency plan for a failed payment gateway, hacked servers, or any critical IT infrastructure.

Usually, the contingency plan requires a detailed and challenging review from the risk and compliance committee and audit committee before being approved by the board. As ALCO is the prime committee for governing the liquidity management, the members of the committee should actively participate in discussing the bank's ALM strategy on funding, lending, and financial risks. However, ALCO may not hold any operational responsibilities, and the operational responsibilities primarily fall to respective executive departments. A Liquidity Crisis Committee may also be formed for liquidity management before potential liquidity stresses and during stressful times. The board should consider in its global agenda a periodic review of ALM and regularly discuss potential events, both internal and external, that may affect liquidity. Sovereign fiscal stresses and crisis as well as geopolitical issues and trade tensions often become a source of financial instability, notably affecting cross-border financial stability.

Topics of the Chapter

The following has been discussed within this chapter:

- The recommendations of Basel Accords, in detail (as summarized in Figure 10.1).
- The recommendations of Capital Requirement Directives IV and V, briefly.
- Supervisory Review and Evaluation Process (SREP), a holistic process that helps banks identify and correct weaknesses related to inherent risks resulting from their business model as well as potential internal and/or external events, as depicted in Figure 10.3.
- The scope of ALM (as depicted in Figure 10.4) includes:
  1. Liquidity Risk
  2. Interest Rate Risk
  3. Currency Risk
  4. Funding and Capital Management
  5. Profit Planning and Growth
  6. Credit Risk

- ALM is supervised by the Asset Liability Committee (ALCO), ensuring adequate liquidity while managing the spreads between the interest income and interest expense.
- Nonetheless, contingencies should be duly established by defining clear lines of responsibility, rules, internal and external communication, and mitigation mechanism.

Part IV—Board Selection, Effectiveness, Independence, Roles and Committees

Chapter 11

Board Selection

Good composition of the board is one of the key conditions to achieve good governance and overall prudent management as well as a corner stone to irradiate the tone at the top. The selection of board members has been a central topic, although recently it has assumed a growing relevance with particular focus on demanding criteria related to the fit and proper profile of board members. The board of directors or the supervisory board must be suitable as a whole to carry its responsibilities. It should be composed in a way that contributes to an effective management and balanced decision-making, keeping in mind the protection of an institution, but also ensuring the financial stability of the entire system in banks, as well as the sustainability of the business model in any organization.

Apart from qualifications, experience, and skills, aspects such as least represented gender and diversity (e.g., geography, age, background, and quotas) are also frequently discussed nowadays, as well as executive development in the governance arena. Also, the psychological profile of directors is highly relevant, as for example non-executive directors should be able to positively and in an optimistically skeptical fashion, to challenge and advise executive directors. The final objective is to promote the trust of the taxpayers on boards and managers.

This chapter discusses what makes a board—and the individuals on it—fit and proper, and how board members should be elected and replaced. This chapter also leverages the guidelines of BIS and ECB about the conduction of the fit and proper process, which can be leveraged by nonfinancial organizations. Also, the principles of ECB are mostly applied transversally in EU outside the eurozone, although some countries apply even more stringent guidelines and roles in the fit and proper assessment process.

There are guidelines establishing principles in the settings of board selection and composition, which are discussed in the subsequent sections. In most jurisdictions, corporates have 4–15 board members, including the chair, non-executive and executive directors, applicable with the governance code or laws. However, the number may vary with corporate needs, complexity of the business model, footprint and governance structure. Currently, the selection process and approval by the supervisors of members of social bodies, both in the financial and regulated nonfinancial systems represents a demanding process. The rationale is to ensure that not only are individuals selected under the fit and proper criteria for the job, but that the board as a whole is fit for the challenges it may face, ensuring there are individuals on board with the relevant competences. A board may incorporate directors who, individually, are fit and proper for the job, but the board itself as a whole does not fit that criteria.

A parallel issue relates to the shareholders. The supervisors—notably in the financial system—have to also assess the fit and proper of large or significant shareholders and ones who potentially can have undue influence over the board of particular members. Both in the US and the European Union, namely in situations involving foreign direct investment (topic expanded in Section 18.3 "Foreign Direct Investment"), the authorities are scrutinizing investors strictly to ensure that the assessment does not raise issues about the ultimate beneficiary owner.

Situations that supervisors believe can provoke financial instability may be reappraised and, if required, European Central Bank

(ECB) or National Competent Authorities (NCA) can block their voting rights or even not authorize the investment, with the philosophical approach for the nonfinancial sector, namely in the US through the Foreign Direct Investment in the United States (FDIUS) or the European Commission through their directorates general.[222] As the board selection can be abstract and does not detail any particular legal structure, as they vary among countries, the aim is that independently of the legal structure adopted, the governance structure should have the same good governance drive. The recently changed guidelines of ECB's Single Supervisory Mechanism (SSM) directive and NCAs does not allow social bodies' members to assume function in social bodies—even when already elected in the general shareholders' meeting—before the supervisor's approval.

11.1 FIT AND PROPER

The fit and proper assessment includes members of the management body (and audit boards, in countries with this legal requirement), both in management function (executives) and supervisory function (non-executives). The Financial Conduct Authority (FCA UK—www.fca.org.uk) informs that the criteria to qualify as "fit and proper" are a benchmark to assess whether an individual is suitable to perform a controlled function, underlying that it is not an exam.[223] When considering the candidate for fitness and propriety, FCA would look at honesty, including openness with self-disclosures, integrity, independence, and reputation; competence and stability; and financial soundness. There are however NCAs that perform interviews with the candidates with the objective of understanding the degree of knowledge and philosophical risk culture approach to business, ability to challenge namely executive directors, independence of mind, as well as detailed technical issues about regulatory matters and areas. It is becoming more common for NCAs to employ psychologists to assess the soft skills of candidates.

The guidelines of Banks for International Settlements (BIS) and the European Central Bank (ECB) are primarily sourced to explain more about fit and proper principles (referenced Section 1.2.3: "Global Financial Crisis 2007–2008 and Increased Governance"). BIS states:

"… supervisors (e.g., ECB) expectations are that the entities (e.g., significant national banks) will take the measures necessary to ensure that managers, directors, and shareholders whose holdings are above specified thresholds or who exercise a material influence on their operations (key shareholders) meet the fitness, propriety, or other qualification tests of their supervisors. Therefore, an effective and comprehensive supervisory regime should include controls designed to encourage the continued satisfaction of the fitness, propriety, or other qualification tests of supervisors and to allow supervisory intervention where necessary."[224]

Therefore, it is possible that over a mandate of a director, an individual for some reason may not comply anymore with the fit and proper criteria, and the supervisor demands that those situations be addressed promptly; they may fall within the fit or the proper criteria. This may result from a supervisory audit or issues affecting a director that may raise potential reputational issues to an organization.

Some of the objectives of fit and proper process include:

- Ensuring that supervisors of entities can exercise their responsibilities.
- Assessing whether those entities are soundly and prudently managed.
- Ensuring that key shareholders are not a source of weakness to those entities.
- Promoting arrangements to facilitate consultation and the exchange of information on individuals and regulated entities.
- Achieving sound and prudent management.

11.1.1 BIS GUIDELINES—FIT AND PROPER ASSESSMENT

Principally, there are two elements—*Fit* and *Proper*. These elements are essentially applicable to the managers and directors, key stakeholders/shareholders, and any other important members on a case-by-case basis considered to exert a material influence.

- **Managers and Directors**

The fitness test seeks to assess the *competence* of the managers and the directors as well as their capacity to fulfill the responsibilities of their positions. On the other hand, the propriety test seeks to assess the *integrity* and *suitability* of the managers and the directors. The components of fit and proper test for the managers and the directors are illustrated in Figure 11.1.

Figure 11.1: Fit and proper

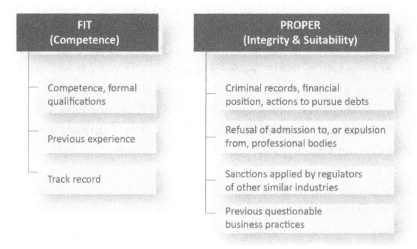

- **Shareholders**

The business repute, financial position, and stake of the shareholders are key considerations in the assessments of fitness, propriety, or other qualifications. For example, bad business reputes of the key shareholders (e.g., financial scandals, money laundering, misbehavior toward the capital markets) may affect the corporate health, both financially and socially. Shareholders are also assessed based on their country or region of origin, as well as the real ultimate beneficial owner of an investment, notably political regimes and political exposed persons, where ultimate control lies with a sovereign (e.g., People's Republic of China, Russia). Because of globalization, geofinance, and geopolitical issues and concerns, this screening process is assuming high relevance.

11.1.2 BIS GUIDELINES—FIT AND PROPER IN FINANCIAL CONGLOMERATES

As conglomerates tend to be larger with several businesses across geographies, supervisors' reach for control and supervision may be limited to their own geographical boundaries, and conglomerates may be subject to supervision in other jurisdictions. For example, Santander Bank is a Spanish multinational financial conglomerate. Within the EU, ECB (European Central Bank) is its prime coordinator. However, outside the EU, such as in the US, Santander may need to further comply with the US Federal Reserve System (Fed) measures in addition to those of ECB and the NCA Bank of Spain.

However, sharing individuals' information from one jurisdiction to another jurisdiction may raise concerns, as stringent privacy laws have come in force such as GDPR (General Data Protection Regulation) in Europe.[225] Moreover, corporates tend to have a unitary board structure in the US and dual board structure in the EU. Thus, the absolute control over the application of fit and proper principles in conglomerates is not achievable. However, BIS has published important guiding principles for attaining the optimal level.[226]

- Fitness and propriety or other qualification tests should be applied to managers and directors of other entities in a conglomerate if they exercise a material or controlling influence on the operations of regulated entities.

- Shareholders whose holdings are above specified thresholds and/or who exert material influence on regulated entities within that conglomerate should meet the fitness, propriety, or other qualification tests of supervisors.
- Fitness, propriety, or other qualification tests should be applied at the authorization stage and repeated thereafter on the occurrence of specified events (i.e., Fit and Proper is a recurring process), or if an issue emerges that has the potential to affect the fit and proper stance.
- An individual who is considered fit for a position may not be considered fit in another institution; therefore, the application of fitness, propriety, or other qualification tests to managers, directors, and key shareholders may vary depending on their responsibilities and the degree of their influence.
- The supervisor of a conglomerate in one jurisdiction should attempt to consult the supervisor in another jurisdiction of the regulated or unregulated entity within the same conglomerate, operating in different jurisdictions, about the fitness and propriety of any managers or directors if they are deemed to exert of material influence; for example, ECB may consult the Fed (US) if they deem that managers or directors in one of the conglomerates of Santander in the US (either regulated or unregulated) exerts a material influence.

11.1.3 ECB GUIDELINES—FIT AND PROPER ASSESSMENT

The ECB—Banking Supervision takes decisions regarding the suitability of members of social bodies of significant credit institutions, while NCAs take the same decision in relation to non-significant banks. The ECB-SSM (Single Supervisory Mechanism) legal framework defines the fit and proper supervision as an exclusive competence of ECB, as stated in Article 4(1)(e) of the SSM Regulation and Articles 93 and 94 of the SSM Framework Regulation, which are part of the supervision responsibilities of the internal governance of credit institutions.

The SSM Framework Regulation imposes direct obligations on supervised entities. Article 93 refers to changes in the management bodies, while Article 94 covers new facts or issues that may impact the permanent obligation to have suitable members in the social bodies. ECB is empowered to collect information, including interviews, imposition of conditions, obligations, or recommendations. Article 91 of the CRD IV deals with the suitability requirements. Essentially, ECB has full control to make the decisions regarding the suitability of the members (e.g., directors or non-executive directors) of significant financial institutions following fit and proper criteria. ECB adopts single rulebook of guidelines and legal frameworks from regulatory agency European Banking Authority (EBA). Also, national law leaves room for the NCAs (National Competent Authorities), as well as for ECB to add further requirements. ECB sets out *six main principles* regarding fit and proper assessment, briefly summarized below, although more detail—including lists of questions to be answered by candidates and banks—can be researched at ECB site (www.ecb. europa.eu), as well as NCAs:[227]

Principle 1: Primary responsibility of credit institutions
The supervised entities have the primary responsibility of selecting and nominating individuals for the management body who comply with the requirements for fitness and propriety (suitability), not only prior to the appointment but also on an ongoing basis, notably in the situation of a significant change to the responsibilities of a member of the management body.

Principle 2: Gatekeeper
Fit and proper supervision must prevent individuals who would pose a risk to the proper functioning of the management body from entering in the first place or from continuing in their role, when an issue regarding their fitness and propriety has arisen.

Principle 3: Harmonization
The ECB's fit and proper supervision seeks to ensure a higher level of harmonization in the assessments of management body members across the eurozone.

Principle 4: Proportionality and case-by-case assessment
The principle of proportionality applies throughout the whole fit and proper process, asserting that the suitability criteria should be commensurate with the size of the entity, the nature, scale, and complexity of its activities, as well as the particular role to be filled. However, experience shows that the fit and proper requirements take less into consideration the proportionality requirement in the assessment process.

Principle 5: Due process and fairness
In case the rights of both the supervised entity and the appointee are affected by a fit and proper decision, both will enjoy all the procedural guarantees.

Principle 6: Interaction with ongoing supervision
The fit and proper assessment feeds into the ongoing supervision of the governance structure of an institution, especially about the composition and functioning of the management body.

11.1.4 ECB ASSESSMENT CRITERIA
ECB mentions that a fit and proper assessment can be triggered in the following cases:

- a new appointment, a change of role, or a renewal (Article 93 of the SSM Framework Regulation)
- new facts or any other issue (Article 94 of the SSM Framework Regulation)

- a licensing (Article 78 of the SSM Framework Regulation) or qualifying holding (Article 86 of the SSM Framework Regulation) procedure

The assessment criteria framework of ECB/SSM in terms of fitness and propriety includes five criteria, as demonstrated below.[228]

The *Experience* criterion includes a deep practical and theoretical experience, requiring proof that the candidate has the relevant knowledge, skills, and experience. It includes experience obtained in previous occupations and theoretical covering knowledge and skills gained through education and professional training to ensure that members of the board understand activities and relevant risks and business drivers, including the stream of revenues and the cost structure. The theoretical banking assessment includes education in relevant areas, namely banking and finance, economics, law, administration, financial regulation, information and technology, financial analysis, and quantitative methods, while practical experience is assessed based on previous positions held, namely the nature of activities involved and their relevance. Areas that should be covered include financial markets, regulatory framework, and legal requirements, strategic planning, risk management, accounting and auditing, assessment of credit approval process ensuring effective governance, oversight and controls, and interpreting financial information.

Particular features are required for directors exercising functions as CEO, CFO, CRO, compliance officer, chief executive auditor, chair of the audit committee, and chair of the risk and compliance committee, as well as of the governance committee, when one is established.

Linked to the proportionality principle, the complexity of an institution demands higher levels of experience, although this principle is seldom accepted, namely when functions demanding segregation of duties (e.g., reporting of internal audit, credit analysis, and approval that requires segregation from risk management function) may be at jeopardy. Another aspect relates to the level and nature of the experience, notably if the function is one of management (executive) or supervision (non-executive), an issue impacted by the governance legal structure adopted (monist or dualist model). Article 91(1) of the CRD IV covers this issue.

As detailed criteria in the assessment of members of boards, experience in public or academic fields can be relevant.[229] A chair of the board (non-executive usually in part-time, depending on the complexity of the business model) or, currently, the chair of the audit committee must exhibit 10 years of continuous relevant experience, including a significant proportion of senior level managerial positions and significant theoretical experience in banking or a similar relevant field, while a non-executive must have three years of relevant experience in banking and/or financial services. A CEO Executive should have 10 years of recent experience in banking or financial services, not dating back more than 12 years, as dramatic changes in the best practice and regulation as well as accounting principles and standards have taken place. For non-executive, if the level of experience is not met, the candidate can still be considered suitable if it can be justified, conducting a "complementary assessment" that considers issues in terms of diversity and the need for a range of experiences, by committing to a training program to overcome the lack of knowledge and/or experience in a particular area.

The second criterion relates to the *Reputation* of the candidate, one where the proportionality criteria are not considered, as a "zero tolerance" approach is adopted. Members of boards must at all times have a good reputation to ensure sound and prudent management. Good reputation should emerge from no evidence that suggests the contrary or no reason that generates doubts regarding the ability to ensure sound and prudent management approaches. Pending legal proceedings, as well as concluded ones, criminal or administrative, have an impact on the reputation, even considering the fact that though legal proceedings are the responsibility of judicial authorities, the fact that an individual is or has been subject to proceedings is relevant. Pending proceedings usually impact the availability to commit adequate time to exercise the responsibilities, and this factor is therefore taken into consideration. Information is required to assess the situation, including the nature of the accusation, particularly if it involves a breach of trust); the phase of proceedings (e.g., investigation, prosecution, sentence, appeal); personal involvement relating to corporate offenses; and mitigating or aggravating factors.

The role of the chair, the nomination committee, and the board in these circumstances is very relevant. The best current practice advocated by a line of thought is that no compromise should be assumed when reputational risk emerges relating to a board member of an internal control function head. Often, codes of ethics deal lightly with this issue, although the best practice's trend indicates the codes to establish demanding provisions in terms of actions to take. This area often raises ethical dilemmas toward a director sitting around the same table; however, the interest of the company and stakeholders should take first priority in the decision, and tolerance should be very carefully balanced with the public image and resulting reputational issues.

The third relates to *Conflicts of Interest*—as well as to potential conflicts of interest—*and Independence of Mind* disclosure, mitigation, management, and prevention of conflicts of interest. Members of social bodies and the board's committees should be able to make sound, objective, and independent decisions and act with independence of mind, which can be affected by conflicts of interest or potential conflicts of interest. The entity should have governance policies for identifying, disclosing, mitigating, managing, and preventing conflicts of interest, whether actual, potential (reasonably foreseeable), or perceived by the public. There is a conflict of interest if the attainment of the interests of a member may adversely affect the interests of the supervised entity.

Having a [potential] conflict of interest does not necessarily mean a candidate cannot be considered suitable. This will only be the case if the conflict of interest poses a material risk not possible to prevent or mitigate under the policies. In the assessment of conflicts of interest, the organization must notify the supervisor of actual, potential, or perceived conflicts of interest. The supervised entity shall assess the materiality of the risk posed by the conflict of interest and, if is considered material, must adopt measures, including the assessment of the situation leading to the decision about preventive and mitigating measures to be communicated to the supervisor for the decision. This is detailed in the Article 91(8) of the CRD IV and Article 88(1) of the CRD IV.

Mitigating measures may include the prohibition from participating in meetings and decision-making concerning a particular disclosed interest such as credit to be awarded to board members and related parties, resignation of a certain positions, cooling-off period, application of the "at arm's length" principle, and approval by the social body for a situation to continue. These situations are assessed on a case-by-case basis.

The *Time Commitment* criteria includes both quantitative and qualitative requirements, as members should be able to commit an adequate level of time to the institution. The time criteria can be affected by several factors, including the number of directorships held, the place or country where they are based, other professional or personal commitments, or even circumstances (e.g., a court case). Holding several positions in social bodies is a relevant factor that may affect time commitment. CRD IV sets a limit on the number of "directorships" in significant institutions.[230] Currently, CRD IV limits to one executive directorship with two non-executive directorships, or four non-executive directorships, although there are two exceptions to this rule. Directorships in organizations that do not pursue predominantly commercial objectives do not count (although it should be declared, as it consumes time), which include the ones stated in

Article 91(5) of the CRD IV: non-profit sports or cultural associations, charities, churches, chambers of commerce, trade unions, professional associations, organizations for the sole purpose of managing the private economic interests of members, and organizations that pursue predominantly noncommercial activities. Also, certain multiple directorships count as a single directorship defined as "privileged counting"; they include positions held in the same group and institutions members of the same institutional protection scheme. The information required includes a specification of the time commitment required for the role; the full list of the mandates and the expected time commitment for each one; and a self-declaration indicating that the candidate has sufficient time to dedicate to all the mandates, as required by Article 91(6) of the CRD IV. Unexpected circumstances may occur and include crisis situations related to the institution but also circumstances where other time constraints that emerge (e.g., court cases or crisis in other directorates).

The *Collective Suitability* is a very relevant criteria when looking at a social body in its full composition, considering the skills of the members, which represents an ongoing governance supervision. The institution should map the skills of the board members to identify gaps in the collective suitability, which should be assessed on an ongoing basis, although this criterion should be assessed during the board constitution process. The motivation should cover the composition of the social body for which the appointee is being assessed, the potential contribution of an individual to the collective suitability profile, as well as a periodic self-assessment, including an analysis of the most recent conclusions of the self-assessment and how the candidate would contribute the status quo and rely on the status quo for particular fields of knowledge, skills, or experience. Under the CRD IV Article 88(2)(c), in systemic institutions, this process should involve the Nomination Committee. The planned proposal to become a member of a specialized committee should be included in the statement.

Interviews are one of the ways to gather information about collective suitability. The relevant information about the appointee can be collected, using the opportunity to probe an appointee from any other source, to test whether an appointee is well informed about the supervised entity and relevant market developments, to explore issues of integrity and propriety, or to verify facts in order to gain more assurance about specific elements of his or her fitness and propriety. Interviews facilitate the competent authority (ECB) to meet the appointee and to set out his or her expectations with regard to the engagement between the appointee, the supervised entity, and him or herself.

ECB states that the aim of the interview is to complement and/ or verify:

1. documentation submitted by the appointee and/or supervised entity
2. information that may have come to the knowledge of the competent authority by another means

Therefore, it takes a proportionate and risk-based approach to the use of interviews in fit and proper assessments, as well as the recent ECB introduced roles that require the documentation and evaluation to be performed by the nomination committee that should issue an opinion on the profile of the candidate, along with the candidate's self-assessment.

New appointments to CEO (or equivalent) and Chairperson positions at stand-alone banks and the top banks of groups directly triggers interviews, as these are considered categories of high-risk. If the business is a holding company, the interview process applies to the largest bank in the group. In the case of cooperatives, the central body or central body association is considered the top entity. In other duly justified cases, the ECB can decide that an interview may not be necessary, such as where an appointee to the position of CEO is already one of the current members of the management body or has been recently interviewed.

An informative interview will cover all elements of suitability, and if required, a second, specific interview focusing on the facts that gave rise to any concerns may be conducted. The ECB may also decide to only hold a specific interview, if it is already clear from the written documentation that there is a specific concern regarding the fitness and propriety of the appointee. The appointee and the supervised entity will be given adequate notice in writing of the date, time, and place of the requested interview. In case of a specific interview, as there is a specific concern regarding the fitness or propriety of an appointee, an outline of the issues to be discussed will be sent to the appointee and the supervised entity in advance. The interview panel will generally consist of a minimum of two and no more than three people, and the chair must have sufficient seniority.

11.1.5 FIT AND PROPER BEYOND FINANCIAL INSTITUTIONS

The applicability of fit and proper principles extends beyond the financial institutions landscape. While the structure of the board differs across geographies, the underlying principles for the assessment remain the same. However, the definition of fit and proper may not be as stringent in unregulated industries (e.g., software development, hotel industry, cosmetic industry, retail) than regulated industries (e.g., financial sector, insurance, telecommunication, commercial airlines, public transportation in general, energy sector, pharmaceutical, health, utilities), and such unregulated industries may voluntarily apply the fit and proper principles to varying degrees for ensuring their prudent risk management and compliance. Additionally, the distinction between regulated industry and unregulated industry may differ slightly from one jurisdiction to another jurisdiction. Usually, banks and financial institutions are heavily regulated in most countries.

11.2 STAGGERED BOARD

Companies tend to have 4–15 board members, although best practice for publicly listed companies recommends that the number should be 7–10, with 12 being the maximum. Assuming that a corporate in the US has a nine-member board. In a normal board, all nine directors can be elected *en masse*. However, in a staggered board, only a fraction of the board of directors can be elected each time instead of *en masse*. The staggered board has been historically popular in the US but is reported to be in the decline. Legislative bodies, central banks, behavior supervisors, insurance and pension funds supervisors, and regulators, multilateral financial institutions (e.g., European Investment Bank, European Investment Fund, the World Bank, EBRD, Inter-American Development Bank, Asia Development Bank) often use staggered elections for *institutional memory*, meaning that collective knowledge and learned experiences of a board are properly transitioned during turnover, ensuring *continuity* in the board that can be important in long-term projects, plans, and policies. In Germany, directors stand election every five years, while countries such as France, the Netherlands, and Belgium usually have a staggered board with a four-year term, so at least a portion of the board is elected each year.

A staggered board is also known as "classified board," meaning that in a nine-member board, three directors may be placed in each class, making three classes in total—Class 1, Class 2, and Class 3.[231] In this scenario, Class 1 board members serve one year on the board; Class 2 board members serve two years on the board; and Class 3 board members serve three years on the board. During each election term, only one class is opened for elections while other two classes are untouched, contrary to the elections held in a normal board. Therefore, the class structure contributes to staggering the number of positions available on the board.

The argument related to the effectiveness of staggered board differs. In some companies or institutions, it may be beneficial; in some, it can be detrimental; and in some, inconsequential. It ultimately depends on the characteristics of the board and the reasons behind the need of a staggered board. Staggered boards can be of idiosyncratic in nature, and a policy dictum applied to all firms may not be appropriate as evidently no one size fits all.

11.2.1 PROS AND CONS OF STAGGERED BOARD

There are advantages and disadvantages in staggered boards. An argument in favor relates to the argument that a staggered board is considered as the strategy for takeover defense, as a staggered board can act as a protective shield for a corporate against a "large investor" looking for quick returns or a hostile bidder desiring to shake up the board and carve out (partial divestiture) the company after taking control of the board. Also, with a staggered board, board continuity is considered more secured, because it is impossible to shake the whole board at once, which may contribute positively to the corporate's long-term vision and strategy. As a result, corporate governance standards are supposed to be of higher quality. Another argument relates to the fact that this model allows the board to retain memory and ensure continuity, if that is desirable, as the change of members is not done at the same time. Boards of regulators and supervisors—notably in the financial industry—as well as in multilaterals and supranational, are examples of boards operating under this model.

Critics argue that the virtue of the staggered board may risk the entrenchment of directors such that any changes are very hard to occur. The directors may not undertake their fiduciary duties as expected, which ultimately underscores the loss of shareholders or stakeholders' interests. Also, not all activist investors or institutional investors have bad intentions; a staggered board may overthrow the bidders who have genuine intentions to boost the shareholder value. One of the studies[232] shows that staggered boards are in decline, with 60 percent of S&P 1500 companies and 80 percent of S&P 500 companies holding annual elections for all directors, and the companies with staggered boards have statistically boasted lower shareholder returns, although they are prevalent namely in central banks and international financial institutions.

Topics of the Chapter

The following has been discussed within this chapter:

- Fit and proper assessment indicates whether an individual is suitable to perform a specific controlled function.
  1. Fit refers to competence
  2. Proper refers to integrity and suitability
- The criteria for fit and proper may vary depending on jurisdiction and supervising body.
- In a normal board, members are elected *en masse*; by contrast, in a staggered board, only a fraction of the members are elected each time. This maintains institutional memory, ensuring continuity.

Chapter 12

Boards' Diversity and Inclusion

A crucial aspect of diversity advocates that organizations should have a balanced and hopefully optimal mixture of skills, expertise, and experience represented in the boardroom. Consultants and advisors may be hired to assess or brief the board in emerging issues when a lack of skills exists. The discussion about diversity and quotas still raises divergent viewpoints, with culture assuming a growing less relevant role,[233] although still influencing some jurisdictions where the best governance practices are only emerging. The inclusion of a diverse pool of talents and backgrounds could extend the existing set with productive perspectives and opinions, leading to a better decision-making process, thus leading to better decisions for the company and for the stakeholders. This chapter discusses diversity—in varied facets—and the way it can be beneficial to a board and its decision-making process.

Gender quotas came in a political context. In the 1970s, only a few countries had electoral quotas system in place, while in 2015, more than 130 countries have one or other form of affirmative action promoting gender equality and balance. This has indirectly influenced the corporate board quotas, particularly in Continental Europe, where stakeholder-centric governance model is more common. Norway has pioneered in effectively implementing the gender quota targets. The current Norwegian law stipulates a minimum 40 percent representation of both males and females needed to be present in the board of publicly listed companies, and the percentages may be slightly lower in cases of boards with less than nine members (i.e., 37.5 percent). Severe sanctions have been implemented as dissuasion for noncompliance; in extreme cases, the forced dissolution of the company can be enforced. These sanctions are viewed as a part of the diversity genre's success in Norway. Nonetheless, commentators also mention that Nordic countries, such as Norway, are driven by trust values and social status, as well as the corporate ownership and control tend to be heavily influenced by the social, political, and industrial environment and also the legislative framework. The same may not be applied across the world, notably due to cultural issues, as no one size fits all.

Another factor is linked to the lack of preparation and planning to ensure diversity, a reality that can be verified in many geographies, resulting in the lack of preparation of the least represented genre to assume senior positions, notably at the board level. This requires a plan to prepare, train, and develop a proper pipeline of talent to ensure an adequate level of representation at senior and top levels. Reality shows corporates still do not dedicate attention and commitment to the issue, with the issue being more aggravated in terms of imbalance at the level of small and medium-size enterprises. This topic should be at the top of the agenda of boards.

As of 2020, only 5.3 percent of board chair positions, 4.4 percent of CEO roles, and 16.9 percent of board seats worldwide is held by women.[234] McKinsey[235] mentions that entry-level women are 18 percent less likely to be promoted than their male peers. Therefore, this level of gender disparity produces a dramatic effect on the pipeline; if entry-level women were promoted at the same rate as their male peers, the number of women at the senior VP level and C-suite levels would be more than double. And so, the debate remains hot and contested. Gender pay gap is another topic that has recently gained momentum. Many reports have shown that women are paid less than men in the same job or position. In the new paradigm, the issues extend beyond gender quotas and gender pay gap, with topics such as discrimination against Lesbian, Gay, Bisexual, Transgender and others included in the concept of LGBT+ or disabled individuals being very sensitive matter, particularly in the US and Europe.

The issue of diversity and inclusion is reflected not only in private institutions but also in the governance of public organizations. The case object of the report published by The Equality and Human Rights Commission[236] is a very relevant example of an inadequate governance framework. The Commission analyzed a sample of complaints under the Equality Act 2006, having identified failings in leadership and inadequate processes for handling anti-Semitism (prejudice, hostility, or discrimination toward Jews) complaints in the UK Labour Party. Having concluded the existence of harassment and discrimination's acts, the organization failed to implement recommendations and measures to change the conduct, reflecting a culture non-aligned with a zero-tolerance approach, concluding that the leadership was ineffective in dealing with discrimination of minorities. The Equality and Human Rights Commission's report required the Labour Party to develop an action plan to address the recommendations—clear, fair, and achievable—which the new leadership committed to implement. The conclusions of the report are strongly related to an organization's culture—"Tone from the Top"—and shows a clear lack of internal control processes, as well as a lack of independent assurance review, which impacts negatively and reputationally, resulting from a lack of a robust governance framework.

The World Economic Forum (WEF)[237] states that half of the global workforce will be Millennials by 2020. Millennials are considered as anyone born between 1981 and 2000, the large portion of the population being tech-savvy and purpose-driven. The Millennials care about ethical, environmental, and social goals, and they would most likely choose the firms that are aligned with those values. Also, age of board members is no longer considered a non-eligible primary factor criterion. Therefore, with the inclusion of Millennials, the current trend is to strengthen the quota reforms, either by implementing them for the first time or consolidating the policies already in place. Nonetheless, the sheer number of countries involved alone means that the spread of gender quotas rivals other major sociopolitical trends, such as the third wave of democracy, the diffusion of neoliberal policies, and the rise of corporate responsibility and ethical values.

Credit Suisse[238] mentions that a diverse workforce promotes wide-ranging expertise and a broad network of contacts, as well as an inclusive and open corporate culture that helps deliver high-quality products and services. Furthermore, research from Credit Suisse Research Institute[239] concluded that companies with at least one female director generate 3.5 percent higher compound excess return than the ones run by male-only boards. Financial Reporting Council (FRC),[240] the accounting regulator in the UK, conducted a research study in 2020 which concluded that over half of FTSE 250 companies (52 percent) fail to mention ethnicity in their board diversity policy, and most of the FTSE 350 do not set measurable ethnicity targets. Just 14 percent of FTSE 100 companies set measurable objectives for board ethnic diversity, while among FTSE 250 companies, the figure is a meager 2 percent. Ultimately, this demonstrates the importance of gender and ethnic diversity.

One of the Research conducted by Duarte Pitta Ferraz, Ilídio Tomás Lopes, and Maria Manuela Martins,[241] to analyze the influence of diversity on boards on profitability of Iberian nonfinancial listed companies, found that some characteristics of board of directors significantly influence the companies' performance, and this could constitute new guidelines for policymakers to establish common corporate governance mechanisms to ensure the desired international comparability. Above all, the issues about the lack of diversity and gender balance, as well as a quota system may threaten sustainability. Sustainability and ESG (Environment, Social, and Governance) is discussed in Section 4.3: "Corporate Sustainability."

Two relevant purposes of good governance are to raise capital from investors—shareholders, bondholders, and the financial system—and to attract talent. The first group of stakeholders linked to capital raising currently considers not investing in corporates and other enterprises that do not comply with the best practice in terms of diversity of their staff pyramids, as well as senior management and social bodies, having policies and algorithms that exclude those from their investment criteria. The latter—attracting talent—should not consider joining a company or firm that is not aligned with the best practice, as it will compromise their careers and very likely do not deserve the talent they can provide to their employer.

Another relevant angle relates to the effort the academic world—not restricted to the business and economics schools—is doing to include in all bachelors' and masters' programs, independently of the nature of the degrees, a mandatory course of corporate governance that would raise the awareness to the topic at an earlier stage and influence a shift change in this area.

12.1 VARIABLES FOR INCORPORATING THE DIVERSITY AND INCLUSION ON BOARD

There are several variables that should be kept in mind when incorporating the diversity on board. Nevertheless, all these variables should be applied in conjunction with one another such that the optimal level is reached.

12.1.1 GENDER AND QUOTAS—DIVERSITY AND INCLUSION CONCEPTS

Gender diversity (having a mix of male and female board members) is one of the emerging topics that in more sophisticated enterprises is better developed and constitutes a top priority in the board's agenda. The best practices of governance trends also consider other elements of diversity, like LBGT+ and people of disability. The acronym LGBT+ stands for Lesbian, Gay, Bisexual, Transgender+. The + represents different sexual and gender minorities that may be difficult to use represented by LGBTQQIAAP[242]—although the acronym is not exhaustive—particularly for North America. In addition, individuals may also identify themselves with more than one of these descriptions.

The #MeToo movement that led a vast number of people to speak about their experiences of sexual harassment and sexual assault, the majority being woman, took the business world by storm. For example, Lloyd's, an insurance market, found that a significant number of staff felt unable to raise concerns about improper conduct.[243] As a result of #MeToo movement, employees are now encouraged to speak up, including through a bullying-and-harassment helpline. Goldman Sachs is believed to incorporate the following entry-level recruitment targets—50 percent female and, in America, 14 percent Hispanic and 11 percent black. Also, in 2020, Goldman Sachs mentioned that it will refuse to take a company public (IPO) unless it has at least one woman or non-white board member, in order to end the era of all-male, all-white corporate boards.[244] Qantas, the flag carrier of Australia, has an ambition to have 40 percent female pilots by 2028.[245,246]

While rules and regulations about diversity and quotas are not mandatory in many jurisdictions for the formation of the board structure, namely the European Commission strongly encourages the member countries to improve the gender balance on company boards, taking measures to balance the least representative genre and have a proactive stance in terms of inclusion, at all levels of the pyramid. It should include a clear and transparent plan to the organization and the involvement and monitoring end-to-end of its development. Diversity and inclusion are characteristics that emerge together, as they are interconnected and overlap in various elements, although they cannot be regarded as the same. A different characteristic between diversity and inclusion is that the first can be defined as a "state of being," while the latter is a cultural compound of the global governance framework of an institution, therefore being "an object of influence and governance."[247] Diversity is related to the presence of individuals displaying a profile of characteristics that may come from birth or developed along their living, which include gender identity (a broader concept of gender than just women and men), ethnicity, LGBT+ status, disabilities, military status, and other minorities that several legal frameworks already recognize. Inclusion is focused on a best practice of an organization being able to ensure that individuals feel comfortable and welcome, being allowed and considered on an equal opportunity stance in terms of their career and being confident about their real self. To achieve the best governance practice, boards of directors should be proactively involved, along with senior management, to ensure and monitor the improvement of diversity, which encompasses a practice of inclusion. This should also include the commitment and involvement of the board with associations' representative of diversity in its broader concept of gender, if they exist at their organization.

Some countries such as Belgium, Germany, France, Italy, and Norway are moving forward with regulatory measures for fulfilling gender quotas in all kinds of companies, and others only applicable to public companies such as the UK, Denmark, Finland, Sweden, Ireland, Greece, Spain, Luxembourg, the Netherlands, Austria, Poland, Portugal, and Slovenia. Other countries have incorporated soft measures such as quotas without sanctions. In the US, there are no specific norms about gender quotas, and policymakers tend to rely solely on voluntary actions. However, new SEC rules require companies to disclose their diversity efforts in the director selection process. Certain states have established their own set of rules that are intended to enhance boardroom diversity. For instance, companies that are publicly listed and headquartered in California need to have at least one female on board by the end of 2019 and at least two females On five members boards or at least three females on six or more members board by the end of July 2021.[248] In 2015, the Canadian Securities Administrators (CSA) introduced the disclosure requirements for the women representation on boards and in executive officer positions. Thus, the concept of gender and quotas may slightly vary across the world, influenced by their own social, economic, or political conditions. Nonetheless, the fundamentals of diversity and inclusion remain the same in all the jurisdictions.

A study conducted by European Women on Boards (EWoB)[249] about the status of gender diversity in 598 European companies that are publicly listed in the STOXX Europe 600 index found that fewer than 5 percent companies are close to gender equality at board and executive level. While gender diversity at board level has improved, women remain under-represented in decision-making roles. Of all the board members in the listed 598 companies, one-third (33 percent) are women, and only 16 percent of the women are in executive level of company decision makers. Also, the representation of women in the C-suite is even lower than at board level. Women represent only 14 percent of all C-level executives, and there are only 41 women in the position of chair of the board in the companies analyzed. Table 12.1 demonstrates the percentage of women on boards and executive levels in the companies analyzed (2019).

In the 2019 report on equality between women and men in the EU published by European Commission, the Commissioner for Justice, Consumers, and Gender Equality of European Commission mentions that the gender gap in employment, pay, or pension may not be closed only by education but also through social behaviors, as gender equalities are socially constructed. Thus, the commission is making sustained efforts to put in place measures that would encourage a change in social behaviors, confront persisting stereotypes, and strengthen women's economic independence and empowerment in decision-making, thus endorsing the concept of diversity and inclusion.[250]

Table 12.1: Percentage of women on boards and executive levels in European countries (EU)

Country	No. of companies analyzed	% Female in Boards	% Female in Executive Levels
Norway	15	39	27
France	88	42	19
Sweden	44	38	22
United Kingdom	153	32	20
Finland	16	32	18
Belgium	16	34	13
Italy	33	35	12
Netherlands	24	34	17
Ireland	9	28	16
Denmark	23	31	16
Portugal	4	24	26
Germany	76	33	12
Austria	7	34	7
Spain	24	24	16
Poland	9	21	9
Switzerland	52	24	10
Luxembourg	1	21	6

12.1.2 GENDER PAY GAP

There are different criteria to define and calculate pay gap, which constitutes a challenge to benchmarking the issue. According to European Parliament,[251] the gender pay gap is the difference in average gross hourly earnings between women and men and is based on salaries paid directly to employees before income tax and social security contributions are deducted. OECD[252] defines gender pay gap as the difference between median earnings of men and women. The UK

Government[253] defines gender pay gap as the difference between the average earnings of men and women, expressed relative to men's earnings—women earn 15 percent less than men per hour. In the US, one survey found that women are making roughly $0.80 for every dollar earned by their male colleagues.[254]

The calculation of gender pay gap may not consider all different factors that may play a role, including education, hours worked, type of job, career breaks, or part-time work. Therefore, interpreting the gender pay gap numbers and equal pay numbers are not the same; a smaller gender pay gap in a specific country does not necessarily mean greater gender equality.[255] A high pay gap is normally seen where women are more concentrated in a restricted number of sectors and/or professions or where a significant proportion of women work part-time. Nonetheless, equal pay is not just a matter of justice and fairness but would also boost the economy, as a line of argument advocates that if women get paid more, they will spend more. This could increase the tax base and would relieve some of the burden on welfare systems. Assessments have shown that reducing the gender pay gap by one percentage point would increase the gross domestic product by 0.1 percent (European Parliament).

The movement against gender pay gap has gained momentum and become a target of scrutiny by stakeholders and society in general. According to Pew Research Center,[256] the gender gap has narrowed since 1980s; however, women earned 85 percent of what men earned in 2018, as concluded in an analysis of median hourly earnings of both full and part-time workers in the US. The gaps are explained by measuring factors such as educational attainment, occupational segregation, and work experience, but other immeasurable factors such as gender discrimination on earnings inequality persist. In one of the 2017 Pew Research Center surveys,[257] it is mentioned that about four-in-ten working women (42 percent) experienced gender discrimination at work, compared with about two-in-ten men (22 percent) who said the same.

The European Commission (EC) has led the *Gender Equality Strategy 2020–2025*.[258] One of the objectives is closing the gender pay gap as there are considerable differences among EU countries. For example, the gender pay gap ranges from less than 8 percent in Belgium, Italy, Luxembourg, Poland, and Romania to more than 20 percent in Czech Republic, Germany, and Estonia. The strategy has the vision where women and men, girls and boys, in all their diversity components, are equal; where they are free to pursue their chosen path in life; where they have equal opportunities to thrive; and where they can equally participate in and lead the European society. The strategy will take a dual approach: (i) Key actions to achieve gender equality and (ii) Strengthening the integration of a gender perspective in all EU policies and major initiatives, namely gender mainstreaming.

The key actions are combating gender-based violence and challenging gender stereotypes; boosting women's economic empowerment and ensuring equal opportunities in the labor market, including equal pay; and giving both women and men the opportunity to lead and participate in all sectors of the economy and in political life. Gender mainstreaming is the inclusion of a gender perspective in all EU policies and processes in order to ensure that these adequately respond to the needs and maximize the potential of women and men, girls and boys, in all their diversity. Gender pay gap reporting can be voluntary or regulated. Nowadays, big corporates often publish the pay gap report and the strategies they have implemented to reduce the gender pay gap. In the UK, since 2017, organizations with more than 250 employees have been required to publish and report specific figures about their gender pay gap. Gender pay gap figures of UK-based companies show that men are typically paid significantly more than women in most UK businesses.[259]

Barclays aims to reach 33 percent female representation in the board and 33 percent across the Group Executive Committee while reducing the gender pay gap (2018). BCG UK mentions that a gap in hourly pay rates and bonus pay arise due to a representation gap (i.e., the under-representation of women in senior positions), and is therefore addressing the under-representation of women in senior roles through a number of specific initiatives in all people processes.[260] In 2018, 49 percent of BCG UK's incoming new joiners were female. Unilever UK claims that women represent 51.1 percent of all management positions (2018) and also introduced programs to help improve balance in the areas where men have traditionally held more roles than women.

The gender pay gap should be a topic in the global agenda of boards to allow for its balance and monitor progress. Companies must act proactively, adopting the best practices and targets issued by international institutions and regulators by setting up demanding targets to keep a balance as well as devising strategies to reduce the gender pay gap if they intend to remain sustainable. Ultimately, this relates to the reputational and ethical stance that may even challenge sustainability.

12.1.3 CULTURE, ETHNICITY, AND RACE

In theory, the main viewpoints advocate different positions defending that the effect of culture, ethnicity, or/and racial diversity on corporate governance can be positive, neutral, or negative. Some argue that board monitoring can be stronger with ethnically diverse candidates, as it leads to higher independence and higher director quality; others say that minorities—heavily regulated in the US—can be pressured to conform and not behave differently. Ethnic diversity means that members in boards with distinct backgrounds in terms of race, geographical origin, age, country of academic background, culture, or religion, regardless of the gender status or any other status. Geographical diversity is a characteristic very relevant in companies with an international footprint, meaning that individuals in the board are chosen from different geographical areas (countries, cultures, regions, or continents). The current mode of globalization has demanded further diversity and inclusion within the scope of culture, ethnicity, and race. Nonetheless, such variables bring new dimensions to corporate governance, as behavioral, political, and psychological aspects are often difficult to identify and quantify; however, they can be examined qualitatively by using a matrix of needs to determine the set of skills required from each individual to build and develop a board globally fit and proper. Therefore, the effort to promote such diversity in boards and executive committees has to be embedded in the talent management strategy and the nomination committee, endorsing the link between diversity and strategy such that the diversity is promoted at all stages of careers to broaden the pool of talent at the executive level. Companies should look forward to recruit executive and independent directors from the widest possible base.

The companies in the UK are struggling to fulfill the ethnicity target even though the UK Corporate Governance Code was strengthened in 2018 to promote diversity including of gender, social, and ethnic backgrounds in UK boardrooms. The topics about ethnic and geographical diversity are frequently debated in the US, European Union, and the UK (probably because they become international earlier than other countries), that soon realized the value diversity brings to the business; understanding local culture, usually leads to a better decision-making process and, very likely, to better board decisions and outcomes. Hence, the companies in the US are endeavoring to achieve ethnic and geographical diversity represented within the corporate boards, even though the standards remain minimal. The European Commission also encourages ethnic and geographical diversity in the board of directors, in addition to gender and quotas. Inclusion of Millennials and other generations, fostering multicultural and multigenerational environment, should also be considered.

McKinsey's affinity networks foster community, mentorship, professional development, and advancement for women, members of the LGBTQ+ community, colleagues from minority ethnic groups, parents of special-needs children, veterans, and colleagues with disabilities. JP Morgan has facilitated programs such as Advancing Black Leaders for attracting, hiring, retaining, and advancing talent within the black community and Women on the Move for advocating the success of women in the firm.[261] Also, it has dedicated Office of Disability Inclusion (ODI), which provides consistent standards and processes to better accommodate employees with disabilities. Lazard has implemented a policy of a diversity and an inclusive, equitable culture regardless of socioeconomic status, race, color, nationality, religion, gender, sexual orientation, physical abilities, and veteran or military status.[262] Currently, 32 percent of its US employees are ethnic minorities, and 44 percent of independent directors are women. Barclays Bank has incorporated five global pillars of focus to build and maintain a diverse and inclusive environment: Disability, Gender, LGBT+, Multicultural and Multigenerational.

Academy Awards (also known as Oscar Awards), which are an international recognition of excellence in cinematic achievements, faced backlash for the lack of racial diversity among the nominees.[263] Critics were also fast to point out that when black actors are nominated, stereotypical roles such as servants, slaves, or criminals are more common. Also, the racial and ethnic makeup of the academy's voting body was questioned due to the presence of largely white members.

The issue often relates to collective inclusion of all participating stakeholders. Historically, the corporates in the US have been shareholder-eccentric, and, in 2020, the change of notion regarding the purpose of corporations came to substantial debate. This trend is emerging to be very relevant for more robust decisions taken in boards, as they are supposed to incorporate diverse viewpoints, although it may involve different requirements, depending on the existence of a certain degree of complexity, the footprint of the organization, and notably on the pipeline of talent. This requires from boards a proactive involvement and supervision that an adequate planning is in place as well as milestones to be achieved.

12.1.4 AGE

Age is often considered a hidden variable. Historically, board members (notably non-executives) have tended to be older and more experienced contributing with different experiences and perpectives, particularly in terms of previous financial and economic crises and other challenges; geopolitical, health, and natural disasters; failure of companies, either because of obsolete business models or governance scandals; or even situations of war and forced migration. Yet, it is widely agreed that a right mix is needed to ensure both an adequate level of expertise and experience from more experienced and older members as well as board members with new and innovative ideas that may emerge from younger members in the age of Millennials (young adulthood around 2000), or even considering the following demographic cohort Generation Z (also known as Post-Millennials, iGeneration, Founders, Plurals, or Homeland Generation, born in 1995 and later). The assumption that advanced age is the most important no longer holds right, as the digital transformation, cyber world, and increased complexity demand new skills and change the nature of decision-making, ultimately transforming the business model—a responsibility of the board—and therefore the way companies operate. The World Economic Forum[264] mentions that companies are becoming more active in promoting gender balance, but age diversity has not been addressed to the same degree, even though more than half of the world's population is aged 30 or under. Thus, companies need to make selection pools diverse and reach those below the radar.

Topics of the Chapter

The following has been discussed within this chapter:

- The performance of the board is expected to improve when it is collaborative, diverse, and engaged with all relevant stakeholders, leading to an improved decision-making process and eventually better decisions.

- Diversity is a "state of being"; inclusion is an "object of influence and governance."
- An increasing number of countries are moving forward with regulatory measures to diversity and inclusion in companies, namely through quotas and reduction of pay gap.
- Boards can be stronger with ethnically diverse candidates, as it leads to higher independence and higher director quality.
- Geographical diversity is very relevant in companies with an international footprint.
- Boards should seek to include younger members such as Millennials with new and innovative ideas.

Chapter 13

Independence and Conflicts of Interests

Independence refers to a mental state of making decisions without the influence of other individual, a concept that is very relevant in the corporate governance framework,[265] while conflicts of interests involve impartiality and objectivity of a decision, opinion or recommendation or, on the contrary may be perceived as being compromised and affected by a personal interest entrusted to an individual. The Organisation for Economic Co-operation and Development (OECD) and the Council of Europe published frameworks to set a mechanism to address conflicts of interests. This chapter discusses factors that can affect the independence of the board, degrees of individual independence in the board, legal and regulatory guidelines' criterion to assess independence, and its pros and cons.

The concepts and definitions of independence and conflicts of interests are critical for board members, notably for the non-executive directors who are bound by law and/or guidelines in being independent—an element intrinsically linked to potential conflicts of interests—affecting all directors and management as well. Institutions should have processes and tools to identify, manage, and mitigate conflicts of interests.

The concept of independence—there advocating "autonomy" instead,[266] although the idea is not widely stated in the literature—can be analyzed from various sources that include the legal framework, internal procedures, codes, or policy documents and guidelines. The broad concept relating to independence encompasses principles relating to behavioral and performing duties with integrity, dignity, care, loyalty, and discretion in compliance with the law, rules, and code of conduct and ethics, adhering to demanding standards of conduct. An individual to be independent, should not either seek, take instructions, or be placed under pressure from a conflicted third party, therefore acting completely free taking a decision for the best of the institution in first place.

Independence is a relative concept involving different levels, a fact that suggests the potentially impossibility of "complete independence." Therefore, when an individual is faced with a requirement of independence, the term should be specified notably to whom it applies (making it specific) and the degree it exists (with the objective of finding ways and actions to mitigate the potential conflict). Consequently, the term "independence" must be interpreted along with other provisions. Board members must avoid situations that may give rise to a conflict of interests or be perceived as such, which emerges when a personal interest has potential to influence the independent performance of responsibilities and/or duties. The definition of personal interests—although not limited to—includes any potential benefit and/or advantage to the decision-maker, spouses, partners, and/or close family members. A former director must respect the obligations arising from their position when active that continue to have an effect at the end of a mandate.

Independence is primarily applicable to the non-executive directors and advisors. Independence may be distorted if board members have a biased professional opinion due to their personal interests or if situations of conflicts of interest, or potential conflicts of interest, are present or emerge.

Independence can be regarded as a state of mind that allows an individual to express a balanced opinion in the best interest of the stakeholders, framing it within the law, regulation, and best practice.

The most common restrictions and limitations that impair independence in the decision-making process include namely: (i) not to be informed and/or prepared about the facts to take a decision and its impact, (ii) not to have a psychological profile that allows optimistically challenging topics for decision, (iii) not have financial independence, or (iv) a desire to renew the mandate in a social body by keeping a low profile in the decision-making process, basically being a "yes-man/woman."

Independence also means not having current or recent relationships or links with an organization or its management that can negatively influence objectivity and balance in judgment. Independence should be exercised carefully and politely, in a fashion that does not create negative dynamics in the board. This process requires articulation with the chairperson that coordinates with the CEO and other non-executive directors.

Adopting a criterion of transparency about potential conflicts of interests and the way they are treated and mitigated is critical for the reputation of an institution. Independence can be analyzed under two subsets of concepts—functional and administrative for the private sector, and functional and institutional for the public sector. Institutional independence is related to a separate legal entity, which includes aspects of organization, budget, staff, and financial independence, while functional independence deals with the principle that no instructions are given from outside the independent entity in the exercise of an individual tasks.[267] Chapter 6: Control Functions and Related Frameworks discuss the concept of administrative and functional independence.

In general, non-executive directors can be categorized into three segments—*insiders, gray,* and *independent.*[268] The insiders are people who work or have worked in the company. The gray directors are individuals who are not directly connected to the firm but have a business relationship with the organization, including bankers, lawyers, consultants, advisors, or suppliers. The interest of such directors is likely or has potential to be biased due to their close relationship with executive directors or management. The independent directors are usually non-executive directors (NEDs), also known as outsider directors, being the ones most likely to have interest aligned with those of the shareholders and stakeholders. The best practice—in the financial system the internal governance rules emanating from regulators—requires a minimum number of independent non-executive directors that should be larger than the number of non-independent directors including executives and non-executives, as some may not qualify as such in the fit and proper process conducted by the supervisors. Those rules establish priorities in dealing with stakeholders, clearly stating that in the banking system the depositors are the priority stakeholders and the shareholders come after those. These guidelines are particular important when a board is making decisions, notably to independent non-executive directors, as they have to consider the priority criteria when deciding matters that put depositors and shareholders into conflict of interest.

Conflicts of interests are intimately related with the concept of independence. Two relevant and inclusive definitions of conflicts of interests were developed by the OECD and the Council of Europe. Conflicts of interests are also discussed in Section 2.1: "The Agency Theory" and Section 8.1: "Business Ethics and Conduct." They have in common the potential emergence of conflicts of interest between the public duties of decision-makers in the public sector and the individual's private interests. A major difference relates to the fact that the definition of the OECD relates to actual or potential conflicts, while the one from the Council of Europe includes actual or perceived conflicts, being the latter more demanding in its scope. Quentin Reed mentions that "conflicts of interest are naturally occurring phenomena, not a pathology—that is, they are an inevitable consequence of the fact that people occupy more than one social role."[269]

OECD states that the definition of the concept of "(...) 'conflict of interest' has been the subject of many and varying approaches, [although] (...) conflicts of interest cannot simply be avoided or prohibited, and must be defined, identified, and managed."[270] The OECD Guidelines follow a simple and practical approach to assist in the effective identification and management of conflicts' situations, defining it as "A 'conflict of interest' involves a conflict between the public duty and private interests of a public official, in which the public official has private-capacity interests which could improperly influence the performance of their official duties and responsibilities." Another view by Quentin Reed defines conflict of interest as "a situation in which a public official has a private or other interest which is such as to influence, or appear to influence, the impartial and objective performance of his or her official duties."

The Guidelines for Conflict-of-Interest Policies in EU Decentralized Agencies[271] structure the elements that constitute a conflict of interest as follows:

A conflict of interest generally refers to a situation where the impartiality and objectivity of a decision, opinion or recommendation of an Agency is or might be perceived as being compromised by a personal interest held or entrusted to a given individual. Relevant personal interest may be of financial or non-financial nature and it may concern a personal or family relationship or professional affiliations (including additional employment or "outside" appointments or former employments or appointments) and other relevant outside activities. Not only actual independence but also perception of independence is important, since it can impact on agencies' reputation by raising doubts about the conclusions reached. The appearance of conflict of interest can constitute a reputational risk to the agency, even if it turns out to be unsubstantiated. Therefore, giving due consideration to proportionality, specific backgrounds, all relevant facts and mitigating circumstances, a risk of perceived conflict of interest should be treated as if it were an actual conflict.

OECD Guidelines for managing conflicts of interest stress that "private interests" are not limited to financial or pecuniary interests, or interests generating a direct personal benefit to an official, as a conflict of interest may involve legitimate private activity (e.g., affiliations, family interests, negotiating employment before leaving public roles is generally regarded as a conflict of interests) in situations where those interests may reasonably be considered to improperly influence the individual related responsibilities.

Both the OECD and the Council of Europe frameworks and guidelines—focused respectively on the private and the public sectors—should be leveraged by boards and directors in the adoption of criteria in addition to the one determined by the legal frameworks of a jurisdiction, setting a robust framework to govern the stance and protect an institution's reputation toward stakeholders.

13.1 SOME CASES OF GOVERNANCE FAILURES

The *Adelphia* case is an example of how the lack of independence could lead to tragic outcomes. Adelphia was a successful family business and one of the largest cable operators in the USA, managed by the Rigas family.[272] In an effort to grow market share as quickly as possible and compete against its major competitor (Comcast) at that time, Adelphia was in a process of making numerous acquisitions in the 1990s, many of them being overvalued, which over-leveraged the balance sheet, growing the debt from 3.5 billion dollars to 12.6 billion dollars in just a few years, as well as placed pressure in the cash-flows. Wirecard, the German payment processor and financial services provider, went bankrupt in 2020 due to its accounting irregularities and due to the senior executives' use of forged and backdated contracts, possibly to inflate revenue.[273]

Rating agencies and shareholders considered it necessary that Adelphia reduced those high levels of debt. The company at that time was managed entirely by the Rigas family and individuals close to them. Even though the company was public, the founding family held significant amounts of voting shares to avoid giving up corporate control. They were accused of submitting fraudulent consolidated financial records[274] and making transactions into subsidiary companies with the objective of inflating earnings and hiding the enormous amounts of debt. Moreover, their external auditors at that time failed to act as independent auditors and to monitor the financial performance of the firm, allowing Adelphia to disclose only parts of their financial situation, thus misleading the financial and capital market. Adelphia subsequently filed bankruptcy in 2002, when the information of their fraudulent behavior became public. The founders were found guilty of bank fraud, conspiracy, and securities fraud, and they received lengthy prison sentences.[275]

In another case, also discussed and referenced in Section 14.2.1: "The Case of Breach of Fiduciary Duties of Care, Loyalty, and Obedience," the senior officials of Tyco, a security systems company, were accused of improperly using corporate funds to the tune of millions of dollars through a racketeering scheme involving stock fraud, unauthorized bonuses, and falsified expense accounts.[276] As the CEO and CFO were accused of stealing millions of dollars, they hid their illegal actions by keeping the numbers out of the accounting books and from the eyes of the board and the shareholders. Later, the CEO and CFO were found guilty in a court of grand larceny, conspiracy, falsifying business records, and violating business law, and they were eventually fined in millions of dollars and subsequently incarcerated. The failure of the board and the audit committee stroked the concern to drive penalties for directors and the board accountability. Factors such as a lack of directors' and board evaluation, management stealing, high-risk culture, improper accounting, directors' networks and collusive environment, lack of accountability, among others, are considered the governance failures at Tyco.

Other cases include the governance failures at companies such as Enron, WorldCom, and Parmalat. The CEO and CFO of Enron, a major American energy companies before collapse, colluded with a staff of executives to develop special purpose vehicles through the execution of accounting loopholes and poor financial reporting in order to hide billions of dollars in debt from failed deals and projects, also deceiving the board and the audit committee.[277] The CEO of WorldCom, telecommunication giant in the US before collapse, was convicted of orchestrating an accounting fraud worth billion dollars through the dubious business strategy of acquisitions.[278] Parmalat, an Italian company specializing in long-life milk, hid its true debt (in billions) using an elaborate scheme of false financial statements and billings tied to shell companies in the Cayman Islands and other tax havens. The CEO and CFO were both seen the architects of the coverup.[279] Ultimately, this explains the importance of having enough independent directors on the board and the committees, which are fit and proper and essentially ensure checks and balances.

The above examples of corporate governance failures resulted from malpractices, where notably non-executive directors as well as boards and audit committees did not exercise their duties and roles in the fields of governance, strategy, and supervision. Also, Enron and WorldCom operated in regulated areas, where the regulators and supervisors seemed distracted and absent from their governance practices.

13.2 CRITERIA AND FACTORS AFFECTING THE BOARD INDEPENDENCE

Best practice and/or legal frameworks require the need to ensure the existence of the independence criteria. However, there are different levels of demand in terms of the legal framing of the concept of independence. This results from the countries' various legal frameworks, notably the governance structure adopted, including if the monist or dualist model; and its specificities in terms of the social body or committee that carries the audit or supervisory responsibility, a matter impacted by the methodology guidelines and empirical evidence. For example, the Anglo-Saxon model adopts generally a functional approach, as the audit committee is formed by non-executive directors, which must be independent because of their duties as members of the audit functions; this approach makes the supervisory and the auditing functions equivalent. Other systems (e.g., Portugal, the Latin Model) establish a model with an audit board constituted by members that have to qualify by the law as independent and cannot integrate the other social bodies. The dualist system requires in many legal frameworks that the supervisory board be constituted by a majority of independent members and that the audit committee (also called Financial Matters Committee) be integrated only by independent members, one of which should be a qualified statutory auditor. Some jurisdictions require the chair of the supervisory board to chair the audit committee, which does not currently represent the best practice, as there is room for conflicts of interest. The best practice recommends that an independent vice-chair or the senior independent director chair the audit committee or the financial matters committee.

Specific regulation, legislations, and guidelines from EBA apply for the financial system, namely European Banking Authority Internal Governance of Banks (EBA/GL/2017/11), which identifies the criteria to qualify as independent, and Directive 2013/36/EU CRD IV, which established the principles adopted by supervisors to usually apply more demanding criteria to determine the independence profile. Joint ESMA (European Securities and Market Authority) and EBA[280] guidelines on the assessment of suitability of members of the management body and key function holders mentions that institutions should differentiate between the notion of "independence of mind" and the principle of "being independent" when assessing the independence of members. Independence of mind is a pattern of behavior, shown in particular during discussions and decision-making within the board, which is required for each member of the board, regardless of whether or not the member is considered as being independent. Being independent means that a member of the board in its supervisory function does not have any present or recent relationships or links of any nature with the institution or its management that may influence the member's objective and balanced judgment and reduce the member's ability to take decisions independently. The non-executive directors are regarded by some jurisdictions' supervisors as "supervisors themselves," which is why guidelines require that members of boards and supervisory boards qualify as independent. Also, guidelines strictly require that the main committees of the board (notably the audit, the risk, and the remunerations committees) always have a majority of independent non-executive directors and be chaired by an independent non-executive director.

Some of the factors that may potentially contribute to a board's independence include:[281]

- *Firm complexity and reach:* Corporates with broader service/ product portfolios typically have greater needs for strategic advisory and independent viewpoints, which may be provided by skilled independent non-executive directors.
- *Firm size:* Larger firms tend to compete in global markets, which may be more scrutinized and exposed to stricter independence requirements. By contrast, smaller and less complex companies with streamlined operations are easier for independent NEDs to comprehend and oversee but may require fewer NEDs.
- *Type of firm:* Firms with extensive research and development and intellectual property investments are relatively difficult for outsiders to understand and require high-quality information. Therefore, they may need fewer independent NEDs in comparison to the banking and financial institutions.
- *Region and market maturity:* Developed markets tend to adopt higher thresholds of board independence than emerging markets. According to International Shareholder Services (ISS), which assessed board governance standards and practices in 50 largest global equity markets under ISS reach, half of the European markets under analysis enforce

a minimum of 50 percent independent NEDs in boards. However, in Latin America, Africa, the Middle East, and the Asia-Pacific, most countries require only 33 percent or less independent NEDs in the board.[282]

- *Ownership structures:* Companies that have roots in family-owned businesses traditionally have lower levels of board independence than listed companies that are owned by a wide group of shareholders.

- *Gender diversity:* The percentage of independent NEDs on the board can be influenced by recommended/enforced gender diversity, regardless of status such as LGBT+ or disability. The percentage of women on the board may vary by geography (discussed in Chapter 12: Boards' Diversity and Inclusion). For instance, Nordic countries tend to have a significant percentage of women on the board, in contrast to other European Union countries.

- *Culture:* Distinct cultural backgrounds may influence the composition and independence of the board. For instance, preferences for formality or informality and sensitivity toward exposing information to outsiders (e.g., recruiting firms, legal counsels, external governance experts) may influence the board's culture. Also, board members' personalities may influence the board culture and, consequently, the board's composition and the independence of speech.

- *Geopolitical context:* Organizations operating in countries facing enormous geopolitics challenges, stressed economic situations, war, or dictatorial regimes are not likely to comply with international standards, codes, or best practices the way neutral democratic countries do (further discussed in Chapter 18: Globalization 4.0).

- *Board size:* To demonstrate the compliance for greater representation of independent NEDs in boards, companies may tend to decrease the number of board members, which may adulterate the original independence rationale. On the flip side, there could be a tendency to enlarge the board to accommodate more independent NEDs, which may create other challenges such as excessively long meetings, increased relationship overload, and heavier decision-making process.

- *Independence requirements:* According to New York Stock Exchange (NYSE) corporate governance guidelines, at least 75 percent of board members must be independent at NYSE traded companies.[283] However, other corporate governance codes and legal frameworks might demand different board independence levels, or perhaps only recommend and not enforce independence levels. There are legal frameworks that demand, for some types of corporates, a chair with an independent status, while others do not require that profile. However, best practice recommends that independent non-executive directors should outnumber the non-independent.

- *Tenure:* ISS governance rating system views "more than nine years as excessive," as it potentially compromises a director's independence.[284] Financial Reporting Council (FRC UK) states that the tenure of NED should be nine years, and the board must justify with reasons why a chair should serve more than nine years. NYSE Corporate Governance Guideline does not demand any limit to a director's tenure. Limits of tenure are a relevant element in keeping directors' independent state of mind. The line of thought that advocates this view argues that if directors know up front that the mandate will not be renewed at the end of a certain number of years, they will tend to keep independence as a decision-making rigorous criteria.

13.3 DEGREES OF THE BOARD INDEPENDENCE

Conceptually, there are four degrees of independence—*zero independence, low independence, balanced independence,* and *full independence* (Figure 13.1).[285]

Figure 13.1: Degrees of board independence

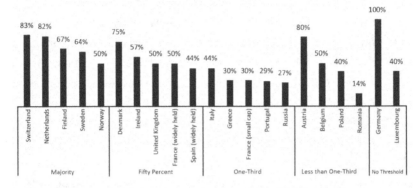

Europe: Market standards do not always correspond to the same practices
median level of board independence by country and recommended best practice, per
company and excluding employee representatives

Source: ISS Analytics, based on profiled boards of companies with meetings from 05/01/2017 to 04/30/2018

Source: (ISS)

Zero Board Independence

Boards with no independence are essentially the boards comprised entirely of executive directors who run not only the company but also the board itself, resulting in a board that can be considered not fit for the job, as the supervisory function is missing. This situation occurs often in family business, principally in Founder's Phase, as well as in companies with concentrated ownership, even involving more than one family. The low degree of independence may have drawbacks for shareholders, notably minority shareholders and stakeholders, as the board's duty to oversee the CEO's and executive directors' execution may be severely impaired, ultimately compromising the protection of shareholder's interests.

Low Board Independence

These are boards that are not fully disproved but have a very low percentage of independent NEDs (less than 33 percent). These board settings are also frequent in private family-owned firms (although it depends on the phase of evolution of the ownership structure, i.e., founder's phase, siblings' phase, or cousins' phase), as the family structure tends to manage the daily business operations while simultaneously defining the strategy and overseeing the executive committee. However, low board independence is not associated only with family-owned enterprises. Research shows that the firms that operate in countries with weak investor protection are less independent than firms with stronger investor protection. Japanese firms are known for low board independence because of the legacy keiretsu model. Despite being pressured by global asset managers, studies show that most of the Japanese firms only have a few outsiders in the board. Nonetheless, the recent business trend show that the Japanese boards have evolved to some degree to accommodate outside directors.[286]

Balanced Board Independence

The concept of a balanced board is well established in main global capital markets, where the board independence best practice requirements typically range from 33 percent to 75 percent of independent NEDs. Balanced board independence is the result of the discretionary or regulated corporate governance requirements, notably in countries with strong capital markets' activity and regulation such as the UK and the USA. In the European Union, rules vary among countries, although in the financial system landscape—particularly in the eurozone—there is an effort to coordinate guidelines and regulations. Also, countries that do not belong to the eurozone have applied generally the same or even more stringent rules to ensure financial stability.

Full Board Independence

These are the boards dominated fully by independent directors—the best practice—having no executive directors as board members. This model reflects the dualist model that encompasses a supervisory board constituted by non-executive directors (supervisory function) and an executive or management board constituted by executive directors (management function). The monist system requires a clear majority of independent non-executive directors to ensure a robust supervision. Section 3.8: "Unitary Board (Monist) vs Dual Board (Dualist)" discusses this issue in more detail, namely in terms of the dynamics both models allow. Under this rationale, a board fully composed of independent directors is able to better oversee the CEO and executive directors as well as the executive committee as a whole, better protecting the interests of the shareholders and other stakeholders and improving the ability to provide supervision and advice to the executive committee.

However, the full board independence, notably in the dualist model, comes at a price. In this setting, asymmetry of information can be extremely high, as is the potential for the CEO or the executive committee—on purpose or not—to introduce systematic risk to the relationship and to the supervision capability of the supervisory board, as the CEO or the executive committee are the main source of information on business operations and on company execution—tactics and operational. There is a line of thought that argues that fully independent boards are likely to become less effective as they are likely to take decisions based on biased information. Another line of thought advocates that this governance model allows for a more robust decision-making process, as non-independent non-executive directors can discuss issues more openly and, in case of doubt, request the presence of the CEO or the full executive committee to provide additional data and information.

Fully independent boards may also be limited in one of their main duties, which is the evaluation of candidates for the CEO role, as they may have insufficient contact with potential internal candidates (i.e., less firsthand information on senior executives) and therefore may be impelled to choose external candidates; this potential limitation is easily overcome by having a process to identify talented candidates by including both internal and external candidates, as well as by hiring an executive search consultant to assist in the process.

Also, as the pool of high-profile independent non-executive directors is scarce, notably considering the time dedication and commitment currently required, the skills that bring independent expertise to a board as well as the fiduciary responsibility that falls on non-executive directors has reflected an increase in the compensation to properly remunerate and attract qualified directors.

13.4 PROS OF DIRECTOR'S INDEPENDENCE

The pros of director's independence are discussed below.[287]

The Independence

Stakeholders of an organization are likely to have opinions and views biased by personal agendas and/or values, even if they believe they act in the best interest of the company. This is likely to happen, as individuals often act in their self-interest intentionally and are also very often to be affected by emotions they are not aware of, which leads to a lack of independent decision-making. Independent members with reputation, financial independence, and flawless stance can possibly identify potential issues affecting the business, the business model and its sustainability, provide advice for the long term, and produce an unbiased, independent view and opinion.

The Compensation and Executives' Agreements Factor

The compensation and remuneration packages are a major factor for incentive alignment within a corporate. Determining the appropriate benefits is usually challenging. If compensation is not sufficient to promote the right level of motivation to executives, it may result in a negative outcome for the firm such as opportunistic and even selfish behavior. Management should not be overpaid or underpaid; the package has to be accordingly linked to fit with the right incentives as well as the profile and responsibilities of a director. The adequacy of packages for both non-executive directors, directors, senior management, and employees can bring a sense of fairness in an organization, decreasing the possibility of biased behavior or lack of commitment.

Credibility

After many accounting and corporate scandals that have been seen in recent history—such as WorldCom, Parmalat, Tyco, Enron, WireCard—transparency and accountability became a very hot topic for investors (both shareholders and bondholders) and stakeholders, notably the staff. This applies to accountability of both correct and transparent financial reporting as well as the way decision-making practices were conducted. Having an independent board with respected members who are fit and proper to the job is critical for potential investors. Although a board member with a good reputation may create a halo effect for the firm—such as by being the chair—it is relevant to have a consistent board in terms of the talent of non-executive directors.

Advice on Competing Interests

Competing interests could arise in many situations and are very common in family-run businesses. An outside director can help in the negotiation process, becoming a facilitator for efficient solutions in competing interests of family members, although the process should not be addressed only when issues emerge in the family, as that can be too late. Succession planning and family members' employment are only two of the critical issues, but there is a series of other governance considerations, like the fit and proper development process of family members or the sustained payment of dividends that should be structured properly and orderly to ensure a robust family governance framework to avoid agency matters among shareholders and the family, which very often causes problems in family businesses, notably resulting in the loss of value and putting the sustainability of the business at risk. Another very relevant consideration relates to the need to respect family members opting for own personal or professional avenues, hinging on family governance framework that protects them from shareholders.

Outside Expertise and Skills

Expertise and skills from different sectors and geographies are often brought from independent directors. Uncommon skills bring diversity to the board, allowing for a better, more thoughtful discussion in terms of the decision-making process.

Formal Board Environment

The presence of outside directors tends to bring a formal stance to the board meetings, which often disappears when outside participation is lacking. Formality could lead to better-structured agendas; adoption of robust formalities can be essential to ensure proper governance and to clearly inform the board in advance on the plan for these meeting in order to allow better preparation from the members.

13.5 CONS OF DIRECTOR'S INDEPENDENCE

The cons of director's independence are discussed below.[288]

Artificial Interests

Compared to executive directors' interests, it may be possible that the outsiders' interests are not as clearly linked to the firm's performance. They can bring independent opinions and views about different topics and alternatives to address them, but their ability to really engage in the process could be questionable. They are paid to serve on the board and bring expertise, but it is likely that they are not really involved and do not give their best commitment and knowledge, as non-executive directors may have an impression that they are not as incentivized as executive directors, which is actually a nonargument. This is a reason why non-executive directors should be paid properly, that is, to compensate for the fiduciary risk they assume and the time they need to invest in preparing and challenging executive directors.

The remuneration of non-executive directors and members of audit boards is an issue that regulators and supervisors should regulate, for example, by indexing it to the remuneration of executive directors. Currently there is a line of thought advocating that non-executive directors' remuneration should be similar to the fixed remuneration of an executive director.

Serving on Multiple Boards and Lack of Equal Effort

The engagement of independent directors in several boards may suggest they may not act at their best when they serve on several boards. One argument relates to the time available to dedicate to all the boards' assignments, while another one raises questions relating to the placement of higher priority on valuable firms to which a non-executive director tends—even involuntarily—to dedicate more attention and effort. For the financial system, ECB regulates that a non-executive director of a significant institution can only hold one executive directorship and two non-executive directorships, or four non-executive directorships, discussed in Section 17.5.2: "Assessment of Time Commitment of Non-executive Directors."

The Lack of Clarity of Extent of Liability

As directors are responsible to govern the institution, non-executive directors may be held legally liable in unexpected stress circumstances. This is one of the reasons why Directors and Officers Liability Insurance (D&O) has come into existence. However, the clarity on this matter varies among jurisdictions and the specific qualification of crimes for decisions or omissions, and its impact in terms of civil responsibility relating to personal liability is often an objective of lawsuits. Increased litigation may possibly lead to risk aversion and heightened conservativeness. It is relevant to mention that the D&O is forbidden in some jurisdictions with the objective of ensuring that the directors, notably non-executive directors, do not refrain from making difficult decisions resulting from the exercise of their supervision powers, roles, and responsibility. There are also companies (e.g., Berkshire Hathaway[289]) that do not allow non-executive directors to integrate the board if they require the D&O insurance; a decision based on the company demands that independent non-executive directors act when they deem necessary by opposition of not acting, as the director has the fiduciary responsibility covered by a D&O policy.

Topics of the Chapter
The following has been discussed within this chapter:

- With regards to members of the board, independence refers to an absence of present or recent relationships or links of any nature with the institution or its management that may influence their objective and balanced judgment.
- Conflicts of interests involve impartiality and objectivity of a decision.
- The degree of independence of a board is defined as:
  1. Zero Independence.
  2. Low Independence.
  3. Balanced Independence.
  4. Full Independence.

Independence of the board can have advantages, as well as disadvantages that should be considered according to the structure and characteristics of the corporate. This may be a challenging but very relevant issue in the family business arena.

Chapter 14

Fiduciary Duties, Board Effectiveness, and Dynamics

Board effectiveness can be harnessed through the adequate knowledge of the principles of the corporate governance, the best practices required for an efficient and effective board, and the knowledge of the fiduciary duties and responsibilities undertaken by the board members and by senior management. This chapter discusses in detail the principles of corporate governance—as defined by G20/OECD and by BCBS—and the fiduciary duties of the board, followed by the concepts of board effectiveness, board dynamics and board agendas.

14.1 PRINCIPLES OF CORPORATE GOVERNANCE

Although the approach for an effective governance varies, according to the size of companies and complexity of business models as well as the cultural environment, it is widely agreed that several guidelines and structures about the principles of corporate governance should apply. Any aspiring chair, non-executive director, executive director, or anyone—like first-line managers—who are connected to a board's activity must be familiar with the fundamental principles of corporate governance and the reason a good corporate governance is vital. Although this responsibility belongs fundamentally to the board members (i.e., keep themselves fit and proper for their responsibilities), there is also a large responsibility that lands on companies to ensure the fitness and propriety of its board members to assume that position and to maintain and develop the required skills, and close the gap, if a particular skill should be improved.

The first includes the conscience for the need to be prepared and updated about emerging trends in corporate governance as well as in the corporate world, and the latter includes the need for a proper organizational structure to support the board activities, a strong induction program for the new members, a robust training program for current and new members, and a clear and transparent succession plan. All these topics are the responsibility of the board, although the chair plays a relevant role leading and dynamizing the process, ensuring that committees of the board develop and propose actions to achieve those objectives.

G20/OECD Principles of Corporate Governance and Financial Reporting Council (FRC UK) Guidance on Board Effectiveness (both referenced in Section 1.2.3: "Global Financial Crisis 2007–2008 and Increased Governance") have proposed detailed recommendations. Also, BCBS Principles of Corporate Governance (also referenced in Section 1.2.3: "Global Financial Crisis 2007–2008 and Increased Governance") include detailed guidelines, namely 13 principles for financial system institutions, which may also be leveraged by the nonfinancial system.

14.1.1 G20/OECD PRINCIPLES OF CORPORATE GOVERNANCE

G20/OECD (www.oecd.org) Principles of Corporate Governance are meant for both financial and nonfinancial publicly traded companies. Essentially, the principles are developed to help policymakers evaluate and improve the legal, regulatory, and institutional framework for corporate governance. Earlier chapters discuss and present corporate governance theories, definitions, and conceptual frameworks, which are relevant to understand the G20/OECD principles.

The G20/OECD principles and sub-principles are designed in six different chapters. Each chapter has one primary principle supported by sub-principles. The titles of the chapters are stated in Figure 14.1.

Figure 14.1: G20/OECD principles of corporate governance

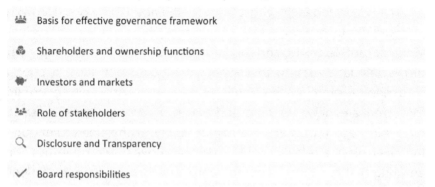

Basis for effective governance framework

Shareholders and ownership functions

Investors and markets

Role of stakeholders

Disclosure and Transparency

Board responsibilities

The chapters, principles, and sub-principals are discussed below, as they constitute a global and general guideline. The fashion in which the guidelines are applied may vary, depending on the legal frameworks. Also, the best practice principles to be applied for a good governance are expected to go beyond the minimum standards required, a factor that can be considered when evaluating the level of governance an institution adopts.

Chapter I: *Ensuring the basis for an effective corporate governance framework*

The first OECD principle relates to the basis for effective governance framework that should promote transparent and fair markets and the efficient allocation of resources, notably talent and capital. It should be consistent with the rule of law and support effective supervision and enforcement. As the corporate governance framework typically comprises elements of legislation, regulation, self-regulatory arrangements, voluntary commitments, and business practices that are the result of a country's specific circumstances, history, and tradition, effective corporate governance requires a sound legal, regulatory, and institutional framework. What works well in one company, for one investor, or for a particular stakeholder, may not necessarily be generally applicable to corporations, investors, and stakeholders that operate in another context and under different circumstances, which is why the characteristics of a business model should be imbibed in the governance framework. While developing a corporate governance framework, national legislators and regulators should duly consider the need for, and the results from, effective international dialogue and cooperation. If these conditions are met, the corporate governance framework is more likely to avoid overregulation, support the exercise of entrepreneurship, and limit the risks of damaging potential conflicts of interest or actual conflicts of interest, in both the private sector and in public institutions.

This principle is supported by several sub-principles, the first being the promotion of transparent and fair markets and the efficient allocation of resources, aligned and consistent with the rule of law and support effective supervision and enforcement. As the corporate form of organization of economic activity is a powerful force for growth, the regulatory and legal environment within which corporations operate is, therefore, critical to overall economic outcomes. Policymakers also have a responsibility to develop a framework that is flexible enough to meet the needs of corporations while remaining focused on ultimate economic outcomes. When considering policy options, they need to undertake an analysis of the impact on key variables that affect the functioning of markets, such as the efficiency of self-regulatory systems and dealing with systemic conflicts of interest when considering the terms of incentive structures.

The second sub-principle relates to the legal and regulatory requirements that affect corporate governance practices, which should be consistent with the rule of law, transparent, and enforceable. Laws and regulations should be designed in a way that makes them possible to implement and enforce in an efficient and even-handed manner covering all parties. Consultation by government and other regulatory authorities with corporations, their representative organizations, and other stakeholders is an effective way of doing this and avoiding overregulation. Public authorities should have effective enforcement and sanctioning powers to deter dishonest behavior and provide sound corporate governance practices. When codes and principles are used as a national standard or as a complement to legal or regulatory provisions, market credibility requires that their status in terms of coverage, implementation, compliance, and sanctions is clearly specified.

The third sub-principle states that the division of responsibilities among different authorities should be clearly articulated and designed to serve the public interest, as corporate governance requirements and practices are typically influenced by an array of legal domains such as company law, securities regulation, accounting and auditing standards, insolvency law, contract law, labor law, and tax law. Also, corporate governance practices of individual companies are often influenced by human rights and environmental laws. There is a risk that the variety of legal influences may cause unintentional overlaps and even conflicts, which may affect the ability to pursue key corporate governance objectives. It is important that policymakers are aware of this risk and take measures to limit it. Effective enforcement also requires that the allocation of responsibilities for supervision, implementation, and enforcement among different authorities is clearly defined, so that the competencies of complementary bodies and agencies are respected and used most effectively. In situations when regulatory responsibilities or oversight are delegated to non-public bodies, it is desirable to explicitly assess why, and under what circumstances, such delegation is desirable.

The fourth sub-principle discusses stock market's regulation, which should support effective corporate governance. Stock markets can play a meaningful role in enhancing corporate governance by establishing and enforcing requirements that promote effective corporate governance by their listed issuers. Also, stock markets provide facilities by which investors can express interest or disinterest in a particular issuer's governance by allowing them to buy or sell the issuer's securities as appropriate. Regardless of the particular structure of the stock market, policy makers and regulators should assess the proper role of stock exchanges and trading venues in terms of standard setting, supervision, and enforcement of corporate governance rules.

The fifth sub-principle relates to the guidelines that supervisory, regulatory, and enforcement authorities should have the authority, integrity, and resources to fulfill their duties in a professional and objective manner. Moreover, their rulings should be timely, transparent, and fully explained.

Supervisory, regulatory, and enforcement responsibilities should be vested with bodies that are operationally independent and accountable in the exercise of their functions and powers and have adequate powers, proper resources, and capacity to perform their functions and exercise their powers, including with respect to corporate governance. Many countries have addressed the issue of political independence of the securities supervisor through the creation of a formal governing body (such as a board, council, or commission) whose members are given fixed terms of appointment. If the appointments are staggered and made independent from the political calendar, they can further enhance independence.

The sixth sub-principle relates to ways in which cross-border cooperation should be enhanced, including through bilateral and multilateral arrangements for exchange of information. International cooperation is becoming increasingly relevant for corporate governance, notably where companies are active in many jurisdictions, through both listed and unlisted entities, and seek multiple stock market listings on exchanges in different jurisdictions. Cross-border ownership and trading require strong international cooperation among regulators, including through bilateral and multilateral arrangements for exchange of information. This issue gained particular relevance, notably in the fight against money laundering, financing of terrorism, and weapons of mass destruction.

Chapter II *The rights and equitable treatment of shareholders and key ownership functions*

This OECD principle states that the corporate governance framework should protect and facilitate the exercise of shareholders' rights and ensure the equitable treatment of all shareholders, including minority and foreign shareholders. All shareholders should have the opportunity to obtain effective redress for violation of their rights, as an equity share entitles the investor to have certain property rights and participate in the profits of the corporation, with liability limited to the amount of the investment. In addition, ownership of an equity share provides a right to information about the corporation and a right to influence the corporation, primarily by participation in general shareholder meetings and by voting. However, the corporation cannot be managed by shareholder referendum.

The shareholding body is made up of individuals and institutions whose interests, goals, investment horizons, and capabilities vary. Moreover, the corporation's management must be able to take business decisions rapidly. In light of these realities and the complexity of managing the corporation's affairs in fast moving and ever-changing markets, shareholders are not expected to assume responsibility for managing corporate activities. Therefore, shareholders' rights to influence the corporation center on certain fundamental issues, such as the election of board members or other means of influencing the composition of the board, amendments to the company's organic documents, approval of extraordinary transactions, and other basic issues as specified in company law and internal company statutes.

Investors' confidence that the capital they provide will be protected from misuse or misappropriation by corporate managers, board members, or controlling shareholders is an important factor in the development and proper functioning of capital markets. Corporate boards, managers, and controlling shareholders may have the opportunity to engage in activities that advance their own interests at the expense of noncontrolling shareholders. In providing protection to investors, a distinction can usefully be made between ex ante and ex post shareholder rights. Ex ante rights are, for example, preemptive rights and qualified majorities for certain decisions. Ex post rights allow the seeking of redress once rights have been violated. Besides, the confidence of minority investors is enhanced when the legal system provides mechanisms for minority shareholders to bring lawsuits when they have reasonable grounds to believe that their rights have been violated. However, there is some risk that a legal system that enables any investor to challenge corporate activity in the courts can become prone to litigation. Thus, many legal systems have introduced provisions to protect management and board members against litigation abuse in the form of tests for the sufficiency of shareholder complaints, so-called safe harbors for management and board member actions (such as the business judgment rule), as well as safe harbors for the disclosure of information. In the end, a balance must be struck between allowing investors to seek remedies for infringement of ownership rights and avoiding excessive litigation. This principle is subdivided into eight sub-principles summarized in the next paragraphs.

The first sub-principle is about the shareholder rights. Basic shareholder rights should include the right to secure methods of ownership registration; convey or transfer shares; obtain relevant and material information on the corporation on a timely and regular basis; participate and vote in general shareholder meetings; elect and remove members of the board; and share in the profits of the corporation.

The second sub-principle relates to shareholders that they should be sufficiently informed about, and have the right to approve or participate in, decisions concerning fundamental corporate changes such as amendments to the statutes, articles of incorporation, or similar governing documents of the company; the authorization of additional shares; and extraordinary transactions, including the transfer of all or substantially all assets, which in effect results in the sale of the company.

The third sub-principle states that shareholders should have the opportunity to participate effectively and vote in general shareholder meetings and should be informed of the rules (including voting procedures) that govern general shareholder meetings. Shareholders should be furnished with sufficient and timely information regarding the date, location, and agenda of general meetings as well as full and timely information regarding the issues to be discussed at the meeting. Processes and procedures for general shareholders' meetings should allow for equitable treatment of all shareholders. Company procedures should not make it unduly difficult or expensive to cast votes. Shareholders should have the opportunity to ask questions to the board (including questions relating to the annual external audit), to place items on the agenda of general meetings, and to propose resolutions, subject to reasonable limitations. Effective shareholder participation in key corporate governance decisions, such as the nomination and election of board members, should be facilitated. Shareholders should be able to make their views known, including through votes at shareholder meetings, on the remuneration of board members and/or key executives, as applicable. The equity component of compensation schemes for board members and employees should be subject to shareholder approval. Shareholders should be able to vote in person or in absentia, and equal weight should be given to votes whether cast in person or in absentia. The principles recommend that voting by proxy be generally accepted. Any impediments to cross-border voting should be eliminated, as foreign investors often hold their shares through chains of intermediaries.

The fourth sub-principle states that shareholders, including institutional shareholders, should be allowed to consult with each other on issues concerning their basic shareholder rights as defined in the principles, subject to exceptions to prevent abuse. In companies with dispersed ownership, individual shareholders might have too small—minority shareholders discussed in the seventh sub-principle—a stake in the company to warrant the cost of taking action or for making an investment in monitoring performance. Moreover, if small shareholders did invest resources in such activities, others would also gain without having contributed, being considered "free riders." In order to overcome this asymmetry institutional shareholders should be allowed, and even encouraged to cooperate and coordinate their actions in nominating and electing board members, placing proposals on the agenda and holding discussions directly with a company in order to improve its corporate governance. Shareholders should be allowed to communicate with each other without having to comply with the formalities of proxy solicitation.

The fifth sub-principle states that all shareholders of the same series of a class should be treated equally. Capital structures and arrangements that enable certain shareholders to obtain a degree of influence or control disproportionate to their equity ownership should be disclosed. Within any series of a class, all shares should carry the same rights. All investors should be able to obtain information about the rights attached to all series and classes of shares before they purchase. Any changes in economic or voting rights should be subject to approval by those classes of shares which are negatively affected. As the optimal capital structure of the firm is best decided by the management and the board, subject to the approval of the shareholders, investors can expect to be informed regarding their voting rights before they invest. After they have invested, their rights should not be changed unless those holding voting shares have had the opportunity to participate in the decision. The disclosure of capital structures and control arrangements should be required. Some capital structures allow a shareholder to exercise a degree of control over the corporation disproportionate to the shareholders' equity ownership in the company. Pyramid structures, cross shareholdings, and shares with limited or multiple voting rights can be used to diminish the capability of noncontrolling shareholders to influence corporate policy. Given the capacity of these mechanisms to redistribute the influence of shareholders on company policy, the disclosure of such capital structures and arrangements should be required.

The sixth sub-principle is about related party transactions. It should be approved and conducted in a manner that ensures proper management of conflict of interest and protects the interest of the company and its shareholders. Conflicts of interest inherent in related party transactions should be addressed. The potential abuse of related party transactions is an important policy issue in all markets, particularly in those where corporate ownership is concentrated, and corporate groups prevail. Jurisdictions should put in place an effective framework for clearly flagging these transactions. They include broad but precise definitions of what is understood to be a related party as well as rules to disregard some of these transactions, when they are not material because they do not exceed ex ante thresholds, and can be regarded as recurrent and taking place at verifiable market terms or taking place with subsidiaries where no specific interest of a related party is present. Once the related party transactions have been identified, jurisdictions set procedures for approving them in a manner that minimizes their negative potential. Members of the board and key executives should be required to disclose to the board whether they—directly, indirectly, or on behalf of third parties—have a material interest in any transaction or matter directly affecting the corporation.

The seventh sub-principle relates to minority shareholders that should be protected from abusive actions by, or in the interest of, controlling shareholders acting either directly or indirectly, and should have effective means of redress. Abusive self-dealing occurs when persons having close relationships to the company—including controlling shareholders—exploit those relationships to the detriment of the company and investors, and it should be prohibited.

The potential for abuse is marked where the legal system allows, and the market accepts, controlling shareholders to exercise a level of control that does not correspond to the level of risk they assume as owners through exploiting legal devices to separate ownership from control, such as pyramid structures or multiple voting rights. Such abuse may be carried out in various ways, including the extraction of direct private benefits through high pay and bonuses for employed family members and associates, inappropriate related party transactions, systematic bias in business decisions, and changes in the capital structure through special issuance of shares favoring the controlling shareholder. In addition to disclosure, a key to protecting minority shareholders is a clearly articulated duty of loyalty of board members to the company and to all shareholders. Other common provisions to protect minority shareholders, which have proven effective, include pre-emptive rights in relation to share issues, qualified majorities for certain shareholder decisions, and the possibility to use cumulative voting in electing members of the board.

The eight sub-principle relates to markets for corporate control, which should be allowed to function in an efficient and transparent manner. The rules and procedures governing the acquisition of corporate control in the capital markets and extraordinary transactions such as mergers and sales of substantial portions of corporate assets should be clearly articulated and disclosed so that investors understand their rights and recourse. Transactions should occur at transparent prices and under fair conditions that protect the rights of all shareholders according to their class. Anti-takeover devices should not be used to shield management and the board from accountability.

Chapter III: *Institutional investors, stock markets, and other intermediaries*
This OECD principle relates to the corporate governance framework that should provide sound incentives throughout the investment chain and provide for stock markets to function in a way that contributes to

good corporate governance. Real world of corporate governance and ownership is no longer characterized by a straight and uncompromised relationship between the performance of the company and the income of the ultimate beneficiaries of shareholdings. It has grown long and complex. The share of equity investments held by institutional investors such as mutual funds, pension funds, insurance companies, and hedge funds has increased significantly, and many of their assets are managed by specialized asset managers. The ability and interest of institutional investors and asset managers to engage in corporate governance varies widely. For some, engagement in corporate governance, including the exercise of voting rights, is a natural part of their business model. Others may offer their beneficiaries and clients a business model and investment strategy that does not include or motivate spending resources on active shareholder engagement. The principles recommend that institutional investors disclose their policies with respect to corporate governance. Voting at shareholder meetings is, however, only one channel for shareholder engagement. Direct contact and dialogue with the board and management represent other forms of shareholder engagement that are frequently used. This OECD principle is subdivided into seven sub-principles summarized in the next paragraphs.

The first sub-principle mentions that institutional investors acting in a fiduciary capacity should disclose their corporate governance and voting policies with respect to their investments, including the procedures that they have in place for deciding on the use of their voting rights. The effectiveness and credibility of the entire corporate governance framework and company oversight depend to a large extent on institutional investors' willingness and ability to make informed use of their shareholder rights and effectively exercise their ownership functions in companies in which they invest. While this principle does not require institutional investors to vote their shares, it calls for disclosure of how they exercise their ownership rights with due consideration to cost effectiveness. For institutions acting in a fiduciary capacity—such as pension funds, collective investment schemes, and some activities of insurance companies—and asset managers acting on their behalf, the right to vote can be considered part of the value of the investment being undertaken on behalf of their clients. When institutional investors have developed and disclosed a corporate governance policy, effective implementation necessitates that they also set aside the appropriate human and financial resources to pursue this policy in a way that their beneficiaries and portfolio companies can expect.

The second sub-principle states that votes should be cast by custodians or nominees in line with the directions of the beneficial owner of the shares. Custodian institutions holding securities as nominees for customers should not be permitted to cast the votes on those securities unless they have received specific instructions to do so. In some jurisdictions, listing requirements contain broad lists of items on which custodians may not vote without instruction, while leaving this possibility open for certain routine items. Rules should require custodian institutions to provide shareholders with timely information concerning their options in the exercise of their voting rights. Shareholders may elect to vote by themselves or to delegate all voting rights to custodians. Alternatively, shareholders may choose to be informed of all upcoming shareholder votes and may decide to cast some votes while delegating some voting rights to the custodian. Holders of depository receipts should be provided with the same ultimate rights and practical opportunities to participate in corporate governance as are accorded to holders of the underlying shares. It should also be noted that this principle does not apply to the exercise of voting rights by trustees or other persons acting under a special legal mandate, including bankruptcy receivers and estate executors.

A recommendation about this second sub-principle covering institutional custodians (e.g., banks) or nominees, relates to the deposit of securities of companies or banks with which an institutional custodian may have potential conflicts of interests. Institutional custodians know the decisions communicated by the securities' owners or the ones communicated by the proxy agencies on their behalf. Although institutional custodians adhere to high ethical standards, there is a risk of a potential conflict of interest to emerge in similar situations (e.g., custody of shares of the selected institutional custodian itself), reason why a due diligence process should be conducted to ensure that the elected institutional custodian is free of potential conflicts of interests.

The third sub-principle states that institutional investors acting in a fiduciary capacity should disclose how they manage material conflicts of interest that may affect the exercise of key ownership rights regarding their investments. Institutions should disclose what actions they are taking to minimize the potentially negative impact on their ability to exercise key ownership rights. Such actions may include the separation of bonuses for fund management from those related to the acquisition of new business elsewhere in the organization. Fee structures for asset management and other intermediary services should be transparent.

The fourth sub-principle states that the corporate governance framework should require that proxy advisors, analysts, brokers, rating agencies and others provide analysis or advice relevant to decisions by investors and disclose and minimize conflicts of interest that might compromise the integrity of their analysis or advice. The investment chain from ultimate owners to corporations does not only involve multiple intermediary owners. It also includes a wide variety of professions that offer advice and services to intermediary owners. Proxy advisors who offer recommendations to institutional investors on how to vote and sell services that help in the process of voting are among the most relevant from a direct corporate governance perspective. In some cases, proxy advisors also offer corporate governance related consulting services to corporations. Other service providers rate companies according to various corporate governance criteria. Analysts, brokers, and rating agencies perform similar roles and face the same potential conflicts of interest, as institutional custodians (e.g., banks).

The fifth sub-principle states that insider trading and market manipulation should be prohibited, and the applicable rules should be enforced.

The sixth sub-principle states that, for companies are listed in a jurisdiction other than their jurisdiction of incorporation, the applicable corporate governance laws and regulations should be clearly disclosed. In the case of cross listings, the criteria and procedure for recognizing the listing requirements of the primary listing should be transparent and documented.

The seventh sub-principle states that the stock markets should provide fair and efficient price discovery as a means to help promote effective corporate governance.

Chapter IV: *The role of stakeholders in corporate governance*
The principle states that the corporate governance framework should recognize the rights of stakeholders established by law or through mutual agreements and encourage active cooperation among corporations and stakeholders in creating wealth, jobs, and sustainability of financially sound enterprises. A key aspect of corporate governance is concerned with ensuring the flow of external capital to companies, both in the form of equity and credit (e.g., bondholders and the financial system). Corporate governance is also concerned with finding ways to encourage the various stakeholders in the firm to undertake economically optimal levels of investment in firm-specific human and physical capital. The competitiveness and ultimate success of a corporation is the result of teamwork that embodies contributions from a range of different resource providers including investors, employees, creditors, customers and suppliers, and other stakeholders.

The first sub-principle relates to the rights of stakeholders that are established by law (e.g., labor, business, commercial, environmental, and insolvency laws) or through mutual agreements (e.g., contracts), as well as in guidelines and recommendations that need to be respected. However, even in areas where stakeholder interests are not legislated, many firms make additional commitments to stakeholders, and concern over corporate reputation and corporate performance often requires the recognition of broader interests.

The second sub-principle states that where stakeholder interests are protected by law, stakeholders should have the opportunity to obtain effective be compensated for the violation of their rights.

The third sub-principle states that the mechanisms for employee participation should be permitted to develop. The degree to which employees participate in corporate governance depends on national laws and practices and vary among organizations as well. In the context of corporate governance, mechanisms for participation may benefit companies directly as well as indirectly, such as through the readiness of employees to invest in firm-specific skills. Examples of mechanisms for employee participation include employee or unions representation on boards and governance processes, such as works councils that consider employee viewpoints in certain key decisions. International conventions and national norms also recognize the rights of employees to information, consultation, and negotiation. With respect to performance enhancing mechanisms, employee stock ownership plans or other profit-sharing mechanisms are prevalent in many countries. Pension commitments are also often an element of the relationship between the company and its past and current employees.

The fourth sub-principle states that where stakeholders participate in the corporate governance process, they should have access to relevant, sufficient, and reliable information on a timely and regular basis, avoiding unjustifiably asymmetry of data and information.

The fifth sub-principle states that stakeholders, including individual employees and their representative bodies, should be able to freely communicate their concerns about illegal or unethical practices to the board and to the competent public authorities, and their rights should not be compromised for doing this. Unethical and illegal practices by corporate officers may not only violate the rights of stakeholders but also be to the detriment of the organization and its shareholders both in terms of reputation effects and an increasing risk of future financial liabilities. It is therefore to the advantage of the company and its shareholders to establish procedures, notably relating to clear and structured mechanisms of whistleblowing, and safe harbors for complaints by employees—either personally or through their representative bodies and others outside the company—regarding illegal and unethical behavior. The board should be encouraged by laws and/or principles to protect these individuals and representative bodies and to give them confidential direct access to someone independent on the board, often a member of an audit or ethics committee.

The sixth sub-principle relates to the corporate governance framework being complemented by an effective, efficient insolvency framework and by effective enforcement of creditor rights. In many jurisdictions, when companies are nearing insolvency, the legislative framework imposes a duty on directors to act in the interests of creditors, who might therefore play a prominent role in the governance of the company. Other countries have mechanisms that encourage the debtor to reveal timely information about the company's difficulties so that a consensual solution can be found between the debtor and its creditors.

In many jurisdictions, the biggest challenges in an insolvency process include the lack of transparency, as well as a lack of strict and clear rules—or its effective and efficient application—to mitigate and avoid conflicts of interests in a typical process that often lacks proper supervision, even with the involvement of courts.

Chapter V: Disclosure and Transparency

The principle relates to the corporate governance framework that should ensure that timely and accurate disclosure is made on all material matters regarding the corporation, including the financial situation, performance, ownership, and governance. Public disclosure is typically required, at a minimum, on an annual basis, though some countries require periodic disclosure on a semi-annual or quarterly basis, or even more frequently, in the case of material developments affecting the company. Companies often make voluntary disclosure that goes beyond minimum disclosure requirements in response to market demand. The Principles support timely disclosure of all material developments that arise between regular reports. Disclosure requirements are not expected to place unreasonable administrative or cost burdens on enterprises, nor are companies expected to disclose information that may endanger their competitive position, unless such disclosure is necessary to fully inform the investment decision and to avoid misleading the investor. A strong disclosure regime—both financial and nonfinancial matters—that promotes real transparency is a pivotal feature of market-based monitoring of companies and is central to shareholders' ability to exercise their rights on an informed basis. Experience shows that disclosure can also be a powerful tool for influencing the behavior of companies and protecting investors. A strong disclosure regime can help attract capital and maintain confidence in the capital markets and the financial system. By contrast, weak disclosure and non-transparent practices, as well as managing asymmetry of data and information, contribute to unethical behavior and a loss of market integrity at great cost to the company, its shareholders and stakeholders, as well as to the economy and society as a whole. This chapter is detailed into five OECD sub-principles summarized below.

The first sub-principle relates to disclosure. It should include, but not be limited to:

- Material information on the audited financial and operating results of the company.
- Company objectives and nonfinancial information, such as relating to business ethics, the environment and—where

material to the company—social issues, human rights, and other public policy commitments (e.g., ESG).

- Major share ownership (including beneficial owners) and voting rights.
- Remuneration of members of the board and key executives.
- Information about board members, including their qualifications, the selection process, other company directorships, and whether they are regarded as independent by the board.
- Related party transactions, fully disclosing all material related party transactions, and the terms of such transactions to the market individually.
- Foreseeable risk factors (risks that are specific to the industry or the geographical areas in which the company operates), dependence on commodities, financial market risks including interest rate or currency risk, risk related to derivatives and off-balance sheet transactions, business conduct risks, and risks related to the environment.
- Issues regarding employees and relevant stakeholders.

Essentially, information should be provided on key issues relevant to employees and other stakeholders that may materially affect the performance of the company or that may have significant impacts upon them.
Disclosure may also include:

- Management/employee relations, including remuneration, collective bargaining coverage, and mechanisms for employee representation.
- Relations with other stakeholders such as creditors, suppliers, and local communities.
- Governance structures and policies, including the content of any corporate governance code or policy and the process by which it is implemented.

The second sub-principle mentions that information should be prepared and disclosed in accordance with high-quality standards of accounting and financial and nonfinancial reporting.

The third sub-principle relates to an annual audit that should be conducted by an independent, competent, and qualified auditor, in accordance with high-quality auditing standards, in order to provide an external and objective assurance to the board and shareholders that the financial statements fairly represent the financial position and performance of the company in all material respects. In addition to certifying that the financial statements represent the financial position of a company fairly, the audit statement should also include an opinion on the way financial statements have been prepared and presented, as well as the key audit matters identified in the audit and the fashion management addressed and/or plans to address matters that may represent future current or future challenges. The independence of auditors and their accountability to shareholders should be required. It is good practice for external auditors to be recommended by an independent audit committee of the board or an equivalent body (e.g., audit board in some jurisdictions) and to be appointed either by that committee/body or by shareholders directly. The audit committee or an equivalent body—in its functional supervisory role—should provide oversight of the internal audit activities and should also be charged with overseeing the overall relationship with the external auditor, including the nature of non-audit services that may or not be provided by the external auditor to the company. This issue should be clearly defined in the rules and procedures; several jurisdictions limit the amount or percentage of non-audit services that the external auditor can provide, with a growing number of organizations do not allowing external auditors to provide non-audit services—basically, consultancy—at all. Provision of non-audit services by the external auditor to a company can significantly impair their independence and might involve them auditing their own work. To deal with the skewed incentives that may arise, the disclosure of payments to external auditors for non-audit services should be required. Examples of other provisions designed to promote auditor independence include a total ban or severe limitation on the nature of non-audit work that can be undertaken by an auditor for their audit client, mandatory rotation of auditors (either partners or in some cases the audit partnership), a fixed tenure for auditors, joint audits, a temporary ban on the employment of an ex-auditor by the audited company, and prohibiting auditors or their dependents from having a financial stake or management role in the companies they audit.

A challenge that has emerged from these rules relates to the need for a company to monitor the amount and volume of non-audit services, for example provided by the big four (Deloitte, PwC, KPMG, and EY), as it may block them from bidding for an external audit assignment, which may pose significant challenges to a company if the desire is to hire one of the big four.

The fourth sub-principle mentions that external auditors should be accountable to the shareholders and owe a duty to the company to exercise due professional care in the conduct of the audit. The practice that external auditors are recommended by an independent audit committee of the board or an equivalent body and that external auditors are appointed either by that committee/body or by the shareholders' meeting directly can be regarded as good practice, since it clarifies that the external auditor should be accountable to the shareholders. It also underlines that the external auditor owes a duty of due professional care to the company rather than any individual or group of corporate managers that they may interact with for the purpose of their work.

The fifth sub-principle states that channels for disseminating information should provide for equal, timely, and cost-efficient access to relevant information by users. Channels for the dissemination of information can be as important as the content of the information itself. While the disclosure of information is often provided for by legislation, filing and access to information can be cumbersome and costly. Filing of statutory reports has been greatly enhanced in some countries by electronic filing and data retrieval systems. OECD recommends that countries should move to the next stage by integrating different sources of company information, including shareholder filings. Company websites also provide the opportunity for improving information dissemination, and some countries now require companies to have a website that provides relevant and significant information about the company itself.

Chapter VI: *The responsibilities of the board*

This OECD principle states that the corporate governance framework should ensure the strategic guidance of the company, the effective monitoring of management by the board, and the board's accountability to the company and the shareholders. Along with guiding corporate strategy, the board is chiefly responsible for monitoring managerial performance and achieving an adequate return for shareholders and stakeholders, while preventing conflicts of interest and balancing competing demands on the corporation ensuring sustainability. In order for boards to effectively fulfill their responsibilities, they must be able to exercise objective and independent judgment. Another important board responsibility is to oversee the risk management system and compliance systems, which are designed to ensure that the corporation obeys applicable laws, including tax, competition, labor, environmental, equal opportunity, health, and safety laws. The board is not only accountable to the company and its shareholders but also has a duty to act in their best interests. In addition, boards are expected to take due regard of, and deal fairly with, other stakeholder interests, including those of employees, creditors, customers, suppliers, and local communities. Observance of environmental and social standards is also relevant in this context. This OECD principle is subdivided into seven sub-principles summarized in the next paragraphs.

The first sub-principle mentions that board members should act and decide on a fully informed basis, in good faith, with due diligence and care, and in the best interest of the company, the shareholders and stakeholders. The board is legally required in most jurisdictions to act in the interest of the company, taking into account the interests of shareholders, employees, and the public good. Acting in the best interest of the company should not permit management to become entrenched. This principle states the two key elements of the fiduciary duty of board members—*the duty of care* and *the duty of loyalty*, to which *the duty of obedience* should be added.

The duty of care requires board members to act on a fully informed basis, in good faith, and with due diligence and care. The duty of loyalty is of central importance, since it underpins effective implementation of other principles in this document relating to, for example, the equitable treatment of shareholders, monitoring of related party transactions, and the establishment of remuneration policy for key executives and board members. The duty of obedience requires directors to be faithful to the organization's mission.

The second sub-principle states that where board decisions may affect different shareholder groups differently, the board should treat all shareholders fairly, notably the minority shareholders that have little or no influence in the management. In carrying out its duties, the board should not be viewed, or act, as an assembly of individual representatives for various constituencies. While specific board members may indeed be nominated or elected by certain shareholders (and sometimes contested by others), it is an important feature of the board's work that board members, when they assume their responsibilities, carry out their duties in an even-handed manner with respect to all shareholders. This principle is particularly important to establish in the presence of controlling shareholders that by default may be able to select all board members.

The third sub-principle states that the board should apply high ethical standards with the "tone from the top". It should take into account the interests of stakeholders. The board has a key role in setting the ethical tone of a company, not only by its own actions but also by appointing and overseeing key executives and consequently the management in general. High ethical standards are in the long-term interests of the company as a means to make it credible and trustworthy, not only in day-to-day operations, but also with respect to long-term commitments. To make the objectives of the board clear and operational, many companies have found it useful to develop company codes of conduct based on, among others, professional standards and sometimes broader codes of behavior and to communicate them throughout the organization. Company-wide codes serve as a standard for conduct by both the board and key executives, setting the framework for the exercise of judgment in dealing with varying and often conflicting constituencies.

On top of the above OECD requirements, the board should ensure the publications of an ethical code should set clear limits on the pursuit of private interests, potential conflicts of interest, issues linked to the risk culture, trading of shares, behavior and as best practice demands respective sanctions for violations. It is also relevant the enforcement of training programs for the board and staff—notably to new hires or in boarding members social bodies—with periodic test and signature by all members of the company conforming their detailed knowledge of its content.

The fourth sub-principle states that the board should fulfill certain key functions, including:

- Reviewing and guiding corporate strategy, major plans of action, risk management policies and procedures, annual budgets and business plans; setting performance objectives; monitoring implementation and corporate performance; and overseeing major capital expenditures, acquisitions and divestitures.
- Monitoring the effectiveness of the company's governance practices and making changes as needed.
- Selecting, compensating, monitoring, and—when necessary—replacing key executives and overseeing succession planning.

- Aligning key executive and board remuneration with the longer-term interests of the company and its shareholders, distinguishing between executive and non-executive directors.
- Ensuring a formal and transparent board nomination and election process.
- Monitoring and managing potential conflicts of interest of management, board members, and shareholders, including misuse of corporate assets and abuse in related party transactions.
- Ensuring the integrity of the corporation's accounting and financial reporting systems, including the independent audit, and that appropriate systems of control are in place, particularly systems for risk management, financial and operational control, and compliance with the law and relevant standards.

The fifth OECD sub-principle mentions that board should be able to exercise objective, independent judgment on corporate affairs. In order to exercise its duties of monitoring managerial performance, preventing conflicts of interest, and balancing competing demands on the corporation, it is essential that the board is able to exercise objective judgment. In the first instance, this will mean independence and objectivity with respect to management with important implications for the composition and structure of the board. Board independence in these circumstances usually requires that a sufficient number of board members be independent of management.

The objectivity of the board and its independence from management may be strengthened by the separation of the role of chief executive—execution—and chair—supervision; current guidelines in banking (EBA/2017/11) are clear about the need to separate both roles. The separation of the two posts is the best practice, as it can help achieve an appropriate balance of power, increase accountability, and improve the board's capacity for decision-making independent of management. The chairperson may, in some countries, be supported by a company secretary, but also by a staff cabinet of the chair, when the complexity and size of the organization requires. In the two-tier board model, consideration should be given to whether corporate governance concerns might arise if there is a tradition for the head of the lower board becoming the chair of the supervisory board on retirement, a practice that the best governance principles discourage for several robust arguments. The variety of board structures, ownership patterns, and practices in different countries will thus require different approaches to the issue of board objectivity. In many instances, objectivity requires that a sufficient number of board members not be employed by the company or its affiliates and not be closely related to the company or its management through significant economic, family, or other ties. However, this does not prevent shareholders from being board members. In others, independence from controlling shareholders or another controlling body will need to be emphasized, in particular if the *ex-ante* rights of minority shareholders are weak and opportunities to obtain redress are limited. This has led to both the codes and the law in most jurisdictions to call for some board members to be independent of dominant shareholders, with their independence extending to not being their representative or having close business ties with them.

Independent board members can contribute significantly to the decision-making of the board. They can bring an objective view to the evaluation of the performance of the board and management. In addition, they can play an important role in areas where the interests of management, the company, and its shareholders may diverge, such as executive remuneration, succession planning, changes of corporate control, takeover defenses, large acquisitions, and the audit function. For them to play this key role, it is desirable that boards declare who they consider to be independent and what they consider the criterion for this judgment.

- Boards should consider assigning a sufficient number of non-executive board members capable of exercising independent judgment to tasks where there is a potential for conflict of interest. Examples of such key responsibilities include ensuring the integrity of financial and nonfinancial reporting, the review of related party transactions, nomination of board members and key executives, and board remuneration.
- Boards should consider setting up specialized committees to support the full board in performing its functions, particularly in respect to audit, and—depending upon the company's size and risk profile—also in respect to risk management and remuneration. When committees of the board are established, their mandate, composition, and working procedures should be well defined and disclosed by the board. When not imposed by law, the set-up of a "board taskforce" to deal with a specific topic will be extinguished in a shorter period than the mandate.
- Board members should be able to commit themselves effectively, by setting time to perform their responsibilities and play their role.
- Boards should regularly carry out evaluations to appraise their performance and assess whether they possess the right mix of background and competences, as well as the contribution to the board of the directors.

The sixth sub-principle mentions that in order to fulfill their responsibilities, board members should have access to accurate, relevant, and timely information, avoiding any sort of asymmetry of data and information. Board members require relevant information on a timely basis in order to support their decision-making. Non-executive board members typically do not have the same access to information as key managers within the company. The contributions of non-executive board members to the company can be enhanced by providing access to key managers.

Although the OECD principles do not specify, best practices—notably in the financial system—require a close relation between non-executive directors and the committees or ad hoc committees of the board to have close interactions with the heads of the control functions—risk management, compliance and internal audit—as well as with external assurance providers—regulators, supervisors and external auditors—as advocated by the IIA's 3 lines of defense model. The recourse to independent external advice represents also a current best practice, which should be at the expense of the company. Where companies rely on complex risk management models, board members should be made aware, as well as monitor and supervise potential shortcomings of such models.

The seventh principle discusses that when employee representation on the board is mandated, mechanisms should be developed to facilitate access to information and training for employee representatives, so that this representation is exercised effectively and contributes to the enhancement of board skills, information, and independence. Procedures should be in place to facilitate access to information, training, and expertise and the independence of employee board members from the CEO and management. These procedures should also include adequate, transparent appointment procedures, rights to report to employees on a regular basis—provided that board confidentiality requirements are duly respected—training, and clear procedures for managing potential conflicts of interest.

14.1.2 BCBS PRINCIPLES OF CORPORATE GOVERNANCE

BCBS Principles of Corporate Governance[290] (referenced in Section 1.2.3: "Global Financial Crisis 2007–2008 and Increased Governance") are focused on financial and banking institutions; however, as they constitute best practices, corporations operating in nonfinancial system may consider leveraging them in their benefit and of its stakeholders. The discussion below is based on the BCBS structure to present guidelines for 13 principles including also a discussion of best practices beyond them and others emanating from other guidelines. There are also inconsistencies and incongruences in the guidelines among regulators, supervisors, and professional associations, some of which result from different legal frameworks, often based on historical background and cultures, or even the establishment of more demanding practices by some. A strong emphasis is placed on the board, governance, and robust risk management culture. Nonetheless, the fundamentals of the principles developed by different institutions remain close to each other, as BCBS Principles often draw from G20/OECD Principles.

Principle 1 discusses and provides guidelines regarding the board's overall responsibilities. Boards are required to ensure compliance to their vast and wide responsibilities, notably the protection of the interests of depositors, shareholders, and other stakeholders, as well as an effective, proactive, and transparent relationship with regulators and supervisors. They also encompass approving and overseeing the implementation of strategic objectives, the establishment of the governance framework, and the way corporate culture is adopted and exercised throughout the entire organization, both locally and internationally. The main topics to address relate to the responsibilities of a board of directors; the corporate culture and values that the board should adopt for an organization under the role of the tone from the top; and the determination of the risk appetite, notably based on the stakeholders expectations, and its management and controls to ensure its monitoring.

The board has ultimate responsibility for the vision, business strategy and financial soundness, key personnel decisions, internal organization, and governance structure and practices, as well as risk management and compliance obligations, and having as an umbrella the exercise of the duties of care, loyalty, and obedience. Duty of care includes the decision-making process by acting in an informed and prudent manner, approaching the affairs as a *prudent individual* (i.e., the way to approach one's own affairs). Duty of loyalty requires an individual to act in good faith in the interest of the company. It prevents individual board members from acting in their own interest, or the interest of another individual/group, at the expense of the company and shareholders entering or being in the limits of raising potential conflicts of interest. These duties bring together the need for the preparation of each board member for the meetings.

Some of these functions may be delegated to the board committees or ad hoc committees, although not the responsibilities and the board required final approval, although jurisdictions may legislate differently. The board should also review the organizational structure to ensure it is adequate to allow them and senior management to carry out their responsibilities and have an effective decision-making process to allow for a good governance, including detailing critical responsibilities and authority, notably involving the control functions in the process.

BCBS clarifies that the word "oversee" has a wider meaning, such that board members are "satisfied with." The board should be involved in the affairs and with any material change in the business model and act promptly to protect the long-term interests of the institution, supervising the development and approval of business objectives and strategy, being involved in it in an end-to-end fashion, and monitoring its implementation. The corporate culture and values represent a relevant responsibility of the board as well as the implementation of the governance framework and its update if relevant changes (e.g., size, complexity, footprint, business strategy, markets, and regulatory requirements) occur or have potential to occur.

The risk area represents another relevant focus of an organization, including the determination of the risk capacity of an institution, the decision of the risk appetite in line with the stakeholders' expectations, and the risk level buffers to ensure a proper risk management of the organization. The types of risk a bank enters is intimately related to the implementation of policies, notably related with capital adequacy assessment and capital and liquidity plans.

The internal control framework should also ensure the establishment of a robust finance function responsible for accounting and financial data and the approval of the financial statements including an opinion of external auditors. It should be added to the responsibilities related to the duty of care and should ensure the timely production of a correct, proper, and transparent set of financial statements is prepared, as a firm's financial statements serve the purpose of providing stakeholders with financial information insight regarding a company's current financial status and the changes expected in the future. The financial statements show the results of the way the executives and non-executives have managed the resources and assets they have been entrusted by stakeholders.

There are other areas that may vary among jurisdictions, particularly resulting from different legal frameworks, different levels of demands from national supervisors, or even among organizations in terms of the governance standards applied. They include, but are not limited to:

- Approval, selection, and performance of the CEO, key members of senior management, and heads of the control functions.
- Oversight of the process for compensation, including the assessment of the alignment with the risk culture and risk appetite.
- Oversight of the integrity, independence, and effectiveness of whistleblowing processes and policies to ensure a free and secure environment for stakeholders to complain and/or inform, protecting both ends of the process.
- Transactions with related parties, including subsidiaries (e.g., price-transfer that should follow the principle of arm's length).

According to BCBS' *Principle 2*, the board qualifications and composition relate to the guidelines that the institutions and eventually the board should adopt to be and remain qualified, individually and collectively, for their positions. They should understand their oversight and corporate governance role and be able to exercise sound and objective judgment about the affairs of the institution.

The board should collectively have appropriate skills and experiences that facilitate effective oversight, through the inclusion of enough independent directors who can bring value to the board. Directors must possess the necessary qualifications that commensurate with the size, complexity, and risk profile of the organization. The collective suitability of the board is determined through its board members having experience of having been exposed in several areas including—though not limited to—capital markets, financial analysis, financial stability issues, financial reporting, information technology, strategic planning, risk management, compensation, regulation, corporate governance, and management skills. Collectively, the board should have a reasonable understanding of local, regional, and global economic and market forces as well as of the legal and regulatory environment, while the attitude of individual board members should facilitate communication, collaboration, and critical debate in the decision-making process, thus helping to promote a friendly and respectful environment in the board.

The selection of board members should be aligned with the fit and proper principles. The board candidates should not have any potential conflicts of interest or conflicts of interest that may impede their ability to perform their duties independently and objectively and subject them to undue influence from management and shareholders, previous or current positions, personal, professional, or other economic relationships with other members of the board, management, or other entities within the group.

The nomination committee, often composed of independent non-executive directors, but there is a model where the members of the nomination and/or remuneration committee(s) not non-executive directors—usually experts in the field of remunerations—should take the aforementioned criteria into account when selecting individuals. A proper induction process and ongoing training program must be developed and facilitated so that board members acquire, maintain, and enhance their knowledge and skills and fulfill their responsibilities.

In situations where an entity as shareholder have to indicate a board member, the board should ensure that such individuals understand their duties. Above all, board members have responsibilities to the institution's overall interests that they should protect, regardless of who recommends and/or elects them. In this respect, it should be stressed that in many jurisdictions, a director when appointed does not represent a shareholder, even when the by-laws establish that a collective entity is the board member—a company or fund that is a shareholder—and, therefore, the individual indicated to represent that collective entity is on its own responsibility and duties resulting from decisions taken.

BCBS' *Principle 3* deals with the board structure and practices and the way it should define appropriate governance structures and practices for its work. It should also implement the means for such practices to be followed, periodically reviewing them to ensure their effectiveness. The board structure and practices include topics regarding the assessment of the constitution and responsibilities of board members, audit committee, and risk and compliance committee.

In order to carry out effective oversight role and other responsibilities, the board should structure itself in terms of leadership, size, and committees (or even ad hoc committees). To support its performance, the board should carry regular individual and collective self-assessments, assessments—alone or with the assistance of external experts—of the board as a whole, its committees, and its individual board members. The board should maintain appropriate records of its deliberations and decisions, such as meeting minutes of the matters reviewed, recommendations made, decisions taken, and dissenting opinions.

Depending on the development of board members' assessment as well as considering the cultural environment, there are other methods that can be adopted progressively. One could be initiating a collective assessment, with the advantage of not focusing on individuals who are notably not culturally adapted to an individual assessment process, using, as its basis, forms that are easily available on consultants' sites. At the same time, the nomination committee may decide to use a consultant agreeing to progress the assessment process in the following year, with the individual self-assessment comprising the view of the individual board members about their contribution to the board and performance as well as the contributions they plan to deliver in the coming year. The next step would be hiring a consultant to perform a 360-degree assessment of each of the board members. The board assessment is a process that implies often a change of culture—at the level of countries as well as at the level of institutions. However, a way that would facilitate its implementation would be to have the process decided and established when hiring board members, notably non-executives, and informing them about this condition (i.e., that each individual will be assessed during the mandate annually). The chair plays an important leadership role in this process.

The chair of the board plays a major role in running the board ("leadership stance"), remembering that the chair runs the board, and the CEO runs the company ("command stance"). The legal framework varies among countries, although a best practice line of thought advocates that, being part of a set of structures whose main objective is the promotion of checks and balances, the chair of the board should be independent (usually non-executive) board member. However, it is common for large companies to have chairs assuming a full-time job. This does not mean that the chair should assume executive duties.

On top of this, the institution should implement measures to mitigate any adverse impact on checks and balances, either by designating an independent lead director—also named senior independent board member—or another similar position, and by having a larger number of non-executives on the board. The role of the independent lead director is usually awarded to the most senior non-executive director (further discussed in Chapter 16: Role of Board Members). The SID (Senior Independent Director) acts as a sounding board for the chair, providing support delivering the objectives. The SID's role becomes critical, working with the chair, directors, and shareholders to resolve significant issues. The SID plays an even more relevant role when the board is under stress. Other responsibilities of the SID relate to the evaluation process of the chair on behalf of the directors and might often take responsibility in the chair's succession process. Board members should have a clear understanding of the role and responsibilities of the SID, as he/she might intervene to maintain board and company stability, notably in moments that may emerge from poor relations and dynamics between the chair and the chief executive officer.

The board committees formed and mandated within the board should increase efficiency and allow deeper focus in specific areas. Each committee should have a charter or other instrument that sets out its mandate, scope, and working procedures, including how the committee will report to the full board, what is expected of committee members, and any tenure limits for serving on the committee. Normally, audit committee, risk and compliance committee, nomination committee, and remuneration/compensation are formed, while other committees or ad hoc committees ("taskforces") can be established depending on the requirements and need.

There are committees required by law (e.g., audit committee), while others may be established as a result of a particular area of focus. An alternative to a permanent committee is the set-up of "ad hoc committees" to deal with a specific topic, i.e., a topic that will lose relevance when decided or resolved. This model will ensure that the members of the board are not tied in a committee that are not required any more.

Although the legal framework may influence the role and constitution of the audit committee of the board, in most jurisdictions, they are compulsory, with some legal frameworks imposing particular skills of its members. Nevertheless, the best practice determines that it must be constituted by following high standards, notably particular characteristics and profile of its members in terms of background (e.g., academic, experience in auditing, qualification as statutory or internal auditor). It should be chaired by an independent director who does not chair any other committee and be composed entirely of independent directors. There is a line of thought that advocates that the position should not be filled by the chair of the board, although some large corporations and banks have adopted this reporting line.

The audit committee is mainly responsible for:

- Framing policy on internal audit and financial reporting.
- Overseeing the financial reporting process and its internal control framework (ICF), providing oversight of and interacting with the internal and external auditors.
- Approving, or recommending to the board or shareholders for their approval, the appointment, remuneration, and dismissal of external auditors.
- Reviewing and approving the multiannual audit plan, scope, and frequency; its performance; and required changes.
- Receive all audit reports and ensure that senior management takes necessary corrective actions in a timely manner to address control weaknesses, noncompliance with policies and laws and regulations, and other problems identified by auditors and other control functions.
- Overseeing the establishment of accounting policies and practices.
- Reviewing the third-party opinions on the design and effectiveness of the overall risk governance framework and internal control system.
- Establishing a proactive interaction with the control functions—risk management, compliance and internal audit.

- Establish an open relation with the external assurance providers—regulators, supervisors, and external auditors.

The risk committee and the compliance committee from the board should be distinct from the audit board required in some jurisdictions and must be formed along with the audit committee in systemically important organizations. The risk and the compliance committees are compulsory in financial institutions, and they should have a chair who is an independent director and not the chair of the board or of any other committee. It should be composed of majorly independent directors with experience in risk management issues and practices. The audit committee is responsible for understanding the stakeholders' expectations to be able to determine the risk capacity of the institution and propose to the board the risk appetite and the buffers to ensure not approaching the risk capacity of the institution. Their responsibilities include the discussion of risk strategies, periodic review of the risk policies (at least annually), as well as oversight and supervision processes that management has in place to promote adherence to the approved risk policies, notably the risk appetite framework. The risk and compliance committee of the board is responsible for advising the board on the overall current and future risk vectors, overseeing senior management's implementation of the Risk Appetite Statement (RAS), reporting on the state of risk culture, and interacting with and overseeing the Chief Risk Officer (CRO).

Regular (ideally monthly) meetings should be held with the heads of risk control functions. A system to ensure effective communication and coordination between the audit committee and the risk and compliance committee(s) is paramount to facilitate the exchange of information and effective coverage of all risks, including emerging risks, and any needed adjustments to the risk governance framework. The committees are further discussed in Chapter 17: Board Committees.

Potential conflict of interests may arise as a result of the various activities and roles of the organization or between the interests of the bank and/or its customers and those of the institution's board members or senior managers, as well as when the organization is part of a group with an extensive geographical footprint and multiple subsidiaries. The board must oversee the implementation and operation of policies to identify emerging potential conflicts of interest. The organization should have a formal written conflict of interest policy and an objective compliance process for implementing and control the policy.

Principle 4 of BCBS provides the guidelines about senior management and the way they must act under the direction and oversight of the board and should carry out and manage activities in a manner consistent with the business model, business strategy, risk appetite, remuneration, and other policies approved by the board.

In a unitary board structure, senior management consists of a core group of individuals, namely the CEO (Chief Executive Officer), CFO (Chief Financial Officer), COO (Chief Operating Officer), and CRO (Chief Risk Officer). They make up the Executive Committee and are therefore the members of the board responsible and accountable to the full board for the sound and prudent daily management of an institution. They represent the management group within the board, while the non-executive directors act as the supervisory side of the board. In a dual board structure, there is a supervisory board, made up of the non-executive directors, from which emanates notably the audit committee in most legal frameworks, and there is an executive board, made up of the executive directors. Members of senior management must be fit and proper and should therefore have the necessary experience, competencies, and integrity to manage the businesses and people under their supervision. They should have access to regular training to maintain and enhance their competencies and stay up to date on developments relevant to their areas of responsibility.

The chair of the board must ensure the collaboration and cooperation with the senior management by setting tone at the top.

Consistent with the direction received from the board, senior management should:

- Implement business strategies approved by the board under the approved business model of the organization.
- Set up and ensure adequate risk management systems and risk culture of the organization at the different hierarchical levels.
- Implement processes, systems, and controls for managing the risks—both financial and nonfinancial—to which the bank is or may be exposed.
- Implement processes, systems, and controls for managing compliance with laws, regulations, and internal policies; this includes comprehensive and independent risk management, compliance, and audit functions (the control functions of an organization) as well as an effective overall system of internal controls under an ICF (Internal Control Framework).
- Keep the board regularly and adequately informed of material or relevant matters in changes in the business model and in the business strategy, risk strategy/risk appetite, performance and financial condition, breaches of risk limits or reaching levels of the prudential buffers, and compliance rules internal control failures, legal, or regulatory concerns, and issues raised resulting of whistleblowing procedures.

BCBS' *Principle 5* discusses the governance of group structures, a highly relevant topic in an organization with international footprint. In a group structure, the board of the parent company has the overall responsibility for the group and for ensuring the establishment and operation of a clear governance framework appropriate to the size and complexity of the structure, business models, and risks of the group and its individual entities. The board and senior management should know and understand the group's organizational structure and the risks it poses.

In a group structure, the board of the parent company should be aware of the material risks and issues that might affect both the organization as a whole and its subsidiaries. It should exercise adequate oversight over subsidiaries while respecting the independent legal and governance responsibilities that might apply to subsidiary board. While parent companies should conduct the group's strategic, group-wide risk management and prescribe corporate risk policies, subsidiary management and boards should have appropriate input to their local or regional application and to the assessment of local risks.

However, the groups' board is entitled to receive information that the board deems necessary, notably to manage the risks at group level. If this is not possible to achieve—even due to legal issues emerging from a particular jurisdiction—then the board may decide to divest in that particular subsidiary or participated company, taking into consideration the inability to provide information to the supervisor on a consolidated basis. A line of thought advocates that this interpretation derives from the spirit of Principle 12 of the Basel Core Principles for Effective Banking Supervision[291] (Consolidated supervision), which considers the ability to supervise on a consolidated basis an essential element of supervision. Therefore, the concept includes the business conducted worldwide, granting the supervisor power to take corrective actions, namely ring-fencing parallel-owned structures and other related entities from parents or subsidiaries in issues that could impair safety and soundness. There are a number of publications that treat the background and basis for this interpretation, including *Home-host Information Sharing for Effective Basel II Implementation* (June 2006), *The Supervision of Cross-border Banking* (October 1996), *Minimum Standards for the Supervision of International Banking Groups and Their Cross-border Establishments* (July 1992), *Principles for the Supervision of Banks' Foreign Establishments* (May 1983), and *Consolidated Supervision of Banks' International Activities* (March 1979).

Therefore, the organization should establish a group structure, including the legal entity and business structure as well as a corporate governance framework with clearly defined roles and responsibilities, including those at the parent company and subsidiary levels, as appropriate based on the complexity, size, and significance of the subsidiary. It should also ensure that the group's corporate governance framework includes appropriate processes and controls to identify and address potential intragroup potential conflict or conflicts of interest while maintaining an effective relationship with both the home supervisor and, through the subsidiary board or direct contact, with the supervisor of all subsidiaries and branches. Subsidiaries' boards and senior management remain responsible for developing effective risk management processes for their entities. The methods and procedures applied by subsidiaries should support the effectiveness of risk management at a group level. The current best practice to address this issue requires that the control functions—risk management, compliance, and internal audit—report centrally. There is a line of thought that also advocates that topics related with remuneration and appraisals should be led by the parent to ensure a robust independent status.

Banks often create structures for legal, regulatory, or/and tax purposes such as units, branches, subsidiaries, other legal entities, or even parallel similar ownership structures that, eventually, have influence over decisions in an entity that is not legally within their consolidation perimeter. In these situations, a line of thought that should be considered is the application of the UBO (Ultimate Beneficiary Owner), even if outside the consolidation perimeter. This has high potential to generate complex situations that may require robust coordination of supervisors to be able to exercise their duties, adding further complexity. Operating through complex or non-transparent structures may pose financial, legal, reputational, and other risks to the bank. Senior management or/and the board should be cognizant of these challenges and take action to avoid or mitigate them.

Principle 6 of BCBS deals with the risk management function, which is one of the three control functions—in conjunction with compliance and internal audit—that should effectively be an independent Risk Management Function (RMF), under the direction of a CRO

(Chief Risk Officer), with sufficient stature, independence, resources, and access to the board, as well as by regulation, in the banking system, access to regulators and supervisors.

RMF (also known as Risk Control Function) belongs to the second line of defense, being the backbone for overseeing and controlling risk-taking activities across the enterprise, empowered with authority within the full organization, that is, on a consolidated basis. The RMF should:

- Identify material individual, aggregate, and emerging risks.
- Assess risks and measure their exposure, subject to the review and approval of the board.
- Develop and implement the enterprise-wide risk governance framework, which includes:
  o risk culture, determination of the risk capacity of the organization, risk appetite (set in accordance with the stakeholders' expectations), and risk limits and respective buffer limits.
  o ongoing monitoring of the risk-taking activities and risk exposures in line with the board approved risk capacity, risk appetite, risk limits, and corresponding capital (ICAAP—Internal Capital Adequacy Assessment Process) or liquidity needs (ILAAP—Internal Liquidity Adequacy Assessment Process) to allow for capital (CAR—Capital Adequacy Ratio) and liquidity (LCR—Liquidity Coverage Ratio) planning.
- Establish an early warning system or trigger system for breaches (or approaching to breach) to risk appetite or limits.
- Influence and challenge decisions that give rise to material risk.
- Report to the board, audit committee, risk and compliance committee, as well as supervisors—when deemed appropriate—including but not limited to proposing appropriate risk-mitigating actions.

Large entities, particularly systemic banks, must have a CRO whose primary responsibility includes overseeing the development and implementation of the RMF. The current best practice requires reporting to an executive board member in the administrative vector with sole responsibility for control functions except internal audit and functionally to the risk and compliance committee, which should be chaired by an independent director. This includes the ongoing strengthening of staff skills and enhancements to risk management systems, policies, processes, quantitative models, and reports, as necessary to ensure that the bank's risk management capabilities are sufficiently robust and effective to fully support its strategic objectives and all of its risk-taking activities. The CRO is responsible for supporting the board in its engagement with and oversight of the development of the determination of the risk capacity, risk appetite, and Risk Appetite Statement (RAS) and for translating the risk appetite into a risk limits' structure. The CRO, along with senior management, should be actively engaged in monitoring performance relative to risk-taking and risk limit adherence. The CRO's responsibilities also include managing and participating in key decision-making processes, including the assets and liabilities committee.

BCBS' *Principle 7* guides the risk identification, monitoring, and controlling, which determines risks that should be identified, monitored, and controlled in an ongoing group and individual entity basis. The sophistication of the bank's risk management and internal control infrastructure should keep pace with changes to the business model, risk capacity, risk profile, external risk landscape, and industry practice.

Risk identification should include both quantitative and qualitative criterion and essentially encompass all material risks, on and off-balance sheet (the financial crisis discovered large amounts of responsibilities off-balance sheet that impacted financial stability) and on a group-wide, portfolio-wise by business line. To perform effective risk assessments, the board and senior management, including the CRO, should regularly and on an ad hoc basis, evaluate the risks and potential risks faced and their overall risk profile. The risk assessment process should include ongoing analysis of existing risks as well as the identification of new or emerging risks. Risks should be captured with the input of all business units and entities. Credit concentration associated with material risks should likewise be factored into the risk assessment. Internal controls should ensure that all key risks have a policy, process, or other measure, as well as a control to ensure that such policy, process, or measure is being effectively applied and works as intended, which should also be verified by internal audit. Also, to avoid actions beyond the authority of the individual or even fraud—notably management collusion—internal controls should also place reasonable checks on managerial and employee discretion.

In relation to quantitative and qualitative analysis, the bank should utilize stress tests and scenario analyses to better understand potential risk exposures under a variety of adverse circumstances in different underlying scenarios, reverse stress testing, among others; and regularly compare actual performance against risk estimates (e.g., back-testing) to assist in judging the accuracy and effectiveness of the risk management process and making necessary adjustments. This includes risk management and approval processes for new or expanded products, services, lines of business, and markets, as well as for large and complex transactions that require significant use of resources or have hard-to-quantify risks. Mergers and acquisitions, divestitures, and other changes notably to the business model in an organizational structure can pose special risk management challenges; in particular, risks can arise from conducting due diligence processes that fail to identify post-merger risks or activities conflicting with strategic objectives or risk capacity and risk appetite. The risk management function should be actively involved in assessing risks that could arise from mergers and acquisitions, notably in geographies that may pose risks emerging from regulators and supervisors applying standards enforced by other regulators and supervisors, for example at parent company, and inform the board.

BCBS' *Principle 8* discusses risk communication, which relates to guidelines to ensure that an institution has in place an effective risk governance framework that contemplates and structures a robust communication within the organization about risk, both across the organization and through reporting to the board and senior management. This issue is linked to the additional requirement of Basel III relating to Pillar 3: Enhance Risk Disclosure and Market Discipline, which in Basel II included only Disclosure and Market Discipline, an enhancement that requires boards to transparently report topics related to risk not only in their quarterly and annual reports but also when potential events may require, a matter that must be evaluated by the board. The goal is to promote a more resilient financial sector, improving its ability to absorb shocks arising from financial and economic stress.

Senior management should actively communicate among themselves and up to the board of directors, consult, and add to their global agenda meetings with the control functions to discuss and monitor the evolution of the business to monitor plans and activities, so that both the board in its supervisory function (non-executive directors) and the heads of the control functions can effectively discharge their responsibilities. Communication about risk issues, including the risk strategy, throughout the organization is a key tenet of a strong risk culture, and a strong risk culture should promote risk awareness and encourage open communication and challenge about risk-taking across the organization as well as vertically to and from the board and senior management. Information, including potential and material risk, should be duly communicated to the board and senior management in a timely, accurate, and understandable manner so that they are equipped to take informed decisions.

Reporting should accurately communicate risk exposures and results of stress tests (which have been made public by regulators and supervisors) or scenario analyses and should provoke a robust discussion of an institution's current and prospective exposures (particularly under stressed scenarios) risk/return relationships, risk capacity, risk appetite, and limits. Therefore, risk reporting systems should be dynamic, comprehensive, and accurate, and it should draw on a range of underlying assumptions. Risk monitoring and reporting should not only occur at the disaggregated level, including material risk residing in subsidiaries, but should also be aggregated to allow for a group and institution-wide integrated perspective of risk exposures. Organizational "silos" should be eliminated, as they can impede effective sharing of information across an organization and therefore result in decisions being taken in isolation from the rest of the organization. Overcoming these information sharing obstacles may require the board, senior management, and control functions to reevaluate established practices in order to encourage greater communication, both internally and externally, according to Pillar 3: Enhanced Risk Disclosure and Market Discipline of Basel III.

In *Principle 9* BCBS states that the board of directors is responsible for overseeing the management of the compliance risk, ensuring the effectiveness of a compliance function, approving policies and processes for identifying, assessing, monitoring, and reporting, and advising on compliance risk, ultimately ensuring the protection of the reputation of an organization. It is accepted that the main two vectors of compliance relate to reputational risk and related financial sanctions. In the last decade, reputational risk has emerged strongly.

The compliance function belongs to the IIA second line of defense framework. It should be independent from management and have sufficient authority, stature, independence, resources, and access to the board. The function is responsible for, among other things, ensuring that the organization operates with integrity and in compliance with applicable laws, regulations, and internal policies. While the board and management are accountable for the organization's compliance, the compliance function has an important role in supporting corporate values, policies, and processes that help ensure that it acts responsibly and fulfills all applicable obligations. The compliance function should advise the board and senior management on compliance with laws, rules, and standards and keep them informed of developments in the area. It should also help educate and train staff about compliance issues, act as a contact point within the institution for compliance queries from staff members and provide guidance to staff on the appropriate implementation of applicable laws, rules, and standards in the form of policies, procedures, and other documents such as compliance manuals, internal codes of conduct, and practice guidelines. More recently, the role of compliance has extended into other areas that emerged as critical after the financial and economic crisis, notably ethics, corporate culture, and whistleblowing.

In most organizations, compliance is also responsible for an area that requires intense training, starting at the board, regarding the regulations that cover Anti-Money Laundering (AML), Combating the Financing of Terrorism (CFT), and financing the Proliferation of Weapons of Mass Destruction (WMD)—discussed in Section 8.4: "Money Laundering— 'The 5 Vectors'." Although the legislation is not uniform, not only of its application but also in terms of its translation into the different legal frameworks of the EU,[292] some relevant acts that directly or indirectly govern the fight against AML-CFT-WMD in the European Union include:

- Directive (EU) 2018/1673 of the European Parliament and of the Council of 23 October 2018 on combating money laundering by criminal law.
- Directive (EU) 2018/843 of the European Parliament and of the Council of 30 May 2018—amending Directive (EU) 2015/849 on the prevention of the use of the financial system for the purposes of money laundering or terrorist financing.
- Directive (EU) 2016/2258 of the European Parliament and of the Council of 6 December 2016 regarding access to anti-money laundering information by tax authorities.

- Directive (EU) 2015/849 of the European Parliament and of the Council of 20 May 2015 on the prevention of the use of the financial system for the purposes of money laundering or terrorist financing.
- Regulation (EU) 2018/1672 of the European Parliament and of the Council of 23 October 2018 on controls on cash entering or leaving the Union.
- Regulation (EU) 2015/847 of the European Parliament and of the Council of 20 May 2015 on information accompanying transfers of funds.
- Commission Delegated Regulation (EU) 2018/1108 of 7 May 2018—supplementing Directive (EU) 2015/849 with regulatory technical standards on the criteria for the appointment of central contact points for electronic money issuers and payment service providers and with rules on their functions.
- Commission Delegated Regulation (EU) 2016/1675 of 14 July 2016—supplementing Directive (EU) 2015/849 of the European Parliament and of the Council by identifying high-risk third countries with strategic deficiencies.

It is relevant to mention that the empowerment of compliance officers is relevant, notably in some jurisdiction in the EU, in the power, privileges, and responsibilities that the function is granted, namely in their independence in reporting suspect transaction without any need for approval of the board or even the board member responsible for the compliance function. However, some jurisdictions require the appointment of a board member (executive or non-executive director) to perform a critical review of operations in the possibility that the compliance officer decided not to communicate to the authorities.

BCBS' *Principle 10* covers the internal audit function (the third line of defense) which should provide independent assurance to the board, as well as support the board and senior management in promoting an effective governance process and the maintenance of a robust ICF (Internal Control Framework) to ensure the long-term soundness and sustainability of the organization.

Internal audit provides an independent assurance to the board of directors and senior management on the quality and effectiveness of internal control, risk management, and governance systems and processes, thereby helping the board and senior management protect the organization and its reputation. There should be no "dual hatting" by the heads of these functions. The board and senior management contribute to the effectiveness of the internal audit function by providing the function with full and unconditional access to any records, file data, and physical properties, including access to management information systems and records and the minutes of all consultative and decision-making bodies. This is required to independently assess the effectiveness and efficiency of the internal control, risk management, and governance systems and processes, requiring internal auditors to adhere to national and international professional standards. This notably includes the standards established by the Institute of Internal Auditors (IIA), requiring that audit staff collectively have or gain access knowledge, skills, and resources commensurate with the business activities and risks of the institution. They also require timely and effective correction of audit issues by senior management and require the function to perform a periodic assessment of the overall risk governance framework and internal control framework, including but not limited to an assessment of the effectiveness of the risk management and compliance functions, the quality of risk reporting to the board and senior management, and the effectiveness of the system of internal controls.

The responsibilities and duties of internal audit are intimately linked to the audit committee of the board, which should be composed in accordance with several regulations and guidelines. The main ones include Directive 2006/43/EC (Article 41), Directive 2006/43/EC of the European Parliament and of the Council of 17 May 2006 on statutory audits of annual accounts and consolidated accounts, which amend Council Directives 78/660/EEC and 83/349/EEC and repealing Council Directive 84/253/EEC (OJ L 157, 9.6.2006, p. 87), as amended by Directive 2014/56/EU of the European Parliament and of the Council of 16 April 2014, as well as by the European Banking Authority on internal governance of banks EBA/GL/2017/11.

World Intellectual Property Organization (WIPO)[293] recommends the development of an Internal Audit Strategy as the tool to enable internal audit to effectively allocate its financial and human resources to meet stakeholders' expectations and achieve its objectives by providing an independent and objective assessment of governance, risk management, and control processes. The definition of a strategic plan and its development is based on the definition of strategy as the means of establishing the organization's purpose, determining the nature of the contribution it intends to make, as well as predefining choices that will shape decisions and actions.[294] Strategy for the internal audit activity enables an adequate allocation of financial and human resources that will support achieving those objectives, as defined in the activity's vision and mission statements, and which also contribute to the achievement of the organization's objectives. This structured process will benefit the internal audit activity through the configuration of resources with the objective of answering stakeholders' expectations, as well as a tool to establish the organization's purpose and determine the nature of the contribution it intends to make, while predefining choices that will shape decisions and actions.

The European Banking Authority, in its guidelines on internal governance (EBA/GL/2017/11: #204-207), recommends the adherence to national and international professional standards, notably the ones recommended by Institute of Internal Auditors (IIA). It indicates that the audit plan should adopt detailed audit programs, following a risk-based approach, which should be approved by the previously by the audit committee and then by the board. It should be drawn up annually (on the basis of the triannual plan) for the coming year to comply with the internal audit control objectives.

The internal audit recommendations should be agreed upon by senior management and the board member responsible for the audited area. The internal audit reports should be formally presented to the audit committee—its functional role of overseeing internal audit—and it should be followed up by the executive director in charge of the area. Finally, the audit committee should present and discuss with the board to ensure their effective and timely resolution. The IIA recommends that the strategic plan of internal audit should adhere to the International Professional Practices Framework's (IPPF) conceptual framework,[295] which guides its development, encompassing two categories—mandatory and recommended. The vision for this approach is that internal audit practitioners would benefit from applying a strategic approach toward developing a strategic plan to achieve their internal audit vision and mission statements and therefore have a structure approach to address expectations of stakeholders.

IIA highlights that internal audit activity must add value to the organization, notably to the board and management, as well as to its stakeholders. This is usually achieved when the internal audit activity provides relevant assurance and contributes to the effectiveness and efficiency of governance and to risk management and control processes.

In *Principle 11* BCBS' guidelines cover compensation and remuneration structure, issues that should support sound corporate governance and risk management. Systemically important financial institutions should have a board's remuneration/compensation committee—or one integrating external experts—as an integral part of their governance structure, although some legal frameworks also allow for the remunerations committee to be appointed directly by the general assembly meeting, which may affect the dynamics of the committee in its relationship with the board of directors. The remuneration/compensation committee is responsible for the overall oversight of management's implementation of the remuneration system for the entire organization. Additionally, the board or its committee should regularly monitor and review outcomes to assess whether the organization-wide remuneration system creates the desired incentives for managing risk, capital, and liquidity. The board or subcommittee should review the remuneration plans, processes, and outcomes at least annually.

The Financial Stability Board (FSB) principles on compensation[296] are intended to apply to significant financial institutions, being especially critical for systemic firms. Nonetheless, banks are encouraged to implement the FSB principles or consistent national provisions based on them. As compensation was also considered by a line of thought one of the factors that contributed to the financial crisis 2007–2008, it needs to be embedded in the broader financial regulatory reform program, built around a substantially stronger and more resilient global capital and liquidity framework. The FSB sound compensation principles highlight the importance of the remuneration committee and the necessity to check executives' variable compensation, namely by taking into account the cost and quantity of capital required to support the risks taken, the cost and quantity of the liquidity risk assumed in the conduct of business, and consistency with the timing and likelihood of potential future revenues incorporated into current earnings.

The remuneration structure should be in line with the business model and risk strategy, objectives, values, and long-term interests of the organization, also incorporating measures to prevent conflicts of interest and potential conflicts of interest. The board or remuneration/compensation committee should approve the compensation of senior executives, including the CEO, CRO, and head of internal audit, as well as of risk management and compliance, and should oversee development and operation of compensation policies, systems, and related control processes. Remuneration should reflect risk-taking, risk outcomes, and risk culture displayed, as well as compliance with applicable laws and regulation, notably the one relating to Anti-money Laundering, Combating the Financing of Terrorism and Weapons of Massive Destruction.

Practices by which remuneration is paid for potential future revenues, whose timing and likelihood remain uncertain, should be carefully evaluated by means of both qualitative and quantitative key indicators. Banks have to set specific provisions for employees with a significant influence on the overall risk profile, known as material risk-takers. The nomination committee should be composed of non-executive directors of the management body in its supervisory function and guided by the FSB sound compensation principles or/and EBA guidelines on sound remuneration policies.[297] EBA defends its policies by stating that appropriate remuneration structures have been a mitigating factor to excessive and imprudent risk taking; therefore, poorly designed remuneration policies have potentially detrimental effects on the sound management of risks, control of risk, and the risk-taking behavior of individuals. Hence, remuneration requirements aim to ensure that remuneration policies are consistent with and promote sound and effective risk management, do not provide incentives for excessive risk taking, and are aligned with the long-term interests of the institutions across the EU.

The guidelines on internal governance (EBA/GL/2017/11, #62) require that the risk and compliance committees must—without prejudice to the tasks of the remuneration committee—monitor if the incentives included in the remuneration policies consider the risk, capital, and liquidity as well as the likelihood and timing of earnings.

BCBS' *Principle 12* discusses disclosure and transparency, which becomes an even more relevant issue after the financial and economic crisis of 2008, becoming the reason why the governance of an institution should be adequately transparent to its shareholders, depositors, and other relevant stakeholders and market participants.

It is difficult for shareholders, depositors, and other relevant stakeholders and market participants to effectively monitor and properly hold the board and senior management accountable when there is insufficient transparency. Therefore, transparency is consistent with sound and effective corporate governance. Institutions—including those for whom disclosure requirements may differ, because they are non-listed—should disclose relevant and useful information to support the key areas of corporate governance.

In general, the institution should apply the disclosure and transparency section of the G20/OECD Principles[298] on top of the disclosures in both the financial statements and the notes to the financial statements, as well as in the quarterly and annual reports. These requirements only represent the minimum standards, which means that the best practice should be applied by the board in order for transparency and disclosure to be in line with them, as the minimum standards may vary among jurisdictions. In an institution with an international footprint, the board should adopt the highest standard.

Accordingly, disclosure should include, but not be limited to, material information on the organization's vision, business model, the strategic plan, objectives, organizational and governance structures and policies (such as the content of any corporate governance or remuneration code or policy and the process by which it is implemented), major share ownership, and voting rights. Related party transactions are an area of particular attention from stakeholders, which is why institutions with relations that may involve relevant transactions between or among the parties should set up a committee of the board to deal with this type of transaction, as it may give rise to potential conflicts of interest. There are jurisdictions that impose ceilings on the total amounts of loans to be possibly extended to shareholders, the sale of a bank's asset, or the acquisition of an asset to a shareholder or related party, as well as the review and opinion about other transactions from a bank, setting up a threshold for transactions with shareholders, notably in credit operations. These operations and transactions, which should be conducted at an arms' length basis and within the same levels of demand and requirements applied to a normal customers, have to be reviewed by the audit board (there are jurisdictions that require this social body), followed by the approval of loans by the board to the shareholders. Relevant banks should appropriately disclose their incentive and compensation policy, following the FSB principles related to compensation or/and EBA guidelines on sound remuneration policies. An annual report on compensation must be disclosed to the public. The reporting structure is further discussed in Chapter 22: Reporting.

Disclosure must be timely, accurate, clear, and presented such that shareholders, depositors, and other relevant stakeholders and market participants can understand the information easily, being a common practice to have the quarterly and annual reports available on the internet site.

Principle 13 of BCBS deals with the role of supervisors that, along with external auditors, represent the so-called fourth line of defense. Supervisors should provide guidance for and supervise corporate governance at banks, including through comprehensive evaluations, and regular interaction with boards and senior management should require improvement and remedial action as necessary and should share information on corporate governance with other supervisors. The Single Supervisory Mechanism (SSM), discussed in Section 9.2: "Single Supervisory Mechanism," grants the ECB sole licensing authority over all banks in participating EU member states (except branches of banks from non-European Economic Area that include Iceland, Liechtenstein, and Norway) and makes it the prudential supervisor of these banks, directly for the significant banks and indirectly for the smaller banks. The SSM operates as a system of common bank supervision in the EU that involves national supervisors and the ECB.

In the UK, Bank of England's Prudential Regulation Authority (PRA) is responsible for the prudential regulation of banks, building societies, credit unions, insurers, and major investment firms whereas Financial Conduct Authority (FCA) regulates the conduct related to the marketing of financial products, with the ability to specify minimum standards and to place requirements on products and power to investigate organizations and individuals. In the Netherlands, besides participating in SSM, the central bank De Nederlandsche Bank (DNB) has introduced Culture and Behavior Supervision applicable to local institutions, building on the top of FSB Guidance on Supervisory Interaction with Financial Institutions on Risk Culture. This kind of supervision looks at the behavior and cultural aspects that impact the performance and risk profile of financial institutions and fundamentally contain risks arising from risk-seeking behaviors of bank board members and managers aiming at crisis prevention in the long run in a forward-looking manner.

How ECB, the banking supervisor, evaluates the business model of banks has been discussed in Section 4.2.2: "Business Model Evaluation." As such, the board and senior management are primarily responsible for the governance, and supervisors should assess their performance in this regard. Supervisors should establish guidance or rules consistent with the principles set forth in this document, requiring banks to have robust corporate governance policies and practices. Such guidance is especially important where national laws, regulations, codes, or listing requirements regarding corporate governance are not sufficiently robust to address the unique corporate governance needs of banks.

Supervisors should have processes in place to fully evaluate a bank's corporate governance. Such evaluations may be conducted through regular reviews of written materials and reports, interviews with board members and bank personnel, examinations, self-assessments by the bank, and other types of on and off-site monitoring. The evaluations should also include regular communication with a bank's board of directors; senior management; individuals responsible for the risk, compliance, and internal audit functions; and external auditors. Supervisors should evaluate whether the bank has effective mechanisms in place through which the board and senior management execute their respective oversight responsibilities, including risk appetite, financial performance, capital adequacy, capital planning, liquidity, risk profile and risk culture, controls, compensation practices, and the selection and evaluation of management. Supervisors should evaluate the processes and criteria (fit and proper) used by banks in the selection of board members and senior management and, as they judge necessary, obtain information about the expertise and character of board members and senior management. Supervisors should also endeavor to assess the governance effectiveness of the board and senior management, especially with respect to the risk culture of the bank, and corporate governance responsibilities of both the parent company and subsidiaries.

Supervisors should regularly interact with boards of directors, individual board members, senior managers, and individuals responsible for the risk management, compliance, and internal audit functions. This should include scheduled meetings and ad hoc exchanges, through a variety of communication vehicles (e.g., e-mail, telephone, in-person meetings). The purpose of the interactions is to support timely and open dialogue between the bank and supervisors on a range of issues, including the bank's strategies; business model and risks; the effectiveness of corporate governance at the bank; the bank's culture, management issues, and succession planning; compensation and incentives; and other supervisory findings or expectations that supervisors believe should be particularly important to board members. The frequency of interactions with the above persons may vary according to the size, complexity, structure, economic significance, and risk profile of the bank.

Supervisors should have a range of tools at their disposal to address governance improvement needs and governance failures. They should be able to require steps toward improvement and remedial action and ensure accountability for the corporate governance of a bank. These tools may include the ability to compel changes in the bank's policies and practices, the composition of the board of directors or senior management, or other corrective actions. They should also include, where necessary, the authority to impose sanctions or other punitive measures. When a supervisor requires a bank to take remedial action, the supervisor should set a timetable for completion. Supervisors should have escalation procedures in place to require more stringent or accelerated remedial action in the event that a bank does not adequately address the deficiencies identified or if the supervisor deems that further action is warranted.

Cooperation and appropriate information sharing among relevant public authorities, including bank supervisors and conduct authorities, can significantly contribute to the effectiveness of these authorities in their respective roles. Such information sharing is particularly important between home and host supervisors of cross-border banking entities. Cooperation can occur on a bilateral basis, in the form of a supervisory college or through periodic meetings among supervisors at which corporate governance matters should be discussed.

14.2 FIDUCIARY DUTIES, ACCOUNTABILITY, AND RESPONSIBILITIES

The term fiduciary is said to come from the Latin word *fiducia*, which means "trust." Hence, fiduciary implies that those who manage other people's money act in their beneficiaries' interests rather than pursuing their own self-interests. Boards of directors, including executive and non-executive, as well as management (that may include levels below the senior one) should implicitly realize their fiduciary duties in three dimensions resulting from the Duty of Care, Duty of Loyalty, and Duty of Obedience. The board and its directors should always be guided by high ethical standards and the firm's value and moral philosophy. Directors must act as the custodians of the corporate and essentially act as fiduciary in holding and managing the assets, not just for shareholders but for all relevant stakeholders. Section 2.1: "The Agency Theory" discusses the principal-agent dilemma, which refers to the potential conflict that may arise between the shareholders (principal) and directors and managers (agent)

Duty of Care

This requires a director to exercise diligence and prudence before reaching a decision, approaching the affairs of the organization as a *prudent person*, as one would approach one's own affairs. They must thoroughly uncover, analyze, and discuss as much information as possible on a given question and be able to show that all reasonable scenarios have been considered and properly vetted. The UK's Companies Act 2006 essentially refers to exercise reasonable care, skill, and diligence, meaning that there is not only a basic level of competence expected from all directors but also a higher standard expected of those with any specific skills, expertise, or experience.[299] For example, an accountant acting as finance director may be evaluated against the standard of a fellow professional with a detailed understanding of the company's finances and the direct and indirect impact they have in other business areas.

Duty of Loyalty

This is a standard of unwavering faithfulness, meaning that a director must always act in the best interests of the company, which requires a director to act in good faith, preventing individual board members from acting in their own interest or the interest of another individual/group as well as at the expense of the company and shareholders and stakeholders. As OECD mentions, the duty of loyalty is of central importance, since it underpins effective implementation of principles and best practice relating to the equitable treatment of shareholders, monitoring of related party transactions, and establishment of remuneration policy for key executives and board members.[300] Directors must identify and disclose all potential conflicts of interest before joining a board. In the US, for example, New York State requires that organizations' bylaws include written conflict of interest policies, to be signed every year by board members. This rule applies in many geographies, notably in the financial system. This principle relies on transparency as the first barrier to potential conflicts of interest and conflicts of interest. The Companies Act in the UK refers specifically for directors to act within their powers by deciding according to the company's policies and shareholders' decisions and in the interests of the company, and not to further their own.

Duty of Obedience

In addition to the duty of care and the duty of loyalty, the duty of obedience requires directors to be faithful to the organization's mission, to ensure that it is upheld and perpetuated, and to enforce compliance with all applicable laws, regulations, and internal policies. Directors are not permitted to decide in a way that is inconsistent with the company's goals and should question any strategies, initiatives, and programs that adulterate a company's mission. The duty of obedience is particularly relevant starting at the board level, that is the decisions of the board as well as those emanating from the executive directors are to be executed and implemented by senior management. This nuance is particularly important in organizations where senior management holds excessive or even undue influence and may not ensure timely execution of the decisions of the board. An internal control system should be in place to ensure that the organization complies with the duty of obedience. Often, the duty of obedience is one of the primary fiduciary duties to be ignored. It is particularly important to understand that the fiduciary duties may be incomplete to legitimize without the duty of obedience.

14.2.1 THE CASE OF BREACH OF FIDUCIARY DUTIES OF CARE, LOYALTY, AND OBEDIENCE

The senior officials of Tyco, a security systems company, were accused of improperly using corporate funds to the tune of millions of dollars through a racketeering scheme involving stock fraud, unauthorized bonuses, and falsified expense accounts. The CEO and the CFO were accused of stealing 170 million dollars from the corporate itself and reaping 430 million dollars more by covertly selling Tyco stock without informing US SEC (Securities Exchange Commission) while artificially inflating the value of that stock.[301] Essentially, they hid their illegal actions by keeping the numbers out of the accounting books and from the eyes of the board and the shareholders. In 2005, the CEO and the CFO were found guilty in a court of grand larceny, conspiracy, and falsifying business records and violating business law. The judge ordered both to pay back 134 million dollars to the company, and to pay a combined 105 million dollars fine, and convicted them to more than 10 years of jail time.[302]

Often, boards fail to act collectively and exhibit fiduciary duties in compliance with their individual duties and responsibilities, which can result from asymmetry of information linked to the fact that individual board members do not have the skills, and more often "the guts," to challenge other board members in the decision-making process, which can also lead to a "herd decision-making process," that is, a decision process that does not involve any process of challenging, finding alternatives, or even making an informed decision, as the group makes a decision based on the first opinion presented at the table. The asymmetry of data and information exists notably between executives and non-executives' directors but also within the executive directors, as the CEO and the CFO are often the most senior executive directors in a corporate and have a higher degree of information that is not available in as much detail to their executive directors' colleagues. Alternatively, there may be a lack of skills among other board members to challenge the senior management, thereby acting like a "rubber stamp board", or even non-executive directors do not prepare for the board meeting. The senior management must always be challenged by the board, fostering end-to-end discussion. The role of independent directors therefore becomes crucial. Other factors may include the failure of the audit committee to oversee the activities of the three lines model over the year, including the interaction between regulators and supervisors and with external auditors in the process of preparation of the financial reporting process and the financial statements audit. The concept of board dynamics and board collusion issues are discussed in Section 14.4: "Board Dynamics."

Some challenges lie in the separation at the board between non-executive directors (supervisory function) and executive directors (management function), as well as of the latter with senior management, accountability process; lines of separation between CEO and chair roles in the board and that of independent and non-independent directors; the need to have more independent directors; and the roles of supervisors or regulatory agencies in establishing the clear guidance, rules, and codes of conduct. In the end, all these factors are crucial components in designing the modern control framework, risk management framework, board selection, board composition, board guidelines, and corporate governance in a nutshell. Therefore, board members understanding of principles of corporate governance is vital for board effectiveness. Fiduciary responsibilities can be somewhat covered by a D&O (Directors and Officers) Liability Insurance, an issue discussed in Section 16.8: "Directors and Officers Liability Insurance."

14.3 UNDERSTANDING BOARD EFFECTIVENESS

In Chapter 3: Models of Corporate Governance, the models of corporate governance in different jurisdictions are discussed. This section elaborates the guidance on board effectiveness and the role of the chair and the directors applicable in most of the jurisdictions. Whether it is a unitary board in the UK, a dual board in the Continental EU, or the mixed board, the underlying principles of fiduciary and board effectiveness remain the same. Contents from institutions such as the European Banking Authority (EBA), Bank for International Settlements (BIS), Financial Reporting Council (FRC UK), among others, are fundamentally sourced to explain the concepts. As the guidance to governance often changes over the time and demand, content will be periodically updated in subsequent editions (Figure 14.2).

Figure 14.2: Board accountability

14.3.1 BOARD SIZE

Most public corporates tend to have 4–15 members in the board of directors, including the chair, executive, and non-executive directors in unitary board or supervisory board alike. Often, legal frameworks require boards to have a majority of independent non-executive directors; however, if that is not the case, the best practice still requires that setup. This was a relevant change in the United Kingdom when the Cadbury Code was improved by Sir Derek Higgs amendments more than 10 years later. The need to have a larger number of non-executive directors emerged based on empirical evidence, so that decisions could ultimately be challenged and influenced by them in the protection of the stakeholders. In private companies, notably in family businesses, it is common to have all executive directors at first, and the inclusion of independent non-executive directors in the board becomes typical once the company starts to grow and when regulation, capital markets, banking system, or stakeholders' interests become relevant. The number of directors on the board is often influenced by the company size, ownership structure, complexity, footprint and the legal and industry regulatory frameworks. The composition and mix of members in unitary boards or in a supervisory board are often different, although the board structure of either model is to achieve a proper and adequate governance. For example, France and Germany tend to have employee representation in the boards, whereas the US, most of Continental Europe and the UK do not contemplate such arrangements. Often, especially in family businesses, shareholders-linked directors are appointed to the board, which does not qualify them an independent member as they should be fit and proper to the position and not only be present to fill a position.

However, the rationale is not to install large boards, as a high number of directors will impact and affect the decision-making ability. It is advantageous for a board to have sector-skilled, financial, and capital markets' competences in an agile and optimal board for well-informed decision-making. The landscape is becoming highly disruptive fueled, with tech impacting the way companies do business and often requiring the need to change or adjust business models, strategy, and tactics within short intervals to remain sustainable. As another example, the impact of COVID-19 was unprecedented. Therefore, having 4–10 members in board is desired, although up to 12 may be entertained if duly warranted. Nonetheless, the number may change, depending on the rules and regulations of each jurisdiction. Board committees are formed within the board to function independently, so that the board accomplishes its task through smaller groups. Boards usually constitute committees such as Executive Committee, Governance Committee, Risk and Compliance Committee, Audit committee, or/ and Ad hoc Committee such as Bylaws Committee and Strategic Planning Committee, which are temporarily formed to meet the specific needs (such as to form a new subsidiary).

14.3.2 EFFECTIVE BOARD

An *effective board* defines the company's purpose and vision, and often the mission as well, and then sets a strategy—the efficient allocation of scarce resources, notably talent and capital—to achieve the vision, underpinned by the values and behaviors that shape its culture, notably the risk culture of the organization and the way it conducts its business (FRC).[303] A fundamental component of good governance is a corporate [risk] culture of reinforcing appropriate norms for responsible and ethical behavior (BCBS Principles of Corporate Governance). The board is definitely not a comfortable place, as the boardroom is the arena for robust and structured debate where challenge, support, diversity of thought, and teamwork are key factors of success. Soft skills that involve the "ability and guts" to challenge, positively confront challenges, establish an environment and climate of teamwork considering opinions and viewpoints resulting from diversity of viewpoints in their differences and components, and the exercise of non-executive directors' duties and responsibilities in relation to the supervision of executive directors are some of the critical factors for an effective board, where the chair plays a major role by proactively interacting and coordinating with each one of the directors.

Various types of skills are expected from board members to constitute to some degree an effective board. They include emotional skills, inspirational skills, rational and logical skills, physical skills (courage and action), emotional intelligence, and availability (Figure 14.3). Emotional intelligence is the ability of board members to recognize, understand, and manage not only their own emotions but also the emotions of other members. It can be agreed that a board with a high level of emotional intelligence can provide motivational oversight to the directors or employees who run the company, essentially garnering healthy relationships with customers, shareholders, or investors.[304] Empathy and self-regulation are fundamentally important. Also, the senior executives with high emotional intelligence are believed to create a stable environment—one of the keys to long-term profitability.

In order to build and foster emotional intelligence, the goal is to build warmer chemistry among directors and board as a team, foster constructive dialogue, and make room—in the room—for diverse viewpoints and voices. Ultimately, this also leads to high levels of creativity, curiosity, and strategic vision in the board.

Figure 14.3: Skills expected in board members

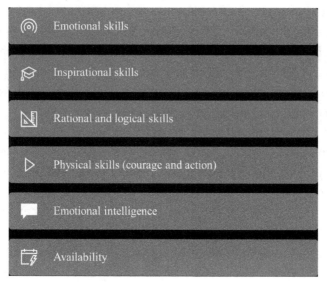

Most importantly, the board must not act as a "rubber stamp board." In other words, the documents being placed on the table should not be approved without the proper screening, challenging, or having alternatives considered before the approval or to benchmark and ensure that the best option is considered. Executive directors in their management function cannot expect the board to approve all the proposals without any meaningful discussion, which would not only reflect a profile that may be questioned in terms of fit and proper but would also provoke a poor performance of a board, therefore revealing a board overall not being fit and proper. Rather, board meetings should be an "end-to-end" process, and the involvement of non-executive directors should be proactive and expected by executive directors. The risk culture of the corporate should come from the top, that being the chair—the prime facilitator and the conscience of the organization. Directors must be aware notably of the corporate policies, such as conflicts of interest, compensation policy, and governance policies. Ultimately, the directors who do not take their fiduciary duties seriously are risking personal liability.

FRC's Guidelines on Board Effectiveness (referenced Section 1.2.3: "Global Financial Crisis 2007–2008 and Increased Governance") enlightens the characteristics of an effective board as follows:

- The board is responsible for setting and reconfirming the company's purpose (vision and mission). A well-defined purpose will help companies articulate their business model—the stream of revenues and the cost structure—and develop their strategy, operating practices, internal control framework, and approach to risk in terms of risk capacity and risk appetite.

- A sound understanding at the board level of how value is created over time is vital in steering strategies and business models toward a sustainable future and growth as well as an adequate return to shareholders and stakeholders. The value may not be just financial but also intangible, such as highly trained workforce, intellectual property, or brand recognition.

- An effective board will manage the conflict between short-term interests and the long-term impacts of its decisions, assessing shareholders' and stakeholders' interests from the perspective of the long-term sustainability.

- Directors are expected to act in a manner consistent with their fiduciary and statutory duties and to uphold the highest standards of integrity and support the chair in instilling the appropriate values, behaviors, and culture in the boardroom and beyond.

- The boardroom should be a place for robust debate where challenge, support, diversity of thought, and teamwork are essential features.
- Openness and accountability matter at every level. Good governance means a focus on how this takes place throughout the company and by those who act on its behalf.

Essentially, a board requires directors who can work as a team in specialized individual roles, such as succession planning, remuneration, mergers, acquisitions and restructuring, and capital allocation.

Harvard Business Review[305] states that boards tend to progress from good-to-great along a four-phase continuum, namely, (i) foundational, (ii) developed, (iii) advanced, and (iv) strategic. The continuum represents a corporate hierarchy of needs that is similar to the famous personal-development hierarchy created by psychologist Abraham Maslow. For instance, a foundational board may focus on survival and provide basic compliance oversight that is comparable to basic survival needs such as food and shelter in the human hierarchy. Directors may be unwilling to take strong positions, make tough decisions or play proactive operational roles. On the other hand, a strategic board may provide prescient forward-looking insights to form a company's foundational strategy and is fully actualized and high performing. Directors take appropriate risk to make significant contributions and lasting impact on enterprise value. So, what hinders the board to grow up the continuum. There are a series of elements and characteristics that when missing in a board's dynamics may involve a poor decision-making process, often leading to less than required decisions. They include:

- Lack of clarity on the roles of individual directors and the board—role ambiguity slows decision-making and causes unnecessary director conflicts.
- Poor process management hinders effective board preparation, meeting management, and communications—results in

indecisiveness and a lack of urgency on critical challenges facing the organization.

- Lack of alignment and agreement on strategy generates disinterest among board members, who then simply default to tackling regulatory and compliance issues. Poor strategic alignment hampers a board's ability to prioritize issues and set their near-term agendas and can cause board disruption sending damaging signals to financial markets.
- Poor team dynamics fracture boards and lead to power struggles. A board should compose of professional peers who respect and work well with each other.
- Board composition can be a serious impediment, if it is not done correctly. As today's challenges require new perspectives and skills, boards often lack the ability to objectively evaluate their makeup to determine if they have the right people and skills at the table.

Effective boards add strategic value, while high-performing boards are usually talent-centric, which evolves through an effective board composition and diversity of its members' expertise and backgrounds spanning across geographies, gender, race, academic background and experience such that to create a whole literally greater than the sum of the parts. At the end, an effective board is the one that not only meets regulatory compliance, but also delivers solid strategic advice and counsel, as well as direction. Therefore, recruiting and developing directors both executive and non-executive who are able to go well beyond the basic needs is the secret to building a high-performing and fully actualized board in a process led by the chair.

Another viewpoint about board effectiveness relates to its building on the following four pillars, which should lead to a robust decision-making process:

1. Individuals' quality, focus, commitment, and dedication
2. Information architecture

3. Structures and processes
4. Group dynamics[306]

In relation to pillar one, although the board may be composed of qualified directors in their respective fields, they may still lack the necessary knowledge to perform tasks as a member of a specific board. Therefore, effective boards establish performance and knowledge standards for individual directors, train and develop their board members, and conduct evaluations and assessments along those standards. Essentially, the quality of the board is enhanced by diversity in terms of industry and professional background as well as diversity of gender, personality, and opinion, regardless of LGBT+ or/and disability status. Boards that are well-focused distinguish the adequate context in which to perform both a supervisory role and a management function to support the management. Dedication and commitment to the firm are also an important elements that go beyond the allotted meeting time.

In summary, the quality of the directors and their focus and dedication are the first pillar for a truly effective board. The typical checklists for self-assessment on the first pillar include namely the following questions:

- How close to the heart of every board member is this company?
- Do I support and contribute to the function of the chair and for outstanding dynamics?
- Where do I truly add value to this board?
- How much confidence do I have in my board colleagues to steer our company the right direction?
- How is our diversity in terms of abilities, personalities, and competencies?
- How clear are we about the role of our board and the role of each committee?

- Is the agenda turned enough toward the future?
- How does my knowledge compare to one of the ideal board members on this company?

Pillar two is about information, which should not only be internal (i.e., information coming from management) but also from external sources, such as social media and press. Sources can be both formal and informal. Formal information architecture is jointly designed to perform board briefings that include financials with forecasts, a CEO report, risks and opportunity maps, analysis of the gene pool, and summary of financial analysts' views, which all contribute to the quality of the information architecture. Regular communication with management and the board and committees' reports are also fundamental. Informal information architecture includes meetings with employees and informal meetings of board members—all need both structuring—to give them potential, some freedom, and creativity, without infringing on management's rights. Communication with stakeholders, notably the capital markets agents and shareholders, is another vector that has to be a part of the global agenda of a board. This includes roadshows, investor relations roadshows (usually under the responsibility of the CEO and CFO), and governance roadshows (under the board leadership) to communicate with the investors—both shareholders and bondholders—typically including the chair, the senior independent director, and the chair of the audit committee. The typical checklist for the second pillar self-assessment includes the following:

- Do I know and intimately track the business and its key value drivers?
- Am I well informed of competitive trends, regulatory changes, technological changes, and shareholder and stakeholder evolution?

- Do I have enough information available independent from executive directors and senior management to build my judgment?
- What informal processes of information do I have?
- How involved was I in designing the information architecture? How involved were my fellow board members?

Pillar three discusses organizational structure and systems and processes, an element discussed in Section 1.3: "Corporate Governance Definition and Concept," as the composition of the board structure contributes to effectiveness. The board independence, a "state of mind," is crucial, with structured access to the right individuals, a process that should be clearly defined including access to the board or to its audit committee. Examples include the reporting line of the CAE (Chief Audit Executive), which recommends reporting should be to the Audit Committee in its functional responsibility or the board. Another line of thought advocates that reporting to the chair, to the CEO, or to an executive director should only include the administrative functions. There are included many processes to run the board effectively and efficiently—evaluation processes, the strategy process, the risk process, the board education process, the CEO and key managers succession processes, the regulatory process, among others.

The board strategy process plays a significant role in increasing effectiveness and strategic involvement occurs in three dimensions, namely co-creation, supervision, and support. Good processes will enrich all the three dimensions. A well-designed strategy process ultimately enables boards to efficiently assess strategic risks as well as strategic opportunities, whereas a poor evaluation process contributes to governance failure. Hence, thriving boards engage in self-assessment or external assessment in terms of their roles, dynamics, and their members' performance. One good practice is to make use of available technology, such as the use of tablets, for board evaluation during meetings, which provides results in real time and thus offers an opportunity for careful and dynamic scrutiny beyond the one-year evaluations.

The checklists for the third pillar self-assessment include:

- What is the list of processes that truly matter?
  - o strategy
  - o sustainability
  - o audit
  - o evaluation
  - o CEO succession
  - o risk
  - o board education
  - o compliance
  - o onboarding/outboarding
- How do I feel about each of these systems and processes? Do I have a clear view of each, or at least the critical ones? Is each one complete and detailed enough?
- Does the board have the right committees and the right people on them?
- Are the reporting lines fool proof?

Pillar four discusses dynamics (also included in Section 14.4: "Board Dynamics") which are linked to the culture of the board and board pathologies. Group-think tendencies—notably the herd decision process—may hinder effectiveness, as do disruptive or dominating members of the board. Boards with lack of energy—the sleepy board—are also common. Their characteristics include distributing information untimely; not making relevant information available; or presenting extensive, poorly structured, long reports, which are examples of intentional practices that hinder governance. Some appoint directors who are close associates of the company founder or its CEO, which can run the risk of sharing common views and heuristics, thus threatening true dynamics, such as constructive dissent, and can safeguard its own governance culture.

The "love board"—the board which believes the CEO can do no bad—is a failing board. One of the most important dynamics is the interaction and communication between the board and senior management. Rivalries and disputes should be minimized, as the board's effectiveness is enhanced. A board that makes rule of engagement clear to all its members, promoting equal participation of its members and their mutual respect, avoids the dominance of a particular board member, which is another key element of effectiveness. Functional board dynamics should ensure that board members are connected to reality, and the role of the chair is the development of a solid and successful board culture.

The checklists for pillar four self-assessment are as follows:

- How energetic is my board?
- How do I feel about the contribution of the different board members? Why?
- Does the culture of my board provide for well-managed meetings and "equal participation" in discussions?
- Do I really listen to the opinions of others? Do I challenge others, respectfully but without conceding, while keeping the relationship professional and not personal?
- Did I prepare for the board meeting by reviewing the documents and exchanging views with other directors before the board is held? Are my contributions short and to the point? Do I make them when I have knowledge or judgment?
- Should I talk to the chair about something that the board does not address well, possibly even his own role?

Broadly speaking, the effective board is destined to provide fervent leadership in the company, developing and promoting the collective vision for the company. The roles of the board and non-executive and executive directors in an effective board include providing direction to senior management; demonstrating ethical leadership; displaying and promoting behaviors consistent with the culture and values defined; creating a performance culture to drive value-creation without exposure to excessive risk, although within the risk appetite limits approved; and establishing the framework to support directors to achieve the statutory duties aligned to shareholders' value and expectations, all elements leading to and allowing for making informed decisions.

14.3.3 BOARD AND COVID-19

The case of coronavirus pandemic (COVID-19) brought unprecedented uncertainty. The COVID-19 is a global crisis never seen before, quite different from the financial crisis of 2007–2008 or influenza. As the sovereigns or supranationals responded with the policy of massive lockdown and social distancing, several businesses were affected, although many governments came with relief package for affected industries. Borders were closed bilaterally or unilaterally on short notice, which severely disrupted the supply chain. Some sectors such as retail, tourism, and energy suffered more than other sectors such as healthcare, groceries, and household. As the government, business, political, or societal leaders have a massive duty to protect people's health at first, health and sanitary issues became a new legal demand to be considered.

Below are some of the actions that a board may follow during a crisis like COVID-19:

- Brief the board/supervisory board of the status.
- Review financial impact and liquidity.
- Present to the board of directors' decisions taken outside the delegated powers by the board, due to the urgency of the situation.
- Review the measures adapted for dividends and share-repurchases.

- Ask for governmental assistance (if it is provided).
- Review the health and safety risks to employees, customers, or relevant stakeholders, as health and sanitary issue is a new legal demand to be considered.
- Review the impact on operations, employees and compensation, and business relationships.
- Review the disruptions or any potential disruptions in supply chain, including the rise of digital supply chain.
- Review the IT infrastructure and cybersecurity policies, as more employees work remotely, and many companies operate in virtual environment.
- Ensure coordinated communication with remote employees, shareholders, or stakeholders with appropriate level of disclosures.
- Convene a Standing Committee or Ad hoc Committee to regularly meet with the management body.
- Create a Crisis Management Team to deal with COVID-19 related risks and reporting.
- Create a contingency and succession plan, in case any board or management member tests positive.
- Address the feasibility of disaster management plan.
- Revisit the vision, strategy and tactics, as well as the business model as a result of COVID-19.

As every crisis has an end, it is essential to frame the post-crisis strategy as well. Often, the executive directors are focused on urgencies and immediate survival or planning, and the non-executive directors should essentially work on shaping future vision and strategy in the post-pandemic era in coordinated collaboration with the management. Tech companies such as Twitter and Shopify announced that they would be switching to digital by default, and many employees would be allowed to work from home permanently, promoting remote work environment

14.4 BOARD DYNAMICS

The dynamics of a board of directors are highly influenced by the chair's leadership, which affects the board members' behavior, dynamics, and performance toward playing the important role of firstly supporting and advising the chair, but more importantly attending board meetings fully prepared and playing and behaving in a way that leads the team to an efficient decision-making process, therefore contributing to sound and robust decisions.

From the chairperson's side, it is very relevant that the expectations of the board members' contribution are set up front in a clear, transparent, and demanding fashion, either during interviews or immediately after the mandate starts, as circumstances may not always allow for dealing with (or are not adequate to be dealt with) over the interviews' process. This should also include the expectations about the works to be conducted by the committees (or ad hoc committees), notably in terms of their global agendas and activities, communication to the board, and commitment in participating in the works. The expectations should include a discussion covering the elements and characteristics of an effective board. Although it is assumed, it is relevant to ensure the relations among the board members are not affected by negative dynamics, including the behavior in and outside the boardroom, where transparency and proper communication eliminate "personal agendas." The assessment process, either the collective or individual self-assessment, is a good structured method to keep this process continuous and keep a healthy pressure on members. The approach should be forward looking.

The problematic dynamics that may occur in a dysfunctional board can be structured and theorized as follows:[307,308]

- *Democracy in Action:* Like voting in the democratic system, the voting of the majority of the board members decides the final outcome. It is possible that the minority may come under immense pressure, even though the result is not desirable. In these types of boards, the dynamics are usually fairly negative, and the division and divergence among board members tends to be wide. Voting is a process of making decisions; however, the more robust decisions are the ones that emerge after sound discussions and through the accommodation of common ground of different viewpoints.

- *Dominated Board:* In a dominated board, the louder or the most erudite dominates. Often, the CEO or former CEO are elected to chairpersonship, imposing as the successor. Not understanding the separation of duties and responsibilities between chair and CEO can bring significant conflicts of interest and negative dynamics. Also, if the chair is not prepared for a new paradigm of chair's responsibilities and roles, there is the risk of often entering the turf of the CEO, even though a CEO is present. As further discussed in Chapter 16: Role of Board Members, "the chair runs the board—leadership role—and the CEO runs the company—command role," a distinction that should be clearly set in the minds of both and the board members.

- *Ratification Board:* The ratification board is dominated by executive presentations, usually with one alternative provoking a rubber stamp decision process; these types of boards also results from a "reverential fear paradigm," where some directors refrain from challenging the chair or other directors due to their seniority or power. The information gap between executive and non-executive directors can be very high, as well as among executives themselves, and few discussions and guidance on priorities, alternative, and dilemmas are carried out. Rubber stamp boards do not ensure the protection of the interest of the shareholders and stakeholders, as the decision-making process is weak, resulting from lack of challenging the proposals and dialogue.

Appropriate guidelines and policies need to be in place for the mitigation of problematic dynamics. The preparation of opinions and positions should be done beforehand. Therefore, "the board begins before the board convenes." After reviewing the documentation, it usually requires bilateral contacts between non-executive directors (often involving the chair) or with the CEO or another executive directors. Board meetings constitute a highly demanding moment, as the board has to discuss a lot of complex materials in a short amount of time, which requires focusing on the essentials and the need for additional clarifications, as well as listening to others' viewpoints. It is also relevant, notably to non-executive directors, to align positions and understand the viewpoints of others about a particular complex or challenging issue or even decide if the information and data provided is enough to make an informed decision. This practice usually avoids unnecessary stresses in the boardroom, which could create negative dynamics and undue stress, resulting from "surprises," a practice that should be avoided, as even "good surprises" do not normally help in establishing good dynamics.

Intuitively, it is a good practice to eliminate any major surprises in the board meetings. Therefore, any significant proposal, disagreements about them, or surprising news (either good or bad) should be shared and discussed with the chair and/or other directors before the board meeting. Some corporates have the practice of setting up one or more "confessional" small rooms, usually with only two chairs, so that board members can meet to discuss situations alone, try to find a common ground, or even align positions. This should happen before the board, but it can also happen when a disagreement emerges during the board, and the directors make an attempt to align positions. Although the intent should be that all the matters placed on the agenda are decided, directors often demand additional information to make an informed decision. In these situations, which should be exceptional, the chair may suggest that the matter should be studied deeper or that other alternatives should be studied and researched. This brings up the question of the involvement of the board on an end-to-end basis in several issues such as changes and adjustments to the business model, the strategic plan, the governance framework, and the internal control framework. The problematic dynamics in the board can be categorized into three segments.

Although directors often do not realize it, the chair always faces the major challenge of ensuring that the board meeting not only deals and makes robust decisions of the full agenda but also finishes on schedule without having to rush discussions and decisions. It is not uncommon to have directors who do not have the cognizance of the time they take to expose their viewpoints or of the moment the matter is exhausted and ready for decision. This topic is of utmost importance to have efficient boards and create good dynamics. A way to control this issue is to allocate an adequate amount of time to ensure proper discussion of each topic of the agenda and consistently enforce the time limit.

There are different views about voting in boards:

1. If there are votes, the board members should always vote; however, this may have the disadvantage of the potentially dividing and breaking the board.
2. Decisions should emerge naturally and pacifically from the discussion; not only is the decision more robust, but it also helps maintaining an environment of good dynamics in the board.

However, the second is not always possible, due to several reasons, and it is a role of the chair to ensure that a good dynamics environment usually leads to better decisions.

The chairperson should establish procedures to ensure that the corporate secretary submits the materials well in advance (two weeks is the best practice) to the board members before the meeting, with the objective of allowing enough time to prepare and reflect on the proposals, the materials for information, and the consequent decisions to be made. The organization should send periodic updates to the board if any crisis or relevant situation emerges (e.g., reputational risk events, COVID-19). Also, the chair should foster an environment where the board members should feel challenged and pressured to contribute to the team. They should engage with executive members and senior management in obtaining the required adequate and proper information about the issues when they consider it necessary.

There are several elements and characteristics that usually indicate a high-performing board.[309] They include:

- Knowledge of their fiduciary responsibility and role as directors.
- Express themselves politely and listen to each other.
- Trust each other to be able to refer to mistakes and less than expected performance.
- Present challenges to proposals and plans.
- Recognize the contributions of the colleagues to the decision-making process and seek advice.
- Participate actively in the board meeting.
- Try to find solutions to problems and challenges that emerge.
- Play as a team even if their viewpoint is not fully considered.

On the opposite, identified characteristics of dysfunctional boards may include:

- Board members criticize each other behind their backs.
- Behave with unnecessary aggressive personalities or even try to dominate the conversation or impose their viewpoint.
- Perception that the contribution of the board members is below the expected standards.

- Do not want to take responsibilities for decisions outside their comfort area.
- Focus on individual goals instead of the ones of the corporation or stakeholders.
- Regularly miss deadlines or continually wish to revisit decisions.

14.4.1 CONFESSION AND COLLUSION IN THE BOARD

As the board is a playground, the board players have the opportunity to confess or collude with each other. For example, two or three directors meet secretly before the board meeting to confess in certain strategic matters, notably to influence decisions in their self-interest or of a third-party interest instead of the interest of the organization, the shareholders, and the stakeholders. This may potentially constitute a collusive environment, resulting in board decisions that are likely to be biased. If the decisions are questionable, it gives a sense of impropriety, though proving improprieties can be very subjective and difficult to investigate.

An article by Peter Vajda[310] mentions that managers and directors may behave differently due to personal reasons and fears such as loss of face, loss of friendships, loss or prestige, loss of a bonus, or the loss of their job, which can be further accelerated by the belief that such unwritten rules are acceptable. As a result, this kind of tacit agreements creates a collusion environment where directors coopt their values and ethics to support their own and others' misdeeds. However, allowing another's collusion, by omission or commission, is another misdeed. It is important to note that collusion environment allows directors and others to engage in unethical, inappropriate, or self-destructive behaviors to gain acceptance, approval, recognition, and security and thereby feel emotionally and psychologically safe. Collusion can be regarded as fraud in some legal frameworks on a deeper level, as it relates to who someone is and how someone conducts relationships with others. Above all, the board culture dramatically influences the potential for the emergence of a collusion culture. Besides the collusion in the board, collusion of management with the board is an issue that can also affect a corporation, breaking the norms of internal controls and corporate functions, particularly in oligopoly situations. This includes the board and the senior management agreeing not to increase the production to keep the price high, or the board and the senior management of two tech firms agreeing not to recruit each other's employees in order to retain talent and keep labor costs down. The New York Times reported that between 2005 and 2009, Silicon Valley industry executives colluded not to poach one another's employees.[311]

In the corporate world, collusion may come with several flavors. Expressions or behaviors include:

- "Keep quiet."
- "You scratch my back, and I'll scratch yours."
- "Going along to get along."
- "One hand washing another."

The following are some examples of collusion:

- When one director withholds honest and forthright comments about inappropriate behavior in a meeting for fear of alienating another director whose work the first director respects or admires.
- When a director pledges allegiance to another director, manager, or co-worker, so that both can feel emotionally safe with each other.
- When one director shares insider information with only a select few directors or managers, so that they are viewed as caring about them and feel they are special.
- When directors lash out on a third party through bullying, sarcasm, or gossiping, therefore experiencing a false sense of connection and camaraderie with other co-colluders at the expense of the third party.

The vital question is: Why do directors—or humans in general—collude? As a human, most of us naturally experience some degree of deficiency. Some humans feel it more and some less. Dealing with such a level of deficiency, humans choose to collude to understand the deficiency and the underlying motives for colluding, and therefore take conscious steps to effectively reduce and eliminate the deficiency so that they can show up authentically with integrity and self-responsibly. Another view is that humans deceive, ignore, deny, or resist telling the truth, hoping to keep their relationships with themselves and others emotionally intact and that the denial will keep the emotional peace. Apparently, collusion is a "progressive drug," as humans lie and collude more and more to maintain the false feeling of emotional safety. This, in return, makes a human vigilant, fearful, worried, and concerned about being found out and about what the co-colluders perceive. Therefore, colluding is exhausting and may require an undue amount of physical, mental, and emotional energy.

Getting rid of a collusive mindset—which is included in the dynamics of dysfunctional boards—is certainly not easy.

Essentially, it requires two-fold processes:

1. To seek understanding of the reasons or excuses someone refrains from or refuses to tell others the truth.
2. To then set the intention to tell the truth when often other individuals would rather resist.

The appetite to tell the truth requires empathy, compassion, acceptance, and courage.[312] Behaving appropriately frees oneself emotionally, physically, spiritually, and psychologically; behaving ethically and appropriately allows oneself to show up authentically, honestly, and in integrity. Therefore, behaving ethically and appropriately is the only way to experience true and real relationships with others. Board members and directors are expected to become knowledgeable in such subject matters and essentially cascade the same tone and risk culture down the organizational structure in a corporate.

As board members and directors are the fiduciary to corporates, they must also be strictly guided by the fiduciary duties of care, duties of loyalty, and duties of obedience, at all the times. The corporate should have a whistleblowing policy, which refers to employee/board member reporting an activity that is dishonest or illegal. It is observed that most corporates these days have a whistleblowing policy to manage their own reputational risk, which is compulsory in the European Union, notably in the financial system, actually being a part of the controls over behavior supervision. *The Guardian* reported that Barclays Bank was hit with 15 million dollar fine by a New York regulator over attempts by its then chief executive and senior management to identify a whistleblower who wrote to the bank's board over the hiring of the head of the bank's financial institutions group in New York, New York in 2016.[313] The chief executive was separately fined to the tune of £642,430 by the UK's financial regulators, which represents just 14 percent of his total compensation.[314]

14.5 GLOBAL AGENDAS, MEETING AGENDAS, MINUTES, AND BOARD MEETING PROCESS

The activities of a board of directors, the executive committee, and the board's committees should be guided and framed by the global agenda of the board. The global agenda can be built down-up (i.e., the committees define the specific topics to be reviewed and discussed along the mandate) or top-down (the board defines the topics and then the committees develop their agendas based on it), following the same approach to ad hoc committees of the board. There are advantages and disadvantages to either process, which can be mitigated by dialogue, interaction, and teamwork among the parties.

It is also necessary to establish the frequency under which the topics are included in the agenda. There are topics that must be included in almost all meetings of both the board and the committees. Other topics should be on the agenda every quarter, every semester, annually, or at an even a wider frequency. The agendas should also be divided into priorities, that is, separate matters for decision, information, investment plan, international operations and subsidiaries, or others, depending on the size and complexity of the business. The appropriateness of the agendas should be reviewed periodically to ensure that there are relevant matters that are added to the global agenda, such as change in regulation and legal framework, adjustments to the business model or strategic plan, unexpected compliance and reputational issues, and geopolitical matters when the operation has an international footprint.

Usually, the topics for global agenda circle around the following matters (although not limited to):

- Review the financial results of the month.
- Report to the board of the results of the work of the board committees and taskforces.
- Oversee the integrity of the financial reporting process.
- Oversee the risk governance model.
- Oversee and review the corporate strategy, if necessary.
- Review of diversity and inclusion issues such as gender balance, pay gap, among others.
- Review sustainability and ESG (Environment, Social, and Governance).
- Ensure that the entity has effective policies and programs to prevent and detect fraud.
- Oversee the entity's communications regarding financial results, notably obtained from rating agencies, analysts, and regulators.
- Promote a culture of ethics and compliance with existing internal and external rules and develop a process of investigation into relevant noncompliance situations.
- Oversee the internal audit and its annual plan.

- Appoint the external auditor and supervise their independence.
- Review of taxation, Foreign Direct Investment (FDI), competition issues, among others.
- Maintain a fluid communication process with the external auditor and/or regulators on matters required by law or regulation and/or required by the applicable auditing standards.

The agenda must be strategic, material, and ripe for decision, something that only the board can handle. Usually, the best practice recommends that six or seven is a reasonable number of agenda items that should be prepared to be discussed in the board meeting, although this can be adjusted depending on their complexity. Before approving the agendas, the chair (via corporate secretary) must request inputs from directors and then circulate a first draft, which should be sent to the corporate secretary to forward it to the services, although only the matters relating to the specific service should be disclosed to the latter. The role of the chair is crucial in designing, conducting, and following up with the meeting (further discussed in Section 16.1.1: "Characteristics of a Good Chair"). Depending on the size and complexity of the organization, boards' meeting should focus their time more on business model issues, strategic plan, financial results, investment plan, talent, IT and cyber security, geopolitics, and pandemic (COVID-19) rather than on operations, which is reserved as the focus of executive directors and senior management.

The old Institute of Internal Auditors (IIA) three lines of defense model advocated that the board should not be involved in the first line of defense (e.g., commercial areas and, in banks, the credit analysis), although IIA released a major update in 2020 acknowledging that this approach is not in line with the best practices, as the non-executive directors and the board as a whole have particular responsibilities in monitoring the adherence to the business model of the organization and facilitating the identification for the need of adjustments to it, namely in relation to provision of products and services to customers as well as managing risk potentially entering the institution.

The board is about deciding, not executing. The board meeting is also not the forum for framing problems. The directors should be aware and informed of any information gap, being always prepared by reviewing the materials distributed, keeping in mind the important decisions they have to make. The chair and the corporate secretary should ensure that all board members receive the final agenda items at least two weeks before the meeting so that they have enough time to review and reflect, possibly even have discussions with colleagues to be able to come prepared.

The minutes are the product of board or committee meetings, which is why they represent a very important document in the life of organizations for the directors who carry their fiduciary responsibility as well as for supervisors to be able to perform their duties, as the minutes support the discussions held and decisions taken in meetings. Directors should have in mind that, independent of the discussions and interactions in the board room, the content of the minutes is usually prevalent over other arguments, depending on the country's legal framework. This may include recalling discussions had in the meeting, details, and background (which are often interpreted in a range of ways) when the need to analyze a particular discussion and consequent decision arises. This is why directors should be very conscientious, careful, detailed, and objective in reviewing minutes of the meetings to which they agreed and signed, as they may be bounded in the future based on the lack of content of the minutes, notably in terms of their fiduciary responsibilities.

Therefore, the minutes of the board and committees' meetings (as well as ad hoc committees if they exist) should be prepared immediately after the meeting, while minds are fresh to remember and recall the debate. A practical and prudent recommendation to boards and committees' members relates to the prudence of keeping in file the minutes reviewed and agreed but not yet signed for all least the number of years the country's legal framework establishes (or countries, when integrating a board of a corporation with international footprint) a board and committee's members can be made accountable under their fiduciary responsibility. A reason for this is that, in practice, many directors are requested to sign the final minute in a moment when it may not be feasible to read and review it in detail before signing. Keeping the minute's draft, a director who gave the "green light" can ensure that the actual content to which agreement was given corresponds to the one reflected in the final version. If turbulent times emerge, either resulting from or into a corporate governance crisis, this mechanism may help the director in case there were changes introduced after the director's review was performed.

Another recommendation relates to the need to maintain in file the signed minutes' PDF of all relevant meetings related to the board, and also of other social bodies, where the legal framework allows, which happens in most jurisdictions in issues that affect the director. Although governance has a fundamental pillar related to trust, and a director should exercise the duties under a trustful umbrella, the director should also maintain in mind and be conscious of individual fiduciary responsibilities and the related risk that may occur by action or omission. When a lawsuit or query by a supervisor is filed, the director should be prepared to provide the lawyers or supervisor evidence, and if that not in his/her possession, it will not make the process more difficult, notably in situations where a conflict has emerged. Although this should not be expected, a director must be prepared for this type of incidents.

The financial system regulation and guidelines require the minutes to reflect the discussions in detail, including the names of the directors and the content of the interventions. There are corporates that, with the authorization of the board members and especially at the beginning of the mandate, tape the meetings to better reflect the content of the discussion under the General Data Protection Regulation (GDPR). After the minute is signed, the best practice indicates that the tape should be destroyed. In the nonfinancial system, in countries that do not require detailed minutes, the best practice of the financial system can then be adopted, reflecting the practice of a good governance framework.

In conclusion, the chair and the corporate secretary must ensure that the minutes of the meetings are delivered to board and committees' members, including justified absentees, as well as the decisions made indicating the results of the voting, on a timely basis and ideally update the same information in the governance section of the corporate's website. This may facilitate information clarity to shareholders and relevant stakeholders. Finally, directors, including the chair and the corporate secretary are suggested to catalog and archive the historical minutes, either using an approved software (e.g., PDF) or physically archiving in a secured place, so that they can always fetch historical information orderly and, most importantly, during disputes. In organizations with an international footprint, consideration should be given to maintain outside the country all or relevant minutes, mainly having in mind the political instability and/or the potential for expropriation of foreign direct investment.

The process of control over the agendas as well as the administrative part of the process, including the control over the documentation to be made available to directors, vary depending on the size and complexity of the business. There are organizations with support staff dedicated to the board (often named Office of the Chair) on a full-time basis, which also includes a group of external advisors and consultants such as specialists in the area of industry, law, and corporate governance. For less complex organizations, it is common to leverage the office of the corporate secretary. This structure and process is very relevant, and the chair should therefore ensure at the beginning of the mandate that an adequate structure is in place to support the board, notably in liaison with the executive committee and the services of the organization to ensure that documents are produced timely and that information requested is provided.

Statistics suggest that organizations hold more than 3 billion meetings per year, and directors spend 40–50 percent of the working hours in meetings, that is, 23 hours per week. 9 out of 10 people daydream in meetings, 25 percent of meetings are spent discussing irrelevant issues, and 73 percent of employees do other work in meetings.[315] Also, a *Fortune 50* company estimates losses in excess of 75 million dollars per year due to poor meetings, and a meeting between several managers or executives may cost upward of 1,000 dollar per hour in salary costs alone. These figures ultimately underscore the importance and cost of effective meeting, which is why the example should start at the top, that is, at the board.

14.5.1 DESIGNING AN AGENDA FOR EFFECTIVE MEETING

An effective agenda sets clear expectations regarding what needs to occur before and during a meeting, allowing enough time for board members to prepare, standard allocation of time, effective discussion, proper identification of when the discussion is complete, and increasing board members' ability to quickly address consensus conflicts, if any. Often, the concept of design thinking is exploited in designing the agenda and the meeting process. Several authors have published guidelines regarding the design of an effective agenda and meeting process. One of such is cited below:[316]

- *Seek input from board members or/and senior management:* It is important that the agenda addresses the needs of the participating members; most likely, the chair of the board would ask members about the agenda items to be addressed in a team setting with proper reasoning. Depending on the needs, the categorization from high priority to low priority may be followed. If any agenda item is excluded, the chair may facilitate the reasoning for the choice to the respective member. This helps in developing the empathy.

- *Select agenda items that affect the entire board:* As scheduling independent non-executive and executive directors at the same time is often difficult, board meeting time is expensive and valuable. Therefore, high priority agenda items that affect all members and require all members to solve must be discussed. In case two departments are interdependent, the board members from such departments may coordinate.

- *List agenda items as questions the boards need to answer:* Rather than setting down agenda items in a phrase, setting them in a question could constitute more clarity. For example, one of the potential agenda items "Increasing profit" may be restructured as "How can we increase profit under current market circumstances?" A question is supposed to assist board members by increasing clarity, preparing the discussion, and monitoring their own and others' comments are on track.

- *Understand the purpose of the agenda item:* The participating board members must clearly know whether the main purpose of the agenda is seeking further information or input for a decision, or it is making a decision. This allows board members to know exactly what the outcome of each agenda item should be. The purpose of agenda items and any updates should be distributed prior to the meeting. For example, if the purpose of one agenda item is to make a decision, then the role of the chair becomes even more crucial. The chair may state at the beginning of that particular agenda item: "The chair looks forward to make this decision by consensus, but if the board is not able to reach consensus after one hour of discussion, the chair reserves the right to make a decision based on the conversation the board had."

- *Estimate a realistic amount of time for each agenda item:* Depending on the number of the agenda items, time may be estimated realistically. Assessing things such as how much time the team will need for introducing the topic, answering questions, resolving different points of view, generating potential solutions, and agreeing on the action items that follow from discussion and decisions is vital. Considering the purpose of the agenda item "How can we increase profit under current market circumstances," the chair may allot one hour to make a decision after discussion in a 10-member board, with each member having approximately six minutes to speak, which may be realistic. Also, within six minutes, the board members are supposed to fit their comments; however, if comments are not fully drawn within six minutes, a little more time may be requested. The idea is not to frustrate the board members since that may lead to poor decision-making.

- *Propose a process for addressing each agenda item:* This is nothing but the formal framework of how the discussion should move, based on the purpose of the agenda item. Often, the board neglects the framework for discussion and participates based on their own process. The chair must set the tone at the top by modeling a learning mindset. If the purpose of the agenda item is to seek input for a decision, the chair may write the detailed process for addressing the agenda and seek consensus from the board. For example, I (chair) suggest the following process to seek input: First 15 minutes to gather all the relevant information on the table; next 15 minutes to identify and agree on any assumptions; another 15 minutes to agree on business interests; and finally crafting a solution that undertakes assumptions adequately and account all the interests.

- *Specify how members should prepare for the meeting:* Again, this depends on the purpose of the agenda. It is important to distribute the agenda with enough time such that the board members can be well prepared for each item. Nowadays, boards often provide directors with secured electronic devices such as iPad or tablets equipped with proper software so that board members can prepare seamlessly and adequately.

- *Identify who is responsible for leading each topic:* Usually, the chair leads and moderates the board meetings. However, directors may also lead particular agenda items, providing context for the topic and explaining data, as they may have organizational responsibility for that area.

- *Review and modify the agenda as needed:* This is to ensure that the team uses its meeting time most effectively, checking if anything has significantly changed before the meeting, even though the agenda items are developed together in consensus.

- *End the meeting with a plus/delta:* Plus/delta is a quick, simple retrospective to improve meetings, planning sessions, or repetitive activities that form the basis for continuous improvement. It is usually done in the last 5–10 minutes of a meeting or activity. Plus refers to the things that brought value and how the board can repeat that. Delta refers to the things the board can change or add to bring more value and ways the board can do better. The board should focus on the process of each particular meeting rather than focusing on people. Questions for plus/delta may include:
  - o Was the agenda distributed in time for everyone to prepare?
  - o How well did team members prepare for the meeting?
  - o How well did we estimate the time needed for each agenda item?
  - o How well did we allocate our time for decision-making and discussion?
  - o How well did everyone stay on-topic?
  - o How well did team members speak up when they thought someone was off topic?
  - o How effective was the process for each agenda item?

A sample meeting agenda is shown in Table 14.1.

Table 14.1: A sample meeting agenda

SN	Agenda Item	Purpose	Preparation	Proposed Meeting Process
1	What changes, if any, should we make to the agenda? **Time:** 2 minutes **Leader:** Chair	Decision	None	The Chair conducts the poll in the board.
2	What deltas from the previous meeting will we focus on the meeting? **Time:** 3 minutes **Leader:** Chair	Decision	Review applicable deltas from the previous meeting notes.	The Chair reviews the area of improvement agreed on this board meeting.
3	Who is going to become the next CFO? **Time:** 30 minutes **Leader:** Chair	Decision	Review the attached CV of three shortlisted candidates and the recommendation from the nomination committee.	Time allotment for each director to give recommendations with reasoning: **3 mins** (considering 10 directors in the board).
4	How do we increase sales and boost profitability? **Time:** 60 minutes **Leader:** CEO-ED	Decision	Identify relevant information, criteria and assumptions that you believe should guide your decision.	Statement of the problem: **5 mins.** The team identifies and agrees on relevant information to consider: **10 mins.** Identify and agree on criteria for acceptable solutions: **10 mins.** Identify and agree on assumptions: **10 mins.** Craft solutions that meet the above constraints: **15 mins.**

SN	Agenda Item	Purpose	Preparation	Proposed Meeting Process
5	Which firm should we select for the horizontal acquisition? **Time:** 60 minutes **Leader:** NED	Seek Information	Read the attached memo recommending three firms with your reasoning.	Time allotment for each director to speak: **6 mins** (considering 10 directors in the board).
6	**Plus/Delta** What did we do well for this meeting? What should we do differently for the next meeting? **Time:** 5 minutes **Leader:** Chair	Decision	None	Members identify pluses and deltas. The team agrees on deltas to work on for the next meeting.

Source: (*Harvard Business Review*—Roger Schwarz)[317]

14.5.2 BUILDING A FORWARD-LOOKING BOARD AGENDA

McKinsey[318] mentions that governance arguably suffers the most when board directors spend too much time looking in the rear-view mirror and not enough scanning the road ahead. The directors of the corporate tend to spend 70 percent of the time on quarterly reports, audit reviews, budgets, and compliance instead of spending time on matters related to the future prosperity and direction of the business. Therefore, there should be an alternative to develop a dynamic board agenda that highlights forward-looking activities so that directors can have enough time over a 12-month period to adjust with the future agenda.

Figure 14.4 demonstrates the activities and agendas forward-looking boards should consider in addition to that of traditional board agendas over the 12-month period.

Figure 14.5 provides a detailed key for the number labeling (1–24).

Figure 14.4: How forward-looking boards should spend their time

Source: (McKinsey)

Figure 14.5: Details on selected activities

Details on selected activities (all others are self-explanatory, as labeled)

Fiduciary
1 Annual accounts
2 Annual budget directives
3 Next year's budget
4 Auditors' report
5 Audit-planning approach
6 Audit-committee reviews

Strategy
7 Set framework for the year
8 Define broad options
9 Outline/select options
10 Approve final strategy approach
11 Review strategic and competitive position, key performance indicators

Investment
12 Engage in ongoing review of investment proposals

Talent
13 Set talent-review objectives for the year
14 Review top 30-50 people

Risk
15 Determine risk-review objectives for the year
16 Conduct annual risk review, including mitigation approaches

Board reinvention
17 Conduct board 360 evaluation
18 Determine approach for board-process enhancement

Decisions
19 Engage in decision making-eg, on budgets, investments, M&A, and key nominations

Board education
20 Travel with sales staff, customer visits
21 Visit R&D facilities
22 Visit new geographies
23 Inspect production sites
24 Attend customer conference

Source: (McKinsey)

461

The foundation to create a forward-looking board is built by the future interpolation and mapping of the appropriate board skills to at least three years, the candidates having appropriate skills for today and for the future, well-defined board roles, and ultimately the hard-working board members with a "get it done" spirit.

Topics of the Chapter

The following has been discussed within this chapter:

- The principles of corporate governance by G20/OECD (summarized in Figure 14.1) and by BCBS are discussed in detail.
- The board's fiduciary duty towards is defined as:
  1. Duty of Care
  2. Duty of Loyalty
  3. Duty of Obedience
     o Failure to uphold these duties can result in significant fines, imprisonment, and damage to reputation.
- Public corporates tend to have 4–15 members in the board of directors; having 4–10 is recommended, with a majority by independent non-executive directors.
- An effective board is one that defines the company's purpose, vision, and mission, then sets a strategy to achieve the vision.
- The following dynamics are indicative of a dysfunctional board and must be resolved:
  1. Democracy in Action
  2. Dominated Board
  3. Ratification Board
- The activities of a board of directors, the executive committee, and the board's committees, as well as ad hoc committees if they exist should be guided and framed by the global agenda of the board.
  1. Table 14.1 and Figure 14.4 offer examples of how board agendas can/should look.

- The board and committees' meetings should be properly documented in the minutes, namely indicating the names of the directors and their interventions, the results of the voting. Also, directors are encouraged to keep the version of the minutes they approved, as well as the PDF duly signed. For companies with an international footprint consideration should be given to keep copies of the minutes outside the country, namely if the foreign investment is in a country or region with political instability.

Chapter 15

Decision-Making

All of the preceding chapters discuss everything the board needs in order to ensure well-informed and high-quality decision-making. This chapter discusses how a board actually makes high-quality decisions and barriers to do so.

The decision-making process is an intrinsic component of a corporate governance framework, as the organizational structure and the processes and systems exist to lead to decisions by boards. Well-informed and high-quality decision-making are critical requirements for the board efficacy and effectiveness. The decision should be structured culminating on an analytical basis. Flawed decisions can be made even with the best of intentions involving competent individuals. Nevertheless, factors that lead to poor decision-making are predictable and preventable in most cases. Boards can minimize that risk by properly designing the decision-making policies and procedures with active participation of selected board committees.

It starts with the conscious establishment of a culture of rigor and risk for the functioning and operational side of boards with a demanding setting of a framework. It also includes an adequate planning and setting of procedures, including the timely distribution of materials to directors and a predetermined structure for the documents submitted to the executive committee and to the board, notably including an executive summary and a short PowerPoint for long documents.

If the goal of the corporation is to become a global leader in digital payment technology, then the board of directors is liable to measure such abilities of the corporate, and therefore facilitate enforcing the adequate policies to reach that goal.

The cultural mindset emerging from the tone from the top and drilled-down the organization pyramid, notably resulting from policies such as code of work, code of ethics and conflicts of interests, diversity policies, and pay gap monitoring directed toward shareholders, customers, employees, and other important stakeholders should be explicitly nurtured to construct a healthy decision-making culture. The board of directors is directly responsible for assuring that their decisions (such as internationalization and new market entry, mergers, acquisitions and divestitures, exiting markets, pricing positions, among others) are aligned with the vision and strategic plan and interests of the corporation as well as its business model. The board should periodically review the standings of the corporate governance framework and subsequently guide the proactive management of the corporate's culture, including ethics stance, risk capacity, risk appetite, risks assumption, speed of decision, among others. The Governance Framework should ensure that people know[319] which decisions have the most influence on corporate's objectives, who should be involved in these decisions, what decision-making process should be used, and how outcomes will be tracked.

15.1 TRAPS AND BIASES IN DECISION-MAKING

Research shows that when decisions go wrong, the fault may lie in the mind of the decision maker rather than in the decision-making process itself, which can be led by decision-making traps and biases. Therefore, there is a risk of directors being a victim to traps and biases, a paradigm that can lead to a dangerous situation for corporate. Therefore, directors are required to become deeply knowledgeable of psychological traps and biases[320] that may undermine decisions in general and business decisions in particular, namely the ones involving the board.

- **The Anchoring Trap**

Sometimes, in decision-making, the mind may give more weight to past event or trend over other factors because of the developed heuristics, such as projecting the sales of the coming year by looking at the sales of the previous year. In the business world, a common anchor is often a past event or trend relying on those to make psychological assumptions. As technological changes and rapid changes in the marketplace are inevitable, relying solely on historical data or long series' anchors can be dangerous and misleading for the corporate standings. It is critical to be open-minded and view issues and challenges from different perspectives.

- **The Status Quo Trap**

Status quo relates to the development of mental dependency from an existing situation, conditioning its questioning. The trap of the status quo lies very deep within our psyches. For example, if A and B are the given options, people may select the traditional status quo A instead of selecting both A and B. Selecting the status quo doesn't require an effort but choosing between A and B may require an additional effort. For example, in corporations, often one status quo is that commission may be more punishable than omission, if things go wrong. Hence, it is very important for directors to become aware and live the corporate's objectives, identify options beyond the status quo, and carefully examine all other options before taking decisions.

- **The Sunk-Cost Trap**

People tend to make choices in ways that justify past decisions, even though the past decisions should be challenged or not considered as valid assumptions, for example, investing hugely in improving an employee's performance who was hired without fulfilling the defined profile for the position (in boards, notably the Fit and Proper process), therefore, not to have been hired in the first place, leading to a stance of not admitting a prior mistake. The business world calls past decisions "sunk-costs," using the metaphor as an expression to define a non-recoverable cost. It may be difficult to become completely free from past decisions, particularly in business, because a bad decision is often a critical matter, inviting comments from colleagues or bosses. Also, if the corporate culture demands severe penalty for bad decisions, managers will be motivated to let failed projects drag endlessly, hoping that they will somehow be able to transform the project into a success. Essentially, it is important for the board and managers to understand that some good decisions can also fail in the future and should therefore not cultivate a failure-fearing culture.

- **The Confirming-Evidence Trap**

Sometimes, the board members can make decisions with "instincts" that support their point of view. They rely solely on information relating to their viewpoint without considering the data and information in relation to other viewpoints. The Confirming-Evidence trap is significantly seen on a preferential viewpoint than the alternative viewpoint. This is why directors should be able to see different viewpoints in equal weight and play devil's advocate to challenge and debate on the viewpoint they deem important. Linked to this issue are the decisions made on proposals to the board that only present one alternative, leading to a rubber stamp decision-making process.

- **The Framing Trap**

In decision-making, the first step should be to frame the question. If the question is poorly framed, this can have a profound and decisive effect on even the best-considered decision. Therefore, directors should not automatically accept the first frame; they should challenge and debate the frame from different angles, eventually leading to the most appropriate decision. Different frames should be challenged until a final frame is decided.

- **The Estimating and Forecasting Traps**

Managers make estimates and forecasts, but they don't have the incentives to get clear feedback about their accuracy versus its execution in continuous intervals. The weather forecasters and bookmakers have opportunities and incentives to maintain judgmental records at all times, but the managers do not. This trap can distort managerial decision-making when dealing with uncertainty. The estimating and forecasting traps lead to three other decision-making traps:

o   The Overconfidence Trap

Directors and managers often tend to become over-confident about the decisions they make. They may have an impression that their judgment and prediction are impeccable and unchallengeable, even though it should be considered that most estimates and forecasts are often influenced by complex environments eventually not being achieved. This results from a process that considers a narrow range of components, perspective, and challenges, which can easily lead to errors in judgment, which is why low and high ends of possible value ranges must be considered.

o   The Prudence Trap

Prudence or overcautiousness is another type of trap. When managers are facing high-stakes decisions, they are likely to adjust their estimates or forecasts to be on the safe side. It is important to note that too much prudence can be dangerous as well as too little. Estimates should always be stated honestly, informing the readers of the assumptions and scenarios that frame the process of estimating and projecting figures into the future, a concept that always involves a degree of uncertainty.

o   The Recallability Trap

People tend to make a decision on future events based on the memory of past events or experiences, even though people are neither very confident nor prudent about it. Therefore, directors and managers should consider and be careful to ensure that their decisions are not unduly influenced by past experiences. It differs from the Anchoring Trap in its basis being in personal memory and not in heuristics.

15.2 COMPARING DECISION-MAKING

15.2.1 DECISION-MAKING VS DEBATE

The board should act as a competitive ground for pursuing constructive debate and positive dynamics among its members. Good decision-making is facilitated by high-quality board data and documentation of support to the process. The board should always consider seeking expert opinions on any doubts.

Hiring third-party consultants is acceptable, as long as the boundaries of stakeholder's interests are not compromised. Such areas may result of gaps in the board collective Fit and Proper matrix of competences. They may include cybersecurity, derivative hedging, hiring an investment firm to launch a bond issue digital, geopolitics and geoeconomy, mergers, acquisitions and divestiture, public offers, activism, remuneration, or corporate governance best practice; or internal areas that the board decides to assess or appraise to ensure they are aligned with the best practice.

A healthy discussion in the board demands the information be analyzed from multiple angles with a willingness to challenge assumptions and bias. Therefore, the board should suitably allow time for debate and challenge, especially for complex, contentious, or business-critical issues, to achieve timely closure. Furthermore, the decisions that the board members conclude should provide clarity on the actions, timescales, and responsibilities.

15.2.2 DECISION-MAKING VS AWARENESS

Board members monitor the evolution of new potential components that impact the business models, namely digital transformation;

environmental, social, and governance (ESG) related risks; or new opportunities or threats that should be addressed. Likewise, board members are expected to be aware of geopolitics and international affairs in jurisdictions where the business operates and, when necessary, where the business may expand. Awareness of such data and information grants board members the skills and ability to make effective decisions. When a board fails to give enough attention to the risk, it is more inclined to adopt a detective approach instead of a preventative approach. As corporate risks can be very punitive, treating the risk should not be just a compliance issue but be well integrated into the early decision-making process. Otherwise, the level of risk involved in a project may endanger corporate stability and sustainability.

15.2.3 DECISION-MAKING VS ETHICS

While the concept of ethics can be very extensive, business ethics are the set of measures that the board members should adequately follow while performing their duties and responsibilities. They may extend beyond the board and the corporate. Ethical values are unveiled in the form of industry best practices, which often forms the basis for nourishing a healthy corporate culture. High ethical values are seldom demanded by the shareholders and the stakeholders. The board members, being fiduciary to the shareholders and stakeholders, should never perform duties for their own self-interest. Sometimes, board politics may lead to reluctance to involve independent directors. The matters may be presented in the board as a sign-off rather than having a constructive debate. Some of the board members may tend to have complacent or intransigent attitude. All these things demonstrate weak organizational culture and low values, and such things may have an adverse effect on corporate's sustainability.

15.3 DECISION-MAKING DYNAMICS IN BOARD

As board members are required to take vital decisions for the well-being of the corporate, it is essential that they excel at decision-making.

A survey conducted by McKinsey[321] found that most companies settle with the trade-offs between velocity (how fast was the decision made and executed?) and quality (how good was the decision?), and faster decisions tend to be of higher quality, suggesting that speed does not undercut the merit of a given decision. Only 20 percent of respondents mentioned their organizations excel at decision-making. Essentially, good decision-making practices tend to yield decisions that are both high quality and fast. The survey also found that quality and speed of decision-making are both strongly associated with overall company performance. The decision types can be—big-bet, ad hoc, cross-cutting, and delegated decisions. *Big-bet* decisions are infrequent. They should be carefully considered, taking into consideration the duty of care components under which board members make decisions. These include high-stake decisions in the board, such as acquisitions and annual resource allocation, which may potentially restructure the company. *Ad hoc* decisions are infrequent and arise episodically, such as decisions taken during the coronavirus pandemic. *Cross-cutting* decisions are like big-bets decisions but more frequent and familiar, and often consist of series of smaller, interconnected decisions made by different groups in the company as part of a collaborative, end-to-end decision process (e.g., pricing decision). *Delegated decisions* are frequent and are narrower in scope, such as HR policy, BYOD (Bring Your Own Device) policy, among others. They are often handled by a single individual or a team that usually requires limited input from others.

As the current era is fueled by the data-driven age, machine learning algorithms are often exploited by the company to make smart decisions that may essentially help in reducing or minimizing the traps and biases in corporate decision-making. Nonetheless, if smart tools are not properly executed, this may result in disengagement (too many reports or presentations), paralysis (confused by too much data), and anxiety (high stakes).[322] Therefore, one of the solutions for the company board or management seeking to untangle the decision-making is to become flatter and more agile while incorporating decision-making and accountability hand to hand.

With corporate scandals in companies such as Enron, Parmalat, or WorldCom, or Disney paying 140 million dollars payout to dismissed President Michael Ovitz, corporate boards are under increased scrutiny by shareholders, stakeholders, and activists. For example, if directors of Disney had obliged with the protocols of compensation committee, they might have stopped Michael Eisner from extending an overly generous separation package to his new hire, or if the directors at Enron had taken the time to request and assess the rationale behind CFO Andrew Fastow's proposal to form off-balance sheet partnerships, they might have prevented the company's downfall. Many corporates these days have more independent directors than there were before. They often develop a formal process for figuring out which decisions should go to the board. Some of the following are presented below:[323]

- *Annual Calendar:* Many corporations are creating a schedule for topics that the board must consider, for example, company strategy in January, business plan in February, capital budget in March, among others. Similarly, schedules may be set for audit, compensation, nominations and governance, or other standing committees. This is meant to ensure that that the board members participate in key decisions.
- *Committee Charters:* Often, corporations develop charters to define the decisions for which the board committees are responsible. Even though the committee decisions need to be ratified by the board, actual decisions are largely made within the committees. For example, the charter of the remuneration committee may need the composition of all independent directors, and the committee charter requires that directors choose independent compensation consultants, review remuneration plans, equity awards, among others.

- *Decision Protocols:* It is important that companies explicitly define which decisions to be taken by the board (directors) and by the management (executives). For example, a rules protocol detailing director decision on financial reporting, risk management, human resources, competitive strategy, acquisitions and divestitures, technology, and governance and compliance may be disclosed to foster transparency and trust.

Sound governance culture is fundamentally important. It is also meant to deal with other unexpected board worthy issues such as regulatory shift, competitor moves, coronavirus pandemic, or technological advancements that the decision protocols may not cover. At times, the chief executive makes the judgment call based on informal norms that have evolved over time. This ultimately reflects the company governance culture and the personality of the CEO and his/her relationship with the rest of the executive team and with the board. The board of directors often hoard the decisions (i.e., not make the decisions objectively and defer them most of the times). Essentially, board hoarders may find it difficult to discern between important and irrelevant details. In Section 14.4: "Board Dynamics," three natures of boards are discussed, namely Democracy in Action, Dominated Board, and Ratification Board.

In *Democracy in Action boards*, the final outcome is decided by the vote of the majority of members. In most cases, voting may not be necessary after having sound discussions and achieving consensus. In *Dominated boards*, the louder or the most erudite dominates, such as when the ex-CEO becomes the chairperson and does not understand the separation of duties and responsibilities between the chair and the CEO. In *Ratification boards*, the board meetings are dominated by executive presentations. The decision-making process may be rubber stamped without end-to-end discussions between independent and executive directors in the board, and this type of boards may also result from a "reverential fear paradigm" where directors may refrain from challenging the chair or other directors due to their seniority or power. Rubber stamp boards cannot ensure the protection of the interest the shareholders and stakeholders, and decision-making process is already weak due to the lack of challenge to the proposals and dialogue.

Because the board is a challenging place and is now being scrutinized more than ever, its appropriate composition is essentially crucial, one that can make decisions objectively without hoarding or acting as a rubber stamp while embodying the appropriate protocols, rules, or charters to set a well-toned governance culture, or norms cascading from the top to the bottom of the organization. The board should be actively involved in high-impact decisions that may shape the future of the company. Essentially, decision-making norms take shape in a common-law manner, incorporating lessons learned from previous applications. Governance culture is what shapes the norm. Improved decision-making can be generative as well as protective, and it can be agreed that good decisions about strategy or products push the business to the next performance level, preserving the value for shareholders and stakeholders.

As the board can be prone to traps and biases in decision-making, this is often amplified by factors such as ambiguity, attachment to organization, approval, familiarity, among others. Essentially, good decision-making depends on good meeting process (i.e., board members having access to the right information at the right time, board members being prepared to ask questions, board members having adequate time for decision-making, among others). The development of effective and efficient board processes that aid decision-making can be enhanced by boards giving specific feedback to management. Ultimately, a board decision should be strategic; informed; smart; balanced and fair; and sustainable, affordable, and legal.

15.3.1 EXAMPLE OF DECISION-MAKING FRAMEWORK

Many companies have developed their own decision-making frameworks. Often, companies' decisions and decision-making are guided by the set of core operating principles. Stripe, an American technology company, has operating principles including—we haven't won yet; move with urgency and focus; think rigorously; trust and amplify, among others. The principles have defined in a way that acknowledges potential tensions and highlights which principle takes precedence in the case of conflict. For example, "think rigorously" is paramount for high-impact and irreversible decisions, whereas "move with urgency" is critical for decisions that are lower impact and potentially tunable. Essentially, the operating principles form the core principle in company decision-making.

Flatiron Health, which ballooned from 4 employees to 135, has developed a decision-making framework also known as "Xanax for decision-making."[324] As start-ups scale, teams grow, perspectives become more diverse, and problems become increasingly complex. In the framework "Xanax for decision-making," it is essential to establish the distinction between good decision-making and good decisions. For example, a good decision can be chaotic if employees are not happy about it. The framework discusses two types of decisions—*Type 1: Irreversible decisions* and *Type 2: Reversible decisions*. The CTO of Flatiron Health mentions that people will expect and accept scrutiny and overhead for Type 1 decisions, whereas streamlining Type 2 decisions makes teams and the people on them happy, allowing things to be accomplished without the usual stress. The framework can be used for either.

The framework matrix starts with a basic chart. It consists of two or more decision options checked against benefits, costs, and mitigations (Table 15.1).

Table 15.1: Xanax for decision-making framework

	Option A	**Option B (or more)**
Benefits	xxx	xxx
Costs	xxx	xxx
Mitigations	xxx	xxx

This can be a quick, stand-alone process or collaborative when working in a team writing on a whiteboard or Google Doc. The leader of the exercise should act as the facilitator rather than placing their own opinions and judgments and should encourage everyone to ideate and include the social considerations or ramifications of each option and not just the cut-and-dried causes and effects on the work. For example, will a boss be made happy by a certain decision? Will a team be energized? Will someone who deserves visibility in the organization be given an opportunity? The cost row should emphasize the risks associated with each choice and how selecting a particular path will play out in reality. Who will be helped? Who will be upset? What are the long-term impacts and short-term impacts? As the company grows, how will these impact change? Therefore, it is really important to dig in and project each choice into the future.

In the mitigations, the facilitator should walk the group through how to soften, allay, or distribute the risks associated with each of the options such that everyone can think through what it would really be like if that option were selected. Essentially, having mitigation conversations elicits opinions and feedback from a wider range of people. This is meant to understand different viewpoints, including those of other departments within the company who might touch or be affected by the decision at hand. The questions can be asked from different angles. What is the root cause of that cost/risk, and can we mitigate it? Can we address this tech-debt/management-debt in other ways? Can we resolve the underlying anxiety through other means? Is there a long-term/short-term trade-off we can make?

Other methodologies that companies often embed in their decision-making process include A/B testing, RACI model (*Responsible, Accountable, Consulted, and Informed*), among others. In the end, good decisions and decision-making are meant to serve for the better purpose of the society that brings positive, sustainable benefits.

Topics of the Chapter

The following has been discussed within this chapter:

- Boards can maximize high-quality decision-making by properly designing the decision-making policies and procedures with active participation of selected board committees.
- When decisions go wrong, the fault may lie in the mind of the decision maker rather than in the decision-making process itself, including one of the following:
  1. The Anchoring Trap
  2. The Status Quo Trap
  3. The Sunk-Cost Trap
  4. The Confirming-Evidence Trap
  5. The Estimating and Forecasting Traps
- The board should act as a competitive ground for pursuing constructive debate and positive dynamics among its members.
- Awareness of relevant data and information grants board members the skills and ability to make effective decisions.
- Board members should adequately follow business ethics while performing their duties and responsibilities.
- The major types of decisions are:
  1. Big-bet decisions
  2. Ad hoc decisions
  3. Cross-cutting decisions
  4. Delegated decisions

Chapter 16

Role of Board Members

The previous chapters discuss the role and characteristics of a board, the process under which it is formed, and the fit and proper and profile of directors. Focus also on the importance, role and leadership of the chairperson. This chapter discusses the expectations from individual board members in their roles to ensure the board—and by extension the organization—functions efficiently, free of conflicts of interests, optimally, and with an objective of ensuring the sustainability of the business model.

16.1 ROLE OF THE CHAIR OF THE BOARD

The chair runs the board (*leadership role*), and the CEO runs the company (*command role*).

The chair of the board (also known as the chairman, chairwoman, or chairperson, depending on the preference of the organization and the individual; or president of the company, in certain jurisdictions) is the head of its board of directors in a unitary board or head of the supervisory board in the two-tier model or other structure.

A chair holds the most power and authority on a board, leading the non-executive and executive directors with the objective of ensuring their duties to shareholders are fulfilled by acting as a link between the board and upper management and setting the tone at the top for the corporate culture. Although currently not considered a best practice and less common, the chair may also hold the title of president or chief executive officer. The accumulation of the chair and CEO roles in one individual was common in the USA 10 years ago; however, current corporate governance best practice recommends a clear separation of roles, as a critical role of the chair is to ultimate oversight of the actions of the CEO and executive directors, and the trend of eliminating that practice has reduced more than half of the accumulation of functions. The titles of president and CEO refer to executives involved in executing strategies approved (tactical level) at board level. Exceptions (which should be temporary) to this rule include situations of the chair accumulating or moving into the CEO position on an interim or permanent basis if a CEO resigns or is dismissed until a suitable CEO is hired. However, if it is on a permanent basis, the best practice recommends that the chair be replaced in that position. The rule of separation of the chair and CEO positions is the common rule in the financial system, notably in the European Union, a change of paradigm that was made almost mandatory after the economic and financial crisis.

The word chair may refer to the place from which the holder of the office presides, whether on a chair, at a stand, or somewhere else more visible (from Robert Rules of Order—manual of parliamentary procedure in the US). European Banking Authority (EBA) states that the chair of the management body (i.e., board) should lead the management body, should contribute to an efficient flow of information within the management body and between the management body and the committees thereof, where established, and should be responsible for its effective overall functioning. The chair should encourage and promote open and critical discussion and ensure that dissenting views can be expressed and discussed within the decision-making process (EBA/GL/2017/11).

In an interview with IMD Business School, Rolf Soiron, the chairman of Holcim, says that the chair should create the corporate tone and the ambitions that the board wants to implement to make the difference. The chair is like the producer of the film who sits in the background but has much influence.[325] That relationship might not be a daily one but is almost a daily one. The relationship with the CEO must be continuous and should be characterized by a high level of communication; transparent, frank and honest, involving and building trust, and mutual respect. The chair cannot allow the board members to come to a meeting without being fully prepared, creating situations that require a conversation at the "confessionary." There should be a respect of opinions at the board. Discussions about individuals and of own wealth of experience do not belong to the board's agenda. The board must solve issues that are on the agenda, and the chair should always stay on the agenda.

The chair, by definition, holds a non-executive role—although the complexity of the business model may require it to be a full-time job—and if the chair is designated to perform temporary executive duties for a valid reason, measures should be adopted to mitigate any adverse impacts, namely involving the senior independent non-executive director.

In Continental Europe, the role of the chair and the role of the CEO are clearly differentiated. As discussed in preceding paragraphs, many companies in the US still have the same individual as the chair and the CEO, but the untangling of the role of the chair and that of CEO has gained momentum in recent times due to the extra push from corporate governance experts, regulators, and relevant stakeholders, including shareholders. There have been some high-profile examples to vindicate the push. US-based Tesla's CEO Elon Musk was propelled to relinquish his chair position. In another high-profile case, Renault board untangled the role of the chair and the CEO after its ex-executive Carlos Ghosn, who previously held both positions, was arrested in Japan in an alleged corporate governance issues relating to the misuse of company assets involving the affiliated company Nissan Motor.[326] Nevertheless, experts state that the separation of chair-CEO roles is just one factor in evaluating a company's corporate governance best practice framework; the consideration of other factors such as the background of independent directors and how long the executive has been on the posts are considered important as well. WeWork, the American commercial real estate company, had to postpone the much-hyped IPO at Nasdaq, because investors were very concerned over its corporate governance framework and valuation.[327] Adam Neumann, the co-founder of WeWork, had to resign from his position as CEO and eventually gave up the majority of voting control. The role of the independent directors and the CEO are further discussed in this chapter.

EBA (European Banking Authority) guidelines on Internal Governance of Banks (GL/2017/11) mentions that the chair of the management body should encourage and promote open and critical discussion and ensure that dissenting views can be expressed and discussed. Where the chair is permitted to assume executive duties, the institution should have measures in place to mitigate any adverse impact on the institution's checks and balances, such as designating a lead board member or a senior independent board member and having a larger number of non-executive members within the management body in its supervisory function. In particular, in accordance with Article 88(1)(e) of the Directive 2013/36/EU, the chair of the management body in its supervisory function must not exercise simultaneously the functions of a CEO within the same institution unless justified by the institution and authorized by the competent authorities.

The chair should set meeting agendas and ensure that strategic issues are discussed, on an end-to-end basis with priority and not acting under a rubber stamp principle. The chair should ensure that decisions of the management body are taken on a sound and well-informed basis and that documents and information are received in enough time before the meeting. The chair should contribute to a clear allocation of duties among the members of the management body (the board) and the existence of an efficient flow of information and data (well-structured and prepared for review and understanding before the board) among them to allow the members of the management body in their supervisory function to contribute constructively to discussions and cast their votes on a sound and well-informed basis.

The Guidance on Board Effectiveness, published by Financial Reporting Council (FRC UK), referenced in Section 1.2.3: "Global Financial Crisis 2007–2008 and Increased Governance," mentions the following about the role of the chair:

- Setting a board agenda primarily focused on strategy, performance, value creation, culture, stakeholders, and accountability, and ensuring that issues relevant to these topics are reserved for board decision
- Shaping the culture in the boardroom
- Encouraging all board members to engage in board and committee meetings by drawing on their skills, experience, and knowledge
- Fostering relationships based on trust, mutual respect, and open communication (both in and outside the boardroom) between non-executive directors and the executive team
- Developing a productive working relationship with the chief executive, providing support and advice, while respecting executive responsibility
- Providing guidance and mentorship to new directors as appropriate
- Leading the annual board evaluation, with support from the senior independent director as appropriate, and acting on the results
- Considering having regular externally facilitated board evaluations

In relation to the agenda, the best practice recommends the preparation of global agendas for the board and the respective committees (and ad hoc committees, if they exist). In terms of the corporate culture, a vector that emerged in the last decade is the need to include in the culture the way the board sets the tone for a robust and conservative risk culture, an issue of particular importance in the financial system. Also, the chair should always ensure that adequate time is available for discussion of the agenda items, particularly strategic issues, and that debate is not truncated, and the decision-making process is rushed. There should be a timely flow of accurate, high-quality, and clear information, with the board determining the nature and extent of the significant risks the organization is willing to embrace (risk appetite) in the development of the strategic plan and its implementation. Directors have to be aware of and able to discharge their fiduciary and statutory duties. The board should consider the views of shareholders, the staff, customers, and other key stakeholders. The induction process is a critical factor for a robust performance and commitment and should be supported by a full, formal, and tailored induction program when joining the board, being the responsibility of the chair and the directors themselves to continually update their skills, knowledge, and familiarity with the operations to fulfill their role on the board and as well as the committees.

EBA and FRC guidelines are apparently influenced from each other with some considering them high-level guidelines that should be considered the minimum basic standards, as they are presented as guidelines—soft law; it is relevant to consider, depending on the size and complexity of the business model, to apply the best practice and consider using the comply or explain rule when not adopting the best corporate governance practice. The guidelines can be leveraged by both financial and nonfinancial institutions, although regulated sectors (notably the financial sector) are more demanding on their application. Additionally, the principles of a good corporate governance are influenced by the cultural, social, political, economic, and legislative framework of jurisdictions. Also, while the characteristics of the role of the chair, executive directors, and independent directors may differ across jurisdictions, the basics remain the same regardless of those elements and the governance structure legal framework.

16.1.1 CHARACTERISTICS OF A GOOD CHAIR

Studies show that the significant number of people who are boards' chairs had at one time been CEOs or executive directors, partners of auditing and statutory audit firms and law offices, or non-executive directors prior to assuming a chairpersonship position. However, the competencies and personal traits that thrived within the vicinity of an individual in those demanding professional positions, namely their activism, may carry little benefit in fulfilling their duties as a chair, as the function demands a different and possibly more sophisticated set of skills.

Stanislav Shekshnia published a very well structured and comprehensive scientific paper in the *Harvard Business Review*,[328] pointing out guidelines on how to become a good chair, which can be inspiring to chairs and aspiring chairs, as well as to any board member. The review maintains the structure of the case study but includes additional viewpoints and comments; they try to bridge and show other views impacted by different cultural environments, as the case study seems to be inspired in practices in the US, although it still presents relevant elements for reflection as well as hints to better perform in a chairpersonship (Figure 16.1).

Figure 16.1: Traits of a Chair

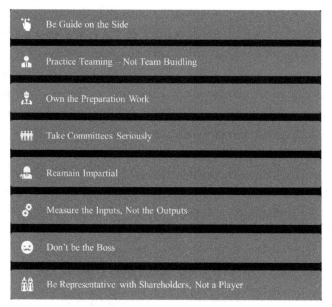

Source: (*Harvard Business Review*—Stanislav Shekshnia)

- **Be the Guide on the Side**

The chair should act as a guide on the side listing three characteristics:

1. *Restraint:* Effective chairs speak little, with interventions on process and people rather than on content and are supposed to be encouraging. Avoid the use of "I" and don't take more than 10 percent of the airtime.
2. *Patience:* Good chairs never rush; they are passionate about their work, but they should have the ability to pause and reflect and to focus on getting things done properly, encouraging introspection and thoughtfulness.
3. *Availability:* Most chairs have part-time contracts, but they should remain committed and dedicate the required time. If the chair has no profound expertise or deep industry knowledge, it is advised to concentrate on the process while other directors share the expertise. Seeing the big picture, making realistic assumptions, and connecting them to solutions are the most important abilities.

- **Practice Teaming, Not Team Building**

Directors are not traditional anymore, as they spend little time together, usually sitting in several boards, leading to a teaming of experts to focus on quick scoping, structuring, and sorting of collaborative work instead of the traditional team norms. One good case for the chair is to have an individual personal interaction with directors before board meetings and consulting with each of them well ahead of time to identify agenda items. Finally, follow up minutes, notes, reports, and phone calls after the meeting. The chair should make sure that each director is given equal airtime to express their views. Unless warranted to get clarification, no directors can take the second time until all directors views are expressed. In the event of disagreements, the chair should facilitate the discussion until consensus is achieved. The chair should focus on arriving at a specific, actionable, clearly formulated resolution and make sure all directors understand and support the resolution. Sometimes, it is possible that consensus may not be achieved, and in such cases, voting may be used as the extreme procedure. However, more robust decisions emerge by consensus.

To reduce the chances of misunderstanding, especially with new directors, it is a good practice for the chair to have a face-to-face conversation and describe and discuss the company, its strategy, its key executives, and its board, but the most important set clear expectations such as attendance at all board meetings—through preparation, not just by management presentation—and development of industry and knowledge. Thus, the chair should oversee the proper acquaintance of novice directors with fellow board members and senior executives, followed by meetings and company visits. In the event a director is not contributing enough and robustly to board discussions, the chair—rather than calling them out in the boardroom—may solicit their opinions before the meeting and present their views to the board and acknowledging the source, such that it could trigger a direct contribution. However, if any director suffers of verbal diarrhea (the quality or habit of talking too much, having no point to the conversation), a three-stage approach could be applied:

1. Direct confrontation in the boardroom
2. A one-on-one conversation offline
3. Another one-on-one with an offer of professional help paid for by the company

If nothing works out, then the chair should consider discussing the topic with the nomination committee or, if there isn't one, ask the director to stop coming to meetings and stand-down from reelection. This process is intimately linked to legal issues and should be carried carefully.

- ## Own the Preparation Work

Inexperienced chairs may often mistakenly believe that the job is all about managing the dynamics in the boardroom, while the experienced chairs take a great share of the work setting the agenda and putting together a briefing package. In the best case, the chair should start preparing meeting agendas a year in advance (a global agenda supports this process), taking inputs from the CEO, other directors, and the corporate secretary. Criteria should be applied when accepting an item in the agenda which must be strategic, material, and ripe for decision, something only the board can handle. It is good to practice limiting six or seven items on an agenda. Before approving any agenda, the chair may circulate a draft among the interested parties.

The chair should make sure the materials in the briefing package are crisp, concise, and with good visuals. As a rule, executive directors should be informed that presentations must have a one-page executive summary, that investment proposals have at least three alternatives, and that presentations should not exceed approximately 15 slides. The chair should make sure that the board meeting contents are sent to all meeting attendees, ideally no later than two weeks before the meeting. Nevertheless, before sending the briefing package, the chair should review the format and standard for materials.

The follow up to the meeting is equally important. The chair should provide the minutes of the meeting to the board members involved and key executives. Use of software can be facilitated. The minutes are supposed to be action-oriented and cover different views and opinions as well as conclusions and resolutions, such that the directors won't forget, ignore, or repeat key positions. The chair should regularly get in touch with the board or corporate secretary to track the implementation of board decisions, and if the implementation of a decision has been delayed, the chair must reach out to CEO for further explanation.

A best practice is the maintenance of a list of decisions by the corporate secretary and the deadline for implementation and the progress made; when completion of decisions is postponed, the list of decisions should indicate the initial deadline and the new one as well as the level of priority.

- **Take Committees Seriously**

Effective and efficient committees (and board's ad hoc committees, if the need arises) are crucial to board success. As committees are small, with individuals having relevant skills and experiences, work may be done progressively with candid discussions and debates. It is often the responsibility of the chair to decide who joins which committees and who serves as their chairs, although when a governance committee or a nomination committee exists, this work should be performed together by the chair and the prospective chair of the committee. The chair should always be on top of the committees' work through monthly calls, during which she/he could take an update on their plans, open issues, and ideas for the future. In case the need for an unplanned meeting arises, the chair may opt for a videoconference, rather than an in-person meeting, thus making it possible for more directors to participate.

The chairs of the committees should present a summary of the matters they have on hand and the proposals to the board. Depending on the jurisdictions' legal frameworks, the committees may have the ability to make decisions or only recommend decisions, which have to be approved by the board. There are exceptions, notably with the audit committee, which may make decisions themselves.

- **Remain Impartial**

The chair should clearly understand the decision-making traps and biases (further discussed in Section 15.1: "Traps and Biases in Decision-making"), ideally refraining from having strong views on a particular issue. This may give a blow to collective productivity. Optimistic skepticism is well regarded, but not behaving anyway like a consultant—such as thinking about ideas, cases, and models that would attract board attention—is recommended. It is ideal to become an onlooker without any stake in the game. Rather than asking "What is the best solution for a problem?" the chair should ask "What the best way is to organize a discussion of the problem?" The chair should listen to each director, observe how that person expresses the view as well as the group's emotions, allow the first speaker to frame a discussion, rephrase what other directors said, synthesize solutions from their opinions, and articulate a proposed resolution. This way, the chair sets the tone of the board and ensures that meetings are dynamic, less noisy, more fun, and altogether more productive. A common trap occurs when the chair expresses her/his views before everyone else's, which can usually limit the discussion and the expression of views that could be relevant.

- **Measure the Inputs, Not the Outputs**

A CEO moving to a chairpersonship position constitutes a difficult and challenging move, notably if the CEO has not prepared for the move. Although chairpersonship may look like a natural evolution from the CEO position, the roles have substantial differences, there-fore requiring different individual profiles. This makes the transition difficult because of the different mindsets of a CEO and a Chair.

CEOs often look for metrics to evaluate the performance of the board. In fact, if an aspiring chair suggests quantitative metrics, that is a "red flag." Boards involve a degree of a "black box" concept, trans-forming certain inputs into outputs (i.e., into decisions). Therefore, if the inputs are good, the outputs will be good. There are five critical inputs, as depicted by Figure 16.2.

Figure: 16.2 Five inputs for board effectiveness

The most crucial input is the people (talent), ensuring the right human capital to deliver the job. The chair may be committed to create the competency maps or descriptions of specific skills and knowledge that the board must possess collectively, as a result of the individual fit and proper profiles of the board members. This can be determined by comparing against online self-evaluations of the directors annually, and companies often opt for external assessments from consultants. In case of gaps, the chair may work with the nominating committee or directly with shareholders, or in family businesses, with the adequate family entity in the family governance structure, to hire new directors; if that does not materialize, the chair may call in the external advisers.

The four other inputs—agendas, materials, processes, and minutes—are also taken into consideration for the assessment, and are assessed through directors' evaluations and consultants' reviews, such as how well agendas cover strategy, executive appointments, compensation, succession, investments, risk, compliance, disclosure, among others; soliciting directors' and experts' views on the quality of board materials and minutes; and asking board members to evaluate the board meetings for length, candor, airtime allocation, engagement level, and resolutions. The chair may also get feedback on own performance, including capacity to frame questions, facilitate exchanges, articulate decisions, conduct reviews, conduct interactions with directors, availability, and proactivity. However, it should be taken into consideration that a monist board includes both executive and non-executive directors. Each group plays a different role and carries different responsibilities in the board. The three main areas under the responsibility of the non-executive directors are governance, strategy, and supervision, while executive directors are responsible for the strategic plan development, its execution, and the supervision of tactics.

Additional options for the recommended process include obtaining the views and feedback, ideally immediately after the induction process. The board members who have just become familiarized with global agendas and documents should be able to provide feedback on their content and structure. Advice from external consultants could complement the views of the new board and adjust the process to improve it and allow for the implementation of best practice. Relating to the own performance of the chair and the board itself, there are other alternatives that may include a survey to senior management and the services about the way they regard and percept the boards' performance and contribution to the organization. This can be done using an external consultant or a former chair or board member.

- **Don't Be the Boss**

The chair must frequently interact with the board members and senior management. Among them, the CEO is the most senior executive director. The chair and the CEO may review board agendas and materials, finalize company press releases, follow up on board decisions, or meet regulators together. Therefore, the chairs may sometimes fall into a trap by assuming themselves as the CEO's boss. The chair should understand that the board is the collective "boss" of the CEO and that the primary task of the chair is to make sure the board provides the goals, resources, rules, and accountability the CEO needs. Building a board-CEO relationship is more crucial rather than a chair-CEO relationship.

As discussed earlier, the chair runs the board, and the CEO runs the company. This is a way to view and separate both roles.

- **Be a Representative with Shareholders, Not a Player**

Here is the thing: if the boss of the CEO is the board, the boss of the board are the shareholders. Regulations for communication between board and shareholders differ according to the jurisdictions, but the chair should ensure equal treatment to all shareholders, not just in public companies but in private companies as well.

Another vector for communication is related to the fact that while the CEO is focused on investors' roadshows (strongly linked to raising capital, notably and to provide financial and strategic data to the capital markets), the chair is focused on the governance roadshows (focused on the governance structure and the way the non-executive directors carry their duties).

16.2 ROLE OF SENIOR INDEPENDENT DIRECTORS AND NON-EXECUTIVE INDEPENDENT DIRECTORS

The concept of independence is discussed in detail in Chapter 13: Independence and Conflicts of Interests. Often, companies make the mistake of limiting the role of independent directors to a ceremonial or/and ornamental level. Most times, this board's profile does not deliver value to the shareholders and stakeholders and often allows to accentuate the Agency Theory (conflicts of interests), notably because non-executive directors do not supervise the executive directors. OECD states in one of corporate governance principles (discussed in Section 14.1.1: "G20/OECD Principles of Corporate Governance") that boards should consider assigning a sufficient number of non-executive board members (NEDs) capable of exercising independent judgment to tasks where there is a potential for conflict of interest. Examples of such key responsibilities include ensuring the integrity of financial and nonfinancial reporting, the review of related party transactions, nomination of board members and key executives, and board remuneration.

In the current landscape, the board is not expected to work as a rubber stamp's board, and instead function as the end-to-end network of coordination and cooperation between non-executive directors (and independent directors) and executive directors, including the senior management. The board (attaining expertise and advice from non-executive directors) must be able to challenge the management in core strategic matters. The independent directors must scrutinize the performance of senior management embedded within the risk management framework, also known as risk framework. Independent directors also play a crucial role in determining the appropriate remuneration of executive directors, being part of the nomination committee or other committees such as governance committee, audit committee, risk and compliance committee, among others. The selection of independent directors must be conducted under a fit and proper rigorous criterion and endorsed by the nomination committee.

16.2.1 SENIOR INDEPENDENT DIRECTOR

The concept of Senior Independent Director (SID) is more widespread in the Anglo-Saxon countries within the unitary board. However, the concept of SID may be equally applicable within a supervisory board under a two-tier structure, and designating SID is even more critical, notably when the chair holds some executive duties in order to check and balance. Also, the role of SID becomes critical when the board is highly stressed. SID should work collectively with the chair and directors, and also with shareholders and key stakeholders to resolve any significant issues. The board should have a clear understanding of the SID, who might intervene to maintain board and company stability.

The examples of the intervention by the SID are mentioned below:

- A dispute between the Chair and the CEO
- Concerns of shareholders or non-executive directors (NEDs) not being addressed by the Chair or CEO
- The strategy followed by the Chair and CEO not being supported by the entire board
- The relationship between Chair and CEO being too close, and decisions made without the approval of the full board
- Assessment of the CEO, which should be led by the SID
- Succession planning being ignored

The FRC UK guidelines for the effective role of the SID are presented below:

- The SID should act as a sounding board for the chair, supporting them in the delivery of their objectives and leading the evaluation of the chair on behalf of the other directors.
- The SID should also be available to shareholders (and if necessary, key stakeholders) if they have concerns that contact through the normal channels of the chair, chief executive, or other executive directors has failed to resolve, or for which such contact is inappropriate.
- When the board or a company is undergoing a period of stress, the SID's role becomes critically important. They are expected to work with the chair and other directors, and/or shareholders, to resolve significant issues.

Therefore, the role played by the SID is very relevant, notably when stressful situations emerge in the life of a board.

16.2.2 INDEPENDENT/NON-EXECUTIVE DIRECTORS

As stated in Chapter 13: Independence and Conflicts of Interests, Independent or Non-executive Directors (NEDs) primarily support the chair and the Executive Directors (EDs) in the board. NEDs play an important role in strategic matters' definition and discussions, risk management, compliance, and audit functions. NEDs are supposed to bring fresh perspectives, along with focus and depth, to challenge the board and take an optimistically skeptical stance, while also serving as key members to be a bridge-builder in difficult conversations such as resolving conflicts of interests. Traditionally, CEO or senior management used to present strategy to the board; however, the paradigm is slowly shifting. When necessary, certain strategic matters can be initiated by the NEDs, leading end-to-end discussion between the senior management and the board. The board is no longer meant to serve as a rubber stamp vehicle, with the independent directors playing their effective role.

In a two-tier structure, such as in Continental Europe, which mandates stakeholder-eccentric model, the NEDs are often labor representatitves, founding family members, national banks, and insurance companies in the supervisory board, as discussed in Chapter 3: Models of Corporate Governance. Sometimes, large shareholders-linked directors are also appointed as NED, although their independence is questionable, and in the financial system, the supervisors rarely qualify them with the statute of independent. The selection of NEDs must be fit and proper, as discussed in Section 11.1: "Fit and Proper." The NED must maintain active communication with senior and middle managers, notably of the control functions; be well informed about the organization and have a strong command of the issues relevant to the business. On the other hand, the chair of the board must ensure that proper induction is appropriated to onboard NED smoothly and swiftly.[329]

As the legal framework differs among countries, in many jurisdictions the chair should be independent, being usually a non-executive board member. However, it is common in large corporates to have chairs assuming a full-time job, but that does not mean the chair should assume executive duties. The board's committees formed within the board or supervisory board should be chaired by an independent director and have a majority of independent directors. Most jurisdictions require the audit committee to be chaired by an independent director who does not chair any other committee as well as be composed entirely of independent directors, such that the committee has the capacity to work independently from the board. Similarly, risk and compliance committees should have enough independent directors and be chaired by an independent director who does not chair any other committee. Other committees formed should also adequately incorporate independent directors.

FRC UK (www.frc.org.uk) guidelines for the effective role of NED are:

- NED should, on an appointment, devote time to a comprehensive, formal, and tailored induction that should extend beyond the boardroom. They should expect to visit operations and talk with managers and non-managerial members of the workforce (always coordinated with the CEO and executive director of the area) in order to gain a better understanding of the culture of the organization and the way things are done in practice and to gain insight into the experience and concerns of the workforce.
- It is vital that NEDs have enough time available to discharge their responsibilities effectively. The time commitment to engage with shareholders and other key stakeholders and to get to know the business can be considerable. NEDs should devote time to developing and refreshing their knowledge and skills to ensure that they continue to make a positive contribution to the board and generate the respect of the other directors. These are reasons that support the requirement for NEDs to be adequately paid, as the time commitment is usually high to perform the job correctly.
- NEDs should receive high-quality information sufficiently in advance so that, they can understand its implications and impact prior to the board meeting; this will allow the exercise of their supervisory and challenging role. NEDs should seek clarification or amplification from management where they consider the information provided is inadequate or unclear. This is also true when the amount of information is huge, and the reports are not structured in a way that allows for their review and adequate preparation.
- It is relevant that NEDs do not operate exclusively within the confines of the boardroom but also have a good understanding

of the business and its relationships with significant stakeholders. NEDs are advised to take opportunities to meet shareholders or stakeholders (mainly over governance roadshows), key customers, and members of the workforce from the different levels of the organization.

A thought relating to a reason for considering changing the designation from "non-executive director" to "governing director." This thought emerged from the fact that, considering their roles and responsibilities—notably in the definition and oversight of the business's Vision and Strategy—their name should be based on the function they should perform rather than based on the function they should not perform as a non-executive director. It would be preferable to create the right, more focused mindset for the governing directorship's holders:

- taking an active stance in leading the definition of Vision and Strategy;
- placing them on a different level to the Executive Directors, that is, also having the responsibility to supervise executive directors; and
- imprinting the need for an active rather than passive stance, moving from a decision-vetting stance to a decision-making approach.

Shareholders should ask themselves the fundamental reason they select governing directors for the board. It is often observed that governing directors are selected based on a need to fulfill a formal criterion—legal and regulatory requirements of their presence and number—leading to the concept of "false independents" or passive directors on the board who add little or no additional value creation. Given the supervisory board's (in a dualist model) or the governing director's (in a unitary model) aforementioned roles and responsibilities, shareholders should be aware of the key capabilities governing directors need to bring to the board, identify candidates who possess such capabilities, and ensure they execute their functions within a defined matrix of competences required by the business model and its challenges.

In situations where Governing Directors are not (i) conscious of their role, (ii) wish to perform it and/or (iii) actively and knowledgeable and add value, a board—and the shareholders and stakeholders—would be in the presence of governing directors who do not deliver the Vision and Strategy required to guide the executive directors and fulfill their role. This void is often filled by hiring external consultants, naturally resulting in a less efficient process—consultants require an induction into the company's internal and external context—a process that leads to incurring additional costs to deliver an output that constitutes the ultimate responsibility of a board in their dual roles of governing directors (non-executive directors) supervising and executive directors developing the strategic plan and executing it.

16.2.3 NEW PARADIGM AND ROLE OF INDEPENDENT/NON-EXECUTIVE DIRECTOR

Under the leadership of the chair and the support of the board committees, the three main responsibilities of a NED are—governance, strategy, and supervision. Shareholders, stakeholders, and notably regulators and supervisors have become increasingly more demanding of NED, a change that requires committing longer hours of dedication (often misaligned from remuneration), establishing as a requirement the ability to challenge the CEO and the executive committee. This new paradigm has influenced the need for NEDs to take their duties seriously, a stance that may influence the view of a large percentage of potential NEDs to turn down appointments. It is also relevant to mention that, in most jurisdictions, they have the same fiduciary responsibility of an executive director, which has led to an accelerated trend with the compensations' best Practices advocating their compensation be compensation be very close to an executive director's fixed remuneration.

Essentially, NEDs should have a stance that can be defined as optimistically skeptical, meaning that NEDs should be able to challenge the corporate's strategy and direction with optimism, but not take what is written, reported, or said at "face-value," which requires an optimistically skeptical stance to be applied. The position of a NED in a board is not a comfortable one, due to the requirements it involves, notably the fiduciary responsibility they take as well as in their function, which requires challenging and supervising executive directors, who are usually high qualified and experienced individuals.

The Institute of Chartered Secretaries and Administrators (ICSA) states the five essential qualities of a NED,[330] as depicted in Figure 16.3.

Figure: 16.3: Five essential qualities of a NED

BIG PICTURE THINKER

ROBUST GOVERNANCE KNOWLEDGE

INDEPENDENT MINDSET

POTENTIAL AMBASSADOR

ENERGY AND COMMITMENT

Being a big picture thinker is very relevant, because while executive directors provide a corporate strategy to the board, the NEDs should be strategic thinkers with the critical evaluation skills to challenge and contribute to it. NED should be effectively able to holistically grab the big corporate picture. Another way to look at this principle of ICSA is to compare the difference between focal vision and peripheral vision. While executive directors should have a focal vision, as they have to execute decisions of the board, the NEDs should display a peripheral vision, looking at the big picture to identify challenges for the corporation that may impact the business model and the sustainability, as well as maintain a radar over elements that usually do not constitute a daily worry to executive directors, like geopolitics, regulatory environment perspectives, and changes in the business landscape.

Having a strong knowledge of corporate governance is very essential for NED. It is the key criteria to appreciate the legal and regulatory framework within which the organization operates as well as the responsibilities and liabilities of directors. This principle of ICSA is particularly relevant for regulated industries and services, notably to the financial system, where the array of new regulations eventually results in high demands from supervisors, not only on shareholders in terms of capital requirements, but also on directors and non-executive directors, both in terms of their compliance but, to the latter, in terms of the supervision they have to exercise. Regulation covers a very wide range of matters, including the areas of control functions, business model, and the culture of the organization and talent.

An independent mindset is critical for NED, leaving aside any personal issues, short-term considerations, or personal preferences in their consideration of the options. NEDs should be focused on the longer-term success of the organization and its sustainability. Looking at the ICSA principle, independence of mind is also seen from the point of view of an individual who is able to make a decision without being biased toward non-relevant issues for the good of the organization as well as take a decision based on a self-personal interest, which may include notably the interest of having the mandate renewed. A way to ensure independence of mind is to limit the number of mandates to two of 3–4 years or limit the mandate to one for a longer period of time (e.g., 5–7 years).

ICSA suggests that all directors must have ambassadorial potential, as they are required to represent the organization to shareholders, stakeholders, regulators, and government departments that may have an interest, and in some cases, to the general public and media. Being a relevant skill for directors, it is also relevant to keep in mind that there are functions of executive and non-executive directors that may be reserved to one or the other group. To have this skill does not mean that any director should, at own initiative and without coordination of the chair or the CEO, initiate contacts on an ad hoc basis, as that may send mixed messages outside the organization.

Energy and commitment are skills (both physical and mental) that the position of NED requires as a result of its demanding profile. Therefore, NEDs should understand their organization, its market and regulatory environment, and competitors and challenges, and they should stay updated on the top of the brief. They also need the energy and resilience to fulfill the role, especially when the going gets tough, so that the board can work effectively through difficult circumstances. On top of the recommendation of ICSA, resilience is a very critical skill, notably in moments of crisis and stressful situations at the board, including moments of confrontation, disputes, or long meetings. This ability is related to emotional intelligence and should help ensuring rationality, even when another board member behaves inappropriately.

16.3 ROLE OF EXECUTIVE DIRECTORS

As the NED should have a peripheral vision, while an executive director (ED) should have a focal vision. The role of ED spreads to the whole business and, therefore, should execute the decisions of the board. This demands greater knowledge, involvement, and commitment at the point of decision. In the US, executive directors are sometimes known as inside directors. The Australian Institute of Company Directors[331] (AICD) mentions that executive directors add value through their deep knowledge of the business, and its strategy and direction;

deep knowledge of the industry and the competitive pressures; technical expertise in their functional area, such as finance, accounting, and law; and greater and deeper access to company information than non-executive directors (NEDs). In a unitary board structure, the EDs sit with NEDs within the same board, while in a dual board model, EDs are present in the management board and NEDs in a supervisory board. In the monist system, a challenge exists regarding the split of roles and responsibilities of NEDs and EDs and the misunderstandings about them. The board essentially sets strategy and management, while executive management implements strategy and reports to the board. Thus, the executive director is both governor and manager. The concept of the principal-agent theory, namely shareholders-directors, is discussed in Section 2.1: "The Agency Theory." Also, in Section 16.1: "Role of the Chair of the Board," it is mentioned that the relationship between the board chair and the CEO is crucial, as is the separation between the role of the chair and CEO.

The chair of the board serves as the liaison between the board and the management, meaning that executive directors may be required to not attend normal board meetings in order to deal with real or perceived conflicts of interests. Also, when required, it is essential to provide the board with feedback on progress toward achieving goals for the strategic plan and budget allocation to fulfill the expected duties. Nonetheless, executive directors are not to be present in cases when the CEO's or executive directors' performance or remuneration are being discussed, or sometimes during board meetings with the external auditor, regulators, or supervisors. As the chair and the CEO work together on most activities of the company, the company benefits substantially when the board chair and the CEO understand and abide by their distinct roles and responsibilities as well as having a mutually trusting relationship. Also, the relationships take time to build and nurture, and the chair and executive directors should be mutually reasonable and give it some time to grow, essentially developing the trust factor.[332]

Therefore, the key to success for EDs is to become clear on their roles (which are different from the ones of NEDs), responsibilities, and purpose of each role, such as between Chief Executive Officer (CEO) and Chief Operations Officer (COO); the latter often carries the title of President, if the position exists. For example, even though a CEO leads the day-to-day management of the company, some of these duties may be shared with a COO. As EDs are expected to serve as the face and public spokesperson for the company, it is needless to say that they should be guided by high ethical and moral standards and have a spotless reputation. Executive directors often make investor roadshows as well as public presentations to the media, members, donors, regulators, community, among others.

The Chief Executive Officer (CEO), Chief Financial Officer (CFO) and Chief Operations Officer (COO) are often the most senior EDs in most cases, and their roles are described in subsequent sections.

In a unitary structure, besides the CEO, EDs such as the CFO or CCO may also be appointed to the board, which demands greater clarity in roles and responsibilities in order to avoid any potential conflicts of interests. Institutions may mandate other functional C-level roles such as Chief Risk Officer (CRO), Chief Risk Officer (CRO), Chief Information Officer (CIO), Chief Strategy Officer (CSO), Chief Marketing Officer (CMO), and other relevant roles as deemed necessary. The CRO functions must have an intrinsically independent status, as discussed in Section 6.2: "IIA Three Lines of Defense Model and Its 2020 Successor," serving on the second line of defense (i.e., risk management and often compliance). Depending on the jurisdiction, the Chief Audit Executive (CAE) may report functionally to the audit committee or audit board or, more recently, to the Chair. The senior management or operating committee or executive committee, or the management board in a dual structure, often consists of CEO, COO, CFO, CRO, CIO, among others. In large corporations, there is usually a position of Chief Legal Office or General Counsel within the group of the corporate officers.

EDs should ask for advice and welcome the constructive challenge and criticism from non-executive directors as an essential aspect of good governance, encouraging their non-executive colleagues to test proposals in light of their wider experience, notably outside the company (FRC). The chair and CEO should ensure that this process is properly followed. In a monist model, though EDs have different roles, they essentially have the same fiduciary responsibilities as non-executive directors, along with duties that extend to the whole of the business and not only related to their executive daily specific responsibilities, although this is not the case in some jurisdictions. Also, it is relevant that EDs recognize they are not a sole member executive committee and therefore have to take a broader view to leverage the advantages of a monist model. However, FRC mentions that EDs are likely to better understand their board responsibilities if they are NEDs on another board, where they are faced with a different set of challenges.

EBA guidelines on internal governance of banks (EBA/GL/2017/11) sets out a model that can be leveraged by nonfinancial institutions, distinguishing the management body in their management function (management board, senior management, or executive function), which has the responsibility to engage actively in business execution, making decisions on a sound and well-informed basis. After the board discussion, with the end-to-end involvement of the non-executive directors, EDs should prepare and develop the strategic plan to achieve the vision and mission and should be responsible for the implementation of the final strategic plan set and approved by the board. They also must present and regularly discuss with the board its timely implementation and the appropriateness of the tactics to implement the approved strategic plan.

This should allow the board/supervisory board to exercise its supervisory function. In its supervisory function, the management board should constructively challenge and critically review propositions, explanations, and information received when exercising its judgment and taking decisions, along with the financial performance and accomplishment of the budget in detail, ensuring a well-informed decision-making process. Also, the management body, in its executive function, should report comprehensively and inform regularly, as well as when necessary, the supervisory board about relevant elements for the assessment of a particular situation, including emerging risks and developments affecting (or which may affect) the institution such as material decisions on business activities and risks taken, mergers, acquisitions and restructuring, international expansion, evaluation of the institution's economic and business environment, liquidity and capital base prudential ratios, as well as the assessment of its material risk exposures. There is a set of good governance and best practice trends that should be reported regularly, notably related to the culture of the organization, pay gap, genre balance, and ESG.

The good practice recommends that the Chair and CEO roles are not accumulated in the same individual, which emerged from a trend over the last decade. However, notably in the USA, there are still a number of large corporations where the Chair and CEO jobs are retained by the same individual, resulting in an executive director—the CEO—chairing the board that supervises the CEO's performance. The potential for the emergence of conflicts of interest is high, as the chair in his chairpersonship role has a lot of influence and power over the agenda of the boards, as well as the power to run the board. This situation may create challenging situations in moments of stress, notably involving the Chair and CEO in his role as CEO. However, these potential situations can be mitigated by the committees of the board, such as during stress moments that involve the Chair/CEO succession process, remuneration, reputational issues, or lack of performance.

Under the board of directors, corporate structures may have an executive committee, management committee, or an operating committee (the designation varies), as well as the Corporate Officers, which usually include the company secretary, worldwide controller, investors relations, corporate communication, general auditor, or compliance officer. Although it is still common to have the general auditor—Chief Executive Auditor, as suggested by the IIA (Institute of Internal Auditors)—as a senior corporate officer, there is a strong emerging line of thought advocating that the general auditor should have a seat in the executive committee. The opposite line of thought advocates that independence is better preserved when the general auditor does not have a seat in the executive committee; however, in this option, the asymmetry of information would naturally be wider, when compared to the members of the executive committee.

16.3.1 ROLE OF THE CHIEF EXECUTIVE OFFICER

The CEO runs the company (*command role*), and the chair runs the board (*leadership role*).

The Chief Executive Officer (CEO) is the most senior ED and the company's top decision-maker and leader in the execution of the strategy plan. A primary responsibility of the CEO is supporting the chair to ensure that the high standards of governance impacting the culture permeate throughout the organization. The CEO leads the group of executive directors that, in most jurisdictions, are constituted under the monist model structured in an executive committee and, in the two-tier model, in a management or executive board to whom first line management reports.

The CEO, with the support of the EDs, has primary responsibility to set the example to the staff; inform the expectations of the board in relation to culture, values, and behaviors (elements that are the basis for a robust internal control framework); ensure that the board is made aware of the views of staff and stakeholders on issues of relevance to the business, based also on other EDs' views, notably on business issues; and ensure that the chair is aware of potential divergence of views among members of the executive committee before proposals are presented for decision at the board.

The CEO is responsible for leading the development of alternative proposals by business segment for the strategic plan, taking into consideration the vision and mission decided by the board under the leadership of the chair. The process of developing the strategic plan should be carried in an "end-to-end process" with the full board, that is, the non-executive directors. This is also true with the executive directors who belong to the board in a monist model but who participate only in the development process of the strategic plan. However, certain strategic matters can also be initiated by NEDs or the chair, fostering end-to-end discussion.

Therefore, the CEO's relationship with the chair is a key relationship that determines the effectiveness of the board. As usual, there are areas of responsibility in the roles of the chair and the CEO that may potentially overlap, and it is relevant to ensure a smooth process that the differing responsibilities of the chair and the CEO should be in writing, structured under a matrix and approved by the board. Any areas of potential overlap should be prudently clarified.

In most cases, the chair has a part-time non-executive role—although the complexity of the business model often requires a full-time chair—while the CEO has a full-time executive role. Leveraging the guidelines of FRC UK, although adjusting them with additional elements, regarding the role of the CEO, they include the following:

- As the most senior executive director leading the executive committee, the CEO is responsible for proposing the basis for the initiation of the discussion of the strategic plan in the board, adopting an "end-to-end" process for developing and building the company strategy, as well as delivering the strategy as agreed by the board. The strategic plan has the objective of structuring the allocation of scarce resources—notably talent and capital—to achieve the vision and mission defined by the board and/or shareholders, depending on the size and shareholders' structure. The CEO's relationship with the chair is a key influence on board effectiveness. When deciding the differing responsibilities of the chair and the chief executive, particular attention should be paid to areas of potential overlap.

- The CEO has primary responsibility for setting an example to the company's employees, for communicating to them the expectations in respect of the company's risk culture, and for ensuring that operational policies and practices drive appropriate behavior. The CEO and senior management are responsible for supporting the chair to make sure that appropriate high standards of governance permeate through all parts of the organization and to ensure the board is made aware of views gathered via engagement between management and the workforce.

- It is the responsibility of the CEO to ensure that the board knows the views of the senior management on business issues in order to improve the standard of discussion in the boardroom and, prior to a final decision on an issue, explain any divergence of view in a transparent and balanced way.

- The CEO is also responsible for ensuring that senior management (or management board, in dual structure) fulfills its obligation to provide board directors with accurate, timely, and clear information in a form and of a quality and comprehensiveness that will enable the board to discharge its duties; the necessary resources for developing and updating their knowledge and capabilities; and the appropriate knowledge of the company, including access to company operations and members of the staff.

As a result of globalization and the rise of middle class in emerging markets with favorable demographics, the CEO should consider in strategic terms to internationalize by going global in a successful and sustainable way.[333]

Therefore, CEOs need to address five dimensions: the company's geographic position, the rapid pace of change, the company's organization model, its culture, the elected model or models of internationalization, and the CEO's own personal leadership.

- Internationalization is a very demanding process, even for companies with some degree of experience, as the results vary widely depending on the regions and countries targeted as well as to which stage of internationalization a company decides to enter (i.e., exporting, joint ventures or partnerships, or establishment of branches of subsidiaries). This decision also requires considering the impact in the strategic plan, notably in terms of the allocation of scarce resources (talent and capital), cost of opportunity, and opening fronts at headquarters of staff involved in the internationalization process. These challenges are usually more difficult in small or mid-size companies without an internationalization structure, which is a key factor to allocate the adequate resources to this process.
- Depending on the geographical locations, companies may follow global or multi-local approach. For example, Coca-Cola has captured the global market brand, whereas companies like Unilever and P&G have developed several brands—at both global or local level—with different price points for different markets, tapping into a variety of global and local supply chains. A local company rooted in one country may ideally follow the path to go regional and subsequently global.
- As the political tensions, technological transformation, trade wars, and pandemics such as COVID-19 are inevitable, foreign markets are ruled by uncertainty, subject to rapid change, and harder to influence on top of the distance imposed by geography, a factor that introduces a high degree of complexity in the business. This essentially necessitates that

companies keep their agility. Strategy may need to be revised in closer intervals than expected. This includes making some quick changes to the setup if local or regional conditions change or divestment of certain operations. In terms of certain industries, it is essential to maintain an extensive network of partners to operate globally; fashion, sportswear, and consumer electronics industries pursue asset-light strategy (i.e., focusing on R&D, marketing, and sales) and outsource the production of their products to local companies, while energy and mining companies enter into joint venture arrangements with local companies, thereby sharing and likely mitigating risks.

- As many companies have been global or spread their activities substantially, managing with one hierarchical structure, one set of headquarters, and one homogeneous leadership team is doomed to fail. Developing a broad array of business units with their own headquarters and decentralized decision-making is very important to increase the odds of achieving the objectives, take effective decisions, and address the need for change and innovation. Nokia was slow to introduce smartphones with dual-SIM cards favored by consumers in India. As a result, it lost out to local competitors. The impact of the introduction of Apple and Samsung phones, through their innovative features accumulated in one "mobile device" such as a number of functions of high quality (e.g., photos, social media apps), led consumers to discard a number of products from their lives in several industries not regarded as their competitors at the first glance, like manufacturers of camera and camera films.

- When companies go global, creating a multicultural environment that reflects the diversity of employees and customers is fundamentally critical to survival. The topic of diversity and inclusion has gained growing importance, though challenges remain to strike the right tone between global and local imperatives. Still, many companies try to foster a single culture by using the same selection criteria for employees around the world, recruiting from the best schools and universities, and training and developing them in the very same way, leading to building a consistent and strong corporate culture. A different view argues that this approach is not the best way to foster corporate culture, as companies need diversity resulting from factors such as different people with different qualities and different ways of seeing the world and dealing with challenges locally, regionally, or globally.

- It is important that the CEO fully understands the developments and trends in the world. As a rule of thumb, if more than half of the company operations are outside the home country, the CEO should be spending at least every other week on the road. The CEO's message must be nuanced and must not shy from asking for feedback, listening carefully to the response, and then adjusting words and actions accordingly. The CEO cannot run a global company oneself but instead build a truly international leadership team that understands the different markets around the world. Many large companies are often criticized over being run by leadership teams dominated by nationals from the home country, showing no diversity in terms of the origin country of the team and therefore not potentially having the skills to make informed decisions about operations in those jurisdictions. Therefore, the composition of the leadership team should ultimately reflect the global structure of businesses, and the CEO should focus on developing the next generation of leaders along with developing his own leadership style.

McKinsey states that "the exact nature of the CEO's role will be influenced by the magnitude, urgency, and nature of the transformation;

the capabilities and failings of the organization; and the personal style of the leader."[334] Also, the consultant suggests that four key functions collectively define a successful role for the CEO in a transformation mode:

- *Making the Transformation Meaningful:* People will go to extraordinary lengths for causes they believe in, and a powerful transformation story will create and reinforce their commitment. The ultimate impact of the story depends on the CEO's willingness to make the transformation personal, to engage others openly, and to spotlight successes as they emerge.
- *Role-modeling Desired Mindsets and Behavior:* Successful CEOs typically embark on their own personal transformation journey. Their actions encourage employees to support and practice new types of behavior.
- *Building a Strong and Committed Top Team:* To harness the transformative power of the top team, CEOs must make tough decisions about who has the ability and motivation to make the journey.
- *Relentlessly Pursuing Impact:* There is no substitute for CEOs getting personally involved when the significant financial and symbolic value is at stake.

16.3.2 ROLE OF CHIEF FINANCIAL OFFICER

Reporting to the CEO and often Vice Chair, or to an Executive Vice President of the executive or management committee in the US, the Chief Financial Officer (CFO) has responsibilities dependent on the size and complexity of the business.

Three relevant roles of a CFO include:[335]

1. Partnering with the CEO to move the business to the next level.

2. Driving sustainable profit, growth, and cash flows.
3. Establishing a strong relationship with the other C-Officers; by themselves, they will not be able to achieve their objectives.

The key difference between the financial controller or treasurer and the CFO is that the controller reports the numbers, whereas the CFO drives the numbers, therefore the role of CFO should be forward-looking toward where the company is heading rather than focusing on where it has been. Essentially, the CFO needs to identify opportunities and initiate solutions that potentially drive financial success. The CFO's involvement with the CEO is crucial, and their partnership is meant to move the business to the next level. The achievement of CFO should not be evaluated based on the accuracy of numbers but on their prudent act with the numbers; the best way to measure is how CFO acted to increase profits in cash flows. A good CFO can grow company profits year by year in favorable conditions. Driving sustainable and profitable growth is the fundamental role of the CFO. However, the CFO alone cannot drive the financial success of the company. It is important that CFO establishes strong working relationships with other C-level officers as well as the sales, operations, and other relevant departments of the company by getting involved in setting prices, managing the profitability, and improving the productivity of the operations. The CFO should strive to increase profits above the costs.

Also, being an essential member of the senior management team or/and board, the CFO is responsible for analyzing and reviewing financial data, reporting financial performance, preparing budgets, and monitoring expenditures and costs involved in the approval of investments, notably international expansion, control over financial risks (e.g., interest rate, exchange rate), leading the capital raising group, preparing and participating in roadshows, control of the preparation and production and the annual report and financial statements, taxation issues. The CFO has a particular responsibility to deliver high-quality information and data to the board on the financial position of the company, including its accuracy in line with the accounting and financial standards as well the analysis of the figures produced, with a strong focus on the business and accomplishment of the strategic plan. The CFO role is wider than just producing the information and should include also its analysis and the impact in the sustainability of the business. The CFO has the most intimate knowledge of the company and its capabilities, namely in developing and presenting proposals, exercising judgment, namely on strategy including issues related to investment, internationalization, mergers and acquisitions, and expansion in general, especially in the international arena. The CFO should also present any issues that may impact cash flows, risk, performance, or reputational risk. While the role of CFO can be rewarding, it may also carry legal or fiduciary obligations that should be strongly adhered to.

The CFO is required to present this information to the board of directors at regular intervals and deliver it to shareholders and regulatory bodies such as the Securities and Exchange Commission (SEC US), European Central Bank (ECB)—Banking Supervision, EU National Competent Authorities, Bank of England (BoE), The People's Bank of China (PBC), Reserve Bank of India (RBI), Bank Indonesia, among others. Also, usually referred to as a senior vice president, the CFO routinely checks the corporation's financial health and integrity. In addition to particular requirements that many jurisdictions expect from the CFO and the three main roles of the CFO discussed above, some other responsibilities are:

- Delivering high-quality information to the board on the financial positioning of the corporate, as well as in many jurisdiction responsibility for overseeing the financial reporting package and information.
- As CFO has the most intimate knowledge of the company and its capabilities, they should actively participate in developing

and presenting proposals and exercising judgment, namely on strategy. The CFO should actively ally with the CEO, directors, and board members in managing banking relations.

- CFO must facilitate their knowledge and experience in the matters of investment, internationalization, M&A (Mergers and Acquisitions), or any expansion in general, and proactively observe any issues that may impact cash flows, performance or reputational risk.
- The perceived role of CFO—quoting Jim Wilkinson—may range from a "technician" role to a "strategist" role. CFOs should act as a driver to the business.

16.3.3 ROLE OF CHIEF OPERATIONS OFFICER

The Chief Operations Officer (COO), being part of the senior management or/and board, is responsible for overseeing the corporation's key operations and issues related to marketing, sales, production and personnel, and research and development. Often more hands-on than the CEO, the COO looks after day-to-day activities while providing feedback to the CEO. The CEO is leader-in-command for the execution of the strategic plan, while the COO is often the second in command, notably in large organizations; the CFO is also often empowered as the number two. In addition to having a strong working relationship with the CEO, the COO should also maintain an effective relationship with the board that reflects confidence and fosters transparency. In the corporate world, the COO may also be referred to as president, having vice presidents leading different departments reporting to the COO. Often, smaller companies, not listed or without subsidiaries or an international footprint may have one person designated to the roles of CEO and chairperson.

Nonetheless, critics argue that there is no single agreed upon description of what the role of the COO entails. For example, in some firms the job may be to "Ms./Mr. Inside" to the CEO's "Ms./Mr. Outside," whereas in others, the mission may be focused on a specific business need. Microsoft filled the long-vacant position of the COO from a retailer, Walmart, announcing that the COO is expected to use the retail experience to lead Microsoft's effort to grow the consumer products business. In order to accommodate such variations and essentially make the role of COO meaningful, the orientation of the COO's role is defined in relation to the CEO as an individual.

The relationship between CEO and COO can take several forms, and the COO's role is to help make the CEO's vision a reality; the COO is expected to make the CEO more effective and complete. Nonetheless, in all these constructs, the CEO is the magnetic force with which the COO must align. Apparently, the decision to have the COO/President position—often seen in the US—in the governance structure comes with reasons and these, essentially, yield different roles vis-à-vis their CEOs. Seven different roles of COO are mentioned below:[336]

- *The Executor:* The fundamental role of COO is to lead the execution of strategies developed by the board and/or senior management, which essentially is a concession to the complexity and scope of the CEO's job, who usually have numerous external commitments particularly in large corporates. As managing large enterprises often requires two sets of hands, the COO typically takes responsibility for delivering results on a day-to-day, quarter-to-quarter basis.

- *The Change Agent:* Companies may hire a COO/President for a specific strategic imperative such as turnaround, major organizational change, global expansion, among others, like the example of Microsoft hiring a COO with experience of retail. In this case, the scope of work may not be as broad as the general execution of strategy, ensuring the implementation of tactics, but the magnitude of the challenge requires the change agent COO to have a degree of unquestioned authority, like that of an executor COO, which is why the title of president often goes together with the one of COO.

- *The Mentor:* It is not uncommon for corporates to bring a COO on board to mentor a young or inexperienced CEO, something that occurs often in family businesses, where the founder assumes that role. The COO might also be an industry veteran or an individual with expertise in a particular area, with experience, wisdom, and a rich network, who can essentially develop both the role of CEO and the expansion of the business. Hypothetically, as the role of CEO develops, it is possible for the COO role to either disappear or be restructured.

- *The Other Half:* Corporates may recruit COO to complement the CEO's experience, style, knowledge base, or penchants but not essentially as a mentor. In this light, observers have closely watched the relationships between Bill Gates and two of his previous COOs, Jon Shirley and Michael Hallman. According to one observer, Jon Shirley provided a calm and self-effacing balance to Gates's brilliant and often intimidating personality. In such cases, the COO role is not meant to lead to a higher position, but it can sometimes be induced.

- *The Partner:* Companies may often create and cultivate co-leadership arrangements. Some CEOs may find themselves being effective working with a partner. Michael Dell, the founder of Dell, who introduced Kevin Rollins as COO, operated in this mode.

- *The Heir Apparent:* In order to test future CEO elect, companies may establish a COO position to groom or to test, as the scope of the job allows an heir apparent to learn the whole company business, environment, and its people. For example, Rex Tillerson was appointed to the number two position at Exxon, and observers noted that it was a deliberate effort to facilitate his succession to CEO Lee Raymond. Another example is John Reed, former Chairman and Co-CEO of Citigroup, a leader who, as COO of Citicorp—and later CEO, many believe as a result of his performance as COO—restructured Citicorp through challenging times, creating a premier global financial services organization, transforming it into an agile bank, namely by leveraging IT and restructuring the back-office and operations' systems and processes.

- *The MVP (Most Valuable Player):* There are situations where some corporates offer the job of COO more as a promotion to an executive considered too valuable to lose, particularly to a competitor. Essentially, by implementing this strategy, the corporate may try to hedge its bets by stopping short of identifying a specific heir or setting a timetable for leadership succession so as not to intrigue its high-potential executives about how the future unfolds for them.

16.4 ROLE OF CORPORATE SECRETARY

The role of the corporate secretary is pivotal for a robust operation and efficiency of a board, although that role varies, depending on the size and complexity of the business as well as on the staff support structure directly allocated to the board or supervisory board. Nevertheless, the corporate secretary is responsible for ensuring that the board adheres to the legal framework and frameworks of the jurisdictions where the company is present or carries business, namely ensuring sending the agenda approved by the chair on time; the documentation for information, discussion, and approval by the board; and ensuring the proper maintenance of the board's minutes, with a high level of detail as required by best practice for nonfinancial industry and by regulation in many jurisdictions for the financial sector.

Setting the agenda and helping the chair in this matter have a major impact on the quality of discussion of the board, and help set the pace of internal governance; its absence creates further dependence from the information provided by management. It is also an important role to advise management of which subjects are more and less relevant for a board meeting and to help non-executives to get the right information.

FRC indicates that the corporate secretary should ensure that board procedures and regulations are complied with, advising the board on governance matters, supporting the chair, and helping the board and its committees function efficiently.[337] Corporate Secretary's responsibility also includes ensuring that governance complies with statutory and regulatory requirements and that decisions of the Board of Directors are well transmitted to the relevant areas of the Company.

It is a kind of unique role, often of neither part line management nor a member of the board itself. Depending on the jurisdiction as well as on the scope of responsibilities and role empowered to the individual on top of the legal requirements, the position of the corporate secretary may also be titled as Company Secretary, the Secretary to the Board, Corporate Governance Officer, or another equivalents. Traditionally, the corporate secretary used to be employed for administrative purposes, but with time, the role of the secretary has evolved to a higher degree. Some jurisdictions consider mandatory a higher education degree in law for the function. The corporate secretary is not only required to have a deep understanding of the law (notably corporate law, public notary regulation, capital markets legislations, foreign direct investment when a corporation has an international footprint and about business) but also of specific regulation of the industry and/or sector and corporate governance, which would help the board achieve optimal performance by fundamentally leveraging two essentials—*Engagement* and *Influence*.

Corporate secretaries (some jurisdictions qualify them as corporate officers) should attend training programs dedicated to board members. Even though the responsibilities of the corporate secretary vary among jurisdictions, they also include being a networker, intellectually honest, a business analyst, and a good communicator, along with having boardroom presence, essentially maintaining a healthy rapport with the chair and also with the board members. The corporate secretary must understand that the resources used by the company and the relationships with its stakeholders are interdependent and interconnected. However, in companies with a structure attached to the office of the chair or the board itself, the role of the corporate secretary becomes more linked to the formalities required by the legal framework and the regulations of the board. In some corporates, the remuneration of the corporate secretary is determined by the remuneration committee. The corporate secretary should report *functionally* to the chair on all board governance matters, as recommended by FRC on the board effectiveness guidance. It is also advisable that they have an independent status, which would require the *administrative* report to be to an executive board member. However, this does not preclude the secretary from also reporting functionally to the chief executive, or other executive directors, in relation to their other executive management responsibilities. However, if this reporting structure exists, then the potential for conflicts of interest and losing the independent status rises. The corporate secretary must have the necessary independence of spirit to perform in the best interest of the company, being important to equally address the different needs of the different non-executive and executive directors, always having a broad vision of the business, along with being the memory of the board.

Under the direction of the chair (within the functional role), the secretary's responsibilities include ensuring good information flows within the board and its committees and between executive and non-executive directors, as well as facilitating the induction process of new directors, arranging board training, assisting with professional development as required, and coordinating fit and proper processes as demanded by regulation. Other duties may include bridging the board with the executive management and also with senior management and keeping a "to do list" of board decisions indicating the milestones and the implementation status; this is a particularly relevant task, as the board demobilizes, and the corporate secretary ensures that proper follow up is performed. A different model would maintain the corporate secretary performing the duties required by Law, hiring a chief of staff for the chair to perform a more administrative role managing the issues of the board of directors. The secretary should arrange for the company to provide the necessary resources for developing and updating its directors' knowledge and capabilities. This should be in a manner that is appropriate to the particular director, and that has the objective of enhancing the director's effectiveness in the board or committees, consistent with the results of the board evaluation processes. It is the responsibility of the secretary to ensure that directors, especially non-executive directors, have access to independent professional advice at the company's expense where they judge it necessary to discharge their responsibilities as directors of the company, and committees (and ad hoc committees, when established) should be provided with sufficient resources to undertake their duties.

Depending on the structure that supports the board or the supervisory board, the secretary may be required to assist the chair in establishing the policies and processes the board needs in order to function properly. The chair, if the board/supervisory board does not have a support structure, together with the secretary should periodically review whether the board and the company's governance process, for example, board and committee evaluation, are fit for purpose, and consider any improvements or initiatives that could strengthen the governance of a company. The effectiveness of the secretary is usually enhanced by building relationships of mutual trust with the chair, the senior independent director (not considered in all jurisdiction, but a best practice due to the role the SID plays in the board), and the non-executive directors, while maintaining the confidence of executive director colleagues.

The Institute of Chartered Secretaries and Administrators (ICSA),[338] a professional body that certifies company secretaries, mentions that the role of company secretary is centered around three main areas:

- *The Board:* Ensure that proper board procedures are in place and are adhered to and that all relevant papers are circulated to board members in advance of meetings. The secretary should also provide practical support and guidance, particularly to non-executive directors, and monitor and guide the company's corporate governance policies.
- *The Company:* Ensure the company's compliance with relevant legislation and codes of conduct specific to the company's business activities. The secretary will often provide a central source of information to the board and senior executives. This role is linked to the structure a company adopts to support the board.
- *The Shareholders:* Act as the primary point of contact for shareholders and institutions, particularly in matters related to corporate and environmental governance.

Depending on the jurisdiction and its legal framework, as well as notably in the financial sector, the secretary is usually the link and point of contact with regulators, supervisors, commercial registry, and other authorities. Often, because of the need to ensure timely upload in platforms of capital markets documentation and information in platforms of capital markets, or even answer to supervisors' reports, this process is also under the responsibility of the secretary.

Despite the variety of internal, legal, and statutory regulation, good governance benefits a lot from an unbiased company secretary that has the right spirit, integrity, and business vision to correctly engage all directors and promote good practices that don't stay solely in the papers but are actually genuinely implemented as a result of decisions taken by boards. In fact, if given some independence, the secretary has the unusual power of framing the context for directors' engagement, managing the agenda, and also working with the chair to include all directors in board discussions and deliberations.

Some examples of a corporate secretary's responsibilities include:

a. Maintaining in order the company books and minutes, the attendance lists, the registration of shares, as well as the file relating to the meetings of the corporate bodies.
b. Certifying the signatures of the members of the board affixed to the company's documents and the representative powers they hold.
c. Ensuring that all copies or transcripts extracted from the company's books or documents archived are true and complete.
d. Satisfying, within the scope of its competence, the requests made by the shareholders.
e. Proceeding to register and centralize the archive of institutional correspondence exchanged with the supervisors and represent the company on all governance matters regarding prudential supervision.

16.5 CRISIS MANAGEMENT—CRISIS? WHAT CRISIS?

To lead is never an easy task; to lead in a crisis, even more so. It applies to chairs and boards. There are several fronts where boards will need to engage on to ensure a company is prepared to deal with crisis reducing a potential negative impact. Most episodes will occur without warning, plunging the organization into turmoil. Some will signal their approach while leaders are left to choose whether they wish to act or go with the flow. A few will choose to stand still—that often fails on all counts—and the organization will suffer or die, dragging along the ultimate value of the board's reputation.

Boards need to act and stand upright considering a renewed scrutiny, and COVID-19 has recently added a dramatic twist to the corporate narrative. Public perception may be key, but the need for rebalance and checking, transparency, and commitment has now gone beyond traditional expectations and should apply in regular times as well as in a crisis mode. In other words, business as usual should go on unaffected—but leaders need to plan for this and keep the ship afloat when on high sea.

Some easy steps will help you lead through crisis:

1. Plan ahead
2. Think strategically
3. Assess damage
4. Make the most of the operations
5. Make the most out of the people
6. Communicate
7. Move on
8. Give back

Planning ahead

No one expects directors to be superhumans, but they will look at the paychecks, where directors live, and which cars they drive, especially when disaster strikes. Every board member, the chairperson, and/or CEO will need to justify their role and act accordingly. Planning all steps of the way is an essential skill for leadership. When at war, Generals will look at the map before the battle. A chair and/or CEO needs to do the same.

Thinking strategically

When lightning strikes, keep the thinking hat on; people will look their way for answers, and the leader may not have them. The power of a team often resides in congregation and certainly in immediate coordination. It also helps to reach out to external, trusted voices.

Advisor roles generally put things into perspective—as an advisor is not directly involved   and can help chairs and boards navigate the immediate steps in a crisis. Independence is important to progress when the road ahead is far from clear.

Assessing damage

Had Albert Einstein been around to advise corporates on crisis, he would have rekindled business with his preferred approach to problem solving—if you've got one hour, do spend 59 minutes understanding the problem, and solve it in the remaining 60 seconds.

Boards afflicted by crisis, be it financial havoc or a behavioral incident, a cyber threat or a reputational episode, will have little time to think but will need to act decisively in the right way. Assessing the impact is very much an important part of that equation.

Sharing responsibilities will be a powerful signal for an organization but also for the stakeholders at large. A chair and eventually a board must be perceived as open and transparent, able to deliver a factual assessment without taking it personally. No blaming, no shaming.

Making the most of the operations

The board needs to understand how the organization is affected—and needs to do it fast. Nobody other than the board is fully equipped to have a 360-degree view on operations and what went wrong. Identifying the weak link and containing the damage can only be done by having the factual feedback and if the board—notably the Chair and CEO—are able to put it in black and white, internally and externally. Trust is key and will reflect on how accurately and promptly a board can collect information.

Making the most of the people

First and foremost, organizations are made of people. They will be there to help when things go wrong. As board's members and leaders know, the staff will look up for guidance, and a board can count on the company's talent for execution. Some will be natural-born solvers, others will be instrumental in supporting the cause, and some will defy. However, overall, no crisis can be solved without the staff.

Communicating

We do not live-in silos. Decisions move in circles, and now they also move remotely. The outside world has come in at unprecedented levels. Board rooms are permeable and exposed to all sorts of scrutiny, collectively and individually. Leaders are more vulnerable in this environment and need to be prepared to face the public before it turns against them.

Spokespeople are useful tools to protect the board when the organization attempts to keep moving while addressing faults. The idea of normality must not evaporate; the Chair or CEO will strive to communicate milestones and progress to keep everyone grounded. Regular updates are the best and may be the only way to keep business going as usual.

Moving on

Putting an end to the story or closing a chapter is also about moving ahead. Doing the right thing is often shunned in the name of higher, more profitable goals. In the long run, leaders and boards will pay the price if they do not resolve the past. Legacy is part of leadership and needs to come across as the sounding board of the organization. If all fails, the structure will still be able to walk and find a new path. Dissociating the organization from personalities can only be possible if it is true to facts and sufficiently robust to stand on its own.

Giving back

Lastly, a Chair, CEO, or the board will be remembered by what they do. If things go wrong, they will be respected by the actions taken. A board sits on top of the decision-making, and there is no other rationale but to justify board members and their actions and goals.

This is the end of Chinese walls. Technology is upon us and leaves no room for opacity. Self-check exercises for the board must act as regular check-ups, and the results must be accessible to all. Crisis mode is all about this state of mind. Coming forward is the only way to give back. One important thing to remember is that boards, just like crises, evolve over time. As technology enters the boardroom, echo-chambers are a thing of the past. Shareholders' meetings will be held remotely and at a distance—as seen during the pandemic—as will key decisions for organizations. No more hush hush. Cyber activism or constructivism will come to you, and your board will need to be part of the crisis-decision-making process in a very visible way. Accountability is clearly an element of corporate governance to stay. There is nowhere to hide, and that is a good thing. This will bring the boardroom to the forefront of transparency and hopefully humanity, as organizations and boards knit collective decisions into the fabric of societies, made more vulnerable by the pandemic but increasingly resilient to change in the name of evolution.

16.6 SOME CRITICAL QUESTIONS FOR DIRECTOR'S SELF-ASSESSMENT

Below is the list of some critical questions that any directors—executive or independent—should ask themselves to self-assess their own capabilities to justify whether they are compliant with the duties and responsibilities at their role. The procedures for assessment of the board and the director are discussed in Section 17.5: "Board and Committee Evaluations."

The answers to all the questions are discussed across the chapters in the textbook.

- Do I understand the dominant constraints to profitability and sustainability?
  - o Understanding the impact of both internal and external dominant constraints to sustainable growth.

- Do I have the necessary skills to grow company organically and through mergers and acquisitions, among others?
  - o Assessment based on fit and proper principles.
- Do I believe I have all the information?
  - o Proactivity and fulfilling the responsibilities of designated roles.
- Do I clearly understand the issues, risks, and uncertainty?
  - o Understanding the issues, risks, uncertainty, traps, and biases in decision-making.
- Is the decision a responsible discharge of my duties?
  - o Compliant to the fiduciary duties of care, loyalty, and obedience.
- Can I explain this in a transparent manner?
  - o A fluid communicator without being dominant.
- Do I have any conflicts in this matter?
  - o Understands the board dynamics and conflicts of interests.
- Objectively, is this a rational business decision?
  - o Understands the objectivity of the decision to the shareholders, the stakeholders, and to the society holistically.

16.7 GOVERNANCE AND INVESTORS' ROADSHOWS

The global economy has never been so connected, with its relevance being briefly discussed in Section 1.5: "The Relevance of Corporate Governance in Raising Capital." Things change fast, stimulated by rapid technological transformation, and so must corporates' strategies to adjust or change their business model toward sustainability. Corporates should take prudent measures to gear for robust compliance and agility to meet any unusual circumstance of uncalculated, unprecedented, and unexpected business needs demand from stakeholders and investors. Figure 16.4 depicts the general global trend in corporate governance.

Figure: 16.4: Trends in corporate governance

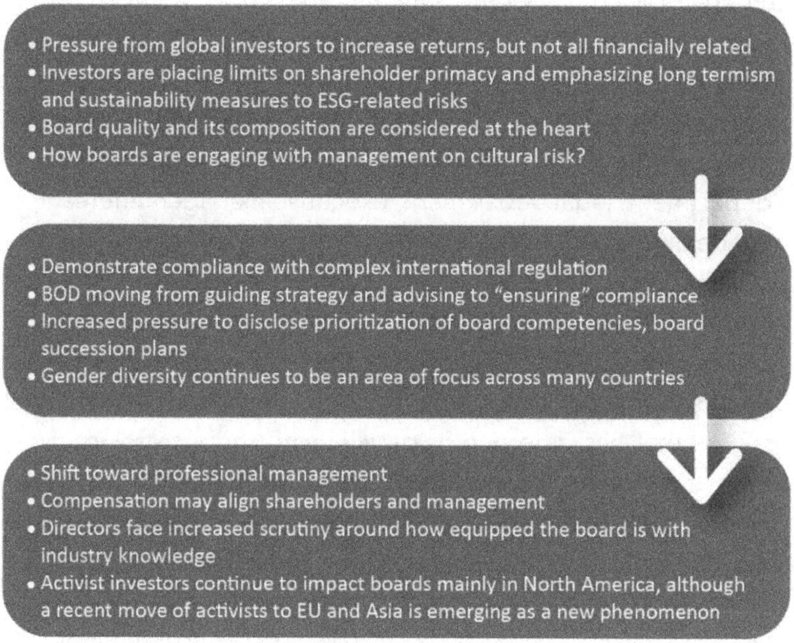

- Pressure from global investors to increase returns, but not all financially related
- Investors are placing limits on shareholder primacy and emphasizing long termism and sustainability measures to ESG-related risks
- Board quality and its composition are considered at the heart
- How boards are engaging with management on cultural risk?

- Demonstrate compliance with complex international regulation
- BOD moving from guiding strategy and advising to "ensuring" compliance
- Increased pressure to disclose prioritization of board competencies, board succession plans
- Gender diversity continues to be an area of focus across many countries

- Shift toward professional management
- Compensation may align shareholders and management
- Directors face increased scrutiny around how equipped the board is with industry knowledge
- Activist investors continue to impact boards mainly in North America, although a recent move of activists to EU and Asia is emerging as a new phenomenon

Critics often argue that the self-serving doctrine of shareholder primacy that is dominant in Anglo-Saxon countries needs to be deconstructed.[339] As these jurisdictions tend to adopt the dominant unitary board, the power is often concentrated in a selected group of insiders.[340] As a result, the dominant unitary board acts as a medium to resist any cultural and institutional changes, which is in contrary to the concept of supervisory board in the EU, notably in Rhineland jurisdictions in Europe. As the supervisory board is expected to reflect the wider social and economic interests of all stakeholders, including employees and society, the board is said to form the basis for having an oversight to the activities of the executive board of management in the realization of these objectives and, hence, foster a strong notion of good corporate stewardship and corporate responsibility. On a positive note, the recent trends suggest that the corporates in the US are more flexible to incorporate the stakeholder notion that have been prevalent in Continental Europe.

Companies usually have an *Investor Relations (IR)* team managing the communication between a company's corporate management and its investors—often the financial information catered to company's financial community. *IR Team works* closely with a company's accounting department, legal department, executive management team, and should be aware of constantly changing regulatory requirements and essentially advising the company on what can and cannot be done from a PR perspective.[341] On top of the *IR Roadshows* usually carried out by executive directors—normally the CEO and CFO—within the scope of shareholder engagement plan, *Governance Roadshows* are a practice that has emerged in parallel with the increasing involvement of activists and hedge funds in the capital of corporations or bondholders, as well as the heightened notion of corporate sustainability. While the focus of the investors relations roadshows is on financial ratios and business development addressed to hundreds of analysts and investors (capital and bonds), the focus of the latter is on the way the non-executive directors supervise and control the overall governance framework and the execution of the strategic plan, as well as the sustainability of the business model. It addresses current shareholders and/or relevant stakeholders—usually long-term investors—whom the supervisory board or the board of directors wants to ensure are apprised of recent developments, including governance arena (e.g., succession plans, diversity, ESG, pay gap), sustainable growth, that will eventually lead to the payment of dividends or reimbursement of bond issues. Thus, each stakeholder should be involved according to their relevant importance and weight.

The *Governance Roadshows (GR)* are led by the chair, having as counterpart the chair of the Visited organization, and should be regarded as a part of a robust, consistent, and ongoing outreach. The best practices of a corporation involve regular and proactive engagement with large shareholders or important stakeholders—notably those that do not participate in the supervisory board—on corporate governance topics, expanding investors relations roadshows beyond portfolio managers and analysts to reach non-executive directors, chairs of governance, audit, strategy and sustainability committees, as well as proxy agencies. While the Chief Executive Officer (CEO) and the Chief Financial Officer (CFO) are often involved in the traditional investor relations roadshows (IR), the board chairperson and often the chairs of the main committees of the supervisory board, or the board of directors, are involved in the corporate governance roadshows.

The primary objective of a corporate governance roadshow is to improve communication between a corporation and its shareholders mainly to governance, as well as to strengthen the overall strategic IR program by enhancing shareholder engagement. On top of these, there are also numerous benefits gained from this activity by establishing dialogue with influential governance groups to promote the corporation's approach to governance and strategy, develop support for a business plan and long-term strategy, and communicate the supervisory board or the unitary board of directors' active engagement in governance matters and its role overseeing strategic and financial plan. In addition, governance roadshows demonstrate openness in understanding stakeholders' perspectives, as well as receiving valuable direct feedback and understanding expectations from relevant investors and third-party governance experts. On the other hand, shareholders that do not have formal governance groups may also be receptive to outreach on governance topics, in which situation, the governance meeting would be with the analyst that monitors the performance of the company.

Members of a supervisory board or board of directors are directly responsible for supervising and monitoring executives. They ensure the execution of the strategic plan in which they have been involved on an end-to-end basis, as well as the existence of a robust governance framework and its effectiveness. Nonetheless, strong cooperation and coordination with senior management is the essential factor to deliver results. As the chair should be the leader of a governance roadshow, the chair must attend all meetings. Other members of the delegation may include relevant members of the supervisory board or a unitary board of directors—chairs of the committees or selected committees—particularly those directly involved in the subject matters of the governance roadshow. Rarely a governance roadshow involves executive directors, namely the CEO, CFO, as their forum is the investors' roadshow. The agenda should be distributed to participating stakeholders such as shareholders and bondholders in advance to grant them the opportunity to be prepared to provide input. The meeting may include a 15-to-20-minute presentation of strategy and governance, although the meeting should be developed as a two-way discussion. The timeframe for governance roadshow is usually during *off-season* (February—July), as the focus is otherwise often on the results, performance, and closing of financial reporting and on shareholders' (or stakeholders') assembly meetings. Instead of in-person meetings, investors may also consider useful video, conference calls or webinars.

16.7.1 STRUCTURE AND CONTENT OF A ROADSHOW

The structure and content of a governance roadshow presentation may vary according to a shareholder or stakeholder profile and whether it has been requested to discuss specific topics. However, a standard governance roadshow would follow a format including overviews of corporate vision, strategy, corporate governance framework, the supervisory board/board of directors, remuneration package, as well as environmental, social, and sustainability practices:

Figure: 16.5: Typical structure of a governance roadshow

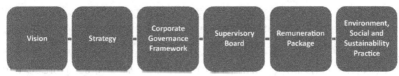

Therefore, in an indicative fashion, the overviews included in Figure 16.5 should include the following:

- The *Vision* statement is the broader or narrowed purpose statement of the corporate that is usually strategic, realistic, and realizable in the foreseeable future. For example, Samsung's broad vision purpose, "create the future," and Wells Fargo's narrowed vision purpose, "we want to satisfy our customers' financial needs and help them succeed financially."

- The overview of *Strategy* usually includes a selection of slides taken from existing IR materials, which as a matter of preparation can be sent in advance to the participating shareholders and stakeholders.

- The overview of *Corporate Governance Framework* should include an introduction and summary of governance norms, laws, and best practices and a description of how they apply in the country or jurisdictions where the corporation operates. It should also include a high-level summary of the governance framework, including recent or planned enhancements enacted under the oversight and supervision of the supervisory board or the board of directors. It should also clearly state the supervisory board's active engagement in governance matters and role in overseeing notably the strategic and financial plan.

- The overview of the *Supervisory Board/Board of Directors* should include short biographies of the non-executive directors in the supervisory board—and also executive directors, in a unitary board—backgrounds and experience, as well as a *skills matrix*, emphasizing the depth, breadth, and diversity of the board members' individual expertise, essentially demonstrating compliance with the Fit and Proper selection principles (further discussed in Section 11.1: "Fit and Proper").

- The overview of *Remuneration Package* should provide a high-level summary of compensation objectives, including how remuneration structure is linked to strategic objectives (further discussed in Section 17.4.1: "Designing Executive Compensation").
- The overview of *Environmental, Social, and Sustainability Practices* should place emphasis on identification of risks and how non-executive directors oversee the management of those risks as well as discuss how the supervisory board identifies and oversees sustainability risks to ensure profitability (further discussed in Section 4.2: "Corporate Sustainability").

The importance of purpose-driven strategy and the concept of broader stakeholder engagement are crucial. The boards are not just meant to lead and manage but also to disseminate the purpose of the corporation linked to the societal, economical, and sustainable dynamics. This not only allows the corporate to better understand the investment expectations and policies but also aids in improving the global reputation and perception of the corporate across a broader spectrum of stakeholders, including institutional investors and shareholders, promoting the virtuous cycle of confidence, goodwill, and long-term relationships, and fundamentally aiming to ensure prudent financial and sustainable stability.

16.8 DIRECTORS AND OFFICERS LIABILITY INSURANCE

Robust advise should be obtained by institutions, board members, corporate secretary, and control functions staff on the available policies and risks covered—an issue that varies widely—its limitations and relevant clauses when potential for an adverse event emerge the requirement for a D&O involvement and use of the policy.

Directors and managers can be subject to lawsuits, notably resulting from the lack (or allegations of the lack) of exercising their responsibilities related to fiduciary duties. Mistakes can happen either knowingly or unknowingly, negligently or not, by action or omission, but mistakes or negligence at a managerial level can be confronting. It must be understood before accepting a position in a board that fiduciary positions in a corporate carry inherent risks. There are also D&O policies that cover managerial positions, namely managers and staff members, that may be a target in a lawsuit for the manner in which they did or did not exercise their role, notably in the way they prepared information for the board, and/or did or did not comply with the statutes or internal regulations.

Therefore, if the jurisdictions or regulatory and/or supervisory authorities do not forbid this type of policies to prevent material loss from such circumstances as well as to attract candidates at a higher level, companies often offer an insurance known as Directors and Officers Liability Insurance (D&O). Allianz, one of the big insurance companies, states that the D&O policies offer liability cover for company directors and officers to protect them from claims that may arise from the decisions and actions taken within the scope of their regular duties. As such, D&O insurance has become a regular part of companies' risk management[342] matrix. Lloyd's, an insurance and reinsurance firm based in the UK, mentions that D&O comes in different forms, protecting individual directors and officers, for example, in cases where they have been accused of committing a wrongful act, and their company is either unwilling or unable to indemnify their litigation costs. Essentially, the insurance cover can also provide balance sheet protection to the corporation in jurisdictions where indemnification is permitted.[343] Some of the insurance companies that provide D&O insurance are AIG, Chubb Limited, Zurich Financial Services, among others.

Usually, the D&O covers the legal fees and other costs the director or corporate may incur as a result of a suit. Nonetheless, intentional illegal acts are typically not covered under D&O policies. The amounts of the policy should be carefully considered, as in lawsuits involving responsibilities, the amounts can reach high values, even for a small or medium-size enterprise.

American Bar Association emphasizes—five points—that should be kept in mind in the current business environment:[344]

- **D&O Actions Commonly Arise in Distressed Situations**

In a period of distress such as by market conditions, fraud, an over-leveraged balance sheet, or another factor, the actions of the company's directors and officers may be scrutinized very closely. One such example would be a quick sale of the company's assets in a distressed situation. It may establish that if sale proceeds are not sufficient to satisfy all constituents, a fiduciary such as a creditors committee or liquidating trustee may initiate the litigation against the directors and officers with the goal of increasing the pool of funds available to creditors. In such circumstances, the directors and officers are more concerned about the company's D&O policy and the coverage for lawyers' fees and satisfy any settlement or final judgment.

- **D&O Policies Are Not Uniform**

It is very often complex to interpret D&O policies and counsels (or advocates) should therefore ensure that clients relying on a policy for risk mitigation understand the operative terms and how similar terms have been interpreted in prior disputes.

- **D&O Policies Are Claims Made**

It means that the coverage exists only for claims made during the time period the policy is in effect. Thus, claims made while no policy or extended reporting period is in effect are usually not covered, although they can be negotiated. Also, when potential for an adverse event emerges, there are policies that require that situation be immediately reported to the insurance company. Familiarization of board's members, corporate officers and company secretary—notably the staff of the control functions risk management, compliance and internal audit—with the specific policy is paramount.

- **Understand Clauses That Can Eliminate Coverage**

The most critical part is the proper understanding of all the clauses that can eliminate coverage. It is very important to learn about wordings and exclusions such as Insured vs Insured Exclusion. International Risk Management Institute (IRMI)[345] mentions that the exclusion may preclude coverage for claims by one director or officer against another. The purpose of this exclusion is to eliminate coverage for four types of situations:

- o   employment practices claim
- o   internal disputes/infighting
- o   claims involving collusion
- o   claims by organizations against their directors and officers for imprudent business practices

- **Negotiate Appropriate Exceptions to Exclusions**

As there is no standard language that would provide the comfort of coverage, directors, and officers would like to ensure that the exceptions would allow coverage for any claims brought by a liquidating trustee, bankruptcy trustee, or similar fiduciary.

Policies for other types of insurance establish monetary limits to the indemnities covered, a feature that varies widely. There are jurisdictions, regulators, and supervisors, as well as some companies, that forbid directors from having the D&O coverage. As it concerns to regulators and supervisors, this line of thought, which is not common, advocates that not allowing directors to have a D&O will demand them to take the right decisions exercising their fiduciary duties, and the view is the same in the case of private or listed companies.

The D&O is an issue that should be carefully considered when accepting a director position, namely performing a proper and demanding due diligence process to ensure consideration regarding potential risks before joining a board that can impact the director's personal wealth. In the case of Tyco scandal, discussed in Section 14.2.1: "The Case of Breach of Fiduciary Duties of Care, Loyalty, and Obedience," its directors and officers were named as defendants in many class-action and related shareholder lawsuits. Even though all of Tyco's directors were sued, the audit committee defendants claimed that the then-auditor did not disclose clear and transparent information to the audit committee. Eventually, members of the audit committee were protected from the financial costs of litigation by D&O liability insurance.[346]

Topics of the Chapter

The following has been discussed within this chapter:

- "The chair runs the board," and "the CEO runs the company."
- The chairperson is primarily responsible for smooth functioning of the entire board, ensure that the best practice and high standards of governance permeate through the organization, empowered into a "leadership role."
- The Senior Independent Director should work collectively with the chair and directors to resolve any significant issues; the role of the SID becomes especially relevant during stressful situations.
- Non-executive directors play an important role in governance, strategy, and supervision; they must scrutinize the performance of senior management and challenge them whenever required.
- The role of the executive directors is to execute the decisions of the board.
- The CEO leads the group of executive directors and supports the chair on the board, empowered into a "command role."

- The CFO identifies opportunities and initiates solutions to drive financial growth.
- The COO takes a more hands-on role in the day-to-day activities of the organization.
- The corporate secretary ensures that the board adheres to the legal framework and frameworks applicable to the organization.
- Corporate leaders need to plan for and be prepared to keep the business afloat during crises, as demonstrated by the COVID-19 pandemic.
- Practices such as governance roadshows help a corporate apprise its shareholders and stakeholders of its supervisory functions, while investors' relations roadshows are directed to the capital markets and analysts.
- Companies often offer an insurance known as Directors and Officers Liability Insurance (D&O) to prevent material loss resulting from the lack (or allegations of the lack) of exercising their responsibilities related to fiduciary duties.

Chapter 17

Board Committees

Committees of the board play a major role in improving the board's effectiveness. They fulfill an important leadership role, similar to that of the chair, with the objective of creating the conditions for overall committee and individual director effectiveness and ultimately of the effectiveness of the board. Committees should regularly report to the board, supporting in its supervisory function. Also discussed are the board's ad hoc committees as an alternative to permanent committees if their remit is not justifiable for a full board's mandate. This chapter discusses the roles of individual committees of the board and the assessment of their performance.

The objective of the committees is to divide the board's work into manageable tasks, providing a robust basis for the process of taking informed decisions at the board. It is relevant to keep in mind that committees' decisions empowerment varies among jurisdictions. However, by definition, committees do not have a delegation of power awarded by the board, and their recommendations should therefore be presented and discussed by the board for decision or ratification, in case the committee makes an urgent decision that cannot wait until the next board meeting. However, in these situations, previous consultation and communication with the chair, senior or even with the CEO, should be considered. Each committee has a charter or other instrument that sets out its remit, composition, mandate, scope, and working procedures as well as reporting lines between each committee of the board and other parties, including how the committee will report to the board, what is expected of committee's members, and what are the tenure limits for serving in the committee. Many jurisdictions indicate that the secretary of the company is responsible to attend, prepare, and keep the minutes of the committees' meetings, providing the drafts in advance of the following board meeting with the objective of the directors signing them before the board meeting. Actually, some jurisdictions require the corporate secretary to attend and prepare the minutes of all social bodies and even in some legal frameworks, along with the meetings of the committees of the board. The best practice requires minutes to be detailed, indicating the discussions and the names of the members intervening in the meeting.

As discussed, there are committees of the board that are required by law, as for example, in most jurisdictions, the audit committee or the nominations committees. Other committees may also be established as a result of the nature and complexity of the business model or a particular area of focus of the board. Usually, a committee should be set up only if its remit is relevant along the full mandate of the board, as otherwise it will not add value. An alternative to the committees, when not imposed by law or that its remit will be relevant along the full board's mandate, is the set-up of "ad hoc committees" to deal with an issue or topic that is very specific and therefore will lose reason for existence along the board's full mandate. This model will ensure that the members of the board are not tied in a committee, which remit is not justified after a short period of time, as it accomplished the objectives before the end of the mandate.

Each non-executive director should serve at least in one committee but in a maximum of three. Committees are teams of usually independent non-executive directors with a particular focus on a specific area. The board committees are usually formed within the vicinities of board members, although they may integrate advisors if a particular area or topic requires expert advice; however, the best practice indicates that an advisor should not have a permanent seat in a board committee. In a unitary board structure, board committees may be formed within the available board of directors, while in a dual board structure, board committees are formed within the supervisory board. The number and the scope of the committees vary among jurisdictions, or even among regulations applicable to the financial and nonfinancial sectors, as well as to the extent of its applicability to private or listed companies. The audit committee and the nominations and/or the remunerations committees are compulsory in most jurisdictions, while in the banking system, the risk committee is also required. The number also varies depending on the complexity, size, footprint, or even by industry, although the best practice recommends that having too many committees can negatively impact the work of the board.

Another element to consider, either by the legal framework or best practice, relates to the independence status of the board members that constitute the committees. Some legal frameworks (regulation notably for the financial sector) and best practice require that committees of the board are chaired by an independent director, therefore being able to exercise objective judgment, and always have the majority of independent directors; however, depending on the status of a company, this may not be the case in some committees.

The board and committees' composition are very relevant in the decision-making processes and structures. This objective may be achieved recruiting non-executive directors (NEDs) with technical skills and knowledge, mainly relating to the committees' scope but also with skills that allow each of the independent non-executive directors to chair committees. To achieve this purpose, the fit and proper process to identify candidates as well as the hiring process should take this requirement and challenge into consideration. The prospective chair should play a major role, establishing the vision for achieving the optimal board composition, usually with the help of external consultants in order to identify the best candidates. The process includes a wide variety of elements; including a rigorous and transparent appointment criteria; a matrix that ensures the presence of the skills required by the business model minimizing and mitigating the skills' gaps; clearly communicating the expectations from NEDs; and informing the established succession planning and process.

The board's committees fulfill an important leadership role, like that of the chair, and create good settings for achieving individual director's effectiveness. Effective and efficient committees are crucial to board success. Because committees are small, with candidates having relevant skills and experiences, things may be done very progressively with frank and honest discussions. European Banking Authority (EBA) states in the guidelines of internal governance for banks that committees should support the supervisory function in specific areas and facilitate the development and implementation of a sound internal governance framework. All committees should be chaired by an independent non-executive member of the management body able to run it independently. Within the EU banking and financial institutions, the institutions that are significant must establish an audit committee, a risk and compliance committee, a nomination committee, and a remuneration committee. Non-significant institutions are not obliged to establish a risk and compliance committee or a nomination and remuneration committee, though it is a good practice to establish these in order for the board to function effectively. The European Central Bank (ECB) uses the criteria depicted in Table 17.1 for classifying the institutions as significant institutions.[347]

Table 17.1: Criteria for classifying the significant institutions by ECB

Size	**the total value of its assets exceeds €30 billion**
Economic Importance	for the specific country or the EU economy as a whole
Cross-border Activities	the total value of its assets exceeds €5 billion and the ratio of its cross-border assets/liabilities in more than one other participating Member State to its total assets/liabilities is above 20%
Direct Public Financial Assistance	it has requested or received funding from the European Stability Mechanism or the European Financial Stability Facility

A supervised bank can also be considered significant if it is one of the three most significant banks established in a country, even holding total assets below €30 billion or banks under a member state intervention.

Institutions can form board committees and ad hoc committees from the available board members to meet their governance needs. Available board members mean that board members consider whether they have sufficient time to dedicate not only to the work of the board but also to that of the committee(s). The real composition of the formation of committees differs across different geographies; however, the best practice requires a balanced inclusion of independent or non-executive directors exhibiting essential skills, expertise, and experience to perform the job. The board may consider the occasional rotation of directors and of the chair of committees in order to avoid undue concentration of power and promote fresh perspectives.

Most common committees in banking and financial institutions or publicly listed firms include:

- Audit committee
- Risk and compliance committee
- Remuneration (or compensation) committee

- Nomination committee
- Governance committee

Other kind committees that can be voluntarily formed include:

- Executive committee
- Ethics committee
- Community relations committee
- Governance committee
- Stock options committee
- Related parties committee
- Asset-liability committee
- Ad hoc committee (for a specific purpose)

The audit committee—compulsory in most jurisdictions—has the prime responsibility to perform the fiduciary duty of care, while other corporate governance committees are responsible to strongly oblige with the duty of loyalty. Nonetheless, the duty of care, the duty of loyalty, and the duty of obedience should be strictly followed by all the board members as a basic requirement to belong to a board.

In non-significant institutions—where the proportionality principle applies—two committees can sometimes be combined, such as the risk and compliance committee and the nomination committee. However, in the financial system, there is an emerging trend that narrows the flexibility toward non-systemic institutions. EBA/GL/2017/11 mentions that whenever non-significant institutions combine committees, those institutions should document the reasons why they have chosen to do so and how the approach achieves the objectives of the committees; and institutions should at all times ensure that the members of a combined committee possess—individually and collectively—the necessary knowledge, skills, and expertise to fully understand the duties to be performed by the combined committee. Private companies have no mandatory requirements to form the committees, but G20/OECD Principles of Corporate Governance recommend as a best practice to at least set up an audit committee and, in large private companies, also a remuneration committee and a nomination committee.

All members of the board should be fully aware of the structure and responsibilities of the committees, as well as the division of tasks between different functions of the board and its committees, to ensure their awareness about the adequate checks and balances implemented, guaranteeing that the decision-making is not being dominated by a single member or a small subset of its members. Executive and non-executive directors should interact effectively with the objective that both functions provide each other adequate data and information to allow them to perform their respective roles. These features and requirements should constitute part of the induction process, under leadership of the chair, and should be revised periodically along the mandate.

17.1 ROLE OF AUDIT COMMITTEE

In many jurisdictions, the establishment of a board audit committee in both the monist model and the dualist model—named financial matters committee in some jurisdictions—is normally compulsory for listed firms as well as for private firms when their dimensions (e.g., revenues, workforce, total assets) reach certain levels. The audit committee should not be confused with an audit board—constituted of individuals not belonging to the board—a requirement of many legal frameworks. While the audit committee of the board intervenes mainly in a supervisory function—as the audit committee also audits—the latter is focused on auditing, therefore a *posteriori*, that is, its main focus is usually to issue an opinion on the financial statements, the internal control framework, and other relevant issues required by law, submitting its opinion at the shareholders' meeting. Depending on the size of the board, the audit committee of the board comprises usually five members, while for the audit board are usually three, one of which in many jurisdiction has to be a qualified statutory auditor.

In the field of international financial institutions (e.g., IFIs, development banks such as The World Bank, European Investment Bank, Asian Development Bank, Inter-American Development Bank, Asian Infrastructure Investment Bank), the remit usually includes broader responsibilities of the audit board beyond issuing an opinion on the financial statements, including an opinion, statement, or conclusion on the compliance with the statutes and compliance with the best banking practices. The rationale is linked to their activity that includes "public policy objectives," and another is linked to commercial banking activities. As IFIs constitute a source for raising capital for the private sector—notably in Public-Private Partnerships, like project finance—the public policy objectives require IFIs or entering into partnerships with the private sector[348] which, depending on the characteristics of the particular IFI involved, presents the challenge of combining pursuing and executing public policy objectives (e.g., alleviating poverty, improve living conditions and standards, support sustainable economic, social and institutional development, as well as promote regional cooperation and integration) with the private sector and commercial or investment banking profitable activities.

The audit committee is generally considered as the most important committees, since the role of the audit is influential. Audit committee responsibilities include the design and development of the pluriannual audit plan to be presented to the board for approval as well as any adjustments that may happen along the mandate. The audit committee also oversees the corporate's financial reporting processes and internal control system over financial reporting, the audit of the financial statements, and the audit of information and cyber security. Currently, the trend is that the functional report of internal audit departments is to the audit committee of the board, and the audit committee also is involved in the selection process of the external auditor. Also, the audit committee has intimate relations with the control functions (risk management, compliance, and internal auditors) as well as with the external assurance providers (regulators, supervisors and external auditors).

The audit committee members should exhibit high standards, notably particular characteristics and profile in terms of background including academic, experience in external auditing, and professional qualification as internal auditor or statutory auditor. It is important that the board or/and audit committee charters (EBA/GL/2017/11) clarify the roles and responsibilities of the board and audit committee in performing the oversight role of the statutory audit and financial reporting processes led by executive directors and management, as well as the robustness of the reporting mechanism.

In most jurisdictions, the audit committee emanates from the board or from the supervisory board, comprising only independent directors or at least a majority of independent non-executive directors being chaired by an independent non-executive director-other than the chairperson. Some countries, such as Portugal, require a social body independent from the board—named "audit board"—appointed by the shareholders' meeting. In the audit board, depending on the legal framework, it is required that at least one member holds the professional qualification of statutory auditor. While the audit committee emerges from within the board of directors, the audit board—with at least one member as statutory auditor—may have supervisory role, the board's audit committee may have an oversight role. In countries where both an audit committee and an audit board have to exist in a corporation, distinction of their functions is important, as the first has a role of overseeing and supervising, and the latter issues an audit opinion. Neither the audit committee nor the audit board can be restricted from accessing any information or data they deem necessary. This naturally results in the overlap of analysis and request of data and information by both. Without limiting the access to data, information, and other issues, the coordination of the activities represents a way to improve synergies in the work of both bodies; supervisors, notably in the financial system, do incentivize this "four eyes" structured process.

Similarly, in the US, the audit committee is composed of independent outside directors, usually three to five; ideally, a minimum of one person qualifies as a financial expert and others have some degree of understanding of finance and capital markets and technical literacy. In the UK, the audit committee should have at least three non-executive directors for listed companies and at least one member of the audit committee should have recent and relevant financial experience. The audit committee should be chaired by an independent director who does not chair any other committee. There is a line of thought that advocates the principle that the chair of the board should not chair the audit committee, as it may hinder the independence and objectivity of audit committee; the best practice indicates this job for the vice-chair, the senior independent director, or a director qualified as a statutory auditor. Even so, some large firms and banks have adopted the same reporting line. On the other hand, if the chair is a former executive director (therefore a member of the board, which role was performed as management function), there should be an appropriate lapse of time before the position of the committee's chair is taken up.

Depending on the jurisdictions, the independent directors of audit committees are restricted from serving in several audit committees. For example, the guidelines by US SEC (Securities and Exchange Commission) and NYSE (New York Stock Exchange) mention that if an independent director simultaneously participates in more than three audit committees, the board must determine if it impairs the ability of the member to effectively serve on the audit committee.[349] Moreover, the director in the audit committee shall not receive any consulting or advisory fees other than the director fees and should not be an affiliated person of the company or its subsidiary, although most jurisdictions allow for extra compensation for chairing or being a member of the audit and other committees, other practice allows members of the committees to receive an allowance for each meeting they attend. As the involvement of audit committee in the oversight of risk depends on the size, complexity, and systemic importance of the firm, the chair of the board should ensure that both the new and the experienced directors facilitate the understanding of the scope of audit committee in overseeing the risk.

Elements to consider during the onboarding of an audit committee member or the committee itself, include:[350]

- Detailed filings of the corporate with the regulator of at least two years.
- Public communications, including disclosures or/and projections, shareholders presentation, analysts' presentation, among others.
- Any related party transactions or/and mergers and acquisitions.
- Materials relevant to company strategy, strategic plan, and scorecards of tracking the plan.
- Materials related to enterprise risk management and internal control functions such as risk, compliance, and internal audit.
- Policies such as conflict of interests' policy, ethics policy, code of conduct, among others.
- Internal audit plan, including information security for the fiscal year and report of previous year.
- External auditor reports and communications held.
- Minutes of the board, executive committee and committees of the board.
- Meeting with the external assurance providers (e.g., national competent authority, external auditors).

Similar to the role of chair of the board for setting the tone and risk culture, the chair of the audit committee plays an influential role in setting the tone, culture, communication, and agenda of the committee. The chair should set clear expectations from committee members, management, and auditors, and should ensure that the right resources are available to all stakeholders to deliver quality reporting. The chair must ensure that all the members are engaged and review the committee charter periodically while smoothening any adjustments if necessary.

As discussed in Section 14.1.2: "BCBS Principles of Corporate Governance," the audit committee is responsible for the following:

- Framing policy on internal audit and financial reporting.
- Overseeing the financial reporting process and its internal control framework, providing oversight of and interacting with the internal and external auditors.
- Approving, or recommending to the board or shareholders for their approval, the appointment, remuneration, and dismissal of external auditors.
- Reviewing and approving the multiannual audit plan, audit scope, and frequency, its performance and required changes.
- Receiving all audit reports and ensuring that senior management takes necessary corrective actions in a timely manner to address control weaknesses, noncompliance with policies, laws and regulations, and other problems identified by auditors and other control functions.
- Overseeing the establishment of accounting policies and practices by the bank.
- Reviewing the third-party opinions on the design and effectiveness of the overall risk governance framework and internal control system.

In the recent times (2020s), the speed at which global and economic volatility generated a high degree of uncertainty,[351] such as during the coronavirus pandemic (COVID-19), which led to a worldwide economic recession, affected globalization; worsened trade relations between the US, China, and Russia; geopolitical tensions, Brexit; high tech and rapid innovation; high level of online connectedness and cyber risk; sustainability (ESG); data protection and privacy (GDPR); data governance, ethics, compliance, and whistleblowing; the supply chain, digitalization; among others, from which new risks emerged, notably operational and cybersecurity risks, as well as posing risks not seen in the past relating to business continuity (growing concern concept). Therefore, the formation and adjustment of the agendas of the audit committee and the board should contemplate these challenging topics be able to meet the legal or/and regulatory compliance, notably the balance between the public health policies and the economy impacting the organization.

Section 14.5.1: "Designing an Agenda for Effective Meeting" discussed how a board can design its global agenda, and the same may be followed by the audit committee and/or the governance committee, if there is one established. Nonetheless, the committee is advised to follow the global trend as discussed while incrementally maintaining or controlling the previous year's agenda in order to have prudent risk oversight. As tech disruption is inevitable, impact of technology while assessing sustainability (ESG criteria, discussed in Section 4.3: "Corporate Sustainability") is also essential; technology seems to have taken a central seat in globalization process, with the potential to have a strong impact in the process. It is relevant to ensure clear expectations from both external and internal auditors. External audit must be aligned with Audit Reporting Standard—IAASB, ISA, among others, detailed in Chapter 22: Reporting. Besides the annual report, the audit committee—as well as the audit board, when applicable—must reassess the scope and quality of other relevant reports (such as sustainability report) and also ensure that internal audit is focused on key risks beyond financial reporting. The audit committee agenda should also include monitoring of the management progress on the implementation of credit standards or other relevant standards, as deemed necessary be the regulators. In banks, the assessment of impairments is of the utmost relevance, as are issues linked to the regulatory levels of capital impacting the CAR (Capital Adequacy

Ratio): ICCAP (Internal Capital Adequacy Assessment Process), and liquidity levels impacting the LCR (Liquidity Coverage Ratio): ILAAP (Internal Liquidity Adequacy Assessment Process).

EBA in GL/2017/11 relating to the internal governance of banks recommends the following about the role of the audit committee:

- Monitor the effectiveness of the institution's internal quality control and risk management systems and, where applicable, its internal audit function, with regard to the financial reporting of the audited institution, without breaching its independence.
- Oversee the establishment of accounting policies by the institution.
- Monitor the financial reporting process and submit recommendations aimed at ensuring its integrity.
- Review and monitor the independence of the statutory auditors or the audit firms.
- Monitor the statutory audit of the annual and consolidated financial statements.
- Be responsible for the procedure for the selection of external statutory auditor(s) or audit firm(s) and recommend for approval by the institution's competent body their appointment, compensation, and dismissal.
- Review the audit scope and frequency of the statutory audit of annual or consolidated accounts.
- Inform the administrative or supervisory body of the audited entity about the outcome of the statutory audit and explain how the statutory audit contributed to the integrity of financial reporting and what the role of the audit committee was in that process.
- Receive and take into account audit reports.

17.2 ROLE OF RISK AND COMPLIANCE COMMITTEE

All companies should have a robust process to identify, monitor, and mitigate the risks their businesses are exposed to, some of which may raise issues of business continuity, that is, constituting a matter of going concern. The board has an oversight responsibility to ensure that a framework and a system is implemented to mitigate them. Therefore, the risk and compliance committee are two of the most important committees of the board, and it is actually compulsory in most jurisdiction for the financial sector and also in the services and nonfinancial sector for many industries. The risk and compliance committees are distinct from the audit committee and must be formed, along with the audit committee, in systemically important organizations as well as significant financial institutions. The concept of the IIA three lines model incorporates the second line of defense the area of risk management and the area of compliance (both discussed in Section 6.2: "IIA Three Lines of Defense Model and Its Successor"), which constitutes a framework for all organizations to consider the identification and the way established to mitigate the panoply of risks to which they are exposed in a structured fashion.

The functions and responsibilities of the risk and compliance committees should be defined in the committees' charter, framing its role in the governance of the risk oversight. The oversight and mitigation of risks is usually more transparent and detailed in the financial sector (disclosure in annual reports and other reporting) due to the demand of regulatory and supervision authorities. However, risk and compliance committees emanating from the board in the nonfinancial and services' sectors is also of the utmost importance, although in many jurisdictions, either not required by law and regulation or based on low standards. Non-exhaustive examples of industries and services that adopt the best practice by setting the risk and compliance committees include commercial aviation, construction, consultants, external auditors, food industry, automotive industry, health care, infrastructures, energy sector, law offices and public notaries, pharmaceutical, technological sectors, telecoms, or transportation in general. Therefore, because of their importance to stakeholders and society in general, risk and compliance committees in corporates operating in nonfinancial industry should have visibility and transparency toward the stakeholders, namely on their websites or in annual reports, providing high standards of transparency and information. The COVID-19 black swan caught most organizations off guard, both public and private, as most did not identify or foresee the impact this risk provoked. This is an example of the complexity of risk identification and mitigation, which is why the board needs to dedicate attention to it.

Nonetheless, some degree of cross-participation between audit committee and risk and compliance committees—as well as with the audit board, if it exists—may be allowed to ensure sufficient flow of information, as they sometimes need to deal with overlapping issues, similar to the case with nomination and remuneration committees. The risk and compliance committee should be composed of a number of independent non-executive directors, with relevant experiences in risk management issues and practices and in compliance matters (e.g., ethics and conduct, conflicts of interest, anti-money laundering, market abuse, and inside information), and should have a chair who is an independent director and not the chair of the board or of any other committee. In significant financial institutions, it should include a majority of independent directors. The audit committee acts as an independent oversight body, being composed of all independent directors with the greater degree of focus, whereas the risk and compliance committee essentially has emphasis on risk management function and on compliance function. Therefore, it is important to form both the audit committee and the risk and compliance committees, with audit committee feeding on the input from the risk and compliance committees and performing an overall oversight role. In non-significant situations or private companies, in addition to the discussion above, the need to establish the risk and compliance committee also depends on factors embedded in the business model, including inherent risk environment, the needs of stakeholders, alignment of risk governance—notably, risk capacity and risk appetite—with strategy, oversight of the risk management structure, scope of risk and compliance committee responsibilities, and communication among committees,[352] as well as risks linked to companies with international footprint or trade with other regions, namely geopolitical, geo-economic, infrastructures, cybersecurity, exchange rate fluctuation, interest rates, foreign exchange controls, money laundering and financing to terrorism, or even corruption. On the other hand, issues such as who is responsible for oversight of management's risk and compliance committee (Chief Risk Officer (CRO), Chief Executive Officer (CEO), the risk and compliance committees, or the full board) and who is responsible for setting the criteria for management's reporting about risk to the board must be well established. The role the risk and compliance committees can play in this is of the utmost importance; when boards have a governance committee, whose role is to focus on the governance framework, that is an appropriate place to deal with this topic.

These board committees are responsible for understanding the stakeholders' expectations to be able to determine the risk capacity of the institution and inform the board about the risk capacity of the organization, and, consequently, propose two or three alternatives to the board, for it to decide the level of risk appetite and the buffers to avoid approaching the risk capacity. Their responsibilities include the discussion of risk strategies, periodical (but at least annual) review of risk policies, as well as oversight and supervision processes that management has in place to promote adherence to the approved risk policies, notably the risk appetite framework.

Essentially, the risk and compliance committees of the board are responsible for advising the board on the overall current and future risk vectors, overseeing senior management's implementation of the Risk Appetite Statement (RAS), reporting on the state of risk culture, and interacting with and overseeing the CRO, and contributing to the design and implementation in the organization of an effective risk and compliance management systems and internal control, reporting regularly its conclusions and recommendations to the board of directors/supervisory board in the exercise of its supervisory function.

Regular monthly meetings should be held with the head of risk control function and with the head of compliance function, residing within the IIA second line of defense model. A system to ensure an effective communication and coordination between the audit committee and the risk and compliance committees is paramount to facilitate the exchange of information and effective coverage of all risks, including emerging risks, and any adjustments needed to the risk governance framework. Therefore, the risk and compliance committee must collaborate with other committees whose activities may have an impact on the risk strategy (audit and remuneration committees) and regularly communicate with the institution's internal control functions, particularly the risk management function and compliance function. In other cases, the risk and compliance committee must, without prejudice to the tasks of the remuneration committee, examine whether incentives provided by the remuneration policies and practices take into consideration the institution's risk, capital and liquidity, and the likelihood and timing of earnings.

EBA details examples of the roles of the risk and compliance committees in the financial sector, which can be adapted and adjusted to the services and nonfinancial sectors (EBA/GL/2017/11):

- Advise and support the management body in its supervisory (board) function regarding the monitoring of the institution's overall actual and future risk appetite and strategy.
- Assist the management body in its supervisory function in overseeing the implementation of the institution's risk strategy and the corresponding limits set.
- Oversee the implementation of the strategies for capital and liquidity management as well as for all other relevant risks of an institution, such as market, credit, operational (including legal and IT risks), and reputational risks, in order to assess their adequacy against the approved risk appetite and strategy.

- Provide the management body, in its supervisory function, with recommendations on necessary adjustments to the risk strategy resulting from, among others, changes in the business model of the institution, market developments, or recommendations made by the risk management function.
- Provide advice on the appointment of external consultants that the supervisory function may decide to engage for advice or support.
- Review several possible scenarios, including stressed scenarios, to assess how the institution's risk profile would react to external and internal events.
- Assess the risks associated with the offered financial products and services and consider the alignment between the prices assigned to and the profits gained from those products and services.
- Assess the recommendations of internal or external auditors and follow up on the appropriate implementation of measures taken.
- Advise and support the board of directors within the control of the effectiveness of the internal quality control system and, therefore, the internal control framework.
- Support the board of directors to oversee the establishment and implementation of internal control systems and the internal control framework, as well as the reporting process on the effectiveness of internal control systems, including anti-money laundering and combating the financing of terrorism and proliferation of weapons of mass destruction (AML-CFT-WMD), which should be reviewed by the internal audit function.
- Support the Board of Directors in monitoring and supervising the Internal Control Framework, anti-money laundering, combating the financing of terrorism and proliferation of weapons of mass destruction (AML-CFT-WMD) reporting processes.

- Advise the Board of Directors on verifying the independence of the internal control functions (risk management and compliance), including the adequate segregation of functions, resources, and necessary powers.

The institutions need to ensure that the risk and compliance committees should at least have access to all relevant information and data necessary to perform their role, including namely information and data from relevant corporate and control functions such as legal, finance, human resources, IT and cyber risk, risk, compliance, and audit; receive regular reports, ad hoc information, communications, and opinions from heads of internal control functions concerning the current risk profile of the institution, its risk culture, and its risk limits, as well as on any material breaches that may have occurred, with detailed information on recommendations for corrective measures taken, to be taken or suggested to address them; periodically review and decide on the content, format, and frequency of the information on risk to be reported to them; and ensure the proper involvement of the internal control functions and other relevant functions such as human resources, legal, and finance within their respective areas of expertise, as necessary.

Additionally, the Committee must hold regular meetings with the board of directors/supervisory board and the statutory auditor and must, mandatorily, meet for the appraisal of the following annual reports of the bank:

1. Control Functions' Reports
2. Internal Control Report
3. Anti-Money Laundering, Combating the Terrorist Financing, and Weapons of Mass Destruction (AML-CTF-WMD) Report
4. Annual Report and Accounts, including the Corporate Governance Report

When a board or the risk and compliance committees do not have expertise in a particular area identified as a risk, then alternatively, they should consider seeking external expert advice.

17.3 ROLE OF NOMINATION COMMITTEE

The appointment of nomination committees varies among jurisdictions. In a model, it may emanate from the board, while in another model, the committee may be constituted by individuals not belonging to the board and therefore be elected by the shareholders meeting. The argument for latter model is linked to the avoidance of potential conflicts of interest, as well as in terms of practicality; when a board reaches the end of the mandate, an independent view about the renewal of mandates is required and aligned with best practice. For example, in the UK, the nomination committee is internal to board composed of independent members, while in Sweden, it is an external committee composed of shareholders representatives in the selection process. Also, institutions often adopt other nomenclatures like "selection and nominating committee" or "nominating and assessment committee," which is why it is relevant to define up front, notably in the governance framework, a charter for it to operate efficiently.

For the banking sector, the EBA guidelines on banks' internal governance suggests that the nomination committee in significant institutions should include a number of independent and be chaired by an independent director. Similar to the risk and compliance committees, the nomination should at least have access to all relevant information and data necessary to perform their role, including information and data from relevant corporate and control functions such as legal, finance, human resources, IT and cybersecurity, risk, compliance, audit, among others, and should also receive regular reports, ad hoc information, communications, and opinions from heads of internal control functions concerning the current risk profile of the institution, its risk culture, and its risk limits. The nomination committee should develop a matrix of competences that should be present in the board, taking into consideration the various components of diversity required by law, as well as by best practice, such that not only are the individuals fit and proper for the job but also the board is is fit and proper to comply with their responsibilities.

A relevant role of the nomination committee is the assessment of the directors, which is a delicate issue in many jurisdictions, though being a relevant process to ensure that the levels of contribution to the board are at least adequate. The role the chair plays in this process is critical, therefore being a matter to be discussed when hiring directors as a condition for them to join the board. Depending on the development of board members' assessment as well as considering the cultural environment, there are other methods that can be adopted progressively. One could be initiating a collective assessment—with the advantage of not focusing on individuals, notably not culturally adapted to an individual assessment process—using as a basis forms that are easily available on sites of consultants, or even hiring a consultant to carry out the process. Alternately, the nomination committee may decide to use a consultant to execute the assessment process in the following year with the individual self-assessment comprising of both the view of the individual board members any of their contribution to the board and performance as well as the contributions they plan to deliver in the coming year. The next step would be hiring a consultant to perform a 360-degree assessment of each board member. This process should be dealt with a degree of confidentiality, as it usually assesses relevant individuals. However, there should be consequences when a particular director does not deliver up to the expectations of the position.

The board assessment is a process that often implies a change of culture, both at the level of countries and at the level of institutions. However, a way to facilitate its implementation is to have the process decided and established when hiring board members (namely non-executives), informing them about the expectations of the company and the board itself, as well as about this condition, that is, each individual will be assessed annually during the mandate. The discussion of this process up front, under the leadership of the chair, usually results in more efficient boards.

Nomination committee must consider the diversity and inclusion targets, as discussed in Chapter 12: Boards' Diversity and Inclusion, as the topics around diversity and inclusion have never been so important. As Millennials and Generation Z (post-Millennials) will be driving the majority of global workforce, age is becoming increasingly irrelevant in the board, as long as a candidate maps with the required skills and experiences. Millennials are those who reach adulthood around the year 2020, while Generation Z (also known as Gen Z, post-Millennials, the iGeneration, Plurals, Founders, or the Homeland Generation) are those born in 1995 or later. It is believed that Gen Z is full of early starters and is very entrepreneurial, and that most of the teens going to workforce between ages 16 and 18 are opting for a traditional route of education while finishing it online. Essentially, the case of COVID-19 has further fueled the shift toward remote learning and working. The difference between these two tech-savvy generations is fundamentally important in order to prepare the business, shift marketing, adjust leadership, and adapt recruiting efforts to stay relevant for the future.[353] Therefore, institutions must look forward to developing the broad and robust talent pool in the long run and, therefore, keep the recruitment base wider in addition to external recruitment process. Ultimately, the chair of the nomination committee plays a leadership role in the nomination process. An article published in Harvard Law School Forum[354] puts the following holistic and structured questions for board and nomination committee to adequately consider in an era of heightened scrutiny from investors and governance specialists:

- Are the company's proxy disclosures adequately showcasing the diverse backgrounds, skills, and qualifications of the directors?

- Is there a robust mix of perspectives—aligned with company strategies and risks—among the current line-up of directors?
- Based on changing company strategies, risks, and challenges, how much board turnover is optimal—in the next one, two, or three years—in order to stay on top of these developments?
- Is the board providing a robust disclosure of the board assessment processes?
- Does the board follow through with board assessments by reviewing key takeaways and implementing an action plan, or with deadlines?
- When was the last time the selection criteria for director nominees was reassessed and updated?

Following are the guidelines from the UK Financial Reporting Council (FRC—www.frc.org.uk) about the role of the nomination committee that should be considered when setting up a nomination committee:

- The nomination committee is responsible for board recruitment and will conduct a continuous and proactive process of planning and assessment, taking into account the company's strategic priorities and the main trends and factors affecting the long-term success and future viability of the company.
- Appointing directors who can make a positive contribution is one of the key elements of board effectiveness. Non-executive directors should possess a range of critical skills valuable to the board and relevant to the challenges and opportunities facing the company.
- Diversity in the boardroom can have a positive effect on the quality of decision-making by reducing the risk of groupthink; with input from shareholders, boards need to decide which aspects of diversity are important in the context of the business and its needs.

- Developing a more diverse executive pipeline is vital to increasing levels of diversity amongst those in senior positions; improving diversity at each level of the company is important if more diversity at senior levels is to become a reality.
- Working with human resources, the nomination committee will need to take an active role in setting and meeting diversity objectives and strategies for the company as a whole and in monitoring the impact of diversity initiatives.
- The nomination committee will want to ensure that the board is composed of individuals who display a range of softer skills.
- Board appointments should be made on merit against objective criteria; the nomination committee should evaluate the skills, experience, and knowledge on the board and the future challenges affecting the business, and, in the light of this evaluation, prepare a description of the role and capabilities required for a particular appointment.
- Skills matrices that map the existing skill set against that required to execute strategy and meet future challenges can be an effective way of identifying skills gaps.
- Publicly advertising board appointments and working with recruitment consultants who have made a commitment to promote diversity are examples of ways in which the nomination committee can access a more diverse pool of candidates from which to appoint.
- Directors are expected to undertake that they will have sufficient time to meet what is expected of them effectively; the role of chair, in particular, is demanding and time-consuming, and multiple roles are therefore not advisable.
- The terms and conditions of appointment of the chair and non-executive directors must be available for inspection.

To ensure access to a wide range of candidates to a director position, namely, to allow the identification of individuals that are "below the radar" or have recently become available for this type of position, the nomination committee usually hires a consultant in the executive search arena to assist in this process. For avoidance of potential conflicts of interest, the assessment of the individual directors and the board should be done by a different firm.

17.3.1 SUCCESSION PLANNING

As the nomination committee is also responsible for succession planning, it must therefore establish a succession planning policy. Bylaws may exist in some jurisdictions, and in such cases, bylaws take precedence over the organizational policies. Prudent succession planning policy aids in achieving the right talent with diversity and inclusion, projecting and ensuring the mitigation of uncertainty; in family businesses, this issue is particularly relevant, notably if the firm is still at the founders' stage. The succession planning is also meant to prevent group thinking, balance of institutional knowledge, balance of power, and continued trust with shareholders and stakeholders, including in moments of changes in the board.

Essentially, board composition and succession planning are about inclusion in terms of skills, knowledge, and viewpoints. While variables such as race, gender, and tenure are important, leveraging unique strengths, perspectives, and experience (inclusion) fundamentally drives collaboration and increases business growth for both the short and long-term. Therefore, to formulate the succession plan, the following questions should be considered beforehand:[355]

- How effective is the board in addressing the key agendas of the corporate? Are directors being recruited with relevant experience, expertise, and education in order to make a collective board?
- Is the board diverse enough to add value? What are the metrics of diversity and inclusion besides gender and ethnicity? Are board members recruited worldwide or within

the same geography or communities to bring a wider skill set to the board?

- Is the diversity effort initiated by the expectations of stakeholders or by regulatory constraints? Is inclusive environment promoted by the board?

Following are FRC UK guidelines for succession planning:

- The chair's vision for achieving the optimal board composition will help the nomination committee review the skills required, identify the gaps, develop transparent appointment criteria, and inform succession planning.
- There are risks of becoming too reliant on the skills of one individual. Discussions on tenure at the time of appointment will help inform and manage the long-term succession strategy. The needs of the company and the board will change over time, so it is wise to manage expectations and encourage non-executive directors to be flexible about term lengths and extensions.
- Executive directors may be recruited externally, but companies should also develop internal talent and capability.
- Talent management can be a strong motivational force for those who wish to develop their career within the company and achieve senior positions. It can provide the nomination committee with a variety of strong candidates.

Regarding the tenure of the chair and non-executive directors, different jurisdictions can have different tenure requirements, as no one size fits all; determining the tenure and/or other factors may impair the independence status of a director. Usually, as a good practice, the maximum tenure of board members lies between seven and nine years. FRC UK advocates that boards will need to justify why they would consider a non-executive or independent director beyond nine years. It is also recommended that the chair be subject to a simi-lar length of service considerations, as non-executive directors and should not stay in post for longer than nine years. For the chair, the nine-year period is calculated from when they were first appointed to the board, therefore years spent on the board prior to becoming chair would be included when considering their total length of service.

Succession planning in a family business, which presents particu-lar specificities, is covered in Chapter 5: Family Business Governance.

17.4 ROLE OF THE REMUNERATION/COMPENSATION COMMITTEE

The roles of remuneration and compensation committee are some-times part of the responsibilities of the nomination committee. Shareholders of listed firms express their views, through participation and voting at shareholders' meetings, namely about the compensa-tion of board members, an issue that gained relevance and has been scrutinized more recently after the 2008 economic and financial crisis. Disclosure of remuneration of board members and key executives is usually presented in the annual or other relevant reports to address the needs to shareholders or stakeholders. In some jurisdictions, remuneration and other forms of compensation of a certain number of the highest paid executives, namely members of the social bodies, has to be disclosed by law, while in others, it is confined to specified positions. Nonetheless, it is important for shareholders and stake-holders to know the remuneration policy as well as the total value of compensation arrangements made pursuant to this policy. Above all, the remuneration of the candidate must be fit and proper to the expected role, follow the current trend of governance, and be appro-priately aligned with bylaws and other such measures, if applicable.

The remuneration committee is fundamentally responsible for the remuneration policy, though it may consult the nomination com-mittee (if it exists) on overlapping matters. The remuneration policy can be established following the guidelines such as EBA Guidelines on Sound Remuneration Policies and FSB Principles for Sound Compensation Practices. Essentially, the remuneration committees are expected to focus on the strategic rationale for executive pay and the links between compensation, strategy, and long-term sustainable success (FRC UK). It is important that the remuneration committee takes steps to counteract the risk of incentives that are detrimental to the long-term success of the company, establishing a method with deferred compensation, or even with clauses and triggers that require executives to return part of the compensation.

Institute of Directors (IoD—www.iod.com), a business organization for company directors, mentions that the members of the remuneration committee should receive a full briefing from fellow committee members, the chief executive, or the human resources director in the following matters:[356]

- The overall remuneration philosophy, namely, the positioning of total remuneration relative to the marketplace, the definition of the marketplace, the approach to short-term and long-term incentives, the benefits policy, etc.
- Contract details, including notice periods, severance arrangements, compensation for loss of office, and special arrangements (if any) in relation to changes of control.
- Details of individual directors' remuneration for the past three to five years, including base salary, bonuses, long-term incentive grants, and exercise values.
- Compliance of current remuneration with any regulatory guidelines.
- Any immediate changes planned, for example, because of the expiry of a share option plan, or a change in the strategy of the business.
- Any special arrangements for individual directors and why they exist; new hires or executives approaching retirement, for example, might have been offered something different.

- The market information provided by advisers.
- How outside advisers were appointed, who they are, and why they were selected.

Following are the roles of the remuneration committee (FRC UK):

- The remuneration committee has delegated responsibility for designing and determining remuneration for the chair, executive directors, and the next level of senior management.
- The remuneration committee is also tasked with reviewing workforce remuneration and related policies.
- The remuneration committee's review is limited to workforce remuneration and related policies in respect of persons engaged under an employment contract or other arrangements to do work or provide services personally.
- The review will include matters such as any pay principles applied across the company, base pay, benefits, and all incentives and aspects of financial and nonfinancial reward that drive behavior.

17.4.1 DESIGNING EXECUTIVE COMPENSATION

Guidelines on Sound Remuneration Policies by European Banking Authority (EBA), Principles for Sound Compensation Practices and Investment Management Association (IMA),[357] and Principles of Remuneration and Financial Stability Board (FSB) are some of high-level guidelines that institutions may follow for designing executive remuneration policy. Companies may also hire consultants from companies such as Korn Ferry, Mercer, or others who specialize in executive search to meet their own requirements.

Incentive mechanisms to align with the stakeholders' interests are discussed in Section 2.1: "The Agency Theory." Because of the management power, self-serving executives can overpay themselves directly or indirectly, and that can induce an agency conflict.

Corporate law in some jurisdictions have a "say on pay" provisions, wherein shareholders have the right to vote on the compensation of their managers and executives. Without a doubt, the say on pay provisions have brought shareholders—mainly institutional, but lately also activists and hedge funds—closer to the boards as a preventive action, and as a result, a new business born and flourished, nowadays known as *proxy advisors* (more in Chapter 20: Proxy Voting Services). For example, *Financial Times* reported, "Deutsche Bank introduced the pay scheme at the beginning of this year. Under the plan, in addition to a basic salary and bonuses linked to the banks and their own performance, divisional heads would also be eligible for a bonus linked to their division's performance. However, in a non-binding vote at Deutsche Banks's annual meeting in Frankfurt, 51.9 percent of shareholders voted against the scheme, with 48.1 percent in favor."[358] Institutional Shareholder Services (ISS), one of the influential shareholder proxy advisors, recommended investors to reject the plan.

While "say on pay" is required by the regulators in the US and UK, it is voluntary in Canada. Nonetheless, the purpose of designing optimal executive compensation has primarily three objectives:

1. Provide strong incentives to increase shareholder or stakeholder value
2. Retaining key talent
3. Limit the cost of the shareholder and key stakeholders[359]

As a principle, the remuneration should be used not to buy loyalties but to promote competence and results. Eventually, the best practice advocates loyalty be obtained through transparent and fair systems. The design of remuneration systems depends on the role profile, not the profile of the person (for example, Executive Director versus Non-executive Director). Remuneration should be viewed as a strategic tool, and the design of incentives should depend on the factors such as responsibilities, performance, and results.

The remuneration policy in organizations should be an inclusive factor and not a divisive factor. For example, if the organization does not have a comprehensive health plan or an inclusive pension plan, it is not justified to exist only for top management. If merit is to be rewarded, it should exist at the level of the whole organization. Essentially, weighing of the levels of remuneration with the market is inevitable. On the other spectrum, excessive remuneration may provoke social disagreement if they are not assumed with transparency and rationality.

Aligning the short-term and the long-term interests of the principal (shareholder) and the agent (management) is probably one of the most challenging tasks. Institutional investors such as pension funds, sovereign funds, societies, mutual funds, small shareholders may be less hawkish than activist investors (further discussed in Chapter 21: Activism) such as hedge funds and short-termism. It is agreed that the former is more likely to work in the best interests of the society, which may later translate into best the best interests of the shareholders. In Continental Europe, the interests of other stakeholders such as employees, banks, society, and environment continue to be represented, and OECD recommendation specifically recognizes the interests of workers and other stakeholders besides shareholders, with long-term remuneration options in order to secure the maximum alignment of interests by creating the sustained value. In G20/OECD, Principles of Corporate Governance mention that the board should fulfill certain key functions, including aligning key executive and board remuneration with the longer-term interests of the company and its shareholders, covering board processes, transparency, and shareholder input respectively. EBA mentions that the specific requirements for variable remuneration of identified staff should be applied in a manner and to the extent that is appropriate to their size, internal organization, and the nature, scope, and complexity of their activities. However, long-term incentive plans have garnered some criticism too.

A survey study showed that executives in the US earn much more than in any region.[360] It seems that US executives are more risk-averse than theory suggests, and that stock compensation plan is a dicey proposition to them. Executives have shown preference to get a one-dollar payout today than two dollar a year later, which the behavioral economists termed as "hyperbolic discounting." The long-term incentive package including deferral of part of the compensation (common in many jurisdictions in Europe) that could be worth a lot in three or four years is valued very little today, mainly due to the uncertainty of markets and global events over which executives do not have influence and/or control, with COVID-19 is an extreme example, as it will likely affect the deferred compensation that is due. Also, the executives are less concerned with absolute earnings and are more motivated by how they are paid in relation to their peers, both inside the company and at competitors. Lastly, the pay package undervalues intrinsic motivation such as achievement, status, power, and teamwork. Extra-large pay packages do not necessarily create stronger incentives (see Figure 17.1). For example, executives are willing to reduce their pay packages by an average of 28 percent in exchange for a job that is better in other respects.[361]

Figure 17.1: CEO average pay around the world

CEO Pay Around the World
Chief executive officers in the U.S. are paid better than their peers abroad and the average American worker

Country	Pay Ratio	CEO Pay	Adjusted GDP per capita
U.S.	265	$14,3M	$53,820
India	229	1,5	6,372
U.K.	201	7,9	39,545
South Africa	180	2,2	12,270
Netherlands	171	8,2	48,177
Switzerland	152	8,5	55,952
Canada	149	6,5	43,469
Germany	138	6,2	45,341
China	127	1,9	14,713
Japan	58	2,2	38,550

Source: (Bloomberg)

The main challenge of a remuneration committee has been to figure out what is the best remuneration model for the firm such that it is favored by both the board and the stakeholders. It is recommended to have at least two non-executive directors (NEDs) in the remuneration committee chaired by a NED, when it emanates from the board, and ideally have one NED with technical expertise in the design of remunerating models; if this is not the case, then hiring a consultant should be considered. Regarding the remuneration structure of NED, the best practice is to have the fixed remuneration appropriate to the different functions in board's committees for which they have been designated and, accordingly, aligned with the market practices for institutions of the sector of equivalent complexity, footprint, type of industry, and size. The best practice determines that a non-executive director should not earn variable compensation. It is an emerging practice related to the fiduciary responsibility (that in most jurisdictions does not distinguish responsibilities between executive and non-executive directors) that the compensation of the non-executive directors should converge to the fixed remuneration of executive directors, with the latter earning an additional variable remuneration.

While designing the remuneration model, the remuneration committee should take the following elements into account:[362]

1. *Trust:* ensuring credibility
2. *Fair:* balanced pay gap and equilibrium
3. *Transparent and simple:* easy to understand
4. *Easy to manage*
5. *Flexible:* adjustable and improvable
6. *Long-term vision:* stability
7. *Well-defined metrics:* what is not measurable is not controllable
8. *Clear responsibilities and assignments*
9. *Written:* evidenced
10. *Empowered*

Issues like pay gap and gender gap have never been as sensitive, and rightly so, which is why the remuneration committee should monitor and oversee, regularly reporting on it to the board and ensuring that it is part of the global agenda of the board.

There is no definitive way to design the remuneration model. However, before starting with the design of the remuneration model, the remuneration committee may start with the analysis of the relevant strategic variables. If the members of the remuneration committee are not fully aware of the business model and the correspondent challenges, as well as financial and economic indicators, the remuneration committee can take support and materials from another committee/department or hire independent external consultants.

Some of the strategic questions can be:[363]

- Does the firm want to increase the international business component?
- Does the firm want to diversify the customer base?
- Does the firm want to be the best in the class at costs?
- Does the firm want to be market leaders and strengthen market power?

It is important to translate answers to strategic questions into annual management objectives, which must be measurable. After measuring the strategic variables of the corporate, the weight to the remuneration package of directors and executives (new or veteran) can be attributed, such as fixed compensation, variable compensation (e.g., bonuses, commission), and any specific compensation plans such as employee stock options (e.g., long-term incentive).

There are also models usually used in large corporations with two compensation committees, one appointed by the shareholders meeting, constituted often by representatives of relevant shareholders or groups of shareholders, whose main role is to establish the global package for the board, detailing non-executive and executive directors, focusing on the variable compensation of the latter; the other emanating from the board or the supervisory board with the main responsibility being the individual allocation of the global package among the executives.

17.5 BOARD AND COMMITTEE EVALUATIONS

17.5.1 EFFECTIVENESS AND EVALUATIONS

The New York Stock Exchange (NYSE) requires listed companies to perform board and committee evaluations. The content from the article *Effective Board Evaluation*,[364] published in Harvard Law School Forum on Corporate Governance, is referred to explain board effectiveness and evaluations. Disclosing the evaluations to shareholders and stakeholders is fundamentally important to demonstrate board effectiveness. Since the financial and economic crisis of 2007–2008, regulators, investors, and stakeholders seek greater board effectiveness and evaluations. The onus is on the board to demonstrate its effectiveness and address the stakeholder interests by enhancing their board evaluation processes and disclosures. High-profile board sight failures, increased complexity, uncertainty, opportunity and risk in business environments globally, pressure from stakeholders for companies to better explain and achieve current and long-term corporate performance, and increased focus on board composition by institutional or/and activist investors are some of the reasons that pressed on board effectiveness and evaluations.

The board and its members should know the goals, objectives, and key performance indicators they are expected to achieve through the evaluation of performance. Essentially, the evaluation process should be for not only demonstrating compliance but for rigorously testing the efficacy of the board's composition, dynamics, operations, and structure for the company and its business environment, both in the short and long-term, by focusing on directors' self-evaluation on actual board or/and committee to agree upon board or/and committee, drawing valuable and candid feedback from each directors about board dynamics, operations, structure, performance, and composition, as well as reaching an agreement among board members on action items and corresponding timelines to address issues observed in the evaluation process. Also, the board should be held accountable for regularly reviewing the implementation of actions based on board evaluations and measuring results against agreed-upon goals and expectation, while adjusting actions in real time to meet the evaluation goals and objectives.

The assessment or appraisal could be seen from two perspectives—the evaluation of individual board members, and the holistic evaluation of board and board committees. In Section 9.6: "Culture and Behavior Supervision," the culture and behavior supervision implemented in the Netherlands is also discussed as a best practice. Financial Reporting Council UK states that the major firms should endeavor externally facilitated board evaluations at least every three years, in addition to the regular internal evaluation. Usually, the nomination committee or/and corporate governance committee performs the board evaluation process, either by itself or along with the senior independent director or the chair. The evaluation process may also involve third parties, internal advisors, and external legal counsel in order to achieve a 360-degree view, which usually requires interviewing superiors, peers, and staff.

The topics on board, committee, and individual director's evaluation should prioritize analysis of board and committee minutes and meeting materials to conclude about the contribution of individual members, using governance documents such as meeting minutes, corporate governance guidelines, committee charters, director qualification standards, conflicts of interest policy. Also, observations relevant to board dynamics, operations, structure, performance, composition, corporate culture, performance, business environment conditions, and strategy are very relevant for the effectiveness of a board and the committees. Another angle relates to the engagement with investors, shareholders, or/and stakeholders on board composition, performance, and oversight.

The topics covered by the evaluation are normally core board duties and responsibilities and oversight functions such as governance, strategy, risk, and financial performance, as well as supervision of executives. Topics should include corporate integrity, reputation, and culture, as well as management performance and succession planning. Board or external consultant may use questionnaires and/or confidential and anonymous interviews to develop the evaluation process, allowing answers to the questionnaire to be provided without attribution, as this can potentially lead to candid and detailed feedback. After fetching the results from the evaluations, the chair should decide, usually with the assistance of the senior independent director, how to brief each individual director and the board, keeping in mind the confidential and anonymous protocol of the assessment. It is relevant that the commitment to demonstrate actions to challenge the weakness and incrementally correct the deficiencies that could hamper the functioning of board and make it more effective.

According to EY Center for Board Matters,[365] the following elements for effective and efficient evaluation should be considered by the board:

- Review the last assessment of the board and directors with the objective of developing actions to improve performance, considering potential needs in terms of the overall fit and proper of the board.
- Ensure an assessment process to validate individual directors to conclude on the fit and proper at that moment.
- Ensure the board's and directors' understanding of the elements of "effectiveness" applied to the board as a whole, its committees, and directors.
- Set up clear goals, objectives, and standards—for the board, committees, and director—to be benchmarked in the assessment.

- Define the periodicity of the assessment process as well as its components.
- Ensure that the assessment process is coordinated and synchronized with the board's periodic governance review, training programs, nomination, succession planning, and stakeholder engagement program.

The guidelines about board evaluations recommended by FRC UK are mentioned below:

- Boards continually need to monitor and improve their performance. This can be achieved through evaluation, which provides a powerful and valuable feedback mechanism for improving effectiveness, maximizing strengths, and highlighting areas for further development.
- Like induction and board development, evaluation should be bespoke in its formulation and delivery. The chair has overall responsibility for the process, and should select an effective approach, involving the senior independent director, as appropriate.
- The senior independent director should lead the process that evaluates the performance of the chair and, in certain circumstances, may lead the entire evaluation process, when the board decides so.
- The chair should consider ways to obtain feedback from the workforce and other stakeholders. Chairs of board committees should be responsible for (or at least involved in) the evaluation of their committees.
- Board evaluations should inform and influence succession planning. They represent an opportunity for boards to review skills, assess their composition, and agree on plans for filling skills gaps and increasing diversity.

- The outcomes from the board evaluation should be shared with and discussed by the board. They should be fed back into the board's work on composition, the design of induction, development programs, and other relevant areas.
- The Code recommends Financial Times-Stock Exchange (FTSE) 350 companies have externally facilitated board evaluations at least every three years. Chairs of smaller companies are also encouraged to consider adopting this process periodically.
- Whether facilitated externally or internally, evaluations should be rigorous. They should explore how effective the board is as a unit as well as the quality of the contributions made by individual directors.

In case of externally Facilitated Board Evaluations, FRC UK recommends that when selecting a board evaluator, the chair needs to be clear about what the board evaluation will offer and needs to be mindful of existing commercial relationships and other conflicts of interests. Also, to ensure a more valuable review, the chair will need to ensure full cooperation between the company and the evaluator. The chair is responsible for making sure that the board gets the most from an externally facilitated board evaluation and should ensure it is not approached as a compliance exercise.

17.5.2 ASSESSMENT OF TIME COMMITMENT OF NON-EXECUTIVE DIRECTORS

The assessment of time commitment to the board and committees may vary across jurisdictions. The Walker Report,[366] recommends measures to improve the corporate governance of banks in UK, suggesting that non-executive directors (NEDs) must not have more than five roles, a standard that is being followed by several regulators and supervisors. However, the number of independent directorships that can be taken, particularly in nonfinancial institutions, may be more, depending on the legislative framework or governance code in each jurisdiction, although the best practice does not allow for a large accumulation of mandates, notably due to the lack of time to commit to an effective non-executive director.

The European Central Bank (ECB) follows the practice of conduct, a benchmarking exercise on the declared time commitment of NEDs in banks in the eurozone. NEDs are expected to commit enough time to their duties and responsibilities within the entity supervised by ECB. Therefore, the ECB requires a minimum set of information from the potential NED and from the supervised entity necessary to conduct the suitability assessment within the scope of fit and proper guidelines. For example, a full list of the appointee's mandates and positions, the number of hours or days dedicated to each mandate or position, any additional responsibilities such as membership of committees, a self-declaration of the appointee judging and ensuring sufficient time to dedicate to all mandates, and a declaration of the financial institution confirming so, as well as a confirmation of adequate buffers for ongoing learning and periods of increased activity.

The time commitment is measured both quantitatively and qualitatively, in line with the fit and proper process discussed in Section 11.1: "Fit and Proper." In the Quantitative Assessment, the ECB sets a limit on the number of directorships that can be held by a member of the board. In other words, the member of a significant institution can only hold one executive directorship and two non-executive directorships, or four non-executive directorships.

The Qualitative Assessment factors considered in the assessment include:

1. Size and circumstances of the entities where the directorships are held and the nature, scale, and complexity of their activities.
2. Location where the entities are based.

3. Other professional or personal commitments and circum-
    stances (for example, a court case in which the appointee may
    be involved).
4. Travel time required for the role.
5. Number of meetings scheduled for the management body.
6. Time needed for necessary induction and training.
7. Nature of the specific position and responsibilities of the
    member (for example, specific role as a CEO, chair, or mem-
    ber of a committee).

According to the ECB (2019),[367] based on the information provided
by supervised entities, NEDs declared on average to devote 22.2
days per year, while chairs declared on average that they devoted 42
days per year to their function in the supervised entity. Essentially, the
amount of time that NEDs said they would devote to their oversight
function was strongly linked to the size of the bank and to their specific level of responsibility on the board.

Topics of the Chapter

The following has been discussed within this chapter:

*   Committees in banking and financial institutions or publicly
    listed firms include:
    Audit committee: designs and develops audit plan; over-
    sees financial reporting processes.
    1. Risk and Compliance committee: oversees and mitigates
        risks.
    2. Nomination committee: recruits and appoints directors;
        assesses performance of directors.
        o   Nomination committee must also establish a
            succession planning policy.
    3. Remuneration committee: establishes remuneration
        policy.

- Boards should continually evaluate and improve their performance; chairs of board committees should be responsible for the evaluation of their committees.
- Time commitment of NEDs is measured both quantitatively and qualitatively, in line with the fit and proper process.
- "Board ad hoc committees" are also discussed as an alternative, when not required by law, to board committees.

Part V—Globalization, Geopolitics, Foreign Direct Investment, and International Financial Institutions

Chapter 18

Globalization 4.0

18.1 GLOBALIZATION

Globalization has emerged as a topic that boards should be concerned with, namely when their companies have an international footprint or are involved in international trade. Globalization interlinks and impacts geopolitics, geo-finance, and geo-economy, areas of knowledge usually outside the matrix of skills required in board members. However, the challenging developments emerging in the geopolitical arena indicate that board members with these skills should have a seat on a board, and the topic should be part of the global agenda of boards. This chapter discusses the concepts of globalization and geopolitics.

Globalization is currently defined as a process by which businesses and other organizations develop international influence or start operating on an international scale. Globalization may constitute both opportunities and threats to the countries, regions, and companies. This is a movement that progressively integrates world economies, businesses, cultures, environment, government, and society challenges, based on more intense relationships and proximity between communities. It results in a systematic transformation, experiencing evolving homogeneity in international trade, foreign direct investment, capital markets, markets, technology, as well as concentration through multiple large-scale merger and acquisition processes.

Globalization involves culture adjustment and a common basis to promote exchanges between groups. Globalization may lead to an increase in competition, efficient capital allocation, dissemination of ideas, information and innovation, technological development, and intellectual capital, as well as improved regulation or deregulation and wider application of international standards. Different countries may have different standards in their jurisdiction, and it is common for corporates to have shareholders and stakeholders spread across the world, even when the corporate image is intimately linked to a particular country or region. For this reason, corporate governance best practices can be seen as constituting a leveling benchmark for the corporate world and also the competitiveness of a country.

Professor Klaus Schwab, Founder and Executive Chairman of the World Economic Forum (WEF), in a paper coined the term "Globalization 4.0."[368] Essentially, there have been three phases of globalization. The first phase was until 1914. At the time, immigration, cross-border capital, and trade flows were larger by contemporary standards, and most people were free to travel from one to another without passports. Only some international economic agreements existed, such as the International Telegraph Union (1865), Universal Postal Union (1874), International Association of Railway Congresses (1884). This period lacked institutional and governance framework. The second phase was the period from Second World War (1939) until late 1990s. This period established much of the modern international economic architecture, namely trade, financial and developmental institutions, and agreements. Multinational corporations emerged and expanded their business gradually across the world, which was aided not only by the policy of liberalization but also by improved communication and transportation. The third phase, that has been existing until today (2020), was fueled by the wider adaptation of internet technology, the establishment of World Trade Organization (WTO), and the formal entry of China into the trading system through its accession to that institution. Other changes continued, such as technological advancement, robustness of banking, financial regulations, along with continued trade and capital liberalization. This was further facilitated by regional free trade agreements and bilateral investment treaties, which constituted the integration of markets and cross-border expansion of value chains. However, in 2019–2020, trade tensions started to emerge, particularly between the US and China.

Globalization 4.0—a concept developed by Klaus Schwab Chairman of WEF—is gradually materializing its structure at the time (2020). However, many of the past assumptions regarding globalization—such as US-China trade tensions, protectionist measures implemented by some countries, the Trump's government shifts in US policy, Brexit, China's Belt and Road Initiative (BRI), tighter immigration controls, automation, remote working, cybersecurity, data privacy and security, among others—may not be valid today. The construct of Globalization 4.0 fundamentally depends on wise governance decisions and technological advancements. Technological disruption is inevitable, and the systems of health, transportation, communication, production, distribution, energy, among others, are poised to change. It is critically important to construct a new synergy between public policy and institutions on the one hand while corporate behavior and norms on the other, enabling humanity to rise above the false choices that are sometimes posed. Nonetheless, current trends suggest that the shaping of Globalization 4.0 may take quite some time, unless the skeptical public becomes assured that global integration and technical change do not inherently pit countries against each other in a zero-sum game. Another vector that emerges from globalization relates to the adoption and achievement of standards of corporate citizenship, a robust legal framework and effectiveness of the judicial system, and regulations that control the internal governance of the corporation and define how power and authority are allocated and exercised. Globalization phenomena have pushed for a more global awareness and consequently an international harmonization of standards. For example, ISO 26000 is concerned with social responsibility and sustainability and offers guidance on socially responsible behavior and possible actions. Similarly, in 2018, COSO published guidelines to ESG (Environmental, Social, and Governance) related risks for managing and maintaining sustainable businesses in a globalized landscape.

As discussed, not all countries are satisfied with the lack of solutions to emerging countries and the potential domino effect of globalization. In an article, EY[369] warns for the erosion of the position of the US in terms of global dominance, resulting from the growth of emerging markets success from globalization. The other side of the coin however shows failures, notably the inability to eliminate or mitigate inequality, poverty, and political instability. There is also a challenge emerging from the strong influence of geopolitical blocks, have defining the rules of the game to maintain and attract new players to their spheres of influence.

The US administration has questioned globalization by advocating protectionism measures, showing signs of opting out of free trade agreements across the world and subsequently raising tariffs on a variety of products imported from China, arguing that China benefits unfairly from an old tariff agreement. China, as a retort, levied extra tariffs against some US-made products. This has given rise to new paradigm in globalized geopolitics that may potentially collaterally affect other economies. A corporation operating in several jurisdictions is likely to fall out if it does not incorporate risk and governance strategies related to globalization and geopolitics. China's foreign direct investment in EU countries has also raised the eyebrows of regulators, notably because it is focused on sectors that are considered geopolitically as strategic, like banking, insurance, healthcare, telecom, energy production and distribution, or commercial aviation.

Cross-border business and investments in recent times, resulting from globalization, raised doubts about their objectives as well as about the lack of the reciprocity rule in foreign direct investment. China has gradually allowed markets to play a role in the business landscape, although claims about privately owned and state-owned enterprises are seen as a more complex challenge, notably the application of the reciprocity rule, which has claimed China does not apply transparently and efficiently for inward investment.

Also, a line of thought argues for evidence of a non-transparent landscape, particularly in terms of the ultimate beneficiary owner (UBO). This relates to holdings of SASAC (State-owned Asset Supervision and Administration Commission) that, at the level of owned companies, are seen as platforms to direct and manage foreign direct investment. Also, there is a line of thought that speculates about the real UBO when private investors are involved, as their board members often belong to high political decision-making structures, which leads to increasing levels of mistrust. This line of thought basically advocates that the state is the actual investor.

In 2020, the trade relations and issues emerging from state aid affecting competition between the US and the European Union resulted in a decision of The World Trade Organization favorable to the European Union for the right to apply punitive tariffs of approximately 4 billion dollars as a result of illegal state help to Boeing as well as a list of US products.[370]

18.1.1 COVID-19 AND GLOBALIZATION

The emergence of the coronavirus pandemic (COVID-19) is another element on top of the geopolitical tensions and trends that led to impact the globalization paradigm. As the case is quite different from trade tensions or protectionist measures, it essentially adds more topics to be dealt with regarding the new globalization landscape phenomenon. Sovereigns' or supranationals' massive policy of lockdown and social distancing measures to protect human life caught business leaders in an unprecedented paradigm as well as with more than one wave of the virus dramatically affecting the balance between the economy and public health discussion. There is an unprecedented impact in the fashion boards run and manage organizations, very likely affecting the fit and proper profile of boards—both individually and as a whole—introducing new elements in the required matrix of the boards' competences, notably in the debate and balance between the business and the employees and their families' health safety as well as the need to add competences in this area.

Although financial assistance was provided by the government in most jurisdictions, the kind of business risk the pandemic constituted was never seen before. Essentially, government, business, political, or societal leaders have a duty to protect people's health at first, although an ethical dilemma has emerged during the first wave—or transition to the second/third wave—that considers the negative consequence in the economy, a challenge that requires a careful balance between the public health and economy. Whenever possible, remote working was endorsed by the governments and many companies followed the same. Nonetheless, global supply chains have become severely affected, and some sectors such as retail, tourism, and energy suffered more than other sectors such as healthcare, grocery, or household. The issue of cybersecurity and data privacy gained high attention, as more people were online than usual. The fear factor is there to stay, particularly regarding social distancing and psychological perception, resulting in higher risk sensitivity not only for individuals but also for the companies. Therefore, the board—being fit and proper—may need to realign the corporate or globalization strategy, fostering an inclusive environment for all stakeholders. WEF[371] actively promoted the "stakeholder" principles for business continuity mentioned below:

- For the employees: The principle is to keep them safe. The organization must do everything it can to protect their workplace and to help them adapt to the new working conditions.
- For their ecosystem of suppliers and customers: The principle is to secure a shared business continuity. The organization

should continue to work to keep supply chains open and integrate suppliers and customers into the business response.

- For the end consumers: The principle is to maintain fair prices and commercial terms for essential supplies.
- For governments and society: The principle is to offer complete support to complement public action with the organization's resources, capabilities, and know-how.
- For shareholders: The principle should be the long-term viability of the organization and its potential to create sustained value.

Depending on the complexity of the business model—notably the international footprint—the board should consider appointing a "Chief COVID Officer" to lead the management of the crisis and coordinate in a transversal fashion the way the organization deals with the pandemic.

18.2 GEOPOLITICS

Geopolitics is increasingly becoming a relevant topic to board rooms. Globalization or impact of events like Brexit, resulting from the United Kingdom leaving decades long economic and political association with the European Union, notably impacting the trade flows in the region and the free movement of capital and EU residents.

Geopolitics may be referred to as the activities of political possibilities and limitations on the global scale. Geopolitics are commonly influenced by the landscape of the country (total area, neighboring countries, oceans or seas), natural resources (e.g., water, oil, coal, natural gas, metals, stone, sand, minerals,), defense budget, number of sophisticated weapons and ammunition, economy (measured by GDP), demographics (population and ethnography), technology (innovation and patents), and available manpower to defend national and economic interests for the purpose of national security, progress, and well-being. Geopolitics should not be confused with geostrategy.[372] Geostrategy is considered a subfield of geopolitics and is often embedded in the foreign policy guided by geopolitical factors. Geopolitics is an evolutionary process, and globalization has further fueled the process. The areas of geopolitical activity cover international relations, security and defense, and corporate governance. Countries such as the US, China, and Russia and the European Union exert significant geopolitical power in the international arena. Geofinance combines the world of global finance with geopolitics—IFIs are often observed to finance infrastructure as a regional or global integration and foreign policy tool.[373]

There are four sides in geopolitics to which a global corporate must be always aware of:

1. Large corporations used by governments to enforce geopolitical interests (e.g., Gazprom in Russia being leveraged for Russian government strategic interests), or SASAC (the State-owned Assets Supervision and Administration Commission of the State Council is an institution directly under the management of the State Council of the Peoples' Republic of China, mandated by the Central Committee of the Chinese Communist Party[374]).
2. Large firms and industrial sectors influencing governments through lobbying to take decisions or to at least follow convenient policies for them (e.g., three large US airlines lobbying against Qatar Airways with the US government for restricting its expansion in US[375]).
3. National intelligence exercised by the government for initiating cyberattack to influence geopolitical activities (e.g., the US Cyber Command's retaliatory cyberattack on Iranian targets in response to drone downing[376]).
4. Sanctions or embargos imposed by the countries (e.g., the US) or supranational authority (e.g., the EU) to another country or corporate for having violated the International norms

and traditions on the grounds of spying, espionage, illegal invasion, human rights, terrorism, illegal production of chemical or nuclear weapons such as uranium (e.g., US sanctions against Iran regarding terrorism and illegal chemical weapon charges, EU sanctions against Russia for invasion of Crimea in Ukraine, US sanctions against the Chinese company Huawei citing spying and espionage[377]).

Huawei reportedly lost billions of dollars in revenues, as the US sanctions effectively banned all the US-based companies from doing business with Huawei and also halting the sales of Huawei produced digital products such as mobile phones in the US market. Any US-based company that is found doing business with Huawei is also subject to a hefty fine. Thus, the sanctions had a profound effect on Huawei business. However, Huawei is considered a big fish with revenues in billions of dollars; it could sustain despite being cut off from the US market (further discussed in Section 18.2.2: "Huawei Case—5G and the New Geopolitics"). However, not all corporates have the privilege to sustain such sanctions. As such, globalized corporates must be extremely careful when doing business in controversial zones or with controversial corporates. Additionally, the globalized corporate must have appropriate geopolitics strategies and contingency plans in unprecedented and heated circumstances.

One may argue that policymakers should be independent of private interests, or that since these interests will always exist, lobbying should be acceptable and regulated. Nevertheless, important geopolitical decisions and outcomes may greatly affect the faith of corporations and result in great social impact. FDI (Foreign Direct Investment), a tool for globalization, often raises concerns with transactions typically associated with mergers and acquisitions of domestic companies. Several countries and regions have passed legislation regarding the scrutiny over foreign deals that may outsource jobs, sharing of sensitive technologies, or impairment of critical infrastructures. The

Committee on Foreign Investment in the United States (CFIUS) is an interagency committee that analyzes transactions involving foreign investment to determine the effect of such operations and transactions on the national security.[378] The Foreign Investment Risk Review Modernization Act (FIRRMA) allows CFIUS to review a wider range of transactions, including any "non-passive investment" that involves critical technology and other sensitive sectors, as well as extends the length of the review period and grants greater power to suspend transactions.[379] The powers of the agency have been reinforced, namely amid the rise of Chinese investment, with other Western countries (e.g., Australia, United Kingdom) increasing scrutiny over foreign investment. In another case in 2020, the US administration blacklisted several Chinese firms from operating in the US (e.g., TikTok), raising capital in the US, and deterring US investors from investing in Chinese firms.[380] Nonetheless, restrictions on FDI may result in retaliatory actions by other countries, which is why OECD and 12 non-members signed a non-binding commitment to treat foreign-controlled enterprises no less favorably than domestic enterprises and defined critical infrastructures.

These policies and political movements resulting from geo-economics and geopolitical arenas involve issues that should be considered by the boards, notably by the non-executive directors, in global companies, as well as by the ones with international trade as part of their business models.

18.2.1 CASE OF RUSSIA'S GAS SUPPLY TO THE EU

Russia exerts quite an influence in the European geopolitics, as the main suppliers of gas to EU countries such as, Bulgaria, Czech Republic, Estonia, Latvia, Hungary, Austria, Poland, Romania, Slovenia, Slovakia, and Finland. These countries imported more than 75 percent of total national imports of natural gas from Russia. Also, Germany imports significantly from Russia. CNBC reported that pipeline projects prompted criticism in Europe and in the US, with Trump administration accusing Germany, the largest buyer of Russian gas, of being captive of this country. EU's relations with the Russia involve stress and have deteriorated with the annexation of Crimea in 2014.[381]

Russia could also see its position challenged in Europe, its main gas market. Though there is a demand for natural gas due to environmental regulations and demands, several European countries are keen to loosen Russia's grip on their energy supplies. To offset slower demand growth and increased competition in Europe, Russia has turned to the Asia-Pacific, and China in particular, targeting new markets. However, Russia is not the only actor in the quest for dominance in the Asia-Pacific, a hotbed of demand growth. Asia-Pacific countries are currently OPEC's main buyers, and the region is becoming more important to OPEC. Beyond OPEC, other exporting nations are also looking to the Asia-Pacific to absorb additional crude oil supplies from the Americas, Russia, and Central Asia.

18.2.2 HUAWEI CASE—5G AND THE NEW GEOPOLITICS

The 5G technology is believed to facilitate high-speed internet connectivity (theoretically increasing from 100 megabytes per second to 10 gigabytes per second) and set-in place certain pre-conditions for telemedicine, driverless cars, and smart cities. 5G is supposed to become 10 times or more faster than the current 4G technology. It seems that there are only four companies in the world that could supply the building components to construct the 5G network, namely China's Huawei and ZTE, Sweden's Ericsson, and Finland's Nokia. Out of all, Huawei had grown very rapidly and was said to possess affordable technology. However, the US government has been quite skeptical about the growing influence and dubious nature of Huawei. On the other hand, the EU countries are observing the business of Huawei very carefully.

Associated Press[382] reported that the US defense and intelligence communities have raised concerns about Huawei being an untrustworthy agent of Beijing's repressive rulers—though without providing evidence. The US sanctions are regarded as a financial tool of pressuring reluctant allies in Europe to exclude Huawei equipment from their networks. Washington presents the arguments of national security and of punishing Huawei for skirting sanctions against Iran.

The US maintains that China may force Huawei to spy on or infiltrate foreign wireless networks or even sabotage critical infrastructure, ultimately imposing sanctions by forbidding US companies from conducting business with Huawei.[383] The effect was immediately felt, as Huawei lost its licensing agreement with Google regarding the provisions of Google Play Services and access to Google Play Store on new Huawei android devices. Since then, both the US and China have been embroiled in heated debate trade war.

Other geopolitical cases include Google Maps and the inclusion of controversial territories such as Crimea and Palestine; Kashmir struggle between India and Pakistan; oil-rich Saudi Arabia and Iran vying for regional influence in the Middle East; and China building military bases in disputed islands of South China Sea.

18.3 FOREIGN DIRECT INVESTMENT

Foreign Direct Investment (FDI) is a topic of the utmost relevance for boards of directors and supervisory boards, notably of companies with an international footprint or with plans to expand their operations into the international arena, as it impacts the business model and the allocation of capital and talent. The topic gained visibility with John Adams,[384] at the end of the tenth century, with the United States' signature of the Treaty on Friendship, Commerce, and Navigation with France that highlights the need for protection of alien property—today, foreign direct investment—under the rules of international law. The plethora of challenges and risks emerging from internationalization, particularly from FDI, involve the allocation of scarce resources, notably capital and talent, and then ensuring that the legal jurisdiction framework of the FDI destination guarantees the protection of foreign property, repatriation of dividends, management fees and royalties, technical assistance, expatriation of proceeds if a divestment occurs, as well as reimbursement of loans in foreign currency. Additionally, it is common for countries to impose foreign exchange controls over the transfer of funds in the local currency to another country, usually through central banks, notably the one that is the source of the investment. Another risk that usually emerges with strong relevance is the regulatory risk, which impacts many industries and should be considered by the board in the due diligence process.

The challenges vary with the stage of internationalization, which impacts differently the involvement of a board. In the process of internationalization, the quote by Charles Darwin, "Ignorance more frequently begets confidence than does knowledge" should be remembered and taken into account in the decision process of the board, as well as another quote of an anonymous author, "(...) when you invest in a foreign country, you contribute with the cash and your local partner contributes with knowledge; (...) when you divest, you bring the back the knowledge and your partner keeps the cash (...)", reason why boards should be involved deeply in foreign direct investment decisions, as well as monitoring their performance and sustainability, namely because of the challenges an international landscape presents. This can be particularly challenging for companies without internationalization experience. Other challenges involve the analysis of the opportunity costs of FDI, the talent that should be dedicated and developed to successfully run an international business resulting from FDI, and the need to adjust to a country or region's cultural environment and related geopolitical, geo-financial, and geo-economic environments. Therefore, in view of the risks, FDI should be considered in the in the governance framework, as well as in the risk appetite framework (RAF) and internal control framework (ICF) of an organization to eventually ensure that the investment has an adequate return in terms of value added.

Companies' boards at advanced stages should be more familiar and experienced with the challenges posed by internationalization.

However, at earlier stages, boards of companies often do not follow a structured decision-making process, instead conducting a robust due diligence process that eventually leads to an informed decision. Assets and businesses located and operating in jurisdictions under different legal frameworks, cultural environments, in developed or emerging markets, or even in regions involving challenging risks. Linked to this emerges a priority issue between good governance principles and the protection of alien property governed by rules of international law.[385]

OECD defines FDI as a category of cross-border investment in which an investor, resident in one economy, establishes a lasting interest in and a significant degree of influence over an enterprise resident in another economy, usually by ownership of 10 percent or more of the voting power.[386] The current mode of FDI is often facilitated through regional agreements, trade agreements, or relevant measures such as North American Free Trade Agreement (NAFTA) signed between Canada, Mexico, and the US. In the EU, a political and economic union of 27 member states ensures the free movement of people, goods, services, and capital within the internal market with common policies on trade, agriculture, fisheries, and regional development. In the past, the FDI flows between countries, such as the US and the EU countries, significantly contributed to the reciprocal development and trade. Today, FDI is seen as one of the policy measures to shore up the economies of the developing world, particularly in Asia and Africa, while others follow the lead. The World Bank[387] defines that FDI net inflows are the value of inward direct investment made by nonresident investors in the reporting economy while FDI net outflows are the value of outward direct investment made by the residents of the reporting economy to external economies.

The corporate governance and the corporate tax rate directly affect the business climate and the prospects of FDI strategic decisions. However, if not handled properly, reputation and litigation are likely to emerge. FDI is a matter that deserves attention, namely in terms of the conduction and implementation of a structured, proper administrative and legal process. This includes—but is not limited to—its registration, the declaration usually with the central bank or FDI agency of foreign currency imported for the investment, an element that most legal jurisdictions require to ensure later repatriation of dividends, potential repatriation of proceeds or indemnities from the expropriation of assets, as well as payment of royalties, technical assistance, and management fees, or even loans contracted oversees in foreign exchange currency (e.g., bond issues, bank loans, or even loans from headquarters or shareholders). These and other issues should be registered and negotiated and should follow other administrative procedures, as well as the inflow of the foreign currency processed through the legal mechanisms—usually through the central bank—ensuring the authorities that there was an inflow to the country, at the time of the request of the payment by the investor.

Boards should also consider buying an insurance policy for FDI. Insurance companies offer insurance in some areas related with FDI, notably to the equity portion. The World Bank, through its subsidiary MIGA (Multilateral Investment Guarantee Agency) offers solutions to protect investments against noncommercial risks, as well as helping investors obtain access to funding sources with improved financial terms and conditions. Their website (miga.org) informs about currency inconvertibility and transfer restriction coverage protection against losses arising from an investor's inability to legally convert local currency (e.g., capital, interest, principal, profits, royalties, management fees) into hard currency (Dollar, Euro, or Yen); protection against losses arising from certain government actions that may reduce ownership, such as confiscation of funds or tangible assets; protection against loss from war, terrorism, and civil disturbance that may include damage; disappearance of tangible assets caused by political acts of war or civil disturbance; business interruption from a covered war and civil disturbance event; protection against losses arising from a government's breach; and protection against non-honoring of financial obligations resulting from a failure by a sovereign, sub-sovereign, or state-owned enterprise to make a payment when due.

18.3.1 THEORIES OF FDI

There are several theories conceptually framing and explaining FDI. With globalization and influence of multinational companies, academicians and practitioners started to explore a proper definition of FDI. Some of the theories are mentioned below, summarizing the working paper *A Selective Review of Foreign Direct Investment Theories.*[388]

Perfect market conditions

One of the early theories of FDI is based on the concept of perfect competition—*perfectly competitive market*. This theory explains that when investment flows from an investment country to a host country, the marginal productivity of capital tends to be equalized between the two countries. Even though the output of the investment country falls, there is no decrease in the national income because the country that invests generates higher income from the investment abroad. However, others are critical of this theory, as history has already demonstrated that the market is not always perfect.

Imperfect market conditions

The *imperfect market* FDI theory is based on the idea of imperfect market conditions. For example, companies that invest abroad must face competition from domestic based companies, which are already in an advantageous position, namely in terms of culture, language, legal system, and consumers' preference. Also, foreign companies or multinationals are exposed to foreign exchange risk. To offset such unbalancing conditions, it requires superior execution at the time of installation and firm-specific advantage such as talent—both local and expatriates—brand names, marketing and management skills, logistics, economies of scale and cheaper sources of finance, and, most importantly, patent-protected technological superiority to facilitate the introduction of new products with new features. As the market is often imperfect, companies can take advantage of their market power to deliver good profits by investing abroad. However, other factors such as geopolitics, licensing/exports, local government policy, local market conditions and size, the reaction of rival firms, among others may affect the decision regarding FDI, and it is up to the firm to take advantage of FDI to the full such that it can capture all the income provided by that control.

The *monopolistic FDI theory* is the extension of imperfect market FDI theory. This theory argues that advantages in the form of superior technology, managerial expertise, patents, among others should encourage the firm to invest in a foreign country with the objective of fully exploit the advantages instead of sharing them with potential competitors in the foreign market. When the opportunity to gain the monopoly is greater in foreign markets, the higher the encouragement for companies to invest. However, jurisdictions often have their own national interests to protect—named protectionism—and not all countries may be open to allow free entry of foreign firms. There are countries with a legal framework that requires entering into a partnership with a local partner or shareholder, an issue that poses additional risks and challenges.

The *internalization theory of FDI* emphasizes on intermediate inputs and technology. The shift of focus is from country-specific international investment theory (or internationalization) to industry-level and firm-level determinants of FDI. The theory discusses the ideas of creation of multinationals on three postulates:

1. Firms maximize profits in a market that is imperfect.
2. When markets in intermediate products are imperfect, there is an incentive to bypass them by creating internal markets.
3. The decision to adopt the internalization of markets across the world leads to multinationals.

For example, a firm may develop new technology, process, or inputs, but these can be difficult to transfer or sell to unrelated firms because of high transaction costs. Therefore, a firm may choose to internalize the integration by following backward and forward approach, meaning that the output of one subsidiary may be used as input to another subsidiary—novel technology developed by one subsidiary may be leveraged by other subsidiary. When this internalization leads to engagement in several countries, it may essentially constitute the definition of FDI. Even so, there exists the risk of host government institution. For example, energy and telecommunication companies may face increased scrutiny, because the societal considerations may require them to balance private objectives with social objectives.

The *oligopolistic FDI theory* argues that firms that are within the industry follow each other's location, and that firms uncertain of production costs in the country to which they are currently exporting run the risk of being undercut by a rival switching from exporting to setting up a manufacturing subsidiary in the host country. Essentially by imitating the rival's FDI, the firm may protect itself from being underpriced. The *Eclectic Paradigm to FDI* amalgamates the oligopolistic and internalization theories with the addition of new dimension, namely location theory. The *location theory* puts forward the question—who produces what goods or services in which locations, and why? They are enumerated on factors such as host country policies, economic fundamentals, firm strategy, and agglomeration economies. The theory explains a firm will involve itself in FDI if the following three conditions are fulfilled:

1. It should have ownership advantages vis-à-vis other firms.
2. It is beneficial to internalize these advantages rather than to use the market to transfer them to foreign firms.
3. There are some locational advantages in using a firm's ownership advantages in a foreign locale.

Essentially, locational advantages of different countries can determine which country will play host to the activities of multinational corporations.

Strength of Currency

The FDI theory based on the strength of currency takes into account the differences in the strength of the currencies in host and source country to take advantage of differences in the market capitalization rate. Often a weaker currency, when compared to stronger investing country currencies, would have a higher capacity to attract FDI. However, this theory garnered criticism that it may fall irrelevant in emerging countries that have highly imperfect or nonexistent capital markets and heavily regulated foreign exchanges.

On the other hand, it should be taken into account in the FDI decision that if a country has high inflation rates, reflecting high depreciation of the local currency versus strong ones, it poses additional challenges in terms of treasury management, regarding both interest rates and currency rates. The use of derivative products to cover those risks is common—if there is a market, as there are many currencies, notably for emerging countries, for which the financial system does not offer derivatives to cover interest rate and foreign exchange rate risks—even when a company adopts a policy of covering these types of risks. Also, it should be taken into consideration that high inflation would very likely negatively impact potential dividends or other payments to send back, as they accumulate along a year and, when converted into hard currency, would represent a fraction of the amount accumulated in local currency along the year. Boards should take these challenges and risks into consideration when making FDI decisions.

International Trade Theory

As the number of international trades has increased—partly because of globalization—researchers have attempted to find the relations between international trade and FDI. It is said that trade will emerge if one country has an absolute advantage in the production of one commodity and disadvantage in the production of another commodity. However, authors have also argued comparative advantage, which means a country will specialize and export that commodity in the production of which it has a comparative cost advantage and import that commodity in which it has the least cost advantage. However, with the rise of multinationals, the existing theories of international trade fell short, and FDI was said to be the reaction to the threat of losing markets as products matured, as well as the need for cheaper factor costs in the face of competition, often coined as *Product Life Cycle Theory*.

This theory also falls short in explaining why it could be profitable for a firm to undertake FDI rather than continuing to export from the home country or by licensing a foreign firm to produce its products. Subsequently, the improvised international trade and investment theory emphasized on two things: (i) When a profit-maximizing firm chooses to serve a foreign market and (ii) the conditions under which foreign market servicing is carried out, either through exporting or local manufacture as a result of direct investment.

FDI is bound to only happen in a world that admits revenue-producing factors being firm-specific on the one hand while the information, communications, and transaction costs that increase with economic distance on the other. FDI that involves international trade may take the shape of horizontal and vertical structure, thus forming cross-border mergers and acquisitions, also known as *Greenfield FDI*. In contrast to horizontal mergers and acquisitions, where a firm often duplicates its home country-based activities at the same value chain stage in a host country through FDI, Greenfield FDI is the type of vertical investment in which a parent company creates a subsidiary in a different country, therefore building its operations from the ground up that may be upstream or downstream. Another concept known as *Platform FDI* is the investment from a source country into a destination country for the sole purpose of exporting to a third country.

18.3.2 THE ROLE OF FDI IN DEVELOPING COUNTRIES

The FDI inflow in China has increased significantly in recent years, which eventually led to its rapid growth, being India another large recipient in Asia, while countries such as Indonesia and Vietnam are also seeing growing inflows. Also, developed countries such as US, Canada, and Western European countries are significant recipients of FDI with reciprocal agreements. The role of FDI is very relevant for developed, emerging and developing countries. The motivation for FDI depends on several factors.[389] including availability of local talent, market size and growth prospects, wage-adjusted productivity of labor (rather than the cost of local labor), infrastructures (e.g., energy, roads, railways, telecommunications, health system, schools), independent and effective judicial and courts' system, political stability, the overall stability of the tax regime, social security and levels of taxation. Other factors that may appeal investors' economic and commercial interests include stable political environment and conditions that support physical and personal security, corruption and governance concerns, legal framework and the rule of law, and risk of confiscation, among others, taking actions to mitigate them through timely measures. Therefore, the board of directors/supervisory board that undertakes FDI decisions must be aware of these conditions and risks and adopt a cautious approach, as the decision of investing, for example, in a corrupt country may provoke the emergence of reputational risks for the organization.

Reduction of regulatory risk for investors is key to strike the FDI inflow. The World Bank[390] has established a database for measuring regulatory risk focusing on three topics: (i) Transparency, (ii) Legal protection for investors, and (iii) Investor access to grievance-recourse mechanisms. Essentially, developed economies need to improve transparency and reduce the bureaucratic discretion to make business outlook more predictable and less risky for companies. Governments of developing countries should look to improve transparency by systematically consulting with the private section and relevant stakeholders. Laws, regulations, policies, or information related to FDI must be publicly accessible with clear articulation. Investment competitiveness and good governance are the most important markers.

International Financial Institutions (IFIs) such as The World Bank, European Investment Bank, Asian Development Bank, African Development Bank and Inter-American Development are established by more than one country to provide financing and professional advice for the purpose of development, particularly in emerging and developing countries. IFIs are further discussed in Section 18.4: "International Financial Institutions and Corporate Governance." As IFIs invest in strategic national or international projects in member or outsider countries through private operations or public-private partnership, they are considered as powerful entities to raise funding and provide advice and technical assistance. The palette of products available includes financing, equity, bond markets, monetary markets, guarantees, trade finance, syndication, credit insurance, equity insurance, among others. For example, the role of Asian Development Bank is to support the transformation of developing cities in the Asia and Pacific region into safe, inclusive, and sustainable urban centers.[391] As such, the bank allocates funds proportionately with the mix of grants, soft loans, equities, among others, depending on the development index of member countries. IFIs often maintain their own index or indicators with country and risk analysis, and other businesses could leverage these to make an informed decision as well. The World Bank follows the same, but its fundamental vision is to end the extreme poverty in the world. Therefore, its strategic decision to invest or fund formulates around same vision. Nonetheless, while allocating the funding, investment competitiveness and good governance are considered especially important benchmarks, while other factors are also adequately considered.

FDI is essentially a robust tool to shore the economy, but it demands transparency and good governance. Many emerging economies often lack the fundamental requirements, but some countries such as India and Indonesia are prime examples demonstrating how FDI can contribute significantly to their developmental economy.

Therefore, the onus is on the country itself to improve the fundamental basis to attract FDI while gradually reforming the status quo.

18.3.3 INTERNATIONALIZATION, DECISION, TYPOLOGIES, AND METHODS

When a board is in the process of deciding to internationalize or expand its international footprint, it should consider several strategic variables, notably the most adequate entry mode. The global strategic motivations involve factors other than entry mode like the establishment abroad for strategic reasons. They include global concentration, market sharing with a limited number of competitors, global synergies or sharing of resources by leveraging technology, logistics, marketing, or regional presence. Language is a criterion often used in electing the destination country. However, this criterion by itself should not be considered a high priority, as the business environment and the culture often does not adapt to the host country. When considering the strategic motivation, there are other highly relevant considerations in the choice of the destination country, notably levels of corruption, legal and judicial systems, protection of foreign assets, and availability of talent.

The three main typologies of internationalization are:

1. Export of goods and/or services (international trade)
2. Cooperation and/or contractual relationships
3. FDI—Foreign Direct Investment

The export business may be direct or indirect, while the cooperation mode may involve exploration licenses, franchising, subcontracting, management contracts, consortium, and joint venture. FDI includes setting up greenfield operations and, through Mergers and Acquisitions (M&A), the acquisition of a majority or minority of an established company, directly or indirectly, at the targeted market, as discussed in the preceding section.

The first alternative, International Trade, is the most common internationalization entry mode, which is used by companies with a limited market knowledge, lack of experience in international markets or in a particular market, lack or scares internationally qualified talent, limited international contacts or contacts in a particular region or market, or even low trading capacity. A relevant challenge of this typology relates to the control over collection and management of foreign exchange risk, which includes the previous authorization for the export from the local authorities (usually the central bank) to ensure that the account receivable will be converted into the currency of the country's exporter. There are tools to mitigate the collection risks involving export and import business. One of the most important is to leverage the banking system's international trade platform, which acts as an independent trusted third party between the exporter and importer. The banks ensure that the documents are properly prepared and approved by the parties involved, and the flows of cash and goods are executed only when that documentation is completed, including the authorization from the authorities (usually the central bank) to convert the local currency and transfer it to the exporter. The banking system only checks and verifies documents, not the characteristics or specifications of the products; there are specialized firms that perform this type of verification before the goods are exported.

The World Bank Group aims at growth that creates jobs, supporting the access to developed and emerging country markets, enhancing their participation in the world economy. Trade is considered an engine to the world economy. The IFC (International Finance Corporation) (ifc.org) offers a Global Trade Finance Program providing guarantees to trade-related payment obligations of approved financial institutions, complementing the capacity of commercial banks to deliver trade finance by providing risk mitigation on a per-transaction basis for more than 200 banks across more than 70 countries. Boards should ensure that a policy exists to address these risks emerging from international trading.

The second alternative for internationalization is a cooperation model through the use of a local partner, which is a hybrid model that allows a company to become familiar with the market and keeps an option of exiting the market. This entry mode usually reduces the risk of entrance as well as the initial investment, helping it reduce or overcome barriers. However, foreign trade still requires any foreign direct investment to follow the defined administrative and existing approval process to qualify as FDI and benefit from its prerogatives. On top of maintaining flexibility, it also allows the development of a partnership, requiring the partner to engage in it and in the business. This mode also allows a company to manage the evolution in terms of ownership of the business. However, even considering the flexibility features, it is recommended that a due diligence process be conducted to ensure the fit & proper profile of the local partner or associated company, as well as the tactics if the decision of exiting the market emerges.

Generally, FDI is classified as Horizontal and Vertical, as discussed in earlier section. The first frames the situation of a company that doubles its home country activities (Origin Country) and at the same stage of the value chain in an FDI recipient country (Host Country). An FDI Platform is a sub-concept when a foreign investment is set up from a country of origin to a destination country for the purpose of exporting to third countries. Often, these situations are linked to free industrial zones or free economic zones (FEZ), also called free zones, which are designated by the trade and commerce administrations of countries—usually areas with low or no taxation and favorable customs' regime on the exported production—to encourage economic activity in a particular area of a country. The World Trade Organization (WTO) has content on conditions and benefits of free zones. However, these models have potential to involve, in some jurisdictions, reputational risks emerging from money laundering issues.

Methods of acquiring voting power may involve purchasing a stake, incorporating a wholly owned subsidiary or company in another country, merger and acquisition of an unrelated company, or through the setup of a Joint Venture under a common equity interest with another investor. Countries are usually focused on attracting FDI as it contributes to growth, job creation, and development. When FDI involves large sums of capital, creates jobs, contributes to growth and development, it is common that a particular investment is negotiated with the authorities controlling FDI. An offer of a basic package of incentives is common, which can take many forms, including the reduction of corporate and other taxes, preferential interest rates, special economic zones, financial investment subsidies, free land, expatriation facilities, and others.

FDI represents a challenge involving risks that should be mitigated to ensure the value creation for the shareholders and stakeholders. Consequently, the involvement of the board, particularly in companies less experienced in the international landscape, should be to challenge the executive directors to consider several options to direct FDI or even to consider options (e.g., acquisitions *versus* greenfield, engage a local partner with clear relationship rules) of entry that do not compromise the value of the investment and the company. The process should be carried professionally and in a structured fashion. Talent represents a key issue to deal with FDI processes, as well as advisors, law offices, and consultants.

18.4 INTERNATIONAL FINANCIAL INSTITUTIONS AND CORPORATE GOVERNANCE

Unlike normal corporates or institutions, International Financial Institutions (IFIs) and Multilateral Development Institutions (MDIs) are financial institutions established by more than one sovereign country and, therefore, the member national governments act as their shareholders. Sometimes, one or more IFIs, MDIs or institutions are also shareholders of another IFI along with the national governments. For example, the European Investment Bank (EIB), the largest IFI by total assets, also owns shares of the European Bank for Reconstruction and Development (FBRD), another CU-based IFI. IFIs are not to be confused with Private Financial Institutions (PFIs), such as retail banks or financial institutions. Usually, the balance sheets of IFIs are in dollars or euros, the result of subscribed capital from shareholder countries and the bond issued in international markets. As most IFIs tend to have good ratings from credit rating agencies, they are potentially able to raise money at low-interest rates.

IFIs tend to invest in strategic national or international projects in member or outsider countries through private operations or public-private partnership—often under a project finance structure—and generally advocate the principles of Sustainable Development Goals (SDGs). Member countries with the greater economy usually own a greater number of shares and voting power and, often, have a larger say, although this is not always the case as majorities may require a percentage of the share capital, but also a percentage of shareholders [countries] voting favorably the proposals. IFIs can be global, such as the World Bank Group (WBG), or regional, such as the Asian Development Bank (ADB), Asian Infrastructure Investment Bank (AIIB), Inter-American Development Bank (IADB) and African Development Bank (AfDB). On the other hand, EIB invests majorly in the EU member countries, and minorly (up to 10% of annual loans) in non-EU countries. International Monetary Fund (IMF), one of the specialized agencies of The World Bank Group, a fund institution formed after World War II, following with Bretton Woods system of monetary management, is also one of the significant global IFIs.

IFIs may also have their own vision and values. The overarching mission of the Washington-based WBG is a world free of poverty. The Luxembourg-based EIB is committed to the creation of jobs in the economy, promote equality, and improve lives for EU citizens and for people in developing countries. In the Asia-Pacific, the Manila-based ADB is committed to achieving a prosperous, inclusive, resilient, and sustainable Asia-Pacific region while sustaining its efforts to eradicate extreme poverty. The Beijing-based AIIB is committed to improving social and economic outcomes in Asia by investing in sustainable infrastructure and other productive sectors in Asia and beyond by connecting people, services, and markets that over time will impact the lives of billions and build a better future. In Africa, the Ivory Coast-based AfDB is committed to spur sustainable economic development and social progress in its regional member countries, thus contributing to combatting poverty.

18.4.1 CORPORATE GOVERNANCE IN IFIS

Contrary to the corporate world, IFIs normally have a Board of Governors (BoGs), with each member being selected from the respective member countries. Eventually, the BoGs appoint the members of the Board of Directors (BoDs)/Supervisory Board (SB), the Management Committee (MC)/Management Board (MB), and the Audit Committee (AC). IFIs may have a different board structure, depending on the jurisdictions, but the fundamental principles of governance remain the same. An additional governance element relates to taxpayers, a relevant stakeholder, as the capital contributed to IFIs and MDMs by sovereigns are sourced national budgets. The governance structure and description at EIB is depicted in Table 18.1.[392]

Unlike in the corporate world, the BoDs are not appointed as individual fiduciaries of all shareholders but as a representative of the several Constituency boards (groups of shareholder- countries). Thus, the board members are there not to serve the interest of individual shareholders (their own countries) but the institution collectively, the objectives and interests of the European Union and of its taxpayers. Essentially, this gives rise to a different type of discussion for board effectiveness contrary to a normal board seen in most corporates. Also, IFIs being global/regional and based in different jurisdictions, being influenced by their own values, priorities and ambitions. Therefore, it is incredibly difficult to absolutely ascertain the effectiveness of IFIs boards of directors. On this respect, a report published by Asian Infrastructure Investment Bank suggests the following additional guidelines[393] on top of the governance guidelines discussed in Chapter 14: Fiduciary Duties, Board Effectiveness, and Dynamics:

Table 18.1: Description of governance mechanism at EIB—European Investment Bank

Board of Governors	Board of Directors	Management Committee	Audit Committee
The BoGs comprises Ministers designated by each of the 27 European Union Member States, usually Finance Ministers. The BoGs lays down credit policy guidelines, approves the annual accounts and balance sheet, and decides on the Bank's participation in financing operations outside the EU, as well as on capital increases. It also appoints the members of the BoDs, the Management Committee, and the Audit Committee.	The BoDs consists of 28* Directors, with one Director nominated by each EU Member State and one by the European Commission. The BoDs has the sole power to take decisions in respect of loans, guarantees and borrowings. As well as seeing that the Bank is properly run, it ensures that the Bank is managed in keeping with the provisions of the Treaty and the Statute and with the general directives laid down by the Governors.	The MC is the Bank's permanent collegiate executive body. It has 9 members. MC is colloquially referred to as management board. Under the authority of the President and the supervision of the BoDs, the MC oversees the day-to-day running of the EIB, prepares decisions for Directors, and ensures that these are implemented. The President chairs the meetings of the MC.	The BoDs consists of 6 members and 3 observers. The AC is an independent body answerable directly to the BoGs. Based on the Bank's Statute and Rules of Procedure, the AC is responsible for the auditing of the EIB Group's accounts, verify that the operations are conducted, and its books kept in a proper manner and verify that the activities conform to best banking practice. At the time of approval by the BoDs, the AC issues its statements.

*Note: United Kingdom left the European Union in 2020

- Allow board input on knowledge, skills, experience, and diversity, and allow the board to have an advisory voice on the matter.
- Lengthen the director tenure following corporate governance guidelines and discourage political motives.

- Allow outside experts to participate in the board, although voting rights should be restricted.
- Evaluate the effectiveness of the board and report key findings in annual reports.

18.5 THE RELEVANCE OF CORPORATE GOVERNANCE IN THE SMART ECONOMY

The *smart economy*, or colloquially *gig economy*, has emerged rapidly as a form of service delivery that challenges existing business models, labor management practices, and regulations.[394] The gig economy is often touted as the free-market system invigorated by technological advances where temporary and freelance job positions are more prevalent, either remotely or on-premises. The gradual fall in computing prices is stimulating the data-driven digital age. Smartphones have never been so pervasive.[395] Novel mobile technologies are on the rise, and a rising number of companies are embedding mobile-first strategy in their overall business strategy. New generations are increasingly looking toward freelance jobs, as technology has made it possible to decouple the jobs and the location. Hence, the gradual shift from traditional employment to temporary or freelance employment with flexibility in location and hours can be expected in some niche digitalized areas. Also, the impact of the COVID-19 pandemic changed already this paradigm and is requiring from companies and boards the reassessment of the use of working at distance using digital means and change dramatically the philosophical landscape and expectations of both organizations and talent. Companies often need to increase their capacity during a short period of time, without long-term investments and without increasing economic pressure on the company to perform. This capacity may just be in working hands or in deep expertise needed that fall outside the current core business of the company, and the level of financial and legal responsibility is much lower than with regular employees

Critics argue that the employers tend to cherry pick the most productive freelance workers—often younger workers—and their employment rights are not well protected. At the end, it is the responsibility of both regulators and corporates to ensure there is proper labor framework to address the working rights of both independent and dependent workers such that freelance work is accepted in the area where it is really warranted. Otherwise, corporates are susceptible to face severe social, reputation, and governance problem that may even threaten their survival. The board members should inevitably understand the benefits and risks associated with hiring independent or freelance workers.

Apart from digitization, *sustainability* is another key measure that should be incorporated into corporate business models in order to achieve sustainable corporate governance and viable business growth. While digitization is related to the virtual world, sustainability involves the human relations with the natural world, to which the pandemic COVID-19 situation is a key element to take into the equation. Nokia mobile phones were at the peak around the 2000s and commanded the global market share of 40 percent at the time, but Nokia befell at the doors of Apple and Samsung soon after. Nokia was too late to incorporate a sustainable business model at the time of swift market change and increasing technological complexity.[396] The topic of sustainability is further discussed in Section 4.3: "Corporate Sustainability." While the past decade was called about the internet of information, the new decade is often referred to as the *internet of value*. There are examples where start-ups have grown into a billion-dollar valuation in a short period. Nevertheless, sometimes, things can go wrong in corporate governance. One such example is the San Francisco based company *Uber*. Embracing sharing economy, Uber grew massively as a ride-sharing platform worldwide after 2009. However, one of the co-founders and former chief executive of Uber, Travis Kalanick, had more voting rights than any other members in the Board of Directors. Kalanick came into intense pressure from investors after Uber's employees reported a prevalence of sexual harassment in the company, misappropriation of trade secrets in a lawsuit filed by Waymo, and the news that Uber had deceived governmental authorities through a tool called Greyball.[397] As a result of unequal voting rights, Kalanick was outweighed in any corporate decisions. This eventually led to the conflict of interests in the board. Kalanick resigned later.

The concept of Decentralized Autonomous Organization (DAO) and DeFi (Decentralized Finance) are being frequently discussed with the advent of *blockchain/distributed ledger technology*, although critics doubt about its wide adaptability (see Figure 18.1), and therefore boards should consider including the topic in their global agendas.

Figure 18.1: Traditional governance models vs DAO

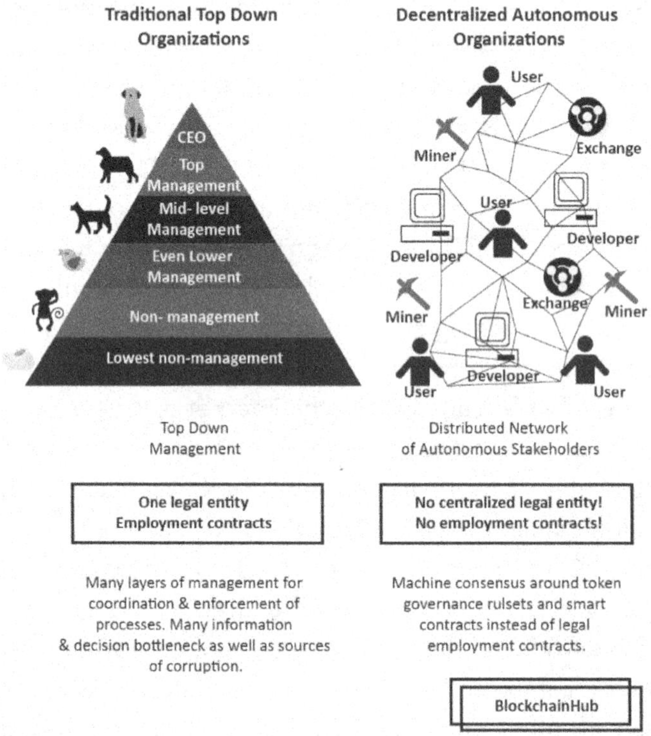

Source: (BlockchainHub)[398]

Cryptocurrencies such as bitcoin or asset-backed digital currencies such as Facebook's Libra are hot topics. Some central banks are reportedly studying the viability of digital currencies and some have already prohibited the practice in some economies and/or established restricted regulation and strong supervision of the topic. Token economy and asset tokenization are on the radar. Machine learning and artificial intelligence have never been more dominant. Internet of Things (IoT)—the extension of internet connectivity into physical devices such as doors, lights—is on the rise. User-generated data is seen as a very important asset class while privacy is the core concern of the regulators. Ultimately, the importance of cybersecurity has grown very rapidly. Measures to mitigate cyber risk have never been more important, and board members must be aware of possible damage of cyber threats, having the topic on the boards' agenda.

The influence the *media gets* is also becoming very instrumental nowadays, with a high degree of online connectedness, particularly through the new forms of social media. Social media management has never been so influential in brand awareness, brand reputation, and brand communication.[399] As a result, the relevance of corporate governance has also started to become driven by corporate's media actions and reputation.

18.5.1 THE CASE OF DUAL-CLASS SHARES IN HIGH-GROWTH COMPANIES

Dual-class shares are especially seen in US-based tech companies listed in New York Stock Exchange or Nasdaq. The main purpose of dual-class shares is to allow the firm's founders and top executives to maintain control. Dual-class shares are controversial, and the topic has been hotly contested namely in the United Kingdom as "one share, one vote" has been a pillar of corporate governance. Nonetheless, it has been learned that the policymakers are discussing the change in listing rules to lure tech start-ups. In a dual-class structure, two classes of shares are usually defined—Class A and Class B. Class B shares are common stocks sold to the public and normally carry 1 vote per share. Class A shares are reserved for founders and insiders, and normally carry 2–10 votes per share, depending on the jurisdiction. Intuitively, it makes an immense difference when voting to select executive directors or/and making decisions. Some US-based companies that have incorporated dual-class shares are Alphabet/Google, Facebook, Snap, and Lyft.

The proponents of dual-class structure agree that the structure gives the founders and insiders more clout in a volatile public market while maintaining desired equity to provide financing, to provide a better defense against events like hostile takeover attempts, and eventually to promote long-termism. As long as the corporate is taking right decisions and fulfilling the norms of corporate governance, it is said to be less of a concern for investors. In most cases, Class A voting shares are not publicly traded. However, they can be converted to Class B shares under some conditions. The opponents of dual-class structure argue that the structure may give further rise to more agency challenges and, potentially, result in problems, discussed in detail in the Section 2.1: "The Agency Theory." For example, a director may prioritize personal goals over the initiatives of the company and seek different ways to cash out Class A shares. Also, the structure may risk preventing other (or minority) shareholders from holding controlling investors to account, like in the case of American real estate company, WeWork, and its founder Adam Neumann. Public equity investors pulled back from WeWork's dual-class share structure, which at one point gave him 20 times the voting power of other shareholders.[400] In another case, there have been concerns that Facebook's Mark Zuckerberg has outsized control of corporate decision-making.[401]

Whether to implement a dual-class structure or not ultimately derives from the trust and values that have been rooted in the business or/and the society. As of May 2020, Novo Nordisk Foundation owns 22.9% of the total share capital and 74.8% of the total number of votes in the Danish pharmaceutical company Novo Nordisk, and following the Nordic model, it has exemplified the benefits of long-term stewardship.[402] Also, Hong Kong changed the rules for dual structure company to list, while the United Kingdom is debating the issue.[403]

Topics of the Chapter

The following has been discussed within this chapter:

- The world is currently moving toward Globalization 4.0; its structure, which depends on wise governance decisions and technological advancements, has been unsettled by trade tensions and protectionism.
- The coronavirus pandemic has led to extensive lockdowns and social distancing measures; business leaders, caught in an unprecedented paradigm, may need to realign the corporate or globalization strategy.
- Geopolitics in the corporate realm refer to the following activities that have political impact on the global scale:
  1. Large corporations used by governments to enforce geopolitical interests.
  2. Large firms and industrial sectors influencing governments through lobbying.
  3. National intelligence exercised by the government for initiating cyberattack to influence geopolitical activities.
  4. Sanctions or embargos imposed by the countries or supranational authority to another country or corporate.
- Foreign Direct Investment (FDI) and Concepts of International Financial Institutions (IFI) are discussed.

Part VI—Rating Agencies, Proxy Voting Services, and Activism

Chapter 19

Overview of Credit Ratings

Credit Rating Agencies evaluate their credit risk based on the current and historical information and data of a corporate. They offer the lender an estimate of the borrower's ability to timely pay back the principal and the interest payments. Proxy Voting Services allow shareholders to gain access to information and analysis of the corporate, evaluate its performance, and allow shareholders to cast an informed vote on the important decisions even when they cannot attend a meeting. This chapter discusses Credit Ratings and Proxy Voting Services, two sets of services that seem to help them interact with corporates in a more informed and empowered way.

19.1 CREDIT RATING

The world of investing, although considered fascinating, is also highly complex. Contrary to the banking world—where deposits of individuals are usually guaranteed up to a certain amount, depending on the legal framework of jurisdiction—stocks, bonds, and other financial instruments are not covered by guarantees. A way for investors to protect their investments is to perform research and ask questions to draw a conclusion about the level of risk involved with the potential investment, as well as to match the level of risk identified with their risk capacity and risk appetite. Laws and rules governing the securities industry derive from a simple and straightforward concept: any investor should have access to certain basic facts, data, and information about an investment prior to the decision. This is a primary concern relating to the disclosure of market-related information, maintaining fair dealing and protection against fraud and asymmetric data. Lately, investors also demand disclosure covering corporate sustainability factors like environmental, social, and governance (ESG).

Credit rating is the classification of a borrower (or the debtor) that evaluates its credit risk. It predicts—but does not guarantee—the borrower's ability to timely pay back the principal and the interest payments and also indicates the likelihood of default. The ratings should be seen as a snapshot, because if conditions of the issuer deteriorate, they may affect the rating extended at the time of the analysis; this is particularly important in moments involving unpredicted financial, economic, and other reasons that trigger impacts in capital markets. In capital markets, the borrowers are primarily sovereigns, municipalities, corporates, banks, or project finance SPVs (Special Purpose Vehicles). A sovereign credit rating refers to the creditworthiness of a country or a sovereign entity (e.g., sovereign funds). The credit rating depends on the macroeconomic conditions, with the economic factor being a prime one, but also considering financial conditions, notably the ability to generate enough cash flow to service the debt and interest payments. In a country, indicators like Gross Domestic Product (GDP) as well as its relation to public expense, public debt, unemployment rates, currency stability, and fiscal policy are critical factors impacting sovereign ratings.

For the business world, sustainability factors in economic and financial terms are relevant, but cash flow sustainability is the element considered in its determination. There is an intimate interconnection between sovereign ratings and corporate ratings, as the first may affect strongly the latter. One of the main objectives behind the establishment of the European Banking Union for the eurozone was to somewhat disconnect those two ratings—sovereign and corporates—by having an authority at the eurozone countries to supervise the financial system, ultimately ensuring financial stability. One of the main vectors of the Banking Union was the establishment of ECB Banking Supervision—with Single Supervision Mechanism (SSM) empowered to supervise systemic banks and National Competent Authorities (NCA) supervising non-systemic banks under a common rule book— ensuring an independent supervision of their economic and financial conditions, notably capital (ICAAP) and liquidity (ILAAP), as well as a governance framework to conduct business in an appropriate fashion that ensured financial stability and a centralized deposits' guarantee fund, whose effective implementation is taking longer than expected.

Credit Rating Agencies (CRAs) play a major role in raising capital— shareholders, bondholders, and financial system—as they basically issue an opinion on the likelihood of default of an organization or the issue of a financial instrument, with investors taking into consideration such opinion. Therefore, this is a relevant topic that boards should have in their global agendas, as CRA can affect significantly the ability of companies—as well as sovereigns—to raise capital and to determine the cost at which they are able to raise capital.

CRAs may assign credit ratings to businesses, corporates, or countries, either at request or at their own initiative. Due to the relevance and impact of their reports, analyses, and opinions on creditworthiness, boards should closely monitor the outcomes of their reports and ensure that organizations provide data and information about for CRA to be able to assess their credit rating. The three main CRAs are firms Standard & Poor's (S&P), Moody's, and Fitch Ratings established in the US. DBRS Morningstar (Canada) and Dagong Global Credit Rating (China) are also firms operating in the ratings business. Credit rating is a highly concentrated industry, as the two largest CRA, namely S&P and Moody's, control 80 percent of the market while the "big three," namely S&P, Moody's, and Fitch Ratings, control approximately 95 percent of the ratings business.

The origin of rating agencies goes back to the days when businesses were close to those who purchased their goods or services, and merchants knew and trusted each other; therefore, it was easy to extend credit, due to their knowledge about their ability to pay them back. However, as trading distances increased, merchants no longer personally knew their counterparts and therefore became more cautious when extending credit. As a result, the hesitation to extend credit to new customers led to the birth of the credit reporting industry in the US, established at the beginning of the nineteenth century amid a financial crisis, then known as Mercantile Credit Agencies—precursors of CRA—that rated the ability of merchants to pay their debts.

The concept of CRA originated in the US in the 1900s, basically when ratings started to be applied to securities, coinciding with the construction of railroads that led to the development of corporate bond issues, with Moody's rating industrial companies and utilities and initiating a letter-rating system to indicate their creditworthiness. Bond markets in Netherlands and Britain were small, revolving basically around sovereign ratings. Although companies provided investors with basic financial information, the financial crisis demanded a new feature related to "independent market information." CRA began charging issuers and investors for their services, as the complexity of financial markets increased, as did their fiduciary responsibility. Later, ratings were also awarded to commercial paper and bank deposits. The CRA introduced levels of gradation to the rating system by adding plus and minus symbols to the letter-rating system, along with some of them using numbers.

The development and growth of the bond market after the end of Bretton Woods led to the liberalization in several jurisdictions of financial regulations and its expansion. In 1975, US SEC rules included credit ratings agencies, requiring minimum capital amounts and regulating smaller reserves for higher-rated bonds, a moment that saw CRA market develop in size and profitability, as issuers accessing the debt markets increased and wanted to have available independent market information to support their investment decisions. As the leading CRA are concentrated in North America, there exists a large gap to the size and visibility of rating agencies with origin in the European Union. This fact raised issues during the financial and economic crisis of 2008, as ratings to sovereigns, banks, and corporates were downgraded by the three largest CRA. The downgrading process raised issues, namely in challenging the process in the arena of geopolitics and geo-economy.

S&P states that credit ratings may play a useful role in enabling corporations and governments raise money in the capital markets, as these entities sometimes borrow money directly from investors by issuing bonds or notes without borrowing a loan from a bank. Investors purchase these debt securities, such as municipal bonds, expecting to receive interest plus the return of their principal. According to Fitch, credit ratings are an opinion on the relative ability of an entity to meet financial commitments, such as interest, preferred dividends, repayment of principal, insurance claims, or counterparty obligations. DBRS mentions that credit ratings are forward-looking opinions about credit risk that reflect the creditworthiness of an entity or security. Dagong states that credit rating service should be able to fully reveal the nature of the all-round risk of a society's credit relations.

Nonetheless, the credit ratings are not an absolute measure of default probability and cannot guarantee the credit quality of an issuer. As future events and developments cannot be exactly foreseen, rating's opinions are not intended as guarantees of credit quality or as measures of the probability of whether an issuer or particular debt issue will default.

19.2 CREDIT RATING AGENCY

CRA (Credit Rating Agency) may assign credit ratings to the entities issuers of financial instruments (e.g., preferred stocks), fixed-income instruments (e.g., government [sovereign] bonds, corporate bonds, municipal bonds, certificate of deposit), and collateralized securities (e.g., mortgage-backed securities, collateralized debt obligations). A credit rating may facilitate the trading of securities in the secondary market and, most importantly, affect the interest rate a security pays out, with higher ratings leading to lower interest rates. Even though corporate ESG ratings and corporate credit ratings are issued separately, credit ratings usually encapsulate the ESG factors to offer a larger picture. Nonetheless, the use of both ratings can effectively facilitate the assessment of the corporate governance standings.

As discussed, the big three CRA, namely Moody's Investor Service (Moody's), Standard & Poor's (S&P), and Fitch Ratings (Fitch), all originating from the US, control most of the worldwide credit rating businesses. The European Central Bank (ECB) recognizes four CRAs—DBRS Morning Start along with the aforementioned three—as the only ECAIs (External Credit Assessment Institutions) to determine the collateral requirements for borrowing from the ECB.[404] In the past, ECB solely used DBRS investment grade credit ratings to lend money to crisis-stricken European countries such as Portugal and Greece. The relevance of the European Union CRAs can be seen by the fact that ECB does not include them in the list of recognized CRAs, therefore demonstrating that the established CRAs in EU continue to not be as visible and relevant as the North American agencies.

The European Securities and Markets Authority (ESMA)—EU securities markets regulator—supervises and performs thematic reviews, including the sovereign ratings process, inspections of small and medium-sized CRAs, and the ratings publication controls, carrying out policy work in the area of CRA in its role as the single direct supervisor of CRAs within the European Union.[405] ESMA mentions that its policy work is carried out in cooperation and consultation with the members of the CRA Technical Committee, which has representatives from the EU national competent authorities. Any CRA internal or external to EU that requires to be certified must pass ESMA's regulations. In the US, CRAs are registered as Nationally Recognized Statistical Rating Organizations (NRSROs) in SEC (Securities and Exchange Commission). Until 2020 in the US, there were 9 registered NRSROs. In the EU, there are more than 40 CRAs either registered or certified. The mission of SEC, as it states, is to protect investors, maintain fair, orderly, and efficient markets and facilitate capital formation. Notwithstanding, the credibility of credit ratings has been questioned in the past. The American subprime mortgage crisis in 2007–08 that lead to the subsequent global recession in 2008–2009 still hangs over the credit rating firms.[406] The article in the *USA Today*[407] states that the agencies' ratings played a critical role in the marketing of risky mortgage-backed securities, such as collateralized debt obligations, which helped bring the United States financial system to its knees. Securities that were given high CRA ratings were downgraded to junk during the financial crisis.

In another case, credit ratings have also been questioned concerning the European sovereign debt crisis occurring since 2008. Financial Stability Board (FSB—www.fsb.org), an international body that monitors and makes recommendations about the global financial system, published *Principles for Reducing Reliance on CRA Ratings* to encourage the businesses, corporates, and governments to reduce the overreliance on credit ratings.

19.3 CORPORATE CREDIT RATING

Ratings are usually expressed as letter grades, from AAA to D, to communicate the CRA's opinion of the relative level of credit risk, AAA being the lowest level of credit risk and D the highest. Usually, the expressions grade investment and non-investment grade differentiate the major classes of risk. However, the grades of each CRA are not the same for a similar type of risk, which is why it is relevant to know and understand the scales of ratings adopted by each one of the CRAs.

The main CRAs broadly follow similar kinds of methodologies. However, the exact methodology of how CRAs rate the corporate is a trade secret to avoid copying. In most cases, the credit rating is measured through both qualitative and quantitative measures. CRAs may follow a similar methodology, although they tend to operate independently from each other and may have different approaches for certain industries, services, or cases.

In another case, the largest domestic credit rating agency in China, Dagong, is controlled by the stated owned administration, which potentially raises the question regarding its independence status.

Essentially, the global CRAs approach the risks through two broad areas, namely business risk and financial risk.[408]

- *Business Risk*: The business risk includes the evaluation of strengths and weaknesses of the rated entity that incorporates factors, such as market position, geographic diversification, sector strengths or weaknesses, market cyclicality, or competitive dynamics. This essentially allows the business to be compared against each other and relative strengths or weaknesses to be identified.
- *Financial Risk*: The financial risk includes the evaluation of financial flexibility of the entity, which incorporates factors such as total sales and profitability measures, margins, growth expectations, liquidity, funding diversity, or financial forecasts. Credit ratio analysis is the backbone of this measure, as the ratio is used to quantitatively position companies of similar business risk against each other.

An example of S&P rating methodology[409] is demonstrated in Figure 19.1. Essentially, to rate a business or entity, business risk profile and financial risk profile are measured, as discussed earlier, and their results are then integrated to determine an issuer's anchor.

The anchor moves through several analytical steps, following forward-looking analysis and analytic judgment to determine the ultimate rating conclusion with the goal of transparency and rating comparability.

Figure 19.1: S&P corporate credit rating framework

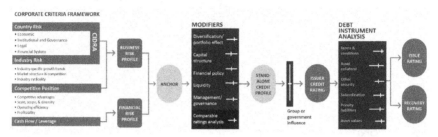

Source: (S&P–www.spratings.com)

Figure 19.2 shows the criteria to determine the grading of anchor. The lower the risk profile, the higher the grade.

Figure 19.2: S&P credit rating anchor

COMBINING THE BUSINESS AND FINANCIAL RISK PROFILES TO DETERMINE THE ANCHOR

Business risk profile	Financial risk profile					
	1 (minimal)	2 (modest)	3 (intermediate)	4 (significant)	5 (aggressive)	6 (highly leveraged)
1 (excellent)	aaa/aa+	aa	a+/a	a-	bbb	bbb-/bb+
2 (strong)	aa/aa-	a+/a	a-/bbb+	bbb	bb+	bb
3 (satisfactory)	a/a-	bbb+	bbb/bbb-	bbb-/bb+	bb	b+
4 (fair)	bbb/bbb-	bbb-	bb+	bb	bb-	b
5 (weak)	bb+	bb+	bb	bb-	b+	b/b-
6 (vulnerable)	bb-	bb-	bb-/b+	b+	b	b-

Source: (S&P–www.spratings.com)

The final credit ratings are designated in two ways—long term and short term (Figure 19.3). Normally, long-term obligation refers to the opinion on relative credit risk with the maturity of one year and more, whereas short-term obligation refers to the opinion on relative credit risk with the maturity of less than one year. Obligor refers to the debt issuer.

Figure 19.3: S&P description of long- and short-term corporate credit ratings

DESCRIPTION OF RATINGS

LONG TERM			SHORT TERM	
Issuer Rating	Description	Issue Rating	Rating	Description
AAA	Extremely Strong	AAA	A-1+	Obligor's capacity is extremely strong
AA	Very Strong	AA	A-1	Obligor's capacity is strong
A	Strong	A	A-2	Obligor's capacity is satisfactory
BBB	Adequate	BBB	A-3	Obligor's capacity is adequate, but vulnerable to adverse circumstances
BB	Less Vulnerable	BB		
B	More Vulnerable	B	B	Obligor's capacity is subject to major ongoing uncertainties
CCC	Currently Vulnerable	CCC		
CC	Currently Highly Vulnerable	CC	C	Obligor's capacity is vulnerable to nonpayment
-	Bankruptcy filing (or similar)	C	SD	Selective Default
SD	Selective Default	-	D	Default
D	Default	D		

Source: (S&P—www.spratings.com)

Also, it is important to note the difference between *investment grade* and *speculative grade*, also named *non-investment grade*—also dubbed *junk bonds*. The so-called Junk bonds have speculative grade ratings (i.e., below BBB−). Junk bonds usually have higher yields than investment grade bonds, as they carry a higher risk than the latter. Junk bonds were one of the most utilized financial instrument to raise capital in the US, notably in the '80s, to finance LBO (Leveraged Buy-Outs) and MBO (Management Buy-Outs). Michael Milken, a senior executive of US Drexel Burnham Lambert Inc., a major investment banking house forced into bankruptcy in 1990 for its involvement in illegal activities, is well-known for the development of market for junk bonds, also referred to as "junk bond king."[410] However, he was later charged by US authorities for several financial misconducts and subsequently sentenced to 10 years in prison and fined 600 million dollars. President Donald Trump pardoned Michael Milken in 2019.

The general summary of the long-term rating is presented in Figure 19.4.

Figure 19.4: S&P detailed description of credit ratings

General summary of the opinions reflected by our ratings

Investment Grade	**AAA**	Extremely strong capacity to meet financial commitments. Highest rating
	AA	Very strong capacity to meet financial commitments
	A	Strong capacity to meet financial commitments, but somewhat susceptible to adverse economic conditions and changes in circumstances
	BBB	Adequate capacity to meet financial commitments, but more subject to adverse economic conditions
	BBB -	Considered lowest investment-grade by market participants
Speculative Grade	**BB +**	Considered highest speculative-grade by market participants
	BB	Less vulnerable in the near-term but faces major ongoing uncertainties to adverse business, financial and economic conditions
	B	More vulnerable to adverse, business, financial and economic conditions but currently has the capacity to meet financial commitments
	CCC	Currently vulnerable and dependent on favorable business, financial and economic conditions to meet financial commitments
	CC	Highly vulnerable; default has not yet occurred, but is expected to be a virtual certainty
	C	Currently highly vulnerable to non-payment, and ultimate recovery is expected to be lower than that of higher rated obligations
	D	Payment default on a financial commitment or breach of an imputed promise; also used when a bankruptcy petition has been filed or similar action taken

Ratings from "AA" to "CCC" maybe modified by the addition of a plus (+) or minus (-) sign to show relative standing within the major rating categories.

Source: (S&P–www.spratings.com)

19.3.1 COMPARISON OF S&P, MOODY'S, AND FITCH

The comparison of S&P, Moody's, and Fitch is demonstrated in Table 19.1.[411]

Table 19.1: Comparison of Moody's, S&P's, Fitch, and DBRS credit ratings

Moody's Long-term	Moody's Short-term	S&P's Long-term	S&P's Short-term	Fitch Long-term	Fitch Short-term	DBRS Long-term	DBRS Short-term	Description
Aaa		AAA		AAA		AAA	R1 (high)	Prime
Aa1		AA+		AA+		AA (high)		High grade
Aa2	P-1	AA	A-1+	AA	F1+	AA	R1 (mid)	High grade
Aa3		AA−		AA−		AA (low)		High grade
A1		A+		A+		A (high)		Upper medium grade
A2	P-2	A	A-1	A	F1	A	R1 (low)	Upper medium grade
A3		A−	A-2	A−	F2	A (low)		Upper medium grade
Baa1		BBB+		BBB+		BBB (high)	R2 (high)	Lower medium grade
Baa2	P-3	BBB	A-3	BBB	F3	BBB	R2 (mid)	Lower medium grade
Baa3		BBB−		BBB−		BBB (low)	R2 (low), R3	Lower medium grade
Ba1		BB+		BB+		BB (high)	R4	Non-investment grade

Manual of Corporate Governance

Moody's								Description
Ba2		BB		BB		BB		
Ba3		BB−		BB−		BB (low)		
B1	Not Prime	B+	B	B+	B	B (high)		Highly speculative
B2		B		B		B		
B3		B−		B−		B (low)		
Caa1		CCC+		CCC+		CCC (high)		Substantial risks
Caa2		CCC	C	CCC	C	CCC	R5	
Caa3		CCC−		CCC−		CCC (low)		
Ca		CC		CC		CC		Extremely speculative
C		C		C		C		Default imminent
/		RD	D	RD	D	D	D	In default
/		SD		D		/		
		D		/		/		

19.3.2 EVALUATING AN INVESTMENT

Investors may use credit ratings as a tool for making investment decisions, such as decisions about purchasing fixed-income instruments or bonds (e.g., corporate, municipal, sovereign), but it should be stressed that ratings are not indicators of investment merit. Ratings are just independent opinion of experts or experienced professionals on creditworthiness, allowing investors to make informed investment decisions. However, the basis for the opinions should be framed within the timeframe of the issuance date, as circumstances and conditions change—often faster than expected—and may strongly impact the favorable opinion and respective rating at the date of issuance. For example, a corporation having AAA rating does not mean it will not default or that the rating will stay as AAA for a long period of time. Ratings are developed with a forward-looking approach while analyzing the current and historical information and data. A corporate or entity that issues the bond may be rated with the predicted ups and downs in the business cycle that can essentially impact the worthiness of credit. Ratings are not meant for "buy, sell, or hold" recommendations, or as a measure of asset value.[412] Furthermore, the ratings are not intended to signal the suitability of an investment, but they do cover one of the aspects of an investment decision—credit quality. The rating may also address what investors can expect to recover in the event of a default. To evaluate an investment, the investor should consider the credit quality, the current makeup of portfolios, the investment strategy and time horizon, tolerance for risk, and estimation of the relative value in comparison to other securities.

As the coronavirus pandemic (COVID-19) has demonstrated, some future events and developments are unprecedented. The ratings are just the relative opinions about the creditworthiness of an issuer or credit quality of an individual debt issue that essentially ranges from the strongest (e.g., for the long-term rating: S&P—AAA, Moody's—Aaa, Fitch—AAA) to weakest (e.g., for the long-term rating: S&P—D, Moody's—C, Fitch—D). Investors and other market operators can use the ratings to screen an issuer or debt instruments with their own risk tolerance, and if necessary, follow the published credit risk guidelines in making own investment and business decisions. As discussed earlier, rating agencies have been the subject of criticisms in the past.

19.3.3 RATING ADJUSTMENTS

The credit rating may potentially vary with the performance and changes in business, as well as with the economic climate, and with actual and potentially emerging risks. The reasons for rating adjustments vary and may be broadly related to overall shifts in the economy or business environment or even more narrowly focused on circumstances affecting a specific industry, entity, or individual debt issue. Unusual circumstances such as the COVID-19 pandemic may also lead to rating adjustments on affected sectors, products, or countries.

In some cases, changes in the business climate can affect the credit risk of a wide array of issuers and securities. For instance, new competition or technology beyond what might have been expected and factored into the ratings may hurt a company's expected earnings performance, which could lead to one or more rating downgrades over time. Growing or shrinking debt burdens, hefty capital spending requirements, and regulatory changes may also trigger rating changes.

While some risk factors tend to affect all issuers (an example would be growing inflation that affects interest rate levels and cost of capital), other risk factors may pertain only to a narrow group of issuers and debt issues. For instance, the creditworthiness of a sovereign or municipality may be impacted by population shifts or lower income of taxpayers, as they may reduce tax receipts and the ability to repay debt.

Another relevant reason relates to downgrading of sovereign ratings, which have an immediate direct impact for adjusting ratings of banks, corporates, and other issuers, mainly because the impact in a sovereign impacts the public finances of the country and its ability, for example, to transfer foreign currency to honor a coupon of a country's corporate or of a sovereign bond issue, potentially impacting the financial stability. The 2008 financial crisis in EU is a relevant example of this paradigm for Ireland, Portugal, Greece, and Spain, which directly impacted the ratings of corporates and banks. Although the sovereign rating is part of the assessment of other rated organizations, it is relevant to monitor the development and robustness, namely of a sovereigns' public finance and fiscal policy as well as the macro environment that may affect the economic conditions of a country or a region.

However, criticisms have also been raised against CRAs that they have too much power over issuers and that downgrades can even force troubled companies into bankruptcy. The lowering of a credit score can create a self-fulfilling prophecy, not only making interest rates on securities rise.

19.3.4 RATING TRIGGER AND DEATH SPIRAL

A rating trigger is a provision in a loan agreement or bond indenture allowing one party or the other to take a certain action if the borrower's credit rating changes for any reason.[413] For example, if the bond issuer's credit rating falls, a rating trigger may release bondholders from certain obligations specified in the indenture. The clause often includes elevated interest rate payments or/and further procedural requirements that the creditor may force the borrower (or the debtor) to fulfill.

The worst-case scenarios of rating triggers can be devastating. The creditor may require the borrower to repay the loan in full, and if the company is unable to pay the loans at once, this may trigger a bankruptcy, also known as the "death spiral." The collapse of companies such as Enron, WorldCom, and Parmalat are some of the hot examples, with similar examples seen in the financial system both in the US and European Union amidst the financial and economic crisis of 2008, with the need of governments to inject taxpayers' money to salvage banks that were too big to fail.

19.3.5 ESG RATINGS

The topics around Environment, Social, and Governance (ESG) have emerged as a highly relevant topic for boards, and therefore should be a priority item in a global agenda. Investors are increasingly making use of Environment, Social, and Governance (ESG) ratings, indices, or metrics to analyze an organization's ethical impact and sustainability exposure. ESG ratings are a supplement to the corporate credit ratings. Investors and relevant stakeholders can take improved decision by incorporating both ESG ratings and corporate credit rating in their strategies. According to Standard & Poor's–S&P, one of the leading credit rating agencies, ESG factors are most often considered when issuing corporate credit ratings.

S&P ESG Index family offers investors to measure the performance of securities meeting sustainability criteria. S&P Fossil Fuel Free Index tracks the performance of companies in the S&P 500 that do not own fossil fuel reserves. Bloomberg ESG Disclosure Scores rate companies annually based on their disclosure of quantitative and policy related ESG data out of 100. Corporate Knights, a Canadian company, publishes an annual index of the Global 100 most sustainable corporations in their Corporate Knights magazine rating out of 100.

MSCI ESG Research provides the corporate ESG ratings from AAA–CCC scale, AAA being the most favorable one. The Dow Jones Sustainability Index (DJSI) family tracks the stock performance of the world's leading companies in terms of economic, environmental, and social criteria out of 100. Thomson Reuters ESG Research provides both percentile rank scores and letter grades from A+ to D–. Sustainability's, formed by the consolidation of Dutch Sustainability Research (Netherlands), Scoris (Germany), and AIS (Spain) rates ESG out of 100. Apparently, a handful number of investors are also developing their own rating methodologies and criteria.

Therefore, in the current business setting, the boards/supervisory boards must ensure that they have enough information regarding ESG-related risks and threats that could possibly compromise the corporate strategy and objectives or its very survival. It is also vital that the boards have fundamental knowledge and experience to analyze the ESG indicators. Studies have shown that high ESG ratings allow for a company to obtain a lower cost of debt and a valued equity. Essentially, sustainability initiatives can lead to improved financial performance and public support. This is a topic that should be part of the global board agenda.

19.4 SOVEREIGN CREDIT RATING

Sovereign credit rating refers to the credit rating of the sovereign state that is considered independent and administers its own government (discussed in Section 1.5.2: "Sovereign Wealth Funds"). As corporate ratings give an opinion on the credit ratings of the corporates and the businesses, sovereign ratings give an opinion on credit ratings of the national governments, states, municipalities, and sovereign-supported international entities. Sovereign borrowers are the largest debt borrowers in many financial markets. Governments in advanced and emerging markets borrow money by issuing government bonds and selling those to private investors, both individual and institutional, either overseas or domestically. Governments may also borrow from other governments and international organizations such as The World Bank, Asian Development Bank (ADB), and International Monetary Fund (IMF).

Sovereigns' credit assessments may reflect long-term perceived default risk as well as short or immediate term political and economic developments. Recent examples included Ireland, Greece, Spain, and Portugal that were close to default, being hastily downgraded by the CRAs, while countries like France, Austria, and Italy were also downgraded during the financial and economic crisis in 2008. Similar— or even worse—conditions seem to be emerging with COVID-19, in spite of policy measures taken by sovereigns, which is why multi-notch downgrades of sovereign ratings are likely to occur again. For example, Fitch downgraded Italy's Long-Term Foreign-Currency Issuer Default Rating (IDR) to BBB—from BBB in April 2020,[414] as the pandemic hit Italian society and businesses significantly.

The big three CRA maintain the rating notation for sovereign ratings similar to that of corporate credit ratings, as illustrated in Section 19.3.1: "Comparison of S&P, Moody's, and Fitch"; though they may have varying evaluation approaches, they may follow a similar methodological approach. National governments may solicit CRAs to generate investors' interest in having improved access to capital markets. Emerging countries often depend on strong sovereign ratings to have access to funding. However, as sovereign governments may be eligible for debt immunity under international law, this may somehow complicate repayment obligations in the event of default. Like corporate credit ratings, sovereign credit ratings cannot be regarded as guarantees or subject or susceptible to change, even in the short term. Sovereign ratings have also come under some criticism, notably as a result of the financial crisis of 2008.

Multi-notch sovereign downgrades are common in economic and financial crises affecting the global economy, as well as the situation credit markets are currently facing. Fitch announced that multi-notch downgrades of sovereign ratings are likely in 2020, due to COVID-19 and the fall in oil prices.[415] In the recent past, 12 developed market sovereigns have experienced 26 multi-notch downgrades, and Latin America has experienced the most multi-notch downgrades, mostly clustered around the global financial crisis in 2008–2009 and the ensuing eurozone crisis in 2011–2012. Fitch announced that nearly 40 percent of multi-notch downgrades started from an investment grade rating (BBB category or higher), including the A and AA categories, which is consistent with the fact that highly rated eurozone sovereigns have also been downgraded during the eurozone crisis.

Topics of the Chapter
The following has been discussed within this chapter:

- Corporate credit ratings are used as a tool for making investment decisions based on the creditworthiness of a corporate; however, credit ratings are not actual indicators of investment merit.

- While the exact methodology is a trade secret, Credit Rating Agencies assign credit ratings based on two broad areas
  1. Business risk
  2. Financial risk
- Environment, Social, and Governance (ESG) ratings, indices, or metrics are used to analyze an organization's ethical impact and sustainability exposure. This topic has emerged as a highly relevant topic of the board's agenda.
- A comparison of the world's leading CRAs is depicted in Table 19.1.
- Sovereign ratings give an opinion on credit ratings of the national governments, states, municipalities, and sovereign-supported international entities.

Chapter 20

Proxy Voting Services

As shareholders are eligible to vote on the important decisions of the public listed companies, this may also have the possibility to impact relevant issues, such as corporate's operations, governance, and social responsibilities, as a result of not all shareholders attending the shareholders' general meeting. These may include resource constraints, traveling to other geographies, sleeping investors, portfolio yield view, or lack of influence of a minority stake, among others. Depending on the legal framework of the jurisdiction and/or the bylaws, shareholders not present at the shareholders' meeting may be considered to have abstained. However, that is not always the case, as their percentage of ownership does not count to the calculation of the "universe" attending the shareholders' meeting. Therefore, in these situations (i.e., when their shares are not considered when calculating the universe of voters at the shareholders' meeting, as the universe is coincident with the ones present or represented), decisions or deliberations consider only this universe. Thus, to mitigate such scenarios, empowering all shareholders (notably minority shareholders and institutional investors), proxy voting came to the existence, representing a tool where those shareholders can express their views through their representation by a proxy firm.

Therefore, proxy voting allows shareholders to vote even when they cannot attend a meeting. Essentially, the proxy advisory firms and asset managers mutually benefit from economies of scale as information production and decision-making scale upward with relatively little additional cost. Because the proxy voting services are not regulated in most jurisdictions, asset managers often say that regulation may lead to greater rather than reduced costs because of heightened regulatory burden.[416]

However, criticism has emerged in the market, notably in the US, as Institutional Shareholder Services (ISS) and Glass Lewis allegedly control "97 percent" of the proxy advisory industry, according to a survey.[417] Often, advisory information is correlated. Though there is widespread competition in asset management, there exists limited competition in proxy advisory. The spotlight on corporate governance and proxy voting carries a great deal of scrutiny, as proxy voting is a relevant compliance activity. For example, ISS recommended the Hewlett Packard (HP) shareholders to support the merger between HP and Compaq. Nonetheless, many large shareholders—including Walter Hewlett, the company's director and son of the company's co-founder—were not in favor of the merger.[418] Eventually, though it went ahead, analysts say that the merger between HP and Compaq has been very controversial. Post-merger HP lost its significant market value and incurred heavy job losses. Analysts questioned the role ISS played acting in alignment with the interests to maximize the value of HP shareholders. This leads to the debate whether proxy advisory firms can formulate robust prescriptions to evaluate the various matters that are considered in the proxy process. The role of proxy voting is arguably among the most crucial for corporate governance yet is subject to little regulation when compared to investment advisers (asset managers) and intermediaries (auditors and credit rating agencies). Analysts and economists believe that appropriate regulation can aid to fill the existing vacuum.

The services incorporated under proxy voting may include agenda translation, voting policy development, provision of vote management software, company research, and review of key governance issues. Essentially, the services can be tailored to each client's needs, such as client-specific voting, template design, and vote execution, along with voting policy consultation service. The services may also encompass the provisions of data covering key governance indicators, such as individual director information and performance, board structure, shareholder rights, remuneration, audit issues, and proxy voting results. Similarly, data ratings and in-depth comparisons of companies and countries can be facilitated.

Some of the services provided by proxy voting services firms are listed below:

- *Engagement services:* Background research and analysis on specific engagement topics and companies.
- *Public affairs services:* Discussions regarding "position papers" and responses to consulting public authorities or private consulting bodies.
- *Corporate governance ratings:* Evaluation of companies' performance and annual updates of companies' ratings.
- *Corporate governance services:* Support institutional investors with global asset portfolios to understand the regulatory diversity and provide corporate governance research and proxy voting advice.
- *Market intelligence services:* In-depth coverage of local market best practices, research studies, and publications on a variety of key governance issues.

the internet and innovation, investors may not only buy or sell equities online, but they can also vote on the proxy statement online prior to the annual meeting. A proxy statement should be filed by a publicly listed corporate before the shareholders' annual meeting to a regulator (e.g., US SEC) and disclose material matters of the corporate relevant for soliciting shareholder votes and the final approval of nominated directors.

A proxy statement is supposed to disclose the company's voting procedure, the candidate nominated for the board, and remuneration of directors and executives. As the proxy statement is one of the very important aspects of the shareholder's meeting, it must be very clear and detailed. A proxy statement can support potential investors in evaluating the qualifications and the remuneration of its management team and board of directors. The trend shows that institutional investors generally post their voting decisions online prior to the annual shareholders' meeting date, either themselves or through proxy voting services; this may provide an individual investor an opportunity to figure out what large investors think about the future standings of the corporate, as there is an understanding that institutional investors conduct in-depth and forward-looking research about the sustainability and profitability of the corporate.

Topics of the Chapter
The following has been discussed within this chapter:

- Proxy Voting Services empower all shareholders, notably minority shareholders; however, lack of regulation can make their services risky.

Chapter 21

Activism

An institutional investor who is considered as "activist" may make substantial use of voting power. An activist investor is a person or group holding a significant number of shares in a public company with the aim of influencing the decisions and structure of the organization.[419] This chapter discusses the predicament of individual shareholders—small and large—along with the themes and trends usually observed.

Activist investors are primarily concerned with underperformance, proper capital allocation, corporate clarity, corporate control, and corporate governance. One of their prime objectives is to profit both activists and their backers. The approach can be good or bad. And the pursuit of profits can show an extreme and obsessive side of people, that is, "mercenary approach" to profit and/or yield at the expense of potentially stepping on the line of ethics' boundaries. The concern fundamentally boils down to the question—Who will better run a company? Professional management and board without rigorous accountability, or a financial investor looking for own interests, with yield and/or extracting value to shareholders taking high priority, instead of an argument based on long-term strategy focusing more on the stakeholders?

The profile and type of shareholders strongly influence one or another approach; a relevant "industry shareholder" usually has a more complacent stance toward efficiency, investment policy, or even dividends than a capital markets' investor like an activist, a hedge fund, or a venture capitalist, whose priorities are often different from the former. The willingness to challenge a corporate management therefore depends on the type of institutions and their investments' objectives, vision, and strategy. Institutions such as insurance companies, private pension funds, and bank trusts may be less willing to challenge the management to protect other business relationships, whereas institutions such as mutual funds, public pension funds, foundations, hedge funds, and sovereign wealth funds may be more willing to challenge the management.

There is also a view of the proponents of activism that argue that companies with active and engaged shareholders are more likely to be successful in the long term—instead of the short-termism criticism—as vigilant shareholders as activists are said to play the role of fire alarms avoiding the "big fires." The opponents argue that shareholder activism and short-termism may weaken strong companies. Overall, practice shows that independent institutional investors with large long-term holdings may influence corporate decisions significantly.

21.1 INDIVIDUAL SHAREHOLDERS ACTIVISM

Individual shareholders with a small number of shares have the right to attend and vote at shareholders' meetings and, depending on the jurisdiction, notably the percentage of the holding, may submit proposals to be voted at shareholders' meetings. They could also make use of proxy voting services or give a power of attorney or another legal instrument, depending on the legal framework, for an activist to represent them, awarding the activist with a larger percentage of votes to impose their viewpoints, or even enter into a lending security agreement with another party. Nonetheless, "empty voting" (i.e., activist borrowing the stock—often through a securities' lending contract—from long-term shareholders to use their voting rights) is regarded by a line of thought as not qualifying as a best corporate governance practice, although another line of thought advocates the practice as an efficient instrument to remove boards that do not perform and protect minority shareholders by operating under the paradigm of the Agency Theory. Empty voting becomes more acute at the time when activist hedge funds exert enormous pressure.

Individual shareholders rarely have success in influencing corporate governance, because the monitoring is costly for individual investors with a small number of shares. It is difficult and expensive for shareholders to navigate the legal framework and procedures that usually favor the management and board, which is why it is unlikely for them to win a proxy fight to change directors or get represented in the board—a right of minority shareholders in many jurisdictions—or get shareholder proposals approved, especially those that go against management, especially with management lobbying against shareholder proposals. Activists often play a role in capturing minority shareholders, putting their voting rights together, and gaining influence.

21.2 LARGE SHAREHOLDERS ACTIVISM

Large shareholders are the ones who own a significant number of corporate shares and actively monitor the firm's management. Depending on the legal framework of the jurisdiction, those who hold more than a certain percentage (e.g., 2–5 percent) of the shares are also referred to as "blockholders." They have influence in a number of matters, depending on the legal framework of the jurisdiction. There are jurisdictions that may give quite some power to the shareholders or syndicates' holding more than 2 percent; usually, 5–10 percent is the celling, and to qualify as a "minority shareholder" (some jurisdictions allow special rights to the so-called minority shareholders), it may impose a ceiling of 10 percent. Their rights and influence may include attending and voting at shareholder meetings, submitting proposals at shareholder meetings, shareholders lawsuits, "voice" (talking/writing to management, privately or publicly), "exit" (initial stock purchase and subsequent trading decisions).

Minority shareholders may often prefer the existence of large shareholders while managers may not, as managers may seek to enjoy smooth navigation and draw individual benefits, an issue related to the agency theory. One line of thought argues that the existence of a large inside shareholder may minimize the agency problem. An inside shareholder may be a founder, director, senior executive, entity, or individual owning a significant amount of publicly traded company's voting shares, more than 10 percent in most cases. For example, Mark Zuckerberg, one of the co-founders of Facebook, owns a large stake at Facebook and has around 20 percent of cash flow rights and 57 percent of voting rights, due to dual class share structure as of 2020.[420] Dual-class shares are commonly seen in US-based tech companies (e.g., Facebook, Alphabet/Google). Shares are normally classified as Class A and Class B shares; Class A shares may only be owned by the inside shareholders (founder or director) with more voting power per share (e.g., 10 per share), whereas Class B shares are common stocks sold to the public and normally carry one vote per share. The concept of dual-class share is also discussed in Section 18.5.1: "The Case of Dual-class Shares in High-growth Companies."

On the contrary, it is argued that the existence of a large outside shareholder (e.g., mutual fund, pension fund, hedge fund, activist) may potentially exacerbate the conflict between managers and shareholders, though this may not always be the case. Nonetheless, minority shareholders benefit in both cases. It is also seen that firms may not always have large shareholders, as some firms can be so large that it would take a lot of wealth to own a significant fraction of it. Also, many investors establish in their investment policies and principles the diversification of their portfolios, adopting a wise "prudent man" approach. Essentially, the concept of activism has been more widespread in Anglo-Saxon countries, namely in capital markets-based economies. However, the influence is gradually being seen in Europe and emerging Asian economies.

21.3 ACTIVISM—CONTROL VS OWNERSHIP

Though the structure with controlling shareholders (e.g., large inside shareholder often more than 50 percent voting rights, such as Zuckerberg, mentioned in the preceding section) may be beneficial for minority shareholders to solve the agency problem, it is also possible that controlling shareholders may "expropriate" minority shareholders and extract private benefits. The risk with controlling shareholders is the potential room to manipulate control/voting rights to exceed cash flow rights through pyramids and cross shareholdings, dual-class shares, or participating in the management of the company. It is more likely to happen when the institution is usually linked to a weak country level governance framework. As mentioned, dual-class shares do exist, notably in some US companies; however, the institutional level governance of the US is "trusted" to be robust.

Elliott Management Corporation, considered one of the largest American activist funds, puts a substantial amount of time and resources into better understanding the opportunities and challenges in the company they have invested or potentially invest, even setting up a dedicated website with presentation, information, research, or letter to the board. As Elliott is often the large outside shareholder, the minority shareholders may essentially benefit from the material it produces. As there are some visible cases where Elliott has openly objected to takeover or buying majority shares. For example, in 2019–20, Elliott held out Capgemini, a French consulting firm, from making a higher bid to acquire Altran, another French consulting firm, arguing that the offer by Capgemini to acquire Altran was lower. Subsequently, Capgemini raised the value of its bid for Altran to 14.5 euros a share from 14 euros. In another case, Elliott openly opposed CTG (China Three Gorges) taking control of majority shares of EDP,[421] a Portuguese utility company with a footprint namely in Spain, the US, and Brazil, mentioning that in the offer was not in the best interest of EDP's stakeholders its current form and may leave company weakened, volatile, and with a less attractive portfolio and diminished growth opportunities. In the general shareholders' meeting of 2019, Elliott, with a holding of 2.29 percent, proposed an item for the agenda that led to the abortion of CTG's public offer to acquire more than 50 percent of shares.

Table 21.1 depicts the control versus ownership status across the world.

Table 21.1: Control vs ownership across the world

Dispersed ownership and weak control	Primarily present in the US and UK; weak monitoring by shareholders; high liquidity (exit); takeovers more likely
Dispersed ownership and strong control	Primarily present in Europe and Asia; moderate liquidity (exit); controlling shareholder monitors; risk of expropriation of minority shareholders; takeovers less likely
Concentrated ownership and weak control	Rarely present (e.g., Swiss firms with voting limits); low risk of expropriation of a minority; less monitoring; low liquidity
Concentrated ownership and strong control	Rarely present (e.g., German firms); controlling shareholder monitors; low liquidity

21.4 THEMES OF ACTIVISM

The five broad themes of activism are—Mergers & Acquisitions (M&As), Assets Divestments/Portfolio Pruning, Change in Business Strategy, Capture Value in the Short-Term, Capital Structure, and Governance (see Figure 21.1).

M&As are the kind of activist strategies that put pressure on the board of directors to entertain discussions with potential suitors. This may spur decision makers to evaluate inorganic strategies to drive share price growth quickly. Though not all M&As are done with bad intentions, decision-making ability (discussed in Chapter 15: Decision-Making) is fundamentally important then.

The activists may demand *corporate asset divestments* or portfolio pruning to crystallize the value in the short-term. Also, other agendas such as reducing exposure to selected markets because of forex/mismatch funding (discussed in Section 10.3: "Asset and Liability Management") can be on the list. The activists may push to *change the existing business strategy* to demand higher profitability. This is said for improving overall risk-return proposition and essentially decrease the risk profile of the target. Also, the revision of executive compensation may be demanded. The activists may engage in *capturing value in short-term* by leveraging the substantial interest generated from market participants. Other things such as reducing capex or outsourcing capex required to fund the project may be examined. The activists may ask to improve the *capital structure* to augment the cash flow generation. Financial ratios involving, among others, debt and leverage such as Net Debt (ND)/EBITDA or Funds from Operations (FFO)/ND are often scrutinized. Other items such as remuneration, perks, dividend policy are closely watched.

Finally, the most crucial factor is the *governance*. Without proper governance, value for shareholders or stakeholders is deemed to fail. Some activists may seek board representation to effect change and pursue the advancement of other objectives. Part III extensively discusses the principles of corporate governance, the concept of board, board size, board selection and composition (fit and proper), diversity and inclusion, the concept of independence, the role of board members, board committees, among others. The profile of executive directors and independent directors to function in the current digital landscape is often questioned. Essentially, activists closely watch the corporate governance practices followed by the board.

Figure 21.1: Themes of activism

Mergers & Acquisitions (M&A)	Agitation seeking a competing tender offer for the company	Put pressure on the Supervisory Board and Executive Board to entertain discussions with potential suitors	Spur decision makers to evaluate inorganic strategies to drive share price growth quickly	Potentially seek to improve deal terms if an alternative offer is presented
Asset Divestments/ Portfolio Pruning	Value crystallisation in the short-term	Continue asset rotation vs. engaging in substantial asset sales	Reduce exposure to selected markets due to compounding effect of hydro volume risk and market risk mainly due to forex/mismatch funding	Likely to require completion of disposals in a defined timeframe
Change in Business Strategy	Revise the Strategic Plan in place demanding higher profitability	Improve overall risk/return proposition. Decrease the risk profile of the target	Overcompensation in a particular country	
Capture Value in the Short - Term	Opportunity for partial or full monetisation, on the back of substantial interest from market participants. Sell down to [51%]	Reduce and/or "outsource" capex required to fund pipeline: development capital to be raised internally vs externally	Oppose potentially pursuing a minorities buyout and delisting of target company as a suboptimal capital allocation	
Capital Structure	Improve leveraged capital structure to augment cash flow generation	ND / EBITDA above the industry average coupled with the lowest FFO/ND. Higher leverage compared to peer group	Proactively address rating attribution (i.e. cash flow going to minorities and structural subordination	Company to uphold dividend policy, with target company having one of the hihest pay-outs in the sector
Governance	Seek Board representation to effect change and pursue the advancement of other objectives			

Source: (Lazard—www.lazard.com)

21.5 TRENDS OF ACTIVISM

Shareholder activism increased amid the 2007–2008 global financial crisis. Investors' groups and hedge funds were vowing to hold executives and corporate board members accountable, notably at annual shareholders' meetings, on issues such as potential conflicts of interests in relation to credit rating agencies (as firms pay for ratings) and auditing firms, executive compensation (say on pay), transparency on succession plans, nonperforming loans in banks, as well as fit and proper profile of directors. Also, as discussed in the preceding section, activists often reject bids arguing the low value of the offer to the stakeholders.

Recently, the activism influence has seen a decline in US targets, through matured markets and growing activity in Europe (starting in the United Kingdom, a corporate governance market based on a shareholder-centric model, the approach adopted in Anglo-Saxon countries, but also moving to Italy) and some parts of Asia. However, notably in Europe, because of the different philosophical issue regarding shareholders and stakeholders, the impact and development of activism is to be seen, as Continental Europe adopts a different approach to corporate governance theories with a communitarian focus based on a stakeholder-centric model. The demand for ESG investing or ESG compliance has continued to grow, and many companies are becoming part of UN Principles for Responsible Investment and essentially contribute to UN Sustainable Development Goals 2030. However, the trend is attracting growing scrutiny over the use of the ESG label and essentially whether the use of the term may be misleading investors.

Studies show that there has been a gradual increase in ownership concentration and passive investing. The increase in concentration is primarily driven by four big investment management institutions who are often seen as passive investors, namely BlackRock, State Street, York Capital, and Vanguard. Research has shown that passive investing may benefit in joint venture and alliances, information transfers, reduction of innovation hold up problem, facilitation in M&As, activity in corporate governance, and increasing supply for equity lending. However, there are costs involved too, such as product market competition and fragility.

The board members and the senior management should be fully aware of the potential activism conduct by the activist investors or their "followers," whose objectives are often coincident. Activist investors may use several tactics to influence the board, such as influencing shareholders to seek common support. This includes actions and tactics like meeting privately with board members, executive directors, management team, and shareholders; leaking and challenging the corporate information to media to support their hypothesis; conducting broad PR campaign to apply pressure on the company to answer back; heightening scrutiny on how corporate responds to such level of hostility, as well as hiring the best law offices and PR firms to block them from being hired by the targeted company.

In meetings with the activist investors, it is advisable to listen to their arguments, which are usually robustly structured and with sound basis, without taking a combative tone. In the case of any material misstatements, it is recommended to correct by proving evidence and factual data. When the stance of board members aligns with the board as a whole or even with executive directors, it is advisable that non-executive directors are briefed and inducted about the way they should conduct themselves if engaged with activists, coordinating the stance to take with the chair, including being knowledgeable about corporate's strategy, internal communications, and press communications and showing commitment to maximizing the shareholder's value.

When a board is under pressure, notably from activists, it is also advisable to consider setting a committee of the board or of the supervisory board to monitor, study, and permanently accompany the activists' developments, as under potentially stressful situations like this, a board having an ad hoc committee focused on the issue makes it more agile and flexible to react, with the committee eventually calling a meeting of the full board, if needed. The activist may throw distorted hypotheses or alternatives to lure the board, but the board must be careful about these types of approach. The board should reflect carefully about commitments and promises on issues with the activist as well as ensure that specific dates and milestones agreed are to be delivered in a timely manner.

Topics of the Chapter

The following has been discussed within this chapter:

- Generally, individual shareholders with a small number of shares rarely have success in influencing corporate governance; however, they can play a role in capturing minority shareholders, putting their voting rights together, and gaining influence.
- Large shareholders have significant rights and influence in a number of matters.
- Dual class votes allow the inside shareholders (founder or director) to have voting power disproportionately greater than their number of shares.
- The broad themes of activism are:
  1. Mergers & Acquisitions (M&As).
  2. Assets Divestments/Portfolio Pruning.
  3. Change in Business Strategy.
  4. Capture Value in the Short Term.
  5. Capital Structure and Governance.
- When a board is under pressure from activists, it is also advisable to set up an ad hoc committee focused on their actions.
- Recently, the activism influence has seen by a decline in US targets through matured markets and growing activity in Europe and in some parts of Asia.

Part VII—Annual Reports and External Auditor's Opinion

Chapter 22

Reporting

Corporate reporting about transparent financial statements as well as about activities constitutes fundamental elements to maintain the dialogue and communication among stakeholders. Reporting has increased in the current paradigm with a more extensive regulatory environment and increased complexity of the accounting and financial reporting requirements, as well as in practice originated by corporate governance best practice.

This chapter discusses annual reports, sustainability reports, and auditor's reports, including why they are important, what they contain, and how they are created.

The main reason why directors should be more committed to quality, transparency, and rigor of the content of their annual report is related to the objective of showing to shareholders, investors, and other important stakeholders (such as regulators and suppliers) the corporation's activities and the results of the decisions and actions taken and implemented over a period of time, thus providing an analysis of the way scarce resources are entrusted to management—linked to fiduciary responsibility—as well as the way they are managed and optimized. The annual report is usually the most piece of information and data about the set of financial statements and its notes, governance structure, and the performance of a board as well as a tool to demonstrate the sustainability of the organization business model.

Capital markets analysts, investors (shareholders and bondholders), the banking system, rating agencies, all critical stakeholders and players in the arena of raising capital use the annual report as a source of data and information to evaluate their investments.

With the annual report being a full responsibility of the board(s), the best practice dictates the active end-to-end way of involvement of the board. Therefore, the process should be led by the board (vision and strategy levels) and not delegated to the services (tactics and operational levels), with the board acting in a rubber stamp mode. The board should communicate to the services the structure and content on time, so that the annual report transmits adequately to the stakeholders not only the activity of the previous year but also a forward perspective for the coming years. At the company level, it is relevant to include the reading of the report in the culture of the organization, as the common culture in many organizations is to believe that the annual report is simply a legally required administrative exercise.

This decade has been fueled by several crucial elements, including sustainability and digitalization, as by the changes in the demand of the reporting structure by the stakeholders. While annual reporting to shareholders has existed for a long time, it now requires a broader scope, meaning that reporting should be designed by default, incorporating not only a shareholder-centric model but also viewpoints of the stakeholder-centric model, notably for companies with a footprint in countries that adopt or operate under those different corporate governance models. Therefore, most corporates publish sustainability reports in addition to annual report, which is also gradually becoming a regulatory requirement. Corporates may also publish separate other reports, such as corporate governance report, pay gap report, nonfinancial disclosure, diversity report, among other. All the reports are somehow meant to be embedded in the annual or sustainability reporting structure.

The governance model adopted—unitary board or dual board— also influences reporting and is required in most jurisdictions to publish different reports from the supervisory board and the executive board, which include subsets of reports, depending on legal frameworks, of independent audit boards, statutory auditors, and specific reports to the capital markets such as if a company issued for financial instruments (e.g., bonds, other debt instruments) or ESG certifications.

22.1 ANNUAL REPORTS

The annual report should be the result of an end-to-end process in its development and preparation and not, as sometimes happens, an adjustment of the previous year. The annual report (and the sustainability report, when prepared in a separate document) has to be approved by each member of the board of directors or supervisory and executive board, before the external auditors (and in jurisdictions where there is an independent audit board) sign their audit opinion/ reports or statements.

Depending on the jurisdiction, publicly listed companies must mandatorily disclose a report quarterly, semesterly, and/or annually, accompanied by audited financial statements and consolidated financial statements performed based on a certain accounting framework (IAS/IFRS, other GAAP); for non-listed companies, the public disclosure is even more restricted. Also, in some jurisdictions, the law could force those companies, when they reach a certain size (e.g., revenues, total assets, and/or number of employees) to have an independent audit board in the monist model or a statutory auditor in the dualist model, with one of the members being professionally qualified and registered with the authorities as a statutory auditor, usually being distinct from the statutory auditor of the company.

Usually, the report starts with a statement of the chair and of the CEO (depending on the governance model they may be in the same document or in separate documents), summarizing the activities of the year and the scenarios and perspectives ahead. A firm's financial statements serves the purpose of providing stakeholders with financial information and insight regarding the company's current financial status (financial position, financial performance, and cash flows) and the changes expected in the future, as well as the notes to the financial statements (considered an integral part of the financial statements), including the legal framework and other regulatory information under which a company operates; details about the accounting policies adopted, in process of adoption, not adopted (if voluntary), or the option elected (if there are alternatives to its adoption); the consistency of application of accounting principles between periods of reporting; and the impact of any changes in the consistency principle. It is also relevant to mention that reporting and/or indicating noncompliance with accounting policies and principles in the accounts does not transform that policy or principle into a proper one. The annual report is accompanied by the external auditors and/or statutory auditors' opinion; the report from the independent audit committee, if one exists, depending on the legal requirements of the jurisdiction; and the notes to the financial statements (which are numbered) to allow an easy cross-reference to the figures shown in the financial statements.

The annual report also communicates the governance model, representing a tool to improve the dialogue with the shareholders and stakeholders (notably bondholders and capital markets), to achieve adequate levels of trust and confidence. Companies maintain a dedicated web page for institutional and investor relations to allow easy access to fetch any such information. Often, the stock markets demand the availability of information to be listed in a transparent manner, and if such does not exist, explain why, under the comply or explain guideline discussed in Section 1.2: "Corporate Governance Guidelines." Comply or explain is a set of code that publicly listed firms may either comply with, or not, explain publicly why not.

In the two-tier structure, supervisory board report and annual report are normally published separately. The supervisory board report is addressed by the chair of the supervisory board and usually details the composition and profile of non-executive directors, indicating the ones qualified as independent; committees' composition; details about the number of meetings, and the attendance, remuneration, budget, functions, and activities of the supervisory board; as well as the board's issuance of opinions and prior opinions on relevant matters. Other issues, such as the vision and mission of the corporation, the main lines of the strategic plan, and the way they are implemented and controlled at the level of tactics are also included. Independent directors and board performance assessment, pay gap, diversity pyramid at all levels of the corporation, ESG, social responsibility, talent attraction and training, and challenges for future may also be included. Details about the control functions (risk control, compliance, and internal audit), the implementation of the Three or Four Lines of Defense structure, the governance framework, and the ICF (Internal Control Framework), as well as company's investments in research and development are also elements that respected corporations disclose to the stakeholders. In jurisdictions where an audit board is required and has oversight authority, it may act as a substitute for the report of supervisory board, although its contents may differ.

The annual report in a unitary structure is addressed in the same report by the chair of the board and the CEO, whereas in a two-tier, the annual report is usually addressed by both the chair and the chief executive; often, dualist model companies that issue separate reports for the supervisory board and the executive board. The annual report is more detailed and presents in depth the company's financial details, risk measures, and corporate governance information. Private companies that are not listed may publish the report voluntarily, which constitutes a welcome practice. However, some jurisdictions may require private companies to disclose certain information mandatorily.

22.1.1 CONTENT OF ANNUAL REPORTS

Usually, the annual report is divided into parts, including but not limited to strategic report, risk review, financial review, financial statements, corporate governance information, and additional information for shareholder/stakeholder.

- *Strategic report* briefly presents director's statement and general corporate information. This part introduces the business model, vision and purpose, measures for stakeholder's engagement, among others.
- *Risk review* part provides the summary of risks, risk types (financial or nonfinancial risks), risk management practices (for example, three or four lines of defense), supervision and regulation of risks such as financial risks and data protection, among others.
- *Financial review* part relates the financial health of the company. The financial health may be indicated by financial ratios such as Cost/Income ratio, Return on Equity ratio, Common Equity Tier 1 ratio. Key balance sheet and income statement figures along with commentary and clarification by the board or directors are usually incorporated in this part.
- *Financial statements part* consists of audited financial statements and, most crucially, the statutory auditors' opinion, which is discussed later in the same chapter. The audited financial statements are consolidated profit and loss statement (also named profit & loss, P&L, income statement or statement of revenues and expenses), consolidated balance sheet (also named statement of financial position), and consolidated statement of changes in equity and cash flow statement.
- *Corporate governance information part* details the governance structure and committees and their opinions and reports. The composition of board and committees along with detailed biographies of board members are presented. Also, the remuneration report justifying the remuneration of chief executive and other directors in the board is added.
- *Additional information for shareholder/stakeholder* is provided and may include information such as key dates, dividends, among others.

The content to be incorporated in the annual report is sufficiently discussed throughout the textbook. A possible non-exhaustive, summary of the contents of the annual report is presented below:

- Strategic Report
  - General corporate information highlights
  - Chair statement
  - Director's report
  - Vision, purpose, and strategy
  - Business model
  - Global trends and strategic advantages
  - Stakeholders engagement
  - Going concern and viability statements
- Risk Review
  - Risk summary
  - Risk management practices
  - Risk performance
- IIA Three Lines of Defense model
  - Risk Control
  - Compliance
  - Internal Audit
- Research & Development
- Human Resources
  - Talent attraction
  - Talent pipeline development
  - Diversity
  - Pay gap
  - Training
  - Supervision and regulation
- Financial Review
  - Financial summary
  - Key performance indicators
  - Consolidated income statement summary, and commentary
  - Consolidated balance sheet summary, and commentary

- Financial Statements
  - o Consolidated financial statements, and notes
    - Consolidated balance sheet
    - Consolidated income statement
    - Consolidated statement of changes in equity
    - Consolidated cash flow statement
  - o Independent auditors report
- Corporate Governance Information
  - o Corporate governance report
  - o Biographies of directors and executive committee
  - o Board committees
  - o Director's report
  - o Remuneration report
- Shareholder/Stakeholder or Additional Information
  - o Key dates
  - o Annual general meeting
  - o Dividends
  - o Forward-looking statements

22.2 SUSTAINABILITY REPORTING

Sustainability report has emerged as a relevant component of the annual report, discussed in Section 4.3: "Corporate Sustainability." Sometimes, the sustainability report may also be colloquially referred to as ESG (Environment, Social, and Governance) report. The sustainability report is, in fact, an opportunity for the corporate to assure its investors and the society about the corporate's stance on environmental, social, and governance issues, showing commitment toward UN Sustainable Development Goals 2030, climate change, workplace safety, well-being of communities, and sustainable economic growth. Essentially, the report demonstrates the organizational values, governance model, and strategy, committing to sustainable global economy.[422] The sustainability report is meant to measure, understand, and communicate the corporate economic, environmental, social, and governance execution; set goals; manage change more effectively; and essentially communicate sustainability performance and impacts, positive or negative. Sustainability reporting is part of the nonfinancial reporting, which is required by the European Union according to the Directive 2014/95/EU of the European Parliament and of the European Council, dated 22 October 2014, amending Directive 2013/34/EU, regarding the disclosure of nonfinancial and diversity information by certain large undertakings and groups, applicable to large public-interest companies with more than 500 employees across the EU, including listed companies, banks, insurance companies, and other significant Public Interest Entity (PIE) or termed as Public Business Entity (PBE) in the US.

Relevant measures included in the EU Audit Reform apply exclusively to PIE. The definition of a PIE under EU law is very relevant, which includes entities governed by the law of an EU Member State whose transferable securities are admitted to trading on a regulated market of any Member State, credit institutions, insurance undertakings, or entities designated by Member States as PIEs.[423] However, the application of the criterion may vary across Member States, particularly undertakings of significant public relevance resulting from their business, size, or number of their employees. The new rules do not apply when an undertaking is not covered by the definition of public-interest entity. Due to the impact of the location of subsidiaries or even branches of PIE—despite the audit reform having no formal extra-territorial impact on companies based outside the EU—all EU-based subsidiaries will be subject to these rules. Another relevant exception relates to its application to branches of non-EU banks located in Member States, which will follow under the definition of a PIEs.

The content of nonfinancial reporting should be in relation to environmental protection; social responsibility and treatment of employees; respect for human rights; anti-corruption and bribery; diversity on company boards in terms of age, gender, educational, and professional background; as well as staff level. The value of sustainability reporting is to ensure that corporates consider their impact on sustainability issues, essentially enabling them to be transparent about the risks and opportunities they are exposed to and face. Sustainability report may include the themes and key issues listed in Table 22.1, adapted from MSCI.

Table 22.1: ESG themes' summary

3 Pillars	10 themes	37 ESG Key Issues
Environment	Climate Change	Carbon emissions Product carbon footprint Financing environmental impact Climate change vulnerability
	Natural Resources	Water stress Biodiversity and land use Raw material sourcing
	Pollution and waste	Toxic emissions and waste Packaging materiality and waste Electronic waste
	Environmental opportunities	Opportunities in clean tech Opportunities in green building Opportunities in renewable energy
Social	Human Capital	Opportunities in cleantech Opportunities in green building Opportunities in renewable energy
	Product Liability	Product safety and quality Chemical safety Financial product safety Privacy and data security Responsible investment Health and demographic risk
	Stakeholder opposition	Controversial sourcing
	Social opportunities	Access to communications Access to finance Access to health care Opportunities in nutrition and health

3 Pillars	10 themes	37 ESG Key Issues
Governance	Corporate governance	Boards (monist and dualist models) Remuneration Ownership Accounting and reporting
	Corporate behavior	Business ethics Anticompetitive practices Tax transparency and compliance Corruption and instability Financial system instability

Source: (MSCI—www.msci.com)

Increasingly, there is an emergent trend resulting from corporates pursuing the broad concept of sustainability reporting rather than just publishing a separate sustainability report. Some accounting firms, including Big 4 (Deloitte, PricewaterhouseCoopers, Ernst & Young, and KPMG), seem to provide assurance service on sustainability reports, relying on assurance frameworks such as ISAE 3000 and AA1000AS. The assurance service may also be provided by sustainability services firms or engineering firms. ISAE (International Standard on Assurance Engagements) is a generic standard for any assurance engagement other than audits or reviews of historic financial information. An assurance report that is in accordance with ISAE 3000 can only be issued by professional accountants, and the assurance provider must also comply with the IESBA Code of Ethics for Professional Accountants. The emphasis of ISAE 3000 is on comprehensive procedures for evidence gathering processes and assurer independence. AA1000AS, the Accountability Principles Standard, is used by some firms to guide their approach to sustainability. The emphasis is on whether the organization and its sustainability reporting respond to stakeholder concerns. One study[424] shows that ISAE 3000 is a bit popular among the audit firms (Deloitte 61.54 percent; EY 50 percent; KPMG 69.23 percent; PWC 47.83 percent), while specialist assurance providers/technical experts seem to favor AA1000AS (76.47 percent, versus 11.76 percent for ISAE 3000).

Some sustainability reporting standards also exist. For example, the materiality map from the Sustainability Accounting Standards Board (SASB) could be beneficial in reporting sustainability issues. Other disclosure frameworks include Global Reporting Initiative (GTI), Task Force on Climate-Related Financial Disclosures (TCFD), Climate Disclosure Standard Board (CDSB), and Climate Disclosure Project (CDP). The broad concept of sustainability reporting may also be colloquially referred to as "integrated reporting." Any material ESG risks must always be in the oversight of the audit and/or risk committee. It is the responsibility of the committees to ensure that crucial ESG and nonfinancial risk factors are integrated with investment and divestment decision-making process, within the scope of audit, and holistically reported in integrated reporting. While nonfinancial reporting is mandatory for PIE, the regulation regarding the auditing of the sustainability report and sustainable financial disclosure is still in discussion, unlike financial reporting. For non-PIE, it is recommended to follow the best practices, incorporating available guidelines.

In 2020, the European Supervisory Authorities, including EBA (European Banking Authority), EIOPA (European Supervisory Authority For Occupational Pensions and Insurance), and ESMA (European Securities and Markets Authority), published a consultation paper in response to the proposed ESG disclosure standards for financial market participants, advisers, and products, covering Sustainable Finance Disclosure Regulation (SFDR). SDFR is broad in scope and covers nearly every sustainable finance product on a cross-sector basis (Figure 22.1).

Figure 22.1: Summary of EU consultation paper regarding ESG disclosure

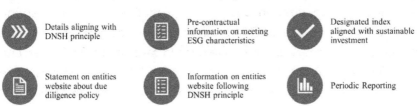

The consultation paper[425] presents six areas of disclosure:

1. Details of the presentation and content of the information to be disclosed regarding the principles of DNSH (Do No Significant Harm).
2. Pre-contractual information on how a product should meet environmental or social characteristics.
3. Additional pre-contractual information, where a designated index acts as a reference benchmark, on how that index is aligned with the sustainable investment objective.
4. A statement to be published on an entity's website regarding their due diligence policy with respect to the adverse impact of investment decisions.
5. Information to be published on an entity's website, including where and how the information should be published, along with a two-page summary document and how the product complies with the DNSH principle.
6. Periodic reporting, under sector specific legislation, focusing on the success of the product meeting sustainable characteristics and objectives, and how the product complies with the DNSH principle.

More sophisticated investors and asset managers consider ESG one of the prominent factors in investment decision-making. Corporate ESG ratings are made available by some entities, although ESG ratings and credit ratings are not the same. While credit ratings may incorporate a broader scope including ESG, the ESG ratings are specific and not as concentrated as credit ratings. For example, Bloomberg ESG Disclosure Scores rates companies annually based on their disclosure of quantitative and policy related ESG data out of 100. MSCI ESG Research provides corporate ESG ratings on AAA–CCC scale, with AAA being the most favorable one. Sustainability rates corporate ESG out of 100. S&P's ESG Index family allows investors to measure the performance of securities meeting sustainability criteria. There may be more global or regional companies providing ESG ratings, including Corporate Knights Global 100, Dow Jones Sustainability Index (DJSI), ISS Quality Score, Thomson Reuters ESG Research Data, among others.

Though big three credit ratings are somehow similar in methodology, ESG ratings methodology, scope, and coverage may vary greatly among providers.[426] Bloomberg rates the companies on an annual basis. It collects public ESG information disclosed by companies through sustainability reports or social responsibility reports, annual reports and websites, other public sources, or through company direct contact. Bloomberg ESG data covers several indicators in ESG theme, including carbon emissions, climate change effect, pollution, waste disposal, renewable energy, resource depletion, supply chain, political contributions, discrimination, diversity, community relations, human rights, cumulative voting, executive compensation, shareholders' rights, takeover defense, staggered boards, and independent directors. For any missing ESG data, the company rating is penalized. MSCI ESG Research looks at three pillars (environmental, social and governance), 10 themes, and 37 ESG key, as depicted in Table 22.1.

Sustainability covers at least 70 indicators and splits ESG indicators in three dimensions:

1. *Preparedness:* Assessment of management systems and policies in place to help manage ESG risks.
2. *Disclosure:* Whether company reporting meets international best practice standards and is transparent in relation to ESG issue.
3. *Performance (quantitative and qualitative):* ESG performance based on quantitative metrics and qualitative assessment based on review of controversial incidents the company may have been involved in.

Regardless, the ratings issued by different entities are meant to form the basis of informal and shareholder proposal-related investor engagement with firms on ESG matters.

22.3 EXTERNAL AUDITORS OPINION

External auditors are considered to belong to the "fourth" line of defense model, along with regulators and supervisors—external assurance providers—which is why they are a very relevant stakeholder for a board or supervisory and executive boards, for its audit committee, as well as to an independent audit board, if required by the legislation. Usually, external auditors engage with the executive management during the performance of the field work as well as with the internal audit, and at the same time have intense interaction with the audit committee of the board and the audit board. Also, depending on the size, reporting periods, complexity of the business, and even emerging issues during the field work should be presented directly to the board, and the frequency of the interaction with the board should be included in the global agenda of the board.

External auditors play a major role in issuing an independent audit opinion to grant a reasonable level of assurance to the readers of the financial statements regarding their preparation, in accordance with the appropriate accounting framework. They also reflect a fair and true view of a company's operations and its economic and financial position. Listed companies must disclose the external auditor report, notably containing an opinion on the financial statements. The term "Statutory Auditor" refers to an external auditor, either individual or entity, whose appointment is mandated by law. The word audit is derived from the Latin term *audire*, which means "to hear."

The current statutory audit legislation in EU, was adjusted, and enacted in 2016, although the legal and guideline' frameworks are permanently improved and updated. EU states that in the case of Public Interest Entities (PIEs), auditors will rotate on a regular basis and will no longer be allowed to provide certain Non-audit Services (NAS) to their audit clients. PIEs are listed companies, credit institutions, insurance undertakings, or other undertakings designated by EU countries to be of public importance.[427] In other words, PIEs cannot make use of the same firm for external audit for a prolonged time, and auditing firms cannot provide certain critical non-audit services to their audit clients. The purpose of an audit is to enhance the degree of confidence of intended users in the financial statements. This is achieved by the expression of an auditor's opinion regarding the preparation of financial statements, in all material respects, in accordance with an applicable financial reporting framework (e.g., IAS/IFRS, US GAAP, UK GAAP). The reporting framework is meant to provide a standard way to describe the company's financial performance such that the company's financial statements are understandable and comparable across international boundaries by investors, regulators, customers, or relevant stakeholders. IAS (International Accounting Standards) and IFRS (International Financial Reporting Standards) are the same; IFRS succeeded IAS and is a set of accounting standards developed by International Accounting Standards Board (IASB), an independent, not-for-profit organization. While IFRS is the international accounting standard and is often the accounting standards of many countries across the world—including the EU countries, which are influenced by IFRS—some major jurisdictions such as US and UK apply another accounting standard for financial reporting, namely GAAP (Generally Accepted Accounting Principles). The US SEC (Securities Exchange Commission) requires domestic public companies to make use of GAAP and does not permit the use of IFRS.

IFRS is said to be principles based while GAAP is said to be rules-based. Intuitively, GAAP has more instruction in the application of standards to specific examples and industries. GAAP has many exceptions and offers guidance targeted toward specific industries. IFRS does not provide any exceptions for industries or specific situations. The preparation of financial statements such as balance sheet and income statements under IFRS and GAAP is similar, but some narrow difference may still exist when presented. In terms of definition and recognition of assets and liabilities, and revenue recognition, there exist some differences due to the differences in structure and standards. However, some components can still be similar. For example, the standards of IFRS and GAAP recognize revenue on the basis of the process that generates the income. Besides, the management and the board of directors are responsible for the preparation of the financial statements. An audit must be conducted by a statutory auditor in accordance with the applicable auditing standards.

However, the exclusive reliance of multinationals' accounting books on the Big 4 Auditing Firms has emerged as a source of concern[428] because of the collapse of some audited clients. On the other hand, the audit firms that are much smaller (difference in revenues in 2020 of more than 20 billion dollars between KPMG, the fourth, and BDO, the fifth[429]) in revenues and size (e.g., BDO, Grant Thornton, RSM, and Crowe Horwath) are usually seen lacking the international reach and depth of service to handle the requirements of large and demanding corporates. The Competition & Markets Authority, a non-ministerial government department in the UK, has taken prudent steps toward acknowledging the barriers to entry for challenger small or mid-sized firms and is therefore pushing the idea of joint audits as a way to "square the circle," an issue that has led to divergent viewpoints in terms of being a viable solution.

The basis for the auditor's opinion is the International Standards on Auditing (ISA), requiring the auditor to obtain reasonable assurance about whether the financial statements as a whole are free from material misstatement, whether due to fraud or error. Reasonable assurance is the highest level of assurance. It is obtained when the auditor has obtained enough appropriate audit evidence to reduce audit risk to an acceptably low level. However, reasonable assurance is not an absolute level of assurance, because there may be inherent limitations of an audit on which the auditor draws conclusions. The concept of "professional judgment" is present in several processes carried during an audit, as well as regarding the efficiency and effectiveness of the internal control system.

22.3.1 CONCEPT OF MATERIALITY

"Materiality" is also a "boundary" applied by the auditor both in planning and performing the audit and in evaluating the effect and impact of potential and identified misstatements in the audit and of uncorrected misstatements, if any, on the financial statements. They are termed "adjustments" when affecting the profit and loss statement or retained earnings and "reclassifications" if they impact entries only in the balance sheet or in the profit and loss statement. Materiality involves both qualitative (nature) and quantitative (amount) components; therefore, both quality (nature) and quantity (amount) of misstatements are relevant to deciding what is material. Application of materiality requirements following ISA standards is often a challenging task. The main purpose to determine overall materiality when planning audit is to identify "performance materiality" in order to help auditors design their audit procedures therefore, estimating a threshold for accumulating misstatements above which becomes material. Materiality is usually determined by selecting the appropriate benchmark—determined by taking appropriate percentage level—and essentially justifying the choice and percentage of benchmark, which usually depends on the types of industries and the relevance of the benchmark. ISA 320 offers examples of benchmarks that can be used, namely profit before tax, total income or total expenses, gross profit, total equity, and net assets. For example, in commercial owner-managed company, profit before tax can be set as the benchmark. Gross or net assets may be used in entities with higher balance sheet values. Nonetheless, the choice of benchmark is largely influenced by the environment and variables where the company operates, and it is the responsibility of the auditor to properly identify the appropriate benchmark.

The process relating to adjustments and reclassification is interactive during the field work, as the external auditors discuss them with management, giving them the opportunity to correct the identified misstatements. If the decision is to correct the entry, then the issue is solved; on the contrary, if management decides not to change or book the identified misstatement, the external auditor accumulates the adjustments and reclassifications with the objective of assessing their impact on the determined levels of materiality for the company and its impact in the audit opinion. The final list of adjustments and reclassifications (i.e., the ones not booked by the company) are discussed with the audit committee, the audit board, and the board.

22.3.2 TYPES OF AUDIT

There are different types of opinion or conclusions resulting from the work of the auditor. The main difference results from the scope of the work—*full audit, limited review,* and *assurance engagements.*

The purpose of a full audit is to enhance the degree of confidence of the intended users of the financial statements (reasonable assurance). This is achieved by the expression of an opinion by the auditor on whether the financial statements are prepared, in all material respects, in accordance with an applicable financial reporting framework. In the case of most general-purpose frameworks, that opinion is on whether the financial statements are presented fairly, in all material respects, or give a true and fair view in accordance with the framework.

In a limited review of the financial statements, the auditor expresses a conclusion that is designed to enhance the degree of confidence of intended users regarding the preparation of an entity's financial statements in accordance with an applicable financial reporting framework. The auditor's conclusion is based on the auditor obtaining limited assurance. The auditors' report includes a description of the nature of a review engagement as a context for the readers of the report to be able to understand the conclusion. The auditor primarily performs inquiry and analytical procedures to obtain sufficient appropriate evidence as the basis for a conclusion on the financial statements as a whole. If the auditor becomes aware of a matter or issue that leads to a belief that the financial statements may be materially misstated, the practitioner designs and performs additional procedures, as the auditor deems necessary in the circumstances, to be able to conclude on the financial statements.

When conducting an assurance engagement, the objectives of the auditor are to obtain either reasonable assurance or limited assurance, as appropriate, about whether the subject matter information is free from material misstatement, and to additionally express a conclusion regarding the outcome of the measurement or evaluation of the underlying subject matter through a written report that conveys either a reasonable assurance or a limited assurance conclusion.

"Assurance" is based on the credibility of the information prepared by the company, based on the auditor evaluation of the sufficiency and appropriateness of audit evidence obtained. The level of assurance awarded by the auditor can be:

- *Reasonable:* high, but not absolute.
- *Moderate or limited:* such as the case of limited review, where the conclusion is presented in a negative format.

The internal control framework (ICF) discussed in Chapter 6: Control Functions and Related Frameworks, affects the extent of the audit work to a relevant degree, as the audit risk determination is based on a judgment, including the materiality and its relationship with the internal controls in force, and the efficacy and efficiency of the way they operate. Nonetheless, the detection of frauds and errors is not the objective of an audit. During audit planning, the auditor should take a "skeptically optimistic" stance, based on the risk that fraud (the objective of a full audit is not to detect fraud, although it may emerge in the auditing work) and human errors may have occurred, or even a judgmental decision about the recording or not of a specific transaction about which the auditor may have a divergent opinion from management. Regarding internal controls, information is material if its omission may distort or influence the decision of the users of the financial statements about the determination of risks and the materiality limits. The auditor may carefully perform the sampling means, depending on the complexity and volume of operations. To obtain sufficient and appropriate audit evidence, the auditor can follow means such as inspection, observation, inquiry, third-party confirmation, recalculation, reperformance, or substantive analytical procedures. The conclusions reached from the process of accumulating audit evidence should be adequately documented to support the audit opinion.

Regarding the preparation of financial statements, the management responsibility should present:

- Financial position in a true and appropriate way.
- Results of the operations and the cash flows.
- Adoption of policies and adequate accounting procedures.
- Maintenance of robust internal controls framework.

22.3.3 MANAGEMENT REPRESENTATION LETTER

Furthermore, it should be followed by the management "representation letter" that recognizes those responsibilities, the content of the financial statements, and the information provided during the audit. A management representation letter is a letter whose minute is written by external auditors, required to be signed by company's board or/and senior management, which attests the accuracy and completeness of the information included in the financial statements that the company has submitted to the auditors. The following things are usually included in the management representation letter:

- Board and/or management is responsible for the proper presentation of the financial statements based on an appropriate reporting framework.

- All necessary information is made available to the auditors.
- All board of directors' minutes are complete.
- Board or/and management has made available all letters from regulatory agencies regarding financial reporting noncompliance
- There are no unrecorded transactions
- Individual and collective effect of uncorrected misstatements is immaterial.
- Management acknowledges its responsibility for the company's internal control system.
- All related party transactions have been disclosed.
- All contingent liabilities have been disclosed.
- All unasserted claims or assessments have been disclosed.
- All liens and other encumbrances on assets have been disclosed.
- All material transactions have been properly recorded.
- Management is responsible for systems designed to detect and prevent fraud.
- Management has no knowledge of fraud within the company.
- Financial statements conform to the applicable accounting framework.

ISA 580: *Written Representations* explains the responsibility of the auditor to obtain written representations from management and, where appropriate, from those charged with governance in an audit of financial statements. The written representation letter is meant to serve as an audit evidence that external auditors require in regards with the audit of financial statements. The external auditor does not allow the board or/and management to make any changes to the content of this letter before signing it, as that would effectively reduce the liability of the company. Also, the auditor will not issue an opinion unless a signed management representation letter is received. The letter essentially shifts some of the risks or blame-game from the auditor to management, in case it is later found that some of the elements of the audited financial statements do not fairly represent the financial results or cash flows of the company. Sometimes, the board members or/and management may be unaware about series of issues relating to frauds, breaks in internal controls, aggressive tax planning, tax optimization schemes, lawsuits, among others, and have told the auditors everything they know; however, the risk is imminent to the company itself and largely depends on the risk culture and risk appetite embedded in the company.

22.3.4 EXTERNAL AUDITOR'S OPINION

The external auditor's opinion is normally included in the annual report adjacent with the audited financial statements. The report should be like a letter where the external auditor expresses an opinion on a company's compliance with standard accounting practices, such as IFRS or GAAP (Table 22.2). The auditor's opinion can be:

- *Unqualified:* It means that the financial statements are free from material misstatements, also known as a clean opinion.
- *Qualified:* It means that there is one or more issues that represent identified material misstatements and/or one or more issues regarding which no sufficient or/and appropriate audit evidence was obtained by the auditor, representing the possibility of non-identified material misstatements (commonly described as scope limitations). Those issues, which are not pervasive to the financial statements as a whole, are described in additional paragraphs and represent exceptions from the cleanliness of the financial statements.
- *Adverse Opinion:* It means that the identified misstatements are not only material but also pervasive to the financial statements as a whole.
- *Disclaimer of Opinion:* It means that the auditor is not able to express an opinion because of an absence of sufficient and appropriate audit evidence that has a pervasive impact on the audit appreciation of the financial statements as a whole.

Table 22.2: Importance of external audit report

Stakeholders	BOD/Management	Supervisory Board
• The auditor provides credibility and reliability to the financial information • The auditor reduces uncertainty and risk associated with the shareholders' decision-making process.	• The auditor helps the board/management on the fulfillment of their responsibilities against shareholders and other stakeholders • Offers a better understanding of the applicable accounting framework, law, and regulation	• The auditor provides relevant information that enables the supervisory board to develop its monitoring activities: risk oversight and supervision of internal control system and financial reporting process

22.3.5 IAASB AUDIT REPORTING STANDARDS

In 2015, the International Audit and Assurance Standards Board (IAASB), an independent standards body, issued the new and revised audit reporting standards.[430] The new changes are meant for:

- Enhanced communications between investors and the auditor, as well as the auditor and those charged with governance.
- Increased attention by management and those charged with governance to the disclosures in the financial statements to which reference is made in the auditor's report.
- Renewed focus of the auditor on matters to be communicated in the auditor's report, which could indirectly result in an increase in professional skepticism.

The revised standards are meant to ensure robust communication between the investors, board, or/and management with the auditors on Key Audit Matters (KAM). The KAM section is believed to provide users of financial statements with an opportunity to engage actively with the board. It is meant to enhance communication, not compliance, and that investors or stakeholders want to learn more about what auditors focused on and why and how the matter was addressed. The new changes are also meant to increase the attention of those charged with governance and management in regard to the appropriate disclosures in the financial statements referred to in the external auditor's report. As KAM are often derived from the matters communicated with the audit committee, the audit committee must carefully review the timings of its meetings and ensure that the audit process and time frame are well facilitated. The audit committee must question the disclosures in the financial statements and annual report, whether the disclosure is reported adequately and fairly to which KAM may exert impact. The committee should also question management response to KAM. Also, the audit committee should scrutinize management's process for assessing the entity's ability to continue as a going concern and examine the relevance and completeness of the entity's disclosures in the financial statements related to going concern. The committee should also determine which documents are meant to be within the scope of "other information," as defined by the ISA, and within the scope of the auditor's responsibilities.

Examples of other information are inclusion of sections that explain management's responsibility for the other information; identify the other information obtained or expected to be obtained; explain the auditor's responsibilities; explain the effort in relation to other information; contain a statement on whether there is something to report in regard to the other information; and contain a statement describing any uncorrected material misstatements. Essentially, the role of the audit committee becomes even more crucial, and the independent directors sitting on the audit committee must be fit and proper to challenge the board and the management.[431]

For listed companies, two sections are deemed as mandatory—Key Audit Matters (KAM) and full disclosure of the name of the audit engagement partner, while they are voluntary for other entities. To determine the KAM, the auditor must consider areas of higher assessed risks of material misstatements or higher risks. Any matter that is considered as KAM must be answered with why the matter was KAM, how was the matter addressed in the audit, and any reference to the related disclosure. Examples of KAM may vary by industries, such as revenue, goodwill, taxation, acquisitions, inventory, investments, and others. The new criteria for full audits reporting structure are mentioned below:[432]

- Opinion section required to be presented first, followed by the basis for opinion section, unless law or regulation prescribe otherwise.
- Enhanced auditor reporting on going concern, including:
  - o Description of the respective responsibilities of management and the auditor for going concern.
  - o A separate section when a material uncertainty exists and is adequately disclosed, under the heading "Material Uncertainty Related to Going Concern."
  - o New requirement to challenge the adequacy of disclosures for "close calls," in view of the applicable financial reporting framework, when events or conditions are identified that may cast significant doubt on an entity's ability to continue as a going concern.
- Key Audit Matters, i.e., the information about audit areas that mattered the most.
- Auditor statement about management responsibilities for the preparation of financial statements and assessment of the company's ability to continue as a going concern.
- Affirmative statement about the auditor's independence and fulfillment of relevant ethical responsibilities, with disclosure of the jurisdiction of origin of those requirements or reference to the International Ethics Standards Board for Accountants' Code of Ethics for Professional Accountants.

- Enhanced description of the auditor's responsibilities and key features of an audit. Certain components of the description of the auditor's responsibilities may be presented in an appendix to the auditor's report or, where law, regulation, or national auditing standards expressly permit, by reference in the auditor's report to a website of an appropriate authority.
- Name of the Engagement Partner.
- Signature, address, date.

Figure 22.2 depicts the new structure of a detailed audit report.

Figure 22.2: New structure of a detailed audit report in most jurisdictions

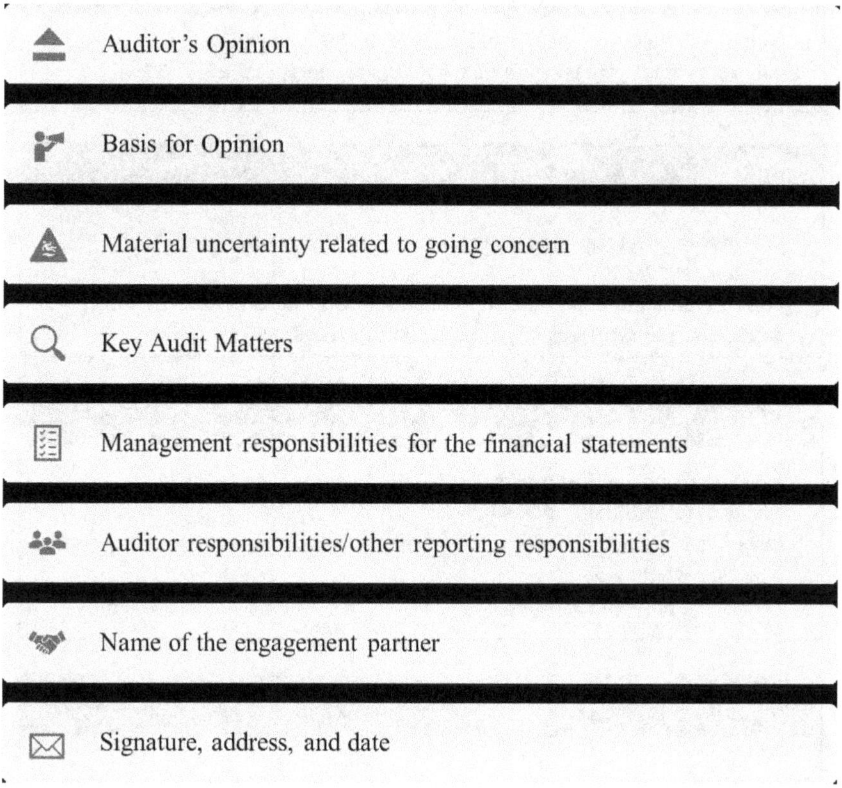

▲	Auditor's Opinion
☞	Basis for Opinion
⚠	Material uncertainty related to going concern
🔍	Key Audit Matters
📋	Management responsibilities for the financial statements
👥	Auditor responsibilities/other reporting responsibilities
🤝	Name of the engagement partner
✉	Signature, address, and date

Evidently, corporates in countries such as the UK and the Netherlands have incorporated remarkably high auditing standards, while other countries are following the lead. The summary of the auditor's report (by KPMG) of the Dutch bank ING is illustrated in Figure 22.3 as an example. The summarized and full audit reports are both usually included in the annual report.

Figure 22.3: Summary of external auditor's report opinion

Audit approach

Summary

Materiality

- Group materiality of EUR 300 milion (2017: EUR 300 milion).
- 4.4 % of profit before taxation from continuing operations (2017: 4.1%).

Group audit

- 90% of total assets by audit procedures performed by component auditors (2017: 87%).
- 80% of profit before taxation from continuing operations covered by audit procedures performed by component auditors (2017: 86%)

Key audit matters

- Estimation uncertainty with respect to the impairment losses on loans and advances to customers and banks.
- Instances of non-compliance with anti-money laundering and anti-terrorism financing acts.
- Risk of inappropriate access or changes to information technology systems.

Opinion

Unqualified

Topics of the Chapter

The following has been discussed within this chapter:

- The annual report presents in depth the company's financial details, risk measures, and corporate governance information.
- An annual report usually contains:
  1. Strategic report
  2. Risk review
  3. Financial review
  4. Financial statements
  5. Corporate governance information
  6. Additional information for shareholder/stakeholder
- Sustainability report is considered a relevant component of the annual report; it is an opportunity for the corporate to assure its investors and the society about the corporate's stance on environmental, social, and governance issues.
- The contents of a sustainability report are listed in Table 22.1.
- The purpose of an audit is to enhance the degree of confidence of intended users in the financial statements.
- The external auditor's opinion on a company's compliance with standard accounting practices can be:
  1. Unqualified
  2. Qualified
  3. Adverse Opinion
  4. Disclaimer of Opinion
- The importance of external audit report is highlighted in Table 22.2.

Part VIII—Framing and Concluding

Chapter 23

Framing and Concluding the Textbook

As stated earlier, the purpose of this manual is to offer a comprehensive and holistic compilation of themes and topics influencing
the corporate governance arena, a branch of study within the business administration field. As a textbook, it is addressed to scholars,
students and decision-makers, notably executive and non-executive
directors as well as to company secretaries and first-line managers
to assist in understanding corporate governance standards and concepts to better contribute to a robust corporate governance framework that makes their board highly efficient.

The World Bank introduced the "Good Governance" concept for
the public sector, advocating that it is a cornerstone to sound economic policies and central to sustain environment to foster equitable
development, while the IMF added more elements and vectors to it
advocating that "promoting good governance includes ensuring the
rule of law, improving the efficiency and accountability of the public
sector, and tackling corruption to ensure economies can prosper."[433]
The World Bank established a mandate to FMI (Financial Market
Integrity)[434] relating to the private sector corporate governance arena
establishing that it would be part of the FMI remit. Teodora de Castro
and Duarte Pitta Ferraz advocate that decision-making benefits from
The World Bank Group concept of "Good Governance" as well as
the Fit and Proper[435] standards applicable to the financial system

are opportunities for the nonfinancial sector to benefit from equally demanding standards, creating a culture that ensures the sustainability of organizations.[436]

The corporate governance concept and definition is consensual among academics and public and private institutions (e.g., OECD, G20, BIS, BCBS, EBA, FSB, IIA) involved in the corporate governance arena. Basically, it is a set of organizational structures (*Structures*), rules, controls, policies, or procedures (*Processes and Systems*) in a way an organization is directed, controlled, and governed (*Decision-Making*). However, no one size fits all, and the governance framework depends on several factors, such as legislative framework of each jurisdiction, company size, public or private status, among others. The corporate governance models across the world are influenced by their own social, economic, political, and cultural values. Things change, tastes change, and governance must adapt with changing time and technology. The board of directors play a crucial role in governance and act as fiduciaries to all relevant stakeholders. Investors, social bodies, and communities value companies with good governance standards that are meant to build and nurture the trust values and promote long-termism and sustainability.

It is often mentioned that the previous era was about internet of information and the present era is about internet of value; sustainability (ESG—Environment, Social and Governance) and digitalization are two core elements every corporate must incorporate in their modern business model to assure sustainable growth and survival. Topics around ESG have emerged as highly relevant for boards, and therefore should be a priority item in a global agenda. Sophisticated investors consider ESG a prominent factor in investment decision-making. While credit ratings may incorporate a broader scope including ESG, the ESG ratings are specific and not as concentrated as credit ratings. Though credit rating agencies are somehow similar in methodology, ESG ratings methodology, scope, and coverage may vary greatly among providers. Public ESG information disclosed by companies is very relevant in sustainability and other reports, as well as in websites. For example, sustainability covers at circa 70 indicators and splits ESG indicators in three dimensions: (i) preparedness, i.e., assessment of management systems and policies in place to help manage ESG risks; (ii) disclosure, including whether company reporting meets international best practice standards and is transparent in relation to ESG issue; and (iii) performance (quantitative and qualitative), namely ESG performance based on quantitative metrics and qualitative assessment based on review of controversial or reputational incidents.

The governance theory discussed in the literature, namely Agency Theory, introduces the dynamics of the relationship between the agent (e.g., managers) and principal (e.g., shareholders) in a publicly listed entity and essentially the incentive mechanisms to align shareholders' or relevant stakeholders' interests. Other theories include the Stewardship Theory, Stakeholder Theory, and Political Theory. The Agency Theory is considered the most notable, rooted on Anglo-Saxon countries where corporates have dispersed ownership, and capital markets play a major role in financing the economy—raising capital. The agent is expected to work in the best interests of the principal without regard for self-interest with the contrary, raising the *principal-agent problem*. Self-dealing may take several forms, and generally involves an individual agent benefiting, from a transaction executed on the behalf of the principal. Also, misstating financial statements, accounting policies applied with aggressive interpretations, or lack of transparency in annual reports are "tools" to manage asymmetry of data and information by agents. In addition, the process of "tunneling"—diluting the shareholders' holdings—is another example.

Agency challenges emerged in the 2007–2008 crisis, particularly in the financial sector, notably in terms of conflicts of interest between the interests of depositors and shareholders. Guidelines addressing this sensitive issue include the guidelines on internal governance—EBA/GL/2017/11, notably awarding depositors' higher priority than to the shareholders, basically because customers' deposits represent a much larger amount of money than the capital of a bank. There are three generic agency problems that include: (i) a conflict between the firm's owners and hired managers, (ii) a conflict between the majority or controlling owner/shareholder and the minority or noncontrolling owner/shareholder, and (iii) a conflict between the firm's owners and the third parties with whom it has contracts, such as employees, creditors, suppliers, manufacturers, and customers. Governance strategies to facilitate relations and the principals' control over the agent's behavior include the process of selection and removal, the initiation and ratification, as well as the trusteeship and reward. The role for a robust development of the process of governance of strategies requires the involvement of the committee of remunerations and/or nominations, as well as the involvement of the chairperson. There are two possible incentives' strategy: (i) the reward strategy—sharing rule and pay for performance, and (ii) the trusteeship strategy.

The topic of family business framework is also addressed, as it poses challenges because of the family or families' involvement. Family businesses are observed to be transitioning from family-first companies to business-first companies, with salary and leadership being based on performance, and only qualified family members being hired in the business. "Legitimacy" emerges as critical factor, as a family does not include only shareholders, and employees may have dedicated their career to the business. Family business generations' stages—founder, siblings' partnership or cousins' consortium—as well as of the business model are relevant considerations. Succession—under frameworks named the "eagle approach" versus the "ostrich approach"—is another of the major challenges and only the ones fit and proper should be involved in running the company, driving its sustainable growth and payment of dividends. Succession should be addressed and structured like in a monarchy, i.e., preparing the potential successor. On the other hand, family business' shareholders must be respected when opting for other professional careers, receiving their share of dividends. Only members of the family that are fit and proper for the job should sit in managerial positions.

Corporate governance models across the world are influenced by their own social, economic, political, and cultural values, as well as by the specific legal frameworks. Corporate law differs among jurisdictions, some allowing both the unitary and the dualist models or only one of them. Principles evolve, and stakeholders—notably shareholders—learn, especially from exceptional negative events, especially and from gaps in the accounting principles and reporting, regulatory environment, risk culture, conflicts of interest, or even the moral fabric of corporate governance frameworks.

While the primary responsibility of the management board is to run the corporate, the responsibility of the supervisory board is to supervise, control, and monitor the management board, including governance, strategy and sustainability of the business model. The most common governance models are the unitary board—(combining executive management and supervisory functions in the same board) and dual board (board of executive directors handling management functions and another board of non-executive directors handling supervisory functions). Usually, the option for the dualist model is followed by companies with a higher concentration of ownership like family companies, state-owned companies, or other having shareholder concentrations. The rules for best practices should adopt and follow business ethics, business goals, strategic management, organizational effectiveness, and corporate communication. Also, practices including governance roadshows help a corporate apprise its shareholders and stakeholders of its supervisory functions, while investor relations roadshows are directed to the capital markets and analysts.

The advantages of the unitary board include a superior flow of information, swift decision-making abilities, effective understanding and participation in the business by the board, as well as reduced bureaucracy—as separate approval from the supervisory board is not required. Independent non-executive directors and executive directors are in the same room, in constant contact, allowing for a better understanding of the business profile and strategy and eventually of a greater prominence of the supervisory function reducing the asymmetry of information and data. It also allows non-executive directors to advise and challenge executive directors, with skilled independent directors adopting an optimistically skeptic stance and bringing experience and expertise to the board. The disadvantages of the unitary board include the possibility of increased agency conflict between the shareholders and the board, as there is no supervisory board to oversee the board since they simultaneously make and monitor the same decisions. This can increase the potential for collusion among directors, reduce neutrality and independence, and also reduce the willingness to discuss issues openly. A last topic relates to the potential for the tone of the board to be overexposed to the personality of the chairperson.

The advantages of the dual board include the effective monitoring through separation—supervisory board with power to challenge and influence management—greater focus on stakeholder inclusion, allowing for an open discussion, clearly defined roles and responsibilities of directors in each board, and strict separation between the chair and the CEO roles, as well as a clear functional report of the control function—risk management, compliance, and internal audit—maintaining independence more robustly. The disadvantadges include increase the increased probability of information and data asymmetry—notably when the supervisory board is solely dependent on the management for its information—and increased possibility of inefficient monitoring due to a lack of information flow between the supervisory and the executive boards.

Governance structures structures are different among countries or regions, with legal frameworks reflecting those characteristics. Japan incorporated the *keiretsu* model being bank centered due to the efforts requiring the banking system to support the reconstruction of the economic fabric after the war, usually adopting the unitary board structure. The South Korean model is known as *chaebol* model reflecting a conglomerate-based economy, with ownership generally held by powerful families, as well as because the government and the chaebol businesses maintain a symbiotic relationship. India is influenced by the Anglo-Saxon model, tending to adopt a unitary board—following a family-centric model—although incentives for shareholders' protection and return are often weak. Some countries' governance models are heavily influenced by government and national strategies and interests; nationalism often emerges in cross-border operations, and job preservation are strong in the continental model. Dominant shareholders have both the incentive and the power to supervise, monitor, and discipline executive management. PRC tends to have a two-tiered structure, as most large corporates—banks, energy, commodities, and transports—are state-owned enterprises (SOE), with the ultimate beneficiary owner (UBO), even in seemingly private groups, being state-owned through holdings, supervised by the State-owned Asset Supervision and Administration Commission (SASAC), having also a strong political and cultural influence and control over the corporate boards. Like in PRC, the big enterprises in the Russian Federation are normally held by state or within the vicinity of state-related members, with national identity and influence being strongly prevalent in state-owned corporates that also have a remit of pursuing national strategic interests—often beyond profitability. Highly concentrated ownership may create a new agency problem, as the interests of controlling shareholders and minority shareholders may not always be aligned.

The business model arena is a very relevant topic for a board. A business model is a structured process that offers the supervisory board/board of directors and senior management a framework to ensure sustainable growth of the business segments and the organization as a whole. The business model is Interconnected with the concept of sustainability and to the principle of an organization's ongoing concern. It should be periodically reviewed, along with its impact on the strategic plan. Vision, strategy, tactics, and operational are the business model's pillars, linking the vision to the business strategy. The "Osterwalder Business Model Canvas" is a tool that can be used to develop a structured process for building a business model segment by segment. Although dynamics in the board vary, it is vital to ensure a robust governance framework and an effective decision-making process.

The business model development initiates with setting—or adjusting—the vision, which may be expanded or detailed into a mission, and emphasize values linked to the strategy, tactics, and operational components of a business model. The current best practices for the strategy development require the involvement of the board (or the supervisory board) in an end-to-end process, contrary to the earlier practice of a rubber stamp process. Non-executives are required to give input, discuss assumptions, review, and give feedback on the first output, and then approve the strategic plan. The concept of strategy applied to the business world can be linked and interlocked to the concept of economy and considered under the Corporate Governance Framework, as advocated by the OECD (G20/OECD Principles of Corporate Governance—www.oecd.org), which promotes transparent and fair markets (linked to raising capital) and the efficient allocation of scarce resources. The third layer of the responsibilities and roles within the governance framework belongs to executive committee relating to the implementation of the strategy defined by the board, moving into the tactics. The tactical plan is developed after crafting the strategic plan, while operational is the process of linking strategic plan goals and objectives to tactical plan goals and objectives, including milestones and conditions for success. Business models should incorporate sustainable development goals, including ESG (Environment, Social, and Governance) vectors as well as the UN

Sustainable Development Goals (UN—www.sdgs.un.org/goals), UN Principles for Responsible Investment (UNPRI—www.unpri. org), expecting corporates and investors to follow these principles to meet their sustainable development goals in order to facilitate in developing a sustainable financial ecosystem, and therefore serving for broader interests of the society.

The internal control functions—risk management, compliance, both second line of defense and internal audit, third line of defense— were always relevant within the dimensions of the Internal Control Framework (ICF). However, their relevance increased significantly after the 2008 financial and economic crisis. This was particularly relevant with a major reformulation and establishment of rules, processes, and systems, as well as empowering with specific responsibilities of the board, senior management, and the heads of the control functions. Regulators and supervisors of the financial systems have as a priority to ensure sustainability of the business models primarily and eventually guarantee the financial stability of the banking system. Major changes and adjustments in the regulation included the empowerment of the control functions through demanding requirements of independence, organization, qualification of talent, and the establishment of "an open line" with supervisors and other authorities, namely judicial entities, as well as requiring from the heads of the internal control functions particular legal obligations in communicating certain types of events and transactions. The rational is to ensure an effective and operating system of internal controls—"Control Functions"—to ensure robust and sustainable prudential ratios and a conduct from the board and senior management aligned with the best practice to avoid the well-known situations that resulted in the financial crisis. Also, the control functions grant their staff a statute of full independence. The relevance of the internal control functions is also strongly linked to the mitigation of asymmetric data and information, notably between executive and non-executive directors, and should be leveraged by non-executive directors to comply with their roles and responsibilities. It is relevant to mention that within the executive committee or executive board, the CEO, the CFO, and the CRO usually have information and data of higher quality and detail than their peers, which places them in a privileged position. Also, BCBS (Principle 10—Internal Audit) stresses that internal audit supports board and senior management should promote an effective governance process and long-term soundness.

The IIA three lines of defense model was updated by IIA in 2020; nonetheless, all of these organizational management frameworks provide a solid fundamental structure to design the governance operating model by following a risk-based approach and incorporating adequate risk vectors from strategic decisions to day-to-day operations. The ICF within the scope of organizational management is meant to achieve assurance in organizational effectiveness and efficiency to achieve corporate vision and goals through the execution of the strategic plan, placing reliability on all kinds of reporting—both financial and nonfinancial events—transparency, and compliance with applicable laws, regulation, and guidelines, informing deviation from the best practice through the comply or explain mechanism. The three internal control cornerstones' functions are risk management functions (second line), compliance functions (second line), and internal audit functions (third line), which should be aligned with the external assurance providers (suggested by Arndorfer and Minto as the "fourth" line of defense; the idea was not incorporated in the 2020 IIA revised three lines of defense model)—regulators, supervisors, and external auditors. Corporates must take decisions within their risk capacity and risk appetite framework, taking into consideration the shareholders' and stakeholders' expectations. The board must review, challenge, and concur with management on proposed strategy and risk appetite framework such that it is realistically aligned with the vision, mission, core values, and objectives. The Asset and Liability Risk Management (ALM) is particularly important to financial institutions, but also to the nonfinancial sector, since a significant portion of their income is often generated from interest income, which can be vulnerable notably to interest rate and foreign exchange risks and mismatches of maturities between deposits and loans, while other factors may also be present and highly influenced in ALM by the international footprint where those areas gain an additional relevance in terms of a headquartered centralized function. On the other hand, financial institutions must abide with the regulatory standards defined by regulators such as European Central Bank (ECB), which supervises the EU-based banking and financial institutions through the mechanism known as Single Supervisory Mechanism (SSM).

Independence refers to a mental state of making decisions without the influence of other individual, very relevant in the governance framework, while conflicts of interests involve impartiality and objectivity of a decision, opinion, or recommendation or—on the contrary—may be perceived as being compromised by a personal interest. The OECD and the Council of Europe have published frameworks regarding the same. Different factors affect the independence of a board as well as the degrees of directors' independence. The concepts and definitions of independence and conflicts of interests are critical for board members—notably for the non-executive directors who are bound by law and/or guidelines in being independent, an element intrinsically linked to potential conflicts of interests—affecting all directors and management as well. Institutions should have processes and tools to identify, manage, and mitigate conflicts of interests. The concept of independence can be analyzed from various sources with a broad concept that encompasses principles relating to behavioral and performing duties with integrity, dignity, care, loyalty, and discretion in compliance with the law, rules, and code of conduct and ethics adhering to demanding standards of conduct. This includes an individual not seeking or taking instructions and acting free. Independence involves different levels, a fact that suggests the impossibility of "complete independence." Therefore, the term and the degree to which it exists should be specified with the objective of mitigating potential conflicts and misinterpretations. Board members must avoid situations that may give rise to a conflict of interests or be perceived as such. A personal interest—although not limited to—includes any potential benefit and/or advantage to the decision-maker, spouses, partners, and/or close family members, as well as involves the fact that a former director must consider the position after the end of a mandate. Adopting a criterion of transparency about potential conflicts of interests and the way they are dealt with is critical for the reputation of an institution. Independence can also be analyzed under two subsets of concepts—functional and administrative for the private sector, and functional and institutional for the public sector.

Conflicts of interests are intimately linked with independence. Relevant definitions of conflicts of interests were developed by the OECD and the Council of Europe. They have in common the potential emergence of conflicts of interest between the public duties of a decision-maker in the public sector and the individual's own private interests. A major difference relates to the fact that OECD's definition relates to actual or potential conflicts, while the one from the Council of Europe includes actual or perceived conflicts. Reed mentions that "conflicts of interest are naturally occurring phenomena, not a pathology—that is, they are an inevitable consequence of the fact that people occupy more than one social role." OECD states that the definition of the concept of "(…) 'conflict of interest' has been the subject of many and varying approaches, [although] (…) conflicts of interest cannot simply be avoided or prohibited, and must be defined, identified, and managed." The OECD Guidelines define it as "conflict of interest involves a conflict between the public duty and private interests of a public official, in which the public official has private-capacity interests which could improperly influence the performance of their official duties and responsibilities." The Guidelines for Conflict-of-Interest Policies in EU

Decentralized Agencies structure the elements that constitute a conflict of interest as more specific and therefore lengthy, mentioning that it generally refers impartiality and objectivity of a decision, opinion, or recommendation, or that it might be perceived as being compromised by a personal interest entrusted to an individual. Personal interest may be of financial or nonfinancial nature, stating that not only actual independence but also perception of independence is important, as it affects reputational risk. Considering proportionality, the risk of perceived conflict of interest should be treated as a conflict.

Boards must be fit and proper to run the corporate, both individual directors and the board as a whole. Boards' composition is critical to achieve good governance and prudent management, as well as to irradiate the tone from the top. Selection of board members assumed growing relevance under the fit and proper (respectively competence, and integrity and suitability) profile of directors to ensure that the board—individually and collectively—is suitable to carry out its responsibilities. Its composition should contribute to an effective management and balanced decision-making, keeping in mind the protection of the institution but also ensuring the financial stability as well as the sustainability of the business model. BIS and ECB guidelines—mostly applied transversally in EU outside the eurozone—are leveraged, recommending its adoption by the nonfinancial sector. Staggered boards are characterized by a board being constituted by the election of only a fraction of the members at each time (e.g., annually, or every three or more years). Staggered boards allow maintaining institutional memory, therefore ensuring continuity. Often, regulators provide guidelines for selection of board members in regulated entities. For example, ECB and National Competent Authorities (NCAs) have established fit and proper guidelines for the selection of board members in regulated banking and financial institutions. OECD has published comprehensive Principles of Corporate Governance guidelines applicable to all public entities, while BCBS Principles of Corporate Governance are customized to banking and financing institutions. Even though the principles are meant for public entities, private companies can potentially leverage the guidelines to varying degrees, as can the nonfinancial sector. Investors seek greater transparency in governance standards. Diversity—e.g., gender, age, generation, region of origin, LBGT+, professional and academic backgrounds—and inclusion on the board has been frequently debated these days, and the onus is therefore on the company itself to manage such opportunities or, by opposition to the leverage of best practice, suffer the resulting reputational risks, notably in the ability to retain and attract talent. Gender pay gap is another topic that has gained traction. The discussion about diversity and quotas raises divergent viewpoints, with the culture assuming a growingly less relevance, although still influencing some jurisdictions where the best practices are still emerging. A diverse pool of talents and backgrounds—younger members such as Millennials and Generations Z and X—enlarges the existing set with different perspectives, potentially leading to better decisions. These topics should be part of the global agenda of a board, as discussed along this textbook.

As the dynamics of a board of directors are highly influenced by the chair's leadership, the chairperson must facilitate to set the tone from the top. "The chair runs the board" (*Leadership role*), and "the CEO runs the company" (*Command role*). The role and responsibilities of non-executive directors are Governance, Strategy, and Supervision, while the role of the executive directors are Strategy Development and Supervision of Tactics. In the dualist model, the division of the roles and tasks of NEDs and EDs are clearer due to the existence of two boards—supervisory board and executive board. IVENS Governance Advisors theorized in a conceptual framework named "IVENS ViSTO": Vision—Strategy—Tactics—Operational (Figure 4.1: IVENS ViSTO framework in Section 4.1: "Vision, Strategy, Tactics, and Operational"). This framework is structured for the different decision-making levels. The ViSTO framework should neither be a top-down nor a bottom-up exercise but rather a co-creation. Co-creating the way forward requires involving, engaging, challenging, and aligning all levels of the organization to create a shared commitment on the way forward among executive and non-executive directors, senior management, managers, and staff. It requires an underlying culture of active participation, risk, growth mindset, and humility, especially amongst its leadership. The framework allows directors, management, and staff to memorize in an organization—as a cultural cornerstone—a framework involving the different organizational levels to ensure the achievement of the vision and objectives and its fast and robust execution. It can be used for the development of the strategic plan, its execution, or even the preparation of a meeting.

The Vision involves the defining the purpose of the organization, although in practice it allows to approach consistently the way a project falls under the "dreams." The Strategy is related to the operationalization of the objectives (Vision) through the allocation of scarce resources—notably Talent and Capital—identifying, creating, and developing alliances and partnerships, with individuals and organizations Tactics require the strategy plan including the specific knowledge about the facts or scenarios, i.e., the premises or assumptions considered, which change and adjustment along the process. Operational relates to the bottom of the pyramid, execution, related to skills, ability, and speed of anticipation—move, meet, influence, win-win approach, and control—to achieve the objectives determined for the Vision of either the organization or a specific project.

The chair must be clear and transparent, and the expectations about the board members' contribution must be set and communicated upfront and appropriately. The board of directors are fiduciary to shareholders and stakeholders and must abide with the duty of care, duty of loyalty, and duty of obedience. The board must envision sustainability and long-termism, notably monitoring and adjusting the business model such that it favors all relevant stakeholders. The role of independent non-executive directors is particularly crucial in exercising independent judgment on tasks where there is a potential for conflict of interest. Essentially, non-executive independent directors should scrutinize the performance of senior management embedded within the risk management framework and, therefore, play a crucial role in determining the appropriate remuneration of executive directors, being part of the nomination committee and/or other committees such as governance committee, audit committee, risk and compliance committee, among others. The boards' committees, as well as the "ad hoc board committees" emanate from the board and play a major role in improving the board's effectiveness. The objective of the committees is to divide the board's work into manageable tasks, providing a robust basis for the process of taking informed decisions at the board. Well-informed and high-quality decision-making is critical for the board efficacy. Board evaluation is equally important and disclosing the evaluations to shareholders and stakeholders is meant to demonstrate board effectiveness. Last but not least, taxpayers have emerged as a relevant stakeholder, notably in the financial system linked to processes of bailouts.

Crisis management is a critical issue for a board in terms of its preparation to lead in a crisis with several fronts that boards need to engage to reduce a potential negative impact. Most episodes occur without warning, propelling the organization into turmoil. Boards need to act and stand upright considering a renewed scrutiny, developing a corporate narrative. Business should go on unaffected—but leaders need to plan for crisis management. Some steps will help lead through crisis: plan ahead, think strategically, assess damage, make the most of the operations, make the most out of the people, communicate, move on, and give back. A Chair, CEO, or board will be remembered by what they do, as a board sits on top of the decision-making, and there is no other rationale but to justify board members' actions and goals. Additionally, technology leaves little room to opacity. Accountability is clearly an element of corporate governance to stay.

Committees of the board/supervisory board should be consti-tuted only by non-executive directors, having a majority of indepen-dent directors, and always chaired by an independent director. The audit committee should not be chaired by the chair of the board. Committees of the board play a major role in its effectiveness, ful-filling an important leadership role—similar to that of the chair—to create conditions for overall committee and individual director effec-tiveness and ultimately of the board. Committees should regularly report to the board, supporting its supervisory function. Most juris-dictions always require an audit committee and a nominations and remuneration committee(s), while for example in the financial sys-tem, the risk committee is also compulsory. Committees (as well as "Ad Hoc Committees of the board" if they exist) should have a global agenda and should meet and prepare for the following board. Committees should meet at least monthly. Also, a clear set of rules and responsibilities—usually stated by law and regulation—should be defined and approved by the board as well as posted on the web-site. Chairs of committees should take lead for the self-assessment or assessment of their committees and members. Certain committees are required by law, depending on the jurisdictions or the area of business being in the financial system or in the nonfinancial system. Other committees may also be established as a result of the nature and complexity of the business model or a particular area of focus of the board. Usually, a committee should be set up only if its remit is relevant along the full mandate of the board, as otherwise it will not add value. An alternative to the committees when not imposed by law or that its remit maintain relevance along the board's mandate, is the set-up of "board's ad hoc committees." Their mandate will deal with a specific issue or topic and, therefore, will lose reason for existence along the board's full mandate. This model will ensure that the mem-bers of the board are not tied in a permanent committee, which remit is not justified after a short period of time, as the objectives were qac-complished before the end of the mandate.

A thought relating to a reason for considering changing the designation from "non-executive director" to "governing director" emerges from their roles and the definition and oversight of the business's Vision and Strategy, based on the function they should perform rather than based on the function they should not perform as a non-executive director. It would be preferable to create the right and more focused mindset for the governing directorship's holders. Shareholders should ask themselves the basic reason they select governing directors for the board, as well as about the "false non-executive independents" who add little or no value creation.

Globalization has emerged as a topic that boards should address and be concerned with, namely companies with an international footprint or involved in international trade. Globalization interlinks and impacts geopolitics, geofinance, and geoeconomics, areas of knowledge usually outside the matrix of skills required in board members. However, the challenging developments emerging in the geopolitical arena indicate that boards may require directors with these skills. Globalization is currently being challenged by opposite views, potentially resulting in deglobalization—process of diminishing interdependence and/or integration—among non-aligned geopolitical actors, a relevant topic, notably for organizations with an international Footprint and dealing with Foreign Direct investment (FDI).

FDI is discussed, indicating decision making frameworks and the challenges it raises to boards, varying with stage of internationalization. The quote by Charles Darwin, "Ignorance more frequently begets confidence than does knowledge" emerges as very true in internationalization and should be considered by the board. Another relevant quote from an anonymous author states "(...) when you invest in a foreign country, you contribute with the cash, and your local partner contributes with knowledge; (...) when you divest, you bring the back the knowledge, and your partner keeps the cash (...)." The deep thoughts of those quotes are reasons boards should be deeply involved in foreign direct investment decisions and its monitoring, which presents a significant challenge and task for those without internationalization experience, notably in terms of risks involved, talent to run the operation(s), and cost of opportunity.

A major topic relates to the control of the assets located abroad—notably cash—and the related risks emerging from FDI, including the registration and approval of the investment, the amounts invested being transferred only through the destination country rules that almost always involve the central bank—notably in countries with strong controls over the transfer of foreign currency to shareholders—repatriation of dividends and proceeds, payment of royalties and management fees, and issues involving the authorization for expatriates' residence. Several of these risks—notably the share capital—can be insured by insurance organizations (e.g., The World Bank Group's MIGA—Multilateral Investment Guarantee Agency) in case of expropriation of assets. It is prudent to maintain critical public notary documents (or legally authenticated copies), notably related to the investment authorization, proof of the amount of the investment having been transferred through the central bank, as well as property registrations. FDI involves risks related to compliance issues. Compliance issues such as tax obligations, aggressive tax planning, tax optimization, use of Special Purpose Vehicle (SPV), and money laundering are often complex and must be adequately dealt with by boards.

Current trends involve the emergence of nationalism, deglobalization, and fractious geopolitics, and boards should incorporate members with the right and appropriate skills. This topic should be a part of the global agenda of boards. Good corporate credit rating—investment grade—may provide assurance on corporate creditworthiness and the ability to lend or borrow funds with favorable interest rates, although credit ratings should not be understood as an absolute assurance—as the previous financial crisis has already shown its weaknesses—or be relied upon in case of non-updated credit ratings for a particular company or security issue.

Taxation is very relevant to boards, notably because many directors do not have enough control over the taxation topic, therefore being unable to identify potential risks. The European Commission researched evidence of aggressive tax planning (ATP) in EU,[437] based indicators at macro and firm-level, which considered together may be regarded as a "body of evidence." ATP structures are grouped into three channels: via interest payments, via royalty payments, and via strategic transfer pricing, classifying multinational enterprises into three targets: where the tax base is reduced; lower tax entities where the tax base is increased but taxed at a lower rate; and conduit entities which are in a group with ATP activities, but no clear effect on the tax base is identified. The EU groups them into country-level and bilateral indicators; multinational enterprises' group-level indicators; firm-level indicators by corporate types; and the combination of firm-level indicators. Cyprus, Malta, and Luxembourg raise more corporate taxes as a percent of GDP, while Ireland attracts a sizable amount of corporate tax base. The United Kingdom, Luxembourg, Estonia, and the Netherlands are central to tax optimal repatriation routes. Taxation requires the engagement and guidance, and monitoring of the board, the organization, and functions of accounting and audit divisions are a critical part of the internal control framework, with taxation (notably those involving tax planning structures), robust and conservative accounting procedures under a process of internal checks and balances (notably with the involvement of internal audit), the dissemination of information and recurrence prevention measures, and highly relevant measures to control inappropriate acts with the tone set at the top—the board.

Credit Rating Agencies (CRAs)—the "Big 3," namely, Standard & Poors, Fitch, and Moody's—and Proxy Voting Services are also discussed, as they have a relevant impact in sovereigns and organizations, therefore representing a topic that should be a part of a board's global agenda. CRAs evaluate credit risk based on the current and historical information and data of a sovereign, a corporate, or even an issue of securities. CRAs offer the lender an estimate of the borrower's willingness and ability to timely pay back the principal and interest payments. CRAs are used as a tool for investment decisions, although credit rating are not actual indicators of investment merit. While the exact methodology is usually not disclosed, CRAs assign credit ratings based on broad areas including country risk, business risk, and financial risk. Sovereign credit rating refers to the credit rating of the sovereign state, providing an opinion on credit ratings of the national governments, states, municipalities, and sovereign-supported international entities. Proxy Voting Services allow shareholders, bondholders, and other stakeholders to gain access to Information of the corporate, evaluate its performance, and allow shareholders to cast an informed vote on the important decisions, notably when they cannot attend a meeting. Proxy Voting Services empower all shareholders, notably minority shareholders. Credit Ratings and Proxy Voting Services provide sets of services and consultancy that seem to help them interact with corporates in a more informed and empowered way.

Activism has been part of the landscape in the US for decades, an activity that however has moved to UK and is spreading to Continental Europe and parts of Asia. An institutional investor who is considered as "activist" usually makes substantial and effective use of voting power. It can be an individual or a holding with a significant (or not) number of shares in a listed company. Usually, activists aim to influence the decisions and structure of a company, having in mind a panoply of actions and measures to improvement of performance and payment of higher dividends, including proactive recommendations to boards to sell non-performing or non-vital areas of the business or even to restructure the governance framework. Individual shareholders with a small number of shares rarely have success in influencing boards. However, activists usually play a role in capturing minority shareholders, putting their voting rights together, and gaining influence. Often, large shareholders have significant rights and influence. Additional challenges may involve dual class votes that allow inside shareholders (founder or director) to have voting power disproportionately greater than their number of shares. When boards are under pressure from activists, they should consider setting up an ad hoc committee focused on activism. As a general rule, a board should have the topic on the global agenda.

Decision-making is a part of corporate governance—on top of organizational and structures and a set of processes and systems—that will lead to decision making running an organization. Boards have to ensure well-informed and high-quality decision-making process and therefore need to understand the elements of high-quality decisions and barriers. Types of decisions may include Big-bet decisions, Ad hoc decisions, Cross-cutting decisions, and Delegated decisions, all of which directors should be aware. To maximize high-quality decision-making, boards should implement decision-making policies and procedures with active participation of selected board committees. A line of thought advocates that when decisions go wrong, the fault may lie in the mind of the decision-maker rather than in the decision-making process itself. The main traps discussed in the textbook is the Anchoring Trap, the Status Quo Trap, the Sunk-Cost Trap, the Confirming-Evidence Trap, and the Estimating and Forecasting Trap. A board should act as a competitive ground for constructive debate and positive dynamics among its members. Therefore, awareness of relevant data and information is an element for effective decisions. Also, directors should adopt high ethical standards.

Annual reports represent one of the most relevant tools to communicate with shareholders and stakeholders, which can take different formats and content, as many jurisdictions do not impose a particular model. Some companies publish, at least once a year depending on the jurisdiction—although listed companies in more demanding markets have to publish audited financial statements every six months or even quarterly—a sole report including notably individual and consolidated financial statements as well as elements required by best practice, law, or accounting principles. Others opt for separate reports, namely for financial statements, for data and information not related with the financial information, sustainability, or, in the case of the dual tier model separate annual reports for the executive board and the supervisory board. Best practice and generally accepted accounting principles, as well as other legislative requirements and the capital markets, demand that financial and nonfinancial reporting should be transparent, as annual reports constitute a fundamental element to communicate with the shareholders, capital markets, and other stakeholders. Reporting has increased in the current paradigm with a more extensive regulatory environment and increased complexity of the accounting and financial reporting requirements, as well as in practice originated by corporate governance best practice. It is very relevant that directors are familiar with financial reporting as well as with the content of the annual reports that are of their responsibility. The audit committee has particular relevance in the process of supervising and reviewing its development.

This textbook discusses, in a summary fashion, the standards of the annual reports' content of a company's financial details, risk measures, and corporate governance information. It also usually includes namely a strategic report, the risk review, the financial review, the individual and consolidated financial statements, and corporate governance structure and information. Additional data for shareholders and stakeholders usually includes a sustainability report, considered a relevant component of the annual reporting. It is an opportunity for the corporate to assure its investors and the society about the corporate's stance on environmental, social, and governance issues. As part of the annual report, the external auditors report—external providers assurance—has the purpose of enhancing the degree of confidence of users in financial statements and financial reporting. External auditor's opinion on the compliance with standard accounting practices can be unqualified, qualified, or adverse opinion or be a disclaimer of opinion. The importance of the external audit report is also discussed. The audit committee of the board—and in many jurisdiction the audit board—has particular responsibilities and roles in dealing with external auditors but also the executive and non-executive directors. Shareholders and stakeholders are entitled to know the corporate's financial standings as well as their stand on sustainability issues. The quality, transparency, and rigor of the content of the annual report is related to the objective of demonstrating to shareholders, investors, and other important stakeholders such as regulators and suppliers, the corporation's activities, and the results of the decisions and actions taken and implemented over a period of time. Essentially, the annual report should result from an end-to-end process in its development and preparation. On the other hand, the sustainability report—when adopted as is still voluntary—is seen as an opportunity for the board/supervisory board to assure investors and society about its stance on environmental, social, and governance issues, namely showing commitment toward namely the UN Sustainable Development Goals 2030, climate change, workplace safety, gender equality, well-being of communities, and last but not the least, sustainable economic growth. At the end, the purpose of corporations should be to stand for the betterment of the society by facilitating the well-being of all relevant stakeholders. Robust governance mechanism is the way to efficiently achieve that purpose.

Organizations may have different governance operating models, depending on their needs, complexity of the business model, and the governance model adopted. The textbook discusses the pros, cons, and dynamics of the different governance models, theories of corporate governance, family business governance, business model, and sustainable growth, ESG-related risks and sustainability, organizational risk management and control (IIA three lines model, internal control framework) risk and compliance concepts, internal audit, supervisory mechanism, board selection (fit and proper, board composition, diversity and inclusion) board effectiveness, board dynamics, board committees, board members' roles, globalization and geopolitics, credit rating agencies, proxy services firms, activism, decision-making, annual reporting, and other aspects of corporate governance. The concepts discussed encapsulate a high-level, holistic governance operating model. The method to establish a governance structure and the reason a start-up should do so varies among organizations. However, there is a discussion based on a Deloitte framework for a governance operating model broken into four components: structure, oversight responsibilities, talent and culture, and infrastructure. The board has to make choices in terms of the components, as no one size fits all." Another topic relates to venture capital firms and start-ups. A start-up is a simple collaboration between similar-minded entrepreneurs to employ a scalable business model that has the potential to grow into great profits. There is a line of thought that advocates that, either from the very beginning or as soon as a start-up starts scaling, a comprehensive governance model should be implemented. Venture capital funds finance start-ups at an early stage, and although venture capital investors are not seen often as hawkish as activist investors, they may have a strong say on the board affairs.

Another important topic relates to the SARS-CoV-2 (COVID-19) "black-swan" that caught most public and private organizations off-guard, as most did not anticipate the pandemic risk, revealing the complexity of risk identification and mitigation, a process that requires careful attention of boards. The case of the pandemic brought unprecedented uncertainty. The COVID-19 is a global crisis very different from financial crisis or previous influenzas, representing another element on top of the geopolitical tensions and globalization as well as a dramatic and challenging ethical dilemma between public health and the economy. Sovereigns' massive policy of lockdown and social distancing caught business leaders in an unprecedented paradigm. As a result, the governance framework requires immediate adjustment under an agile, iterative, and scalable process. Global supply chains are severely affected—borders closed bilaterally or unilaterally with a short notice—and most business sectors including microbusiness, small and medium size enterprises and corporates as well as not-for profit organizations were severely affected. Also, cybersecurity, data privacy, and digitalization gained extreme relevance. COVID-19 has fueled a change toward remote learning and working. The emergence of tech-savvy generations is relevant to prepare the business, shift marketing, adjust leadership, and adapt recruiting efforts. Therefore, institutions must look forward to developing the broad and robust talent pool in the long run and, therefore, keep the recruitment base wider in addition to external recruitment process. Ultimately, the chair of the board and/or the chair of the nomination committee plays a leadership role in the nomination process. As every crisis has an end, it is essential to also frame the post-crisis strategy. Often, the executive directors are focused on urgencies and immediate survival or planning, and the non-executive directors should essentially work on shaping future vision and strategy in the post-pandemic era in coordinated collaboration with the management.

Depending on the complexity of the business model—notably the international footprint—the board should consider appointing a "Chief COVID Officer" or "Chief Health Officer" to lead the management of the crisis and coordinate in a transversal fashion the way the organization is dealing with the pandemic. The unprecedented impact in the way boards run and manage organizations, very likely affecting the fit and proper profile of boards—both individually and as a whole—introducing new elements in the required matrix of a board's competences, notably in the debate and balance between the business and the employees and their families' health safety, as well as the need to add competences in this area. Boards—being fit and proper—will need to realign the corporate or globalization strategy, fostering an inclusive environment for all stakeholders. Some actions a board may follow during the COVID-19 crisis include the establishment of briefs to the board/supervisory board of the status; close monitoring of the financial impact; cash-flows and liquidity position; ratification by the board of decisions taken by executive directors in the emergency state outside the delegated powers by the board; review the payment of dividends and share-repurchases; consider requesting governmental assistance; implement robust processes to protect the health and safety risks to employees, customers, or relevant stakeholders, as health and sanitary issue is a new legal demand to be considered; study the impact on operations, employees and compensation, and business relationships; consider disruptions or any potential disruptions in supply chain, including the rise of digital supply chain; and review the IT infrastructure and cybersecurity policies, as more employees work remotely, ensuring coordinated communication with remote stakeholders. Additionally, consider convening an Ad hoc Committee to regularly meet with the board, as well as a Crisis Management and create a contingency and succession plan, in case any board or management member tests positive. Finally, the board should revisit the vision, strategy, and tactics as well as the operational level and the impact in the sustainability of the business model.

The banking system is currently generally better prepared, in terms of capital and liquidity levels, than before the last financial crisis. Although the crisis started outside the financial system, the economic conditions are certainly negatively affecting cash-flows, and sustainability of businesses and economies will, very likely in the short term, be impacted in the non-performing loans portfolio, an event already observed in the first semester of 2020, with banks reporting losses for the period. Also, this unusual circumstance may also lead to Credit Rating Agencies' ratings adjustments on affected sectors, products, or countries. Similar—or even worse—conditions seem to be emerging, in spite of policy measures taken by sovereigns, that may impact multi-notch downgrades of sovereign ratings, an event that may impact negatively the ability to raise capital from shareholders, bondholders, and the financial system.

Finally, the authors wish this manual could be useful for scholars, students, decision-makers, notably executive and non-executive directors, corporate secretaries, as well as managers who have to prepare and provide data and information to the board on a structured and intelligible fashion, to allow for robust decisions when managing an organization.

INDEX

References

1. PwC, 'PwC's 2019 Annual Corporate Directors Survey', 2019 <https://www.pwc.com/us/en/services/governance-insights-center/assets/pwc-2019-annual-corporate-directors-survey-full-report-v2.pdf.pdf> [accessed 5 May 2020].

2. SEC, 'Institutional Investors: Power and Responsibility', 2020 <https://www.sec.gov/news/speech/2013-spch041913laahtm> [accessed 28 September 2020].

3. A A Berle and G C Means, 'The Modern Corporation and Private Property' (Transaction Publishers, 1932) <https://doi.org/10.2307/3475545>.

4. R Coase, 'The Nature of the Firm', *Economica*, 1937 <https://doi.org/10.3853/j.0067-1975.24.1958.646>.

5. R Coase, 'The Problem of Social Cost', *The Journal of Law & Economics*, 3 (1960), 1–44 <http://www.jstor.org/stable/724810>.

6. P A Samuelson, 'Foundations of Economic Analysis' (Harvard University Press, 1983).

7. P A Samuelson and W D Nordhaus, 'Economics' (McGraw-Hill, 2009).

8. E F Fama, 'Efficient Capital Markets: A Review of Theory and Empirical Work', *The Journal of Finance*, 1970.

9. M C Jensen and W H Meckling, 'Theory of the Firm: Managerial Behaviour, Agency, Costs and Ownership', *Journal of Financial Economics*, 1976 <https://doi.org/http://dx.doi.org/10.1016/0304-405X(76)90026-X>.

10. A D Chandler, 'The Visible Hand: The Managerial Revolution in American Business', 1977 <https://en.wikipedia.org/wiki/The_Visible_Hand:_The_Managerial_Revolution_in_American_Business> [accessed 1 April 2019].

11. A Cadbury, 'Report of the Committee on The Financial Aspects of Corporate Governance, The Committee on the Financial Aspects

of Corporate Governance and Gee and Co. Ltd.', 1992 <https://doi.org/ISBN 0 85258 913 1>.

12. D Higgs, 'Review of the Role and Effectiveness of Non-Executive Directors', *Review Literature and Arts of the Americas*, 2003.

13. ICAEW, 'When Is Comply or Explain the Right Approach?' <https://www.icaew.com/technical/corporate-governance/principles/principles-articles/when-is-comply-or-explain-the-right-approach> [accessed 25 June 2019].

14. T Levine, M Beller, and J T Hancock, 'Dot-Com Bubble', in *Encyclopedia of Deception*, 2014 <https://doi.org/10.4135/9781483306902.n117>.

15. SOX, 'Sarbanes-Oxley Act of 2002', *The Public Company Accounting Reform and Investor*, 2002.

16. Proskauer, 'The New UK Financial Services Act 2010 Makes Significant Reforms; FSA Wins Reprieve From Abolition' <https://www.proskauer.com/alert/the-new-uk-financial-services-act-2010> [accessed 5 March 2019].

17. FRC, 'FRC Guidance for Boards and Board Committees' <https://www.frc.org.uk/directors/corporate-governance-and-stewardship/uk-corporate-governance-code/frc-guidance-for-boards-and-board-committees> [accessed 5 March 2019].

18. BIS, 'Fit and Proper Principles', 2014 <https://www.bis.org/publ/bcbs47c4.pdf> [accessed 5 March 2019].

19. EC, 'Non-Financial Reporting', 2014 <https://ec.europa.eu/info/business-economy-euro/company-reporting-and-auditing/company-reporting/non-financial-reporting_en> [accessed 5 March 2019].

20. BCBS, 'Corporate Governance Principles for Banks', 2015 <https://www.bis.org/bcbs/publ/d328.pdf> [accessed 5 March 2019].

21. OECD, 'G20/OECD Principles of Corporate Governance 2015', 2015 <https://doi.org/10.1787/9789264236882-en>.

22. EBA, 'Guidelines on Internal Governance under Directive 2013/36/EU', 2017 <https://eba.europa.eu/documents/10180/1972987/Final+

Guidelines+on+Internal+Governance+%28EBA-GL-2017-11%29.
pdf> [accessed 26 March 2019].

23. IIA, 'Three Lines Model', 2020 <https://global.theiia.org/about/
about-internal-auditing/Public Documents/Three-Lines-Model-
Updated.pdf> [accessed 2 October 2020].

24. S C Araújo, 'Miopia Estratégica Na Corporate Governance'
(Instituto Superior de Ciências Sociais e Políticas, 2020) <https://
www.repository.utl.pt/handle/10400.5/20158> [accessed 30
October 2020].

25. IMF, 'The IMF's Approach to Promoting Good Governance and
Combating Corruption', 2005 <https://www.imf.org/external/np/
gov/guide/eng/index.htm> [accessed 22 October 2020].

26. T Castro and D P Ferraz, *Fit and Proper—Evitar Um Cisne Negro
Ou Há Um Elefante Na Sala?*, 2018 <https://ifb.pt/wp-content/
uploads/2018/11/IFB-InforBanca-114-NOV2018.pdf> [accessed
22 October 2020].

27. IFC, 'Corporate Governance' <https://www.ifc.org/wps/wcm/
connect/Topics_Ext_Content/IFC_External_Corporate_Site/
IFC+CG> [accessed 5 March 2019].

28. OECD, 'G20/OECD Principles of Corporate Governance 2015',
2015 <https://doi.org/10.1787/9789264236882-en>.

29. FT, 'Audit Committee Definition from Financial Times Lexicon'
<http://lexicon.ft.com/Term?term=audit-committee> [accessed 5
March 2019].

30. L Rathod, '6 Ways Boards Benefit From Good Corporate
Governance', *Diligent*, 2018 <https://diligent.com/en-gb/blog/6-
ways-boards-benefit-from-good-corporate-governance/>
[accessed 19 October 2020].

31. SWFI Institute, 'What Is a Sovereign Wealth Fund?', 2020 <https://
www.swfinstitute.org/research/sovereign-wealth-fund> [accessed
29 September 2020].

32. SWFI, 'Top 89 Largest Sovereign Wealth Fund Rankings by
Total Assets—SWFI', 2020 <https://www.swfinstitute.org/

fund-rankings/sovereign-wealth-fund> [accessed 29 September 2020].

33. Government.no, 'The Government Pension Fund (Norway)', 2020 <https://www.regjeringen.no/en/topics/the-economy/the-government-pension-fund/id1441/> [accessed 29 September 2020].

34. F L Silanes, *Board Committees, Duty of Care and Duty of Loyalty*, 2019.

35. M Brush, 'INVESTING IT;It Keeps Your Pants On. But Can It Fatten Your Wallet?', *The New York Times*, 1996 <https://www.nytimes.com/1996/04/14/business/investing-it-it-keeps-your-pants-on-but-can-it-fatten-your-wallet.html> [accessed 30 September 2020].

36. FundingUniverse, 'History of Velcro Industries N.V.', 2020 <http://www.fundinguniverse.com/company-histories/velcro-industries-n-v-history/> [accessed 30 September 2020].

37. GreenBiz Editors, 'Lessons from Enron on Corporate Governance', *GreenBiz*, 2002 <https://www.greenbiz.com/blog/2002/04/30/lessons-enron-corporate-governance> [accessed 11 March 2019].

38. FundingUniverse, 'History of Velcro Industries N.V.', 2020 <http://www.fundinguniverse.com/company-histories/velcro-industries-n-v-history/> [accessed 30 September 2020].

39. J Armour, H Hansmann, and R Kraakman, 'Agency Problems, Legal Strategies, and Enforcement', *Oxford Legal Studies Research Paper*, 2009 <https://doi.org/10.1136/vr.d7634>.

40. K Amadeo, 'Market Economy: Definition, Pros, Cons, Examples', *The Balance*, 2020 <https://www.thebalance.com/market-economy-characteristics-examples-pros-cons-3305586> [accessed 30 September 2020].

41. O Rusty, G Anthony, and M Melissa, '2019 Global & Regional Trends in Corporate Governance', *Harvard Law School Forum*, 2018 <https://corpgov.law.harvard.edu/2018/12/30/2019-global-regional-trends-in-corporate-governance/> [accessed 21 March 2019].

42. M Fitzgerald, 'Nearly 200 CEOs Say Shareholder Value Is No Longer a Main Objective', *CNBC*, 2019 <https://www.cnbc.com/2019/08/19/the-ceos-of-nearly-two-hundred-companies-say-shareholder-value-is-no-longer-their-main-objective.html> [accessed 20 August 2019].

43. M Sun, 'More U.S. Companies Separating Chief Executive and Chairman Roles', *The Wall Street Journal*, 2019 <https://www.wsj.com/articles/more-u-s-companies-separating-chief-executive-and-chairman-roles-11548288502> [accessed 1 October 2020].

44. S Ross, 'What Are Some Examples of Different Corporate Governance Systems?', *Investopedia*, 2020 <https://www.investopedia.com/ask/answers/051115/what-are-some-examples-different-corporate-governance-systems-across-world.asp> [accessed 1 October 2020].

45. Lexology, 'Corporate Leadership in Norway', 2019 <https://www.lexology.com/library/detail.aspx?g=cf091538-c1c7-47cb-8e01-24a2f1533437> [accessed 9 July 2020].

46. W Kenton, 'Nordic Model', *Investopedia*, 2019 <https://www.investopedia.com/terms/n/nordic-model.asp> [accessed 9 July 2020].

47. A Guluzade, 'Explained, the Role of China's State-Owned Companies', *World Economic Forum* <https://www.weforum.org/agenda/2019/05/why-chinas-state-owned-companies-still-have-a-key-role-to-play/> [accessed 1 July 2019].

48. A Edmans, 'Corporate Governance in China' <http://alexedmans.com/corporate-governance-in-china/> [accessed 19 March 2019].

49. R George and H Dominic, 'Corporate Governance and Directors' Duties in China: Overview | Practical Law', *Thomson Reuters* <https://uk.practicallaw.thomsonreuters.com/4-502-3042> [accessed 19 March 2019].

50. T Evgenia, F Sergey, and G Viacheslav, 'Corporate Governance and Directors' Duties: Russian Federation | Practical Law', *Thomson Reuters* <https://uk.practicallaw.thomsonreuters.com/

5-502-1245?transitionType=Default&contextData=(sc.Default)> [accessed 20 March 2019].

51. The World Bank, 'Corporate Governance in Russia: Report on the Observance of Standards and Codes' <https://www.worldbank. org/en/country/russia/publication/rosc> [accessed 1 July 2019].

52. Mitsubishi Corporation, 'Integrated Report / Annual Report', 2019 <https://www.mitsubishicorp.com/jp/en/ir/library/ar/> [accessed 2 October 2020].

53. MUFG, 'Integrated Report', 2020 <https://www.mufg.jp/dam/ir/ report/annual_report/pdf/ir2020_all.pdf> [accessed 2 October 2020].

54. N Matsunami and K Tatsumi, 'Japan: Corporate Governance Laws and Regulations 2020', *ICLG*, 2020 <https://iclg.com/practice-areas/corporate-governance-laws-and-regulations/japan> [accessed 2 October 2020].

55. Tokyo Stock Exchange, *Japan's Corporate Governance Code*, 2018 <https://www.jpx.co.jp/english/news/1020/b5b4pj000000j-vxr-att/20180602_en.pdf> [accessed 2 October 2020].

56. C Jonathan and J Eun-Young, 'Samsung, Hyundai Chiefs Questioned as Scandal Grips South Korea', *The Wall Street Journal* <https://www.wsj.com/articles/samsung-hyundai-chiefs-to-be-questioned-as-political-scandal-roils-south-korea-1480943777> [accessed 19 March 2019].

57. ICLG, 'International Comparative Legal Guides' <https://iclg.com/ practice-areas/corporate-governance-laws-and-regulations/ korea> [accessed 1 July 2019].

58. S L Hyung and Y K Yoon, 'Corporate Governance and Directors' Duties in South Korea: Overview | Practical Law', *Thomson Reuters* <https://uk.practicallaw.thomsonreuters.com/8-209-5002?transiti onType=Default&contextData=(sc.Default)&firstPage=true&com p=pluk&bhcp=1> [accessed 20 March 2019].

59. The Times of India, 'Satyam's Chairman Ramalinga Raju Resigns, Admits Fraud' <https://timesofindia.indiatimes.com/business/india-

business/Satyams-chairman-Ramalinga-Raju-resigns-admits-fraud/
articleshow/3946088.cms> [accessed 18 March 2019].

60. Vaish Associates Advocates, 'Corporate Governance Framework in India—Corporate/Commercial Law—India', *Mondaq* <http://www.mondaq.com/india/x/456460/Shareholders/Corporate+Governance+Framework+In+India> [accessed 19 March 2019].

61. Proschool, 'Corporate Governance in India—Why Is It so Critical?' <https://www.proschoolonline.com/blog/corporate-governance-india> [accessed 1 July 2019].

62. D Block and A Gerstner, 'One-Tier vs. Two-Tier Board Structure: A Comparison Between the United States and Germany', 2016 <http://scholarship.law.upenn.edu/fisch_2016http://scholarship.law.upenn.edu/fisch_2016/1> [accessed 22 July 2019].

63. Applied Corporate Governance, 'Best Corporate Governance Practice—The Five Golden Rules' <https://www.applied-corporate-governance.com/best-corporate-governance-practice/> [accessed 18 March 2019].

64. A Orencia, '10 Vision Statement Examples To Spark Your Imagination', *FitSmallBusiness*, 2017 <https://fitsmallbusiness.com/vision-statement-examples/> [accessed 15 October 2019].

65. A Osterwalder, Y Pigneur, and C L Tucci, 'Clarifying Business Models: Origins, Present, and Future of the Concept', *Communications of the Association for Information Systems*, 2005 <https://doi.org/10.17705/1cais.01601>.

66. A Hill, 'What Is Economics?—Definition, History, Timeline & Importance Video' <https://study.com/academy/lesson/what-is-economics-definition-history-timeline-importance.html> [accessed 15 October 2019].

67. T W Malnight, I Buche, and C Dhanaraj, 'Put Purpose at the Core of Your Strategy', *Harvard Business Review* <https://hbr.org/2019/09/put-purpose-at-the-core-of-your-strategy> [accessed 29 September 2019].

68. Barclays, 'Barclays Core Values and Purpose', 2019 <https://home.barclays/who-we-are/our-strategy/purpose-and-values/> [accessed 5 October 2020].

69. Bain & Company, 'Management Tools—Strategic Planning ', 2018 <https://www.bain.com/insights/management-tools-strategic-planning/> [accessed 5 October 2020].

70. ClearPoint Strategy, 'Strategic Planning Vs. Operational Planning: The 5 Main Differences', 2020 <https://www.clearpointstrategy.com/strategic-planning-vs-operational-planning/amp/> [accessed 5 October 2020].

71. A G Pateli and G M Giaglis, 'A Research Framework for Analyzing EBusiness Models', *European Journal of Information Systems*, 2004 <https://doi.org/10.1057/palgrave.ejis.3000513>.

72. M W Johnson, C M Christensen, and H Kagermann, 'Reinventing Your Business Model', *Harvard Business Review*, 2008.

73. P Greenberg, 'CRM at the Speed of Light: Social CRM 2.0 Strategies, Tools, and Techniques for Engaging Your Customers', *2009*, 2009.

74. L Schweizer, 'Concept and Evolution of Business Models', *Journal of General Management*, 2005 <https://doi.org/10.1177/030630700503100203>.

75. I T Lopes, D P Ferraz, and A G Rodrigues, 'The Drivers of Profitability in the Top 30 Major Airlines Worldwide', *Measuring Business Excellence*, 2016 <https://doi.org/10.1108/MBE-09-2015-0045>.

76. C Fisher, 'Researching and Writing a Dissertation: A Guidebook for Business Students ', *Prentice Hall*, 2007 <https://books.google.pt/books?id=JaUMkIFiuD0C&printsec=frontcover&source=gbs_ge_summary_r&cad=0#v=onepage&q&f=false> [accessed 5 October 2020].

77. A Osterwalder and Y Pigneur, 'Business Model Generation—Canvas', *Wiley*, 2010.

78. A Osterwalder and Y Pigneur, 'Business Model Generation—Canvas', *Wiley*, 2010.

79. A Osterwalder and Y Pigneur, 'Business Model Generation—Canvas', *Wiley*, 2010.

80. ECB, 'ECB Guides to ICAAP and ILAAP' <https://www.banking-supervision.europa.eu/press/publications/newsletter/2019/html/ssm.nl190213_3.en.html> [accessed 11 July 2019].

81. Y Doz, 'The Strategic Decisions That Caused Nokia's Failure', *INSEAD Knowledge*, 2017 <https://knowledge.insead.edu/strategy/the-strategic-decisions-that-caused-nokias-failure-7766> [accessed 5 October 2020].

82. A Spiliakos, 'What Does "Sustainability" Mean in Business?', *Harvard Business School Online* <https://online.hbs.edu/blog/post/what-is-sustainability-in-business> [accessed 26 June 2019].

83. J Chen, 'Corporate Social Responsibility (CSR) Definition', *Investopedia*, 2020 <https://www.investopedia.com/terms/c/corp-social-responsibility.asp> [accessed 5 October 2020].

84. M Grant, 'Sustainability', *Investopedia*, 2020 <https://www.investopedia.com/terms/s/sustainability.asp> [accessed 5 October 2020].

85. B Barnes, 'Weinstein Company Files for Bankruptcy and Revokes Nondisclosure Agreements', *The New York Times*, 2019 <https://www.nytimes.com/2018/03/19/business/weinstein-company-bankruptcy.html> [accessed 6 May 2020].

86. J M Chua, 'The Rise in ESG Ratings: What's the Score?', *Vogue Business*, 2020 <https://www.voguebusiness.com/sustainability/the-rise-in-esg-ratings-whats-the-score> [accessed 30 October 2020].

87. UN, '17 Sustainable Development Goals' <https://sustainabledevelopment.un.org/?menu=1300> [accessed 26 June 2019].

88. McKinsey, 'Sustainability's Deepening Imprint' <https://www.mckinsey.com/business-functions/sustainability/our-insights/sustainabilitys-deepening-imprint> [accessed 26 June 2019].

89. EU, 'Regulation (EU) 2020/852 on the Establishment of a Framework to Facilitate Sustainable Investment, and Amending Regulation (EU)

2019/2088' <https://eur-lex.europa.eu/legal-content/EN/TXT/?uri= CELEX:32020R0852> [accessed 7 October 2020].

90. EU, 'Taxonomy Technical Report', 2019 <https://ec.europa.eu/ info/sites/info/files/business_economy_euro/banking_and_ finance/documents/190618-sustainable-finance-teg-report-tax-onomy_en.pdf> [accessed 29 July 2019].

91. EU, 'Taxonomy Technical Report', 2019 <https://ec.europa.eu/ info/sites/info/files/business_economy_euro/banking_and_ finance/documents/190618-sustainable-finance-teg-report-tax-onomy_en.pdf> [accessed 29 July 2019].

92. EIB, 'Climate Awareness Bonds', 2020 <https://www.eib.org/en/ investor_relations/disclaimer.htm> [accessed 5 October 2020].

93. FASB, 'For the Investor: Should the FASB Have a Role in Sustainability Disclosures?', 2017 <https://www.fasb.org/cs/Sat ellite?c=Page&cid=1176168752524&pagename=FASB%2FPage %2FSectionPage> [accessed 5 October 2020].

94. T Ko, 'IFRS—Sustainability Reporting and Its Relevance to the IFRS Foundation', *IFRS*, 2020 <https://www.ifrs.org/news-and-events/2020/05/sustainability-reporting-and-its-relevance-to-the-ifrs-foundation/> [accessed 5 October 2020].

95. SASB, 'Materiality Map', 2020 <https://materiality.sasb.org/> [accessed 5 October 2020].

96. HSBC, 'ESG Update 2019', 2020 <https://www.hsbc.com/inves-tors/esg-investors> [accessed 5 October 2020].

97. EDP Portugal, 'Sustainability Is Part of EDP's DNA' <https://por-tugal.edp.com/en/sustainability-1> [accessed 26 June 2019].

98. UN, 'Paris Agreement', 2016 <https://en.wikipedia.org/wiki/ Paris_Agreement> [accessed 28 June 2019].

99. 'European Family Businesses—Facts & Figures' <http://www. europeanfamilybusinesses.eu/family-businesses/facts-figures> [accessed 24 October 2019].

100. EY and University of St.Gallen, 'Global Family Business Index' <http://familybusinessindex.com/> [accessed 22 September 2019].

101. BNP Paribas Wealth Management, 'The Cousin Consortium' <https://wealthmanagement.bnpparibas/ch/en/expert-voices/the-cousin-consortium.html> [accessed 25 October 2019].

102. IFC, 'IFC Family Business Governance Handbook', *International Finance Corporation*, 2011.

103. J A Davis, 'Fundamentals of Family Business System Governance' <https://store.hbr.org/product/fundamentals-of-family-busi-ness-system-governance/807019> [accessed 23 September 2019].

104. J A Davis, 'Fundamentals of Family Business System Governance' <https://store.hbr.org/product/fundamentals-of-family-busi-ness-system-governance/807019> [accessed 23 September 2019].

105. J A Davis, 'Fundamentals of Family Business System Governance' <https://store.hbr.org/product/fundamentals-of-family-busi-ness-system-governance/807019> [accessed 23 September 2019].

106. R L Narva and B G Silver, 'How to Create Effective Governance in a Family Controlled Enterprise?' <http://narvaandcompany.com/how-to-create-effective-governance-in-a-family-con-trolled-enterprise/> [accessed 24 September 2019].

107. K Ramachandran, 'Should You Join the Family Business or Work Elsewhere First?', *HBR Ascend*, 2020 <https://hbrascend.org/topics/should-you-join-the-family-business-or-work-elsewhere-first/> [accessed 20 April 2020].

108. BCBS, 'Corporate Governance Principles for Banks', 2015 <https://www.bis.org/bcbs/publ/d328.pdf> [accessed 5 March 2019].

109. Banco de Portugal, 'Supervision—Corporate Governance and Internal Control System' <https://www.bportugal.pt/en/

page/supervision-corporate-governance-and-internal-control-system> [accessed 5 March 2019].

110. EBA, 'Guidelines on Internal Governance under Directive 2013/36/EU', 2017 <https://eba.europa.eu/documents/10180/1972987/Final+Guidelines+on+Internal+Governance+%28EBA-GL-2017-11%29.pdf> [accessed 26 March 2019].

111. E Larson, '5 Key Elements of Good Internal Controls—Beene Garter', *Beenegarter* <https://beenegarter.com/5-key-elements-of-good-internal-controls/> [accessed 18 November 2019].

112. IIA, 'The Three Lines of Defence in Effective Risk Management and Control' <https://global.theiia.org/standards-guidance/recommended-guidance/Pages/The-Three-Lines-of-Defense-in-Effective-Risk-Management-and-Control.aspx> [accessed 25 March 2019].

113. IIA, 'Three Lines Model', 2020 <https://global.theiia.org/about/about-internal-auditing/Public Documents/Three-Lines-Model-Updated.pdf> [accessed 2 October 2020].

114. D J Anderson and G Eubanks, 'Leveraging COSO across the Three Lines of Defence', *COSO*, 2015 <https://www.coso.org/Documents/COSO-2015-3LOD.pdf> [accessed 2 October 2020].

115. IIA, 'Three Lines Model', 2020 <https://global.theiia.org/about/about-internal-auditing/Public Documents/Three-Lines-Model-Updated.pdf> [accessed 2 October 2020].

116. BCBS, 'Corporate Governance Principles for Banks', 2015 <https://www.bis.org/bcbs/publ/d328.pdf> [accessed 5 March 2019].

117. I Arndorfer and A Minto, 'The "Four Lines of Defence Model" for Financial Institution', *BIS*, 2015 <https://www.bis.org/fsi/fsi-papers11.pdf> [accessed 15 July 2019].

118. COSO, 'Guidance on Monitoring Internal Control Systems', 2009 <https://www.coso.org/Documents/COSO_Guidance_On_Monitoring_Intro_online1_002.pdf> [accessed 6 October 2020].

119. EBA, 'Guidelines on Internal Governance under Directive 2013/36/EU', 2017 <https://eba.europa.eu/documents/10180/1972987/Final+Guidelines+on+Internal+Governance+%28EBA-GL-2017-11%29.pdf> [accessed 26 March 2019].

120. COSO, 'Internal Control—Integrated Framework Executive Summary', 2013 <https://www.coso.org/Documents/990025P-Executive-Summary-final-may20.pdf> [accessed 26 March 2019].

121. S McNally, 'The 2013 COSO Framework & SOX Compliance' <https://www.coso.org/documents/COSO McNallyTransition Article-Final COSO Version Proof_5-31-13.pdf> [accessed 26 March 2019].

122. EBA, 'Guidelines on Internal Governance under Directive 2013/36/EU', 2017 <https://eba.europa.eu/documents/10180/1972987/Final+Guidelines+on+Internal+Governance+%28EBA-GL-2017-11%29.pdf> [accessed 26 March 2019].

123. IIA, 'International Professional Practices Framework ', 2020 <https://na.theiia.org/standards-guidance/Pages/Standards-and-Guidance-IPPF.aspx> [accessed 6 October 2020].

124. IIA, 'Independence and Objectivity' <https://na.theiia.org/standards-guidance/topics/Pages/Independence-and-Objectivity.aspx> [accessed 23 October 2019].

125. IIA, 'Independence and Objectivity—Rotation of the Head of Internal', 2013 <https://www.iia.org.uk/media/419123/rotation_of_hias.pdf> [accessed 18 November 2019].

126. IIA, 'Independence and Objectivity—Rotation of the Head of Internal', 2013 <https://www.iia.org.uk/media/419123/rotation_of_hias.pdf> [accessed 18 November 2019].

127. BCBS, 'The Internal Audit Function in Banks', 2011 <https://www.bis.org/publ/bcbs210.pdf#page=9&zoom=100,0,369> [accessed 18 November 2019].

128. BCBS, 'The Internal Audit Function in Banks', 2011 <https://www.bis.org/publ/bcbs210.pdf#page=9&zoom=100,0,369> [accessed 18 November 2019].

129. IFAC, 'ISA 260', 2016 <https://www.ifac.org/system/files/publications/files/ISA-260-Revised_1.pdf> [accessed 6 October 2020].

130. IFAC, 'ISA 315', 2009 <https://www.ifac.org/system/files/downloads/a017-2010-iaasb-handbook-isa-315.pdf> [accessed 6 October 2020].

131. IFAC, 'ISA 610', 2009 <https://www.ifac.org/system/files/downloads/a034-2010-iaasb-handbook-isa-610.pdf> [accessed 6 October 2020].

132. CIIA, 'Managing Internal Audit', 2019 <https://www.iia.org.uk/resources/managing-internal-audit> [accessed 6 October 2020].

133. BCBS, 'The Internal Audit Function in Banks', 2011 <https://www.bis.org/publ/bcbs210.pdf#page=9&zoom=100,0,369> [accessed 18 November 2019].

134. CIIA, 'Risk Based Internal Audit Plan' <https://www.iia.org.uk/media/408909/201307iaplans-appendix1.pdf> [accessed 23 October 2019].

135. IIA, '1200—Proficiency and Due Professional Care', 2009 <https://www.iia.nl/SiteFiles/IIA_leden/Parktijkadviezen/PA 1200-1.pdf> [accessed 7 October 2020].

136. I Arndorfer and A Minto, 'The "Four Lines of Defence Model" for Financial Institution', *BIS*, 2015 <https://www.bis.org/fsi/fsipapers11.pdf> [accessed 15 July 2019].

137. BIS, 'SRP31—Interest Rate Risk in the Banking Book', 2019 <https://www.bis.org/basel_framework/chapter/SRP/31.htm?tldate=20191231&inforce=20191215> [accessed 7 October 2020].

138. BCBS, 'The Internal Audit Function in Banks', 2012 <https://www.bis.org/publ/bcbs223.pdf> [accessed 15 July 2019].

139. EC, 'Overview: Making Markets Work Better' <https://ec.europa.eu/competition/general/overview_en.html> [accessed 22 January 2020].

140. COSO, 'Enterprise Risk Management', 2017 <https://www.coso.org/Documents/2017-COSO-ERM-Integrating-with-Strategy-and-Performance-Executive-Summary.pdf> [accessed 19 November 2019].

141. COSO, 'Applying Enterprise Risk Management to Environmental, Social and Governance-Related Risks', 2018 <https://www.coso.org/Documents/COSO-WBCSD-ESGERM-Guidance-Full.pdf> [accessed 14 May 2019].

142. B Nauman, 'ESG Money Market Funds Grow 15% in First Half of 2019', *FT*, 2019 <https://www.ft.com/content/2c7b8438-a5a6-11e9-984c-fac8325aaa04> [accessed 29 July 2019].

143. J Peppel, *Board Risk Committee, Risk Appetite and Internal Control Framework*, 2017.

144. Oliver Wyman, 'Streamlining Risk, Compliance and Internal Audit', 2015 <https://www.oliverwyman.com/content/dam/oliver-wyman/global/en/2015/mar/Streamlining_Risk_Compliance_Internal_Audit.pdf> [accessed 12 February 2020].

145. EU, 'Regulation (EU) 2020/852 on the Establishment of a Framework to Facilitate Sustainable Investment, and Amending Regulation (EU) 2019/2088' <https://eur-lex.europa.eu/legal-content/EN/TXT/?uri=CELEX:32020R0852> [accessed 7 October 2020].

146. EU, 'Taxonomy Technical Report', 2019 <https://ec.europa.eu/info/sites/info/files/business_economy_euro/banking_and_finance/documents/190618-sustainable-finance-teg-report-taxonomy_en.pdf> [accessed 29 July 2019].

147. IP Bank B.V., *Bowtie Methodology Manual*, 2016 <https://www.icao.int/safety/SafetyManagement/SMI/Documents/BowTieXP Methodology Manual v15.pdf> [accessed 7 October 2020].

148. EU, 'Regulation (EU) 2020/852 on the Establishment of a Framework to Facilitate Sustainable Investment, and Amending Regulation (EU) 2019/2088' <https://eur-lex.europa.eu/legal-content/EN/TXT/?uri=CELEX:32020R0852> [accessed 7 October 2020].

149. COSO, 'Guidance on Monitoring Internal Control Systems', 2009 <https://www.coso.org/Documents/COSO_Guidance_On_Monitoring_Intro_online1_002.pdf> [accessed 6 October 2020].

150. S Tranchard, 'The New ISO 31000 Keeps Risk Management Simple', *ISO* <https://www.iso.org/news/ref2263.html> [accessed 27 March 2019].

151. Barclays, 'Barclays PLC Annual Report 2019', 2019 <https://home.barclays/investor-relations/reports-and-events/annual-reports/> [accessed 9 October 2020].

152. Barclays, 'Barclays PLC Annual Report 2019', 2019 <https://home.barclays/investor-relations/reports-and-events/annual-reports/> [accessed 9 October 2020].

153. C Boren, 'The NBA's China-Daryl Morey Backlash, Explained', *The Washington Post*, 2019 <https://www.washingtonpost.com/sports/2019/10/07/nba-china-tweet-daryl-morey/> [accessed 6 April 2020].

154. D Bohn, 'US Cyberattack Reportedly Hit Iranian Targets', *The Verge* <https://www.theverge.com/2019/6/22/18714010/us-cyberattack-iranian-targets-missile-command-report> [accessed 16 July 2019].

155. R Daniel, 'FTC Reportedly Approves $5 Billion Settlement of Facebook Privacy Dispute', *TheStreet* <https://www.thestreet.com/investing/stocks/ftc-reportedly-approves-5-billion-settle-ment-facebook-privacy-dispute-15018243> [accessed 16 July 2019].

156. J Croft, 'Hotel Group Marriott Faces London Lawsuit over Huge Data Breach', *Financial Times*, 2020 <https://www.ft.com/

content/d6202d00-a173-4b15-b68a-46764934c76b> [accessed 9 October 2020].

157. BBC, 'British Airways Faces Record £183m Fine for Data Breach', 2019 <https://www.bbc.com/news/business-48905907> [accessed 9 October 2020].

158. K Paul, 'What Is Libra? All You Need to Know about Facebook's New Cryptocurrency', *The Guardian*, 2019 <https://www.the-guardian.com/technology/2019/jun/18/what-is-libra-facebook-new-cryptocurrency> [accessed 9 October 2020].

159. FSB, 'Measures to Reduce Misconduct Risk', 2015 <https://www.fsb.org/2015/11/measures-to-reduce-misconduct-risk/> [accessed 25 June 2020].

160. IRM, 'Risk Appetite and Tolerance' <https://www.theirm.org/knowledge-and-resources/thought-leadership/risk-appetite-and-tolerance.aspx> [accessed 26 March 2019].

161. Deloitte, 'Risk Appetite Frameworks', 2020 <https://www2.deloitte.com/content/dam/Deloitte/au/Documents/risk/deloitte-au-risk-appetite-frameworks-0614.pdf> [accessed 9 October 2020].

162. ECB, 'Risk Appetite Frameworks: Good Progress But Still Room for Improvement' <https://www.bankingsupervision.europa.eu/press/speeches/date/2018/html/ssm.sp180410.en.html> [accessed 27 March 2019].

163. BIS, 'SRP30—Risk Management', 2019 <https://www.bis.org/basel_framework/chapter/SRP/30.htm> [accessed 12 February 2020].

164. J Peppel, *Board Risk Committee, Risk Appetite and Internal Control Framework*, 2017.

165. D Cossin and A H Lu, 'The Four Tiers of Conflict of Interest Faced by Board Directors', *IMD* <https://www.imd.org/research-knowledge/articles/the-four-tiers-of-conflict-of-interest-faced-by-board-directors/> [accessed 5 June 2019].

166. IFRS, 'IAS 24 Related Party Disclosures', 2020 <https://www.ifrs.org/issued-standards/list-of-standards/ias-24-related-party-disclosures/> [accessed 9 July 2020].

167. M Brush, 'INVESTING IT;It Keeps Your Pants On. But Can It Fatten Your Wallet?', *The New York Times*, 1996 <https://www.nytimes.com/1996/04/14/business/investing-it-it-keeps-your-pants-on-but-can-it-fatten-your-wallet.html> [accessed 30 September 2020].

168. FCA, 'DISP 1.3 Complaints Handling Rules', 2020 <https://www.handbook.fca.org.uk/handbook/DISP/1/3.html> [accessed 9 July 2020].

169. S Araki, 'Tax and Corporate Governance: What Tax Authorities Expect of Companies', *CIAT*, 2018 <https://www.ciat.org/tax-and-corporate-governance-what-tax-authorities-expect-of-companies/?lang=en> [accessed 3 June 2020].

170. PwC, 'Conventions for the Avoidance of Double Taxation', 2019 <https://www.pwc.pt/en/pwcinforfisco/tax-guide/2019/conventions-for-the-avoidance-of-double-taxation.html> [accessed 16 July 2020].

171. Iceland Revenue and Customs, 'Double Taxation Agreements', 2020 <https://www.rsk.is/english/individuals/double-taxation-conventions/> [accessed 16 July 2020].

172. OECD, 'Aggressive Tax Planning', 2020 <https://www.oecd.org/tax/aggressive/> [accessed 9 July 2020].

173. R Neate, 'New Study Deems Amazon Worst for "aggressive" Tax Avoidance', *The Guardian*, 2019 <https://www.theguardian.com/business/2019/dec/02/new-study-deems-amazon-worst-for-aggressive-tax-avoidance> [accessed 9 July 2020].

174. R Neate, 'New Study Deems Amazon Worst for "aggressive" Tax Avoidance', *The Guardian*, 2019 <https://www.theguardian.com/business/2019/dec/02/new-study-deems-amazon-worst-for-aggressive-tax-avoidance> [accessed 9 July 2020].

175. F Lucas, 'Ireland Lowered Its Corporate Tax Rate. Here's What Happened', *The Daily Signal* <https://www.dailysignal.com/2018/05/14/ireland-lower-its-corporate-tax-rate-heres-what-happened/> [accessed 24 April 2019].

176. EC, *Aggressive Tax Planning Indicators*, 2017 <https://doi.org/10.2778/822243>.

177. Amundi Asset Management, 'Aggressive Tax Optimisation: What Is the Best ESG Approach?', 2018 <https://research-center.amundi.com/page/Publications/Discussion-Paper/2018/Aggressive-tax-optimisation-what-is-the-best-ESG-approach> [accessed 27 October 2020].

178. J Bogart, 'Tax Planning vs. Tax Optimization (Key Differences)', *Bogart Wealth*, 2020 <https://bogartwealth.com/tax-planning-vs-tax-optimization-key-differences/> [accessed 27 October 2020].

179. EC, 'Antitrust: Commission Opens Investigations into Apple', 2020 <https://ec.europa.eu/commission/presscorner/detail/en/ip_20_1073> [accessed 27 October 2020].

180. CNBC, 'French Court Fines UBS 4.5 Billion Euros in Tax Fraud Case', 2018 <https://www.cnbc.com/2019/02/20/french-court-fines-ubs-4point5-billion-euros-in-tax-fraud-case.html> [accessed 27 October 2020].

181. C Giles, 'OECD Drafts Principles for $100bn Global Corporate Tax Revolution', *FT*, 2020 <https://www.ft.com/content/c269d8ad-11d6-490a-b290-4d3dbf80bd03> [accessed 19 October 2020].

182. EC, *Aggressive Tax Planning Indicators*, 2017 <https://doi.org/10.2778/822243>.

183. PwC, 'DAC6: The EU Directive on Cross-Border Tax Arrangements', 2020 <https://www.pwc.com/gx/en/services/tax/tax-policy-administration/dac6-eu-directive-on-cross-border-tax-arrangements.html> [accessed 9 July 2020].

184. EC, *Aggressive Tax Planning Indicators*, 2017 <https://doi.org/10.2778/822243>.

185. T Castro and D P Ferraz, 'O Governance Internacional No Corporate Governance—Closing the Fence to Besiege Crime', 2019 <https://ifb.pt/wp-content/uploads/2019/10/IFB-InforBanca-117-OUT2019_Separata.pdf> [accessed 18 November 2019].

186. I Wentworth, '5 Basic Money Laundering Offences', *DeltaNet International*, 2018 <https://www.delta-net.com/compliance/anti-money-laundering/faqs/5-basic-money-laundering-offences> [accessed 1 July 2020].

187. E Moskowitz, 'Deutsche Bank Fined for Dealings with Epstein and Money Laundering Banks', *OCCRP*, 2020 <https://www.occrp.org/en/daily/12710-deutsche-bank-fined-for-dealing-with-epstein-and-money-laundering-banks> [accessed 27 October 2020].

188. M Doran and M Janda, 'Commonwealth Bank to Pay $700m Fine for Anti-Money Laundering, Terror Financing Law Breaches', *ABC*, 2018 <https://www.abc.net.au/news/2018-06-04/commonwealth-bank-pay-$700-million-fine-money-laundering-breach/9831064> [accessed 27 October 2020].

189. BBC, 'Commonwealth Bank Offers to Pay Record Fine in Laundering Case', 2018 <https://www.bbc.com/news/world-australia-44351257> [accessed 27 October 2020].

190. EC, 'Action Plan for a Comprehensive Union Policy on Preventing Money Laundering and Terrorism Financing', 2020 <https://ec.europa.eu/info/publications/200507-anti-money-laundering-terrorism-financing-action-plan_en> [accessed 19 June 2020].

191. Banco de Portugal, 'Legislation and Rules', 2020 <https://www.bportugal.pt/en/page/legislation-and-rules> [accessed 26 March 2020].

192. OECD, 'G20/OECD Principles of Corporate Governance 2015', 2015 <https://doi.org/10.1787/9789264236882-en>.

193. FATF, 'Money Laundering', 2020 <https://www.fatf-gafi.org/faq/moneylaundering/> [accessed 19 June 2020].

194. T Castro and D P Ferraz, 'O Combate Ao Branqueamento de Capitais, Financiamento Do Terrorismo e Proliferação de Armas de Destruição Em Massa', 2019 <https://ifb.pt/wp-content/uploads/2019/10/IFB-InforBanca-117-OUT2019_Separata.pdf> [accessed 26 March 2020].

195. BCBS, 'Consolidated Basel Framework', 2019 <https://www.bis.org/bcbs/publ/d462.htm> [accessed 1 July 2020].

196. G30, 'The Structure of Financial Supervision Approaches and Challenges in a Global Marketplace', 2008 <www.group30.org> [accessed 18 February 2020].

197. ECB, 'Single Supervisory Mechanism', 2019 <https://www.bankingsupervision.europa.eu/about/thessm/html/index.en.html> [accessed 19 February 2020].

198. ECB, 'European System of Financial Supervision', 2019 <https://www.bankingsupervision.europa.eu/about/esfs/html/index.en.html> [accessed 19 February 2020].

199. J Chen, 'Contingent Convertibles—CoCos', *Investopedia*, 2020 <https://www.investopedia.com/terms/c/contingentconvertible.asp> [accessed 17 March 2020].

200. ECB, 'Banking Union', 2019 <https://www.bankingsupervision.europa.eu/about/bankingunion/html/index.en.html> [accessed 19 February 2020].

201. ECB, 'Single Supervisory Mechanism', 2019 <https://www.bankingsupervision.europa.eu/about/thessm/html/index.en.html> [accessed 19 February 2020].

202. ECB, 'ECB Will Directly Supervise 117 Banks in 2020', 2019 <https://www.bankingsupervision.europa.eu/press/pr/date/2019/html/ssm.pr191204~45bda0701a.en.html> [accessed 19 October 2020].

203. ECB, 'Risk Report on Less Significant Institutions', 2020 <https://www.bankingsupervision.europa.eu/ecb/pub/html/

ssm.lsiriskreport202001~48ecda4549.en.html#toc1> [accessed 19 October 2020].

204. ECB, 'Single Resolution Mechanism' <https://ec.europa.eu/info/business-economy-euro/banking-and-finance/banking-union/single-resolution-mechanism_en> [accessed 25 April 2019].

205. BCBS, 'Stress Testing Principles', 2018 <https://www.bis.org/bcbs/publ/d450.pdf> [accessed 24 March 2020].

206. EBA, 'EBA Issues 2020 EU-Wide Stress Test Methodology for Discussion', 2019 <https://eba.europa.eu/eba-issues-2020-eu-wide-stress-test-methodology-for-discussion> [accessed 24 March 2020].

207. EBA, 'EBA Publishes 2018 EU-Wide Stress Test Results', 2018 <https://eba.europa.eu/eba-publishes-2018-eu-wide-stress-test-results> [accessed 24 March 2020].

208. FSB, 'Guidance on Supervisory Interaction with Financial Institutions on Risk Culture: A Framework for Assessing Risk Culture', 2014 <https://www.fsb.org/wp-content/uploads/140407.pdf?page_moved=1> [accessed 18 March 2020].

209. DNB, 'Supervision of Behaviour and Culture' <https://www.dnb.nl/binaries/Supervision of Behaviour and Culture_tcm46-380398.pdf?2018122411> [accessed 25 April 2019].

210. ECB, 'The Relevance of the Supervision of Behaviour and Culture to the SSM' <https://www.bankingsupervision.europa.eu/press/speeches/date/2015/html/se150924.en.html> [accessed 25 April 2019].

211. BCBS, 'History of the Basel Committee' <https://www.bis.org/bcbs/history.htm> [accessed 10 July 2019].

212. C B Murphy, 'Tier 1 Leverage Ratio Definition', *Investopedia*, 2020 <https://www.investopedia.com/terms/t/tier-1-leverage-ratio.asp> [accessed 19 October 2020].

213. EBA, 'EBA Report Shows That EU Banks Comply with LCR Requirement of 100% Ahead of Its Full Implementation', 2017 <https://eba.europa.eu/

eba-report-shows-that-eu-banks-comply-with-lcr-require-ment-of-100-ahead-of-its-full-implementation> [accessed 18 February 2020].

214. EU, 'Directive 2013/36/EU of the European Parliament and of Council', 2013 <https://eur-lex.europa.eu/LexUriServ/LexUriServ.do?uri=OJ:L:2013:176:0338:0436:EN:PDF> [accessed 10 July 2019].

215. ECB, 'ECB Guides to ICAAP and ILAAP' <https://www.bank-ingsupervision.europa.eu/press/publications/newsletter/2019/html/ssm.nl190213_3.en.html> [accessed 11 July 2019].

216. European Parliament, 'The CRD V Package', 2019 <http://www.europarl.europa.eu/RegData/etudes/BRIE/2017/599385/EPRS_BRI(2017)599385_EN.pdf> [accessed 2 August 2019].

217. ECB, 'What Is the SREP?' <https://www.bankingsupervision.europa.eu/about/ssmexplained/html/srep.en.html> [accessed 30 April 2019].

218. ECB, 'What Is the SREP?' <https://www.bankingsupervision.europa.eu/about/ssmexplained/html/srep.en.html> [accessed 30 April 2019].

219. BCBS, 'Interest Rate Risk in the Banking Book', 2016 <https://www.bis.org/bcbs/publ/d368.pdf> [accessed 30 April 2019].

220. Oracle, 'Asset Liability Management: An Overview' <http://www.oracle.com/us/industries/financial-services/045581.pdf> [accessed 1 May 2019].

221. BBVA, 'Información Corporativa', 2020 <https://www.bbva.com/en/corporate-information/> [accessed 19 October 2020].

222. H Pamuk and others, 'Exclusive: Trump Administration to Consider Adding China's Ant Group to Trade Blacklist', Reuters, 2020 <https://www.reuters.com/article/us-usa-antfinancial-blacklist-exclusive/exclusive-trump-administration-to-consider-adding-chinas-ant-group-to-trade-blacklist-sources-idUSKBN26Z2UT> [accessed 19 October 2020].

223. FCA, 'Fitness and Propriety' <https://www.fca.org.uk/firms/approved-persons/fitness-propriety> [accessed 1 April 2019].

224. BIS, 'Fit and Proper Principles', 2014 <https://www.bis.org/publ/bcbs47c4.pdf> [accessed 5 March 2019].

225. EC, 'Data Protection', 2020 <https://ec.europa.eu/info/law/law-topic/data-protection_en> [accessed 19 October 2020].

226. BIS, 'Fit and Proper Principles', 2014 <https://www.bis.org/publ/bcbs47c4.pdf> [accessed 5 March 2019].

227. ECB, 'Guide to Fit and Proper Assessments', 2017 <https://www.bankingsupervision.europa.eu/ecb/pub/pdf/ssm.fap_guide_201705.en.pdf> [accessed 2 April 2019].

228. ECB, 'Fit and Proper for Better Governance' <https://www.bankingsupervision.europa.eu/press/publications/newsletter/2018/html/ssm.nl180214_4.en.html> [accessed 1 April 2019].

229. J A Sonnenfeld, 'What Makes Great Boards Great', *Harvard Business Review*, 2002 <https://hbr.org/2002/09/what-makes-great-boards-great> [accessed 19 October 2020].

230. EBA, 'Calculation of the Number of Directorships Held (Privileged Counting of Mandates)', 2018 <https://eba.europa.eu/single-rule-book-qa/-/qna/view/publicId/2018_4158> [accessed 19 October 2020].

231. Investopedia, 'What Is a Staggered Board?', 2020 <https://www.investopedia.com/ask/answers/05/staggeredboard.asp> [accessed 19 October 2020].

232. W Kenton, 'Staggered Board Definition', 2019 <https://www.investopedia.com/terms/s/staggered-board.asp> [accessed 5 March 2020].

233. I T Lopes and D P Ferraz, 'The Value of Intangibles and Diversity on Boards Looking towards Economic Future Returns: Evidence from Non-Financial Iberian Business Organisations', *International Journal of Business Excellence*, 2016 <https://doi.org/10.1504/IJBEX.2016.078705>.

234. Deloitte, 'Women in the Boardroom—A Global Perspective', 2020 <https://www2.deloitte.com/global/en/pages/risk/articles/women-in-the-boardroom-global-perspective.html?id=us:2em:3na:ddbod:awa:ccg:030320&ctr=textlink1&sfid=003a0000025pOnOAAU> [accessed 6 March 2020].

235. J Huang and others, 'Women in the Workplace 2019', *McKinsey*, 2019 <https://www.mckinsey.com/featured-insights/gender-equality/women-in-the-workplace-2019> [accessed 6 March 2020].

236. Equality and Human Rights Commission, 'Investigation into Antisemitism in the Labour Party Finds Unlawful Acts of Discrimination and Harassment', 2020 <https://www.equalityhumanrights.com/en/our-work/news/investigation-antisemitism-labour-party-finds-unlawful-acts-discrimination-and> [accessed 30 October 2020].

237. K Aziz, 'This Is Why Boards of Directors Need Younger Members', *WEF*, 2018 <https://www.weforum.org/agenda/2018/12/boards-of-directors-need-youngsters-millennials/> [accessed 14 February 2020].

238. Credit Suisse, 'Global Diversity & Inclusion' <https://www.credit-suisse.com/corporate/en/responsibility/employer/global-diversity-inclusion.html> [accessed 2 April 2019].

239. Credit Suisse Research Institute, 'Gender Diversification. Europe in the Lead' <https://www.credit-suisse.com/corporate/en/articles/news-and-expertise/gender-diversification-europe-in-the-lead-201706.html> [accessed 2 April 2019].

240. FRC, 'Most UK Companies' Approach to Board Ethnic Diversity Is Unsatisfactory', 2019 <https://www.frc.org.uk/news/february-2020-(1)/most-uk-companies'-approach-to-board-ethnic-divers> [accessed 14 February 2020].

241. D P Ferraz, I T Lopes, and M M Martins, 'The Influence of Diversity on Boards on Profitability: An Overview across Iberian Non-Financial Listed Companies', *Corporate Ownership and Control*, 2016.

242. BBC, 'We Know What LGBT Means but Here's What LGBTQQIAAP Stands For', 2015 <http://www.bbc.co.uk/news-beat/article/33278165/we-know-what-lgbt-means-but-heres-what-lgbtqqiaap-stands-for> [accessed 16 March 2020].

243. BBC, 'Lloyd's Reveals Depth of Sexual Harassment Culture', 2019 <https://www.bbc.com/news/business-49801874> [accessed 19 October 2020].

244. H Son, 'Goldman Says It Will Double Hiring of Junior Bankers from Black Colleges by 2025', *CNBC*, 2020 <https://www.cnbc.com/2020/08/05/goldman-says-it-will-double-hiring-of-junior-bankers-from-black-colleges-by-2025.html> [accessed 19 October 2020].

245. Qantas AU, 'Our People', 2020 <https://www.qantas.com/au/en/qantas-group/acting-responsibly/our-people.html> [accessed 19 October 2020].

246. The Economist, 'How to Make Your Firm More Diverse and Inclusive—Diversity Memo' <https://www.economist.com/busi-ness/2019/11/07/how-to-make-your-firm-more-diverse-and-inclusive> [accessed 21 November 2019].

247. Workable, 'Diversity vs. Inclusion: The Main Differences in the Workplace | Workable', 2020 <https://resources.workable.com/hr-terms/diversity-vs-inclusion> [accessed 19 October 2020].

248. The Corporate Counsel, 'California's Board Gender Diversity Law: How Many Companies Impacted?' <https://www.thecor-poratecounsel.net/blog/2018/10/californias-board-gender-diversity-law-how-many-companies-impacted.html> [accessed 2 April 2019].

249. EWOB, 'European Women on Boards Gender Diversity Index', 2019 <https://europeanwomenonboards.eu/wp-content/uploads/2020/01/Gender-Equality-Index-Final-report-vDEF-ter.pdf> [accessed 19 October 2020].

250. EC, '2019 Report on Equality between Women and Men in the EU', 2019 <https://doi.org/10.2838/776419>.

251. European Parliament, 'Understanding the Gender Pay Gap: Definition and Causes', 2020 <https://www.europarl.europa.eu/news/en/headlines/society/20200109STO69925/understanding-the-gender-pay-gap-definition-and-causes> [accessed 16 March 2020].

252. OECD, 'Gender Wage Gap', 2020 <https://doi.org/10.1787/7cee77aa-en>.

253. GOV.UK, 'Gender Pay Gap Reporting: Overview', 2017 <https://www.gov.uk/guidance/gender-pay-gap-reporting-overview> [accessed 16 March 2020].

254. C Stevens, 'US Gender Pay Gap: Where Do We Stand in 2020?', *Business.Org*, 2020 <https://www.business.org/finance/benefits/gender-pay-gap/> [accessed 19 October 2020].

255. European Parliament, 'Understanding the Gender Pay Gap: Definition and Causes', 2020 <https://www.europarl.europa.eu/news/en/headlines/society/20200109STO69925/understanding-the-gender-pay-gap-definition-and-causes> [accessed 16 March 2020].

256. N Graf, A Brown, and E Patten, 'Gender Pay Gap Has Narrowed, but Changed Little in Past Decade', *Pew Research Center*, 2019 <https://www.pewresearch.org/fact-tank/2019/03/22/gender-pay-gap-facts/> [accessed 6 March 2020].

257. K Parker and C Funk, '42% of US Working Women Have Faced Gender Discrimination on the Job', *Pew Research Center*, 2017 <https://www.pewresearch.org/fact-tank/2017/12/14/gender-discrimination-comes-in-many-forms-for-todays-working-women/> [accessed 6 March 2020].

258. EC, 'Gender Equality Strategy 2020–2025', 2020 <https://ec.europa.eu/commission/presscorner/detail/en/qanda_20_357> [accessed 19 March 2020].

259. O Petter, 'Gender Pay Gap: What Is It and How Is It Different from Equal Pay?', 2020 <https://www.independent.co.uk/life-style/women/

gender-pay-gap-equal-pay-women-paid-less-motherhood-a8856121.html> [accessed 6 March 2020].

260. BCG UK, 'BCG UK Gender Pay Gap Report', 2020 <https://www.bcg.com/offices/gender-pay-gap-report> [accessed 19 October 2020].

261. JPMorgan, 'Advancing Black Leaders', 2020 <https://institute.jpmorganchase.com/about/people-culture/advancing-black-leaders> [accessed 19 October 2020].

262. Lazard, 'People', 2020 <https://www.lazard.com/our-firm/diversity/> [accessed 19 October 2020].

263. E VanDerWerff, 'Oscars 2020: The Nominees' Lack of Diversity Is Disappointingly Familiar—Vox', *Vox*, 2020 <https://www.vox.com/culture/2020/1/13/21063505/oscars-2020-nominations-nominees-so-white-oscarssowhite-diversity-greta-gerwig> [accessed 16 March 2020].

264. C Freeland, 'Millennials Are Starting to Get More Involved in Government, and the Impact Will Be Huge', *WEF*, 2019 <https://www.weforum.org/agenda/2019/01/millennials-are-starting-to-become-involved-in-government-heres-how/> [accessed 19 March 2020].

265. Cambridge Dictionary, 'Independence | Meaning in the Cambridge English Dictionary' <https://dictionary.cambridge.org/dictionary/english/independence> [accessed 22 May 2019].

266. M Everson, C Monda, and E Vos, 'The Theory and Practice of EU Agency Autonomy and Accountability: Early Day Expectations, Today's Realities and Future Perspectives', *SSRN*, 2013 <https://papers.ssrn.com/sol3/papers.cfm?abstract_id=2251027> [accessed 27 October 2020].

267. E Vos, N Athanasiadou, and L Dohmen, *EU Agencies and Conflicts of Interests*, 2020 <https://www.europarl.europa.eu/RegData/etudes/STUD/2020/621934/IPOL_STU(2020)621934_EN.pdf> [accessed 27 October 2020].

268. J Berk and P DeMarzo, 'Corporate Finance, 3rd Edition, Global Edition', *Pearson*, 2013 <https://doi.org/10.2139/ssrn.2779908>.

269. Q Reed, 'Sitting on the Fence: Conflicts of Interest and How to Regulate Them', *Anti-Corruption Resource Centre*, 2008 <https://www.u4.no/publications/sitting-on-the-fence-con-flicts-of-interest-and-how-to-regulate-them> [accessed 27 October 2020].

270. OECD, 'Recommendation of the Council on Guidelines for Managing Conflict of Interest in the Public Service', 2003 <https://www.oecd.org/governance/ethics/2957360.pdf> [accessed 27 October 2020].

271. EU, 'Guidelines on the Prevention and Management of Conflicts of Interest in EU Decentralised Agencies', 2013 <https://europa.eu/european-union/sites/europaeu/files/docs/body/2013-12-10_guidelines_on_conflict_of_interests_en.pdf> [accessed 27 October 2020].

272. S C Gilson and B Villalonga, 'Adelphia Communications Corp.'s Bankruptcy', 2007 <https://www.hbs.edu/faculty/pages/item.aspx?num=35079> [accessed 22 May 2019].

273. R Browne, 'Wirecard Shares Plummet amid Singapore Accounting Scandal', *CNBC*, 2020 <https://www.cnbc.com/2019/02/12/wirecard-shares-plummet-amid-singapore-accounting-scandal.html> [accessed 21 October 2020].

274. US SEC, 'SEC Charges Adelphia and Rigas Family With Massive Financial Fraud', 2002 <https://www.sec.gov/news/press/2002-110.htm> [accessed 3 April 2020].

275. NBC News, 'Adelphia Founder Sentenced to 15 Years in Jail', 2005 <http://www.nbcnews.com/id/8291040/ns/business-corporate_scandals/t/adelphia-founder-gets--year-term-son-gets/#.Xob7XKhKg2w> [accessed 3 April 2020].

276. A R Sorkin, '2 Top Tyco Executives Charged With $600 Million Fraud Scheme', *The New York Times*, 2002 <https://www.nytimes.com/2002/09/13/

business/2-top-tyco-executives-charged-with-600-million-fraud-scheme.html> [accessed 27 May 2019].

277. BBC News, 'Enron Scandal At-a-Glance', 2002 <http://news.bbc.co.uk/2/hi/business/1780075.stm> [accessed 2 April 2020].

278. M Tran, 'WorldCom Accounting Scandal', *The Guardian*, 2002 <https://www.theguardian.com/business/2002/aug/09/corporatefraud.worldcom2> [accessed 2 April 2020].

279. S Weeke, 'Parmalat: The Collapse of an Italian Dynasty', *NBC News*, 2005 <http://www.nbcnews.com/id/4030254/ns/world_news/t/parmas-god-falls-sky/#.XoXNF6hKg2w> [accessed 2 April 2020].

280. ESMA and EBA, 'Joint ESMA and EBA Guidelines on the Assessment of the Suitability of Members of the Management Body and Key Function Holders under Directive 2013/36/EU and Directive 2014/65/EU', 2017 <https://eba.europa.eu/sites/default/documents/files/documents/10180/1972984/43592777-a543-4a42-8d39-530dd4401832/Joint ESMA and EBA Guidelines on the assessment of suitability of members of the management body and key function holders (EBA-GL-2017-12).pdf> [accessed 3 April 2020].

281. OECD, 'Chapter 4. Board Composition, Board Committees and Board Member Qualifications', 2018, pp. 53–86 <https://doi.org/10.1787/9789264307490-7-en>.

282. S Mishra, 'Global Governance: Board Independence Standards and Practices', *Harvard Law School Forum* <https://corpgov.law.harvard.edu/2018/06/01/global-governance-board-independence-standards-and-practices/> [accessed 22 June 2019].

283. NYSE, 'Corporate Governance Guide', 2014 <https://www.nyse.com/publicdocs/nyse/listing/NYSE_Corporate_Governance_Guide.pdf> [accessed 22 June 2019].

284. ISS, 'Governance QualityScore', 2020 <https://www.issgovernance.com/file/products/qualityscore-techdoc.pdf> [accessed 21 October 2020].

285. S Mishra, 'Global Governance: Board Independence Standards and Practices', *Harvard Law School Forum on Corporate Governance*, 2018 <https://corpgov.law.harvard.edu/2018/06/01/global-governance-board-independence-standards-and-practices/> [accessed 3 April 2020].

286. S Masuda, 'Japan's Boards Evolve as Outside Directors Occupy 30% of Seats', *Nikkei Asia*, 2019 <https://asia.nikkei.com/Business/Business-trends/Japan-s-boards-evolve-as-outside-directors-occupy-30-of-seats> [accessed 21 October 2020].

287. W J Holstein, 'The Pros and Cons of Independent Boards', *The New York Times*, 2006 <https://www.nytimes.com/2006/08/27/jobs/27advi.html> [accessed 8 October 2020].

288. O Faleye, 'The Downside to Full Board Independence', *MIT Sloan Management Review*, 2017 <https://sloanreview.mit.edu/article/the-downside-to-full-board-independence/> [accessed 8 October 2020].

289. D Larcker and B Tayan, 'The Management of Berkshire Hathaway', *Stanford Graduate School of Business*, 2009 <https://www.gsb.stanford.edu/faculty-research/case-studies/management-berkshire-hathaway> [accessed 3 April 2020].

290. BCBS, 'Corporate Governance Principles for Banks', 2015 <https://www.bis.org/bcbs/publ/d328.pdf> [accessed 5 March 2019].

291. BCBS, 'Core Principles for Effective Banking Supervision', 2012 <https://www.bis.org/publ/bcbs230.pdf> [accessed 23 March 2020].

292. Banco de Portugal, 'Legislation and Rules', 2020 <https://www.bportugal.pt/en/page/legislation-and-rules> [accessed 26 March 2020].

293. WIPO, 'Internal Audit Strategy 2018–2020', 2018 <https://www.wipo.int/export/sites/www/about-wipo/en/oversight/iaod/audit/pdf/internal_audit_strategy.pdf> [accessed 21 October 2020].

294. IIA, 'Developing the Internal Audit Strategic Plan Practice Guide', 2012 <https://na.theiia.org/standards-guidance/rec-ommended-guidance/practice-guides/Pages/Developing-the-Internal-Audit-Strategic-Plan-Practice-Guide.aspx> [accessed 26 March 2020].

295. IIA, 'International Standards for the Professional Practice of Internal Auditing Standards', 2017 <https://na.theiia.org/stan-dards-guidance/Public Documents/IPPF-Standards-2017.pdf> [accessed 26 March 2020].

296. FSB, 'FSB Principles for Sound Compensation Practices Implementation Standards', 2009 <https://www.fsb.org/wp-content/uploads/r_090925c.pdf> [accessed 26 March 2020].

297. EBA, 'Guidelines on Sound Remuneration Policies under Articles 74(3) and 75(2) of Directive 2013/36/EU and Disclosures under Article 450 of Regulation (EU) No 575/2013', 2015.

298. BCBS, 'Corporate Governance Principles for Banks', 2015 <https://www.bis.org/bcbs/publ/d328.pdf> [accessed 5 March 2019].

299. GOV.UK, 'Companies Act 2006', 2006 <http://www.legisla-tion.gov.uk/ukpga/2006/46/pdfs/ukpga_20060046_en.pdf> [accessed 29 July 2019].

300. OECD, 'G20/OECD Principles of Corporate Governance 2015', 2015 <https://doi.org/10.1787/9789264236882-en>.

301. A R Sorkin, '2 Top Tyco Executives Charged With $600 Million Fraud Scheme', The New York Times, 2002 <https://www.nytimes.com/2002/09/13/business/2-top-tyco-executives-charged-with-600-million-fraud-scheme.html> [accessed 27 May 2019].

302. G Wong, 'Kozlowski, Swartz Sentenced to up to 25 Years in Prison', CNN, 2005 <https://money.cnn.com/2005/09/19/news/newsmakers/kozlowski_sentence/> [accessed 29 July 2019].

303. FRC, 'Guidance On Board Effectiveness', 2018 <https://www.frc.org.uk/getattachment/61232f60-a338-471b-ba5a-

bfed25219147/2018-Guidance-on-Board-Effectiveness-FINAL. PDF> [accessed 3 April 2019].

304. Korn Ferry Institute, 'Director's Toolbox: Emotional Intelligence', 2020 <https://www.kornferry.com/insights/articles/directors-toolbox-emotional-intelligence> [accessed 10 April 2020].

305. A Dutra, 'A More Effective Board of Directors', *HBR*, 2012 <https://hbr.org/2012/11/a-more-effective-board-of-dire> [accessed 17 March 2020].

306. D Cossin and J Caballero, 'The Four Pillars of Board Effectiveness', *IMD*, 2014 <https://www.imd.org/research-knowledge/articles/the-four-pillars-of-board-effectiveness/> [accessed 17 March 2020].

307. L Liu, R Bew, and F Van Der Oord, 'Building Board-Management Dynamics to Withstand a Crisis: Addressing the Fault Lines', *McKinsey*, 2019 <https://www.mckinsey.com/~/media/McKinsey/Business Functions/Risk/Our Insights/Building board management dynamics to withstand a crisis Addressing the fault lines/Building-board-management-dynamics-to-withstand-a-crisis-Addressing-the-fault-lines.pdf> [accessed 21 October 2020].

308. V Bento, *For More Board Effectiveness*, 2019.

309. EY, 'EY Center for Board Matters', 2020 <https://www.ey.com/en_gl/board-matters> [accessed 21 October 2020].

310. P Vajda, 'Collusion, Culture and Bad Management', 2014 <https://www.management-issues.com/opinion/6423/collusion-culture-and-bad-management/> [accessed 25 February 2020].

311. D Streitfeld, 'Engineers Allege Hiring Collusion in Silicon Valley', *The New York Times*, 2014 <https://www.nytimes.com/2014/03/01/technology/engineers-allege-hiring-collusion-in-silicon-valley.html> [accessed 1 April 2020].

312. P Vajda, 'Collusion, Culture and Bad Management', 2014 <https://www.management-issues.com/opinion/6423/

collusion-culture-and-bad-management/> [accessed 25 February 2020].

313. K Makortoff, 'Barclays Hit with $15m Fine over Attempts to Unmask Whistleblower', *The Guardian*, 2018 <https://www. theguardian.com/business/2018/dec/18/barclays-hit-with-15m-fine-over-attempts-to-unmask-whistleblower> [accessed 3 June 2019].

314. C Binham and M Arnold, 'Barclays Chief Staley Fined £640,000 over Whistleblowing Scandal', *Financial Times*, 2018 <https://www.ft.com/content/8a172758-550e-11e8-b3ee-41e0209208ec> [accessed 1 April 2020].

315. E Pidgeon, 'The Economic Impact of Bad Meetings' <https://ideas.ted.com/the-economic-impact-of-bad-meetings/> [accessed 5 November 2019].

316. R Schwarz, 'How to Design an Agenda for an Effective Meeting' <https://hbr.org/2015/03/how-to-design-an-agenda-for-an-effective-meeting> [accessed 4 November 2019].

317. R Schwarz, 'How to Design an Agenda for an Effective Meeting' <https://hbr.org/2015/03/how-to-design-an-agenda-for-an-effective-meeting> [accessed 4 November 2019].

318. C Casal and C Caspar, 'Building a Forward-Looking Board', *McKinsey* <https://www.mckinsey.com/business-functions/strategy-and-corporate-finance/our-insights/building-a-for-ward-looking-board> [accessed 4 July 2019].

319. G Oakes, 'Governance: Nine Steps to Good Decision-making', *Econsultancy* <https://econsultancy.com/governance-9-steps-to-good-decision-making/> [accessed 11 April 2019].

320. J S Hammond, R L Keeney, and H Raiffa, 'The Hidden Traps in Decision-making', *Harvard Business Review*, 1998 <https://hbr.org/1998/09/the-hidden-traps-in-decision-making-2> [accessed 26 May 2020].

321. McKinsey, 'Effective Decision-making in the Age of Urgency', 2019 <https://www.mckinsey.com/business-functions/

organization/our-insights/decision-making-in-the-age-of-urgency> [accessed 26 May 2020].

322. A D Smet, G Lackey, and L M Weiss, 'Untangling Your Organization's Decision-making', *McKinsey*, 2017 <https://www.mckinsey.com/business-functions/organization/our-insights/untangling-your-organizations-decision-making#> [accessed 26 May 2020].

323. M Useem, 'How Well-Run Boards Make Decisions', *Harvard Business Review*, 2006 <https://hbr.org/2006/11/how-well-run-boards-make-decisions> [accessed 26 May 2020].

324. First Round Review, 'The 6 Decision Making Frameworks That Help Startup Leaders Tackle Tough Calls', 2020 <https://firstround.com/review/the-6-decision-making-frameworks-that-help-startup-leaders-tackle-tough-calls/> [accessed 4 June 2020].

325. IMD Business School, 'Role of the Chairman : Interview with Holcim Chairman Rolf Soiron' <https://www.youtube.com/watch?v=My5uJeg2r8k> [accessed 15 May 2019].

326. 'More U.S. Companies Separating Chief Executive and Chairman Roles—WSJ', *The Wall Street Journal*, 2019 <https://www.wsj.com/amp/articles/more-u-s-companies-separating-chief-executive-and-chairman-roles-11548288502> [accessed 29 October 2019].

327. S Fiegerman, 'WeWork Is Postponing Its IPO', *CNN*, 2019 <https://edition.cnn.com/2019/09/30/tech/wework-ipo-postponed/index.html> [accessed 21 October 2020].

328. S Shekshnia, 'How to Be a Good Board Chair', *Harvard Business Review* <https://hbr.org/2018/03/how-to-be-a-good-board-chair> [accessed 25 June 2019].

329. EC, 'COMMISSION RECOMMENDATION of 15 February 2005 on the Role of Non-Executive or Supervisory Directors of Listed Companies and on the Committees of the (Supervisory) Board (Text with EEA Relevance)', 2005 <https://eur-lex.europa.eu/

legal-content/EN/TXT/PDF/?uri=CELEX:32005H0162&from =HR> [accessed 27 October 2020].

330. ICSA, 'The 5 Essential Qualities of a Non-Executive Director' <https://www.icsa.org.uk/knowledge/blog/the-5-essential-qualities-of-a-non-executive-director> [accessed 21 May 2019].

331. Australian Institute of Company Directors, 'Role of Executive Directors', 2012 <https://aicd.companydirectors.com.au/-/media/cd2/resources/director-resources/director-tools/pdf/05446-1-12-mem-director-tools-bc-executive-director_a4_web.ashx> [accessed 10 April 2020].

332. N Price, 'Role of an Executive Director in Board Management', *Boardeffect*, 2018 <https://www.boardeffect.com/blog/role-executive-director-board-management/> [accessed 10 April 2020].

333. H Bürkner, A Bhattacharya, and J Becerra, 'Five Things Every CEO Must Do in the Next Era of Globalization', *BCG*, 2014 <https://www.bcg.com/publications/2014/leadership-talent-every-ceo-must-do-next-era-globalization.aspx> [accessed 8 April 2020].

334. S P Keller, 'The CEO's Role in Leading Transformation', *McKinsey*, 2007 <https://www.mckinsey.com/business-functions/organi-zation/our-insights/the-ceos-role-in-leading-transformation> [accessed 3 April 2019].

335. J Wilkinson, '3 Things Role of the CFO', *StrategicCFO*, 2013 <https://www.youtube.com/watch?v=Bs4Q5FZzL_Q> [accessed 29 April 2020].

336. N Bennett and S A Miles, 'Second in Command: The Misunderstood Role of the Chief Operating Officer', *Harvard Business Review*, 2006 <https://hbr.org/2006/05/second-in-command-the-misunderstood-role-of-the-chief-operating-offi-cer> [accessed 29 April 2020].

337. FRC, 'FRC Guidance for Boards and Board Committees' <https://www.frc.org.uk/directors/

corporate-governance-and-stewardship/uk-corporate-gover-nance-code/frc-guidance-for-boards-and-board-committees> [accessed 5 March 2019].

338. D Armour, 'The ICSA Company Secretary's Handbook', 2016 <https://www.icsa.org.uk/shop/books/icsa-co-sec-handbook-11th> [accessed 20 August 2019].

339. R Tudway, 'Corporate Stewardship and the Rhineland Model', *Financial Times*, 2019 <https://www.ft.com/content/dbf21006-0165-11ea-be59-e49b2a136b8d> [accessed 28 November 2019].

340. D P Ferraz, I L Lopes, and S Hitzelberger, 'The Use of Poison Pills by US Firms over the Period 1997–2015: What Has Been Their Impact on Shareholder Value?', *International Journal of Business Excellence*, 2019 <https://doi.org/10.1504/IJBEX.2019.099450>.

341. E Tarver, 'Investor Relations (IR) Definition', *Investopedia*, 2020 <https://www.investopedia.com/terms/i/investorrelations.asp> [accessed 30 October 2020].

342. Allianz, 'D&O Insurance Explained' <https://www.agcs.allianz.com/news-and-insights/expert-risk-articles/d-o-insurance-explained.html> [accessed 21 May 2019].

343. Lloyd's, 'D&O Consortium Strengthens Lloyd's Position in US', 2014 <https://www.lloyds.com/news-and-risk-insight/news/market-news/industry-news-2014/do-consortium-agreement-strengthens-lloyds-position-in-us> [accessed 11 May 2020].

344. J G Loughnane, 'Five Things to Know About D&O', *American Bar Association*, 2017 <https://www.americanbar.org/groups/busi-ness_law/publications/blt/2017/09/11_loughnane/> [accessed 20 April 2020].

345. J G Loughnane, 'Insured versus Insured Exclusion', *IRMI* <https://www.irmi.com/term/insurance-definitions/insured-ver-sus-insured-exclusion> [accessed 21 May 2019].

346. C A Montgomery and others, 'Tyco International—Case', *Harvard Business School*, 2007 <https://www.hbs.edu/faculty/Pages/item.aspx?num=24223> [accessed 21 October 2020].

347. ECB, 'Criteria for Determining Significance' <https://www.bankingsupervision.europa.eu/banking/list/criteria/html/index.en.html> [accessed 4 April 2019].

348. W Buiter and H P Lankes, *International Financial Institutions-Adapting to a World of Private Capital Flows*, 2001 <https://willembuiter.com/builan.pdf> [accessed 21 October 2020].

349. SEC, 'NYSE Rulemaking: Rel. 34-47672 (Re: Corporate Governance)', 2003 <https://www.sec.gov/rules/sro/34-47672.htm> [accessed 11 May 2020].

350. KPMG, 'Audit Committee Guide', 2017 <https://boardleadership.kpmg.us/content/dam/boardleadership/en/pdf/General/kpmg-audit-committee-guide.pdf> [accessed 1 April 2020].

351. KPMG, 'On the 2020 Audit Committee Agenda', 2020 <https://assets.kpmg/content/dam/kpmg/ch/pdf/on-the-audit-committee-agenda.pdf> [accessed 1 April 2020].

352. Deloitte, 'Risk Committee Resource Guide', 2014 <https://www2.deloitte.com/content/dam/Deloitte/za/Documents/governance-risk-compliance/ZA_RiskCommitteeResourceGuideOnline2014_22052014.pdf> [accessed 1 April 2020].

353. G Beall, '8 Key Differences between Gen Z and Millennials', *HuffPost*, 2017 <https://www.huffpost.com/entry/8-key-differences-between_b_12814200> [accessed 12 May 2020].

354. R Sharma and A Yerger, 'Three Things Nominating Committees Need to Know', *Harvard Law School Forum on Corporate Governance*, 2016 <https://corpgov.law.harvard.edu/2016/02/14/three-things-nominating-committees-need-to-know/#4> [accessed 12 May 2020].

355. M Fucci, 'Board Succession', *Deloitte* <https://www2.deloitte.com/us/en/pages/center-for-board-effectiveness/articles/

board-succession-getting-it-right.html> [accessed 12 May 2020].

356. Institute of Directors, 'What Is the Role of the Remuneration Committee?', 2019 <https://www.iod.com/news/news/articles/What-is-the-role-of-the-remuneration-committee> [accessed 12 May 2020].

357. IMA, 'IMA Principles of Remuneration', 2014 <https://www.ivis.co.uk/media/10277/Principles-of-Remuneration-2014.pdf> [accessed 28 June 2019].

358. J Shotter, 'Deutsche Bank Investors Vote against Executive Pay Packages', *FT* <https://www.ft.com/content/d1c65e1e-1d95-11e6-a7bc-ee846770ec15> [accessed 27 June 2019].

359. S F O'Byrne, 'Say on Pay: Is It Needed? Does It Work?', *Harvard Law School Forum* <https://corpgov.law.harvard.edu/2018/01/25/say-on-pay-is-it-needed-does-it-work/> [accessed 27 June 2019].

360. A Melin and C Sam, 'Highest Paid U.S. CEOs: Top Salaries in 2019', *Bloomberg*, 2020 <https://www.bloomberg.com/graphics/2020-highest-paid-ceos/> [accessed 21 October 2020].

361. A Pepper, 'The Case Against Long-Term Incentive Pay', *Harvard Business Review* <https://hbr.org/2016/10/the-case-against-long-term-incentive-plans> [accessed 28 June 2019].

362. J Talone, *Comissão de Remuneração e Vencimentos*, 2017.

363. J Talone, *Comissão de Remuneração e Vencimentos*, 2017.

364. S Klemash and others, 'Effective Board Evaluation', *Harvard Law School Forum on Corporate Governance*, 2018 <https://corpgov.law.harvard.edu/2018/10/26/effective-board-evaluation/> [accessed 31 March 2020].

365. R Doyle, 'How Companies Are Evolving Board Evaluations and Disclosures', *EY*, 2019 <https://www.ey.com/en_us/board-matters/how-companies-are-evolving-board-evaluations-and-disclosures> [accessed 12 May 2020].

366. ICAEW, 'Walker Report', 2009 <https://www.icaew.com/technical/corporate-governance/codes-and-reports/walker-report> [accessed 12 May 2020].

367. ECB, 'A Closer Look at Time Commitment of Non-Executive Directors', 2019 <https://www.bankingsupervision.europa.eu/press/publications/newsletter/2019/html/ssm.nl190814_4.en.html> [accessed 12 May 2020].

368. WEF, 'Globalization 4.0 Shaping a New Global Architecture in the Age of the Fourth Industrial Revolution', 2019 <http://www3.weforum.org/docs/WEF_Globalization_4.0_Call_for_Engagement.pdf> [accessed 18 May 2020].

369. EY, 'How Companies Can Navigate the Transformative Age in Geopolitics' <https://www.ey.com/en_gl/geostrategy/how-companies-can-navigate-the-transformative-age-in-geopolitics> [accessed 22 May 2019].

370. J Petzinger, 'EU Gets Approval to Slap $4bn Worth of Tariffs on US Imports in Boeing Dispute', *Yahoo Finance* <https://uk.finance.yahoo.com/news/eu-gets-okay-to-slap-4-bn-worth-of-tariffs-on-us-imports-in-boeing-dispute-151006285.html> [accessed 21 October 2020].

371. WEF, 'Stakeholder Principles in the COVID Era', 2020 <http://www3.weforum.org/docs/WEF_Stakeholder_Principles_COVID_Era.pdf> [accessed 18 May 2020].

372. A S Ribeiro, *Análise Geopolítica*, 2019.

373. T Castro, 'Geofinancial Strategy and Governance—Towards Peace by Financial Means', *University of Lisbon*, 2020 <http://ulisboa.academia.edu/TeodoraCastro/CurriculumVitae> [accessed 21 October 2020].

374. SASAC, 'What We Do', 2020 <http://en.sasac.gov.cn/2018/07/17/c_7.htm> [accessed 21 October 2020].

375. Reuters, 'U.S. Restrictions on Qatar Airways Could Lead to Unraveling of Aviation Agreements: Airlines' <https://www.reuters.com/article/us-usa-qatar-airlines/u-s-restrictions-on-

qatar-airways-could-lead-to-unraveling-of-aviation-agreements-airlines-idUSKCN1RT0ZU> [accessed 22 May 2019].

376. J E Barnes, 'U.S. Cyberattack Hurt Iran's Ability to Target Oil Tankers, Officials Say', *The New York Times*, 2019 <https://www.nytimes.com/2019/08/28/us/politics/us-iran-cyber-attack.html> [accessed 18 May 2020].

377. F Bajak and M Liedtke, 'AP Explains: US Sanctions on Huawei Bite, but Who Gets Hurt?', *AP* <https://www.apnews.com/ebc6f2ece653470fb52c665df6219801> [accessed 22 June 2019].

378. CFIUS, 'The Committee on Foreign Investment in the United States', 2020 <https://home.treasury.gov/policy-issues/international/the-committee-on-foreign-investment-in-the-united-states-cfius> [accessed 18 May 2020].

379. J Masters and J McBride, 'Foreign Investment and U.S. National Security', *Council on Foreign Relations*, 2020 <https://www.cfr.org/backgrounder/foreign-investment-and-us-national-security> [accessed 18 May 2020].

380. D Sevastopulo and K Shubber, 'Trump Team Outlines Plan to Crack down on US-Listed Chinese Groups', *FT*, 2020 <https://www.ft.com/content/0d05464a-9f56-421b-8be3-cd72eb04c77b> [accessed 21 October 2020].

381. H Ellyatt, 'Russia and the US Battling over Europe's Gas Market', *CNBC*, 2019 <https://www.cnbc.com/2019/01/08/russia-and-the-us-battling-over-europes-gas-market.html> [accessed 22 May 2019].

382. F Bajak and M Liedtke, 'AP Explains: US Sanctions on Huawei Bite, but Who Gets Hurt?', *AP* <https://www.apnews.com/ebc6f2ece653470fb52c665df6219801> [accessed 22 June 2019].

383. F Bajak and M Liedtke, 'AP Explains: US Sanctions on Huawei Bite, but Who Gets Hurt?', *AP* <https://www.apnews.com/ebc6f2ece653470fb52c665df6219801> [accessed 22 June 2019].

384. J B Scott and J B Moore, 'A Digest of International Law', *The American Journal of International Law*, 1907 <https://doi.org/10.2307/2186316>.

385. R Dolzer and C Schreuer, 'Principles of International Investment Law', *Oxford*, 2012 <https://doi.org/10.1093/law:iic/9780199211753.001.1>.

386. OECD iLibrary, 'Foreign Direct Investment (FDI)', 2020 <https://www.oecd-ilibrary.org/finance-and-investment/foreign-direct-investment-fdi/indicator-group/english_9a523b18-en> [accessed 2 June 2020].

387. World Bank, 'What Is the Difference between Foreign Direct Investment (FDI) Net Inflows and Net Outflows?' <https://data-helpdesk.worldbank.org/knowledgebase/articles/114954-what-is-the-difference-between-foreign-direct-inve> [accessed 2 July 2020].

388. D Nayak and R N Choudhury, 'A Selective Review of Foreign Direct Investment Theories', 2014 <www.artnetontrade.org.> [accessed 2 July 2020].

389. IMF, 'Foreign Direct Investment in Emerging Market Countries', 2003 <https://www.imf.org/external/np/cmcg/2003/eng/091803.pdf> [accessed 2 July 2020].

390. C Pazarbasioglu, 'Reviving FDI Flows Is Crucial to Economic Recovery in Developing Economies', *World Bank*, 2020 <https://blogs.worldbank.org/voices/reviving-fdi-flows-crucial-economic-recovery-developing-economies> [accessed 2 July 2020].

391. ADB, 'About ADB', 2020 <https://www.adb.org/who-we-are/about> [accessed 30 September 2020].

392. EIB, 'Governance and Structure' <https://www.eib.org/en/about/governance-and-structure/index.htm> [accessed 29 November 2019].

393. S Nestor, 'Board Effectiveness in International Financial Institutions: A Comparative Perspective on the Effectiveness

Drivers in Constituency Boards, AIIB Yearbook of International Law', 2018 <www.eib.org/attachments/general/reports/eib_group_corporate_governance_report_2016_en.pdf> [accessed 29 November 2019].

394. J Healy, D Nicholson, and A Pekarek, 'Should We Take the Gig Economy Seriously?', *Labor & Industry: A Journal of the Social and Economic Relations of Work*, 2017 <https://doi.org/10.1080/10301763.2017.1377048>.

395. Intuit, 'Intuit 2020 Report' <www.intuit.com/2020.> [accessed 6 March 2019].

396. Y Doz, 'The Strategic Decisions That Caused Nokia's Failure | INSEAD Knowledge' <https://knowledge.insead.edu/strategy/the-strategic-decisions-that-caused-nokias-failure-7766> [accessed 6 March 2019].

397. K Kuehner-Hebert, 'Corporate Governance: Lessons Learned From Uber's Board—Corporate Board Member', *Boardmember* <https://boardmember.com/corporate-governance-lessons-learned-ubers-board/> [accessed 5 March 2019].

398. S Voshmgir, 'Tokenized Networks: What Is a DAO?', *Blockchainhub*, 2019 <https://blockchainhub.net/dao-decentralized-autonomous-organization/> [accessed 29 September 2020].

399. R E Montalvo, 'Social Media Management', *International Journal of Management & Information Systems (IJMIS)*, 2016 <https://doi.org/10.19030/ijmis.v15i3.4645>.

400. R Molla and S Ghaffary, 'WeWork's Mess and CEO Adam Neumann's Ouster, Explained', *Vox*, 2019 <https://www.vox.com/recode/2019/9/23/20879656/wework-mess-explained-ipo-softbank> [accessed 29 September 2020].

401. The Editorial Board, 'Why Dual-Class Shares Deserve Consideration', *Financial Times*, 2019 <https://www.ft.com/content/6f576e60-0231-11ea-be59-e49b2a136b8d> [accessed 4 December 2019].

402. Novo Nordisk Global, 'Shareholder Rights', 2020 <https://www.novonordisk.com/about/corporate-governance/shareholder-rights.html> [accessed 29 September 2020].

403. E Yiu, 'Hong Kong Stock Exchange's Plan to Attract Tech Listings by Expanding Dual-Class Shares Structures Gains Traction ', *South China Morning Post*, 2020 <https://www.scmp.com/business/banking-finance/article/3086524/hong-kong-stock-exchanges-plan-attract-tech-listings> [accessed 29 September 2020].

404. ECB, 'Eurosystem Credit Assessment Framework (ECAF)' <https://www.ecb.europa.eu/paym/coll/risk/ecaf/html/index.en.html> [accessed 21 May 2020].

405. ESMA, 'Credit Rating Agencies' <https://www.esma.europa.eu/regulation/credit-rating-agencies> [accessed 16 April 2019].

406. M Krantz, '2008 Crisis Still Hangs Over Credit-Rating Firms', *USA Today* <https://eu.usatoday.com/story/money/business/2013/09/13/credit-rating-agencies-2008-financial-crisis-lehman/2759025/> [accessed 16 April 2019].

407. FSB, 'Principles for Reducing Reliance on CRA Ratings' <http://www.fsb.org/2010/10/r_101027/> [accessed 17 April 2019].

408. K Santos, 'Corporate Credit Ratings: A Quick Guide', 2020 <https://www.treasurers.org/ACTmedia/ITCCMFcorpcreditguide.pdf> [accessed 21 May 2020].

409. S&P, 'Corporate Ratings Methodology', 2020 <https://www.spratings.com/documents/20184/774196/Corporate+Ratings+Methodology.pdf>.

410. R Thebault, 'Who Is Michael Milken, the "Junk Bond King" Trump Just Pardoned?', *The Washington Post*, 2020 <https://www.washingtonpost.com/business/2020/02/18/michael-milken-pardon/> [accessed 21 May 2020].

411. Wikipedia, 'Bond Credit Rating' <https://en.wikipedia.org/wiki/Bond_credit_rating> [accessed 16 April 2019].

412. S&P, 'What Are Credit Ratings and How Do They Work?', 2020 <www.UnderstandingRatings.com> [accessed 22 May 2020].

413. The Free Dictionary, 'Rating Trigger' <https://financial-diction-ary.thefreedictionary.com/rating+trigger> [accessed 17 April 2019].

414. Fitch, 'Fitch Downgrades Italy to "BBB-"', 2020 <https://www.fitchratings.com/research/sovereigns/fitch-downgrades-italy-to-bbb-outlook-stable-28-04-2020> [accessed 22 May 2020].

415. The Free Press Journal, 'Covid-19: Multi-Notch Sovereign Ratings Downgrade Likely in 2020, Says Fitch', 2020 <https://www.freepressjournal.in/business/covid-19-multi-notch-sover-eign-ratings-downgrade-likely-in-2020-says-fitch> [accessed 22 May 2020].

416. C S Spatt, 'Proxy Advisory Firms, Governance, Failure, and Regulation', *Harvard Law School Forum on Corporate Governance*, 2019 <https://corpgov.law.harvard.edu/2019/06/25/proxy-advi-sory-firms-governance-failure-and-regulation/> [accessed 25 May 2020].

417. L Tripoli, 'More Companies Pointing Finger at Proxy Advisory Firms', *Compliance Week*, 2019 <https://www.complianceweek.com/surveys-and-benchmarking/more-companies-pointing-finger-at-proxy-advisory-firms/28089.article> [accessed 25 May 2020].

418. ZDNet, 'Worst Tech Mergers and Acquisitions: HP and Compaq', 2016 <https://www.zdnet.com/article/worst-tech-mergers-and-acquisitions-hp-and-compaq/> [accessed 25 May 2020].

419. FT, 'Activist Investor' <http://lexicon.ft.com/Term?term=activist-investor> [accessed 18 April 2019].

420. M Johnston, 'Top 5 Shareholders of Facebook', *Investopedia*, 2020 <https://www.investopedia.com/articles/insights/082216/top-9-shareholders-facebook-fb.asp> [accessed 22 October 2020].

421. Business Wire, 'Elliott Believes in a Brighter Future for EDP', 2020 <https://www.businesswire.com/news/home/20190213005945/

en/Elliott-Believes-Brighter-Future-EDP> [accessed 1 June 2020].

422. Global Reporting Initiative, 'Sustainability Reporting', 2020 <https://www.globalreporting.org/information/sustainability-reporting/Pages/default.aspx> [accessed 27 May 2020].

423. N Clehane, 'What Is a Public Interest Entity (PIE)?' <https://www.bdo.global/en-gb/services/audit-assurance/eu-audit-reform/what-is-a-public-interest-entity-(pie)> [accessed 1 June 2020].

424. S Rao, 'Current State of Assurance on Sustainability Reports', *The CPA Journal*, 2017 <https://www.cpajournal.com/2017/07/26/current-state-assurance-sustainability-reports/> [accessed 1 June 2020].

425. E Khoo and T Baines, 'European Supervisory Authorities Launch Joint Consultation on ESG Disclosures', *Lexology*, 2020 <https://www.lexology.com/library/detail.aspx?g=987777a5-dae1-4377-a1f0-b7a4d1fe223a> [accessed 28 May 2020].

426. B M Huber, M Comstock, and D Polk, 'ESG Reports and Ratings: What They Are, Why They Matter', *Harvard Law School Forum on Corporate Governance*, 2017 <https://corpgov.law.harvard.edu/2017/07/27/esg-reports-and-ratings-what-they-are-why-they-matter/> [accessed 1 June 2020].

427. EU, 'Auditing of Companies' Financial Statements' <https://ec.europa.eu/info/business-economy-euro/company-reporting-and-auditing/auditing-companies-financial-statements_en> [accessed 23 April 2019].

428. FT, 'Big Four Accountants: Catch of the Day', 2019 <https://www.ft.com/content/4308c902-3d35-4dba-9aa9-50938f9e6797> [accessed 28 November 2019].

429. Big 4 Accounting Firms, 'Top 10 Accounting Firms 2020', 2020 <https://big4accountingfirms.com/top-10-accounting-firms/> [accessed 2 June 2020].

430. IAASB, 'Overview of the New and Revised Auditor Reporting Standards and Related Conforming Amendments', 2015 <www.iaasb.org/auditor-reporting.> [accessed 2 August 2019].

431. Deloitte, 'The New Auditor's Report', 2017 <https://www2.deloitte.com/be/en/pages/audit/articles/new-auditor-s-report.html> [accessed 2 June 2020].

432. IAASB, 'The New Auditor's Report', 2015 <www.iaasb.org/auditor-reporting.> [accessed 2 August 2019].

433. IMF, 'The IMF's Approach to Promoting Good Governance and Combating Corruption', 2005 <https://www.imf.org/external/np/gov/guide/eng/index.htm> [accessed 22 October 2020].

434. The World Bank, 'Governance and Development', 1992 <http://documents1.worldbank.org/curated/en/604951468739447676/pdf/multi-page.pdf> [accessed 22 October 2020].

435. BIS, 'Fit and Proper Principles', 2014 <https://www.bis.org/publ/bcbs47c4.pdf> [accessed 5 March 2019].

436. T Castro and D P Ferraz, *Fit and Proper—Evitar Um Cisne Negro Ou Há Um Elefante Na Sala?*, 2018 <https://ifb.pt/wp-content/uploads/2018/11/IFB-InforBanca-114-NOV2018.pdf> [accessed 22 October 2020].

437. EC, *Aggressive Tax Planning Indicators*, 2017 <https://doi.org/10.2778/822243>.

CPSIA information can be obtained
at www.ICGtesting.com
Printed in the USA
BVHW040819201121
622122BV00013B/480